Writing Dangerously

Writing Dangerously

Mary McCarthy *and* Her World

Carol Brightman

Clarkson Potter/Publishers
New York

Published by Clarkson N. Potter, Inc., 201 East 50th Street, New York, New York 10022. Member of the Crown Publishing Group.

Random House, Inc. New York, Toronto, London, Sydney, Auckland

CLARKSON N. POTTER, POTTER, and colophon are trademarks of Clarkson N. Potter, Inc.

Manufactured in the United States of America

Design by Howard Klein

Library of Congress Cataloging-in-Publication Data

Brightman, Carol.
  Writing dangerously : Mary McCarthy and her world
Carol Brightman. — 1st ed. Includes index.
    1. McCarthy, Mary, 1912–1989. 2. Authors, American—20th century—
Biography. I. Title.
PS3525.A1435Z59 1992   92-7180
  818′.5209—dc20 [B]

ISBN 0-517-56400-9

10 9 8 7 6 5 4 3 2 1

First Edition

To Michael, Simon, and Sarabinh,

with love and gratitude,

and

to the memory of Janie Glaeser West

(1939-1981)

Contents

"Only a villain would dare to be true to himself."

—MARY McCARTHY, "THE INVENTIONS OF I. COMPTON-BURNETT"

Introduction

M ary McCarthy belongs with a handful of American writers whose lives embody legends at least as vivid as their prose. One thinks of Hemingway, though Hemingway's adventures were followed by millions of people, while the scandalous sides of McCarthy's career, her slashing wit and amatory wanderings, were the subject of "red-hot gossip" mainly among fellow intellectuals. Nor did McCarthy have any imitators, as Hemingway did, which is not to say she is inimitable, only that she is an original. Her act, most notably a passion for laying bare deception that made her a whistle-blower in the House of Culture, is a hard one to follow, and was for McCarthy herself, who 'mellowed' in middle age, by her own admission—a causality perhaps of the satisfactions of a happy marriage (her fourth) and the ambiguous legacy of a best-selling novel, *The Group*.

If Hemingway comes to mind, it is because both writers, different as they are, mined their turbulent lives for the particular sensations of conflict and pain that fuel their art. One might say they lived their lives (in part) to keep the wick of invention burning: Hemingway, whose risk taking on a wartime assignment, at sea, on safari, was plainly calculated to provide him with the kind of experiences he was used to writing about; and Mary McCarthy, less consciously, whose serial affairs and taste for controversy, her willingness to "step right up to

[life] like a man at a free lunch counter," landed her in precisely the state of excited scruple that occasioned some of her liveliest prose. If Hemingway's 'manly' style masks an aesthetic sensibility of great delicacy, which of course it does, Mary McCarthy's aesthetic sensibility in fiction, memoir, and criticism follows on an inquisitive nature of sometimes Rabelaisian appetites.

The mellowing of Mary McCarthy was much remarked upon by friends in the mid-1980s, when hard into her seventies she began to collect the laurels befitting America's 'First Lady of Letters': the National Medal for Literature and the MacDowell Medal for Literature in 1984, election to the American Academy and Institute of Arts and Letters in the spring before her death in October 1989—none of which conveyed to contemporary readers the "radical turn of her mind. . . . the daring of the self-assertion, the brashness of the correcting tendency," as Elizabeth Hardwick once put it, noting, in later years, how the correcting tendency sometimes expressed an eccentric conservatism, an attachment to a "lost ideal America."

Some of McCarthy's contemporaries found it hard to forget the legendary scandals. "You've got to remember that we don't see Mary as a gray-haired lady," the writer Eileen Simpson reminded me in 1987; "we remember her as she was. . . . When Mary stroked your arm, that was real blood that came out." Which was part of the legend of "Bloody Mary," a woman whose critical performances, in person and in print, frequently filled reviews of her work with references to scissors, swords, and knives.

It was the same with her legendary beauty: the forthright good looks that could still be seen in the gray-haired lady whose ruffled blouses and fine tweed suits, lacy stockings and puritan black pumps, disconcerted her old acquaintances. In his memoir, *The Truants*, William Barrett recalls "the attractive and engaging woman" who arrived at a party in the 1940s "all smiles," and two or three men froze "as if an ogress, booted and spurred, had entered the room brandishing her whips." McCarthy's beauty was accompanied by an uncommon intelligence, which is what may have put the men off; but there was truth in the fear that she had the goods on everybody, and was not above using what she knew. (In her foreword to McCarthy's posthumous *Intellectual Memoirs, New York 1936–1938*, Elizabeth Hardwick "express[es] some relief that her memoirs did not proceed to me and my life . . .") In Barrett's opinion, the "stinging whip" was the "impeccable syntax with which she might lash out in print at any time"; while in Alfred Kazin's judgment, it was a "wholly destructive critical mind" that made Mary McCarthy one of the most dangerous of the rogue intellectuals who cut their teeth at *Partisan Review* in the 1930s and '40s.

Among McCarthy's harshest critics are the wives of New York intellectuals, who, like Ann Birstein, once married to Alfred Kazin, remember her bitterly as "one of the boys," mainly because she ignored the women. "They were all Tootsie Rolls," she seemed to think, in Birstein's recollection. With her appetite for gossip, Mary and her third husband, Bowden Broadwater, reminded Birstein in the 1950s of "a pair of preying mantises. . . . 'Give us Willliam Phillips! Let us have William Phillips!' " she recalls them exclaiming when the name of *Partisan Review*'s editor came up in conversation. Eileen Simpson, who was married to the poet John Berryman, and feared the "younger Mary because I was afraid of the tongue and the quickness of the wit," but became friendly with her later, remembers the scattered voices who privately welcomed Lillian Hellman's $2.25 million lawsuit against McCarthy in 1980—for calling Hellman a liar on "The Dick Cavett Show"—because they thought "Mary should be punished for all the terrible things she said about people all those years."

Such voices harried McCarthy all her life, beginning with the mean-spirited guardians who were put in charge of the four McCarthy children when they were orphaned in 1918. After laying these ghosts to rest in *Memories of a Catholic Girlhood*, Mary McCarthy's classic memoir of a peripatetic childhood, she inured herself to the later voices, which included a legion of angry Catholics misled by the 1957 book's title and the author's Irish-Catholic name into expecting something inspirational.

Toward the end of her life, McCarthy was surrounded by loyalists who were salvaged from every chapter of her career. The long train of friendships lent continuity to a life of multiple households, pyramiding social and professional commitments, constant travel. But there remained a curious gap in the attention paid her over the years. No one ever came forth to give her work—some twenty-two books of distinguished fiction, criticism, art history, political journalism, and memoirs—the same exacting critical attention she gave the writing of others she admired. The reviews might be "friendly," but as McCarthy's publisher, William Jovanovich, noted ruefully of the notices extended *The Writing on the Wall* in 1970, "very few . . . seem to judge the essays for what they say about other writers, about writing and criticism and the conduct of life through letters; rather they tend to rate your degree of approval."

"But do you *like* her?" my editor at *Geo* magazine, David Maxey, wanted to know in 1983, after I had submitted the transcript of a long interview conducted with McCarthy a few years earlier in Castine, Maine. It was an odd question and I never forgot it, whether because it missed all the interesting points about the career of this controversial woman, or because it was one I couldn't answer, I don't know. But for a great many people, there is something in Mary McCarthy that remains unassimilable that keeps this question alive.

Mary McCarthy's work is unimaginable without her life, which fed it like a furnace of the gods. Proust's biographer George Painter is said to have documented much of his biography from *Remembrances of Things Past*, and one can do the same with McCarthy's fiction, which is packed with "real plums," real people and places ("What I really do is take real plums and put them in an imaginary cake," she once explained), whose taste and texture betray their origins in reality. Yet one must proceed with caution, for while McCarthy's 'remembrances' are firmly grounded in experience—indeed, that is their lifeblood and the source of her peculiar faith in writing as an invocation to truth—they also transform experience, as both fiction and memoir are wont to do.

The distinction has not always been observed. And if McCarthy hasn't received the critical attention she deserves, it is partly because her mastery of the art of self-exposure has tended to discourage attempts to assess her achievement, as if she had arrogated the critic's task to herself. Her very notoriety has obstructed a serious assessment of her place in American letters, as if this woman who, following a tragic childhood seemed to 'have it all'—the husbands and lovers, the fearless convictions, the fame and modest fortune, the 'impeccable syntax'—could not, at the same time, possess the talent and competence to create a body of work that stands on its own.

Today, McCarthy's epigrammatic prose, her preference for sense over sensibility, her eye for the perils involved in living for ideas, beckons to new readers precisely because it does stand alone. She remains a "neoclassicist in a country of romantics," as a critic observed in 1968. And yet she was a romantic, too; and her fierce partisanship in both personal relations and politics—another story, explored in the pages ahead—also set her outside the pale.

I was first introduced to Mary McCarthy in the Russian Tea Room in New York in 1967 by Robert Silvers, coeditor of *The New York Review of Books*. McCarthy, the magazine's Vietnam correspondent, was on her way to Hanoi, from where I had recently returned. She had set aside a novel, *Birds of America*, in order to involve herself in efforts to end the war. I had left a fledgling career as a film and book reviewer to start an antiwar magazine, *Viet-Report*, "an Emergency News Bulletin on Southeast Asian Affairs," which picked up where the established media stopped in its coverage of the war.

As a graduate student at the University of Chicago in the early 1960s, I had written a masters thesis on Simone de Beauvoir and Anaïs Nin, titled, with sophomoric pomposity, "Two Women Who Would Write." Mary McCarthy had been added in a postscript after I read *Memories of a Catholic Girlhood* and McCarthy's first collection of stories, *The Company She Keeps*. Perhaps I was moved by certain correspondences with my own history, though I wouldn't have thought of it then. I, too, was raised a Catholic and went to Vassar. I liked McCarthy's deft applications of irony and wit to the wounds of life, and the hint of a wilder current running beneath the taut surface of her prose. When I met her in the Russian Tea Room, however, I had forgotten all this. She was the famous author of *The Group*, a member of the older generation, and I had become a foot soldier in the revolution.

My world had both expanded and contracted, as lives do in periods of transition. I had flown to Phnom Penh, Vientiane, Hanoi; addressed teach-ins and antiwar rallies. I had become an expert in limited war doctrine, with an interest in mapping the corridors of power behind the military/academic complex. The literary world, with its pop-up personalities and fast-food ideas—Norman Mailer on sex, cancer, death; Susan Sontag on 'the pornographic imagination'— seemed faintly seedy in 1967; politics had come to the rescue.

Politics, however, had stolen my memory. And it was partly to get it back that I wrote McCarthy in 1979 to propose an interview, "as a first step in a larger project, a book perhaps," I added, though I don't remember thinking about writing this biography until five years later, after the initial interview was published in *The Nation* in May 1984. Maybe I thought a book would help McCarthy take the interview proposal more seriously, since I had no assignment. But all I remember wondering then was, *Whatever happened to Mary McCarthy?*

What I was also asking was whatever happened to my original interest in writing, writers, and Mary McCarthy, who made the politics, mores, and manners of her literary generation spring to life in stories and essays with a buoyancy I found nowhere else. When I began researching this book and immersed myself in the literature and history of the 1930s and '40s, the period when McCarthy came of political age,

I was more interested in the generation than its scribe. It is, after all, the granddaddy generation: the last one to sustain a critical involvement with the world around it. I wanted to understand how and why its writers pulled back from their early promise; but also, in exploring McCarthy's life and work, along with the visions of others with whom she was intimately involved—Philip Rahv, Dwight Macdonald, Edmund Wilson, Nicola Chiaromonte, Hannah Arendt—I hoped to recreate something of the sturm und drang of an age that seems all too remote from the Siberian nights of our own.

This was before I felt the tug of McCarthy's personality in interviews (around eighteen, conducted in Castine, Paris, and New York in 1980, and from 1985 to 1989), a personality that invariably connected influential events and 'turning points' to social interactions. Mary McCarthy, who lived *in relations* the way other people are attached to things, places, belief systems, helped turn this book into a real biography. With the intensity of her feeling for the people who shaped her life—her 'group,' I came to see it, friend *and* foe—she helped root my own theorizing mind in the material world.

McCarthy was aware of my ulterior interests, and reassured by them, or so she suggested during a panel discussion on biography in which we both participated in New York in 1987. Then she answered a question from the floor about why she had "let [me] in the door," giving me access to her personal papers, and so on, without retaining the usual controls available to living subjects of biographies, by saying (among other things) that insofar as I was "writing about [myself]" in my book about her, she would not presume to interfere. The remark disturbed me, suggesting that our identities had merged, an occupational hazard of biography writing. But it was because I was impelled by my own concerns, McCarthy explained to me later, that the book had acquired "legitimacy" in her eyes. "You would have a reason to write that wasn't commercial exploitation of a 'known' figure or a purely arbitrary fastening on another life," she said. "Most current biographies have no real motive for being. Unless it's an evil one," she added, naming a well-known biographer she hated.

In our interviews, she was often stimulated by the generational theme and by political questions stemming from different premises than her own. My initial curiosity about her indifference to women's issues, for example, triggered a startling peroration on the "self-pity, shrillness and greed" she found in modern feminism, and a tirade against Simone de Beauvoir that sets McCarthy's own paradoxical relations to men, and to her own femininity, in bold relief. My interest in the relationships between writers and their patrons—the Communist party in the 1930s and '40s, the CIA in the 1950s and '60s—was not a burning interest of Mary's; and yet the inquiry that runs through *Writing Dangerously*, and her responses, turn up new information and fresh insights into the complicated mechanisms of mutual deception that often characterize such ties.

"Human beings are too important to be treated as mere symptoms of the past. They have a value which is independent of any temporal processes—which is eternal, and must be felt for its own sake." This is Lytton Strachey in his 1918 preface to *Eminent Victorians*, and he is right, of course; though it takes a "contradictious" character such as General Gordon of Khartoum, one of Strachey's Victorians—or Mary McCarthy—to drive the point home. Nor is a human being's ultimate value revealed with any more perspicacity by reference to psychological processes, the habit of contemporary biographers, than to 'temporal' ones. And yet a critical biography must recreate the web of processes—the multitude of influences out of which an identity is forged—before what is 'eternal' in an individual's character and achievement can be distinguished from what is ephemeral or hostage to the past.

Strachey advises the biographer who would avoid a mere piling up of facts and opinion to "attack his subject in unexpected places," to

> fall upon the flank, or the rear, [to] shoot a sudden, revealing searchlight into obscure recesses . . . [or] row out over that great ocean of material, and lower down into it . . . a little bucket, which will bring up to the light of day some characteristic specimen . . . to be examined with a careful curiosity.

It is a good idea, particularly the bucket approach; and Strachey applies it brilliantly in the four sketches, "haphazard visions," he calls them, that comprise *Eminent Victorians*. I admire this triumph of the 'New Biography,' but as the length of this book attests, I haven't matched its brevity. There are too many stories to tell in the life of a storyteller such as Mary McCarthy, the most tantalizing one being the mysterious arrangement of memory and invention that characterizes the life story the writer tells herself.

CAROL BRIGHTMAN
Walpole, Maine
February 1992

Part One

∎

Seattle/Minneapolis/Seattle: 1912–1929

Prologue

*I*n *How I Grew*, Mary McCarthy remembers being taken to the house of a notorious Seattle bohemian, a lesbian named Czerna Wilson who reads 'advanced books' and presides over a salon. It is 1928, the summer after her junior year at the Annie Wright Seminary, and as always McCarthy is desperate to escape what remains of an orphaned childhood. She has just turned sixteen, and is therefore eligible to "step out" with boys according to the rules that prevail in her grandparents' house, but two years have elapsed since she lost her virginity to a man nearly twice her age in the front seat of a Marmon roadster.

At Czerna Wilson's, McCarthy is exploring new territory. She is not interested in becoming a lesbian, she declares in her memoir, "having been groped more than once by hairy girls who had had me to stay the night." Her heart is set on men and boys, although she doesn't take much physical comfort in them, either. "Sex and love and social conquest were inseparably wedded in my mind with men," McCarthy writes, "even though the male organs were far from beauteous in my eyes."

She is drawn to the notorious Czerna "aesthetically, as a superb foreign object, as a possibility of what one might become, with resolution. . . . It was her insouciance, above all, that I would have wanted to imitate." Czerna Wilson—who appears to be Czech, a onetime dancer, said to have been discovered in a cabaret by her American husband at the end of World War I—is quite simply the most sophisticated person McCarthy has ever met. And sophistication, an air of living dangerously while remaining invulnerable to the blandishments of conscience and the blame and envy of others, is important to McCarthy, more important than either sex or men. Certainly it would be important to her as a writer, although not so important as to preclude a lively sense of truth about herself, as when she observes, in another context, "I was a sucker for style."

It is when McCarthy's crisp, *soigné* prose is put into the service of narrating her sexual history—a history which in somebody else's autobiography might elicit a knashing of teeth—that one grasps the paradox in her method. Naturally the most sophisticated person she would ever meet (at sixteen) would be a lesbian, for whom sex appeared to be a simple dalliance with one's own sex, and not the devil's bargain it often seemed to be with the *opposite* sex. Behind McCarthy's racy prose, in fact, lurks a strangely fastidious reserve on the question of sexuality. In print, she is saucy when depicting a man's seduction of a woman, when all along one senses that her oddly passive heroines are being punished for their own seductiveness. But in a larger sense promiscuity in her writing may have always served McCarthy as a kind of purdah, a place of concealment in a world that regards an intellectual woman, which is what she was, as a freak of nature. As for Czerna, that "superb foreign object," in the end she is more important as an instrument of social ambition than as a model of anything Mary McCarthy will become. One of Czerna Wilson's evening parties is remembered as a "coming-out party—the only one I would have." But Czerna is an early model, nonetheless, of a classic American type, a kind of imposter who in one guise or another will often figure in McCarthy's life and capture her imagination.

With her thick lips and long bronze-colored pigtail, her ashy skin, green eyes, and flared nostrils, from which tendrils of smoke drift lazily (she is "not beautiful," McCarthy writes, but "erotic and dangerous"), Czerna, like Mary McCarthy herself, may not be what she appears, a fact of life typically granted in fiction. In fiction, however, McCarthy herself is more literal-minded, more the moralist, than in either memoir or criticism. In *How I Grew,* she wonders mischievously whether the name Czerna may not have been apocryphal, a borrowing from the "Czerny piano exercises." With her "slow, lazy movements, matching a slow, lazy voice," which carried no accent, she suddenly recalls, Czerna Wilson was probably an "octoroon" (and no doubt she was;

czerna, though McCarthy doesn't say it, is Czech for "black"). For McCarthy, the word slithers off the tongue, suggesting a variant past, dark and sultry and southern, which she doesn't pursue, leaving it to the word *octoroon* to evoke.

Old Seattle was full of such types, like the "baron" Mary McCarthy took up with after she was " 'launched' " at one of Czerna Wilson's parties, a Russian Jew who emigrated after the 1917 Revolution. As a port, Seattle attracted what McCarthy once called "a veritable Foreign Legion of adventurers—soldiers of fortune, younger sons, gamblers, traders, drawn by the money to be made in virgin timber and shipping and by the Alaska Gold Rush." The arrival of one more mountebank on Queen Anne Hill, the site of the city's artistic community, could scarcely have raised an eyebrow. It is sixteen-year-old Mary McCarthy—with her dark glossy hair already drawn into a decisive knot at the nape of the neck—whose presence at the center of Seattle's bohemia invites a closer look.

What was a 'nice girl' like the granddaughter of a prominent Seattle attorney, Harold Preston, doing in a place like Czerna's, anyway? Sixty years later, McCarthy wondered herself, but it wasn't the impropriety of the setting that impressed her so much as her luck in gaining admittance. Thinking back over her first visit to Czerna Wilson's—when she and the friend who brought her had " 'caught' " the famous Seattle hostess in bed with a young woman—McCarthy wonders what "qualifications" might have been offered on her own humble behalf. What did she have to contribute to such storied company? What, she supposes, but her own " 'story,' " and she tosses it off lightly—"orphanhood, my beautiful mother, my grandmother, and the rest"—as if she is not divulging an interesting fact about herself: Namely, that even in 1928, long before she began to spin the raw materials of a tempestuous life into literary gold, McCarthy's 'story' preceded her and opened doors. With the publication of *Memories of a Catholic Girlhood* in 1957, Mary McCarthy's bildungsroman, the 'story' became a legend—but neither story nor legend hold a candle to the life.

1

A Child of Parts

*"She was pretty, she dressed expensively, she
was gay, she made friends, and the only remarkable
thing about her was that she had the air of coming
from nowhere, of having no past."*
—MARY McCARTHY, "GHOSTLY FATHER, I CONFESS"

Seattle in 1912, the year Mary Therese McCarthy was born, was a
city of steep descents and sudden turns. On the water side, the streets
fell away to teeming docks along Puget Sound. It was a watery city,
more watery then than now, and ringed with mountains: the serrated,
snow-covered Olympics to the west, the blue-green Cascades in the
east, and to the southeast, Mt. Ranier, gliding like a ghost ship fourteen thousand feet above the horizon. From his bedroom window on
a clear day Mary's midwestern-born father, Roy McCarthy, enjoyed a
handsome prospect of the mountain. "Mt. Ranier visible all day and
evening," he noted on April 29, 1918, in the leather-bound calendar
that doubled as the family log; it was the most beautiful view he had
ever seen. Lake Washington, nearer the McCarthy's brick house on
Twenty-fourth Avenue, "looked smooth as glass with the moon shining upon it." Mary's father lacked a way with words, but it didn't keep
him from trying to put into words the tender thoughts that other men
might keep to themselves.

Beyond Lake Washington, the harbor, crowded with ships bound
for the Orient, and for the Inland Passage to southeast Alaska, the
Aleutian chain, and the Bering Sea, was still the embryo of a city whose
commerce had leapt the borders of the continental United States.
Seattle, once a tidy settlement of land speculators from the East, who
traded shakes and shingles with the Hudson's Bay Company for sup-

plies, and fought the Yakima Indians, had indeed become the bustling depot that Mary McCarthy evokes in memoir. The settlers' sons and grandsons had become lumber barons and steamship executives, and they had been joined by great trading companies, such as the Northwest Trading Company, for whom Seattle provided the staging ground for the expansion of the fur trade and the fisheries into Alaska.

When Mary McCarthy came into this world on June 21, 1912, Seattle was still a boomtown, pressing hard on the riches of the Northwest and the Alaskan wilderness; pressed from behind, as well, by the private interests of the railroads and the Vanderbilt and Astor trading money from the East. News of Seattle society had not yet reached the gossip columns of *Vogue* and *Vanity Fair,* something Mary noted ruefully in her teens when she scanned the magazines in her Seattle grandmother's sewing room. Inside the great houses overlooking Lake Washington, at the theatre and concert halls, in the dining rooms of the Hotel Washington and the Olympia Club, a kind of Gilded Age was in flower, an age that had already gone by in New York, Boston, and Philadelphia. For McCarthy, however, 'society' would remain a property of the East.

Lawyers such as Mary's grandfather, Harold Preston, commanded positions of influence in Seattle that were hard to match in the older towns they had left behind (Rockford, Illinois, in Preston's case, though both his parents were from Vermont). Their domestic arrangements reflected an easy access to the cheap labor and imported luxuries of an expanding port. Their wives and children, especially their daughters, were petted and indulged to a degree that is hard to imagine today. Among the professional classes, the Victorian ceremonies of the bourgeois household seemed to be exaggerated in Seattle, as if good taste and fashion might compensate them for living in such a rough-and-tumble place.

Fur, timber, fish, and gold, these were Seattle's elements; to extract them, process, and sell them was the business of the city—but it was not notably a business in which either McCarthy's father, who was also a lawyer, with a shadowy partner and a small office downtown in the Hoge Building, or her maternal grandfather, Harold Preston, were directly involved. Years before Mary McCarthy was born, her grandfather's firm, Preston, Thorgenstein and Turner, had established itself as an interpreter of state and federal law in the Seattle region, and Harold Preston more often than not had faced the railroads and the lumber interests from an opposing corner of the courtroom. In 1895, Preston, who had fallen in love with the Northwest when he worked on a geodetic survey during a summer vacation from college, had chaired the commission that drew up the city's second charter, the one that still serves today as the foundation for Seattle's government. From 1897 to 1901, he had been a member of the state senate, and in 1903 he had run for the U. S. Senate on a platform of good government and fair labor practices, and was defeated, as Mary always heard it, by "the interests." In 1911 this staunch Republican lawyer wrote the statute that created the nation's first workmen's compensation law. "The Seattle plutocracy left my grandfather completely cold," McCarthy recalled many years later; "his friends were these old judges and law-yers, maybe a doctor or two." After 1912, however, Preston's career seems to have settled into a more conventional groove of private practice; very little in either his business or his social life exposed him or his family to the turbulent life of the city whose development he had once had a hand in shaping.

It was through Mary McCarthy's Jewish grandmother, Augusta Morganstern Preston, that the family was tied more directly to the material life of the city. Gold had drawn her parents—Mary's great-grandfather Abraham Morganstern and his wife, Therese—to California in 1849. These old German Jews who had joined the historic exodus out of revolutionary Europe in 1848 were gone; but something of their spirit may have survived in the cultivated appetites of their daughter Augusta, or Gussie as she was called, for fine clothes and personal ornament, good food, exquisite decor, and an occasional day at the races. A very young Mary McCarthy saw her grandmother as a "fairy-tale person who lived in an enchanted house, which was full of bulges": the balconies and deep bay windows of the Preston house in the Madrona district of Seattle, where there was a little bulge under the dining room table that summoned the maid. There is a storybook quality to McCarthy's Seattle grandmother, who emerges in the recol-lections of others as one of those pampered creatures who worship at the temple of their own bodies.

By 1912, the western gold was transmuted into lead and steel. And the air near Seattle's harbor was full of the smell of gasoline, fish oil, and fertilizer from the canneries, where Iron Chinks, machines so-called for the Chinese labor they replaced, butchered and cleaned the fish. The port had spawned thousands of industrial plants, though not much of this Seattle enters McCarthy's memories of the city; nothing of the industrial melting pot of Scandinavians and Finns, Irish, Italian, and Balkan construction workers; German, French, and English tradesmen who arrived during the first quarter of the century; and nothing of the migrant workers for whom the Northwest was famous, who labored in gangs in woods and mines and on rivers, and swept into town like roughriders after the breakup of their camps. Only a face picked out of the crowd here and there: an Irish maid who worked for her parents; a Japanese manservant employed for the holidays, who appears in a family snapshot standing stiffly beside a snowman, wearing a sheepskin cap like a small Russian boyar, a McCarthy child in his arms; a couple of "working stiffs" Mary remembers scratching for potatoes in a vacant lot near her house on Twenty-fourth Avenue; something about a dangerous neighborhood called "Coon Hollow" coming from her father.

Seattle's Jewish population was a miniature of European Jewry. Jews who arrived after the 1890s were referred to as "the Israelites" or "the Hebrews" by German Jews who had made some money and established themselves in private clubs. German Jews promoted a notion of "home colonies," a sort of benevolent ghetto to civilize the less fortunate Jews from the Pale, who had often come by way of New York City and regarded themselves as 'labor,' a force to be reckoned with. Like most of the Morgansterns, Gottsteins, and Aronsons, Mary McCarthy's relations on her Grandmother Preston's side, the prosperous Jews patronized the Temple de Hirsch, named after the Baron de Hirsch, who had reformed traditional observances along Anglican lines and fostered programs of cultural uplift for the poor.

In McCarthy's recollections, the Jewish members of her extended family spring to life with a vividness that has not always been welcomed by their direct descendants—one of whom considered suing the author of *How I Grew* in 1987 for defaming the character of her ancestors. "Immense-breasted Aunt Henny" and her children "seemed very alien to me," McCarthy writes, referring to them as "clannish, Temple-going Jews. . . ." Uncle Moses Gottstein, married to McCarthy's Aunt Rosie (who endeared herself to Mary, in part because she 'mixed' in Seattle society), is noted for his "incipient cataracts, full rosy cheeks, raised eyebrows, cigar in teeth, rosy lips showing gums, benign smile." These are almost stock figures, sagging under the weight of caricature—like the fat, waddling women in McCarthy's juvenile fiction, who are not Jewish but *feel* Jewish to the author many years later because they are invested with a repulsion she remembers feeling for the "Jewish quarter" of herself. This was the quarter she "half-tried to disavow—a project all the more tempting," she adds, "in that 'it' did not show."

She "liked Uncle Moses A. (for Abraham?) Gottstein," McCarthy claims in the memoir, but she "did not much like his appearance," which was too 'Jewish.' A similar polarization between 'High German' and 'Hebrew' that existed in the larger society seemed to play itself out inside Mary's own family, or at least in how she herself perceived the family's Jewish component. To maintain contradictory judgments about one's antecedents is sometimes an accommodation to the warring factions in one's own identity—in McCarthy's case, Catholic, Protestant, and Jew each weighing in for a knockout blow. But in typical American fashion, as McCarthy remarks shrewdly, it also allows someone "to be tolerant and prejudiced alternately. . . ."

Actually, in the great chain of being Jewish, Moses Gottstein stood in the middle of a social spectrum even more varied than McCarthy suggests. A woman who worked for Gottstein in the 1920s and 1930s recalls an "immaculately groomed" little man, wearing a battered homburg and a rose in his lapel, who was fond of declaiming passages from William Jennings Bryan, the "silver-tongued orator," and also of embarrassing the German Jewish owners of Schoenfeld's Standard Furniture Company, where he worked as a credit manager, by addressing them in a "Yiddish dialect." Mrs. Gottstein, the former secretary adds, was "a neat, bright little gentlewoman" whose considerable musical abilities (no news to Mary) were originally nurtured in a San Francisco convent.

A bit further out on the social spectrum was Joe Gottstein, Moses Gottstein's brother, a well-known Seattle vice figure. According to one of Mary McCarthy's early friends from Seattle, Jess Rosenberg, Joe Gottstein was rumored to have run the "black and tan district" in the 1920s and 1930s in concert with law-enforcement elements in the city that presided over prostitution and speakeasies during Prohibition. "If you got into trouble in Seattle," Rosenberg remembers, "you got in touch with Joe Gottstein"—who was a kind of 'fixer,' as much at home on the urban frontier of the American West as Moses Gottstein and his musical wife, Rosie. Or Mary's great-aunt Eva Aronson, Augusta Preston's oldest sister, who married a rich Seattle fur importer, lived in a big house with polar bear rugs, and gambled.

The patriarch on the other side of Mary McCarthy's Seattle family was her great-grandfather Simon Manly Preston, who was no less colorful. A Civil War veteran, Preston had retired a brigadier general in the Union Army, in which he had commanded a black regiment in Mississippi. When his wife died in 1890 in Illinois, where he had speculated in real estate, Simon Preston followed his four grown children to the Northwest and started a new career at the age of seventy managing a bank building in downtown Seattle. He died in 1920 at ninety-eight after having acquired a certain local celebrity.

All these figures throw fresh light on provincial society in the Northwest, in which the Jews and Irish both were protected from some of the traditional opprobrium meted out east of the Mississippi, by the presence of large colonies of Scandinavians, Finns, and Orientals who did most of the city's dirty work. Nor would a Yankee such as Mary's grandfather, Harold Preston, have been likely to marry a young woman named Gussie Morganstern in 1888 if he had lived in Illinois— or in Mississippi, where Simon Manly Preston had served as a U.S. claims agent after the Civil War, and where Harold Preston could remember southern ladies drawing aside their skirts in scorn when he and his mother passed them in the streets of Natchez. Seattle, more than San Francisco, carried the dream of the frontier into the twentieth century, and for a certain kind of flatlander who missed the grand opening of the American West a hundred years before, Seattle promised to bring it all back—not only the frontier but a frontier with the lure of a world port.

One wonders what Mary McCarthy might have done with the Morgansterns, Gottsteins, and Aronsons of Seattle if her memories were of a Jewish girlhood. It may be significant that the first real friend she ever made (in 1926) was a Jewish girl named Ethel Rosenberg— Jess Rosenberg's sister, known as "Ted"— and the great friendship of her life was with the political philosopher Hannah Arendt, a German Jew. But McCarthy's relationship to the 'Jewish quarter' in her background remained too ambivalent to allow for much exploration. One is never quite satisfied reading McCarthy on her Jewish connections that one is getting the promised goods. But then neither were Mary's Jewish relations, beginning with her Seattle grandmother, ever eager to confide in her. She was the offspring of a Catholic marriage, after all, one which appeared doomed at the start. When her parents died in 1918, and later, in 1923, she came to live in the Prestons' house, it was with a past that begged to be reinvented.

II

When they were married in 1911, Mary McCarthy's parents each stepped across a line that separated them from more than the single life. Mary's mother, Therese (Tess) Preston McCarthy, reputed to be "the most beautiful woman in Seattle," had adopted the faith of her husband. And Mary's father, a favorite son who seemed to have tapped inexhaustible stores of goodwill in nearly everyone who knew him, despite the fact that he had dissipated most of his adult life in intermittent bouts of drunkenness, had embraced sobriety. It was not a marriage a marriage broker would bet on; but Roy and Tess McCarthy, by all accounts, radiated affection for each other, and for the daughter and three boys who were born to them in such rapid succession that the Prestons worried for Tess's health.

In 1909, at the age of thirty, Roy McCarthy had been sent west by his father, J. H. McCarthy, a wealthy Minneapolis grain merchant, to work for a timber brokerage business in Portland, Oregon. The assignment came at the end of a long chain of abuses of the family trust—after Roy had bounced in and out of jobs and drying-out hospitals for years, once running off with a nurse who had been assigned to his care. The elder McCarthys had nearly given up on this oldest son whose troubles with the bottle may have commenced with the collapse of a promising football career in college, when doctors had discovered a heart severely damaged by an earlier siege with rheumatic fever. Two thousand miles away from his family, however, Roy had surprised them all when he had fallen in love with Tess Preston, a popular University of Washington coed with a husky contralto voice, who even if she was a daughter of "the Chosen" (a favorite McCarthy epithet in Minneapolis) had turned herself into an exemplary Catholic. He had taken his bride back to Minneapolis, to an apartment in the Hotel Maryland, and started to work for McCarthy Brothers, the family grain-elevator business (grain being the 'element' in the McCarthys' lives), and he had promptly fallen off the wagon again. Sadly, J. H. McCarthy had advised Tess McCarthy to return to Seattle alone and leave Roy in Minneapolis, but Tess would have none of it, and she had persuaded her husband that they should both return to Seattle and begin again.

It was after this second start that Mary's father enrolled himself in the University of Washington's Law College, not without encouragement from his father-in-law, one guesses, though as always it would have been his father who footed the bills. Roy McCarthy never made any money, but he had acquired a knack for remaining forever in receipt of funds; and some $40,700 would be expended on his and his family's support from 1911 to 1918 by his father in Minneapolis. In 1915, he graduated from law school at the age of thirty-five, when Mary was three. And it looked as if he really had stopped drinking.

Roy's conversion, for such it appeared, may have been effected with the help of a nun from Mercy Hospital in Portland, Oregon, where he had briefly checked himself in during 1910. Undoubtedly, it owed something to the new regime of family life, or at least to how a rebel from the old regime—the kind that held the oldest son responsible for looking after the business—might respond to a gentler family life of his own devising. Roy, in any event, seemed to turn his participation in the raising of four children into a kind of adventure, an opportunity for endless experiment and observation. Even his bad heart conspired in the transformation of a rogue Irishman to a doting parent, forcing him to take to his bed for increasingly long intervals. At home, he had more time to entertain the "babies," as he called them—Mary, Kevin, and Preston, descending like steps to Sheridan, still in his cradle—and being entertained by them in turn. And yet after Roy McCarthy's apparent conquest of alcoholism, this invalidism in a man so young might be regarded as the crowning blow. And life in the enchanted household may not have been the romp it seems in Mary McCarthy's memoirs, but something more complex.

Roy McCarthy had been a *"romancer,"* a spinner of tales, Mary McCarthy reflects in the preface to *Memories of a Catholic Girlhood.* After the first two chapters of the book appeared in *The New Yorker* in 1948 and 1951, she had been corrected on so many points that she had come to see her father as the kind of person who made people invent stories about him. There was the story of his having been the captain of a University of Minnesota football team, when in fact it was only a Minneapolis high school team; and the more important matter of his supposed literary gift, which unraveled when Mary read his journal, *"a record of heights and weights, temperatures and enemas, interspersed with slightly sententious 'thoughts,' like a schoolboy's. . . ."* [Both the preface and afterword are italicized in the book.] Nothing more than the usual ancestral myths that circulate in families, but for Mary McCarthy, whose hunger for information about a parent she knew so briefly was greater than it is for most people, this evidence of *"mendacity . . . in the McCarthy blood"* was disconcerting.

Most of her memories, she feared, were colored *"by an untruthfulness that I must have caught from him, like one of the colds that ran around the family."* But on one point she would not yield: Her father was not a drunkard, and it was unlikely that he ever was, she argues, even after introducing her uncle Harry McCarthy's convincing testimony to the contrary—perhaps in the interests of a larger truth. Her own argument seems flimsy: She can remember her father trying unsuccessfully to make wine right before Prohibition, and her mother and some friends laughing about " 'Roy's wine.' " If her father had been a dangerous drinker, she maintains, her mother wouldn't have laughed. Moreover, if he had been a *"periodical drunkard,"* as Harry McCarthy, whose job it had often been to run after him, maintained, why was it that no one in her mother's family seemed to have known about it (to which Uncle Harry had retorted: " *'You would think they could have looked up their future son-in-law's history' "*)? She considers the obvious possibility that he had reformed after his marriage, and then immediately dismisses it: *"Periodical drunkards . . . almost never reform, and when they do, they cannot touch wine."* Still, an *"eerie"* mystery remains. An image swims up from the past: her father standing in the doorway, his arms full of red roses for her mother. *"It is a drunkard's appeasing gesture, certainly, lordly and off-balance,"* she observes. *"Was that why my mother said, 'Oh, Roy!'?"*

From the beginning, something was akilter about the McCarthy household, a certain imbalance between the busyness of the nursery and the languor which characterized Roy McCarthy's practical affairs that courted danger. When the whole family came down with colds, as they often did, Mary's Grandmother Preston sometimes tried to take charge. She would appear at the curb in front of the house on Twenty-fourth Avenue in her gray electric, McCarthy recalls, wearing a spangled suit and a hat with a dotted veil stretched tightly across her nose. She had recently been scarred by a plastic surgeon who had pumped too much wax into her face, although Mary didn't know it then; the "strange lady," she assumed, was always veiled.

On one occasion, Mrs. Preston had instructed Tess to assign each member of the family a separate towel, with a name card pasted carefully above the rack. Mary was impressed by the arrangement, which struck her as very stylish. The next day, however, her father spoiled it by using the wrong towel, and soon they were all mixed up again and the labels fell off. It was the only time that Mary McCarthy ever remembers being angry with her father—who seemed to suffer his mother-in-law's interventions with aplomb. During one of her visits, Mary and her brothers had climbed into Mrs. Preston's car, and it had started to roll. Tess had spanked them with her tortoiseshell comb, but her father had boasted of the exploit. " 'How did the little tykes do it?' " he wanted to know.

From the Prestons' point of view, there must have appeared something promiscuous about the Catholicism their daughter had embraced in marriage. It put an immoderate faith in God, which paradoxically seemed to relieve the faithful of full responsibility for themselves. Some of the flavor of this intimate relationship with the deity is captured in Mary McCarthy's memories of her early home, in which *"everything . . . conspired to fix in our minds the idea that we were precious little persons, precious to our parents and to God, too, Who was listening to us with loving affection every night when we said our prayers."* To her mother, being a Catholic was a "crowning treat and privilege"—a privilege that had dismayed her parents, who even after Tess's marriage wouldn't invite a priest or a nun into their home. Seven years and four children later, Tess and Roy seemed to have tossed all cares to the wind.

In *Memories of a Catholic Girlhood*, Mary McCarthy recalls her little diamond rings, beauty pins, an ermine muff and neckpiece; Easter egg hunts, birthday parties with grab bags and fish ponds full of gifts, a tiny electric stove upstairs from which her mother served hot chocolate and cambric tea, and a "glorious May basket" that her father once hung on her bedroom door. The basket appeared in 1917 when she was five. "Mary woke up at 4:20 A.M. to watch for the fairies bringing the May baskets . . ." her father wrote in the family log that year. He was the one who "heard" her prayers, read her *A Child's Garden of Verses*, along with his favorite poems by Eugene Field in the Seattle papers, and taught her to treasure a "treat," such as the small white mountain of sugar into which one dipped a peach. He also took her out to the boulevard near the Sacred Heart Convent to listen to a nightingale in the evening, when, of course, there are no nightingales in North America. Had she grown older with him, she might have come to see him in his relation to other men and the world. But she didn't, and in her memories he is frozen in time, or out of time: tall, handsome, a cavalier, whose walking stick appears like a magic wand; with "queer, lit-up gray-green eyes"—not unlike Mary McCarthy's own—and a wild strain, inherited (she once thought) from ancestors who settled the rocky cliffs of Nova Scotia and became land pirates.

On August 16, 1918, Roy McCarthy noted in his calendar that Tess had enrolled Mary in the Forest Ridge Convent for the fall term. The "babies" were growing up. Kevin was the "cheekiest." " 'Say Mom, who taught the first man in the world to go to the toilet?' " he had asked Tess once, while "enthroned." By 1918, when Mary was six and Kevin was five, he had developed a peculiar voice, rich and deep, which he used to hurl insults at passersby from the family car. It was Kevin who was always ready with a fresh stunt, like the little step he executed while singing "old Mister Jiggerfeller, I love you," reported gleefully by his father in letters to his youngest brother, Louis McCarthy.

" 'Why don't we say "Deliver us to evil",' " Mary once asked her father during prayers, " 'the way Mama does in Frederick and Nelson's when she tells them to deliver it to Mrs. McCarthy?' " The "cute" saying was reported to Mary's Grandmother McCarthy in Minneapolis in the last letter that Tess wrote before her death. Mary may have picked up a cue from Kevin. "There was premeditation behind it, surely; play-acting," McCarthy suggests in *How I Grew*, which casts by far the colder eye on early childhood than *Memories of a Catholic Girlhood*. "I knew perfectly well that children could not pray to be delivered to evil and was only being clever—my vice already—supplying my parents with 'Mary's funny sayings' to meet a sensed demand."

Kevin's pranks appeared less calculated, and sometimes dangerous. When Tess was in the hospital giving birth to Sheridan, it was Kevin who started the "bonfire" in the library on Twenty-fourth Avenue, lighting the first of many forbidden matches to what happened then to be his father's law books. And it was Kevin who was found toying with his father's pistol by his Grandmother Preston after Sheridan was born—*another* brother, whose arrival, Kevin McCarthy speculates today, probably made him jealous. His father, he remembers, never spanked him. Only once, after his father saw him throw a stone at a horse, does Kevin recall hearing him raise his voice in anger, and this was from the bedroom window, which by the spring of 1918 had become Roy McCarthy's vantage point on the world.

Though his doctors had warned him before his marriage *"that he might die at any moment,"* it was only then that Mary's father's health had really begun to fail him. In April 1918, he started taking ten drops of digitalis every four hours for his heart. In June, he was taking terpenhydrate with heroin for a bad cough that wouldn't go away. On June 27, he received a letter from his father, duly reported in the journal, but without comment. Was it the letter that ordered the family to begin their preparations for what would be the fatal trip to Minneapolis? The entry does not say. On September 15, Roy's father wired him that he had bought the family a house on Blaisdell Avenue, two blocks from his own.

On October 5, Roy noted that "the mayor had ordered all theatres, schools, churches, *etc.* closed until further notice, on account of the Spanish Influenza." The great flu epidemic of 1918 was in full swing. On October 8, Tess was very ill, he reported, but on the eleventh she was a little better and they both went out to see a play, oddly enough—one of the few that remained open. It was a red-letter day for Roy, "the first time I've been out in the evening since March 14." Afterwards, he

noticed that his ankles were swollen. Like an elderly heart patient
whose legs swell after the faintest exertion, Roy McCarthy was slowing down. He was thirty-eight, his wife was twenty-nine. They had
only a few weeks to live.

There isn't a hint in the family log of how Roy or Tess regarded
the impending journey. It is unlikely that Roy McCarthy kept his
feelings to himself; perhaps he and his wife considered the move provisional—and Mary's enrollment in the Forest Ridge Convent, and her
brief attendence there, had been a pledge to hold their ground in
Seattle. But all of a sudden, they were gone.

III

*"My parents' death was brought about by a decision on the part
of the McCarthy family,"* Mary McCarthy writes in *Memories of a
Catholic Girlhood. "They concluded—and who can blame them?—
that the continual drain of money, and my father's monthly appeals for
more, had to stop. It was decided that our family should be moved to
Minneapolis, where my grandfather and grandmother could keep an
eye on what was happening and try to curb my father's expenditures."*

At the end of October, the family had disposed of their belongings
and moved into the Hotel Washington (where Simon Preston, then
ninety-six, maintained a residence) to await the arrival of Roy's
brother Harry and his wife, Zula, who were to escort all six
McCarthys across the country. *"[T]hey brought the flu with them,"*
Mary's Grandmother Preston said later. Sheridan and possibly Zula
were already sick when the McCarthys boarded the train on October
31. When they arrived in Minneapolis four days later, it was to a
platform full of stretchers, wheelchairs, nervous redcaps, and dis-
traught officials—"and, beyond them, in the crowd," Mary McCarthy
remembers, "my grandfather's rosy face, cigar, and cane, my grandmother's feathered hat, imparting an air of festivity to this strange and
confused picture, making us children certain that our illness"—for
they had all caught the flu—"was the beginning of a delightful holiday." Four days later, on November 11, 1918, Tess McCarthy was
dead. Roy lived another day.

Mary McCarthy, who was quarantined with her small brothers in
the sewing room of her Catholic grandparents' house in Minneapolis,
tended by masked nurses who bustled around their iron cots like
orderlies in a field hospital, remained ignorant of her parents' deaths
until months later. No adult, no grandparent or guardian, took Mary

or Kevin or Preston on his knee and told them what had happened. Just outside the sewing room, priests and undertakers had come and gone, but Mama and Daddy, the children were informed, had gone to the hospital to get well. In her own way, in a manner that confirmed both the collapse of the family order and the birth of a savagely skeptical consciousness, Mary McCarthy came to learn the facts.

"We became aware, even as we woke from our fevers, that everything, including ourselves, was different," she recalls:

> We had shrunk, as it were, and faded, like the flannel pajamas we wore, which during these few weeks had grown, doubtless from the disinfectant they were washed in, wretchedly thin and shabby. The behavior of the people around us, abrupt, careless, and preoccupied, apprised us without any ceremony of our diminished importance. Our value had paled, and a new image of ourselves—the image, if we had guessed it, of the orphan—was already forming in our minds.

Everything the Seattle children could not understand, everything unfamiliar and displeasing that led them to question their surroundings, or register some faint protest, was now recast by the Minneapolis McCarthys as symptoms of *their* problem, their new condition:

> Before we got sick, we were spoiled; that was what was the matter now . . . we had not known what it was to have trays dumped summarily on our beds . . . to take medicine in a gulp . . . to have our arms jerked into our sleeves and a comb ripped through our hair . . . to be told to sit up or lie down quick and no nonsense about it, to find our questions unanswered and our requests unheeded, to lie for hours alone and wait for the doctor's visit, but this, so it seemed, was an oversight in our training, and my grandmother and her household applied themselves with a will to remedy the deficiency.

Gradually, the idea that their former life had been somehow ridiculous and unsuitable made the memory of it falter—"like a child's recitation to strangers," McCarthy adds. "We no longer demanded our due, and the wish to see our parents insensibly weakened. Soon we ceased to speak of it, and thus, without tears or tantrums, we came to know they were dead."

Mary McCarthy's apprehension of this fact was private, furtive—

even, one gathers from memoir, proud. But now attachment and separation, disappearance and death appeared dangerously entwined.
When Mary's brothers were suddenly removed from their grandparents' house without explanation, she did not wonder what had become
of them; they, too, she presumed, were dead. In actuality, they had
been taken to the house on Blaisdell Avenue by their new guardians,
a middle-aged couple who had materialized in their grandmother Elizabeth (Lizzie) Sheridan McCarthy's sun parlor a few weeks after Roy
and Tess McCarthy's deaths, and to whom all four children had been
presented in a somber ceremony whose significance was probably too
cruel to ponder then. Nor would Mary have wanted to remember it,
for while the man had displayed affection for her brothers, taking
each one on his lap and playing with him, he had paid her no heed at
all. It was a stunning slight, received with a *"queer ebb of feeling
inside. . . . He did not like me."* McCarthy recalls: *"I noticed this with
profound surprise and sorrow . . . not so much jealous as perplexed."*
Her six-year-old heart had grown cold; and when she woke up on the
day her brothers had gone, it had been easier to imagine them dead,
death being in the air, than to consider the possibility that she was
being left behind—as indeed she was, if only for a few months, for
reasons she couldn't understand.

She had thought herself "clever" to have guessed the truth about
her parents, "like a child who proudly discovers that there is no Santa
Claus." The revelation had come in fits and starts. When her Grandmother Preston arrived unexpectedly at her bedside, wearing a black
veil and crying uncontrollably, Mary's reason had been offended by the
fact of her turning up in Minneapolis when she was supposed to be in
Seattle. Her Grandfather Preston had tried to quiet his wife, patting
her and saying, " 'Come now, Gussie,' " which was when Mary had
first heard her grandmother called by her family name. When they
tiptoed away after telling her to be a good girl, Mary understood none
of it and no one enlightened her. "I heard the word 'flu,' " she recalls,

> but it was months before it dawned on me that the occasion had
> been my parents' funeral. Yet when I surmised, finally, that Mama
> and Daddy were not coming back, I felt a certain measure of relief.
> One mystery at least was cleared up: the strange lady had come
> and cried on my bed because her daughter was dead.

Once she knew the truth, however, she would say nothing about
it, or even allow herself to react to it privately. To grieve would be to

admit an inconsolable loss, and even at six she could not or would not appear inconsolable. Or perhaps if she kept the truth to herself, it might still be overruled by the miracle of her parents' reappearance.

It must have been with this hope in mind that Mary McCarthy remembers loitering week after week in the dark well of her grandparents' staircase, "waiting," she writes, "to see Mama when she would come home from the hospital, and then simply loitering with no purpose whatsoever." Anyway, she had come to a decision: " 'I would not co-operate in this loss.' " When her Grandmother Preston cried, it hadn't occurred to her that it might have also been because her grandchildren had lost their mother and their father. Certainly not. Such a show of compassion, too close to pity, was already unimaginable, perhaps impermissible for the oldest among " 'Poor Roy's children,' as commiseration damply styled [them]." To see the tragic turn of events reflected in other people's eyes was to lose one's private grip on the truth; the truth, in this instance, being too important and too uncertain to be entrusted to anyone but one's self.

2

Fall from *Grace*

" 'Say you did it, Mary Therese, say you did it.' "
—MARY MCCARTHY, "A TIN BUTTERFLY"

About cities, Mary McCarthy entertained the same fierce loyalties and stubborn antipathies that she did about people. Seattle appears in memoir as a "port," lively and open to the world, while Minneapolis is a "granary," a place of enclosure; the very word *granary*, with its flat, nasal twang, conjures up images of silos, warehouses, and rodents. Minneapolis, one gathers from nearly everything McCarthy ever wrote about the five years she lived in the city as an orphan, was not a place to be caught dead in.

The character of any town is set by what takes place in it; the dark, icy, municipal pallor of Minneapolis, as it appears in *Memories of a Catholic Girlhood*, is fixed, like the 'humour' of a stock character in an Elizabethan play, by the fact that McCarthy's parents died there. But even if they had survived, and Mary McCarthy had grown up in Minneapolis, the city, one suspects, would not have exercised the same hold over her imagination that Seattle did. In later life, Seattle was recalled in almost pastoral terms: "beautiful when I was a child," McCarthy told a *Life* magazine reporter in 1963, describing the nearby lakes and mountains, "a little in the calendar style, with the sense of the canoe and an Indian who wasn't there." The gleaming metallic city of the present had lost this allure. In Minneapolis, McCarthy might have grown up in a close-knit middle-class Catholic family, married a lawyer herself, she once suggested, and lived a conventional life; and all things considered, she was lucky, she thought, to have ended up "a Puget Sound type who went east to college."

Minneapolis, of course, would always be colored for Mary McCarthy by the conditions that prevailed in the house on Blaisdell Avenue, a boxy "jaundice-colored house," whose rooms she recalls as mere holding pens for furniture and people. More than the house, however—the same house she would have occupied with her parents— it was the character of her new guardians, Margaret and Myers Shriver, the McCarthy children's great-aunt and -uncle on their Grandmother McCarthy's side, that spoiled Minneapolis for Mary McCarthy forever.

In the pecking order that reigns in many extended families, especially Irish American families, Mary's Aunt Margaret and Uncle Myers were the poor relations, the house servants. A childless, middle-aged couple, only recently married, they had already become objects of J. H. McCarthy's charity—as Margaret Sheridan was before her marriage to Myers, a man who seems to have had no known occupation. Myers Shriver, a " 'mountain of blubber,' " as Mary's outspoken Uncle Harry recalled him in the 1940s, was once a pickle-buyer in Elkhart, Indiana; but apart from a brief stint as a traveling salesman for McCarthy Brothers (when, according to Harry McCarthy, Myers ate himself out of the job), he almost never left the yellow house near downtown Minneapolis during the five years that Mary lived with him. Under the circumstances, the Shrivers' appointment as the official guardians of " 'Poor Roy's children' " may have been welcomed, coming as it did with a new house and an annual stipend of $8,200 to feed and clothe the orphans. Such an appointment, however, might have carried with it an air of indentured service; and while Mary McCarthy never says so directly, one reads between the lines of anger and contempt she reserves for these commoners on the family tree, a horror that their inferior status might have rubbed off on her.

"One of the great shocks connected with the loss of my parents was an aesthetic one; even if my guardians had been nice," McCarthy declares, *"I should probably not have liked them because they were so unpleasing to look at and their grammar and accents were so lacking in correctness."* No doubt her attitude toward the Shrivers was colored by the fact that she had been left behind "to roam palely about my grandmother's living rooms," while her brothers went to live with Myers and Margaret. At six, she was judged old enough to " 'remember,' " and so she had been kept on for a few months by herself, "a dangling, transitional creature, a frog becoming a tadpole [*sic*]," after

her brothers, "poor little polyps," were embedded in the new structure around the corner. Memory had interceded on her behalf, as indeed it often would, "like a lawyer [who] represented [her] in court." Memory and her "supposed powers of criticism and comparison," McCarthy adds, entitled her to "a greater consideration"—but there was clearly more to it than that.

At her grandparents' house, Mary McCarthy may have snatched some consolation for a battered ego; but while she lived alone in the grander house, she had been been sent off by herself to a strange "academy," whose wintry classrooms McCarthy never could reconstruct—as if memory, mercifully in this instance, had abandoned the field. On Saturdays, she had been taken to the treatment table of a nearby doctor, where an electric current was run through her small body while she was forcibly restrained. What medical reason existed for this treatment in 1918, she never knew, unless, McCarthy once speculated, it was to help her recover from the flu. Perhaps it had to do with that stony silence of hers, which had led her grandparents to want to keep her with them.

In the end, though, Mary's grandparents' house had seemed a refuge of privilege. When later she ran away from Blaisdell Avenue, it was to return to those starchy parlors and dimly lighted foyers, where nothing could be touched but something of importance could be found—possessions, that is, evoking the wealth and stability of grandparents. "Wealth, in our minds, was equivalent to bounty," McCarthy reflects in her early memoirs, "and poverty but a sign of penuriousness of spirit." It was a lesson first learned in Seattle, where virtue went hand in hand with a certain extravagance. In Minneapolis, at Halloween and Christmas parties, when the grandchildren all assembled at their grandparents' house, Mary found herself on the other side of the fence. The contrast between her own and her brothers' threadbare appearance, and that of their "rosy, exquisite cousins" appeared to confirm the official judgment that "clearly, it was a generous impulse that kept us in the family at all. Thus the meaner our circumstances," McCarthy reflects, "the greater seemed our grandfather's condescension, a view in which we ourselves shared, looking softly and shyly on this old man . . . as the font of goodness and philanthropy. . . ."

Even her Grandmother McCarthy, whose bombastic image was preserved in the dressmaker's dummy standing in the sewing room, its enormous bosom sheeted like a mummy, had appeared likable to the foundling. Many of her grandmother's faults, her provincial contempt for outsiders, her niggardly indifference to her orphaned grandchildren, did not appear to be faults to Mary McCarthy when she was a child. Lizzie Sheridan McCarthy's bloodcurdling Catholicism, for example, could be awe-inspiring. Her father may have been a simple streetcar conductor in Chicago, but in those moments when she grappled with the devil—and also when she sat in her high-decked straw hat in the back seat of her Locomobile—Aunt Lizzie, as she was known in the family, almost appeared a Woman of Parts. It had thrilled Mary as a little girl to hear her rise up against "the Protestants" and the Ku Klux Klan and the "I Won't Work" Wobblies. Whether it thrilled her to hear her grandmother refer sneeringly to "the Chosen," in references to her daughter-in-law's family in Seattle, McCarthy doesn't say, but for a time her grandmother had succeeded in poisoning her childhood memories of Seattle. Seattle, which had elected a Wobbly mayor named Ole Hansen, and whose unions called a citywide general strike in 1919, gradually became "a disreputable place" in Mary's mind, a faraway city with "a dangerous district called Coon Hollow . . . and an 'I Won't Work' Ole for a mayor."

Years later, when Mary McCarthy entered middle age, one could hear an echo of her Grandmother McCarthy in the voice she perfected for her own moments of combat: the note of magisterial self-esteem, struck and held like a spell over the dubious observer, who knew that he or she had somehow strayed into a superior force field. McCarthy's relationship with her Grandmother McCarthy was exceedingly complex. Her own judgment that her grandmother displayed an Antoinettish disregard for her grandchildren's misery is all the more merciless in her memoirs for its frank appreciation of the villain's charms. However, when McCarthy explores the curious bond that sprang up between herself and her grandmother, once the latter had formally conceded Roy and Tess McCarthy's deaths, the importance of this Minneapolis matriarch in Mary McCarthy's development becomes apparent.

" 'She doesn't feel it at all,' " Mary used to hear her grandmother confide to visitors, almost proudly, as if Mary had been "a spayed cat that, in her superior foresight, she had 'attended to.' For my grandmother," McCarthy continues, "the death of my parents had become, in retrospect, an eventful occasion upon which she looked back with pleasure and a certain self-satisfaction." Alongside the curiosity of visitors (a "pornographic curiosity," McCarthy calls it) who whispered, " 'Do you suppose they remember their parents?' " and " 'Do they ever *say* anything?' " her grandmother's dry dismissal of the terror of death seems to have struck Mary as fortuitous in its way.

Lizzie McCarthy appeared unmoved by the emotion of grief, and the last thing she wanted was to arouse it in her wards—a desire she may have realized in the case of her granddaughter, who seems to have equated grief with self-pity. "I had the choice of forgiving those incredible relatives of mine or pitying myself on their account," McCarthy reflects in *How I Grew,* looking back on the interlude in Minneapolis nearly seventy years later as a kind of 'eventful occasion' herself, one which provided her with some of her most risible lines in countless public readings over the years. "Laughter is the great antidote for self-pity, maybe a specific for the malady," she suggests. "Yet probably it does tend to dry one's feelings out a little, as if by exposing them to a vigorous wind, so that something must be subtracted from the compensation. . . ."

A certain idealization of the past, on the other hand, served McCarthy as the antidote for her own grief over the death of her parents; at least it is a possibility suggested by Mary McCarthy's brother Kevin when she was still alive. "Surely she knows, or some part of her knows, that it was probably a difficult life for our parents in Seattle," Kevin McCarthy proposes, "but Mary keeps almost institutionalizing the past: 'the basket of flowers hanging on the door on May Day,' and you say—What a great guy!" Writing, Kevin adds, may have been her way of "getting things straight—of showing how things *should* be, in a perfect world." It is a theory of his that helps him explain the importance domestic ritual and ceremony came to play in his sister's life. "You look to things you can hang on to, *abiding* things that won't go away. There is that *slippage,*" he remarks, "that takes place when people disappear." Kevin also remembers the peach in its mountain of sugar, "like the snow on the top of Mt. Ranier." The things he remembers "were all sort of attractive," but memory in his case leaves room for alternate pasts.

Naturally, there was more to Roy and Tess McCarthy's lives together in Seattle than had met either of their older children's eyes, but if there was anything amiss, it is not explored in Mary McCarthy's memoirs. Life before the flu, life after the flu stood perhaps in too stark a contrast for her to consider that from Roy McCarthy's standpoint life in Seattle with his wife's family may have been more difficult after he grew sicker. The bare facts of his flight from Seattle suggest as much; but while McCarthy rarely hesitates to hazard a theory about someone else's unusual behavior, she leaves her father's motivation for the fatal trip to Minneapolis unexamined.

"The whole idea of traveling with a sick man and four small

children at the height of an epidemic seems madness," she writes in the preface to *Memories of a Catholic Girlhood*, but she understands why the *"risk"* was taken, she adds, from an old clipping saved by her Great-Grandfather Preston. " *'The party left for the East at this particular time in order to see another brother, Lewis McCarthy [Louis], who is in the aviation service and had a furlough home.' This was the last, no doubt, of my father's headstrong whims."* No doubt. But such a trip, beginning with the family's evacuation to a hotel, when theatres, hotels, and public conveyances were much-publicized points of contagion, seems more than "madness." It had courted death.

Mary's Grandmother McCarthy would have been the last to inquire into the circumstances behind the dangerous timing of her son's return to Minneapolis, but when all the children were safely settled with their guardians in the new house on Blaisdell Avenue, she had begun to satisfy their hunger for "mortuary reminiscences." As a special treat when they came to visit, she invited them into the rooms where their parents had died—"for the fact that, as she phrased it, 'they died in separate rooms' had for her a significance both romantic and . . . self-congratulary," McCarthy remembers, "as though the separation in death of two who had loved each other in life were beautiful in itself and also reflected credit on the chatelaine of the house, who had been able to furnish two master bedrooms for the emergency." " 'I turned my house into a hospital,' " was another refrain, reserved for other visitors, which signaled the story of the trays, the special cooking, the laundry and disinfectants, the expensive nurses, called up almost wistfully "like items on the menu of some long-ago ball-supper. . . ." By dying in her house Mary's parents had become "in a lively sense her property," McCarthy relates, "and she dispensed them to us now, little by little, with a genuine sense of bounty. . . ."

Mary and her brothers had begun to beg for these morsels of information, just as they begged for candy, books, movies, and friends to play with, all of which were withheld from them by Lizzie McCarthy's sister Margaret and her husband, Myers. As the memories were doled out they became the children's "secret treasures," McCarthy recalls: "we never spoke of them to each other but hoarded them, each against the rest, in the miserly fastness of our hearts." When the children returned to Aunt Margaret and Uncle Myers, they were "replenished" somehow, and "felt superior to them," even though they also knew that they had no choice but to return to the house whose domestic arrangements seemed to approximate perfectly those of an orphanage. *Knowing their place* was the unspoken premise of the bargain they had struck with their grandparents. "Only by accepting our situation as a just and unalterable arrangement," McCarthy explains, could "we . . . be allowed to transcend it and feel ourselves united to our grandparents in a love that was the more miraculous for breeding no practical results."

When their Protestant grandfather arrived five years later in 1923, and having learned from Kevin and Mary the true nature of their situation in Minneapolis, swiftly moved to change it, his indignation at the McCarthy family surprised the children nearly as much as his actions. "We thought it only natural that grandparents should know and do nothing," Mary McCarthy concludes, "for did not God in the mansions of Heaven look down upon human suffering and allow it to take its course?" Like ninepins, they had all fallen: mother and father, grandparents, a loving God.

Even nature turned ugly when the McCarthy children found themselves penned inside the featureless yard on Blaisdell Avenue on the coldest afternoons of a Minneapolis winter. In the spring, the yard sprouted bridal wreath bushes and a "gross rhubarb plant" that crops up in all of Mary McCarthy's reminiscences of Minneapolis like a telltale stain burning its way through layers of memory. But more than any of these losses, it was the collapse of the child's sense of its own importance, and of the integrity of the family system that responds to its needs, that marked the transformation of both the worldly and the spiritual condition of the McCarthy children as genuinely profound.

"*Read poor for orphan throughout*," Mary McCarthy suggests in the postscript to the first chapter of *Memories of a Catholic Girlhood*, "*and you get a kind of allegory or broad social satire on the theme of wealth and poverty. The anger was a generalized anger, which held up my grandparents as specimens of unfeeling.*" On the contrary, the anger is banked in glistening coals, and it is *never* generalized. But McCarthy's insight into the common nature of both poverty and orphanhood is suggestive. "*We orphan children were not responsible for being orphans, but we were treated as if we were and as if being orphans were a crime we had committed.*" Which is how poverty is regarded in American society: It's a dog-eat-dog world, people say, what do 'they' expect? Uncle Harry brought the point home after reading "Yonder Peasant, Who Is He?" in *The New Yorker*, when he reminded Mary that his mother had only to lift her little finger and she could have cut Mary out of his father's will. "*He wants me to under-*

stand this and be grateful," McCarthy writes in the postscript to the 1946 essay—which is particularly lively because it appears to be privately aimed at him.

But when Mary was six through eleven, she did not blame her grandparents for the myth making that left her in darkness, nor for their indifference to her suffering. What bitterness she felt was reserved for the Shrivers, especially Myers Shriver (or Schreiber: the German name, McCarthy suggests, was Americanized), who Mary and Kevin believed was embezzling the money that J. H. McCarthy had set aside for them. A tidy sum for those years, McCarthy discovered later, some $41,700 for the children's support between 1918 and 1923. As orphans, McCarthy observes, she and her brothers were "too poor, spiritually speaking" to question their grandparents' authority—but far too resourceful, as events would show, to submit to an orderly retirement from the earth's delights.

II

Reading a tale that Mary McCarthy tells about herself, one is struck by the way the message, the moral, the *drift* of the story is nearly always established by the senses, a fact McCarthy's public readings conveyed with special force. Every significant character, event, emotion, or idea is weighed and tested by the *sensation* it arouses in the author's memory; a memory deeply rooted in the tactile world of tastes, sounds, textures. Thus Uncle Myers, with his pigs' feet and banana-topped cornflakes, "his blue work shirt, stained with sweat, open at the neck to show an undershirt and lion-blond, glinting hair on his chest," is "consigned to eternal derision" (McCarthy's words) not for the beatings with hairbrush and razor strop that he administered—which she can still resent "abstractly, as injustice"—but for the "horrible food we were made to eat, the carrots I dumped out the window, the gristle and fat, the chicken necks . . . the prunes, farina and Wheatena. Here there was no compensation," she adds, "no sensibilizing of the palate to shadings of taste: . . ." Bad taste, in short, is the very touch of evil.

In *How I Grew*, Uncle Myers and Aunt Margaret exist as stock figures, amusing to the narrator "for their capacity for being awful. It is a sort of talent," McCarthy remarks lightly, "that people do not have nowadays or not in the same way." But when they first appeared in the memoirs originally published in the *The New Yorker*, when Mary McCarthy, in her thirties, was still awakening from the night-

mare of her dependence upon them, Margaret and Myers embodied in
their driven persons everything dark and dank, scared and cringing and
punishing, which interposed itself like the very shadow of death over
the bright prospects of childhood. To exorcize these demons from her
psyche was no mean feat; and it was not only storytelling that enabled
McCarthy finally to treat her experience with her Minneapolis guardians as an event that was hers to use, rather than an element in her
identity. More than once, she caught herself raving or running scared
like the "underbred Irish offspring" who is recalled in "Ghostly Father,
I Confess"; and as she grew older, with the help of analysis, she came
to admit that she, too, could speak in her Aunt Margaret's voice, or
lose herself in the labyrinth of deceits and self-deceits that had afforded
her some protection as a child.

The scowling, bowlegged child in the worn beaver hat who was
Mary McCarthy in the early 1920s—so like little Mary Lennox in *The
Secret Garden*, whose parents have perished in a cholera epidemic—
was not, by her own admission, a child who thought very much about
her losses. Reason, in fact, had stopped. "I made no effort to subject
the thing that was happening to me to any process of understanding,"
McCarthy writes in *How I Grew*, which, as an "intellectual autobiography," pays special attention to the life of the mind. "Perhaps I was
too stunned to use my intelligence outside of school." In school, at St.
Stephen's, a Catholic elementary school run by the old book, Mary's
intelligence had begun to work. Or at least her imagination was fed
ideas and images from legend that lifted her far afield from the sordid
circumstances at home.

Dreams substituted for thought: dreams of becoming a Carmelite
sister, like St. Teresa of Avila, "effaced, selfless"; or an abbess, presiding over a covey of nuns; or the bride of the pretender to the throne
of France, but fighting side by side with him, commanding her own
troops, *she* would win back the throne. " 'Queen Marie-Therese' "
would be her name. "For me," McCarthy observes, "excess was attractive almost per se. . . ."

She had begun to excel in school: to master elocution and win
spelling prizes and essay contests, such as the prize she won for an
essay on the Irish in American History, for which she had been beaten
by Uncle Myers, lest she "become 'stuck-up.' " Her mastery of the
lines of a play never stopped with her own—an instance of "excess"—
but continued in lip sync with the other actors. She had become a
flaming young Catholic, and enjoyed a privileged relationship with the
parish priest. A venerable American type, the 'flaming Catholic' would

reassert its claims on Mary McCarthy, unsuccessfully for the most part, in the guise of the flaming liberal and fellow traveler of the 1930s and '40s, whose special access to goodness, to right-thinking, appeared mystic or moralistic, like the clergy's.

In Minneapolis, it was the romance of Catholic history, the sensuous rituals of the Mass, as well as the absolutism of the Church—its profession of the One True Faith (which consigned the Lutheran soul of Uncle Myers to eternal damnation)—that led Mary McCarthy to conclude that "*it was religion that saved me. Our ugly church and parochial school provided me with my only aesthetic outlook. . . .*" The flower-bedecked altar, the ornamented prayer books, holy cards, and votive lamps, however debased by mass production, were "*the equivalent of Gothic cathedrals and illuminated manuscripts and mystery plays.*" Thus she remembers a "Catholic girlhood" and not, in the end, an orphaned one. But more likely it is McCarthy's "aesthetic outlook," rather than school or church, which set the parameters for her salvation. A native aestheticism gave her the tools of sensibility to put the tyrannical Uncle Myers in his place—" 'My father was a gentleman and you're not' "—and find in the Roman Church some of the lost sensations of life with her parents.

If Kevin McCarthy were to write his memoirs, one suspects it wouldn't be a Catholic boyhood he would recall, but orphanhood in both its historic and metaphysical dimension. Looking back, he remembers never knowing "what the hell was going on, where I belonged, what I should be doing, where I should be going." School and Church were not the refuge they were for Mary, although Catholicism would impinge more directly on his life. In 1923, when Harold Preston arrived in Minneapolis like an avenging angel—a bit tardy, and a bit partial to his only granddaughter—Mary was taken to Seattle, while Kevin and Preston were sent to a Minnesota convent school for girls, St. Benedict's, where a small cadre of boys was admitted for altar duty. Sheridan remained with the Shrivers for a few more years, moving with them to Indiana. "I was a petty thief," Kevin McCarthy remembers, "I didn't study . . . I saved matches—which meant of course that I wanted to set the world on fire. . . ." In what fashion he never knew. The stage didn't attract Kevin as a boy, as it did Mary. Setting the world on fire seemed to mean making it burn.

During their time with Uncle Myers, it was undoubtedly Mary's temperament, her Seattle pride, that brought out the worst in their guardian, but Kevin's rebelliousness provoked the more pernicious tortures. In *Memories of a Catholic Girlhood*, Mary McCarthy relates that "we were put to bed at night with our mouths sealed with adhesive tape to prevent mouth-breathing. . . ." But it was Kevin (who had enlarged adenoids, though nobody knew it) who provoked Myers to slap the tape across his mouth every night for nearly a year. "I was a mouth breather," he recalls, "and it just irritated the hell out of this man. . . . He said, 'You will breathe through your nose!' " Mary's papal "we" had irked him when he first read her account of the tape in "A Tin Butterfly" in *The New Yorker* in 1951. "Mary, how can you take this—my purple heart—and put it on your breast?" he asked her. But she had reminded him of a long-ago weekend when Uncle Myers thought that she was talking too much, and he had put tape on her mouth, too. It was probably true, Kevin thinks, but for him it was an ongoing punishment, remaining vivid and terrible to him today—as vivid as the memory of the razor strop became for Mary, after a showdown with Myers over a tin butterfly.

There is something apocryphal about Mary McCarthy's tale of the missing butterfly, which Myers had gotten in a box of Cracker Jack and given to Sheridan. Like a Chinese opera in which a single imposture is unmasked, only to reveal another and another, McCarthy's report of her uncle's plot to blame her for its disappearance is subject to alternate interpretations. In the *New Yorker* story, she maintains she never knew who actually planted the butterfly underneath her place at the table. The drama is centered on her uncle's and aunt's attempts to force a confession from her and break her spirit. She is beaten by the fat Uncle Myers until he tires of her fierce resistance, and then by Aunt Margaret, who tires less easily. " 'Say you did it, Mary Therese, say you did it,' " her aunt implores her between blows; and because Mary knows Aunt Margaret only wants to satisfy Myers so the whipping can stop, she complies. But when she is led back to her accuser, the sight of him sprawled in his favorite chair, complacently waiting for her "confession" is too much for her, and the truth flies out again—" 'I didn't! I didn't!' " The beatings are resumed and Mary becomes hysterical, but she refuses to recant. When she is finally released, she limps up to bed "with a crazy sense of inner victory, like a saint's." She is beaten for the usual reasons later (sometimes for the misdeeds of her brothers, on the theory that it was the duty of the eldest to set an example for the younger), but the question of the tin butterfly was closed.

In 1951, in an afterword to the original story, McCarthy sees the event as a turning point. It was only a matter of months before Mr.

Preston arrived, and Myers and Margaret were forced to relinquish their control, and Mary was transported to a more hospitable environment. Later, when she was traveling east to college, she had stopped to see her brothers, who were then reunited in the house of a more indulgent guardian, Uncle Louis McCarthy. All the old people were dead, Grandfather and Grandmother McCarthy, Uncle Myers and Aunt Margaret. Sitting together in the twilight of Uncle Louis's screened-in porch, the orphans looked for a common ground for their reunion "and found it," Mary McCarthy writes, "in Uncle Myers. It was then that my brother Preston told me that on the famous night of the butterfly, he had seen Uncle Myers steal into the dining room from the den and lift the tablecloth, with the tin butterfly in his hand."

The accuser stood accused, and the mystery, it seemed, was solved. Certainly it made a good story; but soon after "A Tin Butterfly" appeared in *The New Yorker,* Mary was led to question the mix of fact and fancy that entered into its denouement. She remembered an unfinished play about her guardians that she had written at Vassar, in which Uncle Myers tiptoes into the dining room and pins the butterfly to the pad underneath her plate. She remembers her drama teacher, the distinguished Hallie Flanagan, suggesting excitedly, " 'Your uncle must have done it!' " Scruple then led McCarthy to consult with her brothers. They all remembered the talk about Uncle Myers on the porch, but Kevin didn't remember Preston saying his uncle put the butterfly there, and Preston (who was seven at the time) didn't remember saying it or seeing it. "Mea Culpa," McCarthy declares. She fears she has *"fused two memories"*—one of what happened, and one of what was imagined, what was written. The latter, the literary truth, had usurped the former, an occupational hazard to which Mary McCarthy, like many a practiced raconteur, was not immune.

"But who did put the butterfly by my place?" she wonders. *"It may have been Uncle Myers after all. Even if no one saw him, he remains a suspect: he had motive and opportunity."* And so she rests her case. Kevin McCarthy, however, offers a different interpretation. "You know, I think we all think we did it," he says. "I think Preston thinks he thought he did it. I think I thought I did it—we were in such intimidation. Mary didn't do it; I don't see that as being part of her, a calculated kind of ploy like that." As for the accused, Kevin McCarthy is sure he *"never* thought that Myers did it."

If it was one of the boys who pinned the goods on Mary—a possibility that Mary McCarthy dismissed, because "the very unfairness of the condemnation that rested on me made me reluctant to transfer it to one of my brothers"—then what was *his* motive? What kind of "intimidation" prevailed in the Shrivers' house that led either Preston or Kevin to wish the agony of that night on Mary? In an ordinary family, it wouldn't be hard to imagine a brother playing such a trick on an older sister. When the prank got out of hand, the culprit might easily become too frightened to confess. Much later, he might even get the facts scrambled in his own mind. But this was not an ordinary family; nor was it an ordinary sister who seemed incapable of imagining this set of circumstances, so much more impressed was she with her guardian's treachery.

3

Coming of Age in Seattle

". . . [T]here went the girl that a Jesuit had failed to convince."
—MARY McCARTHY, "C'EST LE PREMIER PAS QUI COÛTE"

Most lives, upon reflection, tend to gravitate toward certain familiar settings for their moments of revelation. Mary McCarthy's confrontations, her turning points, would often occur on trains—not planes, which she declared herself "against." ("A true conservative," she once said, "one who wants to preserve a golden age, would happily ban air travel.") Sometimes an ocean liner offered McCarthy the mise-en-scène for intrigue, as the *Cristoforo Columbo* would for a bizarre encounter with the German theologian Paul Tillich in 1956. But for moments of genuine illumination, no setting ever served her better than a fast-moving transcontinental train. On a train, anything could happen.

It was on the eastbound Chicago, Milwaukee and St. Paul in 1918 that McCarthy's father either did or did not—depending on whose memory was consulted—pull a gun on the conductor who wanted to dump his family on a platform in Nebraska. The train was the one that had delivered Mary into the arms of "the Catholics," as her brother Kevin would always call the Minneapolis McCarthys. On the westbound train five years later, Mary had been delivered into the hands of the Protestants and the Jews in Seattle. After the tortuous years in Minneapolis, her "escape," she concluded many years later, was her "revenge"—as was memory, and the point of her pen.

The transcontinental train was the holding stitch in the complex weave of Mary McCarthy's early life. So many twists of fate issued from its lower berths, dining cars, and lounges that as she grew older the simple act of boarding a long-distance train carried with it the whiff of adventure—like "the hope that sprang up with the sound of a new step soft on the flowered Pullman carpet," which is memorialized in one of McCarthy's most well-known stories, "The Man in the Brooks Brothers Shirt."

In 1923, when she boarded the Chicago, Milwaukee and St. Paul, wearing a garish red hat and carrying the religious propaganda with which she hoped (at her Grandmother McCarthy's suggestion) to effect a conversion in Seattle, she was, at eleven, on the edge of a personal transformation no less profound for happening at a tender age. Seated in the dining car with her Grandfather Preston, staring helplessly down at the lamb chops and pancakes and sausages that she had ordered and could not eat, she was indeed "the underbred Irish offspring of a genteel New England parent" (as she would say later of the autobiographical heroine in *The Company She Keeps,* Margaret Sargent). "The shabby daughter of a prosperous lawyer," "the Catholic child of a Protestant father"—which fictionalized fact in only a cursory way. In effect, by rescuing her from Aunt Margaret and Uncle Myers, by bringing her *home* in a sense, her Grandfather Preston's star had merged with her father's. And Mary McCarthy had become (once again) a daddy's girl, if now a wayward one.

A fallen star herself, she gyrated between her fear for the prosperous lawyer's immortal soul and her satisfaction that his prosperity, his stolid Protestant gentility, had miraculously become hers. When she reentered the Preston house for the first time since 1918, she was exalted by its "appurtenances." "Everything we had seemed superior to anything anyone else had," she remembers in *Memories of a Catholic Girlhood*: the cabinets with their opaline Tiffany glass, the silk curtains and grass wallpaper, the pretty new clothes that her grandmother's dressmaker made for her; the open shelves in the library, the stereopticon, the new Victrola; the flowers in the garden, the strawberry beds, currant bushes, and homegrown vegetables.

All these luxuries had enlisted her senses in a grand revolt against the tyranny of prunes and dry farina that had prevailed in the Shrivers' household. And yet back at the Forest Ridge Convent in Seattle, where her grandparents had promptly reenrolled her, as their daughter would have wished, something of the dark punitive Catholicism of Margaret and Lizzie Sheridan McCarthy had flared up again. The occasion was the visit of a fiery Jesuit fresh from a mission among the Eskimos, who

delivered a sermon on the perils of Protestantism. A baptized Protestant went straight to hell, he had declared, while a Mohammedan, Jew,
or pagan—who was innocent of God's grace, and therefore unaccount-
able to His Church—was assured a place in limbo. "How could it be,"
Mary had agonized, "that my grandfather, the most virtuous person I
knew . . . should be lost, while I, the object of his admoni-
tion . . . who yielded to every impulse, lied, boasted, betrayed—should,
by virtue of regular attendance at the sacraments and the habit of easy
penitence, be saved?"

The convent's Mother Superior had helped Mary find a way out
for her grandfather, with whom she had established an amicable relation; but it hadn't been easy. God's "infinite mercy" could not be
presumed upon, for its manifestations were too uncertain. Sacred history showed that God's mercy was more likely to fall upon a thief or
a Mary Magdalen than a pillar of the community. This was "the dark
horse doctrine of salvation," an idea that fascinated Mary, who was
beginning to discover that while being the "second most devout" at St.
Stephen's had won her acclaim among the ordinary Catholics of Minneapolis, it was doing nothing for her with the mesdames of the Sacred
Heart and their more select body of students. At the Forest Ridge
Convent, for the first and maybe the last time in her life, she stood
precariously near the edge of eccentricity and obscurity.

In the end, the Mother Superior had found a "loophole" for
Mary's grandfather in a key passage from St. Athanasius. This was the
Benedictine view that an unbeliever could not be damned unless he
rejected the true Church with "sufficient knowledge" of its authority.
"Sufficient knowledge he had not," Mary was certain; her grandfather's knowledge of the true Church was like that of the "heathen
Hiawatha, who had heard strange stories of missionaries, white men
in black robes who bore a Cross." Gratefully, she had flung her arms
around the Mother Superior, resolving to curtail at once the practice
of her devotions at home, "lest the light of my example shine upon [her
grandfather] too powerfully and burn him with sufficient knowledge to
a crisp."

The next weekend home (she was a five-day boarder), Mary had
dismantled the little altar in her bedroom, discarded the religious
pamphlets from Minneapolis, and left off saying grace before meals.
Her grandfather, McCarthy remembers, had warned her against
" 'using the *irreligious* atmosphere of this house as an excuse for
backsliding. There will be time enough when you are older to change
your beliefs if you want to.' " His rebuke had stung her with its

unfairness, but delighted her, too; and as she flounced up to her room, slamming the door behind her, she was flushed with the triumph of the martyr's secret righteousness. If only *he knew* . . .

By 1924, the time of change of which her grandfather spoke was already upon her. Within a year, she had lost her faith. McCarthy recalls the "momentous" event as something that jumped at her "ready-made" out of one of the Mother Superior's discourses. She had no idea at first what it meant. "Lose-your-faith" was merely a string of words, "like the ladder made of sheets on which the daring girl had descended into the arms of her Romeo"—an interesting analogy, quintessential McCarthy, in that it introduces an act of intellectual defiance in frankly sexual terms.

As for the twelve-year-old's virgin faith, she "lost" it, McCarthy tells her readers, originally to call attention to herself. Toward the end of her first year at the Forest Ridge Convent she had decided that if she was "neglected" by the queenly girls and cloistered Ladies of the Sacred Heart, whose "mysterious aristocratic punctilio" both thrilled and baffled her, it was because nobody knew who she was. She had tried to tell a sympathetic desk mate the "truth" about herself in a "dazzling essay" that recounted her triumphs at St. Stephen's, but the girl merely offered her condolences. "I was forced to accept the fact that my former self was dead," McCarthy wrote in "C'est le Premier Pas Qui Coûte," the fourth chapter of *Memories of a Catholic Girlhood*, which first appeared in *The New Yorker*. The summer of 1924 had passed in restless isolation with her grandfather and his companions at a lakeside resort in the Olympic Mountains (her Grandmother Preston stayed in Seattle), and when Mary returned to the convent as a full-time boarder in the fall, she was determined "to get [herself] recognized at whatever price."

No longer would she try to stand first in her studies, or covet the pink good-conduct ribbons that perpetually eluded her. She had once looked upon religion as a "branch of civics and conformity," but now she found herself standing on the edge of "a cult of fashion and elegance in the sphere of religion," whose baroque observances—the spoken French, the curtsies, the curtained beds in the dormitories, the rule of silence at mealtimes, the nun seated behind a screen in the bathroom, dispensing towels—took her breath away. Some dangerous and dramatic act was in order if Mary McCarthy, motherless child, recently of Blaisdell Avenue, Minneapolis, was to take her place beside Émilie von Phul, Marie-Louise L'Abbé, Julia Dodge, and Anna Lyons—convent girls whose names McCarthy could recite like a litany sixty-five years later. "If I could not win fame by goodness," she calculated, "in a cold, empty gambler's mood" in the fall of 1924, "I was ready to do it by badness."

At first she contemplated an affair with the Swedish baron who was the music master—("I grew faint when my laced shoe encountered his spatted Oxford on the loud pedal")—but when reality intervened, she settled on a more serious scandal. " 'Say you've lost your faith,' the devil prompted, assuring me that there was no risk if I chose my moment carefully." Say, on the Sunday before the Monday when the visiting Jesuit commenced a retreat. By Wednesday, when he held confessions, she could regain it, thus exposing her own immortal soul to a window of vulnerability of only four days' duration. In a Catholic milieu that abhored organizational heretics such as Calvin and Luther, but retained a stealthy respect for great atheists and sinners like Marlowe, Baudelaire, and Byron, her scheme was bound to be a showstopper. "It was a miracle that someone had not thought of it already," McCarthy reflects in "C'est le Premier Pas Qui Coûte" ("It's the first move that counts"), "the idea seemed so obvious, like a store waiting to be robbed."

Less obvious was the inner logic of the drama. The faith that Mary McCarthy had inherited from 'the Catholics' may have been right for Minneapolis, where any foundation for hope had to be rock-ribbed, and the only Protestant who mattered was the hated Uncle Myers. In the Preston household, on the other hand, with its gardener, cook, and Kelvinator humming in the kitchen, its library full of Dickens, Tolstoy, Bulwer-Lytton, and Dumas, a faith that owed itself more to the Inquisition than to a belief in divine providence was a clear offense to reason.

II

There is nothing remarkable about an orphan who abandons the religious observances of one set of guardians when she is adopted by another. For Mary McCarthy, however, Catholicism was the lifeline to her dead parents. Much of its holding power derived from the Church's celebration of life after death and the resurrection of the body, two doctrines whose importance to the bereaved child was crystal clear. It was when these heady beliefs no longer bore the weight of need—or perhaps when the memory of her mother and father began to falter—that Mary McCarthy found the "Fortress Rock" of Catholicism heaving underfoot. Behind her celebrated loss of faith, a deeper transformation was under way.

In "C'est le Premier Pas Qui Coûte," one self is dismantled and another born at the moment when McCarthy's heroine searches her memory for "atheistic arguments" to convince the convent chaplain of her defection. Quite unexpectedly, several genuine doubts that she has been harboring, "like contraband in a bureau drawer," reassuringly present themselves. She has always been "a little suspicious of the life after death," for example. "Perhaps it was really true that the dead just rotted and I would never rejoin my parents in Heaven? I scratched a spot on my uniform, watching it turn white under my thumbnail. Another memory was tapping at my consciousness: the question of the Resurrection of the Body."

The idea that she might never rejoin her parents is held at arm's length by a question mark. The doubter still wants to believe. But that spot on the uniform, so uncharacteristically *allusive,* why is it there? "Out, out, damned spot . . ."? A worm of doubt has turned, although the dumb show continues, the play within the play, in which the fraudulent doubter must first assemble her "arguments." "What about cannibals?" her mind pounces. How can *their* bodies leap from their graves to rejoin their souls on Resurrection Day? "God could start with whatever flesh the cannibal had had when he was a baby, before he began eating missionaries, but if his father and mother had been cannibals too, what flesh would he really have that he could call his own?" A thorny question. "At that time," McCarthy continues, sotto voce, "I did not know that this problem had been treated by Aquinas."

As in Shakespeare, the farce anticipates the unmasking—the surprise at the end of all this mummery—by mocking it. The imposter is carried away by her own performance, and elation replaces fear. She can hardly wait to meet the priest to "confront him with these doubts, so remarkable in one of my years." Parallels with the young Jesus, "discoursing with the scribes," float through her head—" 'And all that heard Him were astonished at His Wisdom and His answers.' " Certainly no one at the convent can accuse her of fakery.

When a knock is heard at the door, the doubter has reached the apogee of "doubting the divinity of Christ." Who knows what peak she will scale next? In the "wondering looks" of the girl named Iris who summons her for an audience with the chaplain, Mary sees that already she is "a credit to the milieu." (This Iris, surely invented, is a play on yet another play, a real one at St. Stephen's a few years before, in which Mary McCarthy was cast as the lowly Iris in a pageant of flowers, when she really wanted to be Rose, the heroine. In Minneapolis, she had humiliated herself by prompting the other players with her lips; now she is redeemed. Many of McCarthy's memoirs set the stage for just such an evening of the score.)

At first the convent's chaplain is unimpressed. Nor is this wrinkled old man, "with the hairless face and brown, dead curly hair that looked like a wig," the interlocutor whom our heroine would have chosen for herself. "He had a weary, abstracted air as he turned away from the window, as though he had spent his life in the confessional box. His voice was hollow. . . . As chaplain to Madame MacIlvira [the Mother Superior], he must have become a sort of spiritual factotum, like an upper servant. . . ." As an actor in Mary McCarthy's drama, he is a fortuitous creation. Curtly, he interrupts her soliloquy on the cannibals. " 'These are scholastic questions,' " he tells her, " 'beyond the reach of your years. Believe me, the Church has an answer for them.' " Which makes Mary wonder what the Church is trying to hide.

Father Dennis (his literary name, the real priest's name is long forgotten) appears far more interested in the girl's doubts about the divinity of Jesus Christ; so intensely interested that his young visitor is nearly frightened into withdrawing them. (Because she is "one of those cowards who are afraid not to be brave," she does not.) With this far from scholastic question between them, the interview turns from pretense to real drama. " 'We are supposed to know that He was God because He rose from the dead,' " Mary begins confidently enough. " 'But you can't prove that He rose from the dead. That's only what the Apostles said. How do we know they were telling the truth? They were very ignorant, superstitious men—just fishermen, weren't they?' " She gazes at the priest hopefully, "half begging recognition for [her] doubt and half waiting for him to settle it."

A fatal ambiguousness has crept into her twelve-year-old mind. Now she begins to see everything in doubles. " 'You are calling Our Blessed Savior a liar and a cheat,' " the chaplain replies "in a sepulchral tone," which is not her meaning. " 'He might have *thought* He was God,' " she explains—but Father Dennis only closes his eyes and says, " 'You must have faith, my child.' " The word *faith* touches her for a moment; but he wasn't answering her arguments, and now he watches her with a genuinely troubled expression as if he himself sees an insurmountable gulf between them. For the first time it strikes her—"perhaps I *had* lost my faith. Could it have slipped away without my knowing it?" And that is when she seems to split into two people, "one slyly watching as the priest sank back into the armchair, the other anxious and aghast at the turn the interview was taking."

The test of a first-rate intelligence, as Fitzgerald put it, is the ability to hold two contradictory ideas in mind at the same time. For Mary McCarthy, this doubling of consciousness, this splitting of one mind into two warring halves, is the very breath of life. It often hurts—for the will seems paralyzed, and there is no peace at either pole of consciousness—but in extremis it sheds a cold, bracing light. And in time the double vision usually yields a third way out.

What had slipped away without her knowing it at twelve, of course, was hope as well as faith. She could no longer *hope* for a supernatural way out of the loss of her natural rights: the right to a mother and father and the continuity of childhood. The loss exposed her to the ultimate doubt in the existence of God Himself—which breaks like a thunderhead in the hush of the chaplain's parlor: " 'My child,' " cries the priest, for he has seen "the wild look" in her eyes, " 'do you doubt the existence of God?' 'Yes,' I breathed, in exultant agony, knowing that it was true." Almost immediately upon watching her faith take flight, a sad little dove recalled to the rookery, her mind forks down another path, a less traveled path which will carry her far beyond the hermetic world of the convent.

Listening to the priest recite the five a posteriori proofs of God's existence—the gist of which is that every effect must have its cause—Mary is almost but not quite convinced. "It was as though the spirit of doubt had wormed its way into the very tissue of my thinking, so that axioms that had seemed simple and clear only an hour or so before now became perplexing and murky. 'Why, Father,' " she asks, " 'does everything *have* to have a cause? Why couldn't the universe just be there, causing itself?' " Couldn't the universe be "self-sufficient," as God is (why couldn't *she,* for that matter)? Chance, not order or design, may rule the roost.

In "C'est le Premier Pas Qui Coûte," this idea appears refreshing, like the possibility that has begun to dawn on Mary that Christ really could have been a man. When Father Dennis challenges her to consider how a "mere man" could have been capable of the "wisdom and goodness" that were to be found in the life and teachings of Jesus, she considers it and concludes, " 'Why not?' " Even if history showed that never was there "such a One," she could no longer understand why the simple fact that Christ was an *exception* proved that He was God. " 'There are no exceptions in nature,' " Father Dennis had insisted, but she could think of lots. Her whole life had been a bundle of exceptions, when you thought about it.

As twilight fills the room and Father Dennis lights the lamp, Mary is suddenly glad that she has instigated the confrontation, for she is "learning something new every second. All fear had left [her] and all sense of mere willful antagonism." She has entered an Elysium of unfettered intellect. A good convert, with no hard feelings, she is "intent on showing Father Dennis the new possibilities that opened"; her feelings for him are "comradely."

But once again the old priest cuts her off, ordering her to accept his words because she is too young for understanding. " 'Oh my child,' " he begs her, " 'give up reading that atheistic filth. Pray to God for faith and make a good confession.' " And he makes a hasty exit, leaving her alone with this thing called "faith" which has begun to unravel from too much handling. And with "God"—that "immortal fictional character," Mary McCarthy calls "Him" elsewhere.

Father Dennis's failure made a great impression on the convent, McCarthy relates. Wherever the young agnostic went, she was regarded respectfully: "there went the girl that a Jesuit had failed to convince." "Little queens" who had never noticed her before surrounded her at recess, whispering questions (talk was forbidden during a retreat). The retreat itself heightened the drama of her fall from grace, and it was said that when the visiting missionary preached, he was "pitting his oratory against [her]." It was the reaction of all these others, and Mme. McIlvira's alarm, in particular, that frightened Mary into trying to "feel faith, if only as a public duty." But the harder she tried, the more evident it became that now there was nothing there, nothing at all.

"A sort of uneasiness had settled down over the convent," McCarthy declares, as if the boarding school has metamorphosed into a throbbing metropolis, and the lonely little girl from Minneapolis has become its most prominent citizen. "It was clear to everyone, including me, that I would *have* to get my faith back to put an end to this terrible uncertainty," she states. But a second interview, this time with the fiery Jesuit himself, fails to achieve a rescue. He too is convinced that Mary has been reading "atheistic literature." After she confides that both her father and grandfather were lawyers, he laughs at her, as if her doubts are merely her inherited "gift of gab." Neither priest seems able to imagine that one can figure anything out by oneself; everything is inheritance or reading; and Jesus, of course, could never have been a "mere man." "By failing to convert me and treating my case lightly . . . he was driving me straight into fraud," Mary concluded. The only thing left to do was to enact a "simulated conversion." She had no intention of giving the missionary priest the credit, however. She would be converted in the dead of night, in a dream. The decision sprang from a sense of obligation to others, oddly enough (for it was the first time McCarthy remembered feeling such an obligation), and not to her own soul or to God. Was that proof that 'He' had fled? she wonders (still dangling between faith and reason). "God," she concludes, "(if there was a God) would certainly not be pleased if I *pretended* to regain my faith. . . ."

And so Mary McCarthy had come of age in Seattle. Kneeling in pious simplicity at the Communion rail on Thursday, acutely aware of the nuns rejoicing behind her, and of the girls stirring enviously beside her, Mary's chief sensation had been surprise at how far she had traveled from her old mainstays—"as once, when learning to swim, I had been doing the dead-man's float and looked back . . . to see my water wings drifting, far behind me, on the lake's surface."

The memoir is a tour de force, one of the most supple narratives that Mary McCarthy has spun out of the raw melodrama of her early years. One can read *Memories of a Catholic Girlhood* as a whole for its biographical fact—weighing and sifting the latter is the burden of the italicized commentaries following each chapter—but it is as a gallant propitiation of the dead, and of the byzantine world of childhood, that the episodes achieve their immortality.

"*This story is so true to our convent life,*" McCarthy writes in the commentary, "*that I find it almost impossible to sort out the guessed-at and the half-remembered from the undeniably real.*" The music master, the Mother Superior, the two priests, all have their prototypes in history; and Mary McCarthy *did* pretend to lose her faith, and lose it, and then *pretend* to get it back again, although "*the drama,*" she notes, "*took place during a very short space of time,*" possibly during a retreat (which sounds right because that is when such dramas occur). The retreat, on the other hand, couldn't have been the one when the famous Jesuit preached; according to the memoir's own internal dating, he visited the convent the year before.

Memory, of course, is an act of recreation that borrows as much from the present as from the past; and in 1950, when the memoir was written, McCarthy's memory was supplemented by *The Catholic Encyclopedia*, which supplied her with the a posteriori proofs of God's existence. A good line about the limits of natural reason given to the chaplain—"*There's a little gap that we have to fill with faith*"—was taken from McCarthy's son, Reuel Wilson, then eleven, who brought it home from a sacred Scripture class. Her own youthful questions, she tells the reader, are a mix of memory and conjecture. The conversations are invented, *"but their tone and tenor are right. . . . Even though I wrote this myself,"* she observes with satisfaction, *"I smile in startled recognition as I read it."*

She has made the connection. The ghosts are appeased and spring to life, not only for the author but for the reader. The author has a very good memory, but it is by offering these restless shades good direction, memorable lines, careful costuming and makeup that Mary McCarthy rescues them, her past, and herself from oblivion. The chaplain's "weary, abstracted air" and "half-averted face" are stage directions. McCarthy catches him *in the act* of being a spiritual factotum, just as she catches herself, as an adolescent, *in the act* of thinking and behaving like the mysterious changeling that she is.

"There is no room for the dead in practical life or for the past either," McCarthy once observed in an essay on one of her favorite English novelists, Ivy Compton-Burnett. "That is why people try to suppress it. Yet the past, even when it consents to die, has a feeble sort of immortality owing to its persistence in memory. . . ." Memory, she adds, is a "property of mind." Its immortal part "is attached most vigorously, by common consent, to works of art." Only when the object of memory is converted by *an act of imagination* into something near at hand, into a ghost story maybe, or simply into a good story, does memory yield to art. The proposition (coined in 1966) is a distinctly Compton-Burnettish clue to Mary McCarthy's working method. Works of art are the writer's "brain-children," she states elsewhere in the same essay. Through them a writer may achieve a coveted immortality; through his or her books, the past reenters the present, *becomes* present, thus turning the ordinary course of events into something (shall we say?) *memorable*.

By the late 1940s and early '50s, when *Memories of a Catholic Girlhood* was under way, one might have justly said of Mary McCarthy that something in her own tragic past—the pathos of the orphan—had finally consented to die. After McCarthy's divorce from the critic Edmund Wilson in 1946, she was, as it happened, no longer condemned to reenact the primal scenes of loss, of separation, and flight; to "cry or make disgusting scenes or have cheap tastes or commit adultery (unless she were *very* much in love)," as the heroine of "Ghostly Father, I Confess" confesses. When "C'est le Premier Pas Qui Coûte" was written, she was applying the finishing touches to a bold persona that had grown up in the shadow of more powerful personalities—or personalities that impressed her as powerful so long as she clung to them and ran from them, alternately, in her fashion:

Harold Johnsrud, her first husband; Philip Rahv, a lover and mentor; Edmund Wilson, her second husband, whose power was the most formidable of all.

In *Memories of a Catholic Girlhood*, the exultation of the survivor touches every scene. At the Forest Ridge Convent in 1924, as at the center of the band of New York intellectuals with whom McCarthy traveled after World War II, "It was the idea of being noticed that consumed all [her] attention; the rest, it seemed to [her], would come of itself."

4

Cutting Loose

"Those in whom the true self gets the upper hand,

if only briefly, are dangerous; the true self, like the poor relation,

must be taught to keep his distance. . . . The moral would

seem to be that everyone ought to have something to hide

but they ought to hide it successfully. . . ."

—MARY MCCARTHY, "MORE ON COMPTON-BURNETT"

*T*here was something strange, abnormal, about my bringing up; only now that my grandmother is dead am I prepared to face this fact." So begins the portrait of Augusta Morganstern Preston in "Ask Me No Questions," the last chapter of *Memories of a Catholic Girlhood*. The strangeness is never quite put into focus. Indeed, the darkness that gathers in the corners of the extraordinary portrait of Mrs. Preston, one of the more vivid character sketches in American literature, leaves the reader convinced that something odd really was going on with Mary McCarthy's people in Seattle. Something that sprang from the anomalous circumstances of her ancestry—in which a Jewish belle from San Francisco, Augusta Morganstern, had married Harold Preston, the son of a Yankee colonel in the Civil War. Their only daughter, Tess, had gone on to marry the black sheep of a prosperous clan of Irish Catholic grain merchants from the Midwest. And as if the concert wasn't discordant enough, no one seemed to fit the costumes that they wore.

Everyone, like the fabled Emperor, was naked beneath the clothes that everybody else believed were there. The Jewish grandmother never spoke of being Jewish, at least not in Mary's presence. The Yankee lawyer of impeccable liberal credentials was not so liberal, as Mary discovered in her teens, when young men began to enter the picture; nor so benevolent or fair-minded when regarded from her three brothers' standpoint—for they had been left behind in Minnesota, to be remembered at Christmas and on birthdays with toys and occasional checks, while Mary was raised in the lap of luxury in their mother's house.

And Tess, the beautiful, soft-spoken daughter who had become a "Child of Mary," used to write her Irish mother-in-law in Minneapolis about evenings with "the Hebrews" in Seattle, as Mary was surprised to learn when she read her mother's letters. The doting husband and father, Roy Winfield McCarthy, who turned life into a succession of treats, had been unable to hold on to his own life, or protect the lives of his family. And they were all, as McCarthy once remarked of her Grandmother Preston, "neither in nor out of society." Each one was a kind of recluse. Or if they weren't, as neither Mary's father nor her mother were by nature, death had made them mute.

No wonder that by the time she was a teenager, Mary McCarthy had begun to grow restless in the big house overlooking Lake Washington. The "Preston mansion," as Tess's childhood friends had called it, was not for all its splendor a very happy place. To Mary as a little girl the house had been an extension of the fairyland she inhabited with her father. By 1925, however, after she had left the Forest Ridge Convent, and persuaded her guardians to send her to a public high school, where she hoped to meet some boys, the inflexible routines of another middle-aged household began to close in upon her.

Few writers have drawn a sharper picture of the ennui that can nestle at the heart of a comfortable upper-middle-class marriage than Mary McCarthy in her recollections of her grandparents' reunion at the end of a typical day in the middle 1920s. At quarter to five, wherever she and her Grandmother Preston were, usually in a department store, Mrs. Preston would look at her watch. "It was time to pick up Grandpa, in front of his club," McCarthy remembers in "Ask Me No Questions":

> At five o'clock, punctually, he would be on the sidewalk, anxiously surveying the traffic for us. The car would draw up; he would climb in and kiss my grandmother's cheek; "Have a good day?" he would ask. "All right," she would reply, sighing a little.

At six, they sat down to dinner with Mary's uncle Harold—the "Goose," his friends called him—who occupied a bachelor's suite upstairs. On the table might be deviled Dungeness crab, a young salmon served in a sherry sauce with oysters and little shrimps—

company food, prepared by the cook and eaten in virtual silence. Sometimes there would be ice cream 'turned' by the gardener in an old-fashioned freezer on the back porch. After dinner, Mary's married uncle Frank sometimes dropped in with his wife, Isabel, on their way to a party. More often, her grandparents, having finished the evening papers, played double solitaire. If her grandfather had decided not to return to his club for a rubber of bridge with his cronies, he settled into his armchair, lighted a cigar, and began reading a book that never seemed to change: *The Life and Letters of Walter Hines Page.* "My grandmother would take up her library book, I would take up mine," McCarthy goes on,

> and silence would resume its way over the household. . . . Rarely, the telephone would ring, and I would rush to get it, but it was never anything interesting. . . . Or my grandmother would glance over at me as I lay stretched out on the sofa with my copy (disappointing) of *Mademoiselle de Maupin*: "Mary, pull your dress down."

At ten o'clock, Mrs. Preston closed her book with a sigh and started out to the front hall on her way to bed. " 'Going up, Mama?' " Mary's grandfather would say, "raising his gray eyes with an invariable air of surprise. 'I think so, Harry,' she would reply, sighing again, from the stairs." Soon her grandfather put his book down, too, and offering his cheek to Mary for a kiss, followed his wife up the stairs to the old nursery where he slept.

An early admirer of Mary McCarthy's, Jess Rosenberg, remembers Harold Preston as a pillar of Seattle's establishment, who was nonetheless ostracized by Seattle society because he was married to a Jew. By the mid-1920s, Mr. Preston was living in semiretirement—no longer the figure he once was when he had confronted Seattle's company lawyers as the U. S. government's attorney. He should have been a judge, but a judge's salary was meager, he had once explained to Mary, who always wondered vaguely why her grandfather was no longer *doing* anything. Mrs. Preston, Jess Rosenberg remembers as an eccentric woman who had face-lifts and spent all of her time shopping. She had her own funds, which probably explained the expensive car. She was rarely seen by her children's friends, except when she arrived in the Baker electric to fetch young Harold after he finished a set of tennis at the Olympic Hotel.

When Jess Rosenberg called on Mary—with her glossy hair, white skin, and expressive eyes, she reminded him, at fourteen, of "Hera, the cow-eyed goddess"—he was ushered in by a maid who directed him to the library and served him hot chocolate. On one occasion, he had brought a pocket edition of Rupert Brooke. Mary had upstaged him with her apparent familiarity with more contemporary poets such as Edward Arlington Robinson—and with a recitation of a bawdy poem about " 'John, the Bastard King of England . . . who bound his dong with a leather thong.' " At 8:30 the maid reappeared to see young Mr. Rosenberg out.

There was something ghostly about the household, and by 1925, Mary suspected she wasn't having as much fun as her classmates were. She was forbidden many of the liberties permitted other girls her age, while some of the adventures she did have—her secret life—would have singed the ears of her friends had they known of them. Though she wasn't permitted to go out with boys until she was sixteen, she had already lost her virginity to a local swell in a Marmon roadster when she was fourteen (about whom, more in a moment).

It is characteristic of Mary McCarthy that in her memoirs she identifies with both sides of a contradiction in her experience, aligning herself sometimes with the force of law, sometimes with rebellion, and needing them both. Writing of her popular performance as the rebel Catiline in a school play at the Annie Wright Seminary in 1927, the Takoma boarding school where McCarthy was sent after a single year at Garfield High School, she is quick to point out that behind the "Catilinian poses" there was " 'another' me" who was soon to fall in love with Caesar. And this new sensation, experienced with a rush when she read Caesar's *Commentaries* at Annie Wright, unlike her crush on Catiline, was not a projection of herself, but a brush with an "impersonal reality . . . just, laconic, severe, magnanimous, detached— the bald instrument of empire who wrote not 'I' but 'Caesar.' "

Pondering these schoolgirl tilts in *Memories of a Catholic Girlhood*, McCarthy notes that *"Caesar, of course, was my grandfather: just, laconic, severe . . . [while] Catiline was my McCarthy ancestors— the wild streak in my heredity, the wreckers on the Nova Scotia coast."* (The 'wrecker,' a kind of land pirate who used lanterns to draw ships to their doom, was a reference to Mary McCarthy's great-grandfather on her father's side, John McCarthy, who emigrated from Ireland in 1837 and settled in Newfoundland, where according to record he fished for cod and hunted seals. The fact that the wilder story became the family legend makes its own point.) *"The injustices my brothers and I had suffered in our childhood had made me a rebel against author-*

ity," McCarthy continues, *"but they had also prepared me to fall in love with justice, the first time I encountered it."*

Naturally she had 'loved' her Grandfather Preston from the beginning, but she had to live with him, and the conflicts between them over what she could and could not do often set her in opposition. Caesar, on the other hand, like the Latin language itself, and *"a rigorous code of conduct,"* could be loved abstractly and unreservedly. *"Caesar . . . in real life,"* McCarthy observes, *"would have been as strict as my grandfather ('Caesar's wife must be above suspicion'). . . ."* Later, the transference to literature of moral values impossible to uphold in daily life became a leitmotif of McCarthy's literary vision. The veneration of literature, in effect, endowed the whole business of writing with a rare 'impersonal' power.

Of all this, McCarthy was unaware in 1927—although she had begun to write fiction at this time, and to haunt the local library with her own card, unsupervised. Her stories had titles such as "A Wife and Mother," "The Story of a Suicide," and "What Doth It Profit a Man?" and seem to have been ground out like sausages under the approving eye of a young English teacher at Annie Wright from Vassar College, Dorothy Atkinson. Gloomy satires of fat, waddling, "fleshy" women, wives, mothers, clerks and prostitutes, who deceive themselves most notably in their relations with men, they were cut and sewn along the narrative lines of *True Confessions* and *True Story*—both of which were read by Mary McCarthy during these years, along with *Vanity Fair* and *Vogue*, and were more influential than the periodicals she invokes in her 'intellectual autobiography': *"L'Illustration, The Illustrated London News,* and *Punch,* as well as (I think) *The Virginia Quarterly Review, The Yale Review, Scribner's, The Century."* The presence of these classy journals on the round tables under the central lights of the Seattle library comforted McCarthy during her adolescent years, one guesses, for roughly the same reason that listing them satisfied her in 1987. They strike a dignified note. As for her own stories, even the slightest, "The Story of a Suicide," was 'touched' by greatness: A favorite passage from the New Testament, "I am the Resurrection and the Life," was draped across the title page like a laurel.

II

At home, Mary McCarthy never could put her finger on what was wrong. Nothing in her relations with her Grandfather Preston accounted for the strangeness she felt growing up; only that where her grandfather's history had met and merged with her grandmother's, "hidden chapters" had occurred. Her grandmother was the key.

Her grandmother's father had been a "broker," but what kind of broker McCarthy had never established. "My father had a nice business," was all Mrs. Preston would say. Her sister Rosie's musical abilities—Rose Gottstein was much in demand as a singer at Seattle weddings—suggested private schooling, but Mary could never piece together a satisfactory picture of life among the Morgansterns in San Francisco. Her grandmother had also lost both parents when she was still a relatively young girl, a significant fact in light of Mary's history, but neither McCarthy nor her grandmother seems to have considered it.

Mary liked to think that her Great-Grandfather Morganstern was a political emigré, but Mrs. Preston refused to supply the evidence. "Like many great beauties," McCarthy concluded, "she had little curiosity"—even about the people right under her nose. Her singular fact had been her celebrated beauty, the maintenance of which explained one thing that was different about the Preston household. When other families were sitting down to lunch, Mary's grandmother was in the bathroom with the door shut. A "small complaint," McCarthy calls her memory of the long hours she spent by herself while her grandmother prepared a face to meet her public, "but the clue to everything was there."

The big bathroom, with its couch covered by a worn Oriental carpet, its cupboards and drawers filled with ointments, buffers, and swabs, powders and chin straps and facial masks—the nearby closets hung with silver fox and baum marten, leopard and monkey fur, mink, squirrel, and broadtail—had always been the inner sanctum of the house. Even when Mary's mother was a little girl, and she and a neighbor stole into Mrs. Preston's dressing room while she was out shopping, to parade in front of the mirrors in gowns and furs, the room had a forbidden, haunted air. High on the bathroom shelves, Tessie and her friend Trudy Rigdon, the daughter of a poor Unitarian minister who lived down the street, had once discovered a box of champagne wafers. "The soul of honor," Tessie had been reluctant to touch them, but the clergyman's daughter showed her how to rearrange the remaining sweets to conceal their indulgence. When Trudy was asked to dinner, the experience wasn't pleasant. "Washed and shining," she recalled many years later, "I appeared only to be thoroughly frightened at the austere presence of Mr. Preston. . . ." Mrs. Preston's disapproving eye "followed my every move." The next morning when she returned for a schoolbook, she overheard Tessie's mother reprove her daughter for having chosen this "homely little thing" for a best friend, and Trudy was surprised to hear Tessie say firmly that "I was her best friend, and she wouldn't give me up." Mrs. Preston, the neighbor concluded, was the "beautiful but wicked queen."

Like her mother, Tess Preston also came to be known as "the most most beautiful woman in Seattle." And beauty, of course, would loom large in Mary McCarthy's legend: her actual beauty, the wide-set gray-green eyes, straight nose, triangular smile, the classic profile, which was startling in her youth; but also her attention to beauty, which was sometimes less engaging. "It was not difficult . . . to be the prettiest girl at a party for the sharecroppers," reflects the heroine of *The Company She Keeps,* who like the author is "contemptuous of the men who had believed her perfect, for she knew that in a bathing suit at Southampton she would never have passed muster. . . ." Contemplating her youthful desire to be an actress, McCarthy once suggested that her "stage ambitions were merely the vehicle for a hope to be acclaimed for my beauty." Beauty, albeit a somewhat competitive kind of beauty, and the means to display it, were entwined on the maternal tree.

Certainly it was Augusta Morganstern's beauty that had won her husband's hand, and now its maintenance had become the centerpiece of their married life. "This body of hers was the cult object around which our household revolved," McCarthy recalls. Everything her grandmother touched "became imbued for me with her presence, as though it were a relic," she adds, remembering her grandmother's clothes, "plumped to her shape, hanging on their velvet-covered hangers in her closet, which was permeated with the faint scents of powder and perfume, and the salty smell of her perspiration. . . ."

When her grandmother left to go shopping in the afternoon, Mary, like her mother before her, had flown into the forbidden chamber. There she would examine the jars from Elizabeth Arden, Dorothy Gray, Helena Rubinstein, and Harriet Hubbard Ayer. When she discovered a hidden box of something called Turkish Delight, she left it unopened, not because she was the soul of honor, but because she took it to be a beauty preparation used in harems. In "Ask Me No Questions," the inventory of this dressing room becomes an incantation, as if by *naming* the relics Mary McCarthy will capture the elusive character of the woman whose influence over her own character, once she grew older, came to assert itself with a strange tenacity. ("Did she want to induct you into these pleasures?" an interviewer once asked McCarthy about her Seattle grandmother's love of clothes, food, beautiful objects. "Well, she did! She *succeeded!*" came the prompt reply.)

"She had a cormorant's rapacity for the first fruits of the season: the tiniest peas, the youngest corn, baby beets cooked in their greens," McCarthy relates in the final chapter of *Memories of a Catholic Girlhood.* Mary's father had also cultivated a taste for fine food, hand-picked raspberries, fresh peaches. But Mrs. Preston's fastidious appetite, her emphasis on the *youth* of the garden's produce, struck Mary as almost "cannibalistic, as though she belonged to a species that devoured its own young." Watching her grandmother absently pinch and pluck one apricot after another from a bowl on the table while she read the morning paper, she was reminded of "what Freud calls the primal scene." She herself developed an aversion to apricots which lasted until middle life, when suddenly she, too, grew fond of them. Then, whenever she chose one from a plate, she thought of her grandmother's body, "full-fleshed, bland, smooth, and plump, cushioning in itself, close held—a secret, like the flat brown seed of the apricot."

The care and feeding of the body turned the act of shopping into something of a religious observance. More than anywhere else it was in a department store that Mary's grandmother came into her own. "[P]roceeding at a stately walk . . . peering through her *lorgnon* at the novelties and notions," she would vanish into the elevator to visit her favorite "purlieus"—the lending library, the custom-made, and the hat department. There,

> elderly salespeople, *her* salespeople, would hurry up to greet her, throwing their arms around her, just as though they had not seen her the day before. "Have you got anything for me?" my grandmother would demand . . . surveying the premises with a kind of jesting coquetry, a hand on her hip.

It was the same tone she took with the butcher: ". . . she would even coquette with a piece of meat. . . . To her, every piece of merchandise, suing for her favor, appeared to enter the masculine gender and to be subject, therefore, to rebuff." And yet the salespeople were always happy to oblige her, McCarthy remembers, for she was a very good customer, and "underneath her badinage, always good-humored."

Shopping, McCarthy reflected years later, was her Grandmother

Preston's social life. There was no other; no club meetings or charity
work, no temple observances, no theatrical subscriptions, no entertaining on her husband's behalf; only an annual tea for a few women
friends, with Mrs. Preston and one of her sisters each stationed at
opposite ends of the dining room table at their samovars.

The stillness in the Preston household conveyed a sadness and a
hint of reproof that Mary, as an adolescent, thought was aimed at her.
Was it her own attention-seeking, rebellious nature that sometimes
drove her grandparents into a stony silence? That, and the bad manners and 'common' tastes she feared she carried from Minneapolis like
stigmata? Did she disturb her grandparents' peace because she resembled her dead mother, as some people said? Or because she had her
father's impulsive temperament, as Mary thought herself? She could
never decide, and sometimes when she sensed a wound her grandmother harbored in her solitude, she wasn't sure whether the trouble
sprang from the death of her daughter, the botched-up face-lift (barely
discernible by the time Mary returned to Seattle), or some unpardon-
able social slight suffered deep in the past.

In the end, the aura of mystery surrounding Augusta Preston lingered like a burr under the saddle, reminding Mary McCarthy perhaps,
if she needed reminding, never to take a smooth, well-cushioned ride
for granted.

At Garfield, a big city high school located on the edge of the
Madrona district in what is now a black section of Seattle, Mary
McCarthy threw herself into the business of being a precocious teenager with an abandon not previously displayed. Boys made the difference; the presence of boys in the vicinity—not only at Garfield High
School but upstairs in her young Uncle Harold's rooms—heightened
the senses and bathed the social arena in the bright lights of desire and
anticipation.

The single year in public high school was an eventful interlude,
marking the onset of sexual curiosity, together with the birth of real
friendship—with Ted, Jess Rosenberg's sister. Overlooked in earlier
memoirs, the emergence, in *How I Grew,* of the pennant-waving,
boy-crazy Mary McCarthy compels attention precisely because she is
so unexpected, so unlike the bundle of overexcited scruples one encounters in *Memories of a Catholic Girlhood.* A typical American
adolescent who *hates* to go to the movies with " 'them,' " *hates* to ride
around in the family car on Sunday afternoons, who doesn't want to
look " 'different,' " she clips coupons from cheap magazines for free

samples of nail polish, freckle cream, bust developer, and makes messes in the kitchen cooking candy.

Far from typical, however, is the secret life McCarthy unfurls in her later memoir: the affairs of adolescence, which in McCarthy's case are not with boys—boys, such as the captain of Garfield's football team, Larry Judson, remaining purely objects of fantasy—but with men, who are objects of fantasy, too, but more accessible. There are three. Forrest Crosby, a man nearly twice Mary's age—"medium short, sophisticated, with bright blue eyes and crisp close-cut ash-blond curly hair, smart gray flannels, navy-blue jacket, and a pipe"—is right out of central casting, or the pages of *True Story*. He makes his first pass at the mountain retreat where Mary is vacationing with her grandfather in the summer of 1926, and then deflowers her on a dark wintry afternoon a few months later, when she has secretly met him for a rendezvous in his car.

Forrest Crosby is followed by a painter with a blond mustache named Kenneth Callahan, whom Mary met the following year at the salon of the notorious Seattle bohemian Czerna Wilson. Callahan is remembered for the rickety gangplank that led to his studio, where Mary secretly went to "sit" for him in the afternoons, and for "the things he did in bed [that] made me cringe with shame to think of afterwards." At Czerna Wilson's (where she went secretly, too), McCarthy had also met the older man who was said to be a Russian baron, Mr. Elshin, who owned a stationery shop and designed Christmas cards—one of which featured a ". . . cubic maiden,/ Who had a cubic smile," inspired by Mary, who was said to have a 'crooked smile.' With Mr. Elshin, McCarthy seems to have conducted a Lolita-like affair, though perhaps without the hard-core sex. She remembers how embarrassed she was when he held her hand in the dark at the movies, nearly as embarrassed as when he came to call on her at Annie Wright one Sunday afternoon, wearing cream-colored gloves and carrying a cane. Oddly, neither Crosby nor Callahan, who dispensed with such formalities, seemed to cause her the same embarrassment.

An involvement with older men, who could be expected to keep secrets, was a way of seeming older herself. Even Larry Judson was a senior and Mary a lowly freshman when he was miraculously cast as her "husband" in an acting class scene at Garfield High School. "She was always trying very hard to grow up," a friend from Annie Wright, Barbara Dole Lawrence, remembers of McCarthy during these years, "always looking toward adulthood. . . . We never took her too seriously when she told us about her adventures," she adds, "we thought she was kidding." It wasn't until some of her old classmates read *How I Grew* that they found out how far out on the fringe of convention Mary McCarthy really was. "Mary," Barbara Lawrence exclaimed, wonderingly, after reading the 1987 autobiography, "believes that nothing should be hidden!"

Such candor had its time and place. In *How I Grew,* which revisits a good many scenes from her early life, hidden in previous memoirs, McCarthy reflects upon the habit of deception into which she had fallen during her teenage years. Her grandparents' surveillance, which included prohibitions on everything from wearing silk stockings to going out with boys, she writes, led her to lie as a matter of course about where she had been, and with whom. She lied to her partners in deception as well, inflating her age and her experience for fear they would "despise" her if they knew what a sheltered life she led. And then she lied to other girls "to keep them from knowing . . . all of the above. This lying became a necessity," McCarthy explains, "imposed on me by my grandparents in the first instance, but then the habit was formed, as the wish to appear other than I was . . . dominated every social relation except those with teachers."

The exception was to give birth to a series of passionate attachments to intellectual women, beginning with one or two of the mesdames of the Sacred Heart, and continuing at Annie Wright with Dorothy Atkinson and a Latin teacher named Ethel Mackay (Miss Gowrie in *Memories of a Catholic Girlhood*). In the years ahead, the life of the mind would demand absolute fealty, while the life of the senses compelled surrender—not a devil's bargain but a ticklish one, as time would show. But even at thirteen Mary McCarthy had acquired "disciplined habits of thinking," Jess Rosenberg recalls. "It was all there," he declares, including the fierceness. "When Mary decided to do something, she did it—unlike Ted, who liked to have another cup of coffee and think about it," Rosenberg remarks.

Ted Rosenberg, who served as Mary's spirit-guide through Seattle's bohemia, introducing her to Czerna Wilson as well as to the work of a group of decadent fin-de-siècle authors—Walter Pater, W. H. Hudson, Oscar Wilde—couldn't have been more different. The younger daughter of a large, close-knit family (her father worked in a garment factory) who lived in a tiny house that was often full of young actors, painters, musicians, Ted collected other people's 'stories.' She was "sweet" on Mary's grandmother, whose 'tragic story,' whatever it was, she seemed to know, along with the story of Mary McCarthy's parents; but it was the vibration of a grand and unorthodox passion discovered in literature that teased her own fancy. Mary, on the other hand, was often disappointed in the "one-way traffic in limp leather volumes" that passed between them.

"[W]hat I was hoping for from books described as modern or daring . . . was to see the fig-leaf stripped off sex," McCarthy remarks in her autobiography. The strange vibration Ted picked up in a novel such as W. H. Hudson's *Green Mansions* eluded her. "Now I know its name," McCarthy writes: "literary art"; while she had no trouble perceiving "beauty"—which was what "literary art" was then called—in nature, she had trouble discerning it in books, from which she sought more immediate gratification.

It was in friendship that Ted Rosenberg was the "scout," the "pathfinder," and Mary the "follower." More than literary awareness, it was friendship that Mary McCarthy came to appreciate in her maturity "as essential to intellectuals. It is probably the growth hormone the mind requires as it begins its activity of producing and exchanging ideas," she suggests in *How I Grew*. "You can date the evolving life of a mind, like the age of a tree, by the rings of friendship formed by the expanding central trunk. In the course of my history," she concludes, "not love or marriage so much as friendship has promoted growth."

In social matters, Ted Rosenberg was a scout who nonetheless usually beat a hasty retreat after discovering new territory, while her follower plunged ahead. And yet it was Ted and her gregarious family who introduced the lonely adolescent who was Mary McCarthy in 1925 and 1926 to a larger and more congenial set of people—newspaper reporters, musicians, and actors—than any she had known before, or would again, until after college when she married one of them, the actor Harold Johnsrud, and settled down in New York.

McCarthy's sexual bravado had its own obscure origins, not so different from the circumstances surrounding the habit of deception, but not the same, either. This period in McCarthy's life reminds one of a classic twist in the development of any organism. When growth is arrested or 'dwarfed' in one direction, the impulse behind it bursts forth with enlarged vigor somewhere else. In McCarthy's case, her grandparents' refusal to allow her to pursue a conventional social life probably contributed to the eruption of a certain bawdy streak in her nature, a bawdiness 'thinly'—that is, seductively—disguised by a prose of contrition. Her guardians' surveillance alone does not explain the robustness of her appetite for sexual intrigue, however.

" '*They*' had forced me into clandestinity," McCarthy declares in

How I Grew, arguing the case for her grandparents' complicity in the
events that led to the sensational scene in the Marmon roadster. But
memory intervenes to remind her that on this occasion the Prestons'
behavior was not decisive. "Had they let Forrest Crosby come to the
house, he would have seduced me with greater ease, probably on their
own living-room sofa after they had retired"—because, in fact, *"he did
come to my house,"* she suddenly remembers, and did climb on top of
her on the sofa, whereupon someone was heard at the door, and he
fled. And Mary? How is it that she lands so easily on her back? Is it
the loneliness of the orphan, mixed with revenge against her losses, and
the rock-bottom sense that she is no longer really accountable to
anybody? Or is the prone position simply the 'better side' a much-
photographed model has learned to present to the camera?

It is hard somehow to see even this fourteen-year-old girl as the
helpless victim of a grown man's lust. One of Mary McCarthy's legendary attributes is that no matter how much fire and brimstone she
and her fictional heroines traverse before they see the light, they never
seem to get burned. A McCarthy heroine, beginning with the self she
projects in memoir, is a victim of circumstance, rarely the victim of
malevolence—Uncle Myers being a stark exception, as, in a sense,
Edmund Wilson would become, when McCarthy portrayed him in
fiction and memoir. She is more the student, irrepressibly curious, then
chastened. At the same time, motive and will for whatever reckless
action she enters into with someone else are generally given over to the
other side, and her own interest, the anatomy of her own desire,
remains obscure. Nor do we gather that she takes much pleasure in the
stolen kisses or the sex act.

The rendezvous with Forrest Crosby, like most seductions, begins
in self-deception: Crosby has commenced his lovemaking by making a
crude reference to another Annie Wright girl who was "fucked" by one
of his friends. ". . . I was still trying to think that with me it would be
different," McCarthy writes; "what he was starting to do as he unbuttoned himself and pulled aside my step-ins, would not be that f---ing."
The facts are there, but the feelings have been pruned back to present
an anecdote more shocking for its displacement of emotion. Crosby,
we are told,

> became very educational, encouraging me to sit up and examine
> his stiffened organ, which to me looked quite repellent, all flushed
> and purplish. . . . He must have thought it would be interesting for
> me to look at an adult penis—my first, as by now he must have
> realized. Then, as I waited, he fished in an inside breast-pocket and

took out what I knew to be a "safety." Still in an instructive mood, even with his erect member (probably he would have made a good parent), he found time to explain to me what it was—the best kind, a Merry Widow—before he bent down and fitted it onto himself, making me watch.

The gritty scene is scoured for its farcical properties. Mary sits demurely beside her mentor—one doesn't see whole bodies, only things, like the organ and the " 'safety' "—and takes her instruction with a dainty obedience. Of the actual penetration, she recalls nothing, no sensation; "perhaps a slight sense of being stuffed," and a stray recollection of being told to "keep step as in dancing." What she does remember clearly is "a single dreadful, dazed moment having to do with the condom":

Outside it is almost dark, but he is holding the little sack up to a light source—a streetlight, the Marmon's parking lights, a lit match?—to be sure I can see it well and realize what is inside—the sperm he has ejaculated into it, so as not to ejaculate it in me. I am glad of that, of course, but the main impression is the same as with the swollen penis; the jism is horribly ugly to me, like snot or catarrh, and I have to look away.

It is not a sexy scene.

The second time Mary goes to meet Forrest Crosby at a prear-ranged hour on a prearranged street, he never arrives. She returns the next day at the same hour, but he has abandoned her. When a few weeks later Crosby's letter of rejection reaches the Annie Wright Semi-nary, unsigned, Mary pours her heart into a furious reply, and then writes "I love you" underneath an upside-down postage stamp, which is boarding-school code for Read Me. For nearly a year she looks for the familiar roadster on Seattle's boulevards, sensing Crosby's pres-ence behind the wheel of every automobile whose gray hood juts above a high chassis.

"My love slowly withdrew from him, like a puddle drying up," McCarthy writes, reflecting: "If today there is something 'philosophi-cal' in my attitude to grief or disappointment, it may have been born then." In *How I Grew,* she no longer looks back to Minneapolis, interestingly enough, for the source of the philosophical attitude that is so clearly related, in *Memories of a Catholic Girlhood,* to the death of her parents.

In *How I Grew,* McCarthy puts the finishing touches on a philosophical attitude she herself perfected over the years to handle her losses; one that combines deprecation: "Forrie" ("*Hasta la vista!* . . . Forrie," he signed his letters) was "banal," after all; and self-deprecation: "[i]t was his accessories that seduced me. . . ." The car, the pipe, even the name Forrest Crosby, more harmonious than Burt Gottstein, a second-cousin to whom Mary was briefly attracted, or Jess Rosenberg, or even Larry Judson, who was part Jewish, too.

Still, the reconstruction of memory occasions some interesting reflections. He was a "wolf, but a wolf with consistency of style," McCarthy remarks; ". . . apparently he did not find sheep's clothing becoming." What was unusual about Crosby was not only the triumph of style over substance but also the fact "that he really '*wanted only one thing.*' Most men," she observes, "in the end, want much more." It is on the subject of her own performance that McCarthy is less satisfying. Because Forrest Crosby's organ and sperm repelled her, she wants us to understand that "the attraction did not go deep. . . . It was like a kind of hypnotism." She had obeyed his command to open her legs, having gone too far *not* to complete the "task," but it was only her body that submitted: "my mind held itself apart, not finding him, to my surprise, very interesting."

'Mind' gets the last word. ("You might say *will*, and not intelligence?/ Others go on thinking it mind, mind, mind," writes Robert Lowell in a poem about Mary McCarthy.) But of course she found Forrest Crosby "interesting." The fact that in 1926 this fourteen-year-old girl went out with a twenty-seven-year-old man speaks for itself. It is unlikely that McCarthy ever deliberately sets out to deceive herself about the deeper implications of her affairs, for to do so would cut her off from the pulse of memory, her lifeblood as a writer. Instead, she resorts to a time-honored dualism that is intrinsic to her nature—as it is to the moral world of Catholicism—in which the body proposes, and the mind disposes. Accordingly, the things that happen to the body are mere sports of nature, unclassified and unclassifiable, and only the mind brings order to the chaos of experience.

Such victories can never be more than holding actions, however, as the heroine of McCarthy's last story in *The Company She Keeps* acknowledges, regretfully, after her "analysis" has turned up the unsavory patterns in her loose behavior with men. Gradually, "she too knew what it was to have a sense of artistic decorum that like a hoity-toity wife was continually showing one's poor biography the door." But the 'poor biography,' like the 'poor relation' who is taught to keep his distance, keeps coming back.

Part Two

▪

Vassar: 1929–1933

5

"Touchstone Ambitions"

When I saw that banner on the wall, I asked her,

"If you really went to Vassar, what are you doing in a whore house?"

"Just lucky, I guess," she said.

—VASSAR JOKE

Not everybody's college holds a key to the kingdom of character. Even in the old days when someone 'went away' to school the way people used to marry, in a once-in-a-lifetime way, college occupied the middle, institutional ground in most people's lives. Today the college tie, like an arranged marriage, is often the product of a professional calculation: an investment of time and money against future earning power, divided by a young candidate's test scores, class rank, recommendations, and something ineffable that admissions officers call 'presentability.' Where somebody went to school (and when) tends to tell us more about fashions in schools and counseling offices than about the person who went there. Gone is the opportunity for a *coup de foudre* of the sort that befell Mary McCarthy in 1927, when the image of Vassar College first swam into her ken:

> I myself was an ardent literary little girl in an Episcopal boarding school on the West Coast, getting up at four in the morning to write a seventeen-page medieval romance before breakfast, smoking on the fire-escape and thinking of suicide, meeting a crippled boy in the woods by the cindery athletic field, composing a novelette in study hall about the life of a middle-aged prostitute ("Her eyes were turbid as dishwater") when the name, *Vassar*, entered my consciousness through the person of an English teacher.

The historic moment was recalled in 1951 in "The Vassar Girl"; and the English teacher was Dorothy Atkinson, class of '23. With her ash blond hair, slate blue eyes, folding eyeglasses, and satiric turn of mind, Miss Atkinson symbolized "the critical spirit, wit, cool learning, detachment—everything I suddenly wished to have and to be," McCarthy recalls, "from the moment I first heard her light, precise, cutting voice score some pretension, slatternly phrase or construction on the part of her pupils." In second-year English, Miss Atkinson had introduced her class to the essays of Macaulay and Thomas Huxley, alongside the sophomore's Shakespeare, *As You Like It*. Much later, McCarthy remembered her as "the cool essence of bluestocking." When Dorothy Atkinson suggested she send one of her short stories to the great H. L. Mencken for comment, Mary was struck, like St. Paul, by a divine presentiment: Yes, she was destined to enter the order of scribes—but first she must enter Vassar College.

Mencken never replied; but the idea of going to Vassar "and becoming like Miss A—" took possession of her and began to exact immediate concessions. She spent less time sampling Seattle's bohemia and more time studying. She dropped an easy course in domestic science at Annie Wright and registered for Latin, persuading the formidable Miss Mackay to tutor her in Caesar during the summer of 1928. The sudden change, already a pattern in McCarthy's life, was a foretaste of one of Vassar College's charms, which was that it offered its students a chance to break with the past and envision an idealized future. "A good deal of education consists of un-learning—the breaking of bad habits. This was emphatically true of a *Vassar* education," McCarthy reflects in *How I Grew*. "Vassar remade a girl; other colleges aimed at development, bringing out what was already there like a seed waiting to sprout. Vassar was transformational."

In 1929, the only other college that figured in McCarthy's future was the University of Washington, the "U"—where Ted Rosenberg was going, along with Ted's older brother Dan. Both of Mary's Preston uncles had gone to the U, as had her mother, and later her father. If universities have family plots like cemeteries, Mary McCarthy's soul was already assigned its mortal resting place at the University of Washington—and this was reason enough to bow to an emissary from another, loftier world. What Miss Atkinson represented was a standard of intellectual excellence that was exalted when it was embraced by women. Vassar, with its ancestral traditions of serious scholarship and social eminence, stood in a line of succession that began with the mesdames of the Sacred Heart. There was another side to the college that captured McCarthy's imagination, something she called the Vassar girl's passion for public service, "coupled with a yearning for the limelight, a wish to play a part in the theatre of world events, to perform some splendid action that will cut one's name in history like a figure eight in ice."

In "The Vassar Girl," McCarthy locates the "first note" of this pride in both service and performance in the sovereign pronouncements of the college's founder, Matthew Vassar, a self-taught Poughkeepsie brewer whose farming parents had migrated from England. "Woman, having received from her Creator the same intellectual constitution as man, has the same right as man to intellectual culture and development," he had declared in his maiden speech to the Board of Trustees in 1861, and concluded "that the establishment and endowment of a College for the education of young women" would satisfy his highest aspirations, and be, "under God, a rich blessing to this city and State, to our country and the world."

There was something imperial about the founder's declaration, which had the ring of a manifesto, McCarthy observed, befitting the year that incidentally was the year of Lincoln's inauguration, when the industrializing North set out to 'liberate' the South. The enunciation of a woman's right to "intellectual culture and development" equal to the best available to men evokes a different educational mission than that embodied in the seminarian traditions of the New England sister schools. Vassar's tradition reminded McCarthy of the Renaissance notion of the gentleman of parts. "The acquirement of 'parts,' usually meaning that one's natural gifts were enhanced and cultivated by knowledge of foreign languages, classics, [and] history," she told an audience of graduating seniors in 1976, "became in the high Renaissance a social task imposed on the upper classes, as though to make good for the loss of their function as a warrior caste, they had to become ornaments and shine in conversation."

In her commencement address, McCarthy pointed out that "[i]t was not until the notion that higher education need not be *good* for anything began to prevail that the doors opened to women," a remark not meant to disparage women or liberal education. Women, she suggested, infused new life into the classical liberal arts curriculum. In 1982, she told a group of Vassar students that "Yale boys didn't learn anything in the subjects I knew anything about. We looked down on male education," she remembered.

In her own day, most Vassar students regarded higher education as a more serious opportunity than any vocation: "It was an induction into mental life for its own sake, even into mental athletics, hitherto banned to the sex, like field sports and throwing the javelin. Wrestling with a text," she recalled, "produced a joyful excitment, which lasted into later life. . . ." McCarthy had easily assimilated the Renaissance ideal herself. Trying to assess the worth of the "accumulated bits and pieces housed in my upper story," for her contemporary audience, she wondered:

> If in a lecture on the Gothic given in Leyden, Holland, I am able to say that the architectural style known as English Perpendicular reminds me of Chaucer and evoke from one listener an amused nod of recognition, was it for this that Matthew Vassar brewed his beer?

In "The Vassar Girl," McCarthy had also noted a likeness between the authoritative tone of Matthew Vassar's declaration and the way Vassar students invariably pronounced themselves in favor of this or that school of thought or way of doing things, as if a declaration of preference conferred value. When she asked Vassar undergraduates to define a "Vassar girl" in the early 1950s, she was assured that there was no such thing as a "Vassar *stereotype*"—Vassar was "a collection of very different 'individuals,' " which struck her as "a highly Vassar remark, indicating a certain virtuous superiority. . . ."

When McCarthy entered Vassar's Taylor Gate in the fall of 1929, escorted by two Mrs. Prestons, her grandmother and her uncle Frank's wife, Isabel, she was overcome by feelings of "pride and glory of belonging to the very best class in the very best college in America." The procession of bareheaded Yale boys lounging in roadsters outside the gate; the impeccable Vassar upperclasswomen in pale sweaters, with pearls at the throat; the vaulted library; the catalogue starred for courses like "The Meaning of Morals . . . open to freshmen by special permission"; the row of tea shops and dress shops hugging the northern edge of the campus; the rolling fields and orchards to the east, and the dairy farm to the south (where Vassar's prize Guernseys were bred and milked for the college kitchens); the trolley running downtown to more shops and restaurants, and to the railroad station and New York—"all this," to the outlander from Seattle, "seemed to foretell four years of a Renaissance lavishness, in an academy that was a Forest of Arden and a Fifth Avenue department store combined."

The feeling of "pride and glory," an uncharacteristic one for McCarthy, whose sense of *belonging* over the years would rarely extend beyond a fugitive fringe of like-minded intellectuals, never left her during four years of college. "Vassar," she thought, "has a peculiar power of conveying a sense of excellence." But it was more than excellence, and more than the 'Renaissance lavishness' that held her allegiance in the decades since graduation in 1933, an allegiance that withstood the fury of some of her classmates after the publication of her best-selling novel about the class of '33, *The Group*, thirty years later. By 1976, when she delivered the commencement address, she had begun a triumphal return, which was followed by lectures as a Distinguished Visitor in 1982; the sale of her papers to the Vassar Library in 1984 for $100,000, together with more personal appearances; and in the summer of 1985, incredibly, an invitation to succeed the outgoing president, Virginia Smith, as the new president of Vassar. The letter of invitation from the college search committee was a gesture of recognition and esteem—and the irony was not lost on its recipient, who once confided that her senior rooming group in Main Hall was "practicing tolerance" by including her, "since I was so different from them." By 1985, the prodigal had returned bearing laurels, and while no one could imagine Mary McCarthy, then seventy-three, running a college, a certain score had been settled.

"In a way," Meg Sargent reflects in "Ghostly Father, I Confess," putting the matter in a nutshell, "it was to escape . . . from the whole *unfair* business of having to have a verifiable history, that she had gone east to college. There if you had money and used the right fork, no one could suspect an Aunt Clara in your vague but impeccable background." Vassar supplied Mary McCarthy with a pedigree, by osmosis. After a certain number of holidays (too short to justify the long train trip home) spent in country houses along the Hudson and town houses in New York, she could not help but soak up the materials she needed for that refinement of character that, together with the salting away of arcane knowledge, commanded her respect.

There was another side to McCarthy's tie with Vassar that she herself had forgotten until the early 1980s, when she was sent a packet of letters she had written Ted Rosenberg during her freshman year. In the beginning, she had scorned the "nice little rounded hills and short fat trees" of the Hudson Valley, which she pronounced "too domesticated." She had missed the "geometric lines, points, and angles" of Puget Sound, she wrote Ted in October 1929. Outside the classroom, she had found it hard to establish her footing, and she had made only one friend, a girl from Waterbury, Connecticut, who would leave before the first year was out.

The spectacle of so much wealth and privilege in the hands of girls her own age was unsettling, and it would take her three years before she established her own paradoxical relationship to the bird chorus of debutantes who surrounded her during her freshman year. " 'Cum-cum!' they called, for Comfort Parker, 'Rosil-l-la!' for Rosilla Horn-blower, 'A-lye-dah!' for Alida Davis. A whole bevy of them, trilling and cawing, lived in Davison [as she did] and behaved as if no one else did," McCarthy recalled in 1987. In 1929, she wrestled with her disad-vantage, which had disclosed a new facet. In this "English country-side," she was a "Mick" whose exotic moniker, "Mary McCarthy," drew smiles from boys who opened the doors of their touring cars; her name, they confided, sounded like a little mill worker from Lowell. The smiles surprised her—in both Minneapolis and Seattle the Irish stood on top of a pyramid of Scandinavians. More disturbing might have been the fact of her Jewish grandmother, but throughout her four years at Vassar, McCarthy kept that to herself.

A double vision of haughty contempt for Vassar society, mingled with fascination and with envy, insinuated itself into her early response to college. Vassar was "all right," she wrote Ted, "better than the University of Washington anyway." But there was "too much smart talk, too many labels for things, too much pseudo-cleverness. I suppose I'll get that way, too," she added, "though I'm doing my best to avoid it." And later, after Christmas: "As for me, I do nothing but bewail my fate for being in this damned assured stupid college and write letters even more assured and stupid than the college. What the hell?" Tough talk; but the letters begged for news from her old friend, who hadn't written. Mary had spent Christmas with a girl she hardly knew in Poughkeepsie, she informed Ted, adding, "I wanted to be in some-body's house. . . . The thought of waking up Christmas morning in the Vassar Club was too much for me." For the rest of the holiday she had gone down to New York to meet Harold Johnsrud, the actor she had first seen in Seattle playing a knight in a Magna Charta pageant with her grandparents in 1928, and then met, by arrangement, at a summer dinner party at the Rosenbergs'.

Johnsrud, who had materialized on Fifth Avenue soon after Mary's arrival in New York in September, appeared to be fulfilling his original promise as the Red Cross Knight. He had rescued her from a falling-out with the two Mrs. Prestons at the Metropolitan Museum and taken her to an art exhibit and a downtown play. In October, Mary took her first weekend away from Poughkeepsie to see him in *The Channel Road*, a George S. Kaufman and Alexander Woollcott adaptation of a de Maupassant story. By the second semester she was spending whole weekends with him at 50 Garden Place in Brooklyn Heights, and later on Bank Street in Greenwich Village. The twenty-eight-year-old Johnsrud, who had also been the drama critic for the *Seattle Times,* had begun to offer her the means to hold her own against the mannered voices from the East. With his high-domed forehead and smashed nose, he was a character actor, not a Valentino; but he was also an aspiring playwright, whose "charisma," as one of McCarthy's classmates remembers, "impressed us all." Mary's affair with John, as she called him, evoked a 'past,' a secret life in the adult world about which most freshmen, dutiful daughters still, could only dream.

"We considered Mary McCarthy to be on a level of sophistication we could not attain until marriage, if then," another classmate recalls, remembering a girl who asked, " 'Mary McCarthy says there are perverts who make love to dead bodies. Can that be true?' " and she had responded, " 'Well, if Mary says so.' " This Mary McCarthy was a variation on the image of the siren perfected in Seattle, but the image no more reflected the larger truth of her identity than the teenage vamp reflected the isolation McCarthy remembers feeling in the home of her Seattle grandparents, in *Memories of a Catholic Girlhood.*

An exception to the negative report Mary had offered Ted Rosenberg was Anna Kitchel, an expert on nineteenth-century English literature who taught Freshman Composition. Miss Kitchel was "a joy—homely, raw-boned and middle-aged [at thirty-five], but with a good, heady sense of humor," she wrote Ted. " 'Girls, hand me your effusions,' " she always said when she collected their themes. At her suggestion the students were reading Irish literature on the side, and Mary noted with satisfaction that her classes had turned into "long conversations between her and me." Along with the chairman of the English Department, Helen Sandison (Kitchel's next-door neighbor and close friend), Anna Therese Kitchel, Smith College, University of Wisconsin, was one of a handful of dedicated scholars who dominated the intellectual life of Vassar's more precocious students, much as the celebrated Christian Gauss had done at Princeton nearly twenty years before for Edmund Wilson and F. Scott Fitzgerald—though for McCarthy there was a filial dimension to the apprenticeship.

In *How I Grew*, Miss Kitchel and Miss Sandison evoke the image of "the Mothers" in Goethe's *Faust*: "enthroned beyond the world of place or time." But they were also flesh and blood women with whom Mary and Johnsrud sometimes drank bootleg applejack on the porch behind the faculty dormitory. Both Miss Sandison and Miss Kitchel were fond of Johnsrud, which was important. Like John and Mary, too, in part, they were Midwesterners: Sandison, an Elizabethan scholar, from Indiana; Kitchel from Wisconsin. It isn't hard to imagine a family feeling creeping into the little band, not only for the young woman whose "life [had] been a sad one," as one of McCarthy's Annie Wright recommendations had noted, concluding, "one needs to know something of her history in order to understand her," but for the unmarried professors of English, as well.

McCarthy's account of her favorite teachers is full of unabashed warmth. It is a different matter with her attitude toward the social side of Vassar, which is more ambiguous. Reviewing the long-forgotten correspondence with Ted Rosenberg, she professes surprise at the dissatisfied tone, which runs afoul of established memory. She ponders a line from one of Johnsrud's early letters: " 'I thought you would find Vassar brittle, smart, and a little empty.' " The sentiment, with its suggestion of superior sophistication, flatters her, but had she really looked down her nose at Vassar's smart talk? Perhaps she *had* gotten " 'that way.' " "If I can no longer feel what I felt about the college when I wrote to Ted," she speculates, "it is because I, too, the product of a Vassar education, am now brittle, smart, and a little empty. And oblivious of it."

But maybe the critical stance had been Johnsrud's. In her letters to Ted, she was doing "a bit of mourning plus a bit of impersonation, speaking to her in a soprano rendition of the Johnsrud voice." If such was the case, the mourning may have also been dictated by McCarthy's separation from the first real friend she ever made, and by her departure from Seattle. She had appropriated Johnsrud's judgment for one of those dangerous interludes when, minister without portfolio, she entered a new domain.

II

Vassar's class of '33 began with the Wall Street crash of October 1929, and ended with the closing of the banks in the spring of 1933, and yet the Depression barely enters McCarthy's accounts of her college years, until the election year of 1932. Before that, she recalls merely an onset of "job anxieties" among girls who had to "cut down." Odd jobs on campus like the wake-up job are mentioned. In 1931, she remembers studying Freud's *On the Interpretation of Dreams* in Psychology and hiring a girl "to burst into my room late at night or early in the morning yelling, 'Fire!' which was meant to produce a dream that I could write down, half awake, on a tablet ready by my bedside." The Depression reminds her of funny stories about herself.

In 1976, McCarthy suggested that "what was happening outside in those years . . . was so heavy, sad, and ominous that it seemed better to stay, while we could, with dream-experiments, and with Catullus-Tibullus-Propertius-and Ovid; the condemned man ate a hearty breakfast." In her own case, it would take a literary experience, the discovery of John Dos Passos's *The 42nd Parallel* in Contemporary Prose Fiction, to wake her up to the political upheavals happening outside Taylor Gate. And it would be a literary friendship with the studious poet Elizabeth Bishop (class of '34) that would stimulate an interest in socialism. And both would happen only toward the end of four years at Vassar.

Had anyone asked her in 1930 why she was taking Shakespeare, Medieval French, Philosophy of Nature, and Catullus–Ovid, rather than any of the new courses that were opening up in economics and sociology, the answer would have been "for fun." It wasn't that she was unserious; to summon up grave issues, the mind must be allowed to play; but for the dialectic of sparring, conflict, and 'acting out' between teachers and students to unfold, both text and subject matter were better chosen from among the immortals. And the steamy news of Bonus Marchers in Washington, farmers pouring milk over roads, stockbrokers jumping out of windows, Hitler coming to power, the Japanese entering Manchuria, and banks closing was best left outside the classroom door.

Mary McCarthy's Vassar, nonetheless, really was changing. Other classmates recall the candlelight dinners that were instituted two times a week in 1932 to 1933 to help cut down on the electric bill. Helen Ratnoff Plotz, who with about thirty other members of a class of two hundred went on scholarship in 1932, worked in the campus lunchroom, the Retreat. The poet Muriel Rukeyser, who was offered a scholarship when the family sandstone business went bankrupt, had to turn it down and leave the college. Her parents wouldn't discuss money in front of their children, and Rukeyser's father refused to complete the required financial statement.

While the vital center of the student body undoubtedly remained true to Republican type, the stock market crash shook some apples from the ancestral tree. Vassar largely resisted the vocational impulse that swept other women's colleges, where alarm over the suddenly overcrowded conditions in the 'respectable occupations'—teaching, nursing, stenography, and library work—triggered new interest in the applied sciences, social work, and clinical psychology. The Vassar curriculum, on the other hand, began to reflect a notably businesslike interest in the problems of industrial society. New courses such as The Progress of Social Reorganization, Industrial Development in the U.S., and Labor Problems (taught by members of the New York Department of Labor) testified to Vassar's nearness to the entrepreneurial elite from which it sprang. FDR had been a Vassar trustee, after all, before he became President.

Under lofty hemlocks, earnest young technocrats talked of "better management," of paying people by the "urbs" of work instead of by hours. McCarthy would not have joined them—variations on these themes would be skewered in *The Group*—but the voices of ideologues of every hue set the tone for her tenure at Vassar. By 1932, a few students announced themselves to be Communists; and something called "the Communist system" entered the running debate about how to reorganize society. In Russian History (which Mary didn't take), students watched Miss Lucy Textor, recently returned from a tour of the Soviet Union, draw a pyramidal tree on the blackboard to illustrate the structure of the Communist party. Like students elsewhere, they were asked the traditional question: "Do the results justify the means?"

In the fall of 1932, Vassar students were chastised by a visiting Yale professor for their indifference to the misery of unemployment in the United States; and what did they know of the prison camps in Turkestan, where seventy-five people died every day of starvation? In 1933, Dean Mildred Thompson spoke out for the "right" and the "need" for undergraduates to express opinions on such questions as the IRA and the expanding war abroad. In the 1932 election, most of the left-wing students were Socialists and campaigned for Norman Thomas, like Mary's classmate Eunice Clark, who led a Socialist parade around campus. "We of the 'aesthetic' camp considered them jejeune and naive," McCarthy recalled of the Socialists in "The Vassar Girl." "We were more impressed when we heard, after a poll, that a plurality of the faculty were voting for Thomas that year."

But when a movement of "Concerned Students" with faculty support failed to "Abolish the Senior Prom" and turn the funds over to the Poughkeepsie unemployed, the aesthetes decided to help stage a counterprom for "the poor" (namely, themselves). Tables were set up in Students Building and draped with red-and-white-checked tablecloths; candles flickered in wine bottles; suddenly a smoke bomb went off at one end of the hall, and newspaper vendors poured into the room shouting, "Extra! Extra! . . . J. P. Morgan murdered Karl Marx! . . . Buy the *Mortem Post*!" The handout included a poem by Elizabeth Bishop, which ended: "O victim of th' assassin's shot, the *Mortem Post* forget thee not!" Which was not quite up to the immortal lines that Bishop, as she was called at Vassar, tacked on her door next to the bathroom in Cushing:

> Ladies and gents, ladies and gents,
> Flushing away your excrements,
> I sit and hear beyond the wall
> The sad continual waterfall
> That sanitary pipes can give
> To still our actions primitive.

But it did mark a rapprochement of sorts between the literati and the left.

"The Depression was like an earthquake," Mary McCarthy's classmate Frani Blough Muser recalls today, locating Vassar College some distance away from the epicenter; "it took awhile before the flood got up the Nile." When the tide of radicalism that had already swept City College in New York began to lap at Vassar's gate—via the Drama Department in a torrent of Futurist and proletarian plays—both Frani Blough and Mary McCarthy continued to keep their distance. Not for them a revolving stage with a door leading nowhere, as in the satire *See America Now*, in which a Dance of the Depression was executed by a "bread-line." Frani and Mary, avid stagehands and actors themselves, and from their sophomore year, close friends, were more interested in the Philatheis Society's 1930 production of *The London Merchant* by George Lillo, a revival of a play originally staged at the Drury Lane in April 1731. And it was the Drama Department's American premier of T. S. Eliot's *Sweeney Agonistes* in November 1930, attended by Eliot himself, that gave them, in Frani Muser's words, "the idea of *theatre* as something that was part of the world."

For McCarthy, however, it wasn't politics or theatre but literature that opened doors. "No girl could be the same after Kitchel's English or Sandison's Shakespeare," she asserts in *How I Grew*, adding that even the most complacent student was jolted into a sudden awareness of the contemporaneousness of the classics. What these teachers seemed to offer was something more than an appreciation of great literature; their emotional proximity to the writers themselves ran like a subtext through the lessons a Vassar girl might learn at school. " 'Oh, he was a *rare bird*!' " Anna Kitchel said of Wordsworth, after reviewing his secret affair with Annette Vallon in a course called Blake-to-Keats. Standing up to Miss Kitchel after she declared her fondness for Wordsworth's "Michael," a poem Mary and Frani pronounced "boring," wasn't easy when the teacher's choice was also an affair of the heart. But it was this intimate relationship to the *makers* of literature, so different from the impersonal contemplation of 'great books' practiced in other schools, that fired a girl's imagination and made her bold.

McCarthy recalls her amazement when the soft-spoken Helen Sandison treated her class to a dissertation on the "Platonizing tendency" of the Elizabethan period. Frankness about male homosexuality was unexpected in the classroom, but the novelty was only part of the larger thrill of admission to the private lives of poets. A direct line to the immortals went both ways. A student whose artistically inclined young man was undergoing mental anguish might elicit from Miss Kitchel a sympathetic nod; "Byronism," she would observe knowingly.

This was a life of the mind fairly teeming with romance. Even Horace and Apuleius had their patroness in Miss Elizabeth Hazelton Haight, the tall, white-haired, "Sabine" professor of Latin, whose personal attachment to certain ancients was well known. When Miss Kitchel left Blake-to-Keats in the winter of 1931, she headed for the British Museum to research a book about the famous liaison between George Eliot and G. H. Lewes. Kitchel was an expert on George Eliot, but her original scholarship, like that of many women professors of the day, was devoted to the rescue of minor figures such as George Lewes.

In Mary McCarthy, Kitchel and Sandison seemed to have found a kindred spirit. For her senior thesis with Miss Sandison, a two-part paper, McCarthy chose to write first about Sir John Harington, Queen Elizabeth's worldly-wise godson and the translator of Ariosto. The paper, which was called "Touchstone Ambitions," was published in *The Journal of Undergraduate Studies*, and won first prize for an essay on the Elizabethan period. But it was the second figure she chose to study, Robert Greene, who revealed the special bond she had established with the poet-adventurers of the Elizabethan renaissance.

No doubt Robert Greene caught Mary's eye for his jousting with the mighty Shakespeare—"His tygres heart wrapt in a player's hide. . . . The onely Shake-scene in a county"—as well as for his friendship with the satirist Thomas Nashe. Nor would she have found it easy to resist Greene's deathbed repentance, composed in just such a way that its sincerity could never be ascertained. In her autobiography, McCarthy observes that both Harington and Greene appealed to her for the same reason that King Arthur's nephew, Sir Gawain, attracted her when she discovered him in *The Idylls of the King* at the Annie Wright Seminary. Like Gawain (and perhaps two of her husbands-to-be: Johnsrud and Bowden Broadwater), they were her fatal type: "debonair and disabused." They were accessory lords whose uncertain status may have offered the proselytizer in Mary McCarthy room to show her stuff.

Like Sir Gawain, however, Greene was probably "less a light of love than an alter ego." He provided her with a type whose obscure origins and bright prospects seemed to project her own emerging reality. "Robert Greene," McCarthy wrote in 1933, "had the good fortune to be a scholar at Cambridge during its most brilliant and tumultuous years of intellectual activity." Christopher Marlowe, Edmund Spenser, William Harvey, and Thomas Nashe all passed through Cambridge's St. John's College (where the great Erasmus himself once taught) during Greene's residence. "They were all acutely conscious of their universities, partly from memory of the radiance of learning," she noted, "partly because their universities were their talismans: they served the young writers in lieu of a title or a family name."

Vassar served Mary McCarthy in much the same way. By her senior year when she had moved in with some of the original Davison girls from Chapin and Madeira, she "was delighted to be one of them, even though I was not really one but a sort of guest," she once confided to a stranger. "They amused me, and I, as a Western girl, was impressed by their parents, their houses, their butlers. . . ." A taste for luxury had emerged as a badge of literary sensibility. In *How I Grew*, McCarthy wonders why the plain-dealing Misses Kitchel and Sandison never warned her of "the effect on a girl from the Northwest of exposure to the contagious disease of snobbery. . . . Perhaps my teachers counted on the counter-influence of Johnsrud," she muses. "But it may be, too, that, in their view, social ambition occurred too classically in literature to be regarded as greatly harmful, lying so very close . . . to the passion for excellence, beauty, fine ornament, and to the gift of worship. What English major was—or ought to be—free from the vice?"

McCarthy was also interested in Greene's "sententious novels," which disclosed his decision to become "a journalist, a hack-writer, the first hack-writer of modern times. He could keep a sensitive . . .

finger on the popular pulse, and give it what it wanted." Marlowe and Nashe were themselves, McCarthy wrote, "while Greene was all of them, except Spenser. Had he lived longer he might have been Spenser too. He was Kyd and Shakespeare as well." While Mary McCarthy assimilated 'voices' the way other people assimilate manners, fashion, or ideas from the influences around them, she was neither a hack writer nor an imitator, and never would be; but ambition ran sufficiently strong in her veins to be inseparable from the life force. Greene had it, and, lacking the genius of Kyd or Nashe, knew enough to appropriate their style; just as Mary had assimilated a Latinate turn of phrase from Annie Wright, and at Vassar learned the uses of a kind of Augustan stagecraft in prose. But it was Greene's ability to literally *write* himself into the public eye, to cut a name and a career for himself out of the whole cloth of his prose, that reminds one of Mary McCarthy, and makes this relatively obscure English writer leap to life in her paper.

There was another side to the Cambridge group that attracted McCarthy. Nashe, Marlowe, Greene—all "parodied and satirized one another's writing" and sometimes each other's lives, yet their esprit de corps was never broken. It isn't the Vassar group one thinks of here, but the rogue intellectuals McCarthy would later join in New York. The bickering anti-Stalinists whose 'university' was *Partisan Review*: Dwight Macdonald, Philip Rahv, F. W. Dupee, Lionel Abel—Mary would parody each of them, and most would remain friends; just as she would remain loyal to Elizabeth Hardwick after Hardwick parodied *The Group* in 1963.

At Vassar, with the founding of a rebel magazine named *Con Spirito*, McCarthy had her first taste of the conspicuous clannishness of literary folk. Mary and Bishop originally had the idea for an underground venture in the fall of 1931, when McCarthy wanted to call it "The Battleax," but the first issue, paid for with a three-hundred-dollar bonus that Eunice Clark had gotten for editing the *Miscellany News*, didn't appear until a year later. Eunice Clark recalls *Con Spirito* as "an almost Joycean palimpsest of meanings—we were drinking wine, we were conspirators, and we had a lot of nerve." The maiden issue quoted an editorial from George Jean Nathan's and James Branch Cabell's *American Spectator*: " 'The road to Smith and Vassar is paved with good intentions, the intentions of busy-minded young women to become carbon copies of men,' " to which the editors replied: "We hope that this intellectual venture of ours will no more disturb the all-wise purposes of Jehovah than (we trust) the literary dalliance of these gentlemen has interfered with their lawful begetting of infants." The editors went on to say that *Con Spirito* would avoid "bookishness"—or, as Frani Blough wrote her mother in Pittsburgh, "Nothing tame, arty, wishy-washy. . . ."

With *Con Spirito*, the aesthetes took their stand against the clubby insularity of the *Vassar Review*, which either wouldn't print their avant-garde submissions or altered their sentences to sound like Matthew Arnold. They chose anonymity, tacking up notices for the new magazine on trees in the dead of night, and eschewing a masthead. The stories, poems, and reviews remained unsigned; even the editors—Mary McCarthy, Elizabeth Bishop, Margaret Miller, Muriel Rukeyser, Eleanor and Eunice Clark, and Frani Blough—could never be sure who had contributed what when they met at a Poughkeepsie speakeasy to lay out an issue.

Initially, it was the magazine's anonymity rather than its contents that provoked comment—mostly negative—from the college community. But anonymity also gave the nonliterati a chance to beard the lion. The April 1933 number featured a poem submitted "anonymously" by an inmate of the local mental hospital where Vassar students did volunteer work. "Clinic," which described a woman with "lips . . . like the stoppers of perfume bottles," who tried to knife her husband because he insisted on mashed potatoes for breakfast, was actually written by Helen Ratnoff and a friend, *"con granus salus"* ("with a grain of salt"); but the editors took it for the real thing.

Even today some of the contents remain unidentifiable, like "The Bachae, or Revelling Women," which was neither arty nor tame, but rather gross. "Enter Dionysius H. Lawrence," it began, "Raise aloft the Phallic Symbol," and so on. The Dionysian note was in the air—"Nature in the Raw is seldom *Mild*," declared the Lucky Strike logo in the *Miscellany News*. But the 'Revelling Women' could also be serious, as Mary McCarthy was in *"In Pace Requiescamus."* A prose poem about Hitler and Mussolini—"They say he is an epileptic; they say he is a madman; they say he is Napoleon"—it reached for irony, but communicated instead apprehension over the news drifting in from Europe. McCarthy's review of Aldous Huxley's *Brave New World* and Harold Nicholson's *Public Faces* was more characteristic. Huxley, she pronounced "conceited" for his celebration of the "sensitive man." She much preferred Nicholson's "ribald wit."

Muriel Rukeyser was undoubtedly the author of "Lecture by Mr. Eliot," a poem commemorating Eliot's return to Vassar in 1933 when he first delivered one of the Possum poems. Rukeyser deplored the "cerebral whoredom" of the audience's "homage to prosody as a god," while

> Somewhere beyond these windows,
> China moans . . .
> In Alabama are beat[en] nine dark boys,
> And quenched—while poets practice smiling
> contemptuously at the seventh row.

The "nine dark boys" was a reference to the Scottsboro trial, a contemporary miscarriage of justice that passed McCarthy by. She had just been inflamed by a 1927 pamphlet on the Sacco and Vanzetti case, discovered while wading through Dos Passos in the basement of the Vassar library.

An essay on Surrealism by Margaret Miller, the green-eyed, black-haired art major from Oklahoma, who would later provide Mary McCarthy with a model for Lakey in *The Group*, and Elizabeth Bishop's story, "Then Came the Poor," a black-comic tale of a revolutionary takeover set in the near future, placed *Con Spirito* alongside *The Harkness Hoot* at Yale and the early *Hound & Horn* at Harvard. When Eunice Clark sent the rebel sheet to Lewis Gannett at the *New York Herald Tribune,* he gave it an honorable mention in the *Book Review*. In the summer of 1933, when Mary showed it to the literary editor of the *The New Republic*, Malcolm Cowley, it helped her get her first assignment.

In later life, McCarthy remembered *Con Spirito* simply as a lot of fun. She was less impressed by its literary merit than by a curious lesson in " 'motiveless malignity' " it had to impart. "Because it was unsigned. That was the outrage, the shameful crime, treated as such even by some of the faculty," she recalls in *How I Grew*, who breathed the word 'anonymous' as though it were married to the word 'letter,' denoting something so scurrilous that it dared not sign its name." Nobody stopped to think that the august *Times Literary Supplement* published unsigned articles and reviews. But that wasn't the point. McCarthy never says so directly, but one senses that she thinks *Con Spirito* was too *good* for Vassar. The " 'motiveless malignity' " that it aroused was "touched off by a good or morally neutral deed." The phrase is Shakespeare's and refers to Iago: " 'He has a daily beauty in his life that makes me ugly,' which [Iago] says of Cassio, being the best explanation of his conduct he ever vouchsafes."

Helen Sandison "went to the mat" for the editors, whose identity, McCarthy speculates, she had picked out at once. "It would not surprise me if Miss Sandison had even used her position as head of the English Department to overpower our enemies," she adds. Factionalism was in the air and Mary McCarthy sniffed it out when others might have let it blow over. Truth and beauty never shone so brightly as when they were assaulted by philistines.

Con Spirito's detractors pale beside the figure McCarthy paints of a more serious antagonist in the English Department, Helen Lockwood. In *How I Grew* (as in *The Group*), she cannot resist pitting her favorite teachers against an enemy whose character appears to be their antithesis. While Kitchel and Sandison "were trying to teach us to stand on our own," McCarthy writes, the other Helen, Helen Lockwood "indoctrinated." Miss Lockwood's Contemporary Press "was the scene, almost like a camp meeting, of many a compulsory transformation as hitherto dutiful Republican daughters turned into Socialists and went forth to spread the gospel."

It was Lockwood's means that corrupted her ends, McCarthy suggests. Like an evil stepmother or a jealous guardian, Lockwood "insisted that a girl completely break with her mother as the price of winning her favor. The effect on the girl was a kind of smug piety, typical of the born anew, that could last for years, long after the one-time converts, now alumnae (married, with 2.4 children), had turned back into Republicans." McCarthy, who stayed away from Contemporary Press, prefaces her charges with "we heard" and "it was said." Other classmates who took the course—which is still given at Vassar—remember Lockwood differently.

"She was just as intellectual, just as scholarly as Miss Sandison," Helen Ratnoff Plotz recalls, "but she was interested in social problems." Lockwood had done her dissertation on England's Corn Laws and the literature that followed; in the early 1930s and later, she was active in working women's education. At Vassar, she liked to send her Freshman Composition students down to Main Street in the center of Poughkeepsie to report on what they saw; on other occasions, she assigned papers in Chemistry or Physics (one or the other being required of every Vassar freshman) to teach students how to talk about science in terms that could be understood. She was worldly, more worldly than Anna Kitchel or Helen Sandison, and the world she wanted her students to see and understand during the 1930s was not a comforting one. Indeed, one wonders whether Lockwood's tilt toward the raw materials of life massed outside Vassar's Taylor Gate wasn't part of the grudge Mary harbored against her. "Lockwood made you look at power in a way you never had before," Helen Plotz remembers today—and it is hard to imagine an achievement less congenial to a young woman of the 1930s who was interested in the art of, among other things, addressing a butler.

There is a bitter, unforgiving edge to McCarthy's treatment of Helen Lockwood that hints of buried grief; and indeed there was something in Lockwood's confrontational style (Helen "Intimidation" Lockwood, she was known in the 1940s) that made Mary see red. In her autobiography, McCarthy recalls a moment in the second semester of Blake-to-Keats "when the 'charismatic' Miss Lockwood, who had a mustache and a deep 'thrilling' voice [and was covering the class in Miss Kitchel's absence, much to Mary's dismay] fired an opening question at us in her profoundest bass: 'Girls, what is poetry?' " From the back row, an eager hand went up and a voice answered pertly: " '*Coleridge* says it's the best words in the best order.' " It was Mary, and Miss Lockwood was not amused. The antipathy was mutual. "Amusing," Miss Lockwood scrawled on Mary's papers, in lieu of further comment.

Mary McCarthy and Frani Blough had become pariahs in Blake-to-Keats. Both had been "squelched in class for apparently no reason" so many times, Frani wrote Mrs. Blough, that their predicament had become "the talk of our classmates. Miss Lockwood is famous for her acerbity," she added, "and I suppose two arrogant spirits who failed to be cowed aren't what she is used to. But I am curious about her distemper." After one showdown between McCarthy and Lockwood after class, Mary had broken into tears, and she and Frani had decided to invite Miss Sandison to dinner to "unpack" their hearts. The chairman of the English Department apparently took steps, for the next week's classes, Frani reported, "were exemplary, profitable I am sure, to both Mary and myself."

The truce was short-lived. "We were obnoxious," Frani Blough Muser remarks today, "but my hackles would rise just as much right now if Miss Lockwood was to walk in the door, even in the form of a ghost." The ghost of the terrible Miss Lockwood, of course, was consigned to an eternity of wandering in the McCarthy inferno. Helen Lockwood, whose name now graces the new wing of the Vassar Library that houses the Mary McCarthy Papers, is the first of the female arch-villains with whom McCarthy fought—Simone de Beauvoir, Diana Trilling (more arch than villainous), and Lillian Hellman would follow. With Lockwood, if not with the others, the contest was a contest of wills more closely matched, one guesses, than either would have been likely to admit.

6

Portrait of the *Intellectual* as a *Vassar Girl*

"The relation between life and literature—a final antinomy—is one of mutual plagiarism."

—MARY MCCARTHY, "THE INVENTIONS OF I. COMPTON-BURNETT"

*L*ike most coming-of-age years in an interesting life, Mary McCarthy's sojourn at Vassar has a mythic quality. One thinks of Goethe's eager student Faust in search of the creative power he needs to bring back the lost beauty of Paris and Helen. For McCarthy the Trojan heroes would always remain, in some sense, Roy and Therese Preston McCarthy. And Vassar College, with its turrets and towers, its dark mill-like dormitories, its female scholars who "rejoice in things that long have ceased from being," was her Classical Walpurgis Night. By 1929 when she left Seattle for Poughkeepsie, stopping briefly in Minneapolis for a final audience with her Grandmother McCarthy (who would be dead by graduation), she may have put the longing for her lost parents behind her, but the remembered magic of their lives together was preserved in her reverence for literature. In the perfection of the word, life was redeemed; something like that.

Sooner or later, of course, Vassar's English Department was bound to expose even its fiercest aesthetes to real changes in the world beyond the campus, if not through Contemporary Press then through Contemporary Prose Fiction. For McCarthy, who never was particularly susceptible to political ideas, and would only occasionally prove susceptible to political personalities, the crack in the intellectual armor appeared in confrontation with a new aesthetic. When the seniors in Contemporary Fiction were invited to study "multiplicity" and "stream of consciousness" in *The 42nd Parallel*, the first of Dos Passos's *U.S.A.* trilogy, Mary responded instantly to the book's "unusual weaving of forms." The prose-poem biographies, the Newsreels, the Camera Eye (who was the author, speaking in a wry, embarrassed voice) shattered the conventions of the omniscient narrator in fiction, as well as the Flaubertian ventriloquist—*"Mme. Bovary, c'est moi!"*—who presided over modern realism. Dos Passos's multiplicity of voices, moreover, was dictated by the genuine sweep of his historical imagination.

In the voices of Eleanor Stoddard, J. Ward Moorhouse, Eveline Hutchins, and Charley Anderson, characters who ride hard on the heels of American folk heroes such as the "capitalista yanqui," Minor C. Keith, founder of the United Fruit Company, Luther Burbank, and William Jennings Bryan, McCarthy heard a ring of truth missing in the contemporary fiction she had read before. In the character Mac, a Westerner who becomes a Wobbly, rides the rails, bivouacks in Mexico, and dies young, she felt an unexpected sympathy, while among the biographies it was the sketch of Eugene V. Debs that impressed her most. "I fell madly in love with that book," she wrote many years later. It moved her to action in a way that other "social books," such as Shaw's *The Intelligent Woman's Guide to Socialism and Capitalism*, did not. Action was fresh reading in unexplored pastures, everything Dos Passos had written, including the Sacco and Vanzetti pamphlet and an article about the Tom Mooney case that drew her deeper into the periodicals of the Left. "One thing leading to another, soon after graduation I was writing little book reviews for the *New Republic* and the *Nation*," McCarthy recalled in a 1980 essay, "Politics and the Novel," "and I never looked back. Like a Japanese paper flower dropped into a glass of water, my political persona unfolded, magically, from Dos Passos."

By the end of her residence at Vassar, many streams converged in a torrent of possibilities for the future—not the least of which was McCarthy's affair with Harold Johnsrud, the real-life model for the "intensely self-absorbed young man" in *The Group*, Harold Petersen, who speaks with "a detached impersonal eagerness, as though he were discussing disarmament or deficit spending." With Johnsrud, McCarthy had discovered the New York theatre, the Museum of Modern Art, the Yiddish Café Royal, the uptown speakeasys, and the Staten Island ferry. In August 1932, the first summer she did not return to Seattle, she and John (as he was called) had actually moved in together, taking a dismal furnished room in the East Fifties, which became the site of a battle she would often have with the men in her life who took her in charge, or in whose charge she had placed herself.

It was "the worst month . . . of my life," McCarthy later reflected of this early experiment in conjugal living. Johnsrud, who had probably bitten off more than he could chew when he had agreed to direct eight new plays for a summer-stock company in Scarborough, New York, had returned to the city restless and short-tempered. McCarthy remembers being subjected to streams of abuse; if there was any love-making on the studio couch, she doesn't recall it—only her own tears and shaking shoulders, which exasperated him all the more. "My being there, clearly, was what he resented. Perhaps he had someone else—one of the actresses from the Scarborough company . . ." she speculates in *How I Grew,* "but in that case why had he moved into this room with me?" Her own protests were full of recrimination, for Johnsrud was the reason she had decided to remain in New York.

Mary, nonetheless, had put them both at risk the moment she broke the cycle of return to her grandparents in Seattle. As long as she shuttled back and forth between Poughkeepsie and Seattle, dropping down to the city with Frani Blough to mingle with men in top hats outside St. Patrick's on Easter Sunday, catching the service at Dr. Albert Parker Fitch's Park Avenue Presbyterian Church, meeting another friend for lunch and the symphony, and winding up the day at the Metropolitan Museum; even camping out with Johnsrud on Bank Street, and returning to Vassar to defend a thesis in a Renaissance seminar, she knew where she stood. When this balance was struck, Mary could forget the "whole unfair business of having to have a verifiable history," with parents in place and antecedents known. It was when she began to go through the motions of reinventing a family, as she did, however tentatively, in August 1932 with Johnsrud, that she found herself alone with the ghosts of childhood.

With Johnsrud a new cycle had begun, one that would repeat itself when McCarthy settled down with Edmund Wilson, a much older man. In the first stage of these relationships, the persona of the brash young intellectual began to unravel under the pressure of a darker self, one that McCarthy characterizes in *The Company She Keeps* as "the fugitive, criminal self [who] lay hiding in a thicket" of half-remembered terrors from childhood. The tears with Johnsrud were not so different, one imagines, from the angry cries of a child who has discovered that without its parents it can no longer plead the case of a child, or hope to receive the attention to which it was bred.

The month with Johnsrud had thrown the idea of their "engagement"—an idea that Mary began to suspect was a creature of her need and imagination—into a tailspin of doubt. When John went to Hollywood in October 1932 for a six-month stint as a screenwriter at MGM, for which he was paid the fabulous sum of $200 a week, Mary no longer knew whether they would be married, as planned, after graduation, which meant she had no idea what she was going to do with herself or where she was going after June 1933. Johnsrud's interest in her had always seemed more important than her interest in him, which was a given, or something easily given; and now Johnsrud's interest was on the wane, or so it appeared from his cryptic letters from Hollywood, full of lurid tales of orgies in which he may or may not have participated. After the terrible August in New York, Mary herself had grown numb. "[W]hatever he did, I could not feel it any more. In fact," McCarthy decided later, "he had killed my love for him." When Kay McLean, the Vassar roommate from the South Tower of Main who dated John's brother Byron during the summer of 1932, told Mary that it was *all over*—that she was "just another feather in the Johnsrud cap" (a cruel remark, which McCarthy never forgave)—she was privately convinced it was true.

Yet there was no going back to the Vassar girl's Manhattan, whose tone is captured in an account Mary wrote to Frani Blough of returning to the apartment she shared in July 1932 with three Vassar graduates, to find them gathered around the piano with their young men singing " 'There's a Long, Long Trail,' and, with just the daintiest touch of salacity, 'Hinkey Dinkey Parlay Voo.'. . . Unbelievable," she exclaimed. Unlike them, she had begun to see the city through the eyes of one of the thousands of young job seekers who poured into New York during the early 1930s.

Thanks to a connection at the Scarborough theatre, she had landed a real summer job as secretary to an art dealer, Emmanuel J. Rousuck, who specialized in dog paintings. The job introduced her to a workaday world of unexpected eccentricity: to Cissy, Rousuck's red-haired mistress; Elliot, the young black man who handled the dogs, whose likenesses E. J. Rousuck's Carleton Gallery memorialized in miniatures; Maud Earl, an octogenarian animal painter from London, who produced the miniatures; and to the 'collectors' whose sudden arrivals and departures from the obscure gallery Mary had to monitor—for Mannie, as she called her employer, was always hiding from his creditors. "You see me installed in my position as a member of the proletariat," Mary wrote Frani in July 1932. "My boss is a nice, sweet, battered soul who spends his time skulking about, avoiding the sheriff.

He now owes me eighteen dollars, and there is very little prospect of receiving it," she added, "unless I enlist my grandfather's services and join the ranks of the vultures who are hovering about the poor man. . . . So I content myself with reading the Want Ads everyday in a threatening manner under his very nose."

Johnsrud, who suspected that Mary was lending Rousuck money (which she was), had nothing but contempt for him and the Carleton Gallery. It was a judgment Edmund Wilson later shared, after Mannie moved up in the porous world of society, dogs, and art, and became "Jay" Rousuck of the eminent gallery Wildenstein's, and still commanded Mary's services as a ghostwriter. For Mary McCarthy, the friendship lasted nearly forty years. Rousuck entered her early fiction as Mr. Sheer in "Rogue's Gallery," and McCarthy, in turn, continued to supply him with polished copy for his correspondence and sales brochures throughout the '40s, '50s, and '60s, for which she was well paid. In 1932, Mannie Rousuck was an unprepossessing employer, but they got along, and in his own way he helped see her through a difficult time. In helping him, Mary had discovered resources in herself that neither Johnsrud, her friends at Vassar, nor very likely she herself had known she had.

Still other possible futures seemed to have dried up forever during McCarthy's senior year at Vassar. She would never become an actress Johnsrud told her after seeing her last collegiate performance as Leontes in a modern version of Chaucer's *The Winter's Tale*. She would be wise to pursue criticism, not fiction, Miss Kitchel advised— an estimate she accepted herself. Both Narrative Writing and Descriptive Writing, the 'writer's courses,' had proved disappointing, and she had only herself to blame, she decided, for "frivolously deciding to waste my time writing boring short stories, and still worse, having to read and actually listen to the boring short stories of the other class members, when I might have been in the library reading an author who had something to . . . say."

No doubt McCarthy's writing skills had improved by the end of four years of college, but if her contribution to the freshman *Sampler,* her sole fictional effort published at Vassar, is any indication, her early descriptive powers were not auspicious:

The church was quiet with reverence, and dim with holiness. Far down at the altar, tall tapers burned ardently, but they did not disturb the still twilight of God's house. There a priest moved

slowly back and forth, repeating the solemn words of the most
sacred Mass. . . .

Near the front of the church a window was open. Beyond it
was a patch of blue sky, and the green branch of an apple-tree
waving in the wind. They, too, were expressing the ineffable goodness of God. . . .

After this evocation of "The House of God," a contrasting passage,
entitled "A Survival," presented the same scene perceived without
faith:

Inside there is gloom and unreality; inside, there is a priest.
Around a shadowy altar, a few feeble tapers burn. . . . A few Latin
words drift down toward the worshippers, dead ritual, in a dead
language to a dead God. A thin piece of whitish bread is raised; and
the believers bow their heads and beat their breasts in fear and
adoration.

The spring and the sky and the apple-tree seem more breath-
takingly real. . . . But one notices that the spring shrinks from the
open window; it remains very definitely outside, as the weary
mutterings of a sacred Mass go on.

While these passages bear little relation to what was to come, and
demonstrate the weakness of description that is not grounded in direct
observation, they do reveal several themes dear to the agitated soul of
a renegade Catholic. The opposition of the dim church, "quiet with
reverence," to the bright branch of an apple tree, waving in the wind,
bespeaks the age-old tension between spirit and matter. The spectator
who finds meaning in the Mass, and is at home in "God's house,"
reveres them both, as indeed Mary McCarthy did—though it wasn't
until 1955, when she began the first of two books about the Italian
Renaissance, that she found her way back into the shadowy 'House of
God,' via the worship of beauty embodied in classical architecture,
frescoes, and altarpieces. ("The daily service of beautiful things conduces to decorum; it is a rite, a kind of communion, as we notice
whenever we wash a fine wine glass as opposed, say, to a jelly jar," she
told an audience in Aberdeen, Scotland, in 1974.)

In 1930, when the *Sampler* submission was written, reparations
had not been made for the youthful loss of faith in 'God's house.' The
sad scene suggests a gloom still deeply colored by McCarthy's loss of
her first family, whose Catholicism had been the occasion for celebra-

tion, not the "stale, sour canting mixture of prejudice and ignorance" that she later associated with the priests and nuns in Minneapolis. In the playwriting course she took with Vassar's Hallie Flanagan (who went on to head the Federal Theater Project under Roosevelt), she had tried to confront the experience of loss more directly. The scene she wrote with Uncle Myers stealing into the dining room to pin the tin butterfly underneath her place mat was, in effect, a secular treatment of the loss of faith: the loss of a child's faith in her guardians, and in the reliability of her own innocence. The play, however, remained unfinished.

II

At Vassar, Mary McCarthy made Phi Beta Kappa and graduated cum laude, and yet it never occurred to her to go on to graduate school in English literature. No doubt it was an unlikely commitment for a young woman to make during the Depression, but in any event graduation from Vassar signaled the close of formal learning. With or without the Depression every Vassar girl worth her salt now hoped to make that "*arresting performance* in politics, fashion, or art" for which the college encouraged respect. Only schoolteachers pursued higher degrees. And while one might admire one's female teachers, and assimilate their habits of mind, their tastes for English playwrights and English cigarettes, one didn't expect to *live* like them. One married, as indeed Mary soon did, the first of her class to tie the knot—but not before Johnsrud put her through one more test, and not before her roommates in the South Tower of Main reopened an old wound.

When John came to Vassar to see *The Winter's Tale* in May 1933, he had returned from Hollywood by way of Seattle. The Seattle visit took Mary by surprise. John claimed to have made a conquest of the Prestons, and especially Harold Preston, who brought him little shot glasses of bourbon in the guest room in the mornings. When John gave her his Phi Beta Kappa key from Carleton to hang about her neck (thus saving her the six-dollar purchase price of her own), Mary couldn't help but see the offering as a "convention-defying engagement ring." She was, she remembers, "barely aware of my lack of joy in having him back—smiling ironically, quirking his eyebrows, bowing, being courtly," for there was a triumph in his return that overshadowed the damping off of her own feelings after the quarrelsome summer of 1932. His attentions silenced the "doubters and skeptics," but the triumph alone was insufficient cause to revive the hopes she had pinned on their engagement.

In the spring of 1933, she had begun to see a new set of people in New York, "rather fast and worldly," McCarthy later recalled, who were centered around a young man named Alan Lauchheimer, recently graduated from Yale. Lauchheimer lived with his mother in a New York hotel, where he was trying to write the novel that in McCarthy's experience "so many just out of Yale, Williams, Harvard were trying to write—it was a purely male drive." The affair lasted only a month, but Lauchheimer, who later adopted his mother's name, Barth, and became a well-known editorial writer for the *Washington Post*, and a lifelong friend, took the sting out of Mary's anxieties about John. Before she would decide to marry him now, Johnsrud would have to perform some extraordinary feat—which he did, taking his secondhand car into a nosedive down an embankment of the Delaware River.

Johnsrud's attempted suicide, "if it was an attempted suicide," McCarthy writes in *How I Grew,* "rather than a case of O.U.I.," filled her with respect. She didn't imagine he had tried to kill himself on her account during the weekend they spent together in New Jersey in May 1933. "I felt that he had done it from an immense and wild misery," which she couldn't help but honor, "and if drinking played a part in it, that fitted, for he drank to drown his sorrows, being a Norwegian and Irish, too." She was tired of John, she suggests, but the feelings of awe he inspired in her were revived by the spectacular accident (from which he had escaped unmarked—only some acid holes drilled into his hat from a dripping battery marked the ordeal). He was a "genius," she thought, with a "more than Shavian wit," who was going to win "first the Pulitzer and then the Nobel prize," and then to top it off she had "discovered that he was *colossally* unhappy."

He was also a refuge from the social insecurities that reasserted themselves during Mary McCarthy's final year at Vassar—which was not quite the happy ending to four years of college that *How I Grew* suggests. In the fall of 1932, she had moved into the South Tower of Main with Maddie Aldrich, Rosilla Hornblower, Helen Kellogg, Nathalie Swan, and Kay McLean, a group made up largely of New York society girls whose collective self-esteem was remarkable even at Vassar; but it was a fluke in the rooming system that had led them to approach her in the first place. Together with Frani Blough and Clover Benson, with whom she was originally planning to room, Mary had drawn a low number in the rooming lottery at the end of junior year. The New York group, who wanted the coveted South Tower suite and had drawn a high number, had proposed a merger—which had ultimately won them both the South Tower and Mary McCarthy as a sixth wheel (six beds being in the suite). Frani and Clover, old friends from Walnut Hill School, had joined another group in the North Tower, with no hard feelings. Thus, by the fall of senior year, Mary felt no longer either a contemptuous or an envious outsider, but a member in fair standing of the one group on campus whose social prestige was unrivaled.

The Christmas holiday revealed the shakiness of her position. Privately, McCarthy once acknowledged never losing an awareness of her separateness from the group. "The difference was not a matter of proms, clothes, men," all of which she enjoyed, she confided to a *New York Herald Tribune* editor in 1964, "but was mainly a matter of what [the group] would call 'breeding.' I was not ill-bred," she explained, "but untrained and 'wild,' which meant not just living-with-a-man-before-marriage and drinking (most of them liked drinking too) and breaking the rules, but being very outspoken and extreme in all my enthusiasms and dislikes." These differences didn't particularly concern her. The prep-school voice, for instance, an original dislike, was assimilated to a degree, and one could hear its inflection in McCarthy's own voice half a century later. She had made other friends, moreover, like the more intellectual *Con Spirito* group. The South Tower circle still represented "the East," but the East was also the theatre, books, pictures, and ideas, and most of the New York girls were not interested in those things, except for the beautiful Nathalie Swan ("the Sphinx of the smoking-room," McCarthy calls her), who left Vassar during her senior year to study architecture at the Bauhaus.

When Christmas arrived, Mary had faced the usual problem of where to spend the holiday. Every other year she had been invited to stay with a classmate, or she had stayed with Johnsrud, signing out with a fictitious address; but Johnsrud was in Hollywood. And the unthinkable had occurred: no one invited her home, no one from the group and none of her friends outside of it. "I don't know how this happened," McCarthy wrote in an original draft of a letter to the *New York Herald Tribune* that was never sent, "but to me this was the most horrible thing . . . to have [to] stay on at Vassar, where a skeleton building was kept open for the few pariahs that had to remain. It was as public as being in the pillory." She was much too proud to ask anyone for help, and very likely she had made up some lie about her plans, she recalled; for to say she wasn't going anywhere would have been to beg for an invitation. Maybe her classmates never knew the truth, but Mary didn't think so:

I think the group had decided jointly to be hard, not to let themselves be "used"; society people are capable of this deaf hardness; it is part of their "training." Anyway, the day came; everyone left, very gaily, and I was alone. . . . Then, at the last minute, someone relented toward me.

Margaret Chandler Astor Aldrich, Maddie, the group member she knew the least, called to invite her to spend the Christmas weekend at Rokeby, the family estate on the Hudson. When another young woman invited Mary to her New York town house after Christmas, she went down to the city and eventually wound up her vacation at the Vassar Club. With the holiday broken up like this, it didn't seem as if she was really spending it alone. "I was covered," she noted. But if no one else knew what had happened, she did. She had been *un*covered, at least in her own estimation:

I was used to being popular and rather in demand. But when I knew I was not going to be invited anywhere—and I am a person who has a special feeling about holidays—it was as if this popularity was an illusion or a deceit practiced on me to spare my feelings, and the real me was the proud pariah watching the others carry down their suitcases.

She couldn't blame her classmates, "which would have been to accept the thing that was happening to me as real." In the end she had only blamed herself—"for having been the cause of the heartlessness. . . ." Reliving the experience in 1964, she asked herself, as if for the first time, if she had ever forgiven the group. "Could I have written *The Group* to show them?" she wondered. "Maybe. Who knows? They don't certainly."

"They" had been the occasion for this unflinching reminiscence. After *The Group* went into its second year at the top of the *New York Times*'s best-seller list, the *New York Herald Tribune* had commissioned a front-page story for the *Book Review*: "The Group on Mary McCarthy," in which a handful of embittered alumnae of the class of '33, who didn't like what they saw of themselves in the novel, had pooled some memories of their illustrious classmate for the journalist Sheila Tobias. McCarthy's letter was initially drafted to correct certain distortions in the article, such as the assertion that in Chapter Three (first published in 1954 in *Partisan Review* as "Dottie Makes an Honest Woman of Herself"), that McCarthy had "pursued" the original

Dottie (Dorothy Newton, Vassar '33) into a man's apartment, and then later into a birth-control clinic; Dottie's defloration was wholly imagined, McCarthy stated. Helena Davison ("whose parents . . . lived on the income of their income . . .") was not based on three group members, as Sheila Tobias reported, but on a classmate who wasn't in the group. McCarthy didn't identify her, but the droll little Helena is Frani Blough, while the formidable Mrs. Davison—"simply by clearing her throat, [Helena's] mother could command an audience"—is Mrs. Blough. With her sandy hair and boyish figure, her classical tastes in music, literature, and drama, Helena wears a thin disguise in the novel, and the group's oversight suggests how far removed they were from their controversial classmate.

"It's all there," one of McCarthy's former roommates had conceded of *The Group*, "our parents, our habits, our prejudices, our illusions." But the images the alumnae threw up of Mary McCarthy at Vassar were the images of someone seen through a glass darkly. "She was exciting and terrifying with her skinny figure, her racing around in flats, her verbal performances in class," one remembered. "We were afraid of her brains. . . . We were undergraduates, she was a scholar." And: "Those of us who had known one another at boarding school remained friends after college as well, but we never saw much of Mary. . . ." "The girls were always relieved when she wasn't on hand [for college reunions]," said another classmate, "we were terrified of her sarcasm." A more analytically minded roommate suggested that the crucial fact about Mary was that she "had no family . . . to please. Not having any real reason to cater to adults, she was much less anxiety-ridden than the rest of us. She appeared to be much freer than we were and this fascinated and frightened us."

"I'm afraid mere mistakes and malice are not actionable," McCarthy fumed in a letter to her publisher, William Jovanovich, after seeing the "horrible nasty piece in yesterday's *Tribune*, which moves me, damn it, to want to sue." The mistakes bothered her the most, but what inspired her to draft the long letter to the editor were also recollections of her as a "sort of beatnik . . . unwashed and unbrushed," along with the malice behind remarks such as, "The only thing Mary learned to love at Vassar was the sound of her own voice," which internal evidence tied to Eunice Clark Jessup. Jessup told the reporter she saw herself in Norine Schmittlapp, though she, like everyone quoted in the story, remained anonymous. The short letter that finally appeared in print simply rebutted the mistaken assumptions, but McCarthy couldn't resist noting her surprise that anyone who saw herself as Norine Schmittlapp (the real villain of *The Group,* who speaks in riddles and sleeps with the heroine's husband) would broadcast the fact, though it was the "essence of Norine-ness" not to keep her mouth shut.

> She had been regarded as "nervous" by the medical staff senior year at college, and her abrupt, elliptical way of speaking, as if through a permanent cloud of cigarette smoke, had been developed at the time. When not leading a parade or working on the college newspaper or the literary magazine, she could be found off campus drinking Coca-Cola or coffee and baying out college songs at a table at Cary's with her cronies. . . . Norine's chief interest at college had been journalism; her favorite course had been Miss Lockwood's Contemporary Press; her favorite book had been *The Autobiography of Lincoln Steffens* . . . her favorite painter, Georgia O'Keeffe. Up until senior year, she had been one of the overweight girls, given to Vassar "Devils," a black fudgey mixture that Helena had never so much as tasted. . . .

Helena and *her* friends, on the other hand, "bicycled to the Silver Swan, because the name reminded them of madrigals, or dined with a faculty member at the Vassar Inn, where they always ordered the same thing: artichokes and mushrooms under glass."

From Norine's point of view, such fiction, grounded in material truth, must have seemed full of malice. Still, the harsh judgments McCarthy's classmates made of her in 1964 may not have been so different from how they regarded her in 1933. In the last analysis, there was probably more that was different about the " 'wild' " girl from Seattle than was familiar, more even than McCarthy allows in her candid letter, which can be read as a corrective to "The Vassar Girl," like the postscripts in *Memories of a Catholic Girlhood.*

One looks in vain in the 1933 yearbook for some recognition of McCarthy's presence at Vassar, or her promise for the future. Under the "Lean Year Estimates," the roster of students voted "Funniest," "Has the Best Ideas," "Has the Wildest Ideas," "Most Original," "Most Likely to be a Genius," "Most Likely to Succeed (in Business, in Marriage, in a Profession)," "Most Respected"—the categories in which one might expect to discover an editor of *Con Spirito* and a Star Reporter of the *Miscellany News* (which Mary also was)—McCarthy is not to be found. Eunice Clark takes nearly all the accolades. Reviewing McCarthy's years at Vassar, one glimpses only the rudiments of the literary performance that lay ahead. Perhaps too many secrets were being kept to give her the liberty she later took to play her hand.

If no one had suspected an "Aunt Clara" in her background, the effort of making herself over, of thinking herself "a completely new person" (as Meg Sargent does in *The Company She Keeps*) had perhaps deprived her of a certain flexibility. "Later, when she had grown more sophisticated," Meg Sargent reflects, "Aunt Clara had been converted into an asset. It was amusing to have an aunt who said 'ain't' and 'Jesus, Mary, and Joseph,' and ate her peas with a spoon, amusing because it seemed so improbable that *you* could have an aunt like that." Later, McCarthy would pump Aunt Margaret and Uncle Myers for all that an arresting literary performance would allow. But for Mary McCarthy at Vassar, this history was not amusing.

Nor was it amusing to have a Jewish grandmother, the grandparent who outlived all the others. By the end of the 1930s, McCarthy would find herself very much at home among Jewish intellectuals, a kind of *goyisha* princess, or "a princess among the trolls," as Meg says of herself. To Elizabeth Bishop in the 1960s, McCarthy was "an Irish Jew." (Bishop would have become politically conservative by then, and McCarthy, who traveled to Saigon and Hanoi in 1967 and 1968, would veer close to the New Left.) But in Poughkeepsie, Mary McCarthy was her Grandfather Preston's child, a distaff Yankee at Matthew Vassar's court. In 1934, when Frani Blough and her mother stopped in Seattle to pay a call on the Prestons during a summer trip west, Mary was beside herself with anxiety lest Frani notice her grandmother's "long aquiline nose." Frani never said anything about it, McCarthy notes in the autobiography which is not so 'intellectual' as to ignore a telling social note like this; and Mary, who often stayed over with Frani and Curt Muser in New York in the 1970s and '80s, never asked.

Part Three

■

New York: 1933–1938

7

Stepping Out

*"Rumor had it that there were quite
a few pinks in the publishing biz."*

—MARY McCARTHY, *THE GROUP*

*D*earest Frani in Fountainbleau," the letter begins: "I've written myself dry composing thank-you notes to practically unknown people for small, indefinable objects. Wait till you get married, Frani, and I hope it won't be seven years [which it would be], and you'll see what a variety of strange household furnishings arrive in the mail."

The brand-new watery blue stationery is monogrammed MTJ, suitable for the young matron attending postnuptial chores. The letter, dated July 22, 1933, stops and starts ("Forgive it, for it knows not yet what it does") while Mary and John sleep off the effects of several evenings' entertainments. They were receiving: Corey Ford and Russell Crouse, playwrights whose latest show Harold Johnsrud was directing; Margaret Miller, class of '34, who joined the *Vassar Review* staff when *Con Spirito* merged with its adversary; Earl Blough, Frani's "papa," an executive with Aluminum Ltd. "He seemed cheerful if, at first, a trifle weary, but the cocktail which we gave him as nonchalantly as we could, and which he drank without a quiver, seemed to revive him, and he was very jolly."

Margaret Miller hadn't fared so well. After dinner, she and the Johnsruds had dropped in on Harry Sternberg, an artist friend; and when Margaret, a fine arts major and always a stickler for detail, corrected John for a misuse of the word *empathy*, a "first-class, four-cornered row" broke out in Sternberg's studio. Soon both John and

Harry had become "unbearably boorish and conceited," and Mary told John that she would "never appear in public with him again if he uttered one more word of an argumentative nature," which did the trick and saved the night from one of their "mongoose-and-cobra acts." "Meek and chastened, and suffering from a terrific hangover (which he was convinced was ptomaine poisoning)," Mary wrote, "John telephoned Margaret the next morning and apologized."

Mary was disappointed that Frani's father "was too much enmeshed with the law" to come to the wedding, which had taken place on June 21, Mary's birthday, and even sorrier that Frani—enrolled in a music program at Fountainbleau—was "not among those heaving rice at my hapless form." Elizabeth Bishop hadn't come, either, "chiefly from lack of funds." Mary was hoping to visit her in Wellfleet when John's show opened in Boston in September. But the wedding, she assured Frani, was "all very exciting. Ten of us had breakfast at the Hotel Lafayette, with a swell punch with an applejack base." At St. George's Church on Stuyvesant Square, Mary's "powerful bass voice (last heard in *The Winter's Tale*) changed to a faint, trembling soprano . . . and my knees shook so that I could hardly stand." Dottie Newton and her partner stood up with them and knelt at all the wrong times. It was, in essence, the wedding scene that opens *The Group*:

> It was June, 1933, one week after Commencement, when Kay Leiland Strong, Vassar '33, the first of her class to run around the table at the Class Day dinner, was married to Harald Petersen, Reed '27, in the chapel of St. George's Church, P. E. . . . Paying the driver, smoothing out their gloves, the pairs and trios of young women, Kay's classmates, stared about them curiously, as though they were in a foreign city. They were in the throes of discovering New York, imagine it, when some of them had actually lived here all their lives, in tiresome Georgian houses full of waste space in the Eighties or Park Avenue apartment buildings, and they delighted in such out-of-the-way corners as this. . . .
>
> The sense of an adventure was strong on them this morning . . . they had never been to a wedding quite like this one before, to which invitations had been issued orally by the bride herself, without the intervention of a relation or any older person. . . . There was to be no honeymoon, they had heard, because Harald. . . . was working as an assistant stage manager for a theatrical production and had to be at the theatre as usual this evening to call "half hour" for the actors. This seemed to them very exciting and of course it justified the oddities of the wedding: Kay and Har-

ald were too busy and dynamic to let convention cramp their style. . . . [A]ccording to Helena Davison, Kay's roommate junior year, the two of them had moved right into a summer sublet, in a nice block in the East Fifties, without a single piece of linen or silver of their own. . . .

Which was exactly how John and Mary had begun. The sublet, Helen Sandison's sister's apartment, was on East Fifty-second Street; and improbably enough, given the Johnsruds' precarious finances (slightly augmented by money sent by the Prestons, in lieu of a costly trip to New York), they lived "in state" with a maid who came down from Harlem to clean, wash, and cook dinners: Clara in life, as in *The Group*, "a small, motherly, domineering, conventional character," Mary told Frani, who "will make ladies and gentlemen out of us yet."

In *The Group*, the wedding scene grows steadily darker, more ominous, as it is mentally reviewed by each of the girls, whose eyes are alternately drawn to the bare altar, the sprinkling of guests, the absence of parents, the scuff marks on the back of the bride's black suede shoes. When the curate asks, " 'If any man show just cause, why they may not be lawfully joined together . . .' " every girl held her breath, for there was always something "unsanctioned" about the fact that Kay and Harald (like Mary and John) had already "lived together," and not very harmoniously at that. And perhaps there was a spiritual obstacle to the marriage: Lakey, for one, "considered Kay a *cruel, ruthless, stupid* person who was marrying Harald for ambition."

Like Kay and Harald, Mary and John spent their wedding night at an inn in Briarcliff north of the city. In July 1933, Mary wrote Frani that it was "a lovely place," but because they arrived late, they "did not appreciate its attractions." There was no bystander to review this scene but the bride herself, and Mary McCarthy waited over fifty years to reappropriate one of those shattering self-perceptions that in fiction she would often project onto a heroine's observers. In *How I Grew*, she reports that in Briarcliff, suddenly, she had experienced "an attack of panic."

As we climbed into the big bed, I knew, too late, that I had *done the wrong thing*. To marry a man without loving him, which was what I had just done, not really perceiving it, was a wicked action. . . . Stiff with remorse and terror, I lay under the thin blanket through a good part of the night; as far as I could tell from what seemed a measureless distance, my untroubled mate was sleeping.

In the letter to Fountainbleau, McCarthy assured Frani Blough that she was "happily married. John's character has undergone a remarkable transformation, indeed, a metamorphosis. He is so god-damned nice that he puts me to shame. I am so glad we stopped being sensible and got married." But the voice is a little strained, as if the marriage was willed to follow a path it had not found by itself. Vassar had by no means been left behind. Margaret Miller and Elizabeth Bishop, both seniors, were frequent houseguests whose abrupt departures for Poughkeepsie invariably left Mary feeling wistful. "I find that I am becoming a prey to boredom, the boredom that sends young wives out to join bridge clubs," she wrote Frani later in December, "not boredom with John . . . just a feeling of vacancy that must come with the end of a four years' routine. Housework and a book review or two"—the first, a review of Glenway Wescott's *A Calendar of Saints* for the *The New Republic* appeared on August 2, 1933—"are not effective substitutes for sixteen hours of classes a week. I have decided that I Must Work, and I'm going to ease myself into it gradually by writing a lot of letters."

If Mary looked for a job, nothing came of it. The entertaining continued; and now there was the Johnsruds' new apartment at Two Beekman Place, across the street from J. P. Marquand, to furnish. The rent was high, eighty-five dollars a month, and there was only one medium-sized room, which tripled as kitchen, bedroom, and parlor, but it had real venetian blinds made of wood and an elevator with an elevator man. Mary's bills at department stores began to soar; and an anxious note crept into her correspondence with Frani Blough, who had decided not to move to the city, as McCarthy hoped she would, but to take an editorial job on a Pittsburgh magazine. "John and I are having a strange time," Mary said. A dozen schemes hatched with an eye to financial gain had fallen through, and at the moment they possessed a dollar between them, "but we are hopeful," she added. Someone had commissioned John to put some "clever dirt" into an already-dirty French farce. Together, they had written a movie story about racketeers who triumph over the repeal of Prohibition by going into the art business, an idea probably inspired by Mannie Rousuck, who had been a bootlegger himself before he opened the Carleton Gallery; and the story had just been dispatched to Columbia Pictures. John had finished the first act of a new play. Mary had reviewed Hilaire Belloc's *Charles the First, King of England* for *The Nation*, for which she was paid three dollars.

A certain materialism entered her writing, and she praised Hilaire

Belloc for demonstrating that the "Pyms and Cromwells were not single-minded religious fanatics, disinterested warriors for justice; they were shrewd businessmen with an eye to the future. This throws the whole story of the Great Rebellion into a new and arresting light," she declared. By making both "monarchy and oligarchy a pair of believable and powerful protagonists," Belloc had shown exactly how "in the class struggle a neat balance of power was established." But it was that dollar between them that mattered more. "It is really very amusing," she wrote Frani; she had just gotten "the curse" and run out of Kotex; "if we buy more Kotex we will not be able to eat, so I suppose I shall have to resort to primitive methods." And on that "barbaric note," she signed off, thanking Frani for the "swell" time she and John had enjoyed at the Bloughs' house during a recent visit to Pittsburgh.

There was turkey for the Johnsruds' first Christmas and a fresh round of cocktail parties, where their friends supplied the liquor. McCarthy had sent a story to *Harper's* and something to the *The New Yorker*, and both were rejected; book reviewing was moribund, temporarily, she hoped. John had nearly finished his play, which remained untitled. It was Elizabeth Bishop, still at Vassar and already a protégée of Marianne Moore, who was enjoying what literary success their young circle had. Bishop had just won a prize in a poetry contest and was already corresponding with Yvor Winters, Lincoln Kirstein, and Clifton Fadiman. One young poet was exchanging poetry with her and wanted to meet her in Boston—"just like the Brownings," Mary noted airily in a letter to Pittsburgh. Meanwhile, Mary had begun a "tremendous tome," Sholom Asch's *Three Cities*, and after page 600 it had become quite exciting. "It is a Jewish book," she told Frani, "concerned with the usual sensitive youth, and his struggles with self and world, but it is also all about the Russian revolution, and that is interesting."

Then, in April 1934, John wrote Frani Blough the good news: "I can afford to look down my nose at the rest of you hopeful amateurs, straining away for 'action,' pouring out your song impulses in free verse. ANTI-CLIMAX, or the play of that name which you saw in this very house has been bought for production next season." The producer was Frank Merlin:

> proceeds from the contract: $500 advanced against royalties. . . . The present relations with Albert B. Ashforth, landlord: superb. The present status of Saks-Fifth Avenue, Bonwit-Teller and other bills: paid in full. What followed on the Saturday after the Monday

[when the contract was signed]: a St. Patrick's Day shindig that would have made you turn pale—applejack punch, Irish whiskey, Clara in white apron bustling in and out with caviar and delicately roasted small sausages. State of the guests and hosts after the above: potty.

It was Johnsrud's first break after five years of scrambling for what were usually bit parts and marginal production jobs on plays that seemed to fold in the night before they were ever noticed. Now Merlin and John were scheming to gross at least the eight thousand dollars a week that a comedy such as *No More Ladies* did, and that play had just been sold to Hollywood for fifty thousand dollars.

A week later, Mary sent Frani a "second installment" to John's letter. Frank Merlin had a newly acquired passion for Vassar girls, and she wanted Frani to know that she was reserving her "as a special tidbit for him. He might even give you a job if you would Pay the Price, but I warn you that he is fat and over forty." There wasn't much news. They played bridge with Eunice Clark and Selden Rodman (who together with Alfred Bingham, edited the magazine *Common Sense*), often using them to sober up, "like a Turkish bath." They haunted the theatre, never missing a play featuring their friends, such as *The Children's Hour*, starring Anne Revere and Katherine Emery, which McCarthy enjoyed—but which, strangely enough, was to be the only original play of Lillian Hellman's she ever saw.

With black friends from the theatre world, Nella Larsen and the actress Dorothy Peterson, the Johnsruds went to dance at the Savoy in Harlem, where they did their "uptown slumming," as McCarthy called it. Recently, they had gone up to Harlem to a "pansy joint," Mary wrote Frani, where

> you pay a dollar-and-a-half at the door, and you get as much to drink as you can hold, more usually. The catch . . . was that the only available drinks were gin and ginger ale, gin and white rock, and Martini cocktails, none of which inspire me to gayety. . . . There were Lesbians in tailored suits, fairies with lipstick dating each other up, a foul ladies room, a lot of drunks. . . . The ventilation was almost nonexistent. The evening was unsuccessful, to a degree.

Early one morning, John stumbled out of bed to find an unlikely visitor at the door. It was Mary's brother Kevin. Except for a couple of visits in 1929 and 1930, when Mary passed through Minnesota on her way to Vassar, she had not seen her brother since 1923, when she was eleven and he was ten, and he and Preston were sent to a Catholic boarding school in northern Minnesota. In 1934, Kevin McCarthy was nominally enrolled at Georgetown University—nominally, because he lived in a rooming house off campus, and spent his tuition on pursuits other than the School of Foreign Service. He was discovering the wider world that lay beyond the Catholic enclaves of Minneapolis, including Two Beekman Place in New York.

Almost immediately, he and Mary picked up the broken thread. Something in Mary's icy wit, Kevin McCarthy suggested many years later, always warmed his heart—perhaps because he knew the secret of its origins in their common strife. As for Johnsrud, Kevin found him "a saturnine kind of guy." It wasn't hard to understand why Mary was drawn to him; he was, Kevin thought, a man of the world.

Kevin McCarthy himself was soon to be summoned home after another failure in school. He had not found his direction, and the restless anger and despair that dogged his footsteps through school, and from one guardian to the next, would break out again in 1935 in a desperate attempt to flee 'the Catholics' in Minneapolis for the security that Mary seemed to have found with the Prestons in Seattle.

It happened like this: After Georgetown, Uncle Louis McCarthy set Kevin up in a Minneapolis YMCA, and put him on an allowance of seven dollars a week. It was the middle of the Depression, Kevin couldn't find a job, and soon he began to charge shirts, shoes, and pants to his uncle's account in preparation for the long trip west. Just as he was about to appropriate a car that Uncle Louis had once given him, and then repossessed, the bills were intercepted. His disgrace was complete. The seven-dollar allowance was docked to five dollars to pay back the bills; and suddenly, touching bottom, he realized that there was no one—and probably never would be anyone—who could save him from himself. It was one of those liberating realizations of youth, and only then had he begun to study: not acting, but oddly enough, for a junior in college who had failed to master basic grammar and punctuation, English and Psychology, by correspondence with the University of Minnesota. Quietly, he removed his father's philosophy books from the shelves in his uncle's office and began to really read for the first time. Surprisingly, he got an *A* in Psychology and a *B* in English, and that fall he persuaded his guardian to advance him twenty-six dollars to go back to school, this time as a fully matriculated student at the University of Minnesota, where Preston and

Sheridan McCarthy were already enrolled. There he signed up for everything that sounded hard: History, Philosophy, Psychology, and Shakespeare. Because of the *A* in Psychology, he was separated from the lecture class of six hundred students and put into a special seminar, which was led by a young instructor named B. F. Skinner, the same young man who had graded Kevin McCarthy's correspondence paper.

It was in the fall of 1935 that a theatrically inclined friend dared him to audition for a part in a campus production of *Henry IV, Part 1.* Kevin, who, unlike Mary, had never looked to the stage for an escape from the meanness of ordinary life, protested that in Shakespeare 106 he couldn't even *parse* the lines. " 'Just read *loud,*' " the friend advised, " 'that's all you have to do.' " And so he did, and in a few days discovered he could act. In 1987, he remembered the feeling of being "psychologically unburdened . . . I knew I could do something, and I could do it effectively; it wasn't even a matter of studying. . . . Evidently, I could pretend." Later, others reminded him that he was always pretending as a child. His cousin Jim McCarthy recalled how he was always "dressing up" to run away. But Kevin had no sense of this side of himself—only the feeling of being "isolated, alone and uncertain." Perhaps by 1935, he reflects, he was ready to *"behave* in the safe situations that the theatre seemed to permit."

But in 1934, during his rendezvous with Mary in New York, Kevin McCarthy was very much the dead-end kid. And Mary Johnsrud had begun to launch 'Mary McCarthy' on the literary stage.

She had a new book to write about called *Finnley Wren,* which led her to wonder "what in the world a refined lady reviewer ought to say about it." A resume of the plot would be impossible "without including such tasty little items as a candy box containing one miscarriage sent by a man's mistress to his wife. You might have your mother give a talk on it for her Y classes," she wrote Frani Blough. Frani was directing *The Importance of Being Earnest* for a Pittsburgh dramatic group, and Mary was a little envious. Once again, she wondered why Frani did not follow up on the introduction she had made for her with Miss Linley, the culture editor at *The New Republic*, and get a job in New York. "I should think the work you've done might help you with Miss Linley," she said. "A new dress might go farther with Mr. Merlin. Put it down under professional expenses."

Mary had done a lot of footwork on such matters, but Frani kept her distance, even after McCarthy found a "nice young man" for her, an actor from Harvard. Weekends with the Johnsruds were fun but increasingly frantic. The parties sometimes acquired a funereal edge, like the evening at Eunice's when Mary and John arrived wearing dark glasses, pale and shaken after a fight, like characters in a Greek drama. John was particularly hard to figure, Frani thought, perhaps because he was an actor, he was on stage all the time. He was flippant, and Mary's stock of flippancy was enlarged in his company. As Frani saw it, the side of Mary that was caught up with Elizabethan playwrights and poets at Vassar had succumbed to a kind of tinny sophistication that was the calling card of the New York theatre crowd.

II

Nineteen thirty-four was a bad year for Mary McCarthy (a worse one, as it happened, for Johnsrud), but in Mary's case the hard work of grasping and evaluating a literary text, and relating it to a cultural moment that was itself in turmoil, never ceased. This labor of love simply went underground, to occupy a place not unlike the place that Harold Johnsrud and Johnsrud's New York used to occupy when Vassar supplied the order of the day. Literary work had begun to present Mary McCarthy with the age-old promise, the one that led William Saroyan to take to writing at an early age "to escape from meaninglessness, uselessness, unimportance, insignificance, poverty, enslavement, ill health, despair, madness, and all manner of other unattractive, natural and inevitable things." Unlike the 'four years' routine' at Vassar, the life of an unemployed actor's wife and itinerant book reviewer in New York in the middle 1930s possessed a fathomless aspect. And there was no mentor to ease McCarthy's passage through the waiting rooms of the liberal weeklies.

At *The New Republic* sat Malcolm Cowley, the literary Buddha who first told Mary McCarthy he would give her a book only if she was a genius or starving, and then, on the merits of *Con Spirito*, tossed her Glenway Wescott. Cowley had been at Harvard with Dos Passos, in a French ambulance like E.E. Cummings, in Paris with Hemingway and Aragon. With his clipped mustache and pipe, he still possessed the swashbuckling air of an intellectual officer in the last war. To Alfred Kazin, who also did time on the reviewer's bench in the mid-1930s, Cowley was a conductor

on the great polished coach that was forever taking young Harvard poets to war, to the Left Bank, to the Village, to Connecticut. Wherever Cowley moved or ate, wherever he lived, he heard the bell of literary history sounding the moment and his own voice calling possibly another change in the literary weather.

In 1934, when Malcolm Cowley's *Exile's Return* appeared, the voice had announced a new synthesis between the idylls of the Lost Generation and the imperatives of revolution, and neither pole was one around which Mary McCarthy had rallied.

Alfred Kazin's distaste for a figure who appeared to perfectly embody, in twentieth-century terms, the genteel traditions Kazin would later celebrate in *On Native Grounds* seems strange, but in the 1930s it was a badge of courage for young intellectuals to regard critics such as Cowley, the Van Dorens, Henry Seidel Canby, and John Chamberlain as pretenders to the throne of literary criticism. In Kazin's opinion, Cowley "resembled Hemingway in much the same way that matinee idols once resembled Clark Gable." For Mary McCarthy, it was the whiff of orthodoxy that emanated from both Cowley's person and his position at *The New Republic* that stirred rebellion. "The book-review editors were like kings (and queens)," fancies Libby MacAusland in *The Group,* "holding levees, surrounded by their courtiers, while petitioners waited eagerly in the anteroom and footmen (that is, office boys) trotted back and forth."

In the spring of 1934, when the early promise of the New Deal was receding, it is easy to imagine how the exhortations of these critics might appear abstract and high-handed. McCarthy, like Alfred Kazin, however, was a supplicant on the bench.

Lauren Gilfillan's *I Went to Pit College* was an unlikely assignment for a 'refined' lady reviewer, but maybe Cowley thought the author's recent graduation from Smith College made the book a natural for Miss McCarthy. In a 1989 memoir, McCarthy maintained that with *Pit College* Malcolm Cowley had let her understand "that he was *giving me my chance*," and that she was "supposed to like the book. For the first time, and the last," she states, "I wrote to order." But the reflection is belied by the natural ebullience of the review, which pronounced the book "different from ordinary 'labor' books, and . . . superior to them." Gilfillan had set aside "Economics 305" and gone to a Pennsylvania coal town "simply to see and hear," McCarthy reported. She had dressed as a boy, worked in the mine, and joined strikers on the picket line, singing "The Internationale." But when her typewriter gave her away, the villagers, "fearful and suspicious as badly treated animals, . . . [unable to] believe that a member of the boss class could mean them anything but harm," drove Gilfillan from the town. "Marxian critics may not approve of Miss Gilfillan's book," McCarthy had concluded, "since it is obstinantly impartial and refuses to suggest remedies, but they and all its readers cannot help but feel and admire the terrific reality it gives its subject."

McCarthy's tone was informational and unassuming, exactly what Edmund Wilson had in mind when he wrote in the *Atlantic Monthly* that "the reviewer [should] give the gist of the book in his own words, [and] the reader should be given a chance to judge whether or not he would be interested in the book." But the *New Republic*'s editors were of a different mind, and in a bizarre departure from professional ethics, they appended a "P.S." to the review of "Coalpit College"—which, it seemed, had either enjoyed an unexpected popular success or been repudiated by the magazine's movie critic, Otis Ferguson, a 'real proletarian' who had great influence with Cowley. The Misses Gilfillan and McCarthy notwithstanding, the reader was told the book was not "a gripping social document or even an unstudied humanitarian gesture." The reviewer's reviewer, Mr. Ferguson, let the bourgeois public have it right between the eyes:

> After all, you might as well guess that any unequivocal statement of the truth about these starved and broken creatures—how they get that way because men are *not* brothers . . . and because the all-moving factor of greed is not abstract, but yours and mine—I say you damn well know that any true picture of a mining town would enjoy no great fame and sale among such comfortable consciences as can have sent around . . . for whatever current bit of print may be the proper thing to have sent around, and just put it on the bill won't you.

After that, Mary McCarthy was not to be heard from in the pages of the *The New Republic* again until 1940.

She had more luck with the 'queen' of the *The Nation*, Margaret Marshall. Marshall, the magazine's assistant literary editor, plied her with books whose diversity suggested that Miss McCarthy was not so easily typed. A thoughtful review of Robert Graves's *I, Claudius*, in June of 1934, was followed three weeks later by a not-so-glowing review of Stark Young's best-selling *So Red the Rose*. In December, McCarthy recommended Kay Boyle's *My Next Bride* to "adolescents and curious spinsters [who] ought not to be discouraged by the apparent novelty of [Boyle's] style, for they will find her point of view fundamentally sound"—which was to say, giddily romantic. Given

Clara Weatherwax's *Marching! Marching!*—a January 1935 selection of the Book Union and the winner of a *New Masses* novel contest—McCarthy awarded the book "a pale green orchid as The Most Neurotic Novel of 1935." She had begun to read up on current proletarian literature, and not only Dos Passos but Jack Conroy and Robert Cantwell, she decided, were "taking man-size vigorous strides towards the creation of a proletarian hero and a proletarian epic," while Miss Weatherwax had produced a "pinched, unhealthy, distorted and incidentally dull picture of American proletarian life."

Reading Mary McCarthy on the proletarian novel of the 1930s, one is left with the impression that the literature in question is chiefly a literature for men—or women like herself who relish a muscular prose. Vincent Sheean, whose *Personal History* she reviewed favorably in March 1935, was a "buccaneering young adventurer in the Richard Harding Davis tradition," who had discovered "that in scenes of crisis the current of human affairs runs clearest." McCarthy seems to have been drawn to his "turbulent experience" with the Communist International in China for somewhat the same reasons that Elizabeth Hardwick, writing in the 1960s, is drawn to the "special *vigor* of James, Balzac, Dickens or Racine. . . . Experience," Hardwick notes, "is something more than having the nerve to say honestly what you think in a drawing room filled with men; it is the privilege as well to endure brutality, physical torture, unimaginable sordidness, and even . . . to want, like Boswell, to grab a miserable tart under Westminster Bridge." But Vincent Sheean, in McCarthy's view, was also "a human being of extraordinary taste and sensibility, who [was] primarily interested in moral values." It was not Sheean's decision to work for the classless society that interested her so much as his vivid account of the exemplary young Bolsheviks who inspired him. Something in the "radiant spirit" of Sheean's narrative reminded her of those early Christians who were converted "by Jesus or St. Paul, rather than by their teachings."

At twenty-two, Mary McCarthy had become a regular contributor to the *Nation*'s back-of-the-book, which under Margaret Marshall reflected a more heterodox approach to both politics and culture than did the magazine's editorial pages. McCarthy's response to books as different as H. L. Davis's *Honey and the Horn*, a "folk tale" from her own Pacific Northwest, and Anatolii Vinoguadov's *The Black Consul*, a "living history" of Haiti's liberator, Toussaint L'Ouverture, was sometimes idiosyncratic. As she became bolder in print, one never knew when something moved her to disdain or praise, whether the issue was central to the work or to her own developing consciousness. The sheer intensity of her interest, however, was a refreshing departure from the prevailing habit of reviewers to rate a new book according to preordained ideological categories.

Early in 1935, Harold Johnsrud told Mary that it was only a matter of months before she would be invited to become a *Nation* editor. His own fortunes, meanwhile, had suffered another reversal. In September 1934, *Anti-Climax* had gone back on the market. Frank Merlin, who failed to find a backer for John's play, had picked up another unknown property called *Awake and Sing* by a young man named Clifford Odets. John had finished another play and that one was on the market, too. Mary thought it was "grand, but it may not sell, because it is so strange," she wrote Frani Blough. Together they were having so much bad luck, she added, that she couldn't believe in anything anymore, and she feared that her constant apprehension was bad for John's state of mind.

Being broke was fast losing its Bohemian cachet. Albert B. Ashforth was threatening to evict them again for nonpayment of rent. Disconnect notices from the electric company were piling up in the mailbox, and Mary had become an occasional bench-warmer at both the electric and the telephone companies, where kindly men listened to her earnest assurances that relief was just around the corner. Then one morning late in October 1934, she woke up with severe abdominal pains, and entered the hospital for "observation." After "a fine, full day of pokings about, blood counts, x-rays, studious examination of the 'condition' in the insides of one Mary Johnsrud by a splendid group of physicians and surgeons," John wrote Frani, acute appendicitis was diagnosed, and she was operated on at once.

The interlude offered Johnsrud a chance to take charge. "New York Hospital, the fruits of Payne Whitney's money," he informed Frani, "is a very goddamn fine place and earns from me the kindest thoughts for capitalism I have had in months." He was in constant attendance upon "our daughter, Mrs. Johnsrud," getting her a radio, receiving guests, one of whom was Clara, "looking . . . like a little black Mrs. Payne Whitney herself. The transformation of Clara, when she is done up to pay a call on her 'madam' and see that she is being properly treated in hospital," he noted, "is something to marvel at."

John had little news to report of himself, except to warn Frani that when she got to New York (for Frani was coming, not to *The New Republic* but to Columbia University for a masters in Musicology), she would find them both "leading a very sober life, with . . . midnight closing hours . . . because I am now under a very severe obligation indeed to produce some tangible results out of the theatre or, as the gazettes say, *else*. . . ."

Tangible results, unfortunately, were precisely what eluded Johnsrud and undermined Mary's belief in him. "He was the kind of man who commanded great faith in himself," McCarthy reflected many years later. "He did a great deal of instructing of me, which I responded to very much. . . . I saw myself as Sancho Panzo. He was Don Quixote." It would come as a surprise to her when after their breakup, Frani observed dryly, " 'I've always thought that Johnsrud must have felt terribly *eclipsed* by you.' "

After she returned from New York Hospital, the hard times continued. When her Grandmother McCarthy died a few years earlier, Mary had come into a small inheritance, which began after graduation. Eighteen months later, the dividends from the McCarthy grain elevators totaled twelve hundred dollars, a sizable sum in the 1930s but not enough to support the lifestyle to which the Johnsruds were accustomed. They had turned to the Prestons to cover the hospital bills. And now the phone was cut off, more than once. The midnight closing hours gave way to a new round of parties that attended the marriages, one after the other, of classmates from Vassar. At the Beverly Hotel, Nellie Gray Cheney, '33, gave a cocktail party for Nancy Rodman Macdonald, '32, who had just returned from a honeymoon in Majorca with her husband Dwight Macdonald, Yale '28, a staff writer at *Fortune*. And Mary and John soon became regulars at the Macdonalds' on East Fifty-first Street, where Mary met another Yale graduate, Fred Dupee, who had recently joined the Communist party. McCarthy, Macdonald, and Dupee, who had all been literary aesthetes in college, would soon become comrades at *Partisan Review*. But cocktail parties, not political parties, dominated the Johnsruds' agenda in 1935.

Dressing for a party one night, Mary put on her last pair of stockings, got a run, and collapsed in tears. Overwhelmed by the scramble for funds, she wondered what would happen if, when the money ran out, she and John just stopped fighting and let themselves go. "Would yielding to starvation be as pleasant a lazy death as yielding to cold when you freeze?" she wrote Frani melodramatically. She knew you weren't supposed to utter such sentiments: "The only thing you can do in these circumstances is to be as senselessly cheerful as possible." McCarthy's own cheerfulness bubbled up out of the direst circumstances. She seemed incapable of suffering privation; and down to their 'last dollar,' somehow life retained its charms. Sick in bed with a chest cold, there was always "Clara . . . fluttering around . . . with cups of tea and slices of incredible Harlem cake, which I eat with hypocritical relish." Nor were life's crises ever so serious that one could not be buoyed up by public attention. In the midst of blackouts and dead phones, hangovers, medical crises, and emotional set-tos with Johnsrud—which were increasing—Mary was thrilled when she got her first fan letter for a book review in the fall of 1934. She sent the note to Frani Blough and asked her not to throw it away, "since I want to keep it along with the first of my baby teeth. . . ."

III

Mary McCarthy was not invited to join the staff of *The Nation,* but in the fall of 1935 she was given an assignment that put her name on the literary map for the first time. Part I of "Our Critics, Right or Wrong" appeared under Margaret Marshall and Mary McCarthy's byline on October 23, the day racketeer Dutch Schultz was gunned down in a Newark bar. "A St. Valentine's Day Massacre of reviewers and critics," *Time* recalled the series in a 1942 review of McCarthy's first book, *The Company She Keeps;* and so it was.

Paraphrasing T. S. Eliot, McCarthy and Marshall maintained that while "the purpose of criticism is the elucidation of works of art and the correction of taste," American criticism for a decade at least had contributed to the "debasement of taste." One by one, they exposed the weekly pronouncements of Burton Rascoe, Isabel Paterson, Henry Seidel Canby, J. Donald Adams, and John Chamberlain to a merciless exegesis; all were guilty of perpetuating either an "oracular certainty" based on willful ignorance of modern literature (*namely,* Isabel Paterson: " 'I can't read Joyce and who cares?' ") or an equally unwelcome tendency to reduce criticism "to a quivering jelly of uncritical emotion." J. Donald Adams (whose *Times'* column, "Speaking of Books," would hold the fort for right-thinking literature for forty years) was singled out for both violations of the critical trust. Adams, verbose and otiose, in McCarthy's and Marshall's view, "loves romance, freedom, beauty . . . hates dirty words, class warfare and dictatorships"— whether German, Italian, or Russian, they were all one " 'caster-oil.' "

Proletarian critics fared not much better. The *New Masses'* reviews were distinguished by a "pent-up traditional aestheticism." By treating "questions of content and form [solely] within the context of Marxian dialectics," the authors suggested that reviewers patronized both the book and the book's reader—who was given to believe that by a *correct* reading of the text, "he is right in the midst of the class struggle." Somewhat piously themselves, they hoped that "the new united front will disavow the *New Masses'* critic of a few of his sectarian obligations, and so re-endow him with critical and revolutionary dignity." (In the fall of 1935, the American Communist party had adopted the Soviet Union's new formulation of a "united front from above, which shifted the party's alliance from proletarian literature to the work of established writers.)

In Part V, "The Literary Salesmen," McCarthy and Marshall came down hardest on the reviewers whose "job was not to evaluate literature . . . [but] to sell books." What was original in the argument was not the unmasking of cultural czars, whose influence was even greater then than now, but the documentation of interlocking directorates among the critics, editors, publishers, and book-club executives who presided over the public taste. There were exceptions, particularly among reviewers in the magazines with little advertising, such as *The Nation* and *The New Republic*, but these journals were stylistically too academic to reach a significant public. "In the past ten years," McCarthy (who actually wrote the article) concluded,

> Edmund Wilson, Joseph Wood Krutch, Rebecca West, Frances Newman, Louis Kronenberger, Clifton Fadiman and Robert Morss Lovett . . . in varying degrees [had been] perspicacious, but their faint catcalls have been drowned by the bravos of the publishers' claque. Moreover, none of these critics, with the exception of Mr. Wilson, has made any extended effort to relate what is valuable in modern literature to the body of literature of the past.

For Mary McCarthy, who had assumed responsibility for most of the series when Marshall fell ill, the "exception" was providential. In December 1935, however, when she made her bow to Mr. Wilson—the era's Boswell and Johnson both—he was en route to the Soviet Union on a Guggenheim grant.

Even before "Our Critics" reached the newsstands, Mary and John began to find themselves in new company, less high-hat, more political and literary—which in 1935 amounted to pretty much the same thing. Alongside the *Common Sense* crowd, Selden Rodman and Eunice Clark (now married), Alfred Bingham, Esther and John Strachey (whose lectures on "Literature and Dialectical Materialism" financed the first two issues of *Partisan Review* in 1934), there were new writers and actors visiting Two Beekman Place who were attached, as Johns-rud now was, to the Theatre Union. Led by a Trotskyist named Charlie Walker, and filled with "starry-eyed Stalinists," McCarthy recalled, the Theatre Union was one of the last of the Communist party's cultural organs to unite contending radicals around a common task. Mary's high visibility at *The Nation* also brought the Johnsruds into closer contact with young literary radicals, and now they joined Fred Dupee and Dwight and Nancy Macdonald at a round of benefit parties for southern sharecroppers and striking miners.

In the beginning, both Mary and John regarded their sudden immersion in the left-wing counterculture of New York as a lark: it was something "to which we felt superior, which we laughed at," McCarthy remembered later, "but which nevertheless was influencing us without our being aware of it." For them both, it was a ringside seat at a strange and ambiguous drama heretofore glimpsed only in literature; namely, the enactment in everyday life by ordinary people of revolutionary ideas. When at the end of Clifford Odets's *Waiting for Lefty*, the audience responded to the question from the stage, "Well, what's the answer?" with a thunderous roar of "Strike! Strike!" it was more than a tribute to the play; it was, as Harold Clurman recalls in *The Fervent Years*, the birth cry of the 1930s. Suddenly, the play—not just Odets's but countless others—was the thing, was life at a pitch of sincerity that Harold Johnsrud, with his Shavian wit and English stage accent, could not help but find absurd. But Johnsrud, too, found himself "at the head of a mob," if not in life, then onstage in productions of 'social significance,' such as *The Sailors of Cattaro* and *Black Pit*. In 1936, he appeared in Maxwell Anderson's *Winterset* and Archibald MacLeish's *Panic*, playing, ironically enough, a blind man in both.

Everywhere people seemed to be in the grip of an idea of transformation, both personal and historic, flung up by the unending Depression, sparked by the image of rebirth and reconstruction in Russia, and fueled by the sudden implosion of youthful talent and energy pouring into the city. Edmund Wilson, whose cosmopolitan credentials gave his own conversion to socialism a special authority, provided intellectuals with an apocalyptic vision of the historic moment: "The stock-market crash was to count for us almost like a rending of the earth in preparation for the Day of Judgment," he recalled a few years later in *The New Republic*:

One couldn't help being exhilarated at the sudden unexpected collapse of that stupid gigantic fraud. It gave us a new sense of freedom . . . a new sense of power to find ourselves still carrying on while the bankers for a change, were taking a beating. With a businessman's president in the White House, who kept telling us . . . that the system was perfectly sound, who sent General Douglas MacArthur to burn the camp of the unemployed war veterans who had come to appeal to Washington, we wondered about the survival of representative American institutions; and we became more and more impressed by the achievements of the Soviet Union. . . .

In September 1932, when Mary McCarthy was a junior at Vassar, Wilson had joined fifty-one other prominent intellectuals to declare his support for the Communist ticket of Foster and Ford. The group's reasons were set forth in a pamphlet entitled "Culture and the Crisis," which asserted that both Republicans and Democrats wanted to patch up capitalism, while the Socialists hoped to maintain their respectability and win elections rather than enter into the daily struggles of the working class. Only the Communists were committed to total social, economic, and cultural revolution; intellectuals must choose between a world that was slowly dying and one about to be born. By supporting William Z. Foster, writers could extract concessions from the major parties, expand the Communists' influence among the American people, and prepare the country for a genuine socialist transformation.

An early draft of the pamphlet written by Wilson, Lewis Mumford, Waldo Frank, Sherwood Anderson, and Dos Passos, who wanted to call it "an Appeal to Desk Workers," sounded more 'Communist' than the one finally approved by Malcolm Cowley, Matthew Josephson, and James Rorty. It spoke of the concern of intellectuals for capitalism's tendency to "make eccentric to the mainstream of life [those] creative impulses which are as fundamental . . . as the impulse toward acquisition"; and it also declared the "fundamental identity" of intellectuals with the "interests . . . of the workers and farmers of the nation. . . ."

Very little in the provincial backgrounds of Harold and Mary Johnsrud prepared them for the mixed cast of characters in the new revolutionary movement. Some free-lance research and typing for the labor writer Benjamin Stolberg in 1935 exposed Mary to the 'hard' news of the economic crisis, but for her the big picture remained remote. Her own past stood in stark contrast with that of many revolutionary writers of the period, who were the children of immigrants from Brownsville and the Bronx, one step removed from the poor Orthodox Jews whom Mary used to watch from the Madrona

streetcar in Seattle; pale boys in funny clothes, she remembered, looking old and solemn, seated on the broad porches of wooden tenements.
The brightest among them were destined for "business," it was said in
Seattle, as if "business" was a vocation, like the priesthood. In New
York, a decade later, the brightest had gone 'proletarian,' taking jobs
as cafeteria countermen, and turning to a literature of protest that
celebrated the working man; writing criticism like Michael Gold's,
which saw in the popular novels of Thornton Wilder merely "a short-
cut to the aristocratic emotions."

Alongside proletarian novelists and poets were intellectuals from
Yale and Harvard, for whom it sometimes appeared a point of
honor—given the shame that had befallen their own class—to become
Marxists. In *The New Masses,* they worried about whether Proust
should be read after the socialist revolution, and why there were no
simple proletarians in the intellectually racy novels of André Malraux.
After graduation, some had worked at *Time* (with John Hersey, Robert Fitzgerald, and Walker Evans), or *Fortune* (Robert Cantwell, Louis
Kronenberger, James Agee, Dwight Macdonald), and then, some of
them anyway, moved on to *The New Masses, The Nation, The New
Republic,* or *Partisan Review*—thereby transcending "that great
whore of Babylon and swank journalism," as the poet Delmore
Schwartz called the Luce empire in 1938.

The young writers were a breed apart from the established writers
of the 1920s—Hemingway, Dos Passos, Fitzgerald, Cummings: rebels
from the old nineteenth-century American middle class, for whom the
technique of writing, like the mechanics of bridge building or the
aereodynamics of flight, had been elevated to a fine art. The new
writers cultivated *experience*, "a flourish of dangerous experience," as
Alfred Kazin recalls in his memoir *Starting Out in the Thirties,* which
might transform the art of the novel, if not into a weapon of the class
war, then into a window on the new forces rending the fabric of
American life.

Viewed at close quarters, the "proletarian scowl" that Kazin observed on the faces of the new militants struck Mary McCarthy as
mere affectation when she met the young men at a Webster Hall
dance or a fund-raising party for the Theatre Union in a borrowed
studio, where the drinks were dispensed at long, wet tables, she recalled in "My Confession" in 1953, the liquor was awful, and there
was never enough ice:

Long-haired men in turtle-necked sweaters marched into the
room . . . and threw their overcoats on the floor, against the wall,

and sat down on them; they were only artists and bit-actors, but they gave these affairs a look of gangsterish menace. . . . On couches with wrinkled slipcovers, little spiky-haired girls, like spiders, dressed in peasant blouses and carapaced with Mexican jewelry, made voracious passes at baby-faced juveniles; it was said that they "did it for the Party," as a recruiting effort.

Alfred Kazin walked some of the same corridors as Mary McCarthy, but with a different passkey, which often yielded opposite impressions. The gangsterish young men were sometimes his classmates from City College, whose " 'class' hardness" made him feel ashamed but also jealous:

> In the clattery Saturday night rumble of dances . . . I would find myself envying them for swimming with sure strokes on the surface of chaos . . . the wise types . . . looked as if they had found the right answer. And easy with girls, passing them around at dances with comradely contempt, as if being militant about everything brought immediate advantages.

Kazin preferred the Victorian calm of the New York Public Library, whose spacious reading rooms, with their long golden-oak trestle tables, evoked the nineteenth-century ambience of the American classics. Like a half dozen other young Jewish intellectuals in the 1930s, who wrote the popular American literary histories of the 1940s, Kazin was discovering a more bountiful America in the past.

Both Kazin and McCarthy, nonetheless, were sensitive to the 'immediate advantages' that came with privileged access to the Communist party. For Mary, it wasn't the actors, writers, or the agitators from the Cafeteria Workers Union who caught her eye, but the higher-ups: "dark, smooth-haired owls with large white lugubrious faces and glasses. These were the spiritual directors of the Communist cultural celebrities and they moved about . . . like so many monks or abbés in a worldly salon." She never could resist an argument with the clergy, and she liked to argue with these men, who stood with folded arms, listening to her protesting questions about the murder of the Czar's children, as if they were hearing a confession. " 'The question is of bourgeois origin,' " they suggested gently; and later Mary would shrink in embarrassment, realizing the transparency of her self-exposure; and yet they had not convinced her. Gazing hopefully into their faces, "seeking a trace of scruple or compassion, [she] saw only a marmoreal astuteness."

The superiority that John and Mary felt toward the Communists was, she felt, well-grounded: "it was based on their lack of humor, their fanaticism, and the slow drip of cant that thickened their utterance like a nasal catarrh." Johnsrud, whose political preferences were shaped by exposure to Thorstein Veblen at Carleton College in the 1920s, and by a midwestern populism, remained a skeptic. "Lovestone is a Lovestoneite" he scrawled on the dressing room mirror at the Theatre Union, referring to an American Marxist leader. Both he and Mary knew about Lovestoneites and Trotskyites, even if they were ignorant of the Theory of Permanent Revolution (Trotsky) versus Socialism in One Country (Stalin). Only by the end of 1936, with the onset of Stalin's purge trials, whose most celebrated target was the former leader of the Red Army, Leon Trotsky, would left-wing social life require an opinion on such questions. For the present, it was enough to distinguish the spokesmen and the slogans of the true Church from those of the dissenting sects, whose fanaticism, born of factionalism, was often greater, and to maintain a skeptical but *knowing* detachment from the millenial appeals of them all.

And yet Mary, unlike Johnsrud, was drawn to the Communists. Despite their 'marmoreal' amorality, the impersonal nature of their convictions touched her at a point of vulnerability. "They made me feel petty and shallow," she remembered in 1953; "they had, shall I say, a daily ugliness in their life that made my pretty life seem tawdry." While her interest was a fleeting one, it marked a Rubicon of sorts, which Mary had already crossed—whether she or John knew it yet— alone.

IV

In some "Notes" for a panel discussion on the Thirties in the late 1950s, Mary McCarthy recalls her "Twenties ideology" of this period, which was based on "having fun":

playing bridge, playing ping-pong, discovering new recipes, going to the tennis at Forest Hills, dancing, having cocktails, seeing foreign movies, eating the 85-cent dinner at French restaurants, marching in May Day parades or taking part in demonstrations, which was part of the fun too.

Her own "Twenties" lasted until 1936, she states, which is when the "Thirties" really began for her, and ended, intellectually speaking, around 1945.

In 1935, Mary and John were still 'having fun,' to a degree. At parties John remained "a smoothie" and Mary, very bluestocking in her broad-brimmed hats, eyes flashing, tongue wagging, terrified Dwight Macdonald's wife, Nancy. They had fun on the picket line, too, as when they dressed up in evening clothes to march in support of striking waiters at the Waldorf Astoria with Eunice Clark and Selden Rodman early in 1936 (just like Kay and Harald in *The Group*). But the Johnsruds had begun to replenish a diminishing store of fun in secret liaisons with others. Not only John, who often hinted at his entanglements with "amorous women," and now only thinly concealed the reasons for his frequent layovers at the theatre, but Mary, too, had had a "romantic adventure," which she communicated to Frani Blough's "pink ears only" early in 1935. After that, there was "a little Stalinist" in the Theatre Union, with whom she had a brief affair before she met John Porter at a Webster Hall dance, the "Young Man" memorialized in McCarthy's first short story, "Cruel and Barbarous Treatment," who precipitated the final breakup with Johnsrud.

But it was McCarthy's political adventurousness that signaled the fork in the road ahead. Confronted by the palpable prestige of the American Communist party in 1935, a party that still wore the face of an avenging angel, she no longer felt so superior in her detachment, or so comfortable with Johnsrud's cynicism. When she found herself increasingly at home in Communist circles, however, it was not for political reasons or because of moral vanity but for something more basic. In the end, the Communist party's real influence on Mary McCarthy was established in the one area where she was most open to persuasion: that of social snobbery.

In left-wing society, she found herself, once again, the new girl on the block. It was easy to hide her differences—"lest I find I was that despised article, a 'mere' socialist or watery liberal . . ." McCarthy recalled in the 1950s. Soon she had become adept at reading the hierarchy. "There was something arcane in every Communist," she felt, and the more arcane, the greater her respect, which was why she would always hold the literary Communists in contempt, for they operated in the glare of public opinion, doing the hatchet work:

> An underground worker rated highest . . . next were the theoreti-
> cians and oracles; next were the activists, who mostly worked . . . on
> the waterfront. Last came the rank and file, whose work consisted of
> making speeches, distributing leaflets . . . joining front organiza-
> tions, marching in parades. . . .

The idea of a double life impressed her. "The more talkative comrades seemed to have only one life," like ordinary folk, "but even they . . . had a secret annex to their personality, which was signified by their Party name. It is hard not to respect somebody who has an alias."

For Mary McCarthy, for a little while, the Communist party was *the* party, and while she wouldn't join it, she prided herself on knowing it was the "pinnacle." Only in 1953 when she wrote "My Confession," in the shadow of the McCarthy hearings, did she see the social component in her attitude; "at the time," she noted, "I simply supposed that I was being clear-headed and logical." Today, it is easy to read her "Confession" as a tour de force; she reaches for the arcane herself to skirt the well-worn path. "Most ex-Communists, when they write their autobiographies or testify before Congressional committees," she reminds us, "are at pains to point out that their actions were very, very bad and their motives very, very good." She wants us to understand that for her the opposite was true, without the *very*s. "I see no reason to disavow my actions," which were conventional enough, "but my motives give me a little embarrassment. . . ."

A reviewer of McCarthy's *The Stones of Florence* once observed: "If everybody likes something, Mary McCarthy is sure to say she hates it. She then proceeds by grudging degrees to admit to certain excellences until finally she arrives at the state of enthusiasm in which everyone else began." Something of this psychology is at work in "My Confession." In the 1950s, former leftists often said they had agreed with the Party's ends, but couldn't support its means; they admired the Party's principles, but not its methods of organization, and certainly not its secrecy. The very idea that "a secret annex to [the] personality . . . an alias" should attract an intellectual to the Party, while her own political experience and observations of society remained unexamined, *was* heretical. And yet except for a brief period of activism in 1935 to 1936, McCarthy steered clear of Communist-supported causes. Communist principles, in her opinion, invariably dripped of 'cant.' After the onset of the purge trials, the very presence of Party orchestration behind the scenes of a popular cause (including antifascist campaigns during World War II) could scare her off, if not draw her fire. And this left Mary McCarthy holding pretty much the same opinions as everyone else.

In a strange kind of way, McCarthy's 1953 testimony evokes the more sinister example of Whittaker Chambers, whose case was reviewed by Hannah Arendt that same year. Chambers, too, though a member, had no interest in the political life of the Party: "He looked down on it and escaped it into the inner apparatus where commands were given and obeyed . . . behind the scenes of official Communist politics," Arendt noted. In Mary McCarthy's attraction to the "arcane," the "double life," there is something of this Machiavellian ardor, cold and insubstantial. Yet, while few intellectuals would say as much, it was precisely the Communist party's "inner apparatus," its *secret* life, that made its political authority compelling.

"There was an enormous prestige . . . for people who belonged to the Party," Malcolm Cowley recalled in 1966. "They were listened to as if they had . . . been at meetings where the word was passed down from Mount Sinai." Mount Sinai was Moscow, the administrative capital of another country—whose great size and untold resources have haunted the imaginations of American intellectuals and statesmen alike, as if the Soviet Union was a reverse mold of the United States. Thus, it is not surprising that so many intellectuals who embraced the Communist party in the 1930s, and repudiated it later, could reenter the mainstream of American politics without an ideological hair out of place. To the degree that they attached their loyalty to the Soviet Union, where party and state were one, and not to Marxism, even less to American radical traditions, it required not much more than another leap of faith to shift their allegiance to Roosevelt, Henry Luce, or Jack Kennedy, when new deals, new leaders, and new visions of world order hove into view.

Nancy Macdonald's estimate of McCarthy's flirtation with the Communists is probably just: "She liked the *idea* of being political," Macdonald says, "but I don't think she was terribly serious about it." And yet during the depths of the Depression and the rise of German fascism, *before* the Moscow trials, McCarthy could no more resist the moral authority of the Communist movement than could most of her fellow intellectuals. It would have been strange, in fact, if as an ambitious young contributor to the liberal press she had *not* gone 'proletarian' in her fashion; or that when civil war broke out in Spain, she did *not* support the Lincoln Brigade and protest nonintervention, which she did. Nor was there anything unusual in her having briefly entertained a suggestion by a Communist organizer in 1936 that she join the Party:

> A thrill went through me, but I laughed, as when somebody has proposed to you and you are not sure whether they are serious. "I don't think I'd make very good material." "You're wrong," he said gravely. "You're just the kind of person the Party needs.

You're young and idealistic and independent." I broke in: "I thought independence was just what the Party didn't want." "The Party needs criticism," he said. "But it needs it from the inside. If people like you who agree with its main objectives would come in and criticize, we wouldn't be so narrow and sectarian." . . . He turned to my fiancé [John Porter]. "Not you," he said. "You won't have the time to give to it. But for Mary I think it would be an interesting experiment."

It was like being tapped for Skull and Bones. The experience gave her "quite a new sense of Communism and of myself too; I had never looked upon my character in such a favorable light." But she knew that she was not the person the Party organizer thought she was. It was not idealism that led McCarthy to probe the Party's defenses. She was not then, nor ever would be, one who longed for 'a better world.' What propelled her was a curiosity born of social ambition; for in the world as it was in New York intellectual circles in the mid-1930s, the American Communist party held much the same high ground for her as the New York society girls had at Vassar.

8

A Turn with Trotsky

*"It may be that the whims of chance are
really the importunities of design. But if there is a Design, it aims,
in real lives, like the reader's or mine or Trotsky's,
to look natural and fortuitous; that is how it gets us into its web."*

—MARY MCCARTHY, "MY CONFESSION"

I felt terribly about this business of falling in love with another man,"
Mary McCarthy told an interviewer in 1986, referring to the affair with
John Porter, "but I must have been wanting something to put an end
to the marriage. Of course, he was terribly unfaithful," she said of
Harold Johnsrud. "I didn't know that till afterwards. I was very
unfaithful, but not as unfaithful as he was. I think probably I still don't
know the extent of it." Eunice Clark was only one of Johnsrud's
conquests, as it turned out, but she was as bad as ten. So many
unpleasant facts emerged once Mary broke her private vow of fidelity
to the *rightness* of the marriage—the vow that leads one to expect the
best of life's partners, not the worst—that fifty years later, she had "no
idea what he thought about me." Nor is it clear exactly what Mary
McCarthy thought of her first husband.

Johnsrud wears a succession of masks when he appears in
McCarthy's fiction, as he did in life. In *The Group*, only a letter of his
name is changed; but some of Harald's treachery is borrowed from
Mary McCarthy's second husband. Edmund Wilson, not Johnsrud,
maneuvered his young wife into the Payne Whitney Clinic for psychiatric observation, as Harald does in the novel. In "Ghostly Father, I
Confess," which was written during McCarthy's marriage to Wilson,
the *former* husband, though nameless, appears sympathetic. The heroine, Meg Sargent, who has allowed a psychiatrist "to get his hands on

her beautiful psychology," is the "shady case" in this fiction. On the analyst's couch, she discovers that each time she has married, her past reasserts itself:

> She used to think back over her childhood and marvel, telling herself that it was really extraordinary that "all that" had not left a single trace. Yet as soon as she had married for the first time, she had begun to change back again. The first time she cried, she had said to herself, "This is very strange. I never cry." The first time she . . . heard a torrent of abuse pour from her own lips, she had listened to herself in astonishment. . . . It happened again and again, and always there was this . . . feeling that she was only repeating combinations of words she had memorized long ago. She had been married some time before she knew that she sounded exactly like Aunt Clara.

Aunt Clara, "hysterical, declamatory," is McCarthy's Aunt Margaret, who serves Margaret Sargent as a namesake, a curious and revealing connection (Sargent was the maiden name of Mary's Great-Grandmother Preston), for such borrowings from life are never arbitrary in McCarthy's fiction. "Names have a queer kind of sorcery for me, like guarantees of reality," she once wrote Elizabeth Bishop, explaining why so many characters in *The Group* carried part of the name of the persons who inspired them.

"Ghostly Father, I Confess" is the only one of McCarthy's stories in which she explores the dark side of her personality—"the deeper . . . the tragic notes," which, as she later acknowledged, she tried to expunge from the repertoire of her emotions. In the story, she ensures her heroine's candor by identifying Meg with the real-life guardian whose baleful influence over McCarthy's early life always stood as an affront to her vision of herself as a naturally reasonable person. When the 'usurper' entered Meg Sargent's *second* marriage (as it entered McCarthy's marriage to Edmund Wilson, from the very beginning), Meg is forced to remember how with her "first husband" she was also

> powerless to intervene when this alien personality would start on one of its tirades, or when it would weep and lie in bed in the morning. . . . And when it began to have love affairs, to go up to strange hotel rooms, and try to avoid the floor clerk, she could only stand by, horrified, like a spectator at a play . . . who longs to jump

on the stage and clear up the misunderstanding, but who composes himself by saying that what is happening is not real, those people are only actors.

Turning 'those people'—beginning with herself—into characters in fiction presented McCarthy with one way to 'clear up the misunderstanding.' But another significance of these passages lies rather in the facts they acknowledge from McCarthy's personal history, and in the novelty of their interpretation. In "Ghostly Father, I Confess," she describes Meg's "incredulity and terror" over the alien patterns in her behavior. Her first husband had actually consoled her because he shared her horror:

> It was as if she had lent her house to a family of squatters and returned to find the crockery broken . . . the walls defaced with obscenities, her beautiful, young girl's bedroom splashed with the filth of a dog. And it was as if he had taken her hand and said, "Don't look at it. Come away now. Everything will be just the same; we will send for the cleaning woman, the house painter and the restorer. Don't cry, it has no connection with you." She was glad to believe him, naturally. Nevertheless, before long she began to think him a fool.

And she wonders: "What if she were an imposter?" Perhaps the "false self was . . . the true one."

The question is resolved by a twist of logic that leads Meg to produce "the false self in all its malignancy, [thus] asserting its claim to belief. To say, 'You were wrong about me, look how dreadfully I can treat you, and do it not compulsively, but calmly, in the full possession of my faculties.'" She announces her decision to marry another man; her husband "had grieved over her and let her go, remarking only that her fiancé would never understand her as he did, that she must be out of her senses." Afterwards, she experiences remorse, observing that her first husband's wounds are healed by time, while her own, being self-inflicted, continue to trouble her: "There are other girls in the world, but there is only the single self. . . . [T]he betrayer is always the debtor. . . ."

"Ghostly Father, I Confess" was written during a period of lacerating self-doubt, after Mary McCarthy had entered into a marriage, with Edmund Wilson, that in certain respects reproduced the searing conditions of her childhood in Minneapolis. Wilson, as we shall see, could be both possessive and tyrannical. When McCarthy married him in 1938, she reenacted something of the trauma of orphanhood: she broke with her former friends, quit her first real job, and retired with him to his rented cottage in Stamford, Connecticut, where she promptly became pregnant. Moreover, when McCarthy herself rebelled against these conditions, which were no more tolerable for being self-imposed, Wilson, unlike Harold Johnsrud, regarded her hysterical outbursts as the behavior of a neurotic woman. Mary McCarthy had not come to agree with him, but she could not deny the fact that she was undergoing psychiatric treatment. And by the early 1940s, as "Ghostly Father, I Confess" attests, she was struggling with the possibility that the eternal villain—Wilson, Myers, Margaret—was also the scapegoat; and that she herself continued to give this figure authority over her life, and to settle for an outraged innocence instead of the more arduous challenge of defining and defending her own interests.

In the story, the image McCarthy presents of her first husband is no doubt colored by the explosive and still-unresolved relationship with her second. Johnsrud must have seemed a lamb next to Wilson. Nor is it likely that in the middle 1930s Mary McCarthy would have regarded her behavior with Harold Johnsrud with anything like the uneasiness she felt for her bohemian past in 1942, when the story was written. In 1936, when she started seeing John Porter, the Williams graduate who worked for the Women's International League for Peace and Freedom, whom she met at a Webster Hall dance while Johnsrud was on the road, she was still "returnable," still in circulation—soon to be a gay divorcée.

John Porter figures only briefly in McCarthy's life as a 'fiancé,' but the infatuation inspired her to antic heights in "Cruel and Barbarous Treatment." The first of the stories collected in *The Company She Keeps*, it is as archly sardonic as "Ghostly Father, I Confess" (the last) is unsparingly analytic. It also captures something of McCarthy's affinity for the clandestine life. "She could not bear to hurt her husband. She impressed this upon the Young Man, on her confidantes, and finally on her husband himself:

> The thought of Telling Him actually made her heart turn over in a sudden and sickening way . . . and yet she knew that being a potential divorcée was deeply pleasurable in somewhat the same way that being an engaged girl had been. In both cases, there was at first a subterranean courtship. . . . The concealment of the

original, premarital courtship had, however, been a mere superstitious gesture. . . . One put one's family and . . . friends off the track because one was still afraid that the affair might not . . . lead in a clean, direct line to the altar. . . .

"Cruel and Barbarous Treatment" is McCarthy's anatomy of infidelity, sans retribution, whose sequel, divorce and remarriage, presents the romantic heroine with the usual anticlimax. After the tingling sensations of deception, a public engagement subjects her to second thoughts, mutual distrust, boredom. For McCarthy herself, the affair with John Porter was mainly a passport to the single life, heretofore feared and avoided. The young newspaperman (he also worked for the Paris *Herald-Tribune*) is remembered in later life as "an absolutely worthless person," who was very attractive, "like Fred MacMurray." The episode, nonetheless, led her to pen some interesting speculations about women—about herself and her tangled relations to men, in particular:

> "If the Man," she muttered, "did not exist, the Moment would create him." . . . She had made herself the victim of an imposture. But . . . she had possibly been impelled by unconscious forces to behave more intelligently than appearances would indicate. She was perhaps acting out . . . a ritual which required that, first . . . the Husband be eliminated from the cast of characters. Conceivably, she was designed for the role of *femme fatale*, and for such a personage considerations of safety . . . were not only philistine but irrelevant. She might marry a second, a third, a fourth time. . . . But, in any case, for the thrifty bourgeois love insurance, with its daily payments of patience, forbearance, and resignation, she was no longer eligible. She would be, she told herself delightedly, a bad risk.

In the club car on the train to Reno, "she felt gratitude toward the Young Man for having unwittingly effected her transit into a new life. She looked about her at the other passengers. Later she would talk to them." One of them, as it happened in real life, was a man in a Brooks Brothers shirt who came from Pittsburgh, with whom Mary McCarthy would have her next affair.

John Porter wasn't forgotten. In 1988, in a chapter from the unfinished second volume of *How I Grew*, McCarthy tells what happened to him after she broke their engagement. He had gone to Mexico on an assignment that never panned out, gotten sick, and died, a tragedy for which his mother never forgave Mary (if she had married him, as planned, he would never have left, Mrs. Porter insisted). Fifty years later, McCarthy reviews the sorry tale with a troubled conscience. Like a bulldog, she never let go of a lover, any more than an enemy, with whom there was always unfinished business.

II

In the fall of 1936, after divorcing Johnsrud, Mary McCarthy took a tiny studio at 18 Gay Street in the Village, around the corner from Elizabeth Bishop, who lived on Charles Street. She was indeed on her way to a new life, although little of its literary and political flavor appears in "Cruel and Barbarous Treatment." "A Divorcée on Gay Street: Meetings and Memories," another chapter in McCarthy's unfinished autobiography, later incorporated in *Intellectual Memoirs,* tells more about the tumultuous period. Living outside the matrimonial law, McCarthy soaked up the kind of experience that proved especially amenable to fiction and social commentary. The time she lived in the one-room apartment, with its "teetery bookcase" and "bath suited to a bird"—the site of a succession of one-night stands that allowed her to compare the sexual equipment of an astonishing variety of men, and discover "amazing differences, both in length and massiveness" (this recalled in her seventy-sixth year)—enliven *The Company She Keeps,* the essays in *On the Contrary* (1961), and *The Group.*

The successor volume to *How I Grew* is also reserved for naming names. The overnight affairs, identified in terse one-liners, included the lyricist for an ILGWU musical; a man who made puppets; a married man who worked for a publisher; a truck driver McCarthy met at Chumley's, a West Village bar and restaurant popular with writers. (A more serious lover in 1936, who gave McCarthy the model for Polly Andrews's lover, Gus LeRoy, in *The Group,* was Bill Mangold, who headed up the information committee of the Spanish Loyalists.) When one day she realized that in twenty-four hours she had slept with three different men, she was "slightly scared," but she "did not *feel* promiscuous," she writes; a contention borne out in a backhanded way by the dissection of her lovers' "sexual equipment." "One handsome married man, who used to arrive with two Danishes from a very good bakery," she observes, "had a penis about the size and shape of a lead pencil; he shall remain nameless." Pondering the relation between a man's height and the size of his organ, she muses: "There may be dwarfish men with monstrously large organs, but I have never known one."

McCarthy's early days on Gay Street are remembered as "the harshest months of my life," economically speaking. And yet compared to other struggling writers, she was well-off. The McCarthy grain-elevator stocks had stopped paying dividends for a while, but she could count on twenty-five dollars a week from her Grandfather Preston, augmented by pocket money from the *Nation* reviews. When she finally found a part-time job, it was with Mannie Rousuck, who had established himself in a more respectable gallery (not yet Wildenstein's), specializing in English sporting scenes. Once again, she wrote descriptions of paintings for use in letters to prospective customers (Ambrose Clark, Mrs. Hartley Dodge), for which she was paid fifteen dollars a week. Mannie was on his way to becoming Jay, a well-dressed man-about-town with a fondness for the Boston bull terrier, who would turn up regularly in Cholly Knickerbocker columns. Soon he would be taking Mary to the Colony and Le Voisin, but in 1936 he was still scraping by. With her gilded prose and educated tastes, Mary McCarthy was his Amy Vanderbilt, and Rousuck was one of those odd jobs that free-lance writers collect.

Surprisingly, she continued to go to the theatre with Johnsrud. After the "Our Critics" series, which was still being talked about a year later, *The Nation* commissioned Mary to produce a series on contemporary drama critics. And Johnsrud, with his practical experience in the theatre, helped her achieve the unusual concreteness one finds in the discussion of stagecraft in "Our Actors and the Critics," all the more refreshing in that it seems to be written from an actor's point of view.

McCarthy's social life in these months revolved increasingly around the Sunday open houses that James T. Farrell, whose *Studs Lonigan* she had praised in *Common Sense,* and his wife, the actress Hortense Alden, held in their Village apartment. It was there that she met the cadre of intellectuals—Philip Rahv, William Phillips, Meyer Schapiro, chief among them—who were soon to take an historic leap from the idea of revolution to the idea of literature as an index of civilization. The idea was to be hers, as well, and already was, if what one did without apology, without interference, and before almost everything else was an index to what one really believed in. Writing, in McCarthy's case; reading, and puzzling things out.

In 1936, Mary McCarthy was "just waiting for the world," as James Farrell remembered. And Farrell, whose *Studs Lonigan* was first serialized by *Partisan Review* in 1934, when the magazine was an arm of the Communist party's John Reed Club, was eager to take her in tow, to launch her as a smart little frigate in the shark-filled waters of New York intellectual society. Not unlike Pflaumen in McCarthy's "The Genial Host" (another chapter in *The Company She Keeps*), who offers Meg Sargent access to his own rich social connections, in exchange for her loyal attendance at parties. Pflaumen as a physical type—"the shine of his nails, the whiteness of his sharp, jagged teeth"—was inspired by another host at the time, Robert Misch, an advertising man who was secretary to the Wine and Food Society. It was Misch who introduced Mary to a slightly different crowd, "smart and moneyed, young Communists with a little name, progressive hosts and modernist hostesses"—mostly Jewish, McCarthy noted years later, describing herself as "the only non-Jewish person in the room." It was at such functions, where voices rose "in lively controversy over the new play, the new strike, the new Moscow trials, the new abstract show at the Modern Museum," that Mary made connections for jobs, which, like the fleeting affairs, never seemed to pan out. (One that did was a summer job for H. V. Kaltenborn in Brooklyn in 1937, ghost-writing *Kaltenborn Edits the News*.)

Lillian Hellman, escorted by Louis Kronenberger, was a guest at the party treated in "The Genial Host." Another guest was Leo Huber-man, later the editor, with Paul Sweezy, of *Monthly Review*, who is "the young Russian Jew . . . who wore a rather quizzical, sardonic expression on a pure Italianate face." Seated between a sculpture by Archipenko and the head of the Egyptian queen Nefretiti, Hellman appears as "a woman psychoanalyst who got herself up in a Medici gown and used a cigarette holder." But the substance of her contribution that night is given to a fictional critic, John Peterson, who has been to Madrid, and refuses to countenance any criticism of the Communist cause, either in Spain or Moscow.

In "The Genial Host," Meg Sargent is introduced as "a violent Trotskyist"—although "you knew you were not a violent Trotskyist. It was just that you were temperamentally attracted to unpopular causes; when you were young, it had been the South, the Dauphin, Bonnie Prince Charlie; later it was Debs and now Trotsky that you loved." When she and another guest raise some question about Stalin's treatment of Communist opposition leaders, Peterson calls a halt to the "backstabbing" by invoking the shimmering image of La Pasionaria, whom he has just heard sing in Madrid: " 'What do these petty political squabbles mean to her?' " he demands with a flourish; whereupon Meg, sick of the practiced sentiment, throws back the image of Andrés Nin, a Spanish anarchist suspected of having been murdered by the

Communists. It isn't one of McCarthy's better stories, but it reveals a heart that by the end of 1936 was tense with sympathy for the renegade Trotsky, one of the founding fathers of the October Revolution whose case was soon to be heard in Mexico; at long last, a real human being in the revolutionary movement—not a doctrine, a method of analysis, or a position—with whom she could identify.

McCarthy always dated her conversion to Trotskyism to a publisher's party in November 1936 in honor of the old *Masses* cartoonist Art Young. Jim Farrell took her to the party, performing a role in her life that others would play, the role of sponsor or 'fixer'—Peggy Guggenheim played it for Mary in Europe after the war, and was neatly caricatured as Miss Grabbe in McCarthy's 1947 story, "The Cicerone." "Farrell would write such terrible stuff," McCarthy later recalled of their early years together on the new *Partisan Review*. "PR gave him a column so we wouldn't have to print his pieces. His reputation sank after the Bernard Carr stories." She is right, but the judgment seems unduly harsh for a man who played such a pivotal role in her life; not in terms of literary influence—though the correspondence between Farrell's post-*Lonigan* novels, bristling with dramatized theses about fellow intellectuals, and the fiction Mary McCarthy would soon be writing, is striking.

Novels like Farrell's aspired to contemporary moral history, as did the stories of Delmore Schwartz, which, with the exception of the best one, "In Dreams Begin Responsibilities," about his parents, revolve endlessly around Delmore and his contemporaries. Gossip, the critic Isaac Rosenfeld observed at the time, is really a form of social history. In a story such as Schwartz's "New Year's Eve," or Farrell's *The Road Between*, or Mary McCarthy's "Portrait of the Intellectual as a Yale Man" or *The Oasis*, gossip is elevated to a literary art. Whether it makes a good story, apart from its importance to literary society, is another question.

In "My Confession," McCarthy tells how a "novelist friend"— (Farrell) "dimple-faced, shaggy headed, earnest, with a whole train of people, like a deputation, behind him"—cornered her at the refreshment table and posed a question: Did she think Trotsky was entitled to a hearing? McCarthy blushed. " 'What had Trotsky done?' " And the friend had patiently explained: Trotsky, who had served as Lenin's commissar of foreign affairs, was accused by Stalin of fostering a counterrevolutionary plot in the Soviet Union, and of conspiring with the Gestapo to murder Soviet leaders. Sixteen old Bolsheviks who had

confessed to the conspiracy at the first Moscow trial had implicated
him. It had been in the papers since August. Mary, in the upheaval of
divorce and resettlement, had missed the news.

" 'I don't know anything about it,' " she protested. " 'What do you
want me to say?' " (Writing Jim Farrell twenty years later, McCarthy
added: "I knew you were complimenting me when you asked my
opinion . . . for I really had no title to one. . . .") " 'Trotsky denies the
charges,' " Farrell stated in 1936. " 'He declares it's a GPU fabrication.
Do you think he is entitled to a hearing?' " Her mind had cleared:

> "Why, of course." I laughed—were there people who would say
> that Trotsky was *not* entitled to a hearing? . . . "One thing more,
> Mary," he continued gravely. "Do you believe that Trotsky should
> have the right of asylum?" The right of asylum! I looked for
> someone to share my amusement—were we in ancient Greece or
> the Middle Ages? . . . But nobody smiled back. Everybody waited
> dispassionately, as for form's sake I assented to the phrasing: yes,
> Trotsky, in my opinion was entitled to the right of asylum.
>
> I went home with the serene feeling that all these people were
> slightly crazy.

Four days later, she got a letter from a group called the "Committee for the Defense of Leon Trotsky," with her name among the
signatories. It was the kind of move the Communists often made, and
McCarthy instantly resolved to withdraw her name and write a note
of protest. "Trotsky had a right to a hearing, but I had a right to my
signature." Even if she had been the only one at the party who failed
to understand the import of Farrell's polling, nothing she had said
committed her to Trotsky's *defense*.

The "decision" made, she procrastinated. Probably she didn't
want to offend her novelist friend, who had been "good to her," but
she would have gotten around to it eventually, she thought, if the
phone calls hadn't begun. (In the letter to Farrell in 1957, she wrote:
"I didn't think I was being asked for a signature. But I've never held
that against you; it changed my life—for the better.") Strange calls
came at odd hours from people she hardly knew, and they all said
basically the same thing: The committee was a "tool of reaction," and
liberal people should dissociate themselves from an unwarranted intervention in the domestic affairs of the Soviet Union. They usually hung
up without waiting for a reply. "Behind these phone calls there was a
sense of the Party wheeling its forces into . . . disciplined formations,"

McCarthy remembered; and soon she learned that a telephone campaign was indeed under way.

Almost overnight, an open letter appeared in *The New Republic, The New York Times,* and *The Nation* warning liberals that Trotsky's request for a forum was "a sham." It was signed by sixty prominent intellectuals whose names were familiar signatures on Party petitions: among them, Newton Arvin, Heywood Broun, Theodore Dreiser, Lillian Hellman, Granville Hicks, Corliss Lamont. And the signatures soon grew to eighty-eight—"the most distinguished list of names ever gathered . . . in America in support of the Soviet Union," the American Communist party's leader, Earl Browder, reported to *Pravda.* And one by one, the names of prominent literary figures disappeared from the Trotsky committee's letterhead.

Here was an issue McCarthy understood. She would not suffer intimidation. As for Trotsky, she wrote in 1953: "the only thing that made me think that he might be innocent was the odd behavior of the Communists and the fellow-traveling liberals, who seemed to be infuriated at the idea of a free inquiry." Naturally, she rushed to the committee's defense, which meant going to real political meetings with Jim Farrell, Fred Dupee (who had left the Party), and Philip Rahv, who soon after invited her to join the developing putsch at *Partisan Review.*

III

In "My Confession," McCarthy examines the providential role of chance in her political formation. "The 'great' decisions—those I can look back on pensively and say, 'That was a turning-point'—have been made without my awareness," she reflects. "Too late to do anything about it, I discover that I have chosen. And this is particularly striking when the choice has been political or historic"—or romantic, one might add, thinking of several marriages and affairs. For Mary McCarthy, the very sign of the historic is the nonchalance with which it tosses an individual, like a house lifted by a tornado, into a trend or a destiny marked *personal.* In the 1950s, it was just this play of inadvertence she found missing from the "true confessions of reformed Communists," and she stressed it for that reason. She had also verged on a truth ample enough to live with, one that had interesting implications for a writer.

Not surprisingly, she turned to literature for its confirmation, to Stendhal's hero in *The Red and the Black,* "who took part in something confused and disarrayed and insignificant that he later learned was the Battle of Waterloo"; and to Trotsky, "a man of words primarily, a pamphleteer and orator" (which ignored the Trotsky who was a military leader). Reading Trotsky's *My Life* in 1953, McCarthy noted how one day during Lenin's last illness Trotsky had gone duck shooting on the River Dubna, walked through a bog in felt boots, and contracted influenza. He was sent to Sukhu for the cure, missed Lenin's funeral and the telegram calling him home, and was consigned to bed during the power struggle that raged throughout the rest of 1924. " 'I cannot help noting how obligingly the accidental helps the historical law,' " he wrote. " 'In the language of biology one might say that the historical law is realized through the natural selection of accidents. . . . One can foresee the consequences of a revolution or a war, but it is impossible to foresee the consequences of an autumn shooting-trip for wild ducks.' "

McCarthy commends Trotsky for "[t]his shrug before the unforeseen [which] implies an acceptance of consequences that is a far cry from penance and prophecy," the earmarks of the usual confession. "Such, it concedes, is life. *Bravo*, old sport," she exclaims, "even though the hall is empty"; for by 1953 the name Trotsky had dropped out of sight—along with Lenin and Al Capone, two other desperadoes of an earlier era who intrigued a great many more Americans (who had little to fear from either revolution or organized crime) than historians acknowledge.

When McCarthy went on to speculate that "the whims of chance are really the importunities of design," she formulated a central insight for a writer sensitive to the symbolic events of everyday life. The limitation in the perception lay in its indifference to collective experience, to the unexpected thing that is also happening in one form or another to nearly everyone else.

In the spring of 1936, months before her stumble into Trotskyism, Mary McCarthy, like many other literary radicals, had already discovered something in Trotsky that fired her imagination in a way that Marxist ideas about economics and the class war never could. Reviewing John Steinbeck's *In Dubious Battle* in March 1936, she chided the author for the tedious interior monologues of the two organizers, who reminded her of those tiresome characters in the theatre who chat through the climax of a play. No doubt a successful proletarian novel could be written according to this "classic scheme," McCarthy declared, but Mr. Steinbeck wasn't the man to do it:

If a revolutionary general with the talent for prose—say Trotsky—had cast his reflections upon the technique of class warfare into the form of a novel, though they would fall more naturally, as did Caesar's, into the form of a memoir, the results might have been exciting. Caesar—and doubtless Trotsky—had something to say about the curious and wonderful behavior of embattled human beings. . . .

For James Farrell, the figure of Trotsky had separated itself from the Bolshevik pantheon long before the Moscow trials. Trotsky's "brilliant character vignettes in *The History of the Russian Revolution*," Farrell believed, were "actually social studies in miniature." And for *Studs Lonigan,* he made use of Trotsky in much the same way that the proletarian novelist Robert Cantwell used Henry James—for character study.

The novelist's Trotsky was not the author of theories about Permanent Revolution that inspired men like Farrell Dobbs and James Cannon in the Socialist Workers party. The writers' Trotsky was the 'pamphleteer and orator,' a little bit like themselves; aloof, brilliant but misunderstood, a student of the revolution he had helped to lead; and again like themselves, a failure at politics. Like Garin in Malraux's *Man's Fate,* who states, "Marxism is not a doctrine but a will," this Trotsky combined an almost Nietzschean awe for the power and danger of revolutionary ideas, with a vision of the socialist revolution on a grand scale. Even Malcolm Cowley, who battled Trotskyists throughout the 1930s and '40s, extolled those sections of *The History of the Russian Revolution* where "the author rises above his immediate report into the sphere of universal principles—when he sets out to write a . . . primer of revolutions in general."

For Edmund Wilson, Trotsky's *Literature and Revolution* was one of the Marxist classics, along with Marx's *Eighteenth Brumaire of Louis Bonaparte* and *Das Kapital*. Marxism, after all, was primarily a reading experience for this generation, but it was not to be taken lightly. For Wilson, Marxism *was* literature. Writing the poet John Peale Bishop in 1932, Wilson observed that

although Communism itself . . . has some of the characteristics of a secular church, it corresponds more or less to the literature of the Enlightenment before the French and American Revolutions, and people of our own time can no more afford to be ignorant of it than people of the 19th century could of Voltaire and Montesquieu and Rousseau.

Nor was it a body of dogma, and Wilson reminded Bishop that Marx said he was no Marxist, and that Trotsky's writings were banned in the Soviet Union.

Referring in 1953 to her sudden conversion to Trotskyism in November 1936, McCarthy writes: "I knew nothing about the cause I had espoused; I had never read a word of Lenin or Trotsky, nothing of Marx but the Communist Manifesto, nothing of Soviet history. . . ." Reminded in 1986 of the Steinbeck review, she couldn't remember what she had read that led her to invoke the name of Trotsky before the Trotsky defense committee. Perhaps McCarthy had picked him up in cocktail-party conversation; but the disclaimer of conscious interest in the ideas of the 'revolutionary general' is typical of the memoirs of literary Trotskyists. Something in the ecstatic nature of their apprenticeship to Trotsky made it a private affair, easily forgotten during the Moscow trials, when Trotsky was swallowed up in the showdown with the Communist party. Once Stalin issued the diktat that Trotskyism led objectively to fascism, not Trotsky but anti-Stalinism became the rallying point for a challenge to the Party—one that had been brewing among many liberal intellectuals since the end of 1932, when Edmund Wilson, disabused of his support for William Z. Foster, issued his "A Plea to Progressives" to "take Communism away from the Communists."

When "My Confession" appeared, anti-Stalinism had been eclipsed by the wave of anticommunism that swept through American society in the 1950s. Only a veteran of the literary wars or a former Trotskyist knew what it meant to oppose Stalinism, or official communism, *from the left;* and few stepped forth to set the record straight. In her own way, Mary McCarthy—who repudiated that other McCarthy and *his* trials in a few lectures at the time—had nevertheless accommodated herself to the end-of-ideology ethos that ruled the period. By embracing the role of chance in politics, she had, in effect, reduced her own political "turning-point" to a harmless level of anecdote. Remembering herself as a 'Trotskyite,' "dancing in a nightclub, [while] tall, collegiate young Party members would press me to their shirt bosoms and tell me not to be silly, honey," she had indeed turned the tumultuous history of the 1930s into "a vaguely amorous aspect of her own personality," as an *Esquire* writer observed in 1962. But the truth is that 1936 did mark a turning point for Mary McCarthy, whose repercussions would be felt as late as 1980, when McCarthy's confrontation with Lillian Hellman touched off another round in the civil war on the American Left.

9

Girl Friday Among the Pirates

"The unity of the proletariat,

as a universal slogan, is a myth."

—LEON TROTSKY

Mary McCarthy once corrected an interviewer in the 1960s who assumed that after Vassar she had gone "straight into left-wing politics in New York." Not at all, she said; she was "just there," silent at meetings, argumentative only at parties. "I was much more of a literary girl," she added. "It was only the Moscow trials . . . that put my mind to work." In the early months of 1937, she had plunged into the literature on the trials, reading the verbatim report of the second Moscow trial, Trotskyist pamphlets on the case, the 'bourgeois' press and the liberal weeklies, until she was convinced that the trials, which had sent thousands to their deaths, were a monstrous frame-up.

She mastered the debate, and even the Marxist canon to a degree, but she did not try to become a Marxist or a Trotskyist. "Marxism," she decided, listening to the learned young men at the Trotsky defense committee meetings, "was something you had to take up young, like ballet-dancing." Marxism for Mary McCarthy remained a question of doctrine, not a commitment to an idea of revolutionary change in the power relations of society. Trotsky never appeared to her as a rallying point for a return to classical Marxism, as he did to some others on the Left. Trotsky the heretic, the victim of Stalin's witch-hunts, is the figure who gave her a cause, and turned her into an activist.

In the spring of 1937, McCarthy saw her first action on the anti-Stalinist front. The occasion was the Second American Writers Congress in New York, where Earl Browder shared the speaker's platform with Archibald MacLeish and Ernest Hemingway. Together with Dwight Macdonald, McCarthy teamed up with William Phillips, Philip Rahv, Fred Dupee, and Eleanor Clark to take on Granville Hicks's panel on literary criticism. "Mary got up and spoke, and it was strong and sharp," William Phillips recalled in 1987, "but of course they were smothered by an avalanche of criticism." Both Phillips and Rahv had tried to persuade Macdonald and McCarthy not to attend the Congress, much less participate in its forums, which they insisted were stacked in favor of the party line, but "they browbeat us by making us feel we were cowardly and they were brave," Phillips stated, "and so we went along."

Given the elements of the drama: the confrontation with the chair, the whiff of conspiracy in the wings, the imagery of politics injected like an amphetamine charge in the doughy flank of literature, the Writers Congress couldn't fail but rally Mary McCarthy's interest. In 1949, she would replay the role of outside agitator at the Waldorf Conference in New York, and then again in 1960 in Berlin, when the chair was the anti-Communist Congress for Cultural Freedom. In 1937, the counterset with Granville Hicks over the 'Great Tradition' in American literature was also a warm-up for the collective venture on which she was about to embark with Philip Rahv and William Phillips: the rebirth of *Partisan Review*.

For Mary McCarthy personally the Congress was an introduction to the "manic-impressive" Philip Slav (as Delmore Schwartz called him) in action. " 'They're looking for pimples on the great smiling face of the Soviet Union,' " McCarthy remembered someone objecting when the rebel group had scored a point against the Communists' heavy-handed interpretation of American literature. And Rahv, who had just been expelled from the Party, and was still red behind the ears, had been eager to give her the lowdown on the Communists' debating tactics. Such rejoinders amounted to "waving the bloody shirt," he explained, and were designed to ward off criticism.

By 1937, the party line had changed from what it was when the League of American Writers staged the first American Writers Congress in the spring of 1935. The "capitalist system," which was "rapidly crumbling" when the 1935 Congress took place, was no longer even mentioned; neither was revolutionary writing. The second Congress unfolded in the shadow of the coming world war, and the Communist party had set about mobilizing American intellectuals to press for U.S. intervention against the fascist powers (a program abruptly

revised in 1939 after the Hitler-Stalin pact). "Within the short space of
two years," Rahv noted ruefully, "the 'revolutionaries' of 1935 had
substituted the stars and stripes of New Deal Marxism for 'the red flag
of the new materialism.' " What the new line meant, in his opinion,
was: "Either you become a bourgeois democrat or else the capitalists
will really get sore and bring in fascism."

But it was the realignment of the Party's interest in American
literature—away from proletarian or revolutionary writing, toward
the great traditions embodied in the work of Theodore Dreiser, Jack
London, Sinclair Lewis, Upton Sinclair—that drew fire from the dissident faction. Behind the fanfare for social realism, the dissidents believed, lay a failure to sustain either a revolutionary or a modernist
consciousness of the complexity of American life. The third volume of
Theodore Dreiser's *An American Tragedy* had been announced in
publisher's catalogues for ten years without appearing. Sinclair Lewis,
as Robert Cantwell suggested, had drawn a revolutionary picture of
American middle-class life without coming to revolutionary conclusions about it. No one except Dos Passos had come close to Lewis's
easy familiarity with the small businessmen, country doctors, county
officeholders, village atheists, schoolteachers, librarians, crazy professors, and maddened salesmen—the archetypes of provincial American
society. Sinclair Lewis understood the mechanisms of capitalist control, and satirized them, but he did not challenge the ends to which
they were applied, or envision an alternative except escape into reverie.

As for that other giant, Upton Sinclair, who had seen as much of
the country as Sinclair Lewis, the failure was of a different order.
Upton Sinclair leapt to revolutionary conclusions that Lewis avoided,
but in the opinion of many he merely filled in the picture with social
details that documented the *case* for socialism. The influential critic
Van Wyck Brooks had withdrawn from the ongoing cultural life of the
society that had once inspired him to rebellion in *America's Coming-
of-Age*; now he wrote period histories of Washington Irving, Emerson,
Melville, Twain, and Whitman, which the rebel group disdained.

Even the great American modernists had retreated before the
upheavals in American life. After 1929, Hemingway, Wilder, and Fitzgerald were still cultivating their "little corners," in Edmund Wilson's
opinion. They lacked a sense of the country as a whole, and like so
many in their generation were burdened with an oppressed conviction
of its emptiness, or a dread of its rawness. H. L. Mencken had made
it fashionable to speak of politics as farce; and only Dos Passos, it
seemed to Wilson, writing after the crash, "continued to take the social

organism seriously." By the late 1930s, Dos Passos was in retreat. In *Adventures of a Young Man* (reviewed by Mary McCarthy in 1939), he regarded the political view of reality itself as suspect.

Nor was there much left in 1937 of the early promise of proletarian writing, as embodied in the work of Jack Conroy, Robert Cantwell, and Vincent Sheean. Michael Gold's original vision of "the greater art" that would arise when "there is singing and music in every American street, when in every American factory there is a drama-group of workers, when mechanics paint in their leisure, and farmers write sonnets," struck a sour note as millions of unemployed workers scrambled to take up positions in the vast public works programs that swept the country during Roosevelt's second term. The Communist party, whose historic literary achievement was undoubtedly the simple fact of its having organized American writers *as writers* (through the League as well as the John Reed Clubs), while also inspiring them with a vision of social transformation, had failed to maintain an effective position on literature, as Rahv and Phillips saw it.

By 1937, when Mary McCarthy went to the second Writers Congress, most writers shrank before the increasing complexity of American society. Like the transcontinental plane that vaults overhead at the close of Dos Passos's *The Big Money,* while the lonely hitchhiker stands in broken shoes by the side of the road below, the new behemoth, which was America under the New Deal, appeared to serious literary folk as a socioeconomic mutation whose direction was impossible to fathom. "The upper class has taken to the air, the lower class to the road," Malcolm Cowley suggested; for Dos Passos, they had become "two nations," Cowley believed. After World War II, many American writers would slip easily into the airborne nation, but in the late 1930s, most dangled, like Dos Passos, somewhere in between.

The sense of new forces and classes rising up from the depths to shatter the surface of American life, which caught the imaginations of writers after 1929, now expressed itself in almost religious tones by Archibald MacLeish and Waldo Frank. The once-spirited "will to struggle" was frozen in Marxist time, or had become sentimental, like the message of hope with which Odets ended every play. To the dissident minority, Saroyan's "gentle people," Gold's "singing" proletariat, MacLeish's "hymn to Man," all combined in a populist dirge.

In a strange kind of way, the idea of social commitment in the late 1930s, harnessed to the idea of culture, led not to a revolutionary awareness of the levers of change in American society but to acquiescence. It was a connection Mary McCarthy drew in 1953 when, reflecting on her own experience in the 1930s, she discerned a link between "Stalinism," orthodox thinking, and the mass mind—though the connection probably owed itself more to a preoccupation with 'mass culture' that McCarthy shared with Dwight Macdonald in the early 1950s than to a perception in 1937. In any event, looking back, she saw her own break with Stalinism as a break with "conventional" society. Almost overnight, she stopped playing bridge, doing crossword puzzles, reading popular novels and detective stories—whose pleasures had recently inspired her first front-of-the-book essay in *The Nation,* "Murder and Karl Marx." (Deploring the right-wing tendency in mystery-writing, she had called on "writers of the left-wing once again to borrow the methods of the bourgeoisie and . . . make murder the handmaiden not of [J. P.] Morgan but of Marx"—an interesting idea that has occurred to other novelists since.) Now she "saw less of conventional Stalinists . . . and less of conventional people generally"; her definition of a conventional person being "anyone who could hear of the Moscow trials and maintain an unruffled serenity."

When McCarthy and Macdonald attended the Second American Writers Congress, the Communists were already on the defensive; not because they lacked broad liberal support—they had it—but because the brightest of the literary ideologues had defected to the rebel camp. No one had put forth the Marxist nugget that word and deed, theory and practice, must combine in the proletarian literature of the future more persuasively than Philip Rahv in "The Literary Class War" in 1932. Now Rahv had developed an insurgent point of view; in the wake of the Communist party's 1936 decision to dissolve the John Reed Clubs and pursue a popular front with all antifascist writers, especially famous ones like Hemingway and MacLeish, he and William Phillips had elected to take *Partisan Review* out of the Communist camp altogether. The defection of James Farrell, the decade's most prolific and successful novelist to embrace the revolutionary cause, was even more telling. Alongside such restless minds as these, in which the idea of the European avant-garde came to roost beside the idea of revolution, "Granny" Hicks's vision of *The Great Tradition in American Writing* (the title of his best-known work) no longer stood a chance.

But sectarianism was in the air, even among the anti-Stalinists. New York City, and especially the Village, where the rebels lived, was "a very Russian city," as the critic Lionel Abel used to say: "a metropolis that yearned to belong to another country"—not the Soviet Union as a *place* but the state of mind, real or imagined, of the old "Bolshevik Soviets." The spirit of faction was the lightning rod. One never knew when or where a bolt might strike, or who would catch it on the run from one 'correct' position to another—as Dwight Macdonald discovered when he joined the putsch to liberate *Partisan Review*.

II

Like Mary McCarthy, Dwight Macdonald's evolution from literary aesthete (at Exeter and Yale), to liberal, to Communist sympathizer, to ardent anti-Stalinist was packed into a few years. After graduating from Yale in 1928, he joined the Executive Training Squad at Macy's with the idea of financing a career in literary criticism. After working for six months, he was promoted to the necktie counter at thirty dollars a week, and resigned. Through a college friend, he got a staff job at *Fortune*, whose first issue celebrating the "saga" of American business appeared right after the stock market collapse in October 1929. *Fortune* confirmed an undergraduate suspicion that the men who ran the capitalist system were "narrow, uncultivated and commonplace"; their social and economic theories "childish"; and their Republican party unable to cope with the Depression. Together with other staff writers like Agee, Cantwell, and MacLeish, Macdonald wanted to write about Roosevelt's farm program, the CIO, unemployment, Social Security—anything but business. Luce, who was divided between his probusiness convictions and a journalist's instinct for news, compromised, as did his writers, and for a few years *Fortune* was an interesting montage of liberal muckraking and corporation pieces.

It wasn't a bad place for a political education, and there were tricks to learn, like "the *Fortune* system of getting material," which Wolcott Gibbs exposed in a 1936 parody in *The New Yorker*: "Writers in first draft put down wild gossip, any figures that occur to them. This is sent to victim, who indignantly corrects the errors, inadvertently supplies facts he might otherwise have withheld." Macdonald made good use of the method in a four-part study of the U.S. Steel Corporation, which taught him that the biggest steel company in the world benefited neither its workers (wages were low and trade unionism was forcibly discouraged), its customers (prices were kept high through monopoly), nor its stockholders, who got slim dividends because U. S. Steel was antiquated and inefficient. The final installment in the spring of 1936 began with a cheerful quotation from Lenin's *Imperialism* to the effect that monopoly was the last stage of capitalism. When the article was edited back to earth, Macdonald resigned in protest, aided in this decision by Nancy Macdonald's trust fund.

After Dwight Macdonald left *Fortune,* he tried to turn these articles into a book on the history of the steel industry—a hopeless effort that McCarthy later used in her characterization of Jim Barnett in "Portrait of the Intellectual as a Yale Man." In 1936, she had taken Dwight to lunch with Margaret Marshall to explore the possibility of getting the story into *The Nation*. But economic history had begun to bore him in the wake of a late-blooming passion for politics. Like McCarthy, Macdonald had only begun to read Marx, Lenin, and Trotsky in 1936. But his attraction to the Communist party was deeper and more pragmatic than hers. "I leaned toward the Communists because they alone on the American Left seemed to be 'doing something,' " he recalled in 1957. At *Fortune,* he had organized employees for the Newspaper Guild, and he frequently attended party-sponsored meetings to support the sharecroppers, raise money for strike victims, for *The New Masses,* and the Theatre Union—which is where he and Mary discovered their political affinities. These two, Dwight Macdonald and Mary McCarthy, "a tendril from Yale, a vine from Seattle," Irving Howe called them, would be friends for forty years, if sometimes wary ones, and find themselves more than once a party of two.

When Malcolm Cowley endorsed the essentials of Moscow's briefs against "the Anti-Soviet Center" in *The New Republic* (an endorsement echoed in *The Nation*), Macdonald fired off a letter that was printed in part in May 1937. Instantly, he was invited to join the Trotsky defense committee, which was headed by the eminent philosopher John Dewey, and supported by a variety of public figures and intellectuals, among them Ben Stolberg, with whom Mary had worked as a researcher, and John Chamberlain, whom she had upbraided in "Our Critics Right or Wrong," both of whom joined Trotsky in Coayacán, Mexico. That same spring, Macdonald made his debut as a left-wing journalist with a "now-it-can-be-told" series on the Luce magazines in *The Nation*. Extrapolating from the rightward trend of *Time*, he predicted that Henry Luce's "protofascism" would drop the *proto* when the class war heated up—a prediction that missed the mark. The class war cooled down as the CIO solidified itself in the basic industries—including U.S. Steel, which had also begun to modernize because of the possibility of the coming war. In 1938, with his "Quarantine the Aggressor" speech, Roosevelt launched the interventionist foreign policy that brought back prosperity and reassured the Right. Luce's magazines were reoriented in a more liberal direction. "Extrapolation," Macdonald observed of his prediction twenty years later, "is a dangerous toy for a Marxist, like giving a Sten gun to a baby."

With his appearance in *The Nation,* Macdonald entered the mainstream of radicalism's babbling brook. And presently, together with two Yale friends with whom he had published a 'little' magazine in 1932, *The Miscellany,* Fred Dupee and George L. K. Morris, he found himself in powwows with Philip Rahv and William Phillips. Jim Farrell may have introduced them first, McCarthy speculated, but by then the group was so intertwined by overlapping political and social interests that it is hard to say who introduced whom. Macdonald, however, was not to join the magazine until he underwent a rude initiation at the hands of Rahv and Phillips, the watchdogs of ideological purity. There was his "fellow-traveling Communism" to consider, William Phillips argued at a fractious Sunday meeting in his apartment on East Ninth Street, known in the inner circle, for the abuse it heaped on Macdonald, as "Bloody Sunday." His indefatigable hunger for causes, for organizing committees and writing protests and press releases and getting 'names' to sign them (all of which Macdonald continued, long after the Communist sponsors were replaced by anti-Stalinist ones), came in for attack, along with some Russian bonds that Dwight and Nancy bought after their marriage, and kept. But for Phillips and Rahv—who were always more responsive to Marxism as a method of analysis than a tool for political organization—it was Macdonald's passion for the internecine politics of *parties* that alarmed them most.

The difference was real. Among the so-called 'Trotskyite' editors of the new *Partisan Review*, only Dwight Macdonald actually joined the Socialist Workers party (in 1939). In 1940, he joined Max Shachtman's defecting splinter, the Workers' party, resigning in 1941. Macdonald's taste for faction impressed Trotsky himself, who dispatched a waspish message from Mexico after reading "comrade Macdonald's" attack on his own defense of the Soviet Union's 1939 invasion of Finland. "Back to the Party!" Trotsky's letter thundered:

The opposition leaders seem to have passed over into guerilla warfare. . . . One of the most curious examples is the more valiant than sensible attack of comrade Macdonald on my *Liberty* article. He didn't find . . . in this article an analysis of the contradictory character of the Soviet state and the "progressive" role of the Red Army. With the same logic which he shows . . . in his analysis of the Kronstadt uprising [Macdonald had also criticized Trotsky's suppression of the famous mutiny], he discovers that I am "in reality" a minorityite, a Shachtmanite, or a Macdonaldist. . . . *Partisan Review* is very interested in psychoanalysis and I permit myself to say that the editor of this review, if he analyzes himself a bit, would recognize that he has uncovered his own subconscious.

If Phillips and Rahv were influenced by Trotsky as a theoretician, it was not for theses such as these, but for a different reason. From Coayacán, Mexico, Trotsky also wrote: "Art can become a strong ally of revolution only in so far as it remains faithful to itself." Literature, he suggested in more than one letter to *Partisan Review* after 1937, should not be bent to ideological ends, not even " 'Trotskyist' " ends. It was just this modernist purism on questions of art that made Trotsky a patron for the new program that Rahv and Phillips planned for *Partisan Review*. *"Marxism in politics, and Modernism in art"* was the formula in a nutshell. Between the "two M's," of course, there were deep-rooted tensions, whose resolution would ultimately enshrine Modernism in the place of Marxism.

The attack on Dwight Macdonald was an attack on politics, not only the party politics of recent years but the idea that Marxist intellectuals had a responsibility to articulate the needs of groups and classes other than their own. In the new *Partisan Review,* the intellectual would be addressed neither as a participant of mass movements nor a critic of world politics, but as a member of a vanguard class in its own right, with its own distinctive needs and obligations.

For the moment, Macdonald survived. His critical talent was unproven, but his energy and enthusiasm for the magazine were boundless. He and George L. K. Morris, an abstract painter from an old New York family, who promised to finance the independent monthly (at about three thousand dollars a year), were invited to join the staff, which also included Fred Dupee, who had just left *The New Masses*, where he was literary editor, and Mary McCarthy, who had recently left a husband and a fiancé. Rahv's and Phillips's rift with Dwight would break out again six years later in a showdown over whether intellectuals should support the war effort. Macdonald said no. And the real difference between an editor who wanted to raise embarrassing political questions and others who found that managing the House of Culture was politics enough would result in Macdonald's resignation and the birth of a new magazine: Dwight Macdonald's *politics.*

* * *

From the beginning, *Partisan Review* was surrounded by the kind of controversy that quickened Mary McCarthy's pulse. It was like launching *Con Spirito* in enemy waters, only at twenty-five she signed on with a mutinous crew of men who had left the mother ship for unknown territories. A girl Friday among the pirates, McCarthy had finally taken her stand with that curious product of the urban high school, first glimpsed at Garfield High in Seattle: the self-made intellectual whose contentiousness in the field of ideas was unsurpassed. The association bristled with possibilities. With Rahv and his circle—which included the art critic Clement Greenberg, along with Delmore Schwartz, Lionel Abel, and the art historian Meyer Schapiro—Mary had joined a self-proclaimed elite whose measure was to be taken not by its nearness to money or to established institutions, including Communist institutions, but by its performance as a harbinger of cultural change.

The fact that some of the men in the group owed their ambition to a ghetto experience that was as foreign to Mary McCarthy as her Catholic girlhood and boarding-school education was to them merely invigorated the common enterprise, which was to *discard* the past, to *transcend* one's origins in order to open the future to a wider influence. For Mary, the challenge soon took on an intimate aspect when she and Philip Rahv began to see each other privately in the spring of 1937.

Appearances, as is usual in such affairs, were deceiving. When she first met the tall, dark, thickly built man, who looked more like a prizefighter than an intellectual, at Jim Farrell's, Rahv struck McCarthy as a "pontificating young Marxist," like one of those Puritan pamphleteers named "Zeal, from the Land Busy" whom she and Helen Sandison laughed about when Mary went up to Vassar to report on her adventures in New York. One might think an ideologue like Philip Rahv, who was born in the Ukraine and remembered hiding behind the counter of his parents' shop during the 1917 Revolution, while Red and White troops took and retook the village, wouldn't tie in with a 'literary girl' from Vassar, except for adventitious reasons. When he did, one might have predicted a lopsided relationship in which Rahv, like Johnsrud before him, would play the heavy to Mary's ingenue. Philip was also an older man—only twenty-nine, but he seemed older than his years, he easily dominated the group, and took to himself the preponderant power in shaping the new *Partisan Review*, as he had the old. Rahv, a self-chosen nom de guerre, supplanting Greenberg, meant *rabbi* in Hebrew. There was no doubt where he stood in his legend.

But Mary had stumbled on a review he had written of *Tender Is the Night* for *The New Masses*, and the *tenderness* of the piece, despite its critical stance, had revealed a secret annex to his personality. Fitzgerald was very much 'out' then, but the poetry of the novel had moved Rahv and infiltrated his own prose. The same gentle depth of feeling later overtook his writing about Tolstoy, a figure whose landed experience and communal values appeared even more remote from the urban concerns of a twentieth-century Marxist intellectual, but central nonetheless to Rahv's larger moral scheme. This contrast between the critic's literary sensibility, expressed in prose, and the immigrant's pungent, hard-driving accented speech, with its *dis*'s and *dat*'s, was a revelation to Mary McCarthy. "My dear, I've got the most Levantine lover!" she told Nathalie Swan in 1937. In a reminiscence after his death in 1973, she was more philosophical: "Two persons were married to each other in Rahv," she wrote, "one political, masculine and aggressive; one feminine, artistic and dreamy. And a third, was an unreconstructed child with a child's capacity for wonder."

Only the first person seems to have been visible to his male companions, who, like Delmore Schwartz's friend, the philosopher William Barrett, always found Rahv "menacing." Barrett thought "his authority and power carried a suggestion of masculinity; women were attracted to him." And William Phillips agreed: " 'Yes, he fascinated women, like Jack the Ripper.' " "Philip does have scruples," Delmore Schwartz conceded, "but he never lets them stand in his way." This Rahv was a far cry from the complicated man McCarthy knew, but then many members of her generation viewed heterosexual society in starkly Darwinian terms.

It was something of a shock for the group in the summer of 1937 when they saw Rahv and McCarthy sitting side by side on a sofa at meetings. "They were lovers, and they were living together. That was a daring thing at the time, or at least to the youthful minds of Delmore and myself," Barrett relates in his memoir, *The Truants*. The contrast between Mary's and Philip's public selves and the private understanding they had reached together, and now made public to the world, was startling but probably not surprising in the "sectarian thirties," as McCarthy recalled them, when "the only pleasures that were considered 'serious' were sex and arguing." What set this affair apart from other liaisons was its filial quality—a *fondness* Philip and Mary showed for each other that impressed Nancy Macdonald, the new business manager of *Partisan Review*, as the real thing. (Delmore Schwartz was also impressed: "More and more," he wrote in "The Complete Adventuress," one of several unfinished sketches of Mary McCarthy, "Helena felt an extraordinary admiration as well as affection for Stanislaus. He was superior to her and inferior to her in precisely the way that suited her profoundest need.")

The friendship had begun in the spring, after Mary had obtained a full-time job as a reader for Covici-Friede, a left-wing publisher on East Thirty-second Street. When a German text arrived, she had called on Rahv, who read Russian, German, and Hebrew, for an evaluation. It was free-lance work for a friend whose sinecure with the Federal Writers' Project brought him $21.67 a week, a credit for her, and good for the company; and it also drew her closer to the emerging leader of the anti-Stalinist literary movement. "He had a shy, soft voice (when he was not shouting), big, dark lustrous eyes which he rolled with great expression, and the look of a bambino in an Italian sacred painting. Soon he was taking me out to dinner in the Village, holding my elbow as we walked . . ." McCarthy remembered fondly toward the end of her life. In the summer of 1937, she had persuaded some wealthy friends from the cocktail-party circuit to lend her their apartment on Beekman Place while they traveled in Europe, and she and Philip moved in together.

It was not an auspicious beginning. Rahv, who had spent his first year in New York during the depths of the Depression standing on breadlines and sleeping on benches, declared himself "compromised" by so much luxury. (Greta Garbo lived in an apartment at Two Beekman Place, the Johnsruds' old address; a later tenant would be Antoine de Saint-Exupéry.) Referring to Trotsky's warning about the dangers of "the class war in one country," he proclaimed himself engaged in "a class war in one apartment." In September they rented their own place on East End Avenue, a ground-floor apartment across from Gracie Mansion, where Barrett and Delmore Schwartz saw them at meetings. It was "quite pretty and only moderately expensive," McCarthy recalls in "Divorcée on Gay Street," reviewing the apartment's decor with timeless precision; but it was too far uptown, too close to the German enclave in Yorkville for Philip's taste, she recalls, and he clung to his "Eighth Street ways."

McCarthy herself had undergone a metamorphosis. The figure she cut was almost the reverse of the imperious young woman in cartwheel hats, silk stockings, and Bonwit Teller dresses of a few years before. "How describe her? She was not quite beautiful, and too good-looking to be called pretty; and 'handsome woman' sounds too stiff . . . for her vivid good looks," William Barrett remembers:

there was something wayward and even *gamine* about her. She did not seem to worry about her clothes or appearance generally, and

I noticed—an odd detail to remember now!—that her legs were unshaved. Probably it was no affectation, she had simply been too busy to attend to her toilette; but it reinforced the touch of the gamine about her.

One night when the whole group was there, her hand had rested affectionately on Rahv's knee while he chaired a meeting. Later Delmore turned to Barrett and grumbled: " 'Did you see Mary McCarthy giving Rahv a feel?' " Barrett found the remark strange, a flare-up of Delmore's prudishness; but it was also an early flash of the disapproval that McCarthy's person, as well as her prose, would provoke in the years to come.

When Barrett goes on to say that "Nobody seeing her would have surmised that this striking and vivid girl would prove to be one of the most brilliant women and formidable intellectuals of her time," he suggests another danger McCarthy courted. It wasn't that her good looks distracted attention from her intelligence—hardly. "To make it with these men a woman had to be good-looking," recalls Eve Stwertka, a former student of McCarthy's at Bard, and today a trustee of her literary estate, "otherwise she didn't exist—she was just like an old rug. Mary was pretty. . . ." As was Eleanor Clark, who was briefly married to Trotsky's secretary, and Diana Trilling, who with her dark eyes and flaring nostrils reminded Mary McCarthy of Katharine Cornell. The Trotskyists were said to have " 'all the beautiful girls.' " But this prettiness, and the fact that, as Stwertka notes, "Mary had come in, as all women came in, through a man," also meant she risked being seen in some persistent relation to men.

Intellectuals, of course, were a species of men, not women. An intellectual young woman had to be careful to remain alert to her status as an interloper, particularly if she didn't care to be mistaken for one of the boys, or appear masculine, which Mary emphatically was not. Even more dangerous was to seem to have it all, when one was in reality only at the beginning of a polymorphous career as a femme fatale, a critic of theatre and literature, as well as of society, a satirist and novelist, an art historian, a war correspondent, and a memoirist of the first rank.

In the fall of 1937, when McCarthy began to write her Theatre Chronicle for the maiden issue of the new *Partisan Review*—a field assigned her, she maintained, because she had been married to an actor—she took pains not to "sound bourgeois" and fan the fears of her fellow editors who worried that she might do something, in real life or in print, that would "disgrace *Partisan Review*." "It was often debated whether we should have a theatre column at all," she recalled in the Introduction to *Mary McCarthy's Theatre Chronicles, 1937–1962*. "Some of the editors felt that the theatre was not worth bothering with, because it was neither high art, like Art, nor a mass art, like the movies. But this was also an argument for letting me do it. If I made mistakes, who cared?"

It wasn't as serendipitous as all that. With "Our Actors and the Critics," McCarthy had already turned the peculiar voice of authority she projected in literary reviews to the theatre. Advising the American drama critic, again by name, to "go back to school to learn something of the technique and standards of the profession which gives him his livelihood," she noted in 1936 how with the advent of sound the movies had drained the theatre of "personalities," thus improving the standard of stage acting. Critics, nonetheless, continued to watch the play and ignore the performances. McCarthy's *PR* column would try to do both: review the play as a good reporter covers a live event, with a knowledgeable eye fixed on the stagecraft as well as the text.

In practice, however, it was the period's playwrights—literary moralists, in McCarthy's opinion—who came in for the bulk of her attention. Thus Ben Hecht, with *To Quito and Back*, was "a veteran exhibitionist, and this is perhaps his fullest confession"; while Maxwell Anderson's *The Star-Wagon* (reviewed, alongside Hecht, in the first issue) showed that "once again he has been inspired by a lofty theme and once again the mediocrity of his talent has reduced it to inconsequentiality." Looking back in 1963, McCarthy deplored the "pedantic, pontificating" voice of this earnest young critic, but she found little to modify in her original judgments of the inflated reputations of American realist playwrights—whom she later surveyed in a series of lectures delivered in Poland, Yugoslavia, and the British Isles during a State Department–sponsored tour in 1960. As it turned out, McCarthy's theatre pieces became one of the most popular and durable features of *Partisan Review*, in large part because of their provocative pronouncements.

No doubt she spoke ironically in the Introduction to *Theatre Chronicles* when she compared her early position at *Partisan Review* to George Morris, the "backer," who was so "confused" politically that he once sallied into a "Stalinist bookshop" wearing spats and swinging a cane, to ask for Trotsky's *The Revolution Betrayed*. But if the others accepted her "unwillingly, as an editor because I had a minute 'name' and was the girl friend of one of the 'boys,' who had issued a ukase on my behalf," there was some reason for McCarthy's lack of confidence, if not for theirs. In the ideologically charged milieu of *PR*'s inner office, where the boys hammered out the line of the new American literary Left, Mary McCarthy *was* an outsider. Like the backer, a man of means, she was a woman of parts, whose critical sensibility—trained in Elizabethan scholarship, schooled in close readings of a text, and attuned to the exacting standards of literary expression—was dazzling but faintly suspect. There was no question that she added something to the magazine, but one can hear the boys disputing: *At what price?* Just as one hears Alfred Kazin today—still squirming over old feuds—dispute the significance of her contribution. "Mary McCarthy was the 'bright light' of the *Partisan Review*," he observes. "Why? Because she frightened all those timorous Jews. She didn't scare me."

Reviewing the names lined up for the first two issues, it isn't hard to imagine why McCarthy herself felt like an outsider. Alongside John Dos Passos, André Gide, Ignazio Silone, George Orwell, Wallace Stevens, Edmund Wilson, T. S. Eliot, Pablo Picasso, Lionel Trilling, and Delmore Schwartz—whose "In Dreams Begin Responsibilities" was about to make him "the bright new star in American letters"—who was this girl with the storybook Irish name, who seemed to materialize out of nowhere, always, just as the lightning struck?

10

Seduction and *Betrayal*

"I remember that somebody of the
PR *circle—Delmore or Harold Rosenberg—was widely*
quoted as saying that Mary left Philip for
Wilson because Wilson had a better prose style."

—MARY MCCARTHY, "EDMUND WILSON"

*I*t started late one Saturday morning in October 1937, when Mary McCarthy arrived at *Partisan Review*'s office near Union Square. She wore a slinky black dress and her Grandmother Preston's fox stole, remnants of the Vassar years. Edmund Wilson was there, "short, stout, middle-aged, breathy [he was forty-two, she was twenty-five]," wearing a two-piece gray suit and a white shirt. Introductions were made, and Wilson complimented Miss McCarthy on her reviews in *The Nation,* especially the series on American critics that she had coauthored with Margaret Marshall two and a half years before. But his eyes, faintly bulging in the photographs of the period ("popping reddish-brown eyes," McCarthy describes them), made a swift appraisal. She had been noticed and she knew it.

Wilson had come to discuss plans for the new anti-Stalinist magazine, and the editors—McCarthy, the only woman, included—had taken him to a nearby eatery where Mary's costume, "more suited to a wedding reception than to a business meeting in the offices of a radical magazine," she sensed at the time, must have appeared flamboyantly out of place. Wilson barely addressed her at lunch, but two weeks later he phoned Margaret Marshall to suggest a meeting with the two women over dinner. Marshall, who prided herself on her good looks, was sure Wilson was interested in her. McCarthy knew better.

The boys were anxious that she make a good impression, espe-

cially Philip Rahv; McCarthy, as his girlfriend, had become, in William
Phillips's words, "Rahv's alter-Iago." Wilson's opinion was always
important; only he could observe tersely that "there is no sense in
pursuing a literary career under the impression that one is operating a
bombing plane," as he had a few months earlier in *The New Republic*,
and put both Stalinist and Trotskyist critics in their place. Once again
Mary was made to worry that she might 'disgrace' *Partisan Review*,
being "literary in the wrong way, not really *modern*," she recalls, but
"still interested in graduate-student stuff like Shakespeare and the
Elizabethans." Her political inexperience, moreover, might make the
magazine look foolish to an older critic whose disenchantment with
the Soviet Union, which Wilson visited in 1935 and praised in *Travels
in Two Democracies* (1936), was in full swing, but whose interest in
political history was acute.

The afternoon of the dinner date, Fred Dupee took Mary to the
Hotel Albert bar on University Place for a briefing. Wilson had become
a teetotaler, he warned her, recalling their lunch together on Union
Square when the great man had ordered club soda. Dinner would be
a dry one; perhaps she might loosen up with a few drinks. Mary had
three daiquiries. But dinner was not a dry one. It was, McCarthy
remembered, her "Waterloo."

Wilson, who had been suffering from a hangover on the previous
occasion, ordered several rounds of Manhattans when they took their
table at an Italian restaurant on East Eighteenth Street. A terrible red
wine accompanied the meal. Mary had struggled to hold the high
ground. In American criticism, only "Mr. Wilson made any extended
effort to relate what is valuable in modern literature to the body of
literature of the past." She had written that. Here he was. In her senior
year at Vassar, Edmund Wilson had arrived to deliver a lecture on
Flaubert. After a few sentences, he had floundered, mouth ajar, gasping for air (as he sometimes did in public lectures), and Miss Kitchel
had run for a glass of water. Now his red face bobbed up and down
over their glasses as he filled them again and again. What was valuable
in modern literature was what could keep you talking brightly through
a swarm of inebriate thoughts. Modern literature was failing her.
Margaret, Mary noticed, had fallen into a glassy-eyed silence. And
then, sometime after they left the restaurant, and before they reached
the Chelsea Hotel, Mary passed out.

The next morning, she woke in a strange bed. "There was that
awful feeling. You open your eyes slowly," McCarthy related fifty
years later: "Where am I? With a sinking heart you turn to see who is

sleeping beside you. In the next bed—*Margaret!*" Wilson had checked them into a room at the Chelsea. Margaret Marshall, he assured her later, was his "cover" on the first date, as she would be on the second, when again the two women were invited to dinner, and then up to Stamford, Connecticut, for a providential nightcap at Trees, the Stamford estate of Margaret de Silver (a locomotive heiress, married to the anarchist Carlo Tresca), where Wilson rented the guest house.

The scene at the Chelsea was the apocryphal awakening, a favorite of Mary McCarthy's, in fiction as in life. In "The Man in the Brooks Brothers Shirt," Meg Sargent wakes up with the same sinking feeling. "She knew that she had been drinking the night before, but reflected with satisfaction that Nothing Had Happened. It would have been terrible if . . . She moved slightly and touched the man's body. . . . This can't be, she thought angrily, it can't be." But it was, and it had happened to McCarthy on the train to Reno in the summer of 1936, with the man from Pittsburgh who sold bathroom fixtures. In *A Charmed Life* (1955), Martha Sinnott, another McCarthy alter ego (turned Desdemona in the novel), flashes back to *her* Waterloo with the Wilsonesque Miles Murphy, an ex-husband who is pursuing her. "He started bulldozing her into marriage before she really knew him," Martha recalls. "It was what she needed, he reassured her, appraising her with his jellied green eyes when she woke up, for the second time, in bed with him, after a lot of drinks."

During the first visit to Stamford, after Margaret fell asleep in the guest room, McCarthy had followed Wilson into his study to continue a conversation, whereupon he "firmly took me into his arms, misunderstanding my intention," she writes in the last of her 'intellectual' memoirs, and she "gave up the battle." On the study couch, they had "drunkenly made love," and to the end of her life McCarthy was "convinced that he had me wrong: I only wanted to talk to him." Chance, not choice, governs these insurrections of the flesh, as it does in politics. Love, however, is nearly always 'drunkenly made.' One makes decisions when one chooses to go public: to write and publish. But the ogre depicted in *A Charmed Life*—the husband who Martha Sinnott had married "as a punishment for the sin of having slept with him when she did not love him, when she loved, she still felt, someone else"—is a harsh caricature of the man who began to court Mary McCarthy in the fall of 1937, when she started waking up next to Wilson. Nor was McCarthy so helpless a victim of Edmund Wilson's powerful will as memoir, fiction, and interviews suggest.

* * *

After the first evening with Wilson, Mary had stayed home from her job at Covici-Friede, nursing a hangover. Philip Rahv was reassured that "nothing had happened," as he was after the night McCarthy spent at Trees. On that occasion, incredibly, Rahv had been invited to come out to Stamford the next morning to join Margaret, Mary, and Edmund for lunch, which he did, never suspecting the affair that was already under way. "How shameful a successful deception is," McCarthy reflected years later, wondering, but not too much, over the ease with which she had once again slipped into the clandestine life.

When she had left a book behind after the first visit to Trees, she had written Edmund to make sure he didn't send it to *Partisan Review*, where "everybody opens everybody else's mail and it will provoke a lot of comment that I don't want. I feel too confused to say any more." He must have known not to send it to the apartment she shared with Rahv on East End Avenue. The next day she felt less inhibited, perhaps because Wilson had sent her an affectionate note inviting her back to Stamford, or because the lovemaking had not been as bad as all that. "I am still all shaken up," she wrote. "It's pleasant but painful. I should like to come up some evening. I will need a little while to plan it," she added, for she was dining with prospective Covici-Friede authors every night that week but Friday. "Maybe I will telephone you soon if you want me to. Love to you, too."

A plaintive, girlish note crept into McCarthy's letters to Wilson, which convey a barely suppressed sexual excitement. After their trysts, she was often "*distraite*. My stomach bounces around and does odd, terrifying things, and my movements are jerky, my will relaxed, and I am full of an odd dreamy abstraction. . . . You have dislocated me in a way. I should like to hear from you so as to get some new bearings." She loved to talk shop, to write Edmund Wilson what she called "the letters of a *femme savante*":

Last night I had a wonderful idea for an article for the *PR*. I am going to do a restoration job on Lord Byron, emphasis on political and satirical qualities. . . . This morning I took Byron's letters to work with me . . . making lots of incisive notes. . . . I've felt a sweet affinity with the wicked Lord ever since I was eleven years old and had read "The Prisoner of Chillon," and a nun in the convent, scolding me, said: "You're just like Lord Byron, brilliant but immoral." Elated, I went home and quoted her to my grandfather, who with real Presbyterian indignation, called up the Mother Superior and demanded that the nun retract.

This was one of McCarthy's favorite stories from the Forest Ridge Convent, which would be polished off some years later—"immoral" becoming "unsound"—in *Memories of a Catholic Girlhood*. But the restoration of Byron died a sudden death the next day at Schrafft's over a chopped egg sandwich, when Mary delved deeper into the letters. Byron was disappointing her; he was "a frivolous character," she wrote Edmund, the opposite of what she wanted to prove. An excerpt of "blood-curdling revolutionary invective" from Byron's maiden speech in the House of Lords had been thrown into a different light when she read his letter to a friend: " 'I spoke very violent sentences with a sort of modest impudence, abused everything and everybody, and put the Lord Chancellor very much out of humor; and if I may believe what I hear, have not lost any character by the experiment.' " This was "just *épatant les bourgeois* (or *la noblesse*)," Mary decided. "It's not, to say the least, political idealism. But perhaps his personal motives need not distress me," she reflected, searching for a saving grace. Byron's legend and her own barely conscious one were already entwined. "Perhaps a poseur can be a more incisive social critic than such a desperately 'honest' man as Wordsworth. Simply because the heart is not really involved, only the mind."

But Wilson dampened her curiosity when he noted dryly that Byron "has been written about a lot lately, and I don't think his reputation is low." Byron, he assured her, was always on the side of the rebel, but he "had no politics properly speaking." And he promised to give Mary "a long lecture on the subject if you will submit, and if I ever see you long enough to do so."

Long lectures on the subject of a misunderstood writer were Edmund Wilson's specialty. Particularly with a promising young woman did he extend himself with alacrity. There had been a line of them, starting with that other literary girl from Vassar, Edna St. Vincent Millay, who had refused Wilson's proposal of marriage in 1920 but submitted to his energetic efforts on behalf of her career. In the 1920s and '30s, the women, including two wives, Mary Blair and Margaret Canby, numbered the poets Léonie Adams and Louise Bogan, and the novelist Dawn Powell, who had been plying Edmund Wilson with her books for years.

"Imagine my amazement at discovering how good your novels are, and [to think] that I had been taking you all these years for an incompetent!" Wilson once wrote Dawn Powell, displaying his characteristic instructional style. He was "enchanted" with Powell's two latest novels, he said, but wanted her to know he still thought "there is plenty wrong with them," and he promised to "tell [her] all about it" if she would give him a certain Thursday in New York, starting with breakfast. "Ernest P. Wigmore," he signed his letters to Miss Powell. Later the slightly seedy "Wigmore" was replaced by "Raoul," and Dawn became "Aurore."

In 1937, Wilson was close to Louise Bogan, whose playful mind had some affinities with his own. With Bogan, he was "Pollyano, the Glad Boy," or "Jails Jice" of Truro Center. It was Jails who asked her to return his volume of "Chritipher Ichorword's . . . shy autobuggerphy" in 1938, "pronto-prompto." He wanted to read about "sleek-un Steamin Slender and likely Lewis MacNice and . . . don't be forgetting old W. H. Odd-un, the most glorious of the grope. What hope," he signed off, "they live in despair without dope." With Louise Bogan, Wilson had once played a role he was about to play with Mary McCarthy. When she had first come to New York in 1923, a young Imagist poet from Roxbury, Massachusetts, he had singled her out as a prize. Taking her on as a "star pupil," he had insisted that she write criticism, and, over her strenuous objections, ordered her to sit down at her desk and begin. Bogan, who later became poetry critic for *The New Yorker*, remembered "sitting at that desk with tears pouring down my face trying to write a notice. Edmund Wilson would pace behind me and exhort me to go on. He taught me a great deal," she later concluded, "at a period when I needed a teacher."

Early in 1937, she had suffered a nervous collapse, and Wilson had written her more solemnly. Bogan was a contemporary, and they shared a belletrist regard for literature as an ennoblement of life—the very opposite point of view from the "priestly class of explicators," which was how she regarded critics such as Kenneth Burke, R. P. Blackmur, John Crowe Ransom, and Allen Tate. They had both grown up in one kind of world, Wilson observed, and now had to adjust "socially, sexually, morally" to another, which was itself in a state of flux. And Wilson wanted Bogan to know that, as he wrote, "people like you, with remarkable abilities, even though they're more highly organized nervously than other people's, are under a peculiar obligation not to let this sick society down. We have to take life— society and human relations—more or less as we find them," he added. "The only thing that we can really make is our work. And deliberate work of the mind, imagination and hand, done, as Nietzsche said, 'notwithstanding,' in the long run remakes the world."

By November 1937, when Wilson was courting Mary McCarthy,

Louise Bogan was back on her feet and a houseguest at Trees. Wilson professed his distaste for "Putting to Sea," Bogan's latest poem. And Bogan complained to their mutual friend in Chicago, Morton Zabel, that Wilson was getting "pretty pontifical." When she couldn't accept his "theories," he called her "ignorant"—an abrupt departure from his former sensitivity to her lack of formal academic training. Dos Passos was also visiting that weekend, and Bogan found him "such a Harvard fake. [But] Bunny loves him." "Then I read rather stutteringly extracts from Dante/" Wilson wrote Zabel, of the same weekend: "While the flaming old Fury drank like a Bacchante."

In 1938, Wilson and Bogan assembled a brilliant collection of parodies, which included Wilson's "The Omelet of A. MacLeish" (Bogan called him "MacSlush"), and her own "Evening in the Sanitarium," a poem that set out to parody W. H. Auden, and ended up an Audenesque evocation of modern spiritual desolation. Their relationship had remained platonic except for one night in the middle 1930s when they had gone to bed together; Wilson told McCarthy later that when Louise asked for a glass of water, he had spilled it on the pillow, thus extinguishing their ardor.

By the winter of 1937, Wilson had discovered a new prize in Mary McCarthy. Seventeen years his junior, she nevertheless had literary sensibilities that appeared compatible with his own. Moreover, she seemed to have shaken him out of a self-imposed exile in Stamford. "I hardly ever go to New York and am as rural as any agrarian," he had written Allen Tate from Trees in April 1937. He had spent his first winter there reading, writing—*The Triple Thinkers* was completed, and *To the Finland Station* halfway done—and in the spring he had begun to fish in the river running past the house. "The whole left literary movement got to be a pain in the neck," he wrote Tate:

> and now it has been completely demoralized . . . by the Stalin-Trotsky controversy. I feel, however, that this is clearing the air. People will have to think for themselves, and those who . . . have been hanging on to Stalin's mustaches—also the whiskers of Trotsky—will relapse into the obscurity where they belong—

For awhile Wilson had kept himself out of the fray—which was "straight Russian," in his opinion. The perpetual 'taking of positions' made no sense in the United States, he thought. Still, he couldn't resist suggesting to Malcolm Cowley that if young radicals leaned toward Trotsky, it was because only Trotsky seemed to embody the original ideals of the Russian Revolution. Soon he had joined the Trotsky defense committee—though Mary never saw him at a meeting.

What led Wilson to personally speak out against the purge trials, which shocked him all the more perhaps because he had failed to see them coming, was the religiosity with which fellow-traveling liberals defended the Soviet state. "You sound as if you had read nothing but the official report," he wrote Malcolm Cowley, who was Wilson's successor as literary editor at *The New Republic* and the author of most of the magazine's trial reports. Didn't Cowley recognize "that everything that emanates from the government is pure propaganda, intended to lead simple people and cooked up solely to meet immediate ends . . . ?" The higher-ups, Wilson explained, read the *GPU Bulletin* and *Red Army Star*, the "real" papers, "and simply agree among themselves on what is expedient to tell the boobs." He had seen it himself during his tour of the Soviet Union in 1935. Cowley, Wilson suggested, "ought to read the Trotskyist and Socialist stuff, too."

Wilson, in fact, had moved closer to *Partisan Review*. When he met the editors in September, he had agreed to publish a chapter from *To the Finland Station*, "The Myth of the Marxist Dialectic," in an upcoming issue, and for the maiden issue, the first chapter of *The Triple Thinkers*. This essay, a study of Flaubert's political thought and his relationship to the French Commune, contains the prescient observation that "nothing exasperated [Flaubert] more . . . than the idea that the soul is to be saved by the profession of correct political opinions."

There was another side to Edmund Wilson, a darker side that sometimes alarmed him when he was alone at Trees. One day when he was absorbed in his work he had looked at his hand on the page of a book, "and suddenly saw it as an animal's paw with the fingers lengthened to claws and become prehensile for climbing around, in strange, in incredible contrast to the detached and limitless life of the mind. That was what we were," he noted in his journal, "we still carried with us those animal paws." It was a sensation that often distracted him, and led him to take a "queer pleasure," as the critic Werner Berthoff has observed, in listing the resemblances of animals and insects to men. (Like Ezra Pound, Wilson's lifelong belief in the redemptive power of literature may have been "damagingly related," Berthoff speculates, "to some profound distrust of life and all its disconcerting profusion of motives and appearances. . . .")

Years of remarkable productivity and even domestic tranquillity awaited him—later, with another wife—but in 1937 he was tired and embittered by the political wrangling among writers, and by too many years of hard work, hard drinking, and ill-fated affairs. Both of his marriages had ended badly. His first wife, Mary Blair, was an actress whose chief love was the stage. After three years, they were divorced. Blair, who was consumptive, was now an invalid in a sanitarium, and Wilson's mother in Red Bank, New Jersey, had taken charge of their twelve-year-old daughter, Rosalind, who spent much of her time in boarding schools. Wilson's second wife, Margaret Canby, had maintained a separate residence in San Francisco, where she cared for a child from a previous marriage, and where she died in 1932 in a freak accident two years after their marriage. Since then, he had moved back and forth between furnished rooms and shabby frame houses, like the little house he rented in 1933 for fifty dollars a month on East Fifty-third Street in New York.

On Fifty-third Street, he had turned toward the past to memorialize his mother's ancestors, "the sovereign race of the first settlers of Lewis County [New York]," in the essay "The Old Stone House." He had concluded that he had "actually lost ground . . . having failed even worse than my relatives at getting out of the American big-business era the luxuries and the prestige that I unquestionably should . . . have enjoyed." After moving to Stamford, Wilson had little desire to go home again. (That desire would flare up in the 1950s, when he bought the "old stone house" in Talcotville.) What disturbed him was "to have left that early world behind, yet never to have really succeeded in what was till yesterday the new."

Mary McCarthy was hardly part of the 'big business era,' but she came from a new generation. A cocksure young critic at *Partisan Review*, she was a goyisha princess amidst a squabbling fraternity of bright young men who had been courting Edmund Wilson ever since their break with the Communist party. It was hard to resist this impulsive girl whose lively intelligence seemed to shine only for him, and Wilson was entranced.

Almost immediately, he had developed a program for her literary development, having found McCarthy's theatre reviews too damning, each one "a crushing brief" against a play rather than a disinterested appraisal. Phillips and Rahv failed to appreciate Mary McCarthy's real genius, Wilson thought, which was her gift for storytelling. Her tales of the night train to 125th Street from Stamford showed a promising talent:

> The train was awful, in that dramatically musty way that milk trains have. The seats were upholstered in a dirty olive-green plush that you never see on normal trains, and a half a carful of ex-

hausted people were lying with their clothes disarranged in un-
lovely postures on the seats. I bummed a cigarette from the only
person who was awake, a Jewish man from Springfield, who with
his wife and a collection of relatives was on his way to New York
to his sister's funeral. He had . . . a haberdashery store where he'd
been selling overalls for eighteen years. A man needs education in
this country, he said, and he referred to the females in his party as
"our women." We had quite a talk. He asked me if I worked in a
"shop." He didn't pronounce the "h" and I didn't know what he
meant, and he explained, "a factory." (Maybe you're right. Maybe
my appearance is not . . . as soigné as it should be.) He was curious
about where I'd been. I said to dinner in Stamford, and he rolled
his eyes and said "Youth!" . . . Was I going home to my family
or . . . ? To my family, I said. Ah, he said, it's lucky it's not a husband; a mother always forgives. Yes, I said sentimentally, she does.

McCarthy's naïveté surprised Wilson and delighted him, as did her
sudden outbursts of affection. "You are nice. I like you. I think about
you pleasantly," was how she ended the letter about the haberdashery
man. "I want very much to see you, but no more milk trains!" That
was the night that Edmund had been suffering from a bad cold, and
when they had gone ahead and made love anyway, Mary had missed
her regular train. "One never really wants more than one plans for,
and emotional greediness is always unrewarding," she wrote him afterwards in her Mother Superior's voice. "I am really worrying a little in
a guilty way about your grippe. Do tell me whether it's all right." And
she added: "I have a feeling that you've gotten awfully strong-minded
and sensible and renunciatory after I left. Have you? . . . I should be
very sad if you carried it into stern practice. Oh, very."

With Wilson, Mary sometimes revealed a childlike fear of abandonment, which bubbled up unexpectedly out of a well of loneliness.
"This not-going-to-see-you is very painful," she wrote after he was
suddenly called away on business. " 'You will hear from me,' you said
Saturday, which is a statement that has all sorts of vague and sinister
overtones," she added a few days later. "It's what the head of the
opium ring in detective stories says to the innocent and nervous hero,
and it's what the Man Behind the Desk says to you when he's not going
to give you a job. There's very little security or comfort in it."

She needn't have worried, although she did, especially when other
women visited Wilson in Stamford. She had questioned him about
the girl who inspired his novel, *I Thought of Daisy*, in the 1920s,

and Wilson had assured her that "Daisy was not autobiographical, but . . . synthetic, like most novels." The narrator was a fiction—"and rather a lousy one," he wrote, "partly derived from Proust." But when the woman who inspired Daisy visited him at Trees, he had to reassure Mary all over again. When later he mentioned a dinner he was planning for his neighbors, Franz Hollering, his wife, and their guest Margaret Marshall, Mary had written back, "I want you to know that I am riddled by jealousy. You must write to me and reassure me or I shall languish away." "Sheer intuition" told her that he wasn't coming to New York that week in December, as she hoped he would, and now "logic" told her that she wouldn't hear from him, "because you certainly would not be able to call me in front of your house guest, Miss Marshall."

McCarthy's jealousy of Peggy Marshall, as her friends called her, was evident from the start. On the morning Philip Rahv had been summoned to join them all for lunch in Stamford, Wilson had been affectionate not with Mary but with Marshall, "a good move," McCarthy later surmised, but at the time it had "tried [her] sorely." "When you took Peggy on your lap, something happened to my face that I couldn't stop," she wrote Wilson afterwards. "Philip leaned over to me and said, 'I know something about you,' and I said, 'I know you do,' and he said, 'You're jealous,' and I said, 'Yes.' He attributed it, however, to an extreme coquettishness, and didn't look farther for explanations."

When Mary and Wilson became regular lovers, Wilson wrote her that he was "delighted" whenever she came up to see him, for "nothing exciting" ever seemed to happen when she wasn't there. He was continually writing "innumerable lousy little articles," receiving and dispatching guests, and dreaming improbable dreams. During a trip to Boston when he had seen Thornton Wilder's *Our Town* (and liked it), visited with fellow critics Harry Levin and F. O. Matthiessen at Harvard, and dined with Felix Frankfurter, Wilson confided to Mary that he "thought constantly how I wanted to tell you things, talk over people with you." On his last night in Boston, he had a dream about her "which was so delightful and went on for so long," he wrote, "that two professors with whom I was supposed to be having lunch at one, had to come to rout me out of bed."

Mary had begun to regale Wilson with dreams of her own. One was "a dreadful though extremely intellectual nightmare about Logical Positivism." Another dream, she reported, had unfolded on the return train from Stamford:

I dreamed that there was a train running to Troy, New York, that I very much wanted to get on. This train, it appears, was a special taking only people who were entered in a contest to read *Troilus and Criseyde* out loud in Troy. It was built like a subway, and very crowded, and the doors were closing and the guard wouldn't open them again to let me on. But . . . I reminded [him] that there was a rule . . . by which every contestant could have an essay on the poem read to him before embarking. I insisted on having an essay read to me; a bell boy was dispatched to fetch one; the doors opened and I got on the train. (Of course, I didn't want to go to the contest. I was going somewhere else, maybe to Stamford. . . .)

For Mary McCarthy, *Troilus and Criseyde* was a literary landmark. In "The Man in the Brooks Brothers Shirt," Meg presents her traveling companion with her favorite quotation from Chaucer: " 'Criseyde says it, "I am myn owene woman, wel at ese." ' " And the man responds (after deciphering the Middle English): " 'Golly . . . You are, at that!' " In the dream, the meaning is more transparent. McCarthy doesn't say it, but in Chaucer's tale, the triangle that is created when Criseyde is traded to the Greeks, falls in love with Diomedes, and fails to return to Troilus bears an uncanny resemblance to the drama under way on the New York–New Haven Railroad in the fall and winter of 1937.

Like Troilus, who scorns love until he meets Criseyde, and then is grief-stricken when she leaves him, Philip Rahv was stunned when Mary suddenly announced, sometime after Christmas, that Edmund Wilson wanted to marry her. Up until then, amazingly, Rahv hadn't even known they were having an affair. In the tale, Troilus is finally killed on the battlefield by the Greek warrior Achilles, who evokes another aspect of Wilson, one projected in McCarthy's 1989 "picture of a powerful man trying with various baits and lures to rob a weaker man of his chief treasure. . . ."

The exchange of dreams testified to a kind of intimacy that was all the more exciting because it was forbidden. At Covici-Friede, "only a ferocious Stalinist [who] knows practically all my private life already, and would love to know about . . . you and me" threatened their secret, Mary wrote Edmund around the same time, priding herself on "how poker-faced and calm" she looked in the morning when she opened his letters. McCarthy's "alien personality," the one explored in "Ghostly Father, I Confess," had once again asserted itself, "to have love affairs . . . go up to strange hotel rooms . . . try to avoid the floor clerk," and so on. In this instance, the trick had been to get up to Stamford and back nearly once a week without Rahv knowing where she had been. It helped that she still had Vassar friends with country houses outside the city whom she could say she was visiting, and that Philip Rahv appeared neither interested nor practiced in surveillance. One night, she told him she was going to a prizefight with Mannie Rousuck, and luckily the taxi driver who picked her up at Trees to drive her to the train had followed the match on the radio. He provided a "picturesque account," she wrote Edmund the next day, and she didn't even have to buy a morning tabloid.

Picturesque detail had often provided McCarthy with the lubricant for getting out of a tight spot, as in 1927 when she persuaded her Grandfather Preston to let her visit two somewhat 'fast' girls from Annie Wright who lived in Medicine Springs, Montana, on the grounds (false) that she was going to "tour" Yellowstone Park. Coming home on the train, after having been introduced to both moonshine and a married drugstore Romeo, she met a party of tourists from Yellowstone who rescued her just as the cab driver had (though "they did not have the grasp of detail that my grandfather expected from a narrative," she commented later).

The well-told tale was a social skill, like her ability to "draw a man out," as Meg does in "The Man in the Brooks Brothers Shirt," putting question after question to her traveling companion, "like a happy burglar twirling the dial of a well-constructed safe, listening for the locks to click and reveal the combination." Or like the gifted Mrs. Hazeldean in Edith Wharton's *New Year's Day*—to whom the young Mary McCarthy bears a passing resemblance—who can "turn and twist the talk as though she had her victim on a leash, spinning him after her . . . and leaving him, with beating heart. . . ." There was no question but that Mary had drawn Philip Rahv out. She knew more about his childhood in Russia and his lonely schooldays in Providence, Rhode Island, where he had emigrated with an uncle, than did most of his friends; and it was clear to them all that she had discovered a 'side' to Philip, a reservoir of feeling, that was concealed from others—and that she was exceedingly fond of him.

In one of his unpublished stories about Mary McCarthy, Delmore Schwartz observed that it was hard for their acquaintances to keep a straight face in their company; "for Stanislaus might have remarked merely that the day had been a cold one for early October and Helena then felt compelled to declare that Stanislaus had a consciousness of the external world which disregarded nothing." This ability to turn attentiveness into an act of seduction was a formidable one, which became dangerous only when its possessor believed in the authenticity of her performance, which, by the end of 1937, when Mary finally told Philip Rahv what was going on with Wilson, it seemed she did.

II

"Possibly I hoped that the affair with Wilson would come to an end all by itself somehow," McCarthy speculates in her last memoir, "thus relieving me of having to tell Philip." This dissociation from a self who was, on the face of it, as intent on pursuing Wilson as he was her is remarkable: a case of the left hand not knowing what the right one does, even when the right hand holds the cards. In this case, of course, the left hand doesn't approve of the right hand's motives, especially one that McCarthy waited fifty-two years to disclose: "My own explanation (if I must give but a single one) for my yielding to Wilson," she writes, "is the Marxist explanation. It was the same old class struggle that Philip and I had been waging from the moment we fell in love. Wilson, relatively speaking, was upper class."

When in the late 1980s McCarthy had occasion to read her 1937 correspondence with Wilson, she was "surprised by the intimacy and friendliness" of her letters. "Apparently I liked him much more than I remember, more than I ever would again," she writes. Later, she grew to think of him as a "monster: the minotaur, we called him in the family, Bowden and I," she adds, referring to her next husband, Bowden Broadwater. McCarthy may have felt "a kind of friendship for the poor minotaur in his maze, so sadly dependent on the yearly sacrifice of maidens," she declares, indulging in another classical allusion that conceals a slippery truth. "But if, sensing that need, I warmed to Wilson, solitary among his trees, I did not guess that I would be one of the Athenian maidens with never a Theseus to rescue me."

McCarthy's oral accounts of her courtship with Wilson have a hollower ring. When she left him, Rahv was "brokenhearted, and in some strange way I was brokenhearted that this old ogre had snatched me away," she said in a 1985 interview that stands as a footnote to *A Charmed Life* and a warm-up for "Edmund Wilson." "I felt that I had to pay for the fact of having slept with him when I was tight. . . ." She had offered to live with him, she explains, but Wilson wouldn't permit it. "Marriage was what he wanted. He said to me, 'I've had that.' . . . He wanted to marry and have children . . . and I suppose I was rather interested in eventually having children, but anyway I was *dragooned* into this damn thing." She was "very unhappy about Philip, but when you'd betrayed somebody," she adds, "it seemed to me it meant something." What it meant, McCarthy doesn't say, either in 1985 or later in her memoir, where this curious instance of ex post facto moralizing is not to be found.

She is on firmer ground in "Edmund Wilson" when she introduces the social drama that unfolded when she took Rahv's advice to consult an older person who could be told that he and Mary were living together, and chose the mother of her Vassar classmate, Nathalie Swan. Mrs. Swan, a cofounder of the Junior League, who was "a society woman but rather intellectual," and well aware of Edmund Wilson as a literary figure, was no doubt "flattered to be consulted," McCarthy writes. And the description of the brief excursion to the Swans' country house near Salisbury, Connecticut, in January 1938, "where everything was perfect," allows her to apply a healing balm of self-deprecation to the wound she had given Rahv, and the deeper one she may have sustained herself (as "the betrayor," who "is always the debtor"). She was "excited by the momentousness of it all," she confesses. "It did not subtract from the solemnity of the occasion to be waited on by a butler and maids, to drink Mrs. Swan's society martini (gin and two vermouths) before lunch and Joe Swan's vintage wine with meals. . . ."

Philip and Wilson, meanwhile, waited anxiously in the wings. Mrs. Swan had apparently remained neutral, advising Mary only to " 'Wait a little longer' "—"wise counsel" that she didn't want to hear. After taking the train home from Salisbury, McCarthy remembered nothing "till days later," she writes, "when I was on the train with Edmund, going down to his mother's place in Red Bank"—where they were married on February 10, 1938, in the town hall. She had told Philip Rahv her decision, and they had divided their possessions, an event that *is* remembered: Philip took a tall steel lamp and tweed-covered armchair from Macy's, Mary some Italian plates, her mother's silver, and a red love seat that followed her through two more marriages. "Did we have the 1911 Britannica," she wonders, "or had that gone to Johnsrud?" She quit her job at Covici-Freide, spent a few nights at Trees, and recalls "feeling miserable. I looked at the tall grasses outside the train window and looked the other way, into Wilson's closed face, the narrow lips set in a tight line."

In the end, the literary truth prevailed. Here is Martha Sinnott—as in *sin not*—in *A Charmed Life*:

She had begged Miles merely to live with him, as his mistress. But Miles had held out for marriage . . . he needed a mother for his son [Rosalind Wilson, in life]. She was still hesitating when the knot was tied and Miles was sitting beside her on the train, his chin sunk on his chest, morosely silent, a stranger. . . .

Of all the reasons Mary McCarthy presents for marrying Edmund Wilson, the one that comes nearest to accounting for the psychic turmoil that preceded it is the death of her Grandfather Preston on New Year's Day 1938. It was then that her letters to Wilson betrayed an increasing anxiety about his whereabouts, and, when he offered reassurances, sound most romantic: "Your two letters have made me dreamy. I think I must be a little bit in love." Her grandfather's death (after a stroke) had been "so damned unexpected," she wrote Edmund, adding that while he had written her "some rather touching Elizabethan letters on old age," he was still active in his law work. Mary had been counting on his living another ten or fifteen years—like his father, Simon Preston, who lived to be nearly a hundred. More than any surviving member of the family, he had represented the only stability she had known.

Shortly after his death, she was planning a long-overdue reunion with her brothers in New York, a prospect McCarthy may have dreaded. "It will be trying," she wrote Wilson, "because we have nothing real or natural to talk about." Not her Grandfather Preston, whom they had never really known. How could they guess that with his death, she was orphaned a second time. And that she was alone in a way her three brothers, who had always had each other, were not. "When my grandfather died, it took away some protection that I had always had," McCarthy reflected in 1985. She was "at loose ends," she adds, "and Philip was certainly not going to constitute a new rock," whereas Edmund, "so very established and set in his ways," was.

Philip, in fact, was unmarriageable because he was already married to a woman named Naomi whom he hadn't seen in years. He couldn't afford a divorce, and so it was unlikely he could afford a new wife (though Rahv would resolve that problem in 1940, when he married Nathalie Swan). There was always more to McCarthy's 'daring' affair with Philip Rahv than met the eye. There was his laundry to do and dinner to cook when she came home tired from work. Rahv, who was an intellectual in the pure Russian style, was always reading. "Mary," he used to say, "never stops talking." With the Federal Writers' Project, he was researching an essay on New York's literary history for the WPA's guidebook to the city, and he had recently discovered Poe and

Melville. Then one day he had announced that he was going to stay home all week to read the Bible—the New Testament. It was offered as a concession to Mary, who had just struggled though Marx's *The Eighteenth Brumaire of Louis Bonaparte.* Only once had she turned on Rahv in real anger, and that was after they lived together, and McCarthy learned about a night he had spent with Lillian Hellman (who had tried to seduce *him,* Rahv insisted; he had found her undesirable).

Throughout most of 1937, they seemed to have fun together, like the boxcar kids playing house, but by the fall Rahv had become more deeply embroiled in the paranoid wrangling that passed for left-wing politics in New York, and McCarthy was growing tired of it. In "Portrait of the Intellectual as a Yale Man," she provides Jim Barnett with a perception of the Trotsky defense committee meetings that had grown on her over time: "It seemed to him that every Committee member wore an expression of injury, of self-justification, a funny, feminine 'put upon' look, just as if they were all, individually, on trial." She was tired of the endless anecdotes of persecution, of broken publishers' contracts, personal slander, and betrayal. The fear of ideological error seemed omnipresent. To wake up sweating, " 'What if Stalin were right?' "—a Trotskyist friend had actually confessed to Mary that this had happened to him one night. And if Stalin were 'right,' what would follow? Mary had wondered. Only that he himself had been wrong, which ought not to disturb a 'scientific' thinker, as Marxists claimed to be.

Partisan Review meetings were turning into dialectical tournaments, with one speaker or faction advancing on the other like knights from opposite ends of the field. Rahv especially regarded cultural life in sectarian terms. The imagery of conflict, alliance, betrayal, exclusion was congenital with him. All the *PR* editors seemed to excel in what Irving Howe called (after Hegel) " 'the labor of the negative.' " Their great achievement was to break the hold of *official* thinking in the 1930s—the thinking that celebrated Stalin's dictatorship as a 'higher form of democracy,' and Roosevelt's New Deal as a 'rational' form of socialism. And yet the effort had fostered a kind of counterorthodoxy. In Louise Bogan's opinion, there wasn't much difference between a Stalinist and an anti-Stalinist. Both had their short lists of approved writers and artists—only the anti-Stalinist list was shorter: Proust, Joyce, Mann, Kafka, Eliot. "New works, far from being welcomed, were regarded, almost, with bale," McCarthy recalled in the late 1950s' panel on the Thirties at Columbia.

Politics and literature aside, the social life of *Partisan Review* was a narrow affair, played out, as William Barrett recalls, in a sealed-off circle around Union Square. " 'Midtown' was for us the haunt of middlebrows and philistines of the cultural world." Edmund Wilson had nothing in common with the "ghetto-like mentality" that Barrett describes. And by her own lights, Mary McCarthy, who wrote about Broadway and best-sellers, however loftily, didn't, either. A rising star like Delmore Schwartz, who claimed to have mastered Spengler by the age of fifteen, neo-Thomism by seventeen, and Marxism by twenty, appeared to her as a freak. "He is the most intellectual creature I have ever seen," she complained to Wilson, after taking Delmore out to dinner to discuss a novel he was trying to sell Mr. Covici (who didn't " 'get it' "). "He makes one feel that to admit in his cerebral presense any natural inclination or appetite—for food, company, love, gossip, comfort—would be to commit a most indecent solecism."

In 1959, McCarthy remembered the whole late 1930s radical milieu as paralyzed by "the fear of one's natural self and natural feelings." One was always afraid of being exposed as "a bourgeois 'at heart.' And you were supposed to cut that heart out of you." Ideas became impossibly rigid in every department, not because they had to be implemented in action—"among the anti-Stalinists I knew," she adds, "there was scarcely even a picket-line formed in the late thirties"—but because people feared the possibly unorthodox conclusions that any line of thinking might lead to.

All in all, there was no great mystery to why Mary McCarthy eventually left Philip Rahv. The question was why she deceived him. Was betrayal an easy way out when the heart did not produce the reasons the mind demanded? Or maybe the affair was concealed not only to shield Rahv from the truth of what was happening but to keep McCarthy from facing certain facts herself. Maybe she was ashamed of herself 'at heart' for leading a randy old bird like Wilson to the marriage bed. She thought it the wiser part of valor to deny, even to herself, that she had done it. Later she would 'pay for the fact.'

One might have expected Philip Rahv to suggest that Wilson was Mary McCarthy's prize: The affair and marriage were simply instruments of social ambition. But Rahv, who was very loose-tongued when it came to speculations about other people's lives, kept his mouth shut about his own, and this included his affair with Mary. (Early in 1938, in the shadow of the Moscow trials and Hitler's coming annexation of Austria, Rahv penned one of the most influential political documents of the period. Called "Trials of the Mind," it surveyed the death of revolutionary hope in such starkly despairing tones—"We were not prepared for defeat," etc.—that one wonders whether some of his personal bitterness didn't find its way into the argument.) It is William Phillips who says fifty years later, "I just assumed that [Mary] thought Wilson was a more interesting figure than Rahv."

In the story,"New Year's Eve," Delmore Schwartz introduces the unhappily married Delia, a thinly disguised Mary McCarthy:

> She began to feel miserable because she had not married the man who had courted her for two years before she encountered Oliver. She refused him because when they went out to dinner, he filled his pockets with granulated sugar, a habit contracted during a poverty-stricken and unsweetened childhood. . . ."

Delmore's angle is not so different from one McCarthy sets forth in "The Man in the Brooks Brothers Shirt," when Meg Sargent reflects that all the men she had known had been "handicapped for American life and therefore humble in love." There was the "peculiar-looking" husband, the handsome but "good-for-nothing" fiancé, and

> the serious ones [who] were foreigners . . . or were desperately poor and had no table manners. . . . And was she too disqualified, did she really belong to this fraternity of cripples, or was she not a sound and normal woman who had been spending her life in self-imposed exile, a princess among the trolls?

Edmund Wilson was no Prince Charming. " 'Bunny, how do you get all those dames into bed?' " Louise Bogan's husband, Raymond Holden, once asked him. " 'I talk them into it, of course,' " he had replied, which amused Bogan, on account of his "funny, squeaky voice." For Mary McCarthy, however, Wilson broke a certain spell. Unlike previous lovers, Rahv included, he was not humble in love. And he did have 'a better prose style,' which mattered.

With Eunice Clark, Mary had bemoaned her "economic slavery to Covici," she wrote Edmund in January 1938, and Eunice had said, " 'I'm sure you could do another *Axel's Castle* with no trouble at all.' " Eunice was probably quoted in jest, but the sense of the remark is curious. *Axel's Castle* is Wilson's classic study of the Symbolist movement, unparalleled in its time or since. Did Mary see herself as another Edmund Wilson? Not a *Mrs.* Edmund Wilson—the round-about way of the flesh—but an 'interesting figure' herself, an American literary critic of real stature? If so, she wouldn't have been the first woman to mistake her mentor's attraction for her own; or to confuse the satisfaction of his desires—not to mention the satisfaction of *being* desired—with a more elusive ambition.

A key to McCarthy's impulsive temperament may be found in the character of the 'wicked Lord' himself. "The great object of life is sensation—to feel that we exist, even though in pain," Byron said. "It is this 'craving void' which drives us to gaming—to battle, to travel— to intemperate, but keenly felt, pursuits of any description, whose principal attraction is the agitation inseparable from their accomplishment." For Byron, it was often just such actions that he was also impelled to disapprove, because of his sentimental attachments, and because of a stubborn respect for convention. The same paradox appears in Mary McCarthy. She too cannot resist an 'intemperate' adventure, but only after she has portrayed it in sentimental and conventional terms.

Wilson, she insisted in 1986, enticed her with the serene picture he drew of the life they would lead together: "reading poetry, the Latin classics . . . riding horseback, trout-fishing, [walking] in the woods, hunting for wildflowers—all things that I liked." There was something akin to McCarthy's lifelong attraction to 'deep America' that she remembers as "the positive side of the inducement." As a "White Anglo-Saxon Protestant," Wilson, she remarks, "came from the same tradition I did. His father was a lawyer, once the attorney general of New Jersey." Rahv, of course, "couldn't have been more different, and Johnsrud," she adds, "was not in this vein of tradition either. There was a certain 'coming home' feeling for me in my imagining: my grandfather, Annie Wright, Vassar, the classics, horse-back riding. . . ." All were reborn in the presence of this descendant of American men of law—and men of God, too, if one counts a more remote ancestor of Wilson's, Cotton Mather.

Like Byron, Mary McCarthy is also aware of the division in her nature. At the end of *The Company She Keeps*, the heroine exclaims, "If the flesh must be blind, let the spirit see." And she begs the "Ghostly Father" of the tale to allow her to repossess herself, all of herself, the "sick," impulsive, attention-craving, love-starved side, along with the conscience-stricken side that reasserts itself, coldly reasoning, the morning after. "Preserve me in disunity," she implores. With Edmund Wilson, McCarthy's prayers were not answered. But if she didn't get what she wanted, over time, perhaps, she got what she needed.

Part Four

■

Stamford/Wellfleet/New York: 1938–1945

11

At Home with Edmund Wilson

"The romantic life had been too hard for her. In morals

as in politics anarchy is not for the weak. The small state, racked by

internal dissension, invites the foreign conqueror. Proscription,

martial law, the billeting of the rude troops, the tax collector, the unjust

judge, anything, anything at all, is sweeter than responsibility."

—MARY McCARTHY, "GHOSTLY FATHER, I CONFESS"

I had an extremely cheerful interview with Dr. Ripley last night," Mary McCarthy wrote her husband on June 16, 1938, four months after they were married. "About the pregnancy question, he said the paramount thing to be considered was my feeling about it. If I were anxious to have the baby, an abortion would doubtless be medically more difficult and a successful childbirth medically easier"—which was true enough, for Mrs. Edmund Wilson, twenty-five, was already nearly three months pregnant. "He says, though, that since my own feelings are distinctly pro-baby, the odds seem to be rather definitely on the pregnancy."

Wilson's letter, unfortunately, crossed Mary's in the mail. "About this pregnancy question," it began, "I have thought it all over again and I can't come to any other conclusion but that you mustn't go through with a child at this time. It is a disappointment because we'd counted on having one but, after all, we can always have one; and in the meantime it will land you in a situation that you are really unprepared for." She was, Wilson declared, "somewhat confused about this as about other things."

Mary again: "As for the psychiatric aspect of the matter, [Dr. Ripley] says that observation of My Case indicates that a continuance of the pregnancy will almost certainly not make me worse and possibly even better. He thinks from your point of view the Worst may be over, that you may not have to witness anything like the last thing you did witness"—which "for politeness sake," Mary called "a seizure."

On June 8, 1938, Edmund Wilson, then forty-three, had committed his wife to the Payne Whitney Clinic, Women's Division, of New York Hospital for psychiatric observation. They had fought bitterly in the morning over a confrontation that began the night before, and Mary had broken down in a fit of uncontrollable weeping and vomiting. In rough outline, and mainly from McCarthy's sometimes contradictory review of the events many years later, and a brief account by Wilson in the manuscript of his journals from the 1940s, it happened like this. On the evening of June 7, Allen Tate and his wife Caroline Gordon had come to Wilson's home in Stamford for dinner and what turned out to be a night of hard drinking and endless conversation between old friends with whom Mary felt little connection. She was tired and went to bed early. Later, Edmund had entered their room, and in a pique over some colored bed sheets that Mary had asked the maid to put on that night "as a surprise," he had torn them off with her in them, and she had "bounced" on the floor.

McCarthy was never sure exactly when the fighting began. Perhaps she had "made the mistake of complaining [then], which one shouldn't do when a person is like Edmund, and also very drunk." Or maybe she cried, " 'How *could* you!' " the next morning when he woke up, still drunk. In any event, it was later in the morning, after the Tates had left, she claimed, that Wilson had really hit her hard, striking her breasts and stomach. Hattie, Wilson's maid, had tried to intervene, a point Wilson also makes, while drawing the opposite conclusion.

McCarthy: "Hattie then appeared and tried to calm things down. She *knew* him, of course. And she sent for the doctor. She was alarmed." Wilson: "I did not know what to do about her, but Hattie, who was getting scared, having had the experience of her insane daughter, on her own initiative called a local doctor." (In the original entry from Wilson's journals, probably composed in the 1960s, he had first written "her own insane daughter," as if Mary McCarthy was *his* insane daughter, and then crossed out "own.")

When the doctor came, Mary had calmed down a little, but her face was swollen, she had a black eye, and her arms were bruised. "Of course I wouldn't tell him what had happened. You don't. You cover up. So he thought it was just a pregnancy thing," she maintained. Wilson, too, remembered covering up, albeit for his own reasons.

Mary's "fits of alienation," as he called their confrontations, "at times made life very difficult. I was always having to cover them up. I could not bear to write about it." The doctor proposed a "rest" for a few days in Manhattan's Harkness Pavilion, McCarthy continues, and she had agreed, with the proviso that it be New York Hospital instead, which she remembered fondly from when she had had her appendix out. At this point, there was no psychiatric care implied. She brought that on herself, she insists; she was "such a *consumer* . . . smitten with the yellow roughly woven curtains," she remembered from New York Hospital, "which had a slight line of red running on the edge. . . ." That the Stamford doctor may have transmitted the "psychiatric thing" to her gynecologist in New York, when he first called him to make arrangements for New York Hospital, is suggested in another interview.

The yellow curtains, like the colored bed sheets (light blue), anchor a nightmarish event to the mundane world of surfaces. The details lead one out of the picture—who cares about the yellow curtains and blue sheets?—but they also lend a peculiar weight to the narration. Details like this, one comes to realize from McCarthy's accounts of her life with Wilson, are loaded with the effort of forgetting as much as by the act of remembering. But in this case the details are also stressed to challenge the credibility of Edmund Wilson's assertion that the local doctor, knowing nothing about nervous disorders, had simply assumed that his wife was insane, and sent her directly to the Payne Whitney Clinic in New York.

When Mary and Edmund arrived at the main entrance of New York Hospital on the night of June 8, after an hour-and-a-half taxi ride from Stamford, no one in Admissions had been informed of her coming, McCarthy recalls, and she had been sent around the corner to another section of the hospital, the psychiatric section, where she was duly admitted. The rest is fiction: "Sitting there in the lobby, I was just beginning to wonder where the gift shop was and the florist and the circulating library when a tall doctor came out of an office to talk to me. He seemed awfully curious to know how I got the black eye." This is Kay Petersen in *The Group*, who also arrives at the Payne Whitney Clinic after a marital confrontation gets out of hand: "I laughed and said I'd run into a door, but he didn't get the joke. He kept on pressing me till finally I said, 'I won't tell you.' I didn't see why he should know what had happened between Harald and me. 'We shall have to ask your husband then,' he said." But by then Harald Petersen—like Edmund Wilson—had left.

The admitting psychiatrist assumes that Kay's injuries are self-inflicted, just as in 1938 the first psychiatrist who saw Mary Wilson assumed that she was somehow responsible for her bruises. Kay is led into a small cell-like room, searched and stripped, and left alone in the dark, as was Mary. As soon as Kay realizes that she is not in a regular hospital, she is determined to act as naturally as she can so that she can get herself transferred the next morning; but she keeps getting new shocks, new humiliations—just as Mary did when she sat alone in the locked cubicle where she was first taken, as far from home probably as she would ever get, listening to the click of the tiny Judas window open and shut in the hospital door.

When Wilson returned late the following afternoon, after having gone on a "drinking binge," McCarthy recalls, he confirmed the truthful account she gave the next morning of how she had gotten the black eye, and the room had been changed. In a deposition submitted during their divorce proceedings in 1945, Wilson maintained that Mary had been "confined to the ward for violent cases for a period of time," an account that cannot stand corrected by fiction certainly but that is contradicted by letters. Writing Edmund at home on June 15, Mary noted that she had been on the "out-going" floor of Payne Whitney for a week ("the almost-cured floor," she called it in 1988).

"Tonight we are going to have a Community Sing," the letter continues. "I bet you didn't have that in *your* insane asylum [Wilson had a nervous breakdown in 1932]. I'm learning to play pool. . . . My ping-pong also is improving. There is one woman on this floor who is going to have me in a straight-jacket . . . she thinks that 'Kip' [Clifton] Fadiman is just a *genius*. . . ." Wit, like the hound of intellect, was already moving in to kill the pain.

Like Kay Petersen, Mary had received a perfect zero on the metabolism test, given to incoming patients to measure the energy balance of the body. "Kay glowed as if the machine had paid her a compliment. 'Wait till I tell Harald!' she exulted." Mary wrote Edmund that "the metabolism test came out absolutely normal, which shows how much Dr. Rado knows." (Dr. Sandor Rado, head of the New York Psychiatric Institute, and soon to become the first of several psychiatrists McCarthy would consult during her marriage to Wilson, had apparently suspected a pregnancy-related chemical imbalance before he saw her.) Small victories were important. Payne Whitney's Dr. Ripley, for example, had become more expansive where before he had been secretive—their sessions were now "like conversations," not consultations. When Mary told him that Dr. Rado had written a book about women's castration complex, a theory she had never taken seriously, he had replied, " 'Well, it's a very masculine idea, don't you think?' " "He was very, very reassuring," McCarthy remembered in 1988. "He did not think I was crazy. He thought I was sane."

When Wilson's long letter had arrived the following day, it must have been read with a sinking heart. In summary fashion, this remarkable document introduces the principal issues that Mary and Edmund would fight over for the next seven years: a wife's responsibility to her husband, and to the psychiatrists he has ordered for her; control over the family purse; power. "You oughtn't to be let in for relationships and responsibilities which you're not ready for at the present time, and which might ruin your relationship with me as well as interfere with your psychoanalysis," Wilson maintained. "The psychoanalysis is the main thing, and there's no question that it will go better if you get the pregnancy over.

> There are also the possible difficulties: with a baby you would be badly tied down and the expenses of baby and psychiatrist, too, would certainly be more than we could afford. I think, too, that you and I will get along better with this question out of the way: you won't find your situation with me closing down over you in so oppressive a way as I'm afraid you have. . . .

"Rado," Wilson added, invoking *his* authority in the war of the doctors, "told me . . . today that this question must be settled at once before he could do anything for you. So get the thing over and then you can come out to Stamford and . . . start a gay summer life between New York and the psychoanalyst, and your loving husband."

A week later, Wilson sent Mary a care package from the New Weston Hotel, where he stayed in the city, containing the current *New Republic*, the *New International* with a long article by Trotsky, a card from Louise Bogan, and a note from Nancy Macdonald promising to send the latest *Partisan Review* as soon as it was off the press. "I miss you, dear. I hate to go back there and be without you," he wrote. "The Dr. says you're in good shape. Will see you Saturday. Take things easy."

On June 29, Mrs. Edmund Wilson was discharged. The event is recorded on a slip of paper in the Wilson Collection at Yale. "Diagnosis: Without psychosis; anxiety reaction."

It was not an auspicious beginning to the quiet family life that Edmund Wilson had promised, and Mary McCarthy had embraced, albeit with obscure intent. But Mary was persistent. While Edmund had won a Pyrrhic victory of sorts the moment he had checked her into Payne Whitney—for now their marital problems might be certifiably regarded as Mary's psychiatric problems—Mary won the "pregnancy question." Reuel Kimball Wilson, Mary McCarthy's only child, was born on Christmas Day, 1938.

The large, rustic L-shaped cottage that Wilson leased in Stamford, the first of a series of rented houses, borrowed apartments, and hotel suites that Mary and Edmund would inhabit before and after Wilson's mother helped them buy a house in Wellfleet on Cape Cod, was equipped with a screened-in porch that overlooked the Mianus River. During the day, the porch was filled with sleeping moths that Wilson carefully picked off the screen at night when he was working late. Tiny tree frogs whose jewel-like throats blew up when they peeped also clung to the screens, and these he kept in jars until they nearly died for want of food, and then he let them go. But it was the moths, the Luna and Cecropia who slept by day and awoke fluttering at dusk, that charmed him most. "It is one of the most perfect pleasures I know of," Wilson's friend Vladimir Nabokov agreed: "To open the window wide on a muggy night and watch them come . . . one will settle quietly on the wall to be boxed in comfort, another will dash and bang against the lampshade before falling with quivering wings and burning eyes upon the table, a third will wander all over the ceiling." Nabokov taught Wilson to "sugar" for them: to mix a bottle of stale beer with brown sugar and a little rum, smear it on a score of tree trunks at sundown, and wait. "They will come from nowhere, settling on the glistening bark and showing their crimson underwings . . . and you cover them with a tumbler," he explained. "Try, Bunny, it is the noblest sport in the world."

By day and by night, the thickly wooded ravines reverberated with the clacking of typewriters, Mary's and the machine used by Wilson's secretary. In May 1938, Wilson wrote W. W. Norton to propose a new book of literary essays to be hung on Sophocles' myth of the Wound and the Bow. He wanted to show how the brutalities and terrible anomalies of human existence were the instigators of all important literature—whose task it thus became to help men discover something of value for the control and ennoblement of life. The lead essay, "The Wound and the Bow," was already in the works for the *Atlantic Monthly,* and studies of Dickens, Kipling, and Edith Wharton, who died in 1937, would soon be added. (In "Homage to Edith Wharton,"

which portrays Wharton's early achievement as "the desperate product of a pressure of adjustments," there is something eerie in Wilson's
account of how she began writing serious fiction during the period of
a nervous breakdown, in the midst of an unhappy marriage, at the
suggestion of a psychiatrist who, like Dr. Rado, combined an interest
in literature with a study of "female neuroses.")

He was anxious, as always, about money. In 1938, Mary's dividends from the McCarthy grain elevators totaled thirteen hundred
dollars, which Wilson insisted go into his bank account. His seventeen-
hundred-dollar advance for *To the Finland Station* was already used
up, and he was still struggling with the chapters on Marx and Engels—
"the Owl and the Pussycat," he called them. By the end of the year, he
decided to break a long-standing association with Scribner's, and when
his editor, Maxwell Perkins, had twitted him about a contract that he
had signed with Harcourt Brace, Wilson was moved by the "apparent
assumption that Scribner's has been remarkably generous with me
. . . to expatiate on this subject." Several years before, Scribner's had
refused to extend him a small advance of seventy-five dollars, he
reminded Perkins. When he asked the publisher to help sponsor a bank
loan, he was again refused "at a time when you were handing out
money to Scott Fitzgerald like a drunken sailor—which he was spending like a drunken sailor. Naturally you expected him to write you a
novel which would make you a great deal more money than my books
seemed likely to do. But even so," Wilson remarked, "the discrepancy
seemed . . . somewhat excessive." Then there were the two times that
the bookkeeping department "gypped" him out of monies due on
royalties. And there were the inaccuracies in *Axel's Castle* that remained uncorrected in subsequent editions.

Maxwell Perkins must have quickly smoothed his feathers, for two
weeks later Wilson thanked him for sending the new collection of
Hemingway stories. " 'The Short Happy Life of Francis Macomber' is
as good as *The Green Hills of Africa* was bad," he reported; and he
informed Max that he had just written a notice for *The Nation*. In
1939, Wilson moved Hemingway to the front of his desk, and in a
major essay written for the *Atlantic Monthly*, "Hemingway: Gauge of
Morale," he submitted the collected works of Scribner's best-known
author to a thoroughgoing analysis, one that also found its way into
The Wound and the Bow.

"Edmund was always working his way through the *oeuvre* of some
writer," Eileen Simpson recalls in *Poets in Their Youth*. "He decided
on a writer, read his entire work, wrote a long review, expanded it into

an article, collected the articles into a book: no waste." The practice, one imagines, was the envy of younger literary folk like Delmore Schwartz, R. P. Blackmur, and Eileen Simpson's husband, John Berryman, who were always carrying around a set of incisive notes about some author (listed as a definitive study on their publishers' calendars) for years before burying the corpse in a book review. They were free-lance writers, subject to the usual hazards of solitary work and self-employment; Wilson ran a shop, a one-man shop in which he was both foreman and timeserver, but a shop nonetheless, with a shopkeeper's economy of scale.

A week after their marriage, Wilson had set Mary up in the spare room with a typewriter and shut the door. " 'I think you've got a talent for writing short stories,' " he said, which was a good thing, because she did, and she hadn't known it, and because she had quickly discovered that she had little talent for being the wife of a great man. "Finally, she is less in his light than in his shadow," was how Wilson's close friend, the painter Mary Meigs, later saw it. All the qualities of greatness—"the selfishness, the iron will, the discipline that sets hours and refuses to be disturbed," Meigs observed, depended upon being "coddled and encouraged and excused by the women around them. For every great man needs his slaves, even if one of them, his wife, is a great woman." Edmund, Meigs adds in a memoir, believed from experience that women can't be liberated. " 'They are the way they are, born that way, or they want to be that way,' he would say impatiently." With McCarthy, however, he had used his iron will to instill a kind of discipline, at least in literary matters, which was to become second nature to them both.

Soon after Mary returned from Payne Whitney, they had moved to a larger house on Shippan Point, with fourteen-year-old Rosalind Wilson, who moved in for the summer, and Hattie, who soon left them to work for the owner of Trees. Dr. Sandor Rado rented a house on the same street. Occasionally, they saw friends such as Charlie and Adelaide Walker, who Mary knew from the Theatre Union. Charlie Walker was one of Wilson's cronies from college days, a classics scholar and labor writer, and Adelaide was from Colorado; darkly beautiful, she had been the expatriate Harry Crosby's great love, and she had narrowly missed becoming his 'fire princess' in the October 1929 suicide with which Malcolm Cowley ends *Exile's Return*. After the Wilsons followed the Walkers to Wellfleet in 1941, the ties grew stronger. More than anyone else, it was Adelaide Walker who knew what was going on between Mary and Edmund—"although I never really made a confidante of anybody about Edmund," McCarthy later said, "because I don't believe in it. As long as you're married to somebody, you don't discuss your problems." Except with your psychiatrist, who serves as the outlet—like Dr. James in "Ghostly Father, I Confess," "the hygenic pipe line that kept the boiler from exploding." Rado was followed in 1939 by Dr. Richard Frank, and in 1942 by Dr. Abraham Kardiner, who had been analyzed by Sigmund Freud. In the fall of 1942, Mary McCarthy would rent an apartment on Stuyvesant Square in New York, commuting to Wellfleet on the weekends, in order to keep her daily appointments with Dr. Kardiner.

When the Wilsons saw Mary's friends, it was "somewhat over Edmund's dead body," McCarthy remembered in 1985. But a month after their marriage, Dwight and Nancy Macdonald came to visit. It was a strange evening, an orgy of drinking and shoptalk between Edmund and Dwight; and it was followed by a note from Dwight reminding Wilson of his 3 A.M. promise to review a new Random House edition of Whitman for *Partisan Review*. Nancy, who had often wilted in Mary's presence, was "horrified with how Wilson was dominating her and talking over her head—talking to Dwight as if she wasn't there." But when Mary's old Vassar classmate Frani Blough came up to Stamford after her year in Basel, she saw little of that. "I left her in the arms of Philip Rahv and when I came back . . . she was married to Edmund Wilson," she recalled. "She was moving on awfully fast." The severe little bun at the nape of the neck had been cut, and her shoulder-length hair was waved in the fashion of the '40s. "She had been kind of smoothed up by Edmund," Frani thought, "not that she was unsmooth before, but she seemed a little different."

In October 1938, Scott Fitzgerald and the Hollywood columnist Sheilah Graham came to visit the Wilsons at Shippan Point. Wilson wrote Christian Gauss at Princeton that Scott's "new girl keeps him in better order than Zelda (who seems to be fading out in the sanitorium). But the effect is very queer and disconcerting:

As his personality was always a romantic drunken personality, it is something new for him to have to present to the world a sober and practical one; and he seems . . . rather unsure of himself, and at moments almost banal. There are times when you might almost mistake him for a well-meaning Middle Western businessman. . . .

Mary was impressed by Fitzgerald's "colossal ignorance—it was almost touching." In later life, she was sure that she would have been more indulgent. Fitzgerald, after all, had just written some powerful scenes in *The Last Tycoon*, the descent of the Hollywood moguls on Monticello, for example; but he had misspelled the name of his heroine, Cecilia, a lapse to McCarthy's way of thinking. In Stamford, he talked feverishly of writing a book about Lucrezia Borgia, and sang the praises of Communist screenwriters in Hollywood.

Fitzgerald, who had always called Bunny Wilson his "intellectual conscience," may have found Edmund somewhat disconcerting, as well. It was hard to believe that this portly, red-faced man, who already looked like a cross between W. C. Fields and Herbert Hoover, had once dropped in on their friend Burton Rascoe in the Village in a brown dressing gown and top hat, alongside Mary Blair in pajamas and house slippers, and Tallulah Bankhead in a bathing suit and cutaway coat, to execute a bit of vaudeville of his own devising. He was still funny, signing himself Hiram K. Antichrist on postcards to Katy and John Dos Passos, in which one-liners like "Marxism is the opium of the intellectuals" alternated (in 1938) with "All Hollywood corrupts; and absolute Hollywood corrupts absolutely." And Wilson would never lose his love of pranks and magic tricks. But with his burgeoning household, he was a paterfamilias, often grave and sententious. Scott, he confided to his journal, is only "serious about problems of 'technique' in movies and *The Saturday Evening Post*."

While Mary found Scott Fitzgerald "boring," she was struck by the arrogant condescension Edmund displayed in his company, the same stance she observed when they visited the poet John Peale Bishop on the Cape, the third member of the trio (Wilson, Fitzgerald, and Bishop) who had edited the *Nassau Lit* at Princeton in 1917. "He looked down on them and patronized them," she remembers. Only with Nabokov was Wilson "a bit squared-off."

The next weekend, the Wilsons accompanied Fitzgerald and Sheilah Graham to the Dartmouth Carnival, a mistake, as it turned out, for Scott, for in Hanover he fell off the wagon. The painful scene, McCarthy recalls, was picked up by Budd Schulberg and used in a novel. "He had never before developed a technique for meeting the world sober," Wilson concluded in a letter to John Peale Bishop early in 1939. At forty-three, Fitzgerald was only beginning to evolve one. Apparently, it was too late. In two years, he would be dead; and Edmund Wilson would serve as his memoirist and literary executor.

In the meantime, Wilson was still wrestling with Marx in *To the Finland Station*, which was subtitled "A Study in the Writing and Acting of History." Now that the Moscow trials had thrown a cloud over the Russian Revolution, Marxism itself appeared in eclipse. Wilson seemed loath to let it go, however. For him, the study of Marxism and the Russian Revolution marked the culmination of a decade's involvement with the turbulent politics of his own country. In 1930, he had dropped his literary pursuits to observe firsthand the effects of the Depression on the everyday lives of Americans. Covering a miners' strike in Pineville, Kentucky, early in 1932, he had been run out of town and dumped at the state line by a sheriff who was sure that he was plotting a jailbreak for local Communist agitators. "It seems to me," he had written Allen Tate, "that the world is in for a big struggle between capitalism and Communism"; and he hadn't wanted to miss it. American democracy, he pictured then as a "machine [that] has been running down . . . a life which aims at nothing beyond itself, which is part of no general human effort."

By the end of the 1930s, *To the Finland Station* was Wilson's chance to rescue the idea of "a general human effort" from the wreckage of contemporary left-wing politics, or so he hoped. Lenin's arrival at Finland Station on April 16, 1917, remained the symbolic moment "when for the first time . . . the key of a philosophy of history was to fit an historical lock." This was the moment when man could be seen "to have made some definite progress in mastering the greeds and the fears . . . in which he has lived." Disillusionment was to come, but more than many of his peers, Wilson remained convinced of the grandeur of the revolutionary ideal.

What bedeviled him were the philosophical and economic ideas of Karl Marx. In "The Myth of the Marxist Dialectic," the *Finland Station* chapter first published in the Fall 1938 *Partisan Review,* Wilson had disposed of the ghostly German 'Will' that haunted both Hegel and Marx, and lent the Dialectic its mystic attribute of inevitability. But the materialist dimensions of dialectical materialism eluded him, and he had taken to worrying these questions over with Mary, whose Catholic training, he believed, better equipped her to handle abstract ideas. The labor theory of value gave him particular trouble, McCarthy recalled; "Edmund," she maintained, "didn't have much capacity for theoretical reasoning." He was far more interested in tracking down the psychological or physiological *cause* of an idea than in considering its effects. In *To the Finland Station,* the ideas he didn't like or understand in Marxism, in her view, were too often reduced to "Marx's carbuncles."

In an essay entitled "Is Verse a Dying Technique," written a few years later, Wilson had horrified his poet friends, according to

McCarthy, by "extrapolating from some little things that were happening in certain functions of poetry to the idea that poetry was finished, and that it would change into prose form. It was just the opposite of what was actually happening, but Edmund," she insisted, "not being very well-versed in ideas, when one got hold of him he followed it straight to the cowbarn." It was an opinion sometimes voiced by the boys. " 'Wilson is a good writer,' " Philip Rahv used to say (after Wilson stole his girl), " 'but he has no ideas.' "

II

At her typewriter, Mary continued to write her drama pieces, and an occasional review of books. Her contribution to the Fall 1938 issue of *Partisan Review*—in which Wilson's "Myth" was joined by William Phillips's refutation—was far from ideological (as Dwight reminded Wilson, *PR*'s editors were still "comparatively orthodox communicants of Marx"). "The People's Choice" was a review of current best-sellers. A watered-down sequel to "Literary Salesmen" (Part I of the 1935 *Nation* series on American critics), it noted the absence of any pretense to seriousness in the latest crop of novels. Either there was now a greater meeting of minds between publishers, authors, and the public, she decided, or fiction wasn't taken seriously anymore.

Meanwhile, McCarthy's own first piece of fiction, "Cruel and Barbarous Treatment," was written in a rush of pent-up reminiscence in the spring of 1938. Almost immediately, the story—about the affair that ended her first marriage—was picked up by *The Southern Review*. "Rogue's Gallery" followed soon after. By a flip of the pronoun, the autobiographical heroine of the first story becomes the first-person narrator of the second; and the object of her curiosity, the shady Mr. Sheer, takes center stage. An ex-bootlegger turned art dealer, Sheer is modeled on McCarthy's first employer from the Carleton Gallery, Mannie Rousuck. When Rousuck saw the story in manuscript (after bribing a bellboy to slip him Mary's briefcase at a hotel where they were lunching), he threatened to sue unless she covered his tracks, which she did in a perfunctory way by turning his gallery into a curiosity shop, and by transforming the elderly English dog painter, Maud Earl, into the elderly Monsieur Ravasse, whose tiny canine portraits stare out of crystal cuff links. Mr. Sheer, endowed with Mannie Rousuck's generous talent for imposture, however, remains intact.

"Rogue's Gallery" was rejected by both *The Southern Review* and

Partisan Review. *PR*'s editors had failed to find any "large signifi-cance" in Sheer as a social type. Philip Rahv, who always wanted to know 'who's in it' before he published a story, may have decided that Sheer was too small a fish to fry; or maybe the story ran to too many pages, as Dwight suggested. Mary, in any event, seemed to accept the decision with equanimity; and the story remained unpublished until it appeared in 1942 as a chapter in *The Company She Keeps*. Wilson, however, filed *PR*'s rejection away as another strike against "his wife's magazine," which he had taken to calling "Partisansky Review."

"I've thought there was something wrong in your shop ever since you passed up that short story of Mary's which seemed to me the best thing she had written," he wrote Fred Dupee in 1940, referring either to "Rogue's Gallery" or "The Genial Host," which *Partisan Review* also returned. "You people certainly owed her a chance to develop, since she was one of your original group." Now she was not, Wilson's wording suggested; now Mary McCarthy's literary relations had become, in Edmund Wilson's mind, an extension of his own. *PR*'s rejection reminded him "ominously of the implacable opposition which the *New Republic* boys always put up when one of their num-ber"—such as himself—"showed any signs of trying to write anything but *New Republic* editorials." Complaining to Allen Tate in 1943 of "the dullness and sterility and pretentiousness" of the *Kenyon Review*, Wilson noted: "Mary and I have both sent [John Crowe] Ransom some of the best things we have written of recent years, and he has declined to print any of them. . . . Of Mary's book [*The Company She Keeps*] he published a stupid and impudent review apparently com-posed by the office boy; my books he has not reviewed at all."

In June 1939, six months after the birth of their child, Mary and Edmund took an apartment on South Kimbark in the Hyde Park section of Chicago. Wilson had been hunting for a "regular job" for nearly a year ('regular' meaning academic), and after Christian Gauss failed to turn anything up at Princeton, he had taken a short-term post at the University of Chicago, teaching two ten-week courses for twelve hundred dollars. It was not a happy summer.

Teaching did not come easily to Wilson, as Mary had seen when he lectured at Vassar in 1932. The departmentalization of literature into 'English' repelled him; and the constraints that bound teacher and students in numbered rooms at metered intervals for a preordained transmission of information brought out the worst in him. "I'm no good as a lecturer in the regular way," Wilson had admitted to Gauss, and he had proposed simply to read from several essays in production. At Chicago, as it turned out, Wilson lectured on Dickens *before* writing the essay, and on the social interpretation of literature, drawing on Taine and some of the Marxist texts from *To the Finland Station*. The students were a varied lot, and he was impressed by the fact that many had begun to study Greek in college, unlike at Princeton, where Greek was a dead language. At the end, he had felt "awfully let down and nervous," as he usually did after teaching, he told Mary, but the lectures had gone over well with the students, who paid him "little tributes" when the classes ended. Years later, however, one of his former students recalled how exasperating it was that Edmund Wilson failed to pick up on a cornerstone of the Chicago method of teaching: its love of argument. Confronted by two opposing points of view, he would nod and appear to agree with both, thus depriving his students of the chance to test one idea in confrontation with another in the intellectual arena of the classroom.

At home, however, both Edmund's and Mary's appetite for argument remained irrepressible. Twice their Hyde Park neighbors had to call the police to quiet the noise of their furious voices. But it was only when Mary left Wilson to visit her Grandmother Preston in Seattle that his dissatisfaction with life in Chicago grew acute.

In Seattle, Mary was making a "ritualistic visit," presenting her remarried self and her new baby to Seattle society, such as it was; and for the most part, she was content, she wrote Edmund, "to stay within the forms." Her old labor and newspaper friends didn't even know she was in town, she added, since "they don't read the society section"; but her picture was going to be in the paper Sunday, she noted, "and that will probably elicit something. . . ." As it did. McCarthy's old high school friend Jess Rosenberg remembers a brief reunion in the summer of 1939, when their two children were small enough to share the same playpen.

Her Grandmother Preston, Mary wrote Edmund, was "mad about Reuel," who was no longer to be found "on all fours bucking like a little bronco" in the mornings—"he is standing up eating the paint off the top of his crib. . . ." Mrs. Preston had gotten Mary a fur coat, which prompted Edmund to remark, "Maybe one reason your grandmother has been doing more for you is that you have been so immensely improved under my guidance. Hasn't she mentioned it?" It was the kind of remark that might have passed as ironical during courtship, but married life, one suspects, had worn the irony thin.

The visit was Mary McCarthy's first since her grandfather's death in January 1938. One wonders whether the big house overlooking Lake Washington seemed empty without him. Was her grandmother still mourning? And how did Mary feel now that she was alone with the woman who had always seemed to be withholding something from her, some truth about the past that really mattered? The letters, beginning with a telegram—"INFANT HERCULES AND I ARRIVED SAFELY . . ."—do not say. Her grandmother, Mary wrote Edmund, had been "awfully cute lately, full of wry reminiscences about married life, how grandfather never could remember her birthday, would never go shopping with her, gave blanket approval to everything she wore, how after they had had 'words' he would leave in the morning without saying goodbye to her, and how then she wouldn't speak to him for days. . . ."

The account is a curious one, for it controverts the portrait that Mary McCarthy draws of her grandmother's marriage in *Memories of a Catholic Girlhood*:

> Her marriage had been successful, and she attributed this to a single simple recipe, like one of the household hints in the back of the Temple de Hirsch cookbook. . . . She had never had a quarrel continue overnight. No matter how mad she was at Grandpa, she told me, she always kissed him good night. And . . . no matter how mad she was in the morning, she always kissed him goodbye before he went to the office.

A ring of truth is sounded in the literary version when McCarthy adds that her grandmother had "passed this recipe on to me gravely. . . . [I]f I would just follow it, I would never have any more trouble, she was certain."

Writing in August 1939 about her visit in Seattle, McCarthy sounds like a nervous young wife who has long ago learned to keep some facts to herself. Her letters seem calculated to set Wilson's mind to rest on controversial points—money, for example. "Grandmother is full of ideas for me to spend money"—hats, underwear—"which I devote a good deal of energy to repulsing. Her notion of What You Have to Have and mine have become quite disparate during the years. . . ." But somehow she pressed the wrong buttons. Or she couldn't help but spend, just as Edmund Wilson couldn't keep from withholding access to the family purse, despite the fact that Mary's grain-elevator dividends were a part of it.

When Mary left for the West, Wilson had given her a handful of blank checks signed in advance, making her promise she would let him know about each one when she cashed it. By the middle of August, she was down to her last dollar, and the checks were all cashed. "It's been more expensive out here than I expected," she wrote gamely, "things like Reuel's diaper service and my cleaning bills I hadn't taken into account." And then there was the salary for the girl she had hired to help with Reuel. One assumes the wealthy Mrs. Preston would have picked up her granddaughter's household tabs, but whether or not she did, Mary's poverty more likely owed itself to the fact that her grandmother's notion of "What You Have to Have" and her own were not so far apart as all that. In Frederick's or Magnin's, one imagines the two of them: the elderly little shopper in Cuban heels, raising her onyx and diamond lorgnon to examine a pair of fabric gloves for her granddaughter, who stands to one side like a page, swelling the scene—when suddenly the saleslady, who has always regarded the girl as a prop in her games with the grandmother, beams at the young woman, seeing her for the first time as a customer, a Mrs. Harold Preston in miniature, and invites her to make *her* wishes known.

In any event, Wilson's suspicions were soon inflamed. He, too, was down to his last dollar—"though I hadn't realized how literally till I received your announcement that you had cashed all the checks I gave you," he fumed. "You have very strange ideas of economy," he complained, after reading Mary's account of how her grandmother had "saved" them money by buying her the fur coat—"I shouldn't have been able to buy it now in any case." He reminded her that he still had her psychiatrist, Dr. Richard Frank, to pay, along with moving and storage bills (they were headed for Cape Cod in the fall), gas and electric and other "bills from strange people. . . ." As of August 19, there was nothing left to bring them all—Edmund, Mary, Reuel, Rosalind, and Rosalind's friend Jeanie—back east.

A week later, the storm had passed. Perhaps a relief check had come from Wilson's mother in Red Bank, as it often did when Rosalind's welfare was at stake. Edmund sent Mary a check and instructed her not to cash it until she heard from him. He was bored and exasperated with his colleagues in the English Department, he wrote her, with the exception of Norman Maclean and Morton Zabel, with whom he always had a good time—"delirious," in fact, given the way he had been living lately, which was, he said, "in a painful state of decline. . . ." He had developed a fever and "strange pains in the arms and side," muscular strain, the doctor suggested, brought on from bicycling with Rosalind; but Edmund was sure that "part of my decline has been due to the trauma caused by your departure."

"I miss you," he told Mary flatly. Every time he heard a baby cry, he thought it was Reuel. On August 14, he had dreamed that she was back and that Reuel, who had learned to talk, "was saying rather interesting things." He didn't know how much she meant to him until she was gone, he wrote, and if he was "depressed" it was from "living alone as before marriage." "Celibacy," he noted, "is beginning to tell on me."

"Darling," Mary wrote back teasingly in an undated letter, "I am getting quite excited about seeing you again. . . . Will you be glad to see me?" The answer, which arrived nearly every other day in the mail—except for the slap over money—was obvious, at least in writing.

Mary Meigs, who came to know Edmund Wilson well a decade later, and who was often fearful that he might suddenly turn the "awful words" he frequently applied to others on to her, was reassured whenever she looked back over his long correspondence. She was moved by the "courtly sweetness" that permeated the valentines and letters, "as if he needed the protective medium of the written word to express his most delicate feelings." Wilson's "intuitions" never failed to surprise her, "for his spoken judgements were monolithic and unchangeable." In his letters to Meigs at the very end of his life, she notes, "he was still wistfully writing, 'I miss you.'"

On the Cape, Wilson rented a house in Truro Center, and when Mary and Reuel returned from Seattle in September 1939, they both settled down to a year of hard writing. For Wilson, it was like coming home. The outer Cape was the corner of America he loved best. He and Mary had visited Provincetown briefly in August 1938, staying in John and Katy Dos Passos's house overlooking the harbor, and then he had been overcome with unexpected nostalgia for his old haunts— for the dunes off Race Point, the picnics that wound into the night, the tiny front rooms along Commercial Street, barricaded with books against the river of day-trippers, the Portuguese bakery, and the Atlantic House bar. Nineteen thirty-eight had not seen many tourists and the town had a neglected, seedy look, but Edmund and Mary had spent some lively evenings at Charlie and Adelaide Walker's, talking politics with a wealthy young composer, and music with a "relapsed Communist." There had been the usual conversation stoppers that Wilson collected, like the Portuguese gigolo's remark after hearing one of Wilson's friends tell of someone committing suicide: "I knew a couple of fellows who committed that once." And the Philadelphia matron who was overheard interrupting a denunciation of Hitler to exclaim,

"I think you're going too far—you're talking about him as if he was Roosevelt!"

Mary's being there, Edmund had decided, had unleashed his own nostalgia; he hadn't been so happy when he left Provincetown in 1936 and moved to Stamford. Now it was time to give the Cape another try. Besides, in his old friend Polly Boyden's house in Truro, they could live almost for free. In the fall of 1939, money was even tighter than usual, with Mary's inheritance barely matched by Wilson's irregular receipts from royalties and magazine pieces. In November, Wilson had to go to New York "for the purpose of shaking down editors and publishers," he wrote Morton Zabel in Chicago. He had never seen so many publishers before in his life, and he found them "a very melancholy crew. They have ceased to make any pretense of being interested in publishing books," he noted, "but talk wistfully about religion and the fate of the human race."

World War II had just broken out in Europe—while Mary and Reuel were entrained for the East—but it was not an event that mattered greatly to Wilson or McCarthy. Wilson, in Mary McCarthy's recollection, would have agreed with the Trotskyists (as did she) who argued that an imperialist war never solved anything—fascism could never be defeated by capitalism; and whether or not the Allies won made little difference in the class war. But it was Edmund's intense aversion to all things English, along with his deep isolationism, that made his position on the war resemble that of "an old-fashioned American like Colonel McCormick." When the war heated up and Wilson tangled once again with *The New Republic*'s editors, whose English backer, Richard Elmhirst, was lobbying strenuously for American intervention, he took "a sort of America Firster position," she said (referring to the wartime alliance of conservative isolationists known as the America First Committee), but with "socialist trimmings."

As for McCarthy herself, writing in *The New Republic* in the fall of 1940, she declared: "for most of us, the war has been a rather ghastly kind of entertainment, more heartrending—yes, and more exciting, more dangerous—than the Lindbergh baby or the Johnstown flood." That was before Pearl Harbor, and before the existence of the German death camps became known in the United States; and what she was deploring (in an omnibus review of war correspondents) was the absence of serious investigative reporting. Still, something of the remoteness of the war for American intellectuals during these early years is captured by the questions McCarthy asked in 1940:

Can Hitler survive a victory? Will satisfied fascism retain the same character as hungry fascism? What is the new world-state that Hitler is planning? Is there sabotage? Is there resistance? Is there anything left of the socialist movement? Is there any hope for revolution if Hitler is stalemated?—and what if he is not?

Odd questions, which could only have been asked in the wake of the Hitler-Stalin pact in 1939. German military missions, of course, were advancing across Eastern Europe. Norway had been invaded; Finland from the other side. Leopold of Belgium had surrendered; France had fallen. A scandal had just broken in England concerning a group of British industrialists and financiers who had sabotaged production to keep prices up. And an army of American correspondents had failed to scoop a single "story." They were always "looking the other way," McCarthy noted. Nevertheless, one can't help but be startled today by the relative aplomb with which an American intellectual ceded Europe to Hitler in 1940.

During the winter, McCarthy had put together another Theatre Chronicle for *Partisan Review*, in which the hawk-eyed Dwight Macdonald thought he detected a certain softening. "Please tell Mary I think her Saroyan piece very nice," he wrote Wilson early in 1940 (after informing the latter of a one-third cut *PR* was making in Wilson's essay on the young Lenin), "though personally I could have preferred a little more gall and less honey. . . ." Titled "An Innocent on Broadway," McCarthy's review of two plays by William Saroyan, who was far from popular with intellectuals in New York, was a striking instance of her willingness to bend in the face of theatre that reminded her of 'deepest America.'

Saroyan was an improvement over the "third-rate" talents of Clifford Odets and John Steinbeck, who suffered from "a kind of auto-intoxication," in McCarthy's view; "they are continually plagiarizing themselves . . . and their frequent ascents into 'fine writing' are punctuated with pauses for applause that are nearly audible." Alongside them, William Saroyan, "puerile and arrogant and sentimental" as he often appeared in public, was "the real thing." As an artist, that is. "Saroyan as a public figure does an impersonation of Saroyan, but as a writer he plays straight." Unlike either Steinbeck or Odets, he stood outside what McCarthy called "the literary rackets—the Hollywood racket, the New York cocktail-party racket, and the Stalinist racket," which to her mind had become "practically indistinguishable."

The column is punched out like a wireless, without a Latinate turn of phrase:

> William Saroyan has been in the writing business for eight years. He still retains his innocence. It is as valuable to him as an artist as virginity to Deanna Durbin. To keep it, he has, of course, had to follow a strict regimen. . . . That is, he has had to fight off ideas, Movements, Sex, and Commercialism.

Saroyan's "innocence" was his romance with the "old America"; not the historical past but the theatrical past of vaudeville—which Mary McCarthy, one reads between the lines, is soft on, too. Reviewing *The Time of Your Life*, she revels in the old-time acts: W. C. Fields as Kit Carson, the trapper; Jimmy Durante as Harry the hoofer; the boy out of a job who is the stooge. ". . . [L]ike an evening of vaudeville," she observes, Saroyan's play "is good when it engages the fancy and bad when it engages the feelings."

In this review, McCarthy reveals a side of herself that few contemporaries suspected. She *likes* these sentimental burlesques—especially the "boaster who is both a fraud and not a fraud, an impostor and a kind of saint," who also appears in the second play under review, *My Heart's in the Highlands*. More than William Saroyan's " 'gentle people,' " this character, she suggests, is a genuine national type, one that belonged to the frontier. It was Paul Bunyan and "also the barker. But the tradition is dead now," she concludes (having recently returned from the West). "It died when the frontier closed on the West Coast at some point in Saroyan's childhood." The barker had become "an invisible radio announcer," and the "genial, fraudulent, patent-medicine man" had turned into "a business house, with a public relations counsel"—"for such anomalous human beings could only thrive under nomadic conditions of life."

It didn't occur to her then—how could it?—that the type would reassert itself on the frontiers of the literary world. In American writers as dissimilar as William Burroughs, James Baldwin, Dwight Macdonald, Norman Mailer, and Mary McCarthy herself, there is more than a touch of the 'impostor' who is also, on occasion, 'a kind of saint.'

12

Writing Well Is the Best Revenge

"A proud, bitter smile formed on her lips, as

she saw herself as a citadel of socialist virginity, that could

be taken and taken again, but never truly subdued."

—MARY MCCARTHY, "THE MAN IN THE BROOKS BROTHERS SHIRT"

Your following hasn't forgotten you, be assured!" Dwight Macdonald reminded Mary McCarthy early in 1940. "You must both come down and see us and get 'up' on left politics, which becomes ever more complex." Dwight's invitation must have struck a bittersweet note, for Mary still felt herself to be part of the *Partisan Review* group, but separated now by a burned-up bridge (Rahv), a new baby, and a husband with an overweening desire to manage her affairs.

Reuel was not a problem; despite their uncertain finances, Wilson always insisted that Mary have a nurse. It was his *insistence* on this and other points that was problematical, as when he *insisted* that Mary make up her mind "not to let other things get between you and your writing: otherwise you don't do either your writing or the household to your own satisfaction." Reuel's father, of course, did require tending, but when McCarthy was up against a deadline, as she was, for example, in the fall of 1941 when she was pulling the Margaret Sargent stories together for publication as a novel, Wilson insisted that Mary not "worry about my lunch and breakfast. Just fix what you want for yourself and I'll get along. . . . If we haven't got a cook, we can go out to dinner part of the time."

It was on the question of money that his superintendence had become extreme. In 1980, McCarthy told an interviewer how Wilson made her put both her inheritance from the Minneapolis grain-elevator

stock, then yielding around fifteen hundred dollars a year, and whatever she earned from her writing into his bank account. "I couldn't
have signature power on his account," she remembers; "I had to ask
him for a nickel to make a telephone call." For a while Wilson even
refused to provide her with a regular household allowance. He held the
checkbook and hired and fired the domestic help. Nor would he allow
her to drive, despite the fact, or maybe because of it, that he had never
learned to drive himself. "He was very hard to oppose," McCarthy
said, "because he was so stubborn and so mean and so violent when
drinking"—which was also a problem, especially in the evenings.

"The daytime Edmund was a marvelous companion," Mary Meigs
recalls in her memoir, "with his enthusiasm for everything under the
sun. . . ." It was after he'd been drinking at night, Meigs writes, that
the "Minotaur" came out. Mary and Edmund's Wellfleet neighbor
Adelaide Walker remembers Wilson as the only person she ever knew
who could drink so much and still turn out first-rate writing. More
often, though, he would finish a piece of work after being shut up in
his study for days, and then start drinking " 'in a perfectly civilized
way' " until he'd drunk up everything in the house. He would drink for
days, Walker recalls, and then go to bed and be sick (though Mary
remembers him bouncing back with astonishing rapidity) and not
drink for a while. Only excessive consumption, however, seemed capable of triggering a period of reflection and sobriety. And both states
were bracketed in the end by a steady state of drinking " 'more or less
normally,' " as Walker relates it, but in a way that made him " 'very
mean and satirical.' "

In any event, Mary wanted her own checking account, and so they
fought. "I finally thought this was absolutely mad," she said in 1980;
even her psychiatrist agreed that maybe she was right, which was
significant: "usually they told you to *avoid* change in your life arrangements." She took a stand, "and he gave in, and I had my own bank
account," she recalled, "and that was the end of it." With her income,
she eventually bought a secondhand Ford.

From McCarthy's perspective, there was a little of the pinchpenny
dictator Uncle Myers in Edmund Wilson, though one can see Wilson's
side of the struggle to make ends meet. And once again, writing became
the best revenge, as it had long ago in Minneapolis when Mary had
begun writing little essays and poems. Myers, of course, had beaten her
with a razor strop after she won an essay contest—while Wilson all but
chained her to the typewriter. "I would have never written fiction, I
think, if it hadn't been for him," she stated in 1980. In the early 1940s,

McCarthy's circumstances couldn't have been more different than they were in the early 1920s, but there was something familiar in the extremity of her isolation with Wilson that soon led her to turn her typewriter into a searchlight on herself, her recent past, and the company she kept—including his.

At the end of 1939, something else had happened to cut her loose from her moorings. Shortly after Christmas, a fire had broken out in the room that Harold Johnsrud rented at the Hotel Brevoort in New York. He had fled the building with everyone else, but then returned to rescue the manuscript of a new play, when he collapsed of smoke inhalation. He was rescued by firemen and rushed to the hospital, where he died the next day. Incredibly, John Porter had also just died in Mexico, of a fever after a spell in jail for overstaying his visa. And when Mary took Reuel to Seattle in the summer of 1939, she had learned that her first seducer, Forrest Crosby, was dead, along with a young man named Mark Sullivan, a friend of her uncle Harold Preston's from the University of Washington, who had befriended Mary in her teens and given her her first glimpse of what it meant to be an intellectual. The cortege was crowded with old friends and lovers, and she was only twenty-eight.

Philip Rahv, who was very much alive, suddenly turned up in Provincetown in the summer of 1940, married to Nathalie Swan—an event that McCarthy insisted had come as no surprise. Opinion in New York had it that Philip had married Nathalie on the rebound; and there were some, like William Barrett, who pointed out that in Nathalie, the penniless Rahv, who was always hunting for grants for himself and his magazine, had found "a perpetual Guggenheim." In any event, Nathalie Swan was the first of two beautiful American heiresses whom Rahv—whose taste in women was as aristocratic as his taste in literature—would marry. On the Cape, the Rahvs and Wilsons spent a few tense evenings together, and then Edmund, who pronounced Philip's arrival in extremely poor taste, let it be known that he didn't want his wife to see him.

Wilson had just agreed to return to *The New Republic*, and while he would resign before the next year was out in protest over the editors' promotion of the British war effort (as Edmund called it), he suddenly decided that the job required a return to Stamford. In October, he moved Mary and Reuel back to Trees, and Mary resumed her regular appointments with Dr. Richard Frank. After the death of her Grandfather Preston in 1938, and the other deaths, now there was only Edmund in the suburban fastness of Connecticut, and the ghosts of the self she began to resurrect on the analyst's couch and deploy in fiction.

Somehow, amidst the various lives and double lives that she had led, "the ordinary, indispensable self," as McCarthy put it in the preface to the first edition of *The Company She Keeps*, had been lost. "The home address of the self, like that of the soul," she wrote, was "not to be found in the book." But the book, which had assumed the shape of a novel after Maria Leiper, an editor at Simon & Schuster, first proposed the idea, would show where the 'self' had gone in search of a home, and what it learned each time it failed to find one.

With "The Man in the Brooks Brothers Shirt," the third and, half a century later, still the most remarkable story in the series, Mary McCarthy's search would also reveal a unique ability to depict the human comedy of sex from the standpoint of the hunter and the hunted both—in this case, a young woman who was one and the same.

II

The new man who came into the club car was coatless. He was dressed in gray trousers and a green shirt of expensive material. . . . His tie matched the green of the monogram, and his face, which emerged rather sharply from this tasteful symphony in cool colors, was blush pink. The greater part of his head appeared to be pink, also, though actually toward the back there was a good deal of closely cropped pale-gray hair that harmonized with his trousers. He looked, she decided, like a middle-aged baby, like a young pig, like something in a seed catalogue. In any case, he was plainly Out of the Question, and the hope that had sprung up, as for some reason it always did, with the sound of a new step soft on the flowered Pullman carpet, died a new death. Already the trip was half over.

And so it begins, a crisply tailored drama from the 1940s, as smart and durable today as it was at the creation. The man crowds himself into a seat directly opposite Meg, who is carrying on "a well-bred, well-informed, liberal conversation" with someone else. Immediately, she realizes that he has decided to pick her up, which fills her with contempt. Nevertheless, her voice rises a little in response to him. He makes a few sallies, crude, but still. . . . He claims to know Vincent Sheean (the author of the book she's discussing) "personally." Sheean might not be much—"but in the cultural atmosphere of the Pullman car, Sheean was a titan." And Meg is touched by the man's effort to please her. When she is left alone with him, however, she gets cold feet. He is sure to be tiresome. The monogrammed shirt spells out the self-made man:

> She could foresee the political pronouncements, the pictures of the wife and children, the hand squeezed under the table. . . . It was true, she was always wanting something exciting and romantic to happen; but it was not really romantic to be the-girl-who-sits-in-the-club-car-and-picks-up-men.

Meg shudders at the predatory view of herself that the moment has disclosed. " 'I don't know why you make yourself so cheap,' " she hears her aunt's voice saying. But of course nothing is going to happen; she's on her way to tell her aunt in Portland that she's going to be married again. To the "fiancé" from "Cruel and Barbarous Treatment," John Porter, in life. Mary McCarthy, by the way, was reviewing Vincent Sheean's *Personal History* around the time of her actual affair with the man on the Union Pacific. The story is an omnigatherum: bits and pieces of an old summer harvest, shored up against the winter.

The man's pass, when it comes, is more unorthodox than Meg expected. He asks simply, " 'Can I talk to you?' " And she replies, " 'What have you got to say?' " which embarrasses her—"as if Broadway had answered Indiana." He further surprises her by evincing some knowledge of an "obscure revolutionary novelist" whose advance proofs she is reading. And then he catches her at her own game. She has asked him his business, and when he answers genially, " 'I'm a traveling salesman,' " he sees the panic dart across her face. " 'If it sounds any better to you,' he says, 'I'm in the steel business.' " Meg assures him disapprovingly that it doesn't. " 'You're a pink, I suppose,' he says, as if he hadn't noticed anything. 'It'd sound better to you if I said I was a burglar.' " Which makes her laugh at herself. (George North, the original Brooks Brothers man, worked for American Radiator and Standard Sanitary, a plumbing concern.)

Soon Meg is persuaded to share a bottle of whiskey with the man in his compartment. "In a kind, almost fatherly voice" (irresistible to Meg, who is thankful to him for having "understood and spared her"), he has promised to keep the door open. The golden highballs taste the way they look in the White Rock ads. The white coat of the Negro waiter, the traveling man's smart brown calf luggage, her own bare

arm rising and falling "in short parabolas of gesture," the open door
that allows the other passengers to gaze in at them—all these things
suggest to Meg that a drama is under way.

As it is. While Meg plays the Great Lady, for her companion she
is the Bohemian Girl: a revelation to him. He quizzes her like a wondering provincial. An exquisite foreplay has begun. She begins to see
herself in the man's eyes, and to recover

> a feeling of uniqueness and identity . . . she had once had when,
> at twenty, she had come to New York and had her first article
> accepted by a liberal weekly, but which had slowly been rubbed
> away by four years of being on the inside of the world that had
> looked magic from Portland, Oregon. Gradually, now, she was
> becoming very happy, for she knew . . . in this compartment that
> she was beautiful and gay and clever, and worldly and innocent,
> serious and frivolous, capricious and trustworthy, witty and sad,
> bad and really good . . . all at the same time. She could feel the
> power running in her, like a medium on a particularly good night.

Which recalls Edith Wharton's dazzling Mrs. Hazeldean again: "Yes;
it always amused her at first: the gradual dawn of attraction . . . the
blood rising to the face. . . ."

As these various personalities "bloomed on the single stalk of her
ego," Meg is suffused with "a great glow of charity." The man, too,
must be admitted into the mystery. She begins to question him gently,
spurred on by his mulish shyness ("I'm just a suburban businessman"),
and by the knowledge of her talent, which excels at close encounters
with strangers—"where the cards . . . were laid on the table till love
became a wonderful slow game of double solitaire and nothing that
happened afterwards counted . . . beside those first few hours of
self-revelation." For Wharton's heroine, this talent was her "only
accomplishment!" Meg, of course, is more versatile.

The man begins to talk about his buddies from the war, about the
shirts that he orders from Brooks Brothers by the dozen, about his
wife, Leonie, a Vassar girl and Book-of-the-Month Club member, who
thinks he's stodgy, and about Frank and Joe, his sons. Leonie, he says,
" 'will certainly be excited . . . when she hears that I met somebody
from the *Liberal* on this trip. But she'll never be able to understand
why you wasted your time talking to poor old Bill.' " The girl smiles
at him. " 'I *like* to talk to you,' she said, suppressing the fact that
nothing on earth would have induced her to talk to Leonie."

The slow game quickens when the steel man reveals a sneaking preference for the Socialist candidate, Norman Thomas, in the next election. He talks about the "grand time" he had in the last war, "Mr. Morgan's war," and how there's a new war coming that isn't going to be like that: " 'Because this one will be ideological, and it'll be too damned serious. . . . I'd like to see this country stay out of it. That's why I'm for Thomas.' " Meg's eyes fill with tears, perhaps because of the whiskey. " 'I've never known anyone like you,' " she says. " 'You're not the kind of businessman I write editorials against.' "

Whereupon the man begins to rail against " 'you people' "—the leftists—who are " 'never going to get anywhere in America with that proletariat stuff. Every workingman wants to live the way I do. He doesn't want to live the way he does.' "

By now, Meg has begun to suspect that these lapses in character are willful. The man has made up his mind to thwart her, to drag her down to his level:

> It was like the resistance of the patient to the psychoanalyst, of the worker to the Marxist: she was offering to release him from the chains of habit, and he was standing up and clanking those chains . . . impudently in her face. On the other hand, she knew, just as the analyst knows, just as the Marxist knows, that some-where in his character there was the need of release . . . and there was, furthermore, a kindness . . . which would make him pretend to be a little better than he was, if that would help her to think better of herself.

The little adventure has moved to a new level. Against her better judgment, *"She liked him."* It wasn't sexual; for as the whiskey disap-peared from the bottle, his face acquired a more porcine look, which made her "talk to him with a large, remote stare, as if he were an audience of several hundred people." It wasn't his air of having money, either, which helped but hindered, too. Perhaps it was the homespun quality of his talk "which took her straight back to her childhood and to her father, gray-slippered, in a brown leather chair." Or "his plain delight in her," which was shrewd, she decided, for in a gross sense he was clearly a connoisseur of women. But mainly it was "a vein of sympathy and understanding" she had glimpsed in him, which made him available to any human being, just as he was available to any novelist as a reader. This availability did not proceed from "stupidity," as she had presumed in the club car, "but from a restless and perenially hopeful curiosity" (not unlike her own).

Suddenly, Meg sees the man as "a lonely dinosaur" who has

survived from a bygone American frontier. His imago blurs with her father's and with the images of Roman busts in the Metropolitan Museum, marble faces of businessmen, "shockingly rugged and modern and recognizable after the smooth tranquility of the Greeks. Those early businessmen had been omnivorous, too, great readers, eaters, travelers, collectors, and, at the beginning, provincial also, small-town men newly admitted into world-citizenship, faintly uneasy but feeling their oats."

The little adventure has acquired sublime dimensions. "But Love has pitched his Mansion in the place of excrement," writes Yeats; while sex, as Mary McCarthy suggests, will always pitch its tent in the imagination. In the course of the conversation, Meg has "glided all the way from aversion to tenderness." She sees the man now as "a man without a country, and felt a desire to reinstate him. But where?" He has become boisterously merry, lighted up with memories of the war, Paris, Notre Dame, target practice in the Alps. Outside, the Dust Bowl rolls by, remote as a Surrealist painting. " 'I suppose I'm boring you,' " the man says abruptly, but he hasn't had such a good time since the war, he explains, and so the girl reminds him of it, he doesn't know why. " 'I know,' " Meg says. " 'It's because you've made a new friend, and you probably haven't made one for twenty years. . . . Nobody does, after they're grown-up."

A new stage is reached as the two strangers begin to share confidences about their respective mates. Marriage is not the same as friendship, the man agrees. " 'If you even *think* you'd like to marry a girl, you have to start lying to her. . . . You have to protect yourself. I don't mean about cheating—that's small potatoes,' " he adds. A meditative look crosses his face. " 'Jesus Christ,' he said, 'I don't even *know* Leonie any more, and vice versa, but that's the way it ought to be.' " A wife's job is to have a nice house and nice kids and give good parties. . . . If Leonie understood him, probably they'd both go to pot.

Once again, tears fill the girl's eyes. " 'I was in love with my husband,' she said. 'We understood each other. He never had a thought he didn't tell me.' " The man reminds her that she got a divorce: Somebody must have misunderstood somebody *somewhere* along the line. But Meg rushes on about how touched she always was by her husband's "boyish neck (the face had not been boyish, but prematurely lined) bared like an early martyr's for the sword. 'How could I have done it?' she whispered to herself again, as she still did nearly every day." (Harold Johnsrud, whose face was also prematurely lined, had died not long before this story was written, an event that

might have provoked a reassessment of the marriage. Then again, the
emotion welling up between these lines points to Rahv as the forsaken
one.) But Meg wonders: "Could she not say that all that conjugal
tenderness had been a brightly packaged substitute for the Real Thing,
for the long carnal swoon she had never quite been able to execute in
the marriage bed?"

It grows dark and the waiter returns to serve little brook trout on
crested plates. The conversation dips into ribaldry. Meg is determined
to preserve the decorum of the scene, but she cannot restrain herself.
Everything she says seems to be barbed with sexual innuendo. It was
always like that. When she was a schoolgirl she exchanged dirty jokes
with college boys, who then stopped the car and lunged at her, while
all the time she only wanted to be a good fellow, to show that she was
sophisticated and grown-up, *never* to let them know that her father
didn't allow her to go out with boys! "This freedom of speech of hers
was a kind of masquerade of sexuality," Meg reflects, "like the rubber
breasts that homosexuals put on for drag. . . ." She hopes the man
won't leap at her like other men have when the impersonation succeeded. The response never failed to frighten her: "For it was all
wrong, it was unnatural; art is to be admired, not acted on, and the
public does not belong on the stage. . . ." But once again the man has
spared her. He listens to her as calmly as a priest: "the nightmare lifted;
free will was restored to her."

The next morning, Meg wakes up in a Wyoming station. "Evan-
ston?" she wonders, forgetting the day, the night, the man, herself.
When her naked body brushes his naked body, "waves of shame begin
to run through her, as fragments of the night before presented themselves for inspection." They had sung songs and disturbed other passengers, so the door had been shut. The man had come around the
table and kissed her greedily. She had fought him off for a while, but
she felt tired and kind and thought, Why not? There was something
peculiar about the lovemaking that she couldn't remember. (This was
the hardest scene to write, McCarthy wrote Fred Dupee at *Partisan
Review*: "It kept getting too torrid for the rest of the story." Her
psychiatrist had explained to her why she was having trouble with it,
she told Fred, and after that it was all right.) There was some comfort
in the vagueness, "but recollection quickly stabbed her again:

> There were (oh, holy Virgin!) four-letter words that she had been
> forced to repeat, and, at the climax, a rain of blows on her but-

tocks that must surely (dear God!) have left bruises. She must be careful not to let her aunt see her without any clothes on . . . and [she] remembered how once she had visualized sins as black marks on the white soul. This sin, at least, no one would see. But all at once she became aware of the significance of the sheets. The bed had been made up. And that meant that the Pullman porter . . . She closed her eyes, exhausted, unable to finish the thought.

Perhaps it was not too late—and Meg suddenly envisions herself in a black dress, her face scrubbed and powdered, hair combed, sitting "standoffishly" in her seat, "watching Utah and Nevada go by and reading her publisher's copy of a new *avant-garde* novel. It *could* be done." Stealthily, she climbs out of bed and collects her clothes, including an oft-mended pair of crepe de chine underpants fastened with a safety pin. She gropes around the floor for a missing garter, then "with a final sob" strips off her stockings, steps barefoot into her shoes, and prepares to leave. The man snaps on the reading light above the berth and stares at her in bewilderment: " 'Dearest,' he said, 'what in the world are you doing?' " Meg bends down to kiss him politely good-bye on the forehead. He pulls her down beside him. He looks fat and the short hair on his chest is gray. " 'You can't go,' he said, quite simply. . . . 'I love you. I'm crazy about you. This is the most wonderful thing that's ever happened to me. You come to San Francisco with me and we'll go to Monterey, and I'll fix it up with Leonie to get a divorce.' "

Meg is horrified to see that the man's body is trembling. He is serious. "It was as if some terrible natural force were loose in the compartment." Suddenly, "her own squeamishness and sick distaste, which a moment before had seemed virtuous in her, now appeared heartless, even frivolous, in the face of his emotion."

"But I'm engaged," she said, rather thinly.

"You're not in love with him," he said. "You couldn't have done what you did last night if you were." . . .

"I was tight," she said flatly in a low voice.

"A girl like you doesn't let a man have her just because she's drunk."

She bowed her head. . . .

"Kiss me," he said, but she pulled away.

"I have to throw up."

When she lifts the upholstered toilet seat and vomits, the man watches her evenly from the bed. Meg wipes the tears from her eyes and leans against the wall. " 'Poor little girl,' " he says tenderly. 'You feel bad, don't you?' " And he unpacks a fresh bottle of whiskey from a suitcase. " 'I'll have to save the Bourbon for the conductor,' he said in a matter-of-fact, friendly voice. 'He'll be around later on, looking for his cut.' "

Meg laughs, she can't help it, but she does. The smell of the whiskey gags her, yet her spirits lift. What about the porter? she asks, and the man tells her that he already squared it with him last night. " 'Mr. Breen, you sure done better than most,' ' " was what the porter said. " 'Oh!' " she gasps, covering her face; and the man laughs, and Meg peers up at him shamefaced, and giggles. "The vulgarity was more comforting to her than any assurances of love. If the seduction . . . could be seen in farcical terms," McCarthy writes, "she could accept and even, wryly, enjoy it. The world of farce was a sort of moral underworld, a cheerful, well-lit hell where a Fall was only a prat-fall. . . ."

And not a sentence of marriage, for instance, as Mary McCarthy's affair with Edmund Wilson had become. The more closely one reads "The Man in the Brooks Brothers Shirt," the more one is impressed by the improbable intensity of emotion. Could a Babbitt-like businessman from Pittsburgh *alone* have inspired the tale? Or had something of the misbegotten affair with Wilson—who was also fat and over forty and very 'serious'—spilled over and touched the story with an urgency, however comic, which is nearly without parallel in McCarthy's fiction?

Meg is much taken by the new "atmosphere of the . . . stag line," which is "more bracing . . . than the air of Bohemia." The tips, the bourbon, indicate a certain competence. It was what was missing in the men she knew in New York—"the shrewd buyer's eye, the swift, brutal appraisal." And she thinks about how in one way or another all the men she has known have been lame ducks—"too easily pleased"—and wonders whether she has squandered her life in a kind of self-imposed exile.

When the man puts his arms around her, saying, " 'My God . . . if this had only happened ten years ago!' " Meg is brought back to earth. She has fooled herself about him, too, she sees; time has also made a lame duck out of him. She remains rigid in his embrace, "hard as nails"; but then she begins to *feel* hard, and so she begins to hug him warmly, kissing him carefully on the mouth. A "glow of self-sacrifice" illuminates her. "This, she thought . . . is going to be the only real act of charity I have ever performed in my life . . . it was the mortification of the flesh achieved through the performance of the act of pleasure."

She helps the man remove her dress, and stretches herself out on the berth "like a slab of white lamb on an altar." She waits for him to exhaust himself, "for the indignity to be over," while contemplating the elusive image of herself, "fully dressed, with the novel, in her Pullman seat," and she knew, "with the firmest conviction, that for once she was really and truly good, not hard or heartless at all."

" 'You need a bath,' " the man says sharply, raising himself up on an elbow and looking her over as she lay relaxed on the rumpled sheet. " 'Get up,' he went on, 'and I'll ring for the porter to fix it for you.' " Meg springs to attention, her lips quivering. It was the first wound he had dealt her, an old wound that took her

> back to the teachers who could smoke cigarettes and gossip with you in the late afternoon and then rebuke you in the morning class, back to the relations who would talk with you as an equal and then tell your aunt you were too young for silk stockings, back through all the betrayers, the friendly enemies . . . back to the mother who could love you and then die.

She doesn't want a bath, she tells him, but the man presses the bell, and, when the bath is ready, shoves her into the corridor in his Brooks Brothers dressing gown with a cake of English toilet soap in her hand.

It is in the ladies lounge that Meg feels a spasm of "genuine socialist ardor":

> For the first time in her life, she truly hated luxury, hated Brooks Brothers and Bergdorf Goodman and Chanel and furs and good food. . . . By a queer reversal, the very safety pin in her under-wear . . . came to look to her now like a symbol of moral fastidi-ousness. . . . A proud, bitter smile formed on her lips, as she saw herself as a citadel of socialist virginity, that could be taken and taken again, but never truly subdued. The man's whole assault on her now seemed to have had a political character; it was an inci-dental atrocity in the long class war.

But some morbid competitiveness will not allow her to let the man outdistance her in feeling, and she remains in his compartment. Later, after a breakfast of corned beef hash and fish cakes, served by the waiter of the night before on the collapsible table, she finds herself rising to the occasion again. "There was to be no more love-making, she saw, and from the moment she felt sure of this, she began to be a little bit in love." The long day passes in a desultory, lingering conversation. "Dreamy confidences were murmured, and trailed off . . . like the dialogue in a play by Chekhov." The sagebrush country slips by the window, reminding Meg sweetly of the contemporary wasteland. Once again, "the man's life lay before her; it was almost as if she could reach out and touch it, poke it, explore it, shine it up, and give it back to him."

She could not change it, however. As Meg listens to the man talk about his childhood, his first affair, the war, his job—which is the nexus of his personal friendships—his family, she knew that the actual sharing of his life was no longer a question. He was at peace with himself, and with her. "She had brought it off, and now she was almost reluctant to leave him."

"I love you," she said suddenly. "I didn't before, but now I do."

The man glanced sharply at her.

"Then you won't get off the train . . . ?"

"Oh, yes," she said, for now at last she could be truthful. . . . "I'll certainly get off. One reason I love you, I suppose, is because I am getting off."

"And one reason I'm going to let you do it," he said, "is because you love me."

She lowered her eyes, astonished, once more, at his shrewdness.

Naturally they meet again. On Meg's return trip the train stops in Cleveland for a few hours and Mr. Breen gets on with a corsage of purple orchids and a bottle of whiskey, *"in memoriam."* He was still begging her to marry him, but a business conference prevented him from riding with her to New York. When he drops in to see her in her tiny Village apartment later during a business trip to the city, he has become more critical of her, more the businessman and less the suitor. A little later, she receives a duck he has shot in Virginia. The last time she sees him in New York, his friendliness returns over double martinis at Longchamps—"and he begged her with tears in his eyes to 'forget all this red nonsense and remember that you're just your father's little girl at heart.' " When her father died, he must have seen the notice in the papers. "SINCEREST CONDOLENCES," he wired. "YOU HAVE LOST THE BEST FRIEND YOU WILL EVER HAVE." She tore the telegram up immediately. How banal, she thought: "It would have been dreadful if anyone had seen it."

* * *

"Tidings from the Whore," was how Delmore Schwartz referred privately to "The Man in the Brooks Brothers Shirt" when it was published in *Partisan Review* in the summer of 1941—after having been turned down by Robert Penn Warren at *The Southern Review*. (The story was full of "brilliant writing," Warren wrote Mary, "but . . . the sex episode probably makes it unusable for us," a judgment the editors communicated "with some humiliation.") At first, there had been sentiment among *PR*'s editors against printing the story on the grounds that it was journalism, not fiction; but it was too good to be true. A rumor was started by James Laughlin at New Directions, which circulates still (Lionel Abel for one believes it), that Mr. Breen was really Wendell Willkie. The mythmaking had begun. And Delmore Schwartz was not the only one who tended to regard Mary McCarthy as a fallen woman. But all things considered the story broke like a comet over the heads of McCarthy's literary generation; and it established her reputation as a writer, a *rough* writer, and as a woman, a *tough* woman— neither of which she was at all.

To Barrett, Meg Sargent was "almost a dramatized thesis" of McCarthy's chosen motto from Chaucer: I am mine own woman well at ease. But Mary McCarthy uses the motto ironically, just as she regarded her own bohemian celebrity in the Village ironically. In "The Man in the Brooks Brothers Shirt" the line from Chaucer marks an ironic transition from Meg Sargent's relief that "the nightmare [had] lifted" to her rude awakening in the steel man's berth the next day. For that moment, she had become, in effect, the *man*'s woman, and she was *not* at ease.

"We did not know it then," Barrett continues in *The Truants,* "but [McCarthy] was in fact firing the first salvo in the feminist war that now rages within our society." But that was not quite true, either. Such episodes in *The Company She Keeps* are no more a "salvo in the feminist war" than William Burroughs's *Naked Lunch* is a blow against drug addiction. Barrett's accolade, if it is an accolade, seems just as misplaced as Alfred Kazin's denunciation, in *Starting Out in the Thirties*, that McCarthy's stories display "that bleak, unsparing, suspicious view of human nature which is so much admired by reactionaries because it leaves the lower classes so little reason to rebel." As if either 'reactionaries' or the 'lower classes' read Mary McCarthy's fiction (or anyone else's) for reasons to rebel.

"You don't have to tell anybody it's a book written by a woman," William Carlos Williams wrote Simon & Schuster in 1942, after the publisher had sent *The Company She Keeps* to the celebrated poet for comment; "Women smell and think differently from men." The book disturbed Williams for "its plodding murderousness." He couldn't say more "than that Mary McCarthy, as Mary McCarthy, is something to be surmounted—and a man had better be feeling fit when he takes her on," which was a curious kind of literary criticism. McCarthy's male reviewers have often displayed the liveliest fascination for the men in her fiction, as if a Mr. Breen or a Jim Barnett, the hero of "Portrait of the Intellectual as a Yale Man," are sorely handicapped surrogates for themselves. William Carlos Williams suggested that McCarthy's fiction "is written principally for those it attacks," a plausible observation—although "attacks" hardly describes the fun she has with the men in her fiction. "The men are pretty foul," Williams concluded, "but she really likes them, they complement her."

Female reviewers have also projected themselves into McCarthy's trysting spots with unseemly results. "[F]rom the embarrassing safety pin in her underwear to the dirty words [Mr. Breen] asks her to repeat during her copulation, to the literal vomit in her mouth the next morning, to the bath he insists she take because she smells, Miss McCarthy spares the reader nothing," the critic Eleanor Widmer laments, as if reading Mary McCarthy is akin to being molested in a health club. "Is her easy virtue to be held for or against her?" Miss Widmer wonders, reminding the reader darkly that "the gains of the sexual revolution of the 60s had not permeated the 40s and 50s, and that McCarthy ran the risk of appearing as a loose woman."

When reviewers question a novelist's virtue, smell, or suspicious view of human nature, something is up. With "The Man in the Brooks Brothers Shirt," Mary McCarthy stepped on the lion's tail, that stricken sad-eyed beast of public opinion, with the thorn in its foot. But it was too soon for her to ponder the meaning of her reviewers' agitation, or to see the opportunities that a critical reception committee bristling with high priests and priestesses might pose for her.

There were three more stories to write: two raids on the literary rackets, "The Genial Host" and "Portrait of the Intellectual as a Yale Man," and the intensely introspective "Ghostly Father, I Confess," which would illuminate the preceding five stories—and, in the opinion of McCarthy's old editor from the *New Republic*, Malcolm Cowley, "save" *The Company She Keeps* "from the ruck of novels." "Mr. Cowley had no intention of being patronizing toward the author," Mr. Cowley assured a *New Republic* reader who complained of his patronizing review of *The Company She Keeps* in June 1942. "He doesn't write that way, with pin pricks; he tries very hard to say what he thinks. . . . He thinks in this case that the heroine is presented as a perfect bitch," Cowley continued, "redeemed—and for god's sake why not say redeemed?—by her honesty. That's what the heroine thinks too: 'And yet, she thought, walking on, she could still detect her own frauds. . . .' All this on the last page, where she tries to sum up her character."

At home with Wilson, meanwhile, married life retained its unquiet side. Every year added a new address to Mary and Edmund's comings and goings: Stamford, Chicago, Truro, Wellfleet, Stamford, New York, Wellfleet. . . . After the summer of 1941, when for four thousand dollars, mostly borrowed from Edmund's mother in New Jersey, Wilson bought an old house on Money Hill in Wellfleet, and for another thousand, borrowed from his publishers, winterized it, the Wellfleet address remained the same. But now their trips to New York grew more frequent, especially for Mary—who took an apartment by herself on Stuyvesant Square in the fall of 1942, when she began to see a new psychoanalyst, Dr. Abraham Kardiner, Dr. Frank having been drafted into the army. Reuel then remained on the Cape with his father, a nurse, and sometimes Rosalind, in a ménage à quatre with which Edmund Wilson was growing increasingly familiar.

13

War Babies

*"In my youth I thought that life
was Shakespearean, but it becomes more and more
obvious to me that it is Dostoyevskian."*

—DELMORE SCHWARTZ (1942)

N   ew York in the early 1940s was not as much fun as it had been
in the 1930s. For Mary McCarthy, the city soon became a home away
from the home she made with Edmund Wilson, and one where she
could still lose herself. But there was no mistaking the change in the
atmosphere, especially at parties, where anything might happen—as in
February 1942, when Mary and Edmund found themselves at a party
with Dawn Powell and the poet Rolfe Humphries, along with Lionel
Abel and Delmore Schwartz, and the Surrealist painter Matta had
suddenly proposed a game of truth or consequences in which everyone
was to take off their clothes.

Wilson, who William Barrett recalls was "truculantly silent" on
such occasions, had paid "Mr. Schwartz" a good deal of attention on
this particular night, calling him Schwartz after the second highball,
Delmore after the fifth, and Mr. Schwartz again after the eighth.
Delmore, for his part, had been thrown into an "immense depression"
by how "paralyzed" everyone seemed that evening, he wrote his wife,
Gertrude Buchman, in Cambridge. Nobody had anything to say or
only "foolish things" to say; no one was "going forward with their
work." The group was still haunted by what he called the period's
"post-Munich sensibility": a "complete hopelessness of perception
and feeling." In Eleanor Clark and Mary McCarthy, he thought he
discerned a "withdrawing attractiveness, mostly in a flattening out of

their features"; as if the new Zeitgeist that had followed first England's and then the Soviet Union's accommodation with Hitler had aged the generation prematurely, and tarnished the bright image of its women.

After his own brilliant debut in 1937, Delmore Schwartz's work was not going very well, and by 1943 his marriage was on the rocks. He was much preoccupied with Scott Fitzgerald's reflection about how in American lives there are no second acts. Probably he saw his own deteriorating fortunes playing themselves out in everyone around him. ("Am I coming up or are you going down?" he inquired of Mary McCarthy at a party at the Rahvs', after the two of them ran into each other at the door without their respective spouses for three weeks in succession. And the fact was that Mary had left him far behind.)

Looking back on these years as they are filtered through the letters, memoirs, and recollections of American intellectuals, one is struck by a common despairing note, a mood anticipated by Auden toward the end of 1939, when he found himself sitting alone in a Fifty-second Street dive in New York:

> Uncertain and afraid
> As the clever hopes expire
> Of a low dishonest decade. . . .
> All the conventions conspire
> To make this fort assume
> The furniture of home;
> Lest we should see where we are,
> Lost in a haunted wood,
> Children afraid of the night
> Who have never been happy or good

For Louise Bogan, Auden's dive might have been a wartime cocktail party at Philip and Nathalie Rahv's, where "the rooms were crowded with such an assortment of talent, stupidity, ugliness, beauty, sects, spies, *agents provocateurs* and just plain hangers-on, as was seldom seen. . . ." Writing Edmund Wilson in 1940, Malcolm Cowley conjured up a nightmare world run by intellectuals in which "all the naked egos that would be continually wounding and getting wounded, all the gossip, the spies. . . . the careerists, the turncoats" sounded like one of these parties. "Remember too that the character assassinations now so much in vogue . . . are nothing less than symbolic murders," Cowley added somewhat menacingly, considering that Wilson had just charged him with practicing "Stalinist character assassination of the most reckless and libelous sort" in *The New Republic*. "They would be real murders," Cowley concluded, "if the intellectuals controlled the state apparatus."

By the early 1940s, a few intellectuals, Cowley included, had begun to enter the state apparatus via Archibald MacLeish's new Office of Facts and Figures (soon renamed the Office of War Information). When the Dies committee began to go after fellow-travelers in government, in a burst of 'premature' anticommunism around 1941, Cowley left the OFF and joined the Rockefeller Foundation. With Lionel Trilling and the Princeton critic R. P. Blackmur, he formed the troika that directed the Rockefeller Foundation's wartime investments in American literature. For the Guggenheim Foundation, another Cowley 'hat' in the 1940s, he teamed up with Allen Tate—whose enthusiasm for the aristocratic traditions of the antebellum South made him no less useful to the Guggenheim fortune than did Cowley's battered allegiance to the Soviet Union. In 1943, Delmore Schwartz was approached by the State Department on behalf of his friend Will Barrett—whom Delmore "compared to Aristotle and Kant"—when Barrett was moving into Army intelligence.

By the start of the new decade, the 'conventions' of which Auden spoke were unraveling, not only the ideological ones but the more fundamental convention that American intellectuals had traditionally observed of maintaining a critical independence from established institutions. "When the Depression came two roads were left,/ War or Socialism: knowing the populace,/ can we be surprised at War's selection?" Delmore wrote in his journal, and he was right: More than anything else it was the war that dealt the coup de grace to the radicalism of the 1930s. It was the war that buried the idea of socialism, together with the New Deal, once the United States entered a military economy. And it was the war that gutted the concept of internationalism that was basic to Marxism.

For Jewish intellectuals, World War II, which was not just another imperial conflict like World War I, opened the door to the legitimization of nationalist feelings, as William Phillips has observed in *A Partisan View*. It also opened the door to Zionist impulses, once the reality of Hitler's war of extermination against the Jews became known; and Zionism, as opposed to the millenial social thought that flourished in the Diaspora, is intrinsically nationalist. And all these impulses accelerated the anti-Stalinism of the period, giving it a new coloration, a nationalist coloration, and turning it ultimately into a crusading anticommunism in the hands of a core of American intellectuals which became as fierce and unforgiving as any Cold War doctrine that emanated from Congress or the White House.

But this moves ahead of our story. It would be a few more years before the plaintive note sounded in Auden's poem turned mean, and the disappointed rebels of the 1930s began their counterattack on Marxism, the 'God that failed.' In the early 1940s, most writers in Mary McCarthy's circle were still governed by the beliefs of the 1930s. Especially during the early war years, *Partisan Review*'s editors were united in opposition to an American entrance into the European conflict. "We loathe and abominate fascism as the chief enemy of all culture, all real democracy, all social progress," declared a statement issued by the League for Cultural Freedom and Socialism in 1939, and published in *Partisan Review* with the endorsement of the editors. "But the last war showed only too clearly that we can have no faith in imperialist crusades to bring freedom to any people. Only the German people can free themselves of the fascist yoke." American writers and artists were advised to "help make articulate the strong opposition which the great majority of the American people still feel to our entry into the war. . . ."

"The psychology of the 1930s spilled over into the 1940s," Mary McCarthy observed in 1959. "You were supposed to be wised up about the War and not let yourself be a victim of propaganda," she explained, echoing the characteristic response of intellectuals to the Communist party a few years before. "When people like me (who were just liberals, not even Marxists) resisted the truth about the War, it was simply because we were afraid of making a mistake, of being 'taken in,'" she said. "We were in terror of being 'soft.'" When Philip Rahv broke ranks early in 1941, editorializing, "And yet in a certain sense this is *our* war," McCarthy, along with Dwight Macdonald and the critic Clement Greenberg, argued that Rahv was capitulating to bourgeois thinking.

Four years later, she would find herself crying in the dark during a British war documentary, watching the British army triumph over Rommel in the Africa campaign. And then she would give a blood transfusion "to relieve my feelings," just one—"to give regularly would have been to be a 'patriot.'" But it wasn't until the summer of 1945, when the war was over, that she would leave the 1930s behind and suddenly say what she "really thought," which was that "the war had had to be supported because the death camps had to be stopped and none of us had had a program for doing this."

In the meantime, McCarthy's early skepticism about the war made her a sharp-eyed critic of the manipulations of Hollywood propaganda, which transported the burning issues of history to a world of pure melodrama. At bottom the war movies revolved around the same old struggles of the "household deities," she stated in an omnibus review in 1944: "Bogart, Huston, Randolph Scott *vs.* character actors like Erich von Stroheim left over from the last war." Commenting on *The Purple Heart,* "unquestionably the worst war movie I have ever seen, but . . . the apotheosis of a type," she marveled at Hollywood's habit of converting the conflict in the Pacific into a "struggle between five or six Oriental character actors of terrifying physical aspect . . . and seven or eight recurrent American actors" who represent the forces of democracy, namely, "the Irishman, the Italian, the Jewish boy from Brooklyn, the farm boy from the South or the Middle West, and the upper class boy from the East, who is inevitably cast as the hero." Of *North Star* (whose screenwriter, Lillian Hellman, goes unmentioned), she deplored the romantic depiction of the Soviet Union as an "idyllic hamlet . . . that might be labeled Russian Provincial and put in a window by Sloane."

Reviewing wartime news broadcasts and the books of foreign correspondents, McCarthy made the prescient observation that "the closer we are brought by technical means to events, the less we know about them. . . . Americans were better informed about the progress of the Kaiser's war," she thought, "than they were about Franco's or are about Hitler's." The passion for undigested war news, she suggested, was a little bit like the passion for broadcast baseball. You could get a sounder digest of the game from the morning paper, but the fans are more interested in "the kinesthetic sensations . . . the sense of vicarious life and struggle." Referring to the "I can hear it now" genre in war reporting, she argued that the newsreels didn't make the war more "real," only "more familiar."

In the end, however, it was the British documentary *Desert Victory* that alerted McCarthy to her own "true feelings" about the war—which were that she was "horrified by the Luftwaffe and the Panzer divisions and pulling ardently for England to survive. If only England could survive without implicating us," by which she meant not the United States but "us personally as detached minds." After the Norway invasion and the Africa campaign indicated that England might *not* make it alone, then something like those "kinesthetic sensations" had taken over: "one's spontaneous feelings, oscillating between joy and despair," she recalled in 1959, could no longer be reconciled to the "rigid, learned ideology."

In Mary McCarthy's circle, only Dwight Macdonald, who resigned from *Partisan Review* in 1943 in protest over the magazine's
turnaround on the war, remained opposed to the participation of
American intellectuals in the general mobilization. Once intellectuals
tied themselves to "the bourgeois war machines," Macdonald warned
in the early 1940s, they gave up the "privilege" and the "duty" to
criticize "class values." Intellectuals only fooled themselves if they
believed they could pick up their progressive goals and resume the role
of an effective political or cultural opposition after the war. "In politics," he pointed out, "the mask molds the face. You become what you
do and say; you don't become what your reservations are."

And yet it was Macdonald who first opened the eyes of American
intellectuals to a disturbing implication of Hitler's death camps, one
that would further erode their faith in Marxism. Europe's Jews, he
observed in "The Responsibility of Peoples," were "murdered to grat-
ify a paranoid hatred, but for no reason of policy or advantage that I
can see." And he concluded that "the German atrocities in this war are
a phenomenon unique in modern history." Among Jewish intellectuals, only the émigré political philosopher Hannah Arendt had begun
publicly to ponder the implications of this fact; namely, that "systematic mass murder" strained "the framework and categories of our
political thought. . . ." German fascism was not just a monstrous
variation on capitalism, Arendt suggested, but the product of a complex and infinitely darker constellation of forces than any materialist
interpretation of history allowed. For this reason, she concluded,
"there is no political method for dealing with German mass crimes."

Insights such as these would take a few years, and the publication
in 1951 of Hannah Arendt's classic study, *The Origins of Totalitarianism*, before they settled into the common ground; but the writing was
on the wall. It was no time for politics, Trotskyist or otherwise. With
the expiration of political hopes, the claim of 'pure literature' had
begun to assert itself with its own peculiar vengeance. " 'I want to live.
I want to travel. *I do not want to become a fountain pen*,' " Cocteau
had exclaimed in the 1930s, and Delmore Schwartz had warmly
agreed; but in the 1940s when Delmore was holed up with a naval
commission at Harvard, teaching literature to sailors, he told Mark
Van Doren that "now these words hardly impress me, perhaps because
I have become a fountain pen, and it is a pleasant enough thing to be."
After left-wing intellectuals were buffeted first from one side by the
Hitler-Stalin pact, and then from the other by the Communist-hunters

on the Dies committee, even Malcolm Cowley laid claim to feeling "politically amputated, emasculated," but relieved, after all, that now he could get back to his "proper field of interest"—which "was and had always been the contemporary history of American letters."

'American letters,' nonetheless, had quickly become another proving ground for the intelligentsia, as it had in 1937. Among Mary McCarthy's friends, the enemy was a new kind of literary man, typified by Archibald MacLeish, John Steinbeck, Van Wyck Brooks, and the playwright Robert Sherwood. Writing Maxwell Geismar in 1942, Edmund Wilson sounded the general alarm when he criticized Geismar's *Writers in Crisis* for inflating the importance of the "social consciousness enthusiasms" of the 1930s, on which the fortunes of so many members of the wartime literati were built. "Aren't MacLeish and Sherwood . . . as well as Steinbeck . . . really second and third-rate writers?" Wilson wondered, echoing his wife's published assessments. "May it not possibly turn out to be true that they represent merely the beginning of some awful collectivist cant which will turn into official propaganda for a post-war state socialist bureaucracy?" With MacLeish heading up Roosevelt's OFF and Robert Sherwood attached to the White House, Wilson professed himself "rather uneasy."

To poets such as Delmore Schwartz and Louise Bogan, whose sensibilities were easily overcharged in the presence of any offending stimuli, the influence of "national" poets like "Foxy Grandpa Frost" and "Arch MacSlush" was equally alarming. It was one thing for a poet of modest talent—"his whole subject being the nostalgic echo of an unclear memory of an imprecise feeling about Nature," Delmore wrote of MacLeish—to condemn an interest in modernist poetry and prose as politically "irresponsible," as MacLeish did in a controversial address delivered at the end of the 1930s. It was something else when the same poet was the Librarian of Congress, as well as the author of a phantom air raid staged on national radio (in 1939) to awaken the populace to the fascist threat.

Reviewing MacLeish's twenty-page poem "America Was Promises" in *The New Yorker* late in 1939, Bogan called it "political poetry, even a kind of official poetry," whose danger, she thought, lay not in the advancement of this or that opinion but in the absence of "the strict checks and disciplines of poetry written for itself (as a result of reality making a direct emotional impact upon the temperament of a trained and exacting writer)." Writing Fred Dupee as "Butch Bogan, the Dorchester Dreadnought," she was less restrained: MacLeish was the "Missing Link between the White House and the red-light districts of

Art." He "buttered 'em up. He smeared marmalade on Baudelaire and Chocolate frosting on Rimbaud. He made a peach melba of 'The Waste Land.' . . ." (McCarthy didn't care for Archibald MacLeish, either, and associated him with his ardent admirer Helen Lockwood.)

For *PR*'s editors, Van Wyck Brooks represented a more sinister direction in wartime literature. In a widely quoted paper delivered at Columbia in the fall of 1940, entitled "Primary Literature and Coterie Literature," Brooks had argued that "primary literature"—by which he meant Socrates, Erasmus, Goethe, Milton, Dickens, Tolstoy, Emerson, Whittier, Thomas Mann, and *not* Joyce, Proust, Valéry, Pound, Eliot, James, Hemingway, Dos Passos—"is a force of regeneration that . . . conduces to race survival." A "primary" writer was "a great man writing," who "bespeaks the collective life of the people" by celebrating "the great themes . . . by virtue of which the race has risen—courage, justice, mercy, honor, love." A "primary" writer believed in "the idea of progress." The "secondary" or "coterie" writer, on the other hand, as Dwight Macdonald noted scornfully in a *PR* symposium on the Brooks-MacLeish thesis:

> is a thin-blooded, niggling sort of fellow, whose work reaches "a mere handful of readers." His stuff has brilliant "form" but lacks "content." He is "a mere artificer or master of words," who perversely celebrates the "death-drive" instead of the "life-drive." He is a doubter, a scorner, a skeptic, expatriate, highbrow and city slicker. His work is pessimistic and has lost contact with The People and The Idea of Greatness. He is, above all, secondary.

The coterie writer, naturally, was likely to be a contributor to *Partisan Review*. Like Mary McCarthy in her 1943 review of Thornton Wilder's *The Skin of Our Teeth*, he had scant patience for the "perennial nostalgia" of the American stage, especially when the orgy of nostalgia was expressed "not for the past but for an eternal childhood, for the bedrock of middle-class family life." And he certainly would have rapped Wilder, as McCarthy did, for the play's affirmation of "the eternity of capitalism, which it identifies with 'human nature.' " But what Dwight Macdonald found disturbing in Brooks's thesis was the echo of German fascism in the emphasis on "race survival." Goebbels, too, was a foe of "degenerate" modern art and a promoter of the Idea of Greatness. In Brooks's polarization of "form" versus "content," "pessimism" versus "optimism," "intellect" versus "life"—in his confusion of social values with literary values—Macdonald also heard the drumbeat of Soviet-style "social realism."

And so the lines were drawn, and the war brought home to a more familiar turf for American writers than the killing fields of Europe and the Pacific. (" 'What did you do in the war to make the world safe for the lesser evil?' " Delmore once imagined a grandchild asking; and he would say, " 'I was in the Navy, defending the English language.' ") "The old battles must be fought again, the old lessons learned once more," Macdonald concluded, somewhat wearily, for he agreed with Van Wyck Brooks that Eliot, Joyce, Proust, James, and Valéry represented the end, not the beginning, of a cultural awakening. Nevertheless, without the "new social and political forces which alone can bring into being a new esthetic tendency," he believed the modernist school (Eliot, Joyce, etc.) was "still the most advanced cultural tendency"; in a "reactionary" period it had come to represent, once again, "the same threat to official society as it did in the early decades of the century."

There was nothing weary about Macdonald's call to arms, however. "It's your business, I suppose, but I think you're making a mistake in keeping silent on this Brooks [affair]," he wrote Edmund Wilson in November 1941:

> it would seem the responsibility of writers on *our* side of the fence to stick their necks out now. . . . Personal letters don't do the job at all. (You'll recall we had the same disagreement at the time Cowley made his smear attack on PR in the New Republic—and I still think the personal letter you wrote him at the time . . . was the wrong tactic.)

Wilson had "an especial responsibility to repudiate Brooks publicly," Macdonald argued, inasmuch as Brooks had actually invoked him as a supporter of his ideas. But Wilson kept out of the fray. Perhaps his silence was to be explained by the "radically different conceptions of the relationship of the author to his audiences" that Dwight Macdonald said each of them had always had. Very likely he was put off by the stridency of Macdonald's repudiation. For Wilson, literature was not the pursuit of politics by other means.

However, Macdonald had caught him in a moment of uncharacteristic reserve. Following Wilson's showdown with *The New Republic* in the fall of 1940—which ended with his threat to report Richard Elmhirst to Washington as a British agent—Edmund Wilson had retreated into semiretirement. After nearly a decade's involvement with the revolutionary ideas that became the subject of *To the Finland Station*, he now watched the book slip into a kind of instant oblivion. (The first edition, oddly enough, made a greater impact in England, but only in the 1960s did a new paperback do well at home.) He was depressed, moreover, by Scott Fitzgerald's death, which arrived like a thunderclap in a reign of deaths. "It's extremely depressing to me that Joyce should have died, too—even though I suppose his work was finished," Wilson wrote John Peale Bishop in January 1941. "Yeats, Freud, Trotsky, and Joyce have all gone in so short a time—it is almost like the death of one's father."

Some sort of midlife crisis seems to have shadowed these years for Wilson, years which for his young wife were crowned by growing recognition. While *The Company She Keeps* got mixed reviews from Christopher Isherwood in *The Nation* and Malcolm Cowley in *The New Republic*, and a hostile notice from Clifton Fadiman in *The New Yorker* (who charged McCarthy with indulging in "high-grade back-fence gossip"), the book won praise in unexpected corners: in *Time*, for instance, and in the opinion of Vladimir Nabokov, who wrote Wilson that he found "Mary's book . . . a splendid thing, clever, poetic and new." Wilson wrote back to say that "Mary was cheered by what . . . you said . . . as she has been getting pretty dreadful reviews. Almost nobody has said that the book was well-written. I don't think people notice the difference nowadays," he added. But Randall Jarrell had also written him in praise of *The Company She Keeps*: "writing intelligent instead of sensitive stories is a new idea in our time," he commented. After finishing "Ghostly Father, I Confess," he had "felt good all afternoon," Jarrell added. Wilson himself let it be known that he thought his wife might be a "female Stendahl." The book, meanwhile, sold a respectable ten thousand copies in 1942.

Wilson, however, despite his extraordinary productivity during his marriage to Mary McCarthy—five books, three of them, *The Triple Thinkers, To the Finland Station*, and *The Wound and the Bow,* major critical works—had entered a period of uncertainty. In a benchmark essay published in 1943, when he was forty-eight, "Thoughts on Being Bibliographed," he noted ruefully that he "had arrived at middle age under the illusion that he had not yet really begun to write." He still saw his work in a continuum from the eighteenth century on, but now he was troubled by a new fear about literature, which was that it would one day be absorbed by "the academy" and "corporate journalism." With Macdonald, he agreed that for the moment it was the war that posed the greatest danger to independent political discourse. The socialists had become "merely patriots," as they inevitably became in wartime, while the Communists were "Russian nationalists who would not recognize a thought of Lenin's if they happened by some mistake to see one," and the liberal weeklies were "false phantoms" puffed up by "an alien mixture of the gases of propaganda injected by the Stalinists and the British. All this press of the Left," Wilson lamented, "has been losing its best talent through its own mediocrity and timidity, to the Curtis and Luce organizations."

But it was Mary McCarthy, in the fifth episode of *The Company She Keeps*, who presented her readers with the period's most extended meditation on the Left/liberal/Luce connection. With "Portrait of the Intellectual as a Yale Man," she also began to take a more serious look at the rootless urban intelligentsia whose company she had once again begun to keep in New York.

II

"The intellectual is the only character missing in the American novel," Philip Rahv observed in an influential essay of the time. An intellectual "might appear in his professional capacity—as artist, teacher, scientist," he noted, "but very rarely as a person . . . who transforms ideas into actual dramatic motives instead of using them as ideological conventions. . . . Everything is contained in the American novel except ideas." It was an arresting idea in itself, this notion of turning ideas into motives, and it was to be put to use by Mary McCarthy in a way that Rahv might not have imagined.

Of the Yale Man who has just taken a big bite of *Das Kapital*, and can't resist spreading the news:

> He would buttonhole a classmate after a few sets of tennis down at the old Fourteenth Street Armory. "You know, Al," he would say, twisting his head upwards and to one side in the characteristic American gesture of a man who is giving a problem serious thought (the old salt or the grizzled Yankee farmer scanning the sky for weather indications) . . . "I never thought so at college, but the Communists have something. Their methods over here are a little operatic, but you can't get around their analysis of capitalism."

" 'I think the system is finished,' " Jim Barnett would say, " 'and it's up to us to be ready for the new thing when it comes.' And Al, or whoever it was, would be doubtful but impressed." He might pick up a copy of the Communist Manifesto on his way home, the "little Socialist classic" enjoying a popularity in the middle 1930s nearly as great as the *Reader's Digest*, McCarthy reminds us. At night, he would tell his wife that maybe it was a good idea to lay in a stock of durable consumers' goods—"in case, oh, in case of inflation, or revolution, or anything like that." His wife would interpret this in terms of cans and place a large order with the grocer the next morning for Heinz's baked beans, Campbell's tomato soup, and so on. "This," writes McCarthy, "was the phenomenon known as the dissemination of ideas."

The lure of a fresh idea appears frankly sexual in McCarthy's early fiction; and in "Portrait of the Intellectual as a Yale Man," the mind itself becomes an erogenous zone. The unmasking of ideological convention or social routine offers the intellectual a thrill not unlike the thrill of physical or sexual conquest. For the mythical Yale Man, schooled in a measure of intellectual prodigality, "systems of thought had a certain wanton, outlawed attractiveness; and Marxism," McCarthy observes, "was to become for Jim's generation what an actress had been for the youths of the Gilded Age." Like "The Man in the Brooks Brothers Shirt," "Portrait of the Intellectual as a Yale Man" sparkles with innuendo. The sight of John Dewey nodding at an extravagant statement made by a Trotskyist ideologue such as Max Shachtman reminds the narrator of "finding your father in bed with a woman." In the liberal magazine Jim Barnett works for before he turns to safer shores, left-wing ideas "emerged in his writing in a state of undress that made them look exciting and almost new. . . ." The analogies are brazen, perhaps because in "Portrait of the Intellectual as a Yale Man," Mary McCarthy, qua narrator, impersonates a man, though it is a feminine touch that allows her to strip ideas of their abstract character and return them to the social world from whence they come.

The story's reigning idea, and the 'motive' behind the Yale Man's character development, is the dying out of the belief in socialist revolution. By the time McCarthy resumed her comradely relations with the boys, the Marxism of both anti-Stalinists and Stalinists ("anti-Hitlerites," was the term Cowley preferred) was not much more than a ceremonial language. The functional vocabulary was the language of fable, of "children afraid of the night," moralizing and psychoanalytic: the language McCarthy employs in the final chapter of *The Company She Keeps*, when Meg Sargent reflects: "Now for the first time she saw her own extremity, saw that it was some failure in self-love that obliged her to snatch blindly at the love of others, hoping to love herself through them, borrowing their feelings, as the moon borrowed light." Politics, too, proved susceptible to the analyst's knife: "It was unfortunate . . . that the radical movement had inherited Karl Marx's cantankerous disposition together with his world-view," observes the narrator in "Portrait of the Intellectual as a Yale Man"; "[t]he 'polemical' side of Marxism was its most serious handicap: here in America, especially it went against the grain."

This was straight Wilson, as is the more autobiographical reflection that follows:

> Unfortunately . . . the bad side of Marxism was precisely what attracted warped personalities of the type of Miss Sargent, who had long lists of people she did not speak to, and who delighted in grievance committees, boycotts, and letters to the editor. So that the evil multiplied a thousandfold. It was like an hereditary insanity that is perpetuated not only through the genes but by a process of selection in which emotional instability tends to marry emotional instability and you end up with the Jukes family. Or you begin with Marx's carbuncles and you end with the Moscow trials.

But "Portrait of the Intellectual as a Yale Man" is quintessential McCarthy. It mirrors the rancorous New York milieu of the late 1930s and early '40s, whose analyst she was fast becoming. And it is suffused by an almost fin de siècle sense of destiny closing in on the radicalism of the 1930s—a sense that McCarthy herself may have helped usher into public consciousness. At least it is for the ease with which she convinced "the sick, deluded ex-utopians" of her generation of their "easy credulity," in Alfred Kazin's view, that some of McCarthy's contemporaries never forgave her.

"It was impossible to believe that Mary McCarthy had ever been a believing Socialist," Kazin declares in *Starting Out in the Thirties*; "she could belong to a radical movement only when it was in decay and objectively ridiculous." Her "authority," he maintains, expanded in perverse relation to "the growing conviction of meaninglessness in the air . . ."; "bewilderment in the 'movement' . . . set her up exactly as the pathos of the 'emancipated' woman of the 20s had made a world for Dorothy Parker." Alfred Kazin makes no brief for socialism, which appears in his memoirs as someone else's lost Elysium. What provokes him about McCarthy's fictional postmortems is the "discipline of style . . . [the] show of classical severity and subtler manners . . . that pointed up her *right* to take such a very large bite of her victim." But it is more than 'style' or 'manners' that McCarthy deploys in her deft probe of the troubled psyche of American intellectuals.

* * *

In "Portrait of the Intellectual as a Yale Man," *Destiny* is the name of the slick, Luce-style magazine that gobbles up Jim Barnett after he resigns from the *Liberal,* and renounces his brief affair with Miss Sargent, along with independent political thought and action, and the promise of writing a great book—all three somehow merging in the ex-radical's mind as part of the same lost historic moment. "Destiny" is also why Miss Sargent herself will not try to write a book: "A fortune teller told me I was born to fritter away my talents. I wouldn't want to go against my destiny." "Destiny," in other words, is time and life in America. And the story, combining as it does McCarthy's peculiar reverence for the whims of chance, with a sensitivity to the romantic impulse in American radicalism, has about as much to do with Yale men as the famous seduction on the train is about Brooks Brothers. The college tie, along with the shirt, exist mainly to establish verisimilitude. They identify the class of persons that McCarthy treats.

The story is about the seduction of American intellectuals by "the scarlet woman of the steppes," and about the sinners' comeuppance, their return to the fold. Not just Ivy league intellectuals but others, as well. "Most men had come to socialism by some all-too-human compulsion," McCarthy writes:

> they were out of work or lonely or sexually unsatisfied or foreign-born or queer in one of a hundred bitter, irremediable ways. They resembled the original twelve apostles in the New Testament; there was no real merit in their adherence, and no hope either.

It is an odd formulation, setting sexual frustration on a par with unemployment as equally hopeless reasons for embracing socialism. Only if a man comes to consciousness through some *inhuman* compulsion, presumably, is his commitment valid.

And so it is with the Yale Man, who "like the Roman centurion or Saint Paul . . . came to socialism freely, from the happy center of things, by a pure act of perception which could only have been brought about by grace; and his conversion might be interpreted as a prelude to the conversion of the world." The original model for the Yale Man, John Chamberlain, once claimed that he had never seen himself in Jim Barnett's shoes, ironically enough, because his "own identification with the Left in those days was purely out of a depression-induced pessimism. . . ." Socialism, Chamberlain maintained, possessed only a "stomach appeal." In this regard, McCarthy's "centurian" is probably autobiographical.

"To look at him, you would never have believed he was an intellectual," the story begins. "With his pink cheeks and sparkling brown eyes and reddish brown hair that needed brushing . . . he night have been any kind of regular young guy, anywhere in America." And continues:

> He made you think of Boy Scouts and starting a fire without matches . . . and skinning the cat and Our Gang comedies and Huckleberry Finn. . . . He might have done very well as the young man who . . . looks up happily from his plate of Crunchies, saying, "Gee, honey, I didn't know breakfast food could taste so good!"

With his pink cheeks and brown eyes, Jim Barnett, of course, is a first cousin to Mr. Breen, who looks like "a young pig, like something in a seed catalogue." Barnett, in fact, is one of those Babbitts to whom McCarthy's heroines, as Louis Auchincloss has observed, are so frequently drawn. But he is also an intellectual of a classic American type.

In the story, which begins in the middle 1930s, the young man has been hired by a tired old liberal magazine (*The Nation* or *The New Republic*) to dress things up. When Miss Sargent, a free spirit despite her grievance committees, is taken on as an assistant editor, she promptly rocks the boat with her principled defense of Trotsky, throwing the Yale Man into a primal quandary. He is drawn to the girl for the usual reasons: His wife is about to deliver a baby and he feels entitled to one last fling; the girl is pretty, young, and patently unencumbered. But he is also impressed by the seriousness and intelligence of her unconventional convictions. Defending Trotsky's decision to publish a criticism of the Moscow trials in a popular magazine, Miss Sargent argues, "You know, you might not think so, but it's quite as possible for a revolutionist to make use of Hearst as it is for Hearst to make use of a revolutionist." And she makes Barnett laugh when she exclaims, "What would you have him do? Hold up his hands like a girl, and say, 'Oh no! Think of my reputation! I can't accept presents from strange gentlemen!'" (Which is borrowed from one of Trotsky's letters to *Partisan Review*: "You defend yourselves from the Stalinists like well-behaved young ladies whom street rowdies insult," the old man wrote in 1938. "'Why are we attacked?' you complain; 'we want only one thing; to live and let others live.'")

Miss Sargent's iconoclasm reminds Barnett painfully of how easy it has been for him to put his own ideas over at the *Liberal*: "It was like having a girl give in too quickly; you felt that she did not take you, as an individual, seriously—she only wanted a man." And so when

Miss Sargent is fired from the magazine, Barnett resolves to leave it himself, and almost in the same breath, to "take" the girl: twice, in her funny little apartment—but only after he has decided to give her up: ". . . and indeed it seemed to him that if he did not have her he could not give her up. . . ."

McCarthy's anatomy of a certain kind of sexual obsession, one in which the charisma of a dangerous idea (the girl's Trotskyism, not to mention the idea of risking the good life at home with one's wife) mingles with the temptations of the flesh, is here rendered flawlessly. In theory, that is. In reality, nothing really *happens*. The Yale Man, who has been reassembled from bits and pieces of a half-dozen men—Chamberlain, yes, but chiefly as "a good-looking clothes hanger" (McCarthy), along with telltale tinctures of Dwight Macdonald, Malcolm Cowley, and Robert Cantwell—is indeed a "broad type," as McCarthy suggests, whose singularity is what makes him representative of a class. As a character, however, he is not a free agent; he does not develop in time, but only unfolds as time works him over. The narrator holds all the cards.

III

"Portrait of the Intellectual as a Yale Man" was first conceived as another magazine piece, a character study in which Margaret Sargent initially had no part. That she appears at all as Jim Barnett's love interest is thanks to the editor at Simon & Schuster who saw a successful novel in the affairs of Miss Sargent. The story, unlike the others in the collection, is not centered on significant events in McCarthy's own life, but is a compilation of experiences, which may explain why the seduction scene is so wooden:

> In the apartment, he took her twice with a zeal that was somehow both business-like and insane, and then rolled over on his back and sighed deeply, like a man who has completed some disagreeable but salutary task. . . . As if she, too, knew that it was finished, she got up at once, with an air of apology for being naked in unsuitable circumstances. She picked her clothes off the floor. . . . Without a word, he took his own clothes off the chair. . . .

"*Why the hell,* he said to himself now, had he not at least taken her to a decent restaurant for dinner . . . ?"

The foreplay occurs the night before, when Barnett tosses and turns in bed beside his wife, lusting after Miss Sargent. As for McCarthy's heroine: "It was as if she were his sister, his twin, his tormented Electra; it was as if they were cursed, both together, with a wretched, unquenchable, sterile lust that 'ran in the family.' " But we never sense Miss Sargent's lust, only Barnett's appraisal of it.

Margaret Sargent is here revealed through the eyes of an intellectual like herself, a fellow traveler on love's sterile couch, but a man, nonetheless, who when the time comes to end the affair brushes her off in a mist of sentiment:

> "Margaret," he said, "I can't explain, but the set-up wasn't right before. Working in the same office. . . ."
>
> "Yes," she agreed. "It would have been a terrible mess." She smiled.
>
> "It hasn't been any picnic for me, Margaret," he said in an aggrieved tone. "I still feel the same way about you."
>
> "That's wonderful," she said with her first touch of sharpness. "I would like to feel the same way about you . . . but I can't. I don't seem to be able to bank my fires. That's a man's job, I suppose."

Telling the story from Jim Barnett's point of view allows McCarthy to explore a different side of Margaret Sargent, and of herself as well, as others may have seen her. Miss Sargent belongs to that "tiresome class" of intellectuals, "the unsuccessful, opinionated, unknown intellectuals," Barnett reflects later, after settling in at *Destiny*, "who had nothing, so far as he could see, to say to him." Barnett has been introduced to a larger world, the world of Curtis and Luce. Outsiders imagine that his radicalism keeps him in hot water in his new job, but it isn't so. "He wrote about American youth, farm security, South America, musical comedy, and nylon . . ." the narrator informs us (evoking Macdonald's menu at *Fortune*); "if the article seemed too 'strong,' it was given to someone else to modify. He was not obliged to eat his own words." Barnett, in fact, was "not so much a writer as a worker on an assembly line," who performed his tasks "conscientiously," and anyway, "since the finished product was always several removes away from him, it was, in a certain sense, not his concern."

McCarthy's characterization of the inner workings of corporate journalism holds up well a half century later. As control over his own work passes from his hands, Jim Barnett, like many a well-paid hack today, learns to covet information instead:

Jim liked the facts that were served up to him daily by the girl
research workers, liked the feeling that there was nothing . . . that he
could not find out by pressing a bell, sending a telegram, or taking a
plane . . . he had only to mention the name of the magazine and he
would be whisked into a farmer's homestead, an actress' dressing
room, a Fifth Avenue mansion, a cold-water flat . . . a girls' college,
an army camp . . . a great hotel. . . . [N]obody but a tax assessor had
ever had such freedom, and where the tax assessor was detested,
Jim's subjects welcomed him. . . . It pleased them that someone
should know *all about them* and write it down and publish it with
pictures. It pleased Jim too; it gave him a great feeling of responsibility, as if he were a priest or God.

Among Barnett's friends, there were those who thought the villain
was Nancy, Jim's wife—Dwight's, too (though the Nancy "who had
gone and had two more children . . . who needed a house in the country . . . who kept [Jim's] nose to *Destiny*'s grindstone" was a far cry
from the hardworking business manager of *Partisan Review* and *politics*.) If Jim Barnett fostered this illusion, it was not only because it
sheltered him from responsibility, but because "it permitted him to
enjoy what was really a success story secure from the envy of the less
privileged." The truth is that Jim Barnett *liked* working at *Destiny*,
and *loved* the children, the garden, the new appliances, quite as much
if not more than his wife did.

It was a different truth than most of McCarthy's contemporaries
drew from the lives of such men. The burned-out radical who had put
the "faith and foolishness" of the 1930s behind him, and now punched
a clock for Curtis or Luce, was a tragic case in the opinion of Edmund
Wilson, who wrote feelingly about those "members of the professional
classes" whose consciences were awakened by Marx and Lenin, and
who were then seized by "the conception of the dynamic Marxist will"
and suffered a kind of "snow blindness." Wilson, one suspects, had
experienced the "moment of seizure" himself, when Marxism seemed
to provide "the key to all the mysteries of human history," while Mary
McCarthy had not. But Wilson didn't delve into the social realities of
mass culture to solve the mystery of why so many onetime Marxists
would lead the armies of reaction in the 1950s; and McCarthy did.

Privately, Wilson had voiced some Barnettish speculations about
the career of Robert Cantwell, whose apartment he and Mary had
sublet in New York in the winter of 1941 when "Portrait of the
Intellectual as a Yale Man" was being written. Cantwell, then working

for *Time*, had worked at *The New Republic*, which is where Mary met him in 1934 when he was Cowley's assistant, and he had written some very good criticism and fiction both, in Wilson's opinion. After the Moscow trials, he had suffered a kind of mental breakdown, and when Fred Dupee ran into him later on in the 1940s at a party in New York, "Bob was like a stranger, an amnesiac," he reported. Many of his friends, and especially Edmund Wilson, "thought Cantwell a tragic victim of Stalinism, the anti-Stalinism of [Whittaker] Chambers, the Luce publications ambiance, and his marriage to the fiercely possessive little Betsy."

In a nutshell, this is the continuum McCarthy explores in "Portrait of the Intellectual as a Yale Man." Even the anti-communism of Whittaker Chambers, whose tainted testimony would later send Alger Hiss to jail, is prefigured in the "aggressive stage" that Jim Barnett reaches whenever he drinks too much, when he tells anyone who is still a socialist "how he had waked up to himself back in 1937 and what a fine thing it had been for him." Where McCarthy's perspective departs from Wilson's view is in its refusal to portray the intellectual as a tragic victim. The key to McCarthy's intellectual is the *ease* with which he slips in and out of his relationship to events, people, ideas (not unlike Mary herself in these years); and so there can be no tragedy when he feels himself to be a failure in the midst of plenty—which of course in the end he does. By withholding pity, by honoring the weight and worth of convention in American life, Mary McCarthy uncovers a deeper truth about the way in which American intellectuals handle the revolutionary dreams of youth, and why they so often turn on them and learn nothing from them.

Barnett, like any interesting character, is of two minds. Thinking about his old flame from the security of his senior post at *Destiny*, he marvels over how "That single night and day when he had been almost in love with her had taught him everything. He had learned that he must keep down his spiritual expenses—or else go under." It is the lesson McCarthy's political generation drew from its early romance with Marxism. 'Going under' for ex-radicals in the 1940s meant going over to the other side—or losing one's credibility with the only side that mattered, the one in power. There is no doubt in Barnett's mind about the wisdom of *his* choice. He can never "envy" the girl who had once moved him, however briefly, to raise his expectations of himself, not to mention his expectations of a woman, for her hands are empty: "she was unhappy, she was poor, she had achieved nothing, even by her own standards. Yet she exasperated him. . . ."

Similarly, there were few second thoughts among the ex-Marxists of the 1940s about the wisdom of their embrace of Literature (with a capital *L*) over politics: 'pure' literature stood faithfully by the door like the good wife awaiting her errant husband. And there was not much doubt in the minds of the same men when the time came (in 1952) to 'choose the West' in the Cold War—in the words of Dwight Macdonald, of all people. Mary McCarthy could hardly have foreseen all this in 1941, but it would be some of the same intellectuals (Macdonald excluded) who were infuriated in the 1960s by the New Left, as if they were reminded of that 'single night and day' when they had chosen to step out with the 'scarlet woman.'

In his unhappy letter to Edmund Wilson, Malcolm Cowley confessed that left-wing politics reminded him of a night in the 1920s "when he went on a bat with a lot of noisy and lecherous people," whom he "thoroughly despised," while realizing that he was "one of them." Nineteen forty was early for this note of moral fastidiousness to enter the confessions of Marxist intellectuals, but soon it was common enough. McCarthy, in effect, had put her finger on an impulse in the American character that would always ascribe something promiscuous to the radicalism of youth.

In memory of old times, Jim Barnett still talked to Miss Sargent when he ran into her at parties, but now "her sarcasm bored him. . . ." It irritated him when he heard she had applied for a job at *Destiny*; "he was perfectly justified in telling the publisher that she would not fit in." Still, he cannot put his finger on why it is that only Margaret "had the power to make him feel, feel honestly, unsentimentally, that his life was a failure, not a tragedy exactly, but a comedy with pathos." What does he regret? If he had it to do all over again, he would make the same moves. "What he yearned for perhaps was the possibility of decision, the instant of choice, when a man stands at a crossroads and knows he is free," McCarthy suggests, turning the scalpel gently but firmly as she probes her metaphor.

"Still, even that had been illusory. He had never been free," of course,

> but until he tried to love the girl, he had not known he was bound. It was self-knowledge she had taught him; she had showed him the cage of his own nature. He had accommodated himself to it, but he could never forgive her. Through her he had lost his primeval innocence, and he would hate her forever as Adam hates Eve.

Barnett's affair with Miss Sargent evokes something rarely acknowledged in the legacy of the American Left. Marxism, too, seemed to put a man at the crossroads. The idea that men and women make history, the very idea of 'history' as something to be known and shaped, the idea that 'ideas' really matter is heady stuff. And it had all been proved illusory. Stalin proved it. Deep down, of course, even anti-Stalinists knew that Stalin hadn't proved anything about the capabilities of American intellectuals. Along with the well-advertised absence of 'objective conditions' favoring a socialist revolution in the United States, there was some failure of will and imagination, some rock-bottom fear of change among the men and women who first tasted the forbidden fruit, then advanced the idea of revolution in a 'bourgeois' society, and then withdrew from the fray without ever really putting up a fight.

McCarthy's story touched a raw nerve on the Left. Unlike "The Man in the Brooks Brothers Shirt," "Portrait of the Intellectual as a Yale Man" was about somebody important to intellectuals: themselves. And yet one looks in vain in the 1940s, or later for that matter, for a critical discussion of its content. Maybe it was because the story was not published independently before it appeared as a chapter in *The Company She Keeps*, and Jim Barnett's tale was overshadowed by Margaret Sargent's adventures; or maybe Mary McCarthy's own emerging notoriety had already begun to distract her reviewers from what she was saying. The ideas McCarthy put forward also seemed to emerge in a "state of undress," as they did for the Yale Man; "in the end, it was not the ideas that counted so much, as the fact that Jim Barnett held them," McCarthy observes; and the same, alas, might be said of her.

14

The Wife of Bunny's Tale

*"It's harder to write fiction. I probably
feel closer to my fiction. When fiction is finally
done, it has more of oneself in it."*

—MARY McCARTHY, VASSAR VIEWS

"Everything is real until it's published."

—ROBERT LOWELL, THE DOLPHIN

A literary marriage never ends. Whether it is made in heaven, like
the Brownings', or in hell, which is more or less where Mary McCarthy
consigns her round with Edmund Wilson, it acquires a kind of immortality that other unions lack. Even the marriages of celebrated person-
ages—princes, presidents, movie stars, famous novelists, whose
spouses are not literary—are like dead planets alongside a literary
union, drawing their celebrity from the attention of others. Only a
literary tie permits its partners the gratification of playing the match
out forever on a multitude of screens, in fiction and in memoir, in a
poem, an interview; long after separation, divorce, or death has separated one mate from the other.

Immortalizing an object of desire (or rage or envy) has always been
a prerogative of poets. Dante memorializes his Beatrice, his Muse, and
in the *Inferno* consigns his fickle friends and Florentine enemies to an
eternity of bad press notices. In our own time, the immortalizing
tendency has become more narcissistic; the attraction of one sensibility
to another doubles back on itself in a kind of self-love. Robert Lowell
worries that a brother under the skin may have his way with him in
words. "I used to want to live/ to avoid your elegy," Lowell wrote in
his own terse elegy for the poet John Berryman in 1972, after Berryman
jumped to his death from a bridge over the Mississippi River.

Yet really we had the same life,
the generic one
our generation offered. . . .
    We asked to be obsessed with writing,
and we were. . . .
    You got there first.

While Lowell, it should be noted, got the last word.

Yet the poems, the words, outlive them all—and there's the rub. ". . . [A]uthors have a double life," Mary McCarthy observes of the fertile novelist Hereward Egerton, the antic hero of Ivy Compton-Burnett's *A God and His Gifts,* "and a double chance of survival, through their brain-children, who will certainly outlive them (that is the vexing part) and may attain a fabulous age." The "creative" writer who "breeds best sellers," as McCarthy says of Egerton, "begetting them on his wife, his wife's sister, his son's fiancée," in a succession of amorous adventures that supply him with his material, is not vexed so long as the value of his literary stock goes up. It is the wife, the sister-in-law, the fiancée, and sometimes *their* progeny, who may discover in the mutant 'child' a defective gene of their own perhaps; a secret terror flushed to the surface of the immortal page; a 'distinguishing characteristic' such as only the precinct officer, the medical examiner, the analyst, or the coroner knows is there in the flesh.

The great and awful power of the pen is magnified when both subject and object are writers, begetting their brainchildren on each other, in a sense, incestuously. A certain competitiveness creeps in which is different from the connubial strife that may have fired the creative process in the first place. "Whose will-shot arrow sings cleaner through the pelt?" Robert Lowell wonders, this time writing about Mary McCarthy. Even among friends, the competitive edge is aphrodisial: "I slip from wonder into bluster; you/ align your lines more freely, ninety percent on target—/" Lowell tells Mary—and posterity: "we can only meet in the bare air."

During two writers' lifetimes, who is the more discreet? Whose intimate exposures are packaged more deftly: inviting inspection, even evoking the spirit of the original through the animism of 'detail,' but repulsing the prying eye of the lawyer, and the public; foiling identification? And who writes the last word?

Writing long after the death of a contentious spouse, the survivor may conclude that he or she has published the last word—when suddenly the long arm from the grave erupts into print. Mary McCarthy, who began drawing from the well of her marriage to Edmund Wilson long before the pump stopped running, putting Wilson into two stories before their divorce, was confronted with just such a nightmare in 1982, when the third volume of Wilson's posthumous journals, *The Forties*, was about to be published. While McCarthy maintains that between the two of them it was considered "fair play" to use one's private life in fiction—Wilson had done it with *I Thought of Daisy* and *Memoirs of Hecate County*—only Mary had written publicly about their private lives together. In "Ghostly Father, I Confess," Wilson appears as Meg Sargent's second husband, Frederick, a shadowy but overbearing presence who is given to sudden outbursts of reason:

> "For God's sake," her husband said, "give up worrying about your imaginary sins and try to behave decently. You use your wonderful scruples as an excuse for acting like a bitch. Instead of telling yourself that you oughtn't to have married me, you might concentrate on being a good wife." "But I do try," she said sadly. "I really do."

In this long story, which first appeared in *Harper's Bazaar*, Wilson is disguised as an architect—"after all, I was living with him," McCarthy remarked in 1985. The fiction is a repository for her resentment over the 'therapeutic' course that marriage to Edmund Wilson took from the very beginning:

> When she had wept and cursed and kicked at him, he had not known how to "cope with" her (the phrase was his), and out of . . . a certain sluggishness, an unwillingness to be disturbed, to take too much spiritual trouble, he had done what the modern, liberal man inevitably does—called in an expert.

And later:

> That was what he had sent her to the doctor for—a perfectly simple little operation. First comes the anesthetic, the sweet, optimistic laughing-gas of science (you are not bad, you are merely unhappy, the bathtub murderer is "sick," . . . and that dirty fornication in a hotel room, why, that, dear Miss Sargent, is a "relationship"). . . . Then the patient takes a short rest and emerges as a cured neurotic; the personality has vanished, but otherwise he is perfectly normal. . . .
>
> Already, in her own case, the effects of treatment were notice-

able. . . ."You are not so tense as you used to be. You don't get so excited about causes." It was true, she was more subdued. . . .

One can see this young woman seated demurely beside her husband in the photographs of Mary McCarthy and Edmund Wilson in Wellfleet around 1942. They have just bought the old house on Money Hill, which Reuel Wilson owns today with his half sister Helen Miranda Wilson. In her seersucker blouse, Mary looks fresh and a little rumpled at the same time; her shoulder-length hair, which is curled, is pulled back from her heart-shaped face and secured in barrettes on the side. She is smiling and the smile dimples her cheeks and crinkles her eyes, which are averted, as if she is following the movements of a child off camera. Wilson's hand rests on her shoulder. He wears a buttoned-down shirt, no jacket, a tie knotted snugly under his double chin. He is short-waisted and his pants ride up and over his bulky stomach, giving him the appearance of a man with no middle, no bend. His eyes, which are unsmiling, are fastened on the photographer. For him, one feels, the portrait, a variation on the American Gothic, is an occasion, a small but important triumph.

"She did not assert herself in company; she let her husband talk on his own subjects, in his own vein," McCarthy continues in "Ghostly Father, I Confess." "She learned to suppress the unpleasant, unnecessary truths: why let an author know that you do not like his book, why spoil a party by getting into an argument . . . ?" Which was Mary McCarthy being a good girl, as she was when a critic such as Maxwell Geismar—whose book *Writers in Crisis* she did *not* like, and who she thought Wilson was grooming to run against the boys at *Partisan Review*—dropped in to discuss social consciousness in American fiction. Or when Alfred Kazin, another greenhorn from *PR*'s point of view, was summoned to hear Wilson's pronouncements on Kazin's popular *On Native Grounds* in 1943. McCarthy suspected that Wilson was courting Alfred Kazin for the same ignoble reason; although as Kazin remembers it, Wilson seemed piqued with the younger man's survey of nineteenth-century American literature, as if Kazin was poaching on the master's turf.

When Vladimir Nabokov and his wife, Vera, suddenly arrived in Wellfleet with their butterfly nets for a visit of uncertain duration, Mary might throw herself into preparations for an elaborate cherries jubilee—"new then, you only had them at someplace like '21'," she recalled later. Nabokov would let out a terrible whinny; "he made fun of one's desserts," she says. Hot cherries and brandy on cold ice cream shocked his sensibility, as did the Wilsons' noisy Frigidaire, which kept him awake at night, and which he memorialized in a poem published in *The New Yorker,* which Mary found "amusing."

Then there were the times when she and Edmund went down to Chatham to have dinner with the "stuffed shirts" (Wilson's phrase) who gathered at John Peale Bishop's—although at the Bishops' Mary McCarthy could not always hold her tongue. In *The Thirties,* Wilson recalls a dinner party when Mary sat beside a man who kept joking about how many cats—"Katzes"—there were in the Bronx. Didn't Mary think that was funny? Not very, she replied, since her own "maiden name was Katz," which had drawn a chilly curtain of silence across the table. As for John Peale Bishop, he was "a pretty good poet," McCarthy declared, "but a dreadful, dreadful bore, a monologuist." She could have "*died* of boredom" listening to him tell her how to grow sweet peas.

Evenings with Katy and John Dos Passos in Provincetown were easier. They were also fond of gardening and elaborate cooking; dinners prepared in the basement kitchen on Commercial Street, McCarthy remembered, never got on the table in any time frame related to when the guests arrived. John Dos Passos, of course, she had admired ever since reading *U.S.A.* in Contemporary Fiction at Vassar in 1932, but to be left alone with the man while his wife labored over dinner, could be "terrifying" because he was so "terribly hard to talk to and very shy."

Unlike either Mary or Edmund, Dos Passos was the kind of writer who was articulate only in prose, and even his fiction, when it was most autobiographical, as in the Camera Eye passages in the *U.S.A.* trilogy, was agitated by a collision of impulses that made it more like poetry. No one caught the tremors of ambiguity in the American intellectuals' original commitment to revolutionary politics better than John Dos Passos in *The Big Money,* when he remembered his "first stuttering attempt" at soapbox oratory:

> and then the easy climb slogan by slogan to applause (if somebody in your head didn't say liar to you and on Union Square . . .)
> you suddenly falter ashamed flush red break out in sweat why not tell these men stamping in the wind that we stand on a quicksand?

By the 1940s, Dos Passos's own doubts, especially his disillusion with the Communist party's role in the Spanish Civil War, had all but quenched his political imagination. His writing had begun to drift from the sharp vernacular of the common man to a kind of baby talk that barred the admittance of ideas of any kind. "An intellectual, to Dos Passos, is always a phoney," Mary McCarthy complained in her review of *Adventures of a Young Man*. The book was a chronicle of his disillusionment with left-wing politics, but in McCarthy's opinion, he had packed the intellectual scene of the 1920s and '30s "with a group of harsh and repulsive caricatures." (Wilson was more disturbed by the many landscapes and street scenes in the book, and the thinness of the hero's interior life. "I think you really ought to take some exercises to correct your extraversion," he told Dos Passos in a letter.) But despite these reservations about the vitality of Dos Passos's current work, both Edmund and Mary valued his company.

Katy made it easier. She was the reason Dos Passos had come to Provincetown, even though he had always scoffed at the place as a middle-class artists' colony. For Wilson, Katy and Dos were the center of a network of cronies anchored on the outer Cape. Charlie and Adelaide Walker were part of it, along with the White Russian émigrés Nina and Paul Chavchavadze, the writer Mary Heaton Vorse, Frank and Edie Shay, Eben Given, and Chauncey (Bubs) and Mary Hackett. Before them, there had been Jig Cook, Hutchins Hapgood, and Edna St. Vincent Millay, Wilson's Provincetown friends from the 1920s. The 1940s' group had become "a community" in Wilson's eyes, "more closely bound up together than we had realized or perhaps wanted to be." The summer parties, the drinking, the flirtations; the typewriters clacking on kitchen tables; the cold winter afternoons by the stove, living on trickles of income that ran dry one year and bubbled up the next—all this seemed to satisfy the survivalist's instinct, which was also the artist's, to seek the perimeters of society and eschew the center, to make do.

For Wilson the Cape Cod setting was steeped in nostalgia. When Katy Dos Passos died in a car accident in 1947, and the old group reassembled to bury her in the Truro cemetery, he was overwhelmed with sadness, "not only on account of Katy," he reflected, "but because it reminded me of Mary." With Mary McCarthy, Wilson would bring up a child "long enough to feel grounded . . . and to have become molded to some solidarity," and yet only a few years after their final separation he would find her "just as much gone, just as much destroyed, as Katy." For him, the Cape was the kind of place that conferred meaning on every inhabitant, and he was the kind of man for whom a woman, even a wife, was not quite real once she fell outside the boundaries.

The same place had looked very different to Mary. There was

something of the retirement community in the artists' towns along the New England seaboard that was bad for business when you were still young, still looking around, still capable of an original blunder or a fresh adventure. With her lengthening visits to New York, Mary was already on the run, though it was a few more years before she felt strong enough to declare herself unable to be Edmund Wilson's wife.

Old Provincetown bohemians like Mary Heaton Vorse, Harry Kemp, and Heaton Vorse, were remembered by McCarthy in the 1980s as "joke figures." With prim satisfaction, she recalled the morning Katy Dos Passos visited Mary Heaton Vorse and removed a lamb chop, "cooked, I believe," from the sofa before she sat on it. Katy and Dos, together with the Walkers, remain "positive" figures in McCarthy's arcanum. "But the rest of these people on the Cape were these terrible hacks," she told an interviewer, "beat-up people," who had maybe published something once and now drank too much and had messy affairs. "Rusting freelancers," she called them in *A Charmed Life*, a novel whose baleful sense of *place* (New Leeds for Wellfleet/Truro) induces a kind of claustrophobia in the reader, in that it admits of so little variation on the theme of human dissipation on the outer banks of an artistic community.

At the start of the 1940s, Wellfleet and Truro had been invaded by psychoanalysts, many of them refugees from Nazi Germany, whom McCarthy remembered as "the white-nosed people" because their noses were always coated with Noxzema. On the beach, where they undressed under giant striped towels, their portable radios were turned up loud to the war news. " '*Hallooo Dr. Bloomberg!*' " they called to each other across the sands, " 'like natives,' " the Wilsons' neighbor Herbert Solow noted mischievously. Wilson ignored the invasion of the analysts, who were just tourists in his opinion, peripheral to the local community, which for him—not for Mary—had always included genuine natives from the Portuguese fishing families.

In the summer of 1942, the Stamford psychiatrist who had written a book about women's castration complex, Dr. Sandor Rado, turned up in Provincetown, as well. It was during a visit with Dr. Rado that Mary McCarthy, who had become pregnant again, had begun to bleed and actually did miscarry across the street at the Dos Passoses' house. A bizarre event, when one recalls that as Edmund Wilson's adviser in 1938, Rado had counseled Mary to have an abortion. When she miscarried in 1942, Edmund accused Rado of having induced it.

Shortly before going to the Dos Passoses' she had been up on a ladder washing windows, "a fatal mistake," McCarthy ventured many years later. ("Dos and Katy thought she'd planned it and were not happy about it," Wilson's daughter Rosalind, who brought Mary home in the car, recalled in 1989.) She had gone to see Dr. Rado "socially," McCarthy relates, in what is meant to be a comic anecdote about the "terror of being left alone with Dos," but which is really about something else. As is often the case with such stories, a nightmarish experience is narrated in just such a way—"I had this awful thing of having a *miscarriage* in Dos Passos' house"—as to induce laughter and forestall sympathy or further questioning. It is "Dos, who was terribly shy about anything that had to do with sex," who is presented as the victim of the tale.

How McCarthy felt about becoming pregnant for the second time with Wilson, how she felt about miscarrying, she doesn't say, not at first telling. Such ruminations are locked in a safe-deposit box of the mind marked DOS PASSOS: SHY. "I was disappointed by the miscarriage, as I should have liked to have another child," McCarthy suggested at a later date. The visit to Sandor Rado, she repeats, was "just an afternoon social call." Rado, "an amusing, intelligent Hungarian," was really a kind of ally in her rejection of Freudian analysis, which remains "all myth and superstition," she insists, "the religion of our time." She remembers him saying once that the human race might not recover from the effects of the industrial revolution, "a very un-Freudian notion," she thinks, "and probably true." Rado's theory about the existence of a castration complex in women is reassessed: It is "a fear of castration in people who have nothing to lose . . . a typical Rado paradox, quite ingenious."

McCarthy's pregnancy might not have been treated so lightly in 1942, however. In 1989, shortly before her death, it came out that she had sold her rights to *The Company She Keeps* to RKO Radio in 1942. She had forgotten about it, and when she learned that she would get no royalties from an HBO production of "The Man in the Brooks Brothers Shirt" in 1989, she was greatly dismayed. "Her selling the rights so incautiously makes me think that in 1942 she needed money badly, and must already have been planning to leave Edmund Wilson," one of McCarthy's literary trustees, Eve Stwertka, suggests. Perhaps it was this pregnancy, less welcome than the first, which had prompted the sale around precisely the time she would have contemplated an abortion.

In McCarthy's own recollections nearly a half century later, there isn't much left of the desperado who was married to Edmund Wilson—the young woman who could give as well as she got, who once set fire to a sheaf of papers and swept them under the locked door of Wilson's study during a fight, when he wouldn't come out to confront her. The person remembered, one begins to think, is not unlike the 'cured neurotic' cited in "Ghostly Father, I Confess," or maybe it always takes a cured neurotic to reconstruct the past.

II

It is in fiction that a writer opens an account in which all kinds of troublesome experiences, unfit for daily consumption, are deposited. For Mary McCarthy during her marriage to Edmund Wilson, fiction, more than any psychiatrist, provided the outlet that 'kept the boiler from exploding.' Sometimes the transfer is a direct one, as in "Ghostly Father, I Confess" when McCarthy disposes of the lost opportunities of youth:

> She could no longer go back into circulation. . . . The little apartment in the Village, the cocktail parties, the search for a job, the loneliness, the harum-scarum, Bohemian habits, all this was now unthinkable for her. She had lost the life-giving illusion, the sense of the clean slate, the I-will-start-all-over-and-this-time-it-is-going-to-be-different.

And sometimes the deposit is coded, as when Meg Sargent discovers that her *rational* faculties are more limited than she supposed: "Up to the day that Frederick had sent her to the doctor, she had believed herself indestructible. Now she regarded herself as a brittle piece of porcelain. Between the two of them they had taught her the fine art of self-pity." What was dangerous about this lesson was that it confronted McCarthy's heroine with "the fact of her illness, a fact she could not talk away, since she went to the doctor daily, this fact was invaluable to [Frederick] as a weapon in their disputes. He was always in a position to say to her . . . 'You are not a fit judge of this because you are neurotic.' "

For Mary McCarthy, who really was haunted by Edmund Wilson's ability to use her regular visits to the analyst against her, the fiction, one imagines, is meant to function like the picture of Dorian Gray, which grows old while its subject stays forever young. In *The Company She Keeps*, McCarthy creates a self-portrait to carry the unbearable burden of being, in this instance, a little crazy, so that in 'real life' the subject appears indisputably sane, which is to say, *right;* blameless;

free of the hollow wrenching sense of guilt that the losses of childhood, especially, seem to inflict.

In the making of such a work, in this case a work of language, the words are drawn from the well of pain; from that part of life, the burdensome part, least susceptible to reason—reason being, for Mary McCarthy, what one covets in life. Thus the devil takes the hindmost. The portrait, the literary image, takes up a burden of truth that, as Meg Sargent puts it airily, is, in actuality, "all too apropos for acceptance."

"She was a real Freudian classic, and as such faintly monstrous, improbable," Meg admits at the close of *The Company She Keeps*. Both she and Dr. James try to avoid lengthy discussions of her childhood from "a distaste for the obvious," but also because the subject frightens them both; "for it suggested . . . that the universe is mechanical, utterly predictable . . . and this in its own way is quite as terrible as the notion that the universe is chaotic." Nevertheless, only after Meg unburdens herself of this monstrous childhood on the analyst's couch (the altar, where sacrifices are heaped) does the narrator summon the voice to dismiss it. Only after Meg has told the story of how that "elegant little girl" whose "mamma did not come home from the hospital" was transformed into "a stringy, bow-legged child with glasses and braces on her teeth, long underwear, high shoes, blue serge jumpers that smelled, and a brown beaver hat two sizes too big for her" can she "reject the whole pathos of the changeling, the orphan, the stepchild . . . [and] this trip down the tunnel of memory which resembles nothing so much as a trip down the Red Mill at Coney Island. . . ."

"Yet what were you going to do?" Meg reflects coldly, with the author, who by 1942 has arrived at the same question herself. "You could not treat your life-history as though it were an inferior novel and dismiss it with a snubbing phrase. It had after all been like that." The effort is made, just as it was often made in life, with a jab of wit and a shrug, or a stab at self-analysis: "Her peculiar tragedy (if she had one) was that her temperament was unable to assimilate her experience," the narrator observes hopefully; "the raw melodrama of those early years was a kind of daily affront to her skeptical, prosaic intelligence." And a little later: "If only she could have been disinherited in some subtle, psychological way. . . ." But it is impossible. The hysterical Aunt Clara, for example, a hybrid of both Aunt Margaret and Uncle Myers, "could be bodily left at home but her spirit presided over her niece like a grim familiar demon."

* * *

Indeed, something of Aunt Clara's punitive spirit continued to dog Mary McCarthy's footsteps, even after the demon was consigned to fiction. To John Berryman, who often saw McCarthy at parties at Allen Tate and Caroline Gordon's in the mid-1940s, she was the incorrigible Phi Beta Kappa student who couldn't keep from scanning the conversations around her for lapses in taste and erudition. She knew more than Tate, more than Wilson, Berryman used to say. She was always correcting somebody's diction or pronunciation—or addition. "Mary wants me to call your attention to the fact that the sum you were doing in the margin of your letter is not correctly worked," Wilson noted in a postscript to Nabokov early in 1944.

In "Ghostly Father, I Confess," however, McCarthy's nagging demon seems to trouble her less than the fear that she has been swallowed up in marriage to an older, overbearing man; that she has, in fact, been "cured." "What Frederick had not foreseen was that the good would vanish with the bad," Meg reflects, sadly:

> Poor Frederick . . . he did not see . . . that his spirited termagent of a wife would be converted into a whimpering invalid who no longer raged at him so often, who no longer wept every morning and seldom threatened to kill him, but who complained, stood on her prerogatives. . . . And yet . . . Perhaps he had seen it, and accepted it as a lesser evil to living with her on terms of equality or allowing her to leave him. . . .

"Poor Frederick" can be glimpsed in the figure that Edmund Wilson cut for many people during his years with Mary McCarthy. To Berryman's wife, Eileen Simpson, Wilson looked like Mary's father, "an old man," she thought at the time, "because he was so prematurely heavy and bald. . . ." Simpson didn't see enough of the Wilsons to form an impression of their relationship, but she retains an image of how McCarthy, whose beauty was softer then than it would appear a few years later, looked in a certain kind of dress. "She dressed like the wife of a man with a certain amount of money," she recalls; the dress was an expensive-looking evening dress, "but it wasn't quite put in focus." It was as if the young Mrs. Wilson was dressing up, "like that grandmother who was interested in style and clothes and buying expensive things," Simpson suggests, referring to Augusta Preston in *Memories of a Catholic Girlhood.*

When Arthur Schlesinger, Jr., first met Mary McCarthy at the critic Harry Levin's in Cambridge around 1943, he remembers feeling "outraged at the fact that Edmund Wilson seemed to be such a terribly old man married to this young and attractive girl." Wilson was only forty-eight, hardly an "old man," Schlesinger reflects, but he never could rid himself of the impression that something was amiss in the alliance. Even Alfred Kazin, who writes harshly of McCarthy in two memoirs, and recalls both Edmund and Mary from the 1940s as "tremendous egos," remembers how "vivacious" Mary appeared alongside Edmund: a "brilliant active personality, that would have seemed like a great gift from some young woman." But Edmund, Kazin adds, was accustomed "to being taken very seriously. No woman would have found him easy to live with." He was "a bit of a dictator," in Kazin's opinion, "entirely bookish and intellectual"—and yet, "despite his girth, also a bit of a lecher."

This was another side of Wilson about which Mary McCarthy is more reserved. There isn't a hint of it in the fiction published during their marriage—not in *The Company She Keeps*, and not in "The Weeds," a story Wilson did not like, which begins: "She would leave him, she thought, as soon as the petunias had bloomed." In "The Weeds," Wilson appears again as the architect husband, whom the heroine wishes dead, even though "he would leave her nothing. . . . What he would do for her by dying would be to relieve her of the necessity of decision," and she wonders, "How many women . . . had poisoned their husbands, not for gain or for another man, but out of sheer inability to leave them. The extreme solution is always the simplest. . . . Murder is more civilized than divorce; the Victorians, as usual, were wiser." McCarthy had given Wilson this story to read in 1944, as she did all her fiction whether he was portrayed in it or not. He made no comment, and she had sent it off to the magazines. When it appeared in *The New Yorker*, he had become "very angry and agitated," McCarthy remembered. "I said, 'but you've already read that.' And he said, 'Damn it, you've *improved* it!' "

It was ten years after their divorce before McCarthy made a fictional pass at Wilson's energetic appetite for sex. An appetite, we learn in Wilson's journals, that could turn the sight and sound of a pretty young violinist into an extended meditation on how the "sawing motion" of the arm and bow "represents the feeling for a woman of the underpart of the penis lingeringly passing in and out and eliciting exquisite music." Members of Wilson's audiences at the Ninety-second Street Y later in the 1940s, who listened to him read the sexually explicit "The Princess with the Golden Hair" from *Memoirs of Hecate County* ("probably the best damn thing I ever wrote, at least, it has given me more satisfaction . . . ," he wrote Morton Zabel), were sometimes disturbed by Wilson's palpable excitment. "He appreciated himself so much that it was a joy to listen to him," the harpist, Daphne Hellman, remembers, but she "hated his attitude about sex . . . it made [her skin] creep. It was a very ugly male chauvinist thing," she adds, though she wouldn't have put it that way then. Even Nabokov led Edmund to believe that with this story, he "had made an unsuccessful attempt to write something like Fanny Hill."

"Old, soured, boiled as an owl a good deal of the time, bored to desperation except when he was working," Mary McCarthy wrote of Miles Murphy in *A Charmed Life*, "he nevertheless had passions . . . that let him know that he was a man still, among senile adolescents. Like an old lion, he nursed the wound Martha had given him," by leaving him, because "he held sex sacred." Strangely enough, Wilson seems never to have objected publicly to this character who embodies an intimate side of his nature more explicitly than the anemic Frederick, and wears his disguise—"He was a fat, freckled fellow with a big frame, a reddish crest of curly hair, and small, pale-green eyes"— thinly, like Groucho Marx wearing a false mustache and stick-on eyebrows that wiggle when he leers. When McCarthy wrote Wilson shortly after publication to assure him that she had "*not* intended" to put him into the novel, he had assured her that while he hadn't read the book, he assumed the character was just "another one of your malignant, red-haired Irishmen" (referring to Henry Mulcahy in *The Groves of Academe*, published three years before).

"I am not freckled and do not have 'small, pale-green eyes,' " he wrote the publisher of Doris Grumbach's 1966 book about Mary McCarthy, *The Company She Kept*, after Coward-McCann sent him the proofs that contained the statement that Miles Murphy not only behaved like Edmund Wilson, he looked like him, as well. "Cf. Wilson's letter: there is no resemblance," McCarthy added in the proof's margin: "Miles has been a boxer, E. is utterly nonathletic. Miles is a sort of mongrel; he talks a ghastly jargon. . . . Miles smokes; E. doesn't. . . ." The publisher was convinced, Grumbach stood corrected, and caveats were inserted.

To Arthur Schlesinger, Jr., in 1955, however, McCarthy revealed the false bottom in her argument. Miles was not really meant to be Edmund, she insisted—for Schlesinger, like most of their friends, had spotted him immediately—"but a modern type quite different . . . the type of modern 'compleat' man who is always a four-flusher like a piece of imitation Renaissance architecture." Nevertheless, "to the extent that Edmund is a boor and a four-flusher (and he really is, Arthur," she interjected, "I could a tale unfold and so could all his wives and his servants and his progeny)," Miles was "a kind of joke extrapolation of him—minus the talent, minus the pathos, for Edmund is pathetic," she added, "probably because of the talent, which creates a kind of hopeless chasm . . . between the man and the quill."

She had drawn on her own feelings "quite directly" in the chapter where Martha remembers her marriage, McCarthy conceded, and she "used certain episodes, altered, from my married life with E., as the raw material to create him," but it was all changed around and new events added—most notably, Miles's blustering into Martha's house to seduce her—"not for purposes of disguise," she explained, "but to make a new whole." If Miles didn't exist in his own right, perhaps he was a failure as a character, she suggested, a possiblility she "refuse[d] to entertain," though others were free to. And then in one of those swoops that recalls Whitman's immortal lines—"Do I contradict myself? Very well, I contradict myself. I am large, I contain multitudes"— she wondered how Schlesinger could have ever thought that "Miles is my idea of Edmund, since Miles is his share of those events."

It was like an earlier occasion when Mary had explained to Dwight Macdonald that the former husband in A Charmed Life couldn't be Edmund because Miles was tall, and Edmund short, Miles wrote successful plays, and while Wilson had written a few little plays, "everybody knows that Edmund never had a successful play in his life." True, true, Macdonald had shrugged helplessly, one must be reading something into it. . . .

In The Company She Kept, Wilson, McCarthy, and Coward-McCann entered into one of those official fictions in which the principals conspire to hide the body from the public. Doris Grumbach played into their hands when she rested her case for the autobiographical core of A Charmed Life on a literal transmission of fact into fiction. The truth, she might have guessed, is nearly always masked; how else does it gain admittance to the play? Still, if there was ever any doubt about where the truth lay in this particular fiction, McCarthy herself set the record straight in an interview with Grumbach, quoted in The Company She Kept. Asked to account for the fact that despite the differences between Miles Murphy and Wilson, their resemblance had been universally recognized, she replied, "In some sort of joking way, it was as if I were saying to Edmund: 'Look what would happen to you if you were transposed by an evil fairy into this ghastly red-haired, self-analytic, jargon-speaking Irishman. This is what you'd be like. Can you recognize yourself?' " The actual circumstances borrowed from their marriage operated in the novel like "a piece of animism," McCarthy suggested, adding "the likeness to him would be something only he would recognize."

One is reminded of William Carlos Williams's insight that Mary McCarthy's fiction is "written principally for those it attacks," in which case *A Charmed Life* may have been written, in part, for an ex-husband who rarely listened to what he was told but thought twice about what he read. Assuming that Wilson did get around to reading his by-then-famous ex-wife's novel about Wellfleet, what, one wonders, did he make of scenes like the following?

Standing face-to-face with Miles Murphy for the first time in years at the home of some mutual friends, Martha Sinnott struggles to suppress her nervous excitement:

> As she named Tern Pond, she colored and hurried on with her exposition, for she and Miles used to picnic there . . . and once or twice, after bathing, they had made love, over her protests, on the sand. . . . Martha had claimed that somebody would come and catch them; she had had a lot of sexual defenses, though she always liked it, in the end.

In *The Forties*, Edmund Wilson memorializes one of these picnics himself, which begins with Mary packing a wicker basket of boiled eggs, bean salad, and cucumber sandwiches. At Wellfleet's Gull Pond, they set a jar of white California wine to cool in the water, not far from a network of moated castles that Reuel has constructed earlier while playing with his nurse. Together they explore the distant shore, admiring the lady's slippers and the tiny white violets growing along the sandy beach—which for Wilson is a Lawrentian pastorale. The violets, whose "long slim purplish stalks [grow] with thready roots in the damp sand," have a "faint slightly acrid pansy smell," he notices; their lower lips are "finely lined as if with beards."

When they arrived, the lake was roughened by a brisk wind, but at the end of their walk the air has grown still and the water appears limpid and lovely. They clear a spot in a grove of pine trees for lunch. Wilson examines a sweet-smelling cluster of baby pine cones, which he finds "embarrassingly soft, almost like a woman's nipples." Beyond the perimeter of their blanket he discerns the deep, divided hoofprints of deer, and out over the pond a yellow and black butterfly—"a monarch?"—flutters above the water. "Mary," he recalls, "looked very pretty and white . . . ripened by the summer sun where her face and neck and arms had been exposed while working on her garden. . . ." The pink tints in her pale skin were in harmony, he thought, with her blue overalls.

The afternoon in this precious corner of Wilson's world is a success; a memory he has pressed into service for posterity, like a moth wing pressed between the pages of a book.

And sex, one senses in scenes like this (from which the actual lovemaking had been cut, at McCarthy's insistence, when she read the first proof), is an unexploded bullet in the wall of fiction that McCarthy erected around her marriage. In *A Charmed Life*, an otherwise talky, over-narrated novel, the scene where Miles seduces Martha on the Empire sofa in her parlor fairly dances off the page. Only when these formidable antagonists are shown "heaving and gasping" in the dark do they come alive as characters. Why? Perhaps because Wilson's "capacity for behaving *incredibly*" (as McCarthy puts it in the letter to Schlesinger) was nowhere more pronounced than in his sexual appetites.

McCarthy runs the seduction scene forward and backward, first from Miles's point of view, then from Martha's, a dramatic device that allows her to give full play to her own robust sexual imagination, and to a nearly inexhaustible appetite for remorse and self-castigation. Miles:

> He followed her back into the parlor, observing the motion of her hips, which pranced a little as she walked, with short, incisive steps, in her high-heeled shoes. Up to that moment, he had not been sure whether he wanted to dally with her or not. But now the old Adam in him sat up and took notice. They were alone, hubby was gone—why not?

The scene is set with a few deft strokes. McCarthy gives us the devil, who tosses off a highball, wipes his lips, glances at his watch, and darts across the room:

> She had struggled at first . . . when he flung himself on top of her on the sofa. But he had her pinioned beneath him with the whole weight of his body. She could only twist her head away from him, half-burying it in one of the sofa pillows while he firmly deposited

kisses on her neck and hair. . . . [H]e did not let her little cries of protest irritate him as they once might have done. . . . She wanted it, obviously, or she would not have asked him in.

Miles has no intention of "raping" Martha, the author states, and it hurts his feelings when she crosses her thighs, "when all he wanted, for the moment, was to hold her in his arms." This is when her hair slips from its pins, and he seizes it, "pressing his mouth into it and inhaling deeply. From the sofa pillow came a muffled cry of disgust. . . ." Miles lumbers on, planting kisses on cheek and ear, nuzzling his ex-wife's neck, growing "almost worshipful" and therefore "lax" in his grip. Martha scrambles over onto her stomach, and lies stiffly, "as if waiting." Encouraged, Miles fumbles for her zipper, but she turns around and presses her fists into his chest. She is wearing a high-necked black dress of thin wool, and his eyes are drawn to her small, firm breasts, straining against the material, "like ripe pears." He bends to kiss them through the wool, but her hands spring up again to block his approach. He kisses her white neck and the hollow of her throat, but whenever he tries to reach her mouth, she pulls away.

And then he gets the idea: "The thing was to respect her scruples. She did not seem to mind if he kissed her arms and shoulders; it was her breasts and mouth she was protecting, out of some peculiar pedantry." It is obvious to Miles that Martha is neither frightened nor opposed to his advances, not very deeply opposed, at any rate. She doesn't scream or try to scratch him; what opposition she offers exercises his wits (and his organ, which Martha can now feel grinding into her pelvis); and he, for his part, doesn't try to lift her skirt. The struggle proceeds in silence, "as if they were afraid of being overheard." There is only their breathing and an occasional muffled " 'Stop!' " from Martha. A string of beads snaps and clatters across the floor. " 'Sorry,' " Miles says as he dives for her left breast. And he hears Martha laugh faintly as she pushes his head away, the humor of the situation overcoming her.

The scene is vintage McCarthy; a send-off to intramural sex (within the family, between consenting adults) that only could have occurred *before* the sexual revolution made sex seem like something men do to women, and that women are henceforth free to 'do' to men, too. The critic Eleanor Widmer is dead wrong to conclude that in her risqué fiction of the 1940s and '50s Mary McCarthy anticipated the sexual revolution of the '60s, when nothing was forbidden and anything could happen. McCarthy is the doyenne of pre-revolutionary sex; there is no fear of flying in her bedrooms, only of getting caught. For young readers today, there must be something kinky about these two has-beens 'heaving and gasping' on the couch, like a couple of adolescents listening for their parents at the door.

To return to the parlor: Miles concludes that Martha now realizes that "one screw, more or less, could not make much difference, when she had already laid it on the line for him about five hundred times." His hunger for her, he thinks to himself, is really a "compliment" in that he is "so well fixed up at home." But that was what was wrong with intelligent women, he reflects, "there was always an *esprit de serieux* lingering around the premises. They lacked a sense of proportion." And he whispers in Martha's ear, " 'You want it, say you want it'." But still she procrastinates.

When he finally gets the zipper started down its steel track, and the dress falls open, and his hand slips in and begins moving along her spine, she stiffens; but when he bends down and kisses her shoulder blade, Martha doesn't try to stop him, her back apparently not being covered by the prohibition. It is when Miles ventures to pull her dress up over her shoulders that he triggers her response:

> "Don't," she cried sharply, as the material started to tear. She sat up in indignation, and his hand slipped in and held her breast cupped. "Take it off," he urged, speaking of her dress in a thick whisper. "I can't," she whispered back, as his other hand stole in and grasped her other breast.

They begin to argue in whispers. Martha mentions Miles's wife, their friends, the town, but not—"and this was curious"—the name of her husband, John Sinnott. The prose heats up, more like *True Confessions* than 'literary' prose, but then McCarthy, here as elsewhere, writes *in character,* and the point of view remains that of Miles Murphy:

> "Please don't," [Martha] begged, with tears in her eyes, while he squeezed her nipples between his fingertips; they were hard before he touched them; her breath was coming quickly. She had caught his lower lip between her teeth, and there was a drawn look on her face, which meant that she was ready for it. "Stop, Miles, I beg you," she moaned, with a terrified air of throwing herself on his mercy. "It won't make any difference," he promised hoarsely.

Still arguing, she lets him slip her dress off her shoulders. "He freed her breasts from her underslip and stared at them hungrily. Martha's eyes closed and she took a deep breath, like a doomed person. 'All right,' she said."

The scene, which is funny partly because the author has such a good time with it, is all the funnier when one considers the misguided view of Mary McCarthy as a scout in the "feminist war that now rages within our society" (Barrett), a sex-critic like Marge Piercy or Margaret Atwood. In fact, the seduction scene is a vamp on reality—though the reality was a lot closer to the fiction than even Mary and Edmund's closest friends supposed. At least in bed, the "ghastly . . . jargon-speaking Irishman" *was* Wilson, as this passage from *The Forties* suggests:

> Sunday afternoon—full of lust. . . . E. came and lay in bed with me . . . and when I abandoned the notion of postponement, my appetite and passion mounted. We did 69 first. She responded to it, flushed darkly—which is rare with her—legs up so that I could push it down into her. I was terrifically swollen and hot—"You were so big!" she said afterwards—and got that green wolfish look in her eyes that is so unlike her ordinary blue-eyed and sweet expression.

It was "our most strongly animal encounter," Edmund Wilson wrote of the February 1947 afternoon with his fourth wife, Elena Mumm Thornton. He had gone on a long time without coming, he added, as in dreams he sometimes had about his "old girls," such as Edna Millay and Anna, the Ukrainian cocktail waitress whose affair with Wilson in the early 1930s inspired "The Princess with the Golden Hair," and in the end he had never "come" (though "she came"), and he had "laid off in a perspiration." Later, Wilson noted, he had gone down to his study and drunk a bottle of ginger ale and eaten what was left of the party nuts after a dinner with his friends Bubs and Mary Hackett. Elena curled up on a love seat with "her beautiful bare feet" to read Francis Perkins on Roosevelt, and then quickly went to sleep. Wilson went back up to bed, where he began to "straighten out" an unpublished manuscript of John Peale Bishop's (then deceased), "wonderfully quiet, clear-minded, content."

Such is life. Fiction only sometimes holds a candle to it.

In the novel, Martha has returned to New Leeds to write a play, a fact that angers Miles, a former playwright, because it reminds him of "that pattern of imitation. She had not changed in the least," he concludes, "she had come back here to compete with him again." Of course, when Mary McCarthy returned to Wellfleet in the spring of 1953 with her third husband, Bowden Broadwater, it was not to put Edmund Wilson in his place in a novel, or to compete with him in the marketplace of notoriety, but that, in effect, is what happened. Moreover, McCarthy succeeded, figuratively speaking, in putting herself in Edmund Wilson's place, at least with the night of stolen kisses, thus creating one of those portraits (again like Dorian Gray's) that might relieve her of some of the burden of feeling she had inherited from the marriage, "the dread and creeping apprehension" that concerned Arthur Schlesinger when he noticed it in the book in 1955.

The scene on the Empire sofa rings true not because it ever took place after McCarthy and Wilson's divorce in 1946 but because it was in just such a contest of wills, in which desire was pitted against fear, that McCarthy was able to bring out something essential in the psychology of her characters, something that had haunted her about her 'surrender' to Edmund Wilson on the couch in Stamford in 1937. Over to Martha:

> Miles had not enjoyed it much either, Martha said pensively to herself, as she picked up the beads from the parlor floor. It had been like an exercise in gluttony. . . . But she did not feel especially bad for what they had done. Now that it was over, it appeared to have been inevitable.

The climax was an anticlimax. After the fleeting moment of desire ("the only thing that shamed her . . . the fact that her senses had awakened under Miles's touch"), Martha had tried to give Miles a good time; or at least that was how Miles saw it, and he had regretted the whole business halfway through. Martha: "She could not take it seriously. All the while she was struggling, she had been suppressing a smile, at his ridiculous searching for her zipper. . . . Her chief worry . . . had been that he would break the sofa."

When she moves into the character of Martha, McCarthy displays that reductive sensibility so annoying to readers like William Carlos Williams, Malcolm Cowley, and Alfred Kazin. Martha, however, displays a telltale passivity: "She had not been alarmed for her virtue, feeling certain that she could free herself once he grasped the sincerity of her objections." She was "disgusted" with Miles for "slavering" over her hair, "but since she could not stop him, she resigned herself—that was the way he was, and his enjoyment could not harm her. This inability to feel outrage was of course her undoing." And there it is, the leitmotif of McCarthy's later account of why she had let 'this old ogre,' Edmund Wilson, steal her away in the first place: "It was like that thing in law [Martha reflects], where if you let somebody cross your property without hindrance, they finally secure a right of way."

But Martha Sinnott, who has thought it all over in the bathroom, where she retreats to sober up (for they're both tight) and wait for Miles to leave, decides she has really brought the night on herself. She shouldn't have asked him in because she *knew*—how could she not? she had been married to him—that Miles would seduce her. Why? Because Miles is the master of her sexual vanity, her need to be desired, something that the reader is never told but infers. And also because the occasion "had been one of those challenges that she always rose to, like a fish to the bait—the fear of being afraid."

A Charmed Life is a continuation of marriage to Edmund Wilson by other means. Even the novel's flashback to Miles and Martha's breakup is lifted almost verbatim from a deposition McCarthy filed in *Wilson* vs. *Wilson,* testifying to her husband's cruelty. The actual deposition describes a showdown in the summer of 1944, when Mary and Edmund were cleaning up after a party they had just given for about eighteen guests:

> Everybody had gone home and I was washing dishes. I asked [Edmund] if he would empty the garbage. He said, "Empty it yourself." I started carrying out two large cans of garbage. As I went through the screen door, he made an ironical bow, repeating, "Empty it yourself." I slapped him—not terribly hard—went out and emptied the cans, then went upstairs. He called me and I came down. He got up from the sofa and took a terrible swing and hit me in the face and all over. He said: "You think you're unhappy with me. Well, I'll give you something to be unhappy about." I ran out of the house and jumped into my car.

In the novel, McCarthy redistributes the blame:

> Their penultimate quarrel . . . had exploded in the middle of the night, after a party, when she was carrying two overflowing pails of garbage and he refused, with a sardonic bow, to hold open the screen door for her. There she was, manifestly the injured party, but instead of leaving it at that, and taxing him with it the next day, when he was weakened with a hangover, she immediately

distributed the guilt by setting down one pail of garbage and slapping him. . . .

Sometime in the 1960s, when Wilson prepared his journals from both the 1930s and 1940s for posthumous publication, he made his counterattack. He found his wife "an amusing and provocative companion, and I really, till the very end, never ceased to be extremely fond of her," he wrote in *The Thirties*. She had "a child-like side," he believed, which made him feel sorry for her, and he had invariably wanted to "rescue" her. "I suppose that I reacted neurotically, too, as I usually do with women I live with, in rebelling against her at intervals, as I used to do against my mother," he added. "Our life—though we had also a great deal of fun—was sometimes absolutely nightmarish."

The picnic at Gull Pond and these afterthoughts hardly exhaust Wilson's reflections on this tumultuous relationship, but they were nearly all that remained after his editor, Leon Edel, showed Mary McCarthy the pages about her in the manuscript of Wilson's journals. Surprisingly, for Edmund Wilson was not given to public hangings where personal relations were involved, he had dug up the oldest bone of contention between them: the question of his ex-wife's sanity. "It was very, very bad stuff," McCarthy told an interviewer afterward, remembering the horror she felt when she discovered "those terrible charges" resuscitated in the manuscript of *The Forties*. "It was like that bomb that Hemingway placed under Scott Fitzgerald," she said, referring to a story Hemingway tells in *A Moveable Feast* about Fitzgerald once wanting to be reassured about the size of his penis. For McCarthy, who knew that people will believe anything if it appears under the right cover, the thought that Edmund Wilson had peppered his journals with shot that would be heard in certain influential literary circles made her eyes roll.

In *The Forties'* manuscript, in language nearly identical to a deposition that Wilson had submitted before their separation hearing in March 1945, he presented the case for his wife's "sinking deeper and deeper into insanity." The original deposition was his defense against the charge of cruelty that McCarthy had brought against him, a charge that came bristling with affidavits of its own. And until his own lawyer talked him out of it, the deposition had been the foundation for Wilson's demand for custody of Reuel, as well. It read, in part:

Plaintiff is the victim of hysterical delusions and has seemed for years to have a persecution complex as far as I am concerned. She seems to believe that I have attacked her and struck her on occasions when nothing of the sort has happened.

In 1945, Wilson's deposition collapsed for lack of support from the doctors he had hired to treat his wife. Sandor Rado, Major Richard Frank, and Abraham Kardiner all submitted affidavits testifying that Mrs. Edmund Wilson had been treated for "psychoneurosis" (Kardiner), and that she exhibited no signs of insanity. For Mary McCarthy herself, however, such fine distinctions made little difference. In 1945, 1982, and to the end of her life, the charges hurt.

15

The Breakup

"There is no question [but] that you have been very much better this

last year. There have been long stretches when you seemed to

me to handle things better and to be a great deal happier

than at any time since we have been married—isn't that true?

and I am sorry that I have sometimes been demoralized myself

and let you down when you were doing your best."

—EDMUND WILSON TO MARY McCARTHY, 7/13/44

*L*ike all things held together by force of fear and habit, a bad marriage, when it breaks and becomes a divorce, shows its worst colors. So it was with the seven-year marriage of Mary McCarthy and Edmund Wilson, which culminated in the separation suit filed by McCarthy in New York in February 1945, and in divorce in December 1946. In ending the thing, both parties played the villain of each other's fantasies.

In late January 1945, with the aid of Mannie Rousuck, whom Wilson despised, Mary took the 'baby' and ran. Rousuck loaned her two hundred dollars to hire a lawyer, and helped her coordinate her flight to the Stanhope Hotel with six-year-old Reuel to coincide with the arrival of a process server at 14 Henderson Place, the mews near Gracie Mansion where she and Edmund had rented an apartment, so that her husband would not be forewarned and refuse to be served with a subpoena. Filing suit for "extreme cruelty," McCarthy sought a legal separation that would set the stage for divorce, the only other grounds for a New York divorce in the 1940s being adultery, and she had no evidence of adultery.

"Dear Edmund," ran the runaway note:

I'm afraid I don't see what else there is to do. Perhaps the fighting is mostly my fault, but that's not a reason for our stay-

ing together. . . . I'm sorry. This could probably all be managed
with less eclat, but the only way I can ever break off anything is to
run away.

At the end of the summer of 1944, Wilson had finally agreed to
draw up a separation agreement, but then he had broken it off. It had
happened like this. After the confrontation over the garbage cans in
July, Mary had run off to New York, and to get her back, Edmund had
promised that he would "not drink anything all summer. I think it is
hard on Reuel to wreck the family in the middle of the summer like
this," he wrote her at the New Weston Hotel, where she had fled
before when their quarrels grew violent. "It would be easier for you
and me to set up separate establishments in the autumn when he will
be going to school," he continued, arguing the case for a "modus
vivendi for the next two months." And Mary had agreed. For the rest
of the summer, Wilson had gone on the wagon, but in the fall they had
gone down to the city together, and, ensconced in a comfortable
brownstone in Henderson Place (a nineteenth-century mews named
after one of Nathalie Rahv's ancestors on her mother's side), and with
Reuel enrolled in St. Bernard's School, Wilson had changed his mind.

Instead, McCarthy recalled years later, he demanded that she return to the analyst. Psychiatrists usually don't want you to change your
life situation while you are in analysis, something she figured Wilson
was counting on. "And all the time he was threatening what he would
do if I would leave him," she added, "use all his pull, influence, and
money—" To harm her career? No; "to keep Reuel." Reuel was her
Achilles' heel.

Wilson, who had recently taken over Clifton Fadiman's job reviewing books at *The New Yorker,* had acquired some new clout. "I
am going to be all right for money," he wrote Mary on January 17,
1945, from Red Bank, where he was visiting his mother. He had had
lunch with the *New Yorker*'s editor, William Shawn, who was sending
Wilson to Europe in March as a *post*war correspondent, as it were; and
he would be paid the grand sum of one thousand dollars for a three-
thousand-word article every other week. Shawn even promised "a
couple of thousand" in advance. Mary's funds from both grain-
elevator stocks and writing had dwindled around this time to almost
nothing. In any case, she had gone back to Dr. Abraham Kardiner, but
she had insisted he tell Wilson that returning to analysis did not
commit her to staying with her husband—which Dr. Kardiner had
done. And Wilson, according to McCarthy, had responded by saying

" 'the deal is off,' " and by tearing up the separation agreement they had put together in the fall. It was then that she had bolted and filed a hostile suit for separation.

Wilson's January letter throws a slightly different light on the events leading to the breakup. He didn't "want to sign a separation agreement now for reasons I have already explained," which almost certainly included his impending trip. "I wish you would go to Kardiner," he urged, "not because I want him to talk you into any different course of conduct, but because I think you really need it." Kardiner, he said, "was still holding a place for you. . . . I think he thought you might change your mind, and I think you probably ought to call him up and let him know if you're sure of not going."

If Mary went to see Abraham Kardiner at this late date, it must have been only to have him relay the message about analysis not tying her to the marriage. Or maybe Edmund's letter was the last straw. After reiterating his refusal to honor the separation agreement, he had insisted that all she had to gain from his signing it then was "the satisfaction of feeling that you have somehow scored off me. Later on, we can separate, or divorce, if you want to. I will sign a paper . . . agreeing to do this," Wilson had added in what may have become a familiar litany, "when I get back."

Before the month was out, in any event, he was asking the writer Anaïs Nin to accompany him while he bought his "uniform" and sleeping bag for the trip to Europe. ("The war must be really over . . . if *The New Yorker* is sending Wilson out as a correspondent," William Barrett reflected when he ran into Edmund's "short and pudgy figure, above which the face of Herbert Hoover looked intently at you, dressed in the khakis of a military correspondent" a few months later in Rome, where Barrett was serving as an information officer with the U. S. Army.) Wilson had praised Nin's *Under a Glass Bell* in an omnibus review in *The New Yorker* in 1944; and now he invited her to lunch. "Even though not an intimate friend," Nin wrote in her diary in January 1945, "Wilson senses my sympathy and turns toward it. He is lonely and lost." They talk, and he tells her about his "suffering" with Mary McCarthy—who reminds Anaïs Nin of Lillian, one of the three women in her new book, *This Hunger*, "the one who seeks liberation in aggression."

When he returned to the United States in August, Wilson had read *This Hunger* and pronounced it lacking in "form. It is not concrete enough," he told Nin. In Lillian, however, who unlike Mary "never drank or went to the icebox," he found much to remind him of his wife. In August, he portrayed himself to Anaïs Nin as a man who suffered because he loved clever women; " 'clever women are impossibly neurotic,' " he told her as they sat rocking in the two chairs that remained in the apartment on Henderson Place after Mary had cleared it out. "There is a paradox in Edmund Wilson which interested me," Nin noted; "[c]ontrary to his academic, formal, classical work, and the cold intellectual criticism, he himself is fervent, irrational, lustful, violent." Wilson's house, his books, the Hogarth prints hanging on the otherwise empty walls, remind her of her father ("bourgeois . . . classical"), and she senses "nameless dangers. But Wilson clings. He has a book for me. He has a review of *This Hunger*." Wilson wanted Nin "to help him reconstruct his life, to help him choose a couch," she writes, "but I wanted to leave," which was probably a good thing. "Wilson, if he ever tastes of me," Anaïs Nin concluded, accurately enough, one suspects, "will be eating a substance not good for him. . . ."

By February 1945, the war of the depositions between Mary McCarthy and Edmund Wilson had begun. McCarthy's charge that since the birth of their son she had "been compelled to suffer physical and mental humiliation at the hands of the defendant," and that this happened in the presence of both strangers and family, including Reuel, was followed by Edmund Wilson's startling assertion:

> At no time did I ever attack her. I have found it necessary to protect myself against violent assaults by her in the course of which she would kick me, bite me, scratch me and maul me in any way she could. She has even gone so far as to break down a door to my study to get at me and she has on other occasions pushed paper under the door of my study to set fire to it.

According to Wilson, the faithful Hattie had been a witness to more than one of these assaults, for it had been "necessary on occasion for the maid to intervene between us," he added, "to stop a threatened attack against me."

Hattie, who had left Wilson's service six years before, didn't testify. Nor did anyone else testify in support of Wilson's claim that his wife was "a psychiatric case," who had developed "a progressively aggravated condition of hysteria, which resulted in violent outbursts toward me"; although years later, Rosalind Wilson said that it was only to protect Reuel that she hadn't stepped forth. McCarthy "bamboozled" her father, she suggests today; she was "mentally ill" when

she married him, "and did not tell him . . ." Philip Rahv is remembered
telling Rosalind, at twenty, that he never intended to divorce and
marry Mary because of her illness." In 1945, nonetheless, Wilson was
advised to drop the charge. What the deposition did reflect, however,
was the rapid deterioration of relations between Edmund and Mary
after their return to the city the previous fall.

In her deposition, McCarthy pointed to the fact that Wilson had
publicly accused her of infidelity—once in the presence of Reuel—as
an instance of "mental humiliation." As a complaint, this one had
some foundation in Wilson's well-known jealousy of Mary's friendships with the boys from "Partisansky Review." And indeed, the depositions that McCarthy's lawyer gathered on his client's behalf are most
convincing on the issue of Wilson's "violent temper [and] ridiculous
jealousy. . . ." All but one were submitted by people who had known
Edmund before he married Mary McCarthy—such as Adelaide
Walker, who recalled the time in the fall of 1941 when she and Mary
had driven their children up to Boston to see a doctor, and after they
had returned late that night, Edmund, who had been drinking heavily,
pounced on them, accusing Mary of having had a "clandestine meeting" with a man, and Adelaide Walker with having connived in her
deception. And yet Wilson had reason to be jealous, for sometime
during Mary's numerous furloughs to New York, she had established
a liaison with Clement Greenberg.

II

It is impossible to guess what Edmund Wilson actually knew about
his wife's affairs, but they would probably remain Mary McCarthy's
secret today if it wasn't for Mary McCarthy—who couldn't resist a
stirring confession after the fact. "I had an affair with Greenberg, and
I did not enjoy this affair and did not like him. You know when you
have an affair with some man you don't like," she said in 1987,
"somehow they're the hardest to break with." Like her marriage to
Wilson, which the Greenberg affair resembled in being regretted from
the beginning, it did prove hard to forget. As late as 1960, when
McCarthy wrote Hannah Arendt that she had revived the whole sorry
interlude during a night of shared confidences with a man she really
loved, she was still squirming on a bed of hot scruples.

Actually, Mary McCarthy's liaison with Clement Greenberg—"Sir
Clement Greenberg (O.M., Ph.D., D. Litt [Horizon]., W.C. [Oxon.],
PMLA, DT)," Delmore Schwartz billed him in a letter to Dwight

Macdonald—was a poorly kept secret in the 1940s; not much more than a "fling," William Phillips remembers, but one followed almost immediately by an animosity on McCarthy's part whose bitterness Phillips never could understand. Greenberg, an art critic with a taste for ideological discourse, had made his mark in *Partisan Review* as early as 1939 with the appearance of one of those ground-breaking essays, "Avant-Garde and Kitsch," which, whether you agree with it or not, wears its years with astonishing lightness because it is so prophetic. In it Greenberg noted the demise of public support of the visual arts following the collapse of the WPA-sponsored Federal Arts Project; and he voiced his concern for the absence of new patrons who, he declared, could only come from the "ruling class." The avant-garde had been "abandoned by those to whom it actually belongs—our ruling class. . . . No culture can develop without a social basis," he explained, by which he meant "a source of stable income." In Europe, traditionally, support was provided by "an elite among the ruling class of that society from which [the avant-garde] assumed itself to be cut off, but to which it had always remained attached by an umbilical cord of gold." In the United States, where a new avant-garde was arising, Greenberg argued that a similar system must prevail.

It was as clear a triumph of the elitist principle in modernism, and its separation from Marxism, as could be heard in these years. And Greenberg promulgated it without any loss of caste as a Marxist intellectual of Trotskyist persuasion. In this essay and others, he went on to launch an "historically inevitable" course for what he called "American Style Painting," painting that had outgrown its dependence on the pictorial world; "pure painting," whose object would henceforth be the projection of its own formal elements: color, "significant form," and so on. He launched a prophet: Jackson Pollock, just as Harold Rosenberg, Greenberg's competitor in the selling of Abstract Expressionism after World War II, would launch Willem de Kooning. By the early 1940s, when Mary had begun to see him privately, Greenberg was a force to be reckoned with. Like Philip Rahv a few years before, he was a power broker in the all-important, all-American realm of marketing the '*new*': in this case, the new American painting.

There isn't much evidence that McCarthy interested herself in Greenberg's theories about art. "Theory, in artists, did not matter to him, only results," she writes of Miles Murphy in *A Charmed Life*; and in this instance Miles probably speaks for the author. "Warren seemed to think that progress was mandatory in art and bubbled about advances and setbacks," Miles observes of his friend Warren Coe, whose electrifying portrait of Martha he is about to buy. "Most artists talked that way nowadays . . . and most of them had a father-figure in the background who supplied the motor-ideas," he reflects, evoking for the cognoscenti of the 1950s the imposing figures of Greenberg and Rosenberg. "They were all boy scouts in their cordorary fashion, eager beavers, following the leader, some jackleg critic or straw-boss philosopher."

What did interest McCarthy about Clement Greenberg is hard to say. In her personal inferno, he is presented as "very sadistic," an overbearing man who used to volunteer to come around and "spank Reuel" after she had left Edmund. A few years later she remembered hearing that Greenberg had told someone that the reason she hadn't put him in *The Oasis* was because " 'Mary knows that if she put me in I'd come and beat up Bowden' " (McCarthy's third husband).

Clement Greenberg represented a return to the squabbling fraternity from which McCarthy had come to feel exiled by her marriage to Edmund Wilson. If she decided later that "inwardly . . . I just loathed that smarmy man," it may have been partly because in choosing Greenberg she had actually set herself farther away from the one figure in the group who really mattered to her, Philip Rahv. In any case, it was nearly always as an enemy of Rahv's that Greenberg was remembered by McCarthy in later years; that is: "Clement Greenberg always *hated* Philip Rahv, and was consumed with envy . . . and he organized internal opposition on the magazine . . . he wanted to overthrow him, like a dictator." And he nearly did in 1948 when Greenberg and Phillips set up a lunchtime confrontation with Rahv over Rahv's penchant for malicious gossip, and for monopolizing the editorial affairs of *Partisan Review*.

In later years, McCarthy came to see even the 1941 confrontation that she had entered into with Dwight Macdonald and Clement Greenberg against Philip Rahv, over the latter's support of the war, in a new light. "That may have been *against Rahv*," she concluded, a power play. "We didn't realize it then, or I didn't anyway, but it might have been the first symptom—" She could still hear Greenberg's triumphant words buzzing in her ear: ". . . *his hands* [Rahv's] *were shaking like autumn leaves*," when Greenberg told her about the restaurant showdown in 1948. And suddenly a whole string of confrontations at *Partisan Review* strikes her as an outbreak of "male rivalry," of which the innocent Rahv was largely unaware.

As for McCarthy's own affair with Greenberg, whatever else it was it set her at odds with herself, or with an image of herself; and while she could not keep from bringing it up, she couldn't help but drop it either, and leave unanswered the question of why this business of falling in with the man of one's nightmares was such an oft-told tale.

The breakup of the marriage to Edmund Wilson, meanwhile, proceeded like the labor of birth over many months. The war of the depositions was but a late stage along the way, as was the interlude with Clement Greenberg, which flared up and subsided once the separation of the principals was complete. The real turning point in McCarthy's life with Wilson had been the violent quarrel in July 1944 that led her to run away from Wellfleet and hide out in New York, and then, like the heroine of "The Weeds," to return for another go-round when she had exhausted her alternatives, and her husband had sued for a reconciliation. In this swift sequence of events, all the elements of the unraveling of McCarthy's second marriage are revealed. The violence had erupted after a party, when both Mary and Edmund had been drinking, and Wilson's penchant for jealous outbursts was at its height. The confrontation, moreover, took place when Wilson's teenage daughter was in residence; and Wilson was not alone in observing, as he wrote Mary in hindsight, that it was "always true that Rosalind upsets the balance of the family when she comes. . . ." McCarthy also remembered feeling the pinch when Wilson's daughter was with them (something not lost on Rosalind Wilson herself; she would have much preferred Dawn Powell as a stepmother, she remarks today).

Nothing threw Wilson into a greater imbalance than when he perceived that Rosalind and Mary were in league against him, as a passage in *The Forties'* manuscript shows he did. Rosalind, Wilson wrote, "needed an older woman who could set her an example of dignity. Margaret [Canby, Wilson's second wife] had always been perfect with her and Rosalind had been very fond of her," he recalled. "But since Mary was such a strong personality she [Rosalind] imitated her shrewish ways. I had to deal with two children." On the night of the famous quarrel, Mary had been joined in her flight by Rosalind, who was not really in league with her—later, in a memoir, Rosalind Wilson attributed Mary's "abortive leavetakings" to her "brief involvement" with a "complicated Jewish intellectual" in New York (Greenberg), adding, "She was Anna Karenina without the warmth. . . ."

The exchange of blows over the overflowing garbage pails might seem to confirm Wilson's assertion that it was Mary who was the aggressor in their physical conflicts. She had slapped him first; perhaps

it was this unexpected behavior in a wife that triggered his own rage
and gave him a rationale for excusing his violent behavior later on the
grounds that it had been "necessary to protect myself. . . ." But the
blows McCarthy had sustained, at least by her own account, exceeded
all bounds.

Wilson, she related years later, had chased her "blind drunk" into
Reuel's bedroom, where a good part of the beating he gave her that
night actually occurred. When she and Rosalind had run out of the
house and jumped into the car—which ran out of gas at Gull Pond—he
had pursued them and crashed through a window in the front door,
cutting his arm. McCarthy didn't remember how she and Rosalind got
home; maybe they borrowed some gas from Adelaide Walker; but
when they returned, Rosalind went in and "negotiated." Wilson was
to leave Mary alone, "not engage in any more fisticuffs," and "stay in
his own part of the house," which he did. Mary had gone to bed, Reuel
had gotten back to sleep, and her exodus, when it occurred, happened
the following day after an intricately "hi-larious" chain of events
that (as a narration) perfectly satisfies Mary McCarthy's taste for the
ridiculous.

The next morning the Wilsons' housekeeper, Miss Forbes, whom
McCarthy refers to, in an interview, as the "nursery governess," as if
she was only one of their numerous servants, had arrived to take
charge of Reuel. Seeing blood on the kitchen floor, she had followed
the trail upstairs to Wilson's room and demanded that he get up and
show her where he had cut himself. After some dispute, Wilson had let
Miss Forbes bandage the wound and call the doctor, but when the
doctor arrived, he had thrown him out, which was when "I decided to
get out of there, yes!" McCarthy exclaims. Miss Forbes, however, had
informed her that she could not stay in the house alone at night with
Mr. Wilson, "not because of his conduct," McCarthy continues, "but
because she had promised her mother when she went into service that
she would never stay alone with a man." Mary called Adelaide Walker
to see whether Miss Forbes could sleep there, and Adelaide had agreed;
but she had forgotten that she was going away herself that night, and
Miss Forbes, that "valiant Scotswoman," had been left alone with
Charlie Walker. A few days later, when Mary was installed in the New
Weston Hotel, and Edmund Wilson was at home with Miss Forbes,
Reuel, and Rosalind, a huge salmon had appeared at the door in
Wellfleet, a present to Mary from Mannie Rousuck, who was fishing
on the Gaspé Peninsula. "And Edmund"—McCarthy smiles her
crooked smile—"had to cope."

In "The Weeds," the runaway wife descends the hotel elevator, reviewing the sentences she will serve up to acquaintances who ask her why she has left her husband (" 'I would have left him long ago if it hadn't been for those damned petunias,' " strikes the right note, she thinks, avoiding vindictiveness and piety, and introducing some humor into a tough situation), when the elevator door opens and she sees her husband sitting in the lobby. The narrator is wise to the wife's "native patois, where jest masks truth but does not deny it," and there is more than a little of this masking in McCarthy's later account of her ordeal with Wilson. Life really had been like that, though.

"The problem of providing a chaperone for Miss Forbes has proved a considerable nuisance," Wilson wrote Mary in New York. He had persuaded Adelaide Walker and some other women friends to spend alternate nights with him and the housekeeper, but Adelaide had "never turned up." Someone else "let me down late at night," he complained, and finally he had had to resort to spending the night with Herbert Solow. The next day Wilson had sent for Vladimir and Vera Nabokov, who were not good company; and the day after that he had asked another friend, who was forced to leave when his estranged wife turned up for cocktails, whereupon Wilson had "to get Vladimir out of a sound sleep to come over here with Vera." From that night on, he informed Mary, he was arranging to have "Miss F. herself go over to the Walkers to sleep. . . . She is capable, kindly and well-intentioned," he concluded, "but she is really of a formidable stupidity."

"Any woman who has ever had her wrist twisted by a man recognizes a fact of nature as humbling as a cyclone to a frail tree branch," Elizabeth Hardwick once remarked in a review of Simone de Beauvoir's *The Second Sex*, and wondered, "How can *anything* be more important than this?" "Lots," one imagines Mary McCarthy replying; and yet something like this fact of nature certainly operated in her dealings with Edmund Wilson. Wilson seemed to shrink from his violence himself when he wrote Mary on July 13, 1944, that among the other circumstances surrounding the "mess" he had caused during the fateful night in Wellfleet were his own "bad habits," which, he concluded, "did the rest." "Bad habits" is his shorthand for heavy drinking, which often accompanied his desire to lash out at a woman who was both loved and resented with a passion he felt for no one else.

Back and forth he could swing on this point, sometimes in the same letter:

I have really loved you more than any other woman and have felt closer to you than to any other human being. I think, though, that it is true that, as lovers, you and I scare and antagonize each other in a way that has been getting disastrous lately (though sometimes I have been happier and more exalted with you than I have ever been with anybody). And when you make me feel that you don't want me, all my fear of not being loved, which I have carried all my life from childhood, comes out in the form of resentment.

At least in letters, Wilson revealed an awareness of the differences between them that was more sensitive than his overbearing actions suggested. The difference in their ages, for example, was "a real difficulty between us," he conceded in July. "I prevent you from doing things that are no longer to my taste but that are perfectly natural for you to want to do," he wrote, while Mary, for her part, did not "sympathize with the miseries—like the death of old friends, bad habits and diseases of one's own, and a certain inevitable disillusion with the world that has to be struggled against—that hit you when you get on in your forties." (In the spring of 1944, Wilson was stunned by the death of John Peale Bishop, who had undergone a shocking deterioration in his last years, seeming almost senile when he died, Wilson wrote Christian Gauss. He had been thinking about the old group from Princeton: Bishop, Fitzgerald, Stan Dell, Teek Whipple, all but one dead; and in certain ways, he suggested to Gauss, "Princeton did not serve them very well. I said this to Mary, who has had considerable opportunity to observe men from the various colleges," he added, "and she said: 'Yes, Princeton didn't give them quite moral principle enough to be writers.' Instead, it gave you too much respect for money and country-house social prestige. Both Scott and John," he thought, "fell victims to this. . . ."

When McCarthy recalls the stark contrast between the Wilson she called "the Princeton gentleman," who came to get her when she ran away—"the person who wrote the articles," and letters like the above—and "the person that you'd been living with . . . a kind of monster," one senses she wasn't very happy or exalted with either side of Wilson. She was married; happiness or exaltation had nothing to do with it. She was married to Edmund Wilson, and she was Reuel Wilson's mother. These were positions of consequence, more difficult to sustain than that of critic, fiction writer, or bohemian girl.

Nothing conveys the pathos of McCarthy and Edmund Wilson's relations with each other better than Edmund's efforts to reassure her:

"I want you to know . . . I know that you have made an effort to keep house for Reuel and me," he wrote her at the New Weston Hotel, "and that we all appreciate it. You have been wonderful except at those times when you turn the whole thing into a kind of masochism that is calculated to make other people as uncomfortable as you are." In an unpublished passage from *The Forties*, however, Wilson's condescension leaps to the fore when he complains that one of "Mary's childish traits" was that she was never able to decide things herself, even with Reuel—"but then would oppose objections to all my suggestions. . . ." Nevertheless, "she would always accept my decisions," he declared. "Though so positive in her opinions, she did not want to take this kind of responsibility. And yet Mary all through this was making an effort to do her duty. . . . She was capable of much dignity of character, and this made her collapses tragic."

A mortuary reminiscence, one might say. And the survivor's displeasure is not hard to comprehend. "One of the strangest things, for me, reading these charges," Mary McCarthy wrote her lawyer in 1982, after reviewing the manuscript entries pertaining to their marriage, "is that while they were being penned Wilson and I were on excellent terms." Long after the reason for their getting together, Reuel, had grown up and married, Edmund was "suggesting lunches, drinks, etc., whenever he was in my vicinity," McCarthy added, "sending me his annual 'Christmas letter.' . . . So that I never suspected, not for a second, the time-bomb he was fashioning."

But Wilson's vengeful temper was always unpredictable, as Nathalie Rahv reported in a deposition she submitted in March 1945. After noting that Wilson "always took the attitude . . . that all of Mrs. Wilson's friends should be made to feel unwelcome in his household," an understatement as far as she and Philip Rahv were concerned, Nathalie went on to say that he

> appeared to take delight in scolding and upbraiding his wife for petty matters. He humiliated her in my presence and in the presence of other friends by attempting to belittle her efforts at running the household and performing her wifely duties. He was constantly asking where his things were when it was perfectly obvious where they were.

In a transparent reference to Wilson's charge that his wife was psychologically unfit to take custody of their child, she suggested "that any nervousness that Mrs. Wilson suffered was the direct result of her husband's difficult manner . . ." It was Wilson who was "temperamentally unbalanced," in Nathalie Rahv's opinion, "and his crude conduct and rude demeanor was such as would induce nervousness in anyone closely associated with him."

None of McCarthy's several deponents testified to having witnessed the physical violence she alleged in her own deposition, but the statements create a context in which such charges can be believed. Still, reviewing the case many years later, one is struck by the vigor with which Mary McCarthy went to the mat with this formidable man, seventeen years her senior. ("Formidable and obnoxious looking," Kevin McCarthy thought at the time: "not friendly.") In the letter she wrote her lawyer in 1982, she set forth her own version of the "fits of alienation" described by Wilson. While most of the accounts were "almost entirely fabricated," she claimed, the story of her setting fire to some papers and shoving them under the locked door of his study was not. "And that does sound crazy," she conceded. "My defense is that one of his favorite ploys was to hit me and then run into his study and lock the door to escape retaliation. Wouldn't that drive you mad?"

The scrapper's pulse still races between these lines. "Do you try to treat a domineering person the same as he treats you?" asked one of the questions on the "Personality Inventory" Mary had been given at the Payne Whitney Clinic in 1938, and the answer, which would never change, was "Yes." With Wilson, nonetheless, McCarthy was up against a power she did fear. Wilson's influence, his "pull," frightened her and persuaded her to return again and again after their confrontations.

Edmund Wilson was just a literary man, but inside the kingdom of letters he was the Red Queen. " . . . [A]n established old resident," the critic Warner Berthoff writes: "we picture him on a balcony . . . overlooking the town, a county seat perhaps (for he is a man of the world)—beset by uneasiness at some of the changes taking place before him but not compelled to add them all up and arrive at a genuinely new sum. . . ." The same posture carried over into personal life, and woe be it for the recalcitrant servant or wife who opposed his will. Naturally McCarthy was afraid Wilson would use his influence to keep Reuel, and her fear of this possibility partly explains her vivid fear of his power to declare her a "psychiatric case," and thus unfit to be a mother. "Mary was very much alone, and in many ways much weaker than you," Adelaide Walker reminded Edmund in 1947, when he still refused to forgive Walker for testifying on Mary's behalf in 1945. McCarthy was the weaker party. Yet there is something excessive about her fear of the insanity charge, as if it is rooted in her own imagination as well as in Wilson's. Or maybe this was one fight she would not or could not undertake: the fight to defend her right to break down, to foul the nest in combat with the demons of childhood, to participate in a Jekyll and Hyde drama far from unusual among writers, without being branded an 'hysteric.'

For the mature Mary McCarthy, the most offending passage in the manuscript of *The Forties* was the one in which Wilson called her "an hysteric of the classical kind who makes scenes. . . . In her spells of hysteria, she would be likely to identify me with the uncle by marriage whom she had hated and with whom she and her brother Kevin had been sent to live after her parents' death," he stated. "She would accuse me, in her fits, of imprisoning her and of other offenses which were quite inappropriate." In his 1945 deposition, Wilson had given as one of the problems which the psychoanalysts had confronted "this imagined terrorism by me and her identification of me with her aunt's husband who had treated her terribly during her childhood."

In the fiction written most directly out of her experience with psychoanalysis, McCarthy makes the same connection (Meg Sargent's "father" representing Harold Preston):

> "Finally . . . your father dies, and you are free to make a real marriage. You at once marry Frederick and imitate, as much as it's possible for a grown woman, your own predicament as a child. You lock yourself up again, you break with your former friends, you quit your job; in other words, you cut yourself off completely. You even put your money in his bank account."

This is Dr. James speaking, who would have been Dr. Richard Frank at the time. The physician addresses the patient, who shares the analysis with the reader—thereby securing some dispensation from the horror of living it out in practice. The "Ghostly Father" of the tale is really posterity; and the unknown reader, as always, holds the key to posterity's judgment. Dr. James continues:

> "You are alone: if you cry out, no one will listen; if you explain, no one will believe you. Frederick's own weaknesses contribute to this picture; they affirm its reality. His own insecurity makes him tyrannical and over-possessive; his fear of emotional expenditure makes him apparently indifferent."

Thus had McCarthy taken her own case to the typewriter, to fiction; but she had not been absolved.

In the story, Meg Sargent regards her own "bad habits" with incredulity—"as if she had lent her house to a family of squatters. . . ." She would like to be assured that none of the ugly scenes she has played out with men will stick. Everything will be "just the same" after certain repairs are made—which is where psychoanalysis comes in, restoring reason to the throne, reestablishing continuity between an "analyzed" past and a desired future. Indeed, psychoanalysis had been made to work for Mary McCarthy—a truth one comes to appreciate grudgingly, in spite of her own arguments to the contrary. Analysis of an old-fashioned Freudian kind helped her discover the importance of her years with Uncle Myers and Aunt Margaret. The ritual on the couch allowed her to overcome a bondage to the past. And it is in the analytically charged fiction of *The Company She Keeps* that McCarthy begins to 'try on' the illustrious roles she will play in years to come.

In "Ghostly Father, I Confess," Meg recalls the excitement and gratitude she felt when she learned (at twelve) that her Protestant father was going to let her leave the convent. Losing her faith was a rite of passage, and she had resolved that "she would repay his confidence in her by having a brilliant career." She would be "a great writer, an actress, an ambassador's gifted wife."(James West, McCarthy's fourth husband, was not an ambassador, but he was the public affairs officer at the American embassy in Warsaw in 1960 when they met.) Meg had also wondered whether her guardian "would like it best if she were to study for the bar"—and in 1952, in the heyday of government loyalty oaths and security checks, McCarthy came close to doing that, too.

"A great lady of some sort who spoke six languages fluently . . ." That was something else to be. A few years after putting the idea of law school behind her, McCarthy had hobnobbed with Bernard Berenson at his villa in Tuscany, and added Italian to the French and Latin she already knew (German coming later), in order to research two lavish volumes on the art and architecture of Venice and Florence. After leaving politics, little magazines, and law behind her in the mid-1950s—temporarily, in the case of politics—the image of a "great lady" snapped into focus in sittings for Cecil Beaton. Only the person who made disgusting scenes got left behind on the cutting-room floor. But the chemistry of self-improvement being what it is, this party, of course, would find its way back.

PRECEDING PAGE:
Mary McCarthy, 1916.
LEFT: *Harold Preston,*
Mary's maternal
grandfather.
BELOW: *Augusta*
Morganstern
Preston, Mary's
grandmother,
on the Seattle house
porch with children,
Harold Jr. and
Therese (Tess), Mary's
mother, and Mrs.
Preston's sister, Rose
Gottstein, around 1910.

TOP LEFT: *Tess Preston
and Roy McCarthy on
holiday in Oregon, 1911.*
TOP RIGHT: *Roy and Tess,
before their marriage.*
RIGHT: *Four generations
in Seattle (left to right):
Mary, Simon Manly
Preston (great-grandfather),
Kevin McCarthy, Harold
Preston, and Tess McCarthy
with baby Preston, early 1916.*

PRECEDING PAGE: *Three generations of McCarthys: Roy McCarthy, Kevin, J. H. McCarthy, Mary, Lizzie Sheridan McCarthy with Sheridan, Tess McCarthy, and Preston, late 1917.*
ABOVE: *In Minneapolis, Aunt Margaret (Shriver) with Preston, Mary, Kevin, and Sheridan McCarthy, 1921.*
LEFT: *Mary in Dutch costume for school play, 1923.*

RIGHT: *In Seattle, the teenage Mary McCarthy at the Annie Wright Seminary, 1928.*
BELOW: *Annie Wright's graduating class of 1929. (Mary, first row, second from right)*

LEFT: *Vassar's Taylor Gate.*
BELOW: *Main building,
with the porte cochere
(demolished in 1961) intact;
the South Tower, home of
McCarthy's rooming group,
is in the background.*

*Mary McCarthy, dressed for
a prom in 1931, a far cry
from the "skinny
figure, . . . racing around
in flats," whose terrifying
"verbal performance in
class" some bitter classmates
recalled in 1964 after reading
The Group.*

TOP *(left to right): Mary's close friend, Frani Blough; classmates Eunice Clark and Kay McLean, who partly inspired* The Group's *heroine, Kay Strong Petersen.*
LEFT: *Mary's favorite teachers, Helen Sandison, chairman of the English Department, and Anna Kitchel.*

ABOVE: *The 1932 Hall Play,* Uncle's Been Dreaming, *was adapted from a Dostoevsky story. Elizabeth Bishop, LEFT, is the little man in the center; Mary stands in profile, immediately stage left.*

ABOVE: *Harold (John) Johnsrud and Mary McCarthy were married on Mary's birthday, June 21, 1933, when this picture was taken.*
RIGHT: *Mary and her second husband, Edmund Wilson, on the porch of their Wellfleet house, 1942.*

LEFT: *Mary and her son, Reuel Wilson, born on Christmas Day 1938, with the Wilsons' dog, "Wrecky," 1943.* BELOW: *Mary McCarthy and Edmund Wilson strike an "American Gothic" pose.*

ABOVE: *Among the literati on Wellfleet's beaches, Edmund Wilson and Arthur Schlesinger, Jr., pictured here in 1948, were familiar figures.*

PRECEDING PAGES: *Bowden Broadwater,*
McCarthy's third husband, and Mary shown
at Westport Harbor, c. 1952.
Mary and her brother, the actor Kevin McCarthy,
ABOVE, *at Westport Harbor, c. 1952.*
LEFT: *Mary confers with her old employer, E. J.*
(Mannie)Rousuck, around the same time.
BELOW: *Reuel and his mother at the Lobster*
House, Newport, R.I.

A "natural mistress of rich
and delicious desserts,"
Broadwater once said of his
wife, whose Rhode Island
kitchen, ABOVE, was a
treasured retreat.
LEFT: Robert Lowell, Mary,
Reuel, Elizabeth Hardwick,
and Bowden gather in a
Boston restaurant, 1956.
BELOW: McCarthy, Nicola
Chiaromonte, and Dwight
Macdonald in New York, 1948.

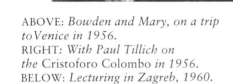

ABOVE: *Bowden and Mary, on a trip to Venice in 1956.*
RIGHT: *With Paul Tillich on the* Cristoforo Colombo *in 1956.*
BELOW: *Lecturing in Zagreb, 1960.*

Part Five

■

Truro / Bard / New York / Paris / Newport:
1945–1953

A *Time* of *Liberation*

"When the instruments are broken and unusable, when plans are

blasted and effort is meaningless, the world appears with a

childlike and terrible freshness, suspended trackless in a void."

—JEAN-PAUL SARTRE, AFTER WORLD WAR II

"Ideology crumbled, personality bloomed."

—IRVING HOWE, *A MARGIN OF HOPE*

*T*he summer of 1945, "Hiroshima summer," Mary McCarthy called it—"wonderful, strange, bittersweet"—was another turning point in her life, like the fall of 1936, only happier. Referring to it in an unpublished manuscript as "a dividing-line," she keyed the second *d* in *dividing* over the first *n* in *divining*, so that a deeper meaning seeps into print.

The summer when McCarthy returned to Polly Boyden's house in Truro alone with Reuel divides two grand periods of her life. Life with Edmund, life after Edmund is part of the change; but so, too, is the end of the "Thirties ideology," which she traced to the evening on the Cape in August 1945 when she suddenly said aloud to a group of friends what she had not even admitted to herself: " 'But I supported the war all along; we all did.' " Then she had been visited by a sense of boundless freedom: "It was not too late to begin over again and start thinking what you really thought," she remembered musing. And for a moment she had felt "rather small, which was a salutary thing," but she was not therefore "driven to the conclusion that from now on it was best to follow the majority. This one time they had been right, but that did not make a rule." Only after this moment of revelation had the 1940s become for Mary McCarthy, though not necessarily for the rest of the group—many of them contributors to Dwight Macdonald's *politics*—a "time of liberation [and] genuine radicalism."

Most of the family circle assembled on Polly Boyden's porch that night had denied they were pulling for the British and the Americans to win the war. Some had been leaning toward a pacifist "plague on all your wars" position, even before the atomic bombing of Hiroshima and Nagasaki; while others still saw the war from a Trotskyist perspective as just another big power conflict. After the enormity of Hiroshima began to sink into consciousness, partisan passions of any kind seemed irrelevant. But even in August 1945 it wasn't the onset of a fresh political vision so much as the company of the group, and in particular its central figure, Nicola Chiaromonte, an Italian anarchist who had flown with André Malraux in the Spanish Civil War, that helped McCarthy draw a curtain on the recent past. The new group, with some old friends and familiar faces: Fred Dupee, Jim Agee, Dwight and Nancy Macdonald, Lionel Abel, Niccolò Tucci, another émigré intellectual, and the new man, Chiaromonte, gave her a sense of belonging that Wilson's community on the outer Cape never had.

Nicola Chiaromonte was first introduced to intellectuals on the East Coast by Dwight Macdonald, who had "discovered and adopted" him, in William Barrett's recollection, shortly after Chiaromonte arrived in New York via Casablanca in 1941. Macdonald had been roughly handled in intraparty disputes among the Trotskyists, and if he had not abandoned Marxism altogether, he was open to suggestion from other quarters. Chiaromonte, with his belief in the power of small self-supporting groups to pioneer change, easily commanded a hearing. His credentials were irresistible. He had fought in Spain; he was classically educated—in Malraux's *Man's Hope* he appears as the gunner, Scali, who is always reading Plato. He was connected to resistance movements in France, Italy, and North Africa; and he worked as a journalist.

Mary had first met him in the summer of 1944; and he and his American wife, Miriam, who taught English at Washington Irving High School in New York, had turned up at Henderson Place, and then later at Kevin McCarthy's apartment on East Fifty-sixth Street, where Mary had established a temporary residence for herself and Reuel after leaving Wilson (Kevin being in the Army, and his new wife, Augusta Dabney, an actress, on tour with a play). But it wasn't until the summer of 1945, when Mary found herself passing the Chiaromontes' cottage while taking Reuel to the beach in Truro, often joining them for picnics and long talks that wound into the night, that Mary got to know him well. Her friendship with Chiaromonte, which "was not a love affair in any respect," McCarthy maintained, "was probably *the* crucial event in my life," she said. Hannah Arendt would soon become "the other person who made a change—but not so dramatic."

Chiaromonte, the hint of a tonsure in his classic Roman profile, seemed to embody in his compact person as much as in anything he wrote (reviews and essays for *The New Republic, Commonweal, Atlantic Monthly, Partisan Review,* and *politics*) the Platonic idea of the *political man.* What he wrote, in fact, was less instrumental in establishing his peculiar influence than was his personal character, his apparent disregard for his own career and reputation, and his interest in ideas for their own sake. "He represented some sort of moral force for Mary and others," William Phillips recalls, "some ideal of honesty," which also satisfied Mary's need "to break away from the rational and antimoralistic politics that Marxism had introduced."

Unlike other people Dwight and Mary knew who talked politics with an intensity largely unknown today, Chiaromonte seemed disinterested; practical politics frightened him, perhaps because politics in the ordinary sense invited mass manipulation, or because the masses frightened him. But he asked the big questions, while fending off the big answers, the discredited ideologies and programs of the 1930s, which was why his charisma came in handy. It was still dangerous in 1945 to fly without visible ideological instruments—to sweep the table clean of Marxist debris left over from the past without sounding like a convert to the Managerial Revolution, or an anti-leftist.

In a 1960 tribute to Albert Camus, who shared Chiaromonte's profound distrust of ideology, Chiaromonte remembered "being totally obsessed by a single thought" after the war: "we had arrived at humanity's zero hour, and history was senseless; the only thing that made sense was that part of man which remained outside of history, alien and impervious to the whirlwind of events. . . ." Such a thought would have appeared anathema to Dwight Macdonald had it presented itself in religious trappings—indeed, the very idea that anything *conscious* exists 'outside of history' runs against the intellectual grain of these years. But Chiaromonte's political consciousness was essentially an ethical consciousness, not an otherworldly one. And even if it did touch the part of both Mary and Dwight that sometimes seemed to turn politics into "a groping for salvation" or a "leap towards the Absolute," as Barrett remarks of Macdonald, Chiaromonte's own history—his intimate exposure to the "whirlwind of events" that had reshaped the modern world—gave his utopian leanings a weight that the hard-boiled realism of many New York intellectuals lacked.

Along with Camus, Chiaromonte had appeared in New York like

a man risen from the dead. " 'We were born at the beginning of the first World War,' " he remembered Camus telling a rapt American audience in 1946: " 'As adolescents we had the crisis of 1929; at 20, Hitler. Then came the Ethiopian War, the Civil War in Spain, and Munich.' " This was their common history, and the history of their generation in Europe—the " 'foundations of our education. . . . Next came the Second World War, the defeat, and Hitler in our homes and cities. Born and bred in such a world,' " Camus wondered, " 'what did we believe in?' " The answer was Nothing. The world they inhabited was an "absurd world," and there was no other to take refuge in—as there had been for American writers, who rendezvoused with Pure Literature during the war, though neither Camus nor Chiaromonte said as much. " 'The world of culture was beautiful, but it was not real,' " Camus suggested. And then he had made a point with which Chiaromonte stood in agreement: " 'The facts showed that men deserved what was happening to them. Their way of life had so little value,' " Camus stated, that the violence of Hitler " 'was in itself logical. But it was unbearable,' " he added, " 'and we fought it.' "

The idea that people 'deserve' their masters is an idea that flares up like an ague in the postwar thought of both European and American intellectuals, though a review of what writers such as Camus, Chiaromonte, Ignazio Silone, Andrea Caffi, Alberto Moravia, and Arthur Koestler were saying in *Partisan Review* and *politics* during and after the war argues for rooting this influential proposition with the Europeans. For them, the idea conceals a lordly quotient of despair and contempt for the body politic, which is only partly mitigated by the fact that confronted by fascism, most of these writers had fought it. For New York intellectuals, a variation of the idea attached itself to the 1950s' critique of "mass society," where together with Daniel Bell's later concept of the 'end of ideology' it helped maintain the status quo. (Mary McCarthy preferred D. H. Lawrence's "notion of the little couple and the marriage [as] the beginning of mass-society." As evidence of the phenomenon, she cited the Dick and Pat show during the vice-presidential Nixon regime, but also the sight of "the favored couples arrayed on the Bauhaus furniture" in the Rahvs' drawing room.)

In August 1945, however, when McCarthy remembered feeling with her comrades "very quick in the Biblical sense," Nicola Chiaromonte's despair and isolation were not visible. Nor would these qualities ever stand out in McCarthy's perception of her friend, probably because nothing in her own relation to ordinary society, distant to an extreme, led her to question his reserve. When she recalled their long talks on the beach in Truro, what impressed itself on memory was "a kind of thoughtfulness," particularly in regard to literature. With Chiaromonte's help, she had begun to perceive the act of reading as well as writing in a completely new light.

At thirty-three, Mary McCarthy had just been offered her first regular job, teaching literature at Bard College, where Fred Dupee was also teaching. One of her assigned classes was going to be the Russian Novel, and she had taken to talking about Tolstoy and Dostoevsky with Chiaromonte, who had written eloquently on Tolstoy and the 'idea of history.' "And the *change* from someone like Edmund and his world and most of the *Partisan Review* boys was absolutely stunning," she recalled in 1980. Chiaromonte hadn't liked Dostoevsky, but he had a passion for Tolstoy, as much for Tolstoy's ethical precepts as for his literary achievement; as of course Mary did, too, along with Philip Rahv and also Hannah Arendt—Tolstoy worship filling in, one suspects, for the breakdown of the old relationship with the Russian Revolution. "It never occurred to me before to think of these two writers as anything but two writers, as *Edmund* would have looked at them," McCarthy explained; to say

that Tolstoy of course was a much better stylist and Dostoevsky wrote bad Russian, and so on—[which was] an empty literary point of view. . . . It really didn't involve thinking about what these writers were saying! . . . It never occurred to any of those people [Edmund, the 'boys'] that there should be any connection . . . between how they were living and what they believed in.

The realization that one's personal life could itself be an arena for the enactment of a revolutionary drama seems to have hit Mary McCarthy in 1945 with the force of revelation. It didn't mean that "you had to shut the rest of the world out," she suggests, but only that "you had to start with [your own] integrity as a point of departure"; to shore it up in countless private rectifications of behavior, so that you were not defenseless in the face of public opinion. "Tolstoy calls it 'living for your soul,' " she remarks; and the idea also appears in the writing of Kierkegaard and the French social philosopher Simone Weil, both of whom she also read that summer.

It was the "little ethical points" she discovered in these writers that McCarthy remembered in 1987: "If one is alone in a room one must behave as if one is not alone in a room"; and, "in one's relations with others one should have the same standards as one would have alone. . . . In other words, don't have a 'little private self' . . . don't pick your nose." (This was Simone Weil, updated by Mary McCarthy.) The breaking of bad habits applied to mental habits as well; for someone in the process of shedding an old skin—a woman between husbands, a writer between books, an intellectual between wars—these little Franklinesque precepts couldn't have been more to the point.

Not many people Mary knew could stand up to an exposure of their private selves, or sleep peacefully at night with their public selves, without much papering over; and Weil's proposition became a "test" of character she began to apply to others as well as to herself. In this kind of thinking she was joined by Jim Agee, whose *Let Us Now Praise Famous Men* was also informed by a drama of personal ethics. Dwight Macdonald, on the other hand, "could not have understood any of it," McCarthy adds. Dwight, who once said that if nobody had ever mentioned the idea of God to him he would never have thought of it, "would have been too eminently practical."

As for the religious component in such concerns, McCarthy supposed that behind it all "was some religious training that one had had as a young person, and that one was in some sense referring back to"—which was an understatement. Nothing is more Catholic than turning an examination of conscience, where 'living for one's soul' begins, into an opportunity for an invigorating spiritual workout. Catholicism, with its vivid concept of the soul, has also developed a concept of sin that arises from overindulging one's desire to be good: the sin of scrupulousness—in a secular sense, a sin one feels Mary McCarthy might have been guilty of if it wasn't for her appetite for mischief.

Later in the summer of 1945, the connection between life and literature was brought home in a more somber fashion when she sat down to translate Simone Weil's "The Iliad, or the Poem of Force"—looking the way a woman novelist should look, Eileen Simpson recalls, with her black hair "coiffed like Virginia Woolf (while the wildly gesturing Dwight, wearing eyeglasses and a goatee, looked the way a radical should look)." Mention of this translation crops up in all McCarthy's fond recollections of the summer, although it is the image of herself sitting on the beach in the illustrious company of Homer and Simone Weil that stands out most vividly. And yet Mary McCarthy seems to have been genuinely moved by Weil. Not by her embrace of

Christianity and her never-to-be-consummated affair with the Church ("I tended to act as if that didn't exist"); more likely it was the passionate intensity of Weil's moral consciousness. She was also moved by Homer's epic poem; when another series of essays on the *Iliad,* also written by a Frenchwoman, Rachel Bespaloff, appeared somewhat later, McCarthy translated them, too.

Chiaromonte had first read Simone Weil's essay in *Cahiers du Sud* in January 1941, while he was hiding out in Marseilles after the fall of France, waiting for passage to Algeria and Morocco. Weil (who died of malnutrition and tuberculosis before she was thirty-five) was writing under the pseudonym of Emile Novis; Chiaromonte didn't know who Novis was, but the remarkable essay told him that "the author was certainly neither an academic nor a *littérateur,* but someone who had suffered in spirit and had purged through intellect the sense of defeat that had been hanging over Europe for at least four years." That the author had chosen to cast 'his' anguished meditation on the spread of fascism in a modern reading of the *Iliad* impressed Chiaromonte at the time as "a sign that 'humane letters' could still yield vigorous thought." And he was happy to claim a hand in having gotten the essay published in the United States—in *politics,* where Mary McCarthy's translation appeared in November 1945.

Many years afterwards, Dwight Macdonald singled out "The Iliad, or the Poem of Force" as the best thing that ever appeared in his magazine. With his knowledge of Greek, he had also had a hand in the translation, helping Mary compare her rendering from the French with Homer's original. In 1945, McCarthy's translation stood apart from the rest of her work, from the fiction and memoirs that had begun to appear regularly in *The New Yorker,* and from the feisty Theatre Chronicles in *Partisan Review.*

Of force, Simone Weil says: " 'it is that *x* that turns anybody who is subject to it into a *thing*. Exercised to the limit, it turns man into a thing in the most literal sense: it makes a corpse out of him. . . .' " This was the " 'summary, gross form of force,' " with which both the *Iliad* and modern Europe were overrun; but " 'how much more surprising in its effects is the other force,' " Weil proposed, " 'the one which does not kill . . . just yet.' " This kind of force allows its agents

to turn a human being into a thing while he is still alive. He is alive; he has a soul; and yet he is a thing. An extraordinary entity this—a *thing* that has a soul. And as for the soul, what an extraordinary house it finds itself in. Who can say what it costs it, moment by moment, to accommodate itself to this residence, how much writhing and bending are required of it?

Like any human experience sharply observed by a capable mind, Simone Weil's meditation on force was, and remains, subject to countless applications. More than anything Chiaromonte or Camus themselves wrote, "The Iliad, or the Poem of Force" put flesh on the old bone about the part of man that remains outside the whirlwind of history, 'alien and impervious.' When, looking back at the summer of 1945 thirty-five years later, McCarthy suddenly exclaimed, "that was Europe! . . . what I was listening to on the beach was Europe," it was Chiaromonte she had in mind; but listening over her shoulder, the voice of Simone Weil is what touches a contemporary reader with the truth of what 'Europe' had to say to America after the war.

II

In spite of Weil, Homer, Tolstoy, the end of the 'Good War,' as only Americans call World War II, and the atomic bomb, Mary McCarthy's bittersweet summer closed with the start of a new novel inspired by a more evanescent theme. "A satire, it was to be, on the literary life and the thirst for fame, just as dangerous to self-respect as the thirst for alcohol . . . ," she recalled in 1979. The thumbnail sketch is intriguing, but probably it was the wrong summer for such an inquiry; and McCarthy was not yet on a first-name footing with the truth of the proposition, a precondition for her fiction.

"The Lost Week," as the novel was to be called, was inspired by the arrival on the outer Cape of a hot contemporary novelist named Charles Jackson (author of *The Lost Weekend*). In the first heat of inspiration, and spurred on by friends who thought the subject was "made" for her, McCarthy had begun writing, and then had packed her bag and typewriter, and taken a series of trains and a ferry to Yarmouth, Nova Scotia, where she hoped to put up at one of those rustic inns that exist more often in a writer's imagination than in actuality, and "freshen [her] invention" in solitary walks upon the beach. Yarmouth struck her instead as a featureless commercial town, and she never did find her way from the traveling salesman's hotel to the harbor. At the end of seven days, despite the eighty pages she had to show for what turned out to be her own " 'lost week,' " she knew she had a dud.

When she returned to Truro, McCarthy's friends let her know they suspected a "romantic episode" lay behind the trip, not an unlikely conjecture. There was a new party on the horizon: Bowden Broadwater, a tall, loose-limbed young man who spoke with a Harvard drawl, which he came by honestly, having grown up in Maryland and graduated from Harvard in 1941, where he had distinguished himself as "Pegasus" on the Harvard *Advocate*. Mary had first met Bowden the night she left Edmund Wilson in January 1945, at a dinner party at Niccolò Tucci's on Mother Cabrini Boulevard in Queens, and he had visited her on several occasions on the Cape. By August, when she was laboring over her translation of Weil, he knew her well enough to commend her for her struggle "to lead a hermit's life in Truro and turn your back on all the world save the McDonalds [*sic*], Nathans, Dos Passos, Jeanie, Lawrence Ubel, Clement . . . and Reuel."

If there was another agenda behind the trip to Nova Scotia, it wasn't Broadwater, however, but Edmund Wilson, who had just returned from Europe, and whose visit with Reuel, McCarthy presumed, would be better served if she was away. When she returned, she was met by an angry letter from Wilson—who, unannounced, had taken Reuel to New York—rebuking her for assuming that the court had awarded her custody of their son pending final hearings: "that is not the case, and you have no right to choose a school for him or do anything about him without consulting me," he snapped, referring to McCarthy's upcoming appointment at Bard, which would require enrolling Reuel in a Red Hook elementary school.

"You will have to see me and discuss these problems before I will allow you to take him," Wilson stated. Then he had introduced the "conditions" under which he would agree to give Mary a divorce:

> You can take Reuel this winter and I will give you money for him while he is with you. Later I will take him to Europe for a whole year. Otherwise, we will share him six months and six months. Of course, I shan't insist on having him for the whole of my six months if I'm not in a position to give him a proper home or I think it's undesirable for other reasons. I decide all matters of his education.

Looked at in hindsight, Wilson's peremptory terms appear to contain more bluster than serious intent. After all, he had just returned from a tour across war-ravaged Europe to a now ex-wife who from all appearances had summered happily in his old haunts on the Cape. Moreover, as some of his traveling notes reveal, the air war in Europe may have unhinged him. Surveying the wreckage of Europe's cathedrals, palaces, and railway stations from a plane, Wilson was stunned by the fragility of civilization. The human habitations looked "like wasp-cells stuck in the slit of a blind . . . mere shells which men have knocked together in order to crawl inside them and which a bomb dropped casually from above can shatter or annihilate in a moment."

He couldn't help but notice the difference between his point of view and Mary's, noting that "she has never known a time when there weren't planes." There was something terrifying but poignant in the knowledge that he was witnessing the passing of an older, more expansive universe. "We are probably on the brink of a new construction by man of a conventional world for himself," he had confided to the journal from which *Europe Without Baedecker* is drawn. ". . . [T]he network of air travel and radio, instead of a precarious extension, will be part of the self-contained human house. Already 'ceiling' means not only . . . the roofs of a few feet above our heads," he observed, "but also the cloud formation above our heads under which our airplanes range."

But the contemplation of Europe's destruction had unleashed a monstrous satisfaction in Wilson. "It must be a temptation . . . to blow up whole cities from the air without getting hit or hurt oneself, and while soaring serenely above them," he marveled from a plane. "Many must feel vicariously as I do the thrill of doing this . . ." as he had, for example, "when the Germans were bombing London, before we had begun bombing them." This was no jeremiad; Wilson was excited by "the liberation of some impulse to wreck and to kill on a gigantic scale without caring and while remaining invulnerable oneself. . . ." And for this reason, for the bursting of the "conventions and codes that we live under," he had even discovered "an element of exhilaration about the whole Nazi exploit. . . ." Little of this would find its way into either *The New Yorker* or *Europe Without Baedecker*.

Nor would another reflection, inspired by war-torn Naples, which was the kind of thinking that drove Mary McCarthy wild:

> I have had moments when I have felt, 'Let the Americans take it over and make it into something which will be much better if it is only as good as Stamford' . . . All the little sections of Europe, like Italy—why should anyone take them seriously as countries: Italy and Greece might be kept on as quaint and picturesque old places as New Orleans is with us. The great mistake about Europe is taking the countries seriously and letting them quarrel and drop bombs on one another.

At the end of the summer, Wilson's mood was the very opposite of Mary's. A staggering heat wave had descended on New England, "suffocating, stultifying . . ."; it was "queer getting back here," Wilson wrote a poet friend; "a lot of things that used more or less to interest me now seem . . . unbearably boring. With the great role that we seem to be called upon to play, I don't see that we are doing much of anything to supply inspiration or ideas," he added, in a cryptic reference to America's postwar euphoria: "Our only great contribution has been the atomic bomb."

Wilson was used to giving orders, however. "You will have to see me . . ." was probably the operative sentence in his angry letter to Mary, but it isn't hard to imagine why she took his threatening "conditions" at face value, which she did, convincing Adelaide Walker that Edmund really did mean to take Reuel to Europe for a year; and thereby winning Walker's support as a witness in a preliminary suit for *sole* custody that McCarthy launched at Foley Square in the fall of 1945. (In the final divorce agreement, Edmund took Reuel in the summers, retaining the right to choose his schools, while Mary had him for the rest of the year, sharing holidays. Wilson paid her a weekly "maintenance" of eighty-five dollars.)

No doubt it was his abrupt departure for New York with Reuel that gave a twist to the knife he seemed to hold at her back; and years later McCarthy recalled the event as a "kidnapping." She had gone to Nova Scotia "to leave the coast clear for Edmund," and he had responded by "kidnapping Reuel"—by taking him down to his mother's in New Jersey. Judging from the date of Wilson's letter, September 11, and Mary and Reuel's eventual arrival in Red Hook on September 15, Reuel wasn't out of sight for very long. But Edmund's impulsive action must have frightened McCarthy, for her account has the earmarks of a cover-up. "It was just like the O. Henry story, 'The Ransom of Red Chief,' " she begins merrily, "in which some kidnappers, having kidnapped a child who is a real terror, offer a reward to his parents if they will come and get him." When Mary went down to Red Bank to get Reuel, "the old lady . . . was happy to return him," she relates; and she had taken him on up to Bard and second grade, and commenced a new career without a hitch.

17

Bard, Bowden, and Broadway

"Dearest, divinest Mary, Mother of Jesus, Have

you thought about wearing a hat in class?"

—BOWDEN BROADWATER, LETTER TO MARY McCARTHY, 1945

Tiny Bard College, numbering some eighty students when Mary McCarthy arrived, was more isolated in the mid-1940s than it was before the war. The train to New York City from Red Hook took four hours, and hardly anybody had a car. It was an insular community where the maids, left over from the years when Bard was a men's college, gossiped over the affairs of the nine-member faculty. "Miss McCarthy has taken Mr. Dupee from that nice Miss Ginsberg," one of McCarthy's students remembers hearing in 1945, although Vita Ginsberg, an attractive young drama teacher from Bennington, who remained a longtime friend of Mary McCarthy's, was not a girlfriend of Fred Dupee.

Dupee, however, tweedy, debonair, at forty-one a celebrity on the small upstate campus, had helped Mary get the job at Bard. At three thousand dollars a year, it wasn't a bad one for a fledgling instructor in 1945. Before she arrived, he had politicked vigorously on her behalf among the students, telling them what a "terrific woman" she was, though Dupee wasn't Mary McCarthy's lover, either. He was a close friend who shared an important piece of Mary's past in New York. His friendship was the rock-ribbed kind that would withstand an unflattering portrait of himself in 1952 as Howard Furness in *The Groves of Academe* ("a cow-country version of one salient of yourself," McCarthy later confessed, after Dupee assured her he was not offended).

Among the faculty, where opinion about McCarthy's arrival was divided, she needed no introduction. " 'It was something fearful to think of her coming here,' " a faculty wife remembers. " 'We had all read *The Company She Keeps,* and knew how devastating she could be. . . .' " The book had made the best-seller lists, and yet it was not as a 'famous author' that McCarthy was coming to be known so much as a dangerous one. In *Partisan Review,* her work appeared alongside stories by Delmore Schwartz, Eleanor Clark, Elizabeth Hardwick, Saul Bellow, and Jean Stafford; but she was the only one who had also started appearing regularly in *The New Yorker,* and whose literary style made room for autobiography, social comment, and a biting humor that set it apart from the prevailing fiction of urban malaise. *The Company She Keeps* had introduced a new voice and a new candor about sex into American writing that made the young Norman Mailer, for example, regard Mary McCarthy as a "guiding light." But at Bard her reputation for 'back-fence gossip' preceded her, like a page bearing the severed head of the last guest.

She was "very vivacious, extremely pretty," and disarmingly nervous in front of her first few classes, a student remembered; but the seed of suspicion was sown that here was a woman who remained loyal only to her muse, forgivable, even admirable in a man, disturbing in a woman. There was some rumbling about qualifications. Thanks to McCarthy's regular contributions to *Partisan Review,* she had kept her critical skills intact, but she held no advanced degree. "In those days, writers didn't teach and teachers didn't write," another one of McCarthy's former students, Eve Stwertka (then Eve Gassler), remarks, "except maybe on Shakespeare and the like, but that wasn't the same thing." Neither Robert Lowell nor Jean Stafford, then Lowell's wife, had succeeded in landing a teaching job at Bard when they had applied the year before. McCarthy was breaking new ground, which wasn't easy; teaching at Bard placed her at the edge of an established academic community in which she couldn't help but feel a threat of ostracism. A *voyageur sans bagages,* she was looking in once again on a world of insiders where she didn't entirely belong. No wonder that at Bard she also earned a reputation for being a slightly "pushy" woman.

Eve Stwertka, who became a lifelong friend, remembers sitting in McCarthy's office waiting for her first appointment while leafing through a stack of children's books lying on the desk. McCarthy had swept in and out; she was surrounded by people, and there was "a tremendous air of excitement around her." And then she heard her voice, "a little strident, rather louder than the other voices," announce:

" 'One of my students is in my office reading *The Little Red Hen,* ' " and everyone had laughed. "It was the sort of thing she would say, that she would notice, that would amuse people and have people collected around her to hear," Stwertka observes.

McCarthy's tutee didn't take the very popular Russian novel course that Mary offered that year, though Eve's friend Ellen Adler, Stella Adler's daughter, did, along with Barbara ("Andy") Anderson, who later married Fred Dupee. But McCarthy directed her reading and independent study, the heart of a Bard education. Together they ploughed through Chaucer, Dante's *Inferno* (as did Bowden Broadwater, "holding tight to Dante's hand"), and a book called *The Golden Hind,* a collection of the essays and poetry of minor Elizabethans such as Robert Greene and Thomas Nashe, whom McCarthy loved.

Stwertka was one of seven students of widely varying interests and abilities whose core studies McCarthy supervised. Another was a young woman with whom she read the Stoic philosophers; while with a third, a student who appeared to be almost retarded, lying in bed nearly every day with a huge dog the college let her keep in her room, McCarthy had gone back to the basics. Together they read Cinderella and discussed it as literature—"a stroke of genius," in Stwertka's opinion, for no one else had succeeded in drawing the girl out. Far from giving up on such a young woman—handicapped students at Bard being common during the war when students were hard to get— McCarthy had been curious about her, and she had undertaken her intellectual development with the same intensity of purpose that she devoted to her more gifted charges.

At home with Reuel in the rambling old house she rented in Upper Red Hook, McCarthy had begun to put together the rudiments of a life more to her taste than the one she had lived as Edmund's wife or Philip's girl. Meeting her tutorial responsibilities, preparing lectures on both Russian literature and the novels of Jane Austen, George Eliot, and Henry James, she worked alone late into the nights. More than anything she "loved this business of studying," McCarthy told a Bard audience in the middle 1970s, when she returned to accept an honorary degree. "It was all quite mad," she remembered, especially since under the tutorial system the students were always in a position to see whether the professor had done her homework; but it was "exciting and fun," and it offered an amateur scholar like herself a chance to forage in new fields. While the cost might be a good deal of midnight oil, for the students, the Bard system guaranteed a faculty "perforce fresh and perennially inexperienced, that is, alive. . . ." So far as she knew in 1976, Bard was seldom "boring . . . and boredom, highly contagious, is the great malady of education." It was high praise for an unconventional college, unconventional by Harvard, Yale, or Vassar standards; Oxford instituted the tutorial system centuries ago.

Living alone with Reuel, she had also begun to regain a sense of mastery over her personal affairs that she had lost with Wilson. With her son she appeared very much at ease, managing him, a student baby-sitter remembers, the way single working mothers often manage an only child today: including him in conversation, treating his opinions with almost professional consideration. "Reuel was a very charming child," Eve Stwertka recalls, although he had his critics among people who found him a nuisance because he interrupted his mother and was "always sort of around in social situations. . . ." Stwertka thought he was very well behaved, "not mischievous, never naughty, didn't cry, wasn't demanding. The only thing was that he wanted to talk or he wanted you to talk to him," not what one expected of a seven-year-old in the 1940s.

In domestic affairs, McCarthy had once again taken a cue from literature. This time it was a "Kierkegaardian law" that got her through a day that began with getting Reuel up and fed and off to school in time to meet an 8 A.M. class on campus, and ended with making his dinner, reading him a story, putting him to bed, and getting her own supper—"and then, what? *the dishes!*" McCarthy recalled in 1987, all before she could sit down and go to work. It was the sight of the disorder in the kitchen that unnerved her more than anything else, until (like Dear Abby) Kierkegaard came to the rescue. Kierkegaard's "law" was suggested by the nineteenth-century philosopher's decision not to marry his fiancée because only by *not* marrying her would he then be free to 'choose' her over and over again. "There may have been some self-deception on the part of Kierkegaard," McCarthy conceded, "but I took [the 'law'] as just a practical thing. . . . I'd look at those dishes and make a Kierkegaardian decision not to wash them. As soon as I decided not to wash them, I could wash them. . . . they would just start beckoning." It was a trick she never stopped using, though not with the dishes; "you can't cheat," she said, "you have to really decide not to do the thing you have to do." Like much of her daily existence at Bard, the homely illustration of Kierkegaardian freedom would be ploughed into *The Groves of Academe* in 1952. Domna Rejnev, a White Russian émigré in the literature department, and the novel's Mary McCarthy character ("a smouldering anachronism," with dark, glossy hair, "pure ivory skin," rosy lips, gray eyes "queerly lit from within, as by some dangerous electricity, . . . she had the temperament and vocation of a *narodniki*"), is always asking herself, "What would Tolstoy think?"

Life in Red Hook was by no means all work and no play. It was at Bard in 1945 to 1946, with Bowden Broadwater increasingly in attendance on the weekends, that Mary McCarthy began to acquire a reputation for serious entertaining, for planning elaborate dinner parties, costume parties, and garden parties, with snippets of poetry baked into little cakes. At the end of the first semester, she gave a Russian Novel party to which everybody came dressed as their favorite character; Mary choosing Anna Karenina. Forty-two years later, this party was repeated in a sense, when McCarthy, back at Bard as the Charles Stevenson Professor of Literature, and teaching the Russian Novel once again, had all her students to an end-of-semester buffet dinner of turkey and Indian pudding in the off-campus house on Allandale Road which the college loaned her. No one was in costume, but as the students filed into the living room for a brief discussion before dinner, Mary's fourth husband, James West, impeccably attired in a three-piece suit, circulated with bottles of champagne.

In New York, still the center of intellectual society, Bowden Broadwater had become McCarthy's eyes and ears: spying, "unobserved, Cousin [Allen] Tate—in the most faun-colored of suits—taking cocktails in the Algonquin lobby with Mad Lowell . . ."—who "likes you *very* much," he assured Mary, after having had drinks with Lowell himself. At *The New Yorker,* where Broadwater covered art galleries for the "Goings on About Town" column, he kept her posted on Edmund Wilson: "Le Monstre is lunching Wystan Hugh Auden today . . ."; and, "Monster's girl-friend's name is Frankie: I haven't seen her. Wondered myself if Monster is as well posted about you as vice-versa; and through *whom?*" After they were married, he would sometimes call Wilson "my father-in-law."

Bowden's listening posts now included *politics,* where he volunteered his services to Dwight Macdonald as a French translator, and to Nancy as a kind of secretary, one of a group—he called it the "Sewing Circle"—that helped the dedicated Nancy Macdonald manage the benefits and forums that *politics* sponsored during these years. His letters out-McCarthy Mary McCarthy:

Last night was Sewing Circle, a positive throng. Atmosphere of the Lady of the Manor presiding over the village wives at the Belgium

bandage-roll: Much Mrs.-Macdonalding, How is Mr.-Macdonald-
ing. . . . A young man, not myself . . . breezy, flip . . . is flirted with
by a drudge from *Mademoiselle*. . . . There is a rather nice French
girl, a little frightened at this unexpected glamour and clamor, and
a salty old woman who has taken the name Francine. By next
week, I shall be . . . in love with them all.

At Niccolò Tucci's Bowden ran into Chiaromonte, and was able
to report that "the Master does not have a cold. . . ." When Chiaromonte smiled, he revealed "two beautiful golden bridges," between
which were "twice the number of teeth, neat as a row of print, that
you, I, or other mortals have. The Master's costume" was also worth
mention: "a spot of off-red in the cravat, a dark coat buttoned high,
and cordorary pants of a soft, delicate green." Fred Dupee was referred
to as "Onc-due-pee," a witticism of Reuel's. (Dupee, who was well
aware of Bowden's tongue wagging, was of all McCarthy's friends the
most put out over his arrival in her life.)

Bowden was not nice; he had a fork in his tongue that could gore
an ox. (Anaïs Nin peddles pornography to a senator in Washington, he
informed Mary; Bowden had just read about a hundred pages of the
material that Nin had subcontracted to his friend George Barker at a
dollar a page—some of Barker's "best stuff," he thought.) Later, when
Bowden and Mary "got on to somebody," as one of their acquaintances recalls, still shuddering, "it was murder . . . they were ferocious!" But in 1945, Bowden Broadwater was a twenty-five-year-old
researcher at *The New Yorker,* who looked "very much like Christopher Robin turned twenty and rather wicked in his exquisitely cut
Brooks Brothers suits." He was having an affair with one of the
magazine's most-talked-about authors, a woman eight years his senior
and twice divorced, most recently from the formidable Edmund Wilson, who stood at the center of a largely admiring circle of New York
intellectuals. No wonder he kept a sharp tongue. He would need it.

In his letters to Mary, nonetheless, in which an exuberant affection
flows unabashedly, Broadwater revealed a more complicated sensibility. Running into the poet Weldon Kees on a Madison Avenue bus in
1946, he was treated to a blow-by-blow account of Clement Greenberg's fight with Lionel Abel: "Pvt. Greengroin's latest battle," Kees
had called it, and with gusto Bowden had passed it on to Mary. The
"warrior" had bounced down to Abel's with a bundle of the latest
French magazines, and engaged the latter in a heated argument over
Jean-Paul Sartre—then beginning to become known in New York.
Abel, who defended Sartre, had drawn himself up to his full height (a

foot shorter than Greenberg) and ordered him to " 'go back to Brook-lyn, where you came from. . . .' " Greenberg swung, and "Dear Lionel, when he rose," Bowden wrote, "protested that fisticuffs were not his specialty, that he was recovering from a *malaise*." The fight spilled out on to the sidewalk, where Abel was trounced. Reactions among the intellectuals were mixed. "Dwight (Free-and-Equal) Macdonald wrote Clem [and] said it was time for the warrior to stop settling his disputes in this rough manner—and sent a copy of the letter to Mr. Abel"; Chiaromonte, who was "furious," did the same. Weldon on the other hand, "hopes [Greenberg] will flatten out Philip [Rahv]." Broadwa-ter's reaction was different. "Poor Clem," he concluded, "I really feel quite sorry for him; it seems a nightmare, anyway, to *me*." (In McCarthy's transmission of the story years later, it is Chiaromonte who is commended for saying, " 'I would hate to be Clement Green-berg,' [while] everybody else was criticizing him.")

In these early months of courtship, Broadwater followed the affairs of the boys like a hawk circling its prey, not out of hunger for himself as for his mate confined to the nest. In the fall of 1947, he took a short-lived job as production editor at *Partisan Review*, thus entering the lion's den. By then, he and Mary McCarthy were married; Mary had returned to the maelstrom of New York literary politics; and Bowden had a job to do, an unglamorous one that he did well, accord-ing to William Phillips, who writes in his memoirs that of all the people who worked for the magazine during its halcyon years, Broadwater was "by far the best." His interest in the plots and counterplots of the New York literary scene, at bottom an interest in personalities and manners in the eighteenth-century sense, never ceased; in 1949, it was simply displaced when he and Mary moved to Portsmouth, Rhode Island, and Bowden assumed a more congenial perch overlooking Newport society.

"I think Bowden had a certain liking for some kind of vicarious existence which didn't therefore require too much commitment on his part. On the other hand, he didn't like being out of things," Mary McCarthy reflected in 1985. With Mary, of course, he would rarely find himself out of things, not until after 1955, when McCarthy's trips to Europe grew more and more frequent. One understands why some of their contemporaries regarded their marriage as a great catch for Broadwater, and for Mary a kind of slip. But McCarthy lent little credence to this view. Bowden Broadwater's great commitment was to her, and there was nothing vicarious about it.

In the years to come he would take a fervent interest in McCarthy's career, protecting her against intrusion while she put in her daily time at the typewriter. While Mary wrote about Minneapolis and Seattle and the Convent of the Sacred Heart (*Memories of a Catholic Girlhood*), along with the politics of the intelligentsia (*The Oasis*), the politics of academic life (*The Groves of Academe*), the manners and morals of bohemia, and marriage to Wilson (*A Charmed Life*), the art and architecture of the Italian Renaissance (*Venice Observed, The Stones of Florence*), Vassar and marriage to Johnsrud (*The Group*), not to mention countless reviews of plays and books, Bowden Broadwater fixed the leaky faucets, deployed the hated vacuum cleaner, screened the calls and callers, restored one house (Portsmouth, Rhode Island, 1949 to1953), caretook another (Wellfleet, 1954 to 1955), and remained throughout a steadfast companion to Reuel. He left dinner to Mary, however ("Dear Mary, natural mistress of rich and delicious desserts . . ."), who could not have been kept out of the kitchen, anyway.

Until 1955, when Bowden took a job at St. Bernard's, a prep school in New York, he slipped in and out of employment on the fringes of journalism, without exhibiting much apparent concern about his own career. Mary's income met most of their expenses. He wrote some fiction but suffered prodigiously from writer's block, lacking no doubt that 'will-shot arrow' that Robert Lowell observed in McCarthy's quiver. Mary always sang his praises as a writer. "He was gifted and original," she said, "but he was not original in any expected way (like Donald Barthelme . . .); he was original in an unexpected way, and that doesn't go." She remembered his unpublished stories appreciatively, especially one he wrote about a party at the Rahvs' in which Philip and Nathalie, "the Dogma and the Dogmatesse," hold down opposite ends of an enormous "*Rahvian*" sofa. In 1961, Broadwater published a story, "*Ciao,*" about the early days of his marriage to "the d.w." (the dear wife) in *Paris Review;* but his best writing seems to have gone into his letters, and his best efforts into his marriage.

For the young Broadwater, as for Mary, too, perhaps, life seemed to shade magically into Great Books. "You are unique," he wrote her in 1946, "in all literature no comparable figure, creator or created, really exists. . . ." In himself there was "only a little Dickens," he thought, "mostly hyperbole. . . ." And yet the paradox that seemed to make the relationship work was the obvious delight that Mary took in Bowden; obvious to Bowden at any rate, who would sorely feel the pinch in 1960 when "the shoe passed to the other foot" (Mary having fallen in love with James West), and Bowden became, as he wrote her sadly from New York, "the lover rather than the loved one."

There was something childlike about the pleasure McCarthy took in his company. "Sweet Bowden," she wrote him from Bard; when the train took him away, it was as if she had been visited by an "angel" who had suddenly, courteously "dematerialized." "What a relief he must have been from Wilson's ponderous ways—young, spritely, and ever so *slim*," Stwertka suggests. As for Bowden himself, when Mary showered him with little gifts and Valentine's Day poems, he was transformed: "so surrounded by my collection of totems of your personality," he wrote her in 1946, "that I am on the edge of turning into a transvestite out of sheer love." For the first time in her life, McCarthy had found a man who believed in her performance absolutely.

Eileen Simpson saw something maternal in the quality of the attention McCarthy gave Bowden Broadwater (an assessment with which Stwertka disagrees). "He was her *son*, you know," Simpson says, remembering a night long ago when they were all at a party at the Macdonalds' and Bowden had fallen asleep on the couch, looking "like a pouty late adolescent, hair touseled. . . . It was time to go, and Mary tried to wake him up," Simpson relates; "it was like waking a sleeping child, and she would be so patient, tender . . . I couldn't believe it!" But Broadwater was probably more like a younger brother to Mary McCarthy. When she married him in December 1946, within a few weeks of Edmund Wilson's marriage, his fourth, to Elena Mumm Thornton, she not only acquired the husband she would always need to hold down the other end of her own 'sofa,' she also got a playmate, as time would show.

When toward the end of her second semester at Bard, McCarthy was asked to teach another year, she declined, partly because teaching left her little time to write—and it was to the order of scribes, not the order of scholars or teachers that she belonged—and partly because she had decided to return to New York with Bowden Broadwater.

II

From 1945 to 1946, Mary McCarthy published two stories, "The Friend of the Family" and "The Unspoiled Reaction," neither up to the standard set by *The Company She Keeps*. The first ran to heavy-handed metaphor: "In the long war of marriage, in the battle of the friends, Francis Cleary was an open city. . . . an inconspicuous white flag fluttered in his sharkskin lapel." Because it is in the mood of "The Weeds," "The Friend of the Family," originally published in *Town and Country*, was probably begun while she was still married to Wilson, and only finished at Bard. "Appropriately *nobody* suggested

Francis Cleary—a zero person, who grows out of . . . the dislike married couples feel for each other's friends," McCarthy recalled many years later. But the story contains a nugget from McCarthy's continuing meditation on bourgeois marriage: "What passes for love in our competitive society is frequently envy," she writes; "the phlegmatic husband who marries a vivacious wife is in the same position as the businessman who buys up the stock of a rival corporation in order to kill it. . . . We cannot, in the end, possess anything that is not ourselves."

Throughout 1945 and 1946, McCarthy published only two Theatre Chronicles, but the theatre continued to offer her a medium for reading society's pulse, middlebrow society in particular. After noting the passing of the war plays and musicals, and the arrival of the great "play doctors," George Kaufman and George Abbott, McCarthy's 1945 review, "We Must Have Faith," went on to examine three "patients" who exhibited acutely escapist symptoms. *Harvey, The Streets Are Guarded,* and *A Bell for Adano* couldn't have been more different, but each in its fashion asserted the reality of an unreal world, whose objects (a six-foot rabbit, a Christ-like marine, a miracle-working bell, respectively) were objectively delusional, McCarthy noted, but whose *subjects,* the believers, were ennobled by pretending they weren't. Belief in the little town of Adano's bell, for instance, conveyed "the feeling of democracy" after the substance has fled; *feeling* is all.

Such plays wouldn't last very long on the American stage, she predicted; it was unlikely that the theatre could ever turn itself into a vehicle for supplying the public with fantasies and secular myths because the drama was "incorrigibly concrete." Unlike the movies— whose stock was always tainted in McCarthy's eyes—the theatre couldn't "deal in shadows, or in reverie . . . It demands that its conflicts be settled; it cannot . . . dissolve them away, as the camera can." It was the only art whose medium was the "living flesh," and thus limits were set to belief: "one is always more conscious of what is excessive in a stage performance than one is . . . in a movie or a novel," she argued, 'excess' in art (as in life) representing something unclean to an aesthetic sensibility. And she concluded: "the very plainness . . . and realism of the stage have unfitted it to deal with this period of irresolution, evasion and ambiguity."

It is a somewhat wooden vision of the theatre, in which Anglo-Saxon stage conventions appear as inexorable as the revolving seasons, while what lies beyond the marquee is full of murk and mire. One is reminded unexpectedly of Edmund Wilson, declaiming the virtues of books: "O indispensable books! O comforting alternative worlds, where all discords are finally resolved, if not by philosophy, then by art. How without you should we reconcile ourselves to this troublesome actual world . . . ?" The idea that the theatre's concreteness protects it from fantasy and myth has hardly borne the test of time. But perhaps Mary McCarthy can be forgiven her odd romance with the stage, in view of the novelty of her observations.

When a little life returned to the theatre after the war, her commentaries grew positively rosy. "The G.I.'s have gone home and Broadway is at peace," she declared at the end of 1946, delighting in the reappearance of the Rolls-Royces, "like large perambulators," gently depositing "their muffled elderly couples before the lighted marquees. . . ." Culture had emerged from its wartime bunker; Oscar Wilde and Eva Le Gallienne were finding "the enemy departed." For the first time in a long time, New York theatregoers could "step into almost any theatre lobby with that sense of virtuous expectation . . . that the drama peculiarly awakes and that makes the theatre for New York what the cafe is for Paris," she told her readers: "a pleasure and also a pride, a habit and a ritual, a diversion and a duty. To the extent that America has any communal life at all," she added, "it is centered in the New York theatre"—a parochial observation that showed where McCarthy felt most at home.

The reasoning behind her lifelong passion for the stage would never again be stated as guilelessly as in the January-February 1947 *Partisan Review*. Speaking up for "the ordinary middling man," who is "annihilated" by the movies, and unmoved by great symphonies, McCarthy praised the theatre as the only art form he can "approach with his faculties alert and unabashed; he sees it as a kind of courtroom and himself as a qualified juror whose verdict is, from moment to moment, solicited."

The return of Eugene O'Neill and George Kelly, a popular drawing room satirist of the period, along with a string of classical revivals, set the tone for the coming season: "an old man's season, garrulous, unsentimental, reasonable, pessimistic, and, in the manner of Lear and the late Yeats, contradictory, willful, and adventurous." McCarthy's own criticism was becoming more robust and saucy. "To audiences accustomed to the oily virtuosity of George Kaufman, George Abbott, Lillian Hellman, Odets, Saroyan," she noted in a review of Eugene O'Neill's *The Iceman Cometh* in 1946, "the return of a playwright who—to be frank—cannot write is a solemn and sentimental occasion."

There was a wild streak in O'Neill that led him to bow down to inarticulate love and inarticulate rage, which both disturbed and attracted Mary McCarthy. Plays such as *The Iceman Cometh, Desire Under the Elms,* and *A Moon for the Misbegotten,* "reddened by whiskey, like a bloodshot eye," seemed to stir dark ancestral memories. In the latter two, she saw "behind the pagan facade of Irish boasting, drinking and ribaldry . . . a wheyey sentimentality and retching hatred of sex." In *The Iceman Cometh,* whose characters are the derelict habitués of a cheap downtown bar circa 1912, she chided O'Neill for subtracting precisely that "thing that is most immediately striking and most horrifying in any human drunkard, the sense of the destruction of personality. Each of O'Neill's people," she went on, "is in perfect possession of the little bit of character the author has given him. The Boer is boerish, the Englishman english, the philosopher philosophizes, and the sentimental grouch who runs the establishment grouches and sentimentalizes in orderly alternation."

Such didacticism and predictability were also the besetting sins of Saroyan, Sean O'Casey, Thornton Wilder, and Maxwell Anderson, if not of the entire so-called American realist tradition, in McCarthy's opinion. But in reviewing O'Neill in the mid-1940s, and then later in 1952, she seems more offended by the lapses in O'Neill's grasp of American "drinking *moeurs* [habits]" than anything else. Her own sharp evocation of the "rancorous, semi-schizoid silences . . . obscurity of thought . . . dark innuendoes . . . flashes of hatred," the hallmarks of the actual drunkard, betrays more than dramatic interest.

Perhaps Edmund Wilson's drinking inspired the sharpness of these passages, although Wilson's drinking lacked some of alcoholism's customary sour breath. He had rarely gotten sick or had bad hangovers (maybe because he didn't smoke, McCarthy thought, cigarettes and alcohol combining to produce the worst hangovers). Edmund's hard drinking had usually begun after the guests had gone and the house was quiet. Alone in his Wellfleet study, he had put his favorite records on the phonograph—Beethoven, Mussorgsky, Schönberg—and read over his old diaries and published works, sometimes writing in the former if he wasn't too much the worse for wear. When he finally went to bed, it was to a tiny attic chamber above the study in the rear of the house, and when he awoke, usually late the following afternoon, he disappeared into the bathroom "to perform his ablutions," McCarthy recalled in 1988, emerging in his BVD's "like a reborn God, all scrubbed, and ready to call for his tray in the study," which was brought to him by a maid if they had one, by Mary if they didn't.

The allusions to 'dark innuendoes . . . flashes of hatred,' and the 'wheyey sentimentality' discerned in *A Moon for the Misbegotten,* are more suggestive of Irish drinking. And the peculiar intensity of McCarthy's observations of O'Neill probably owes itself to experiences closer to home.

With the publication of "Yonder Peasant, Who Is He?" in 1948, Mary McCarthy had begun to dig into her own Irish Catholic past, and to uncover in herself a well of bitterness about the events that had happened in Minneapolis so long ago. Her findings had taken a dramatic turn when shortly after the memoir came out in *The New Yorker,* the ghostly figure of Uncle Harry had turned up in New York. Harry McCarthy, Roy McCarthy's younger brother, and the white hope of the clan, a graduate of Andover and Yale who made a million dollars before he was thirty, had escorted Mary's family across the country in the fall of 1918. In his early sixties he had come to bear a striking resemblance to her dead father, a resemblance that wasn't apparent when he was younger; his white hair stood up in a pompadour, and he had the same gray-green electric eyes and the same animal magnetism.

He was also a "terrible drinker," McCarthy noted in a 1988 interview. "It was almost inevitable that it would happen," she said of the night in 1948 when they "all got absolutely plastered—Bowden, Aunt Zula, Uncle Harry and I." And Mary and Harry had engaged in "a lot of drunken self-accusation"; Harry exclaiming, " 'Oh, and when I think about how I was living it up at the Minneapolis Club, instead of doing something about you children!' " And Mary, feeling sufficiently chastened by the shock the first installment of her memoirs had caused her aunt and uncle, promised not to rake over any more coals.

Writing his niece a few years later in his stripped-down vernacular, Uncle Harry called up another side of the evening: "remember the night you and i got drunk in the cold water walk up where you lived in new york . . . we probably both talked at the same time but my recollection was that you questioned the amount of money furnished your family thruout the years, you insisted that mr preston most certainly furnished a good share." After he got home in 1948, Harry had checked the family records, which showed that his parents had allocated $41,700 to the orphans from 1918 to 1923, while Harold Preston had sent two checks totaling $300. "To complete the picture" was a receipt for $23,250 that Mary had received in 1947, when the Capitol Elevator Company was sold. In 1948, he had decided to drop it: "We liked you so why start the bitterness again," he explained, "it would lead no place in fact would turn back on itself, it is the eternal cul de sac. [But] you ripped it open again and i have to answer."

In 1951, Mary had published another memoir in *The New Yorker,* "A Tin Butterfly" (harder on her Grandmother McCarthy than the first), and Harry McCarthy could no longer restrain himself: "one glance at the title and author, i told zula, another scream of persecution for profit by our niece, she replied 'it couldn't be, mary promised me in new york the peasants ["Yonder Peasant . . ."] was her last on that subject, furthermore she was sorry she wrote that.' . . ." The rancor included a slice of pungent anti-Semitism: "you definitely are a throw back to the maternal side of your breeding which explains your inability to resist this urge," Uncle Harry had written, referring to the "scream of persecution for profit." "[m]any jews have told me and it is recognized by all who stop to wonder, why all this race creed and color lament, it is because they most of all owe their present position of advancement to the constant cry of persecution. . . ."

"I don't remember 'promising' Zula not to write any more about the family," Mary wrote back in April 1952. "But I probably did say . . . that I didn't intend to write further about it; I felt through with the subject at the time. . . ." And she had gone on to defend her Grandfather Preston, despite the evidence that upon the death of his only daughter he had abandoned responsibility for his four grandchildren, and then, after making amends with his granddaughter, continued to ignore the three boys. "No doubt, your own feeling for your mother has the same basis as mine for him," she declared of the gratitude she still felt toward Harold Preston; "it is a case of direct experience which no argument will budge." And then she lamented her uncle's "terrible anti-Semitism. As I told you that night, rather drunkenly, 'God will not forgive you for that, Uncle Harry.' "

It was a revival of the tug-of-war Mary had felt as a child when she was caught between the colliding values of her Minneapolis and Seattle grandparents. Yet "in some strange way" it had been "a pleasure" to get his letter, McCarthy wrote her uncle Harry—as the whole rancorous reunion had been a pleasure, one senses, including the drinking— "perhaps just because of your vitality, which I admire." And she hoped he and Aunt Zula wouldn't "treasure this grudge up against me." Uncle Harry's objections and corrections continued to come in, refueling both memory and pain, supplying the adversarial spark to keep the boilers of inspiration hot. Thanks to Harry, memory was jogged on the question of Lizzie McCarthy. When the Minneapolis chapters appeared in *Memories of a Catholic Girlhood* in 1957, they were appended by the postscript in which McCarthy states that she has been unfair to her Grandmother McCarthy by *"looking back at her and judging her as an adult. . . . [A]s a child, I liked my grandmother; I thought her a tremendous figure. . . ."*

Probably Uncle Harry's most significant contribution was the firsthand account he gave Mary of the years he spent chasing her father before Roy McCarthy's marriage, when Roy, an incorrigible alcoholic (though of course the word was never used in the family), had fled the various nurses and drying-out facilities provided for his care. As Harry saw it, her parents' marriage was simply the most ingenious of all his drunkard's schemes for extracting money from his father, a theory McCarthy discounted as an expression of her uncle's pique, but that she reports nonetheless in a speculative spirit. As for the rest of Uncle Harry's portrait, "I more or less believe it," she volunteered in 1988; including the likelihood that her father had never completely stopped drinking when he settled down with her mother in Seattle.

In New York in the late 1940s, her mind had begun to roam across the same troubled waters that she discovered in the Irish family sagas of Eugene O'Neill. Uncle Harry, a self-professed "belligerent catholic," for whom the "greatest thing was to have been born into the Catholic faith," is vintage O'Neill; to wit: "i am also one of the usual sort of irish lads, who just naturally has the greatest inherent respect and love for my mother [as he informed his niece in 1952], and if any one tosses a slur at an irishman's mother, he dont cry persecution or police, he licks them or gets licked trying."

There is a touch of Harry—and maybe a touch of Roy McCarthy—in James Tyrone, Jr., the middle-aged alcoholic of educated pretensions who is unstrung in the final apocalyptic scene of *A Moon for the Misbegotten*. And one can't help but suspect that McCarthy's sudden immersion in the Irish Catholic stream of her ancestry is what lends a peculiar urgency to her treatment of O'Neill in 1952. The great theme of O'Neill's drama, the death of feeling in a man, is not calculated to offer her an easy critical occasion; and yet it is precisely the tragic dimension of O'Neill's vision, his queerly romantic classicism, that wins her over in the end. ". . . [D]espite the tone of barbershop harmony that enters into all O'Neill's work," McCarthy writes, "this play exacts homage for its mythic powers, for the element of transcendence jutting up woodenly in it like a great home-made Trojan horse." The play's emotions ring true because they are true to forms she understands.

In *A Moon for the Misbegotten*'s last scene, the raw-boned daughter of a miserly old bootlegger is to be married off to the Broadway Rakehell (Tyrone); it is their wedding night and Tyrone unburdens himself of a monstrous crime he has committed against his dead mother: while escorting her body home on the train, he entertained a prostitute in his drawing room; and now he sobs himself chastely to sleep on his intended's lap. This moment when the daughter discovers that Tyrone "is really 'dead,' emotionally speaking—an exhausted mummified child," McCarthy observes, "is a moment of considerable poignancy." Tyrone, the fallen man of the world, is a study in regression; and the outsized young woman (who is known for her "herculean sexual prowess," but in actuality is a virgin with a fierce maternal heart) is a study in something else:

> The defeat of all human plans and contrivances is suddenly shaped in the picture of the titaness sitting staring at a stage moon with a shriveled male infant drunkenly asleep at her side. The image . . . takes on a certain grotesque epic form; the woman, stage center, like a gentle beached whale, appears for an instant as the last survivor of the world.

As a note from a critic who regards the theatre as "incorrigibly concrete," this passage tells a different story. The image of the "titaness" is alive with ambiguity. If its power appears "mythic" to Mary McCarthy, it is very likely because the image draws its meaning less from the "living flesh" of the New York stage than from the tangled roots of her own family tree.

18

Intellect Abroad

*"Morality did not keep well; it required stable
conditions; it was costly; it was subject to
variations, and the market for it was uncertain."*

—MARY McCARTHY, *THE OASIS*

America, I think, was greatly improved thanks to Hitler and Mussolini," McCarthy once ventured in an interview. "The whole character of New York was changed by the appearance of the refugees," among whom were the European intellectuals who entered her own circle during and after the war: Chiaromonte, Arthur Koestler, Hannah Arendt and her husband, Heinrich Blücher; along with others who traveled in wider orbits—among them, Paul Tillich, Thomas Mann, Bertolt Brecht, Albert Einstein, Arnold Schönberg, Fernand Léger, and Marc Chagall. The Europeans had "a certain wisdom," McCarthy thought, which was lacking in the "crude society" of American intellectuals—whose crudeness reflected itself on occasion in her own rude tongue.

It was at one of Philip and Nathalie Rahv's parties in the spring of 1945 that McCarthy dropped her bomb on Hannah Arendt's toes. A conversation about the hostility of French citizens to the Germans occupying Paris had been under way, and Mary remarked that she felt sorry for Hitler, who was so absurd as to long for the love of his victims. It was pure Mary McCarthyism, a remark not calculated to offend Arendt, who was part of the group, but Hannah was incensed. "How can you say such a thing in front of me—a victim of Hitler, a person who has been in a concentration camp!" she exclaimed; and McCarthy's attempt to make amends had gone unheeded. A few years later, after the two women kept finding themselves in a minority together at meetings to discuss the future of *politics,* Arendt turned to McCarthy on a subway platform where they both stood silently waiting for a train: "Let's end this nonsense," she said. "We two think so much alike." Mary had gratefully apologized for the Hitler remark, and Hannah confessed that she had never been in a concentration camp, only an "internment" camp in France. And to a degree rare among intellectuals, male or female, their friendship prospered ever after.

Hannah Arendt was not yet the imposing figure she would become in the 1950s, after the publication of *The Origins of Totalitarianism* and *The Human Condition* established her as a political philosopher of uncommon range. In the mid-1940s when she and Heinrich Blücher lived with Hannah's mother in a rooming house on West Ninety-fifth Street, and she worked as an editorial assistant at Schocken Books, and wrote primarily on Jewish affairs for Jewish periodicals in New York, many of her new American friends were dazzled less by her thought than by her style of thinking, by "her astonishing expressiveness as an expounder," Alfred Kazin recalls, which was "already inseparable from her charm as a woman." It was Arendt's passion for discussing Plato, Kant, Nietzsche, Kafka, along with her explorer's interest in the political foundations of her adopted country, that set her apart from other intellectuals. With her wiry salt and pepper curls and piercing eyes, her razored gestures and dangling cigarette, her *"Szee here"* tossed out with a toothy smile, "meant both to subdue and to solace," she was not attractive in any conventional way. If she had been, she might not have succeeded in charming her admirers—"by no means unerotically," Kazin notes—quite so unforgettably.

"Hannah Arendt was [Mary McCarthy's] first real love," Kazin declares today. "I always knew Mary as a harsh, sort of pointy person," he says, "but with Hannah she was almost humble, deferential." The attachment would bloom later, however. In the 1940s, by her own account, McCarthy found the outspoken Arendt more amusing than anything else. When they first met at the Murray Hill Bar in 1944, Hannah and her feisty Berlin-born husband, both not long off the boat, had presented her with their discovery that there was no such thing as America: It hadn't " 'jelled' " yet. McCarthy, who was accompanied by Clement Greenberg, wasn't sure exactly what they meant—maybe they had found a nation of shopkeepers and peasants, more old-world than new; but "they filled me with delight and wonder," she recalled. Later she would discover "some great similarity" between herself and

Hannah Arendt, "not biographical, certainly." Arendt, a student of Martin Heidegger and Karl Jaspers, was born in Königsberg, East Prussia, in 1906 of educated Jewish parents—"but we would have the same thought on either side of the Atlantic; letters would cross with this same thought." And long after the sun set on the radicalism of the 1930s and the postmortems of the 1940s, after the witch-hunts of the 1950s, Arendt reminded McCarthy that a life of the mind divorced from a love of the world was not worth living.

When McCarthy returned to New York with Bowden Broadwater in the second half of the 1940s, however, Hannah Arendt was only one of the refugee intellectuals to catch her eye. The dashing Hungarian-born British novelist, Arthur Koestler, was another. More well known than either Chiaromonte or Arendt, Koestler, author of *Darkness at Noon* (1940) and *The Yogi and the Commissar* (1945), was less a man of conscience than an "anti-Stalinist celebrity," in William Phillips's opinion. He was not one of Mary McCarthy's heroes, though his postwar celebration of the idea of small libertarian groups—"oases"—gave her the title of her next book. But with his soldierly experience as both an antifascist and an anti-Communist, his air of having seen it all, and his dark, vaguely gangsterish good looks, he was a romantic figure who couldn't help but attract her.

And so he had, albeit briefly; first at a party at Arthur Schlesinger, Jr.'s, in New York, and then later at one of those meet-and-get-met functions that *Partisan Review*'s editors were forever hosting—this one, a dinner party in the spring of 1948 at William and Edna Phillips's apartment on West Eleventh Street. Mary McCarthy, Hannah Arendt, Elizabeth Hardwick, Dwight Macdonald, Delmore Schwartz, Sidney Hook, and William Barrett were all in attendance, but not Philip Rahv. For Phillips and Rahv, "the Potash and Perlmutter of literary criticism," as Kazin called them, referring to an old vaudeville duo, the honeymoon was over; and their separate parties had themselves become an expression of the competitiveness and jockeying for position that increasingly characterized their stewardship of the magazine. If Phillips had Koestler, and among the other editors, Barrett, Schwartz, and Greenberg in his corner, Rahv had his stable of fresh talent: Robert Lowell, the critic Isaac Rosenfeld, Saul Bellow, the Kentucky-born Elizabeth Hardwick, a fiction writer and critic who was also "incredibly beautiful," a contemporary recalls. Until 1949, when *The Oasis* appeared with its humiliating portrait of Rahv as Will Taub, he could also count Mary McCarthy. Between Rahv's parties and Phillips's, however, there wasn't much comparison. Rahv's Friday-night affairs, where Hardwick and McCarthy first met, served New York's intelligentsia as a kind of Oriental bazaar. "Here alliances were struck up or down, deals clinched, quarrels reheated," Irving Howe recalls; while across the "Turkish boundaries" that separated the men from the women, only the writing women might cross and "share in intellectual conversation." Here, too, Barrett probably sat beside the two older men he describes in his memoirs who "suddenly froze" when Mary McCarthy came in the door, all smiles, "as if an ogress, booted and spurred, had entered the room brandishing her whips." But the smaller receptions on West Eleventh Street contained their dramatic moments, as well.

At the dinner for Koestler, McCarthy had turned in a peak performance, regaling the group with her parodies of New York literary life; and Koestler had made his play. When a few days later he asked Mary to meet him in his hotel room at One Fifth Avenue, she agreed on condition that there be no lovemaking, and their "contract" had become a much-talked-about joke around town. "He made a pass, and I resisted," McCarthy later reported. "I said, 'I just got married,'" but Koestler had pinned her down in the manner of a "garage mechanic," and she had just barely "succeeded in extricating [herself] from his clutches. It really was an attempted rape." Afterward, he made the same move with Elizabeth Hardwick, she added, "with more success."

Hardwick's affairs often shadowed Mary McCarthy's, as if there weren't enough desirable men to go around, or enough women of their caliber to save them the awkwardness of sharing lovers. In the mid-1940s, Hardwick was involved with Philip Rahv, long after McCarthy had finished with him; but at the end of her life, Mary couldn't resist letting an arrow fly in her direction. "Lizzie was in love with Philip," she told an interviewer; "don't let her tell you otherwise." Hardwick had even asked Nathalie Rahv to give him up, she said, and when the affair ended she wanted to think it was because Philip was married. Philip, however, "didn't care for her much in bed," McCarthy said, noting that "he told me a lot of things like that later when we became friends again. . . . But [Lizzie] also described their sexual commerce rather negatively," she recalled, warming to the story's theme, "the disinclination" that doomed the affair, but also (between the lines) Rahv's loyalty to her. (Twenty years later, at a party at Sue and John Marquand's, Rahv had his say. "'Mary got no tits. Lizzie got no tits. Theo,'" he exclaimed, referring to his third wife, then standing in the next room, "'she got tits!'")

At William Phillips's party, meanwhile, Koestler faced a challenge in Mary McCarthy, whose anti-Stalinism, unlike his own, didn't go very deep. When he launched a discussion of passive resistance (Gandhi then being one of her heroes), the conversation had aroused the hard-core rationalist and much tougher anti-Communist Sidney Hook—"who never let social considerations stand in the way of his intellectual principles" (Phillips). Koestler and Hook had jumped into the ring to settle a point of dogma, but also to best each other in the presence of Mary. And then Koestler had broken away, snapping at Hook: " 'I didn't come three thousand miles to hear this nonsense.' "

The dinner party had been greatly enlivened by the guest of honor's mistaken assumption that *Partisan Review* and the writers associated with it stood at the very pinnacle of American culture. Koestler was extrapolating from the situation in Paris and London, where magazines such as Jean-Paul Sartre's *Les Temps Modernes* and Cyril Connolly's *Horizon* really were central to intellectual life, and intellectual life was central to culture. Not so in New York, and even less in the country at large, where only the tatters of a genuine opposition culture survived from the 1920s and '30s, and among writers there was little of the creative ferment that was under way among painters after the war.

In 1948, *Partisan Review* seemed to occupy a no-man's-land between its adventuresome youth and the stillness of respectability to come. But Koestler's expectations presaged a break in the weather. For Western intellectuals, Barcelona, Paris, Marseilles, and Casablanca were the great wartime cities, but New York was their postwar city: a demilitarized zone where artists and writers jettisoned state, nationality, even ideology for a while, to find in each other's company the promise of something new. In the midst of the ferment, *Partisan Review* became itself an oasis, and for a good many European intellectuals, among them Sartre, Malraux, Camus, and Simone de Beauvoir, a state visit to its offices, like the postwar tour of the United States, was de rigueur.

As for the flirtation between McCarthy and Koestler, such encounters were part of the folklore of intellect abroad. In 1946, Sartre had met the famous "M" in New York, and Camus had taken up with a pretty young translator named Patricia Blake. In 1947, Simone de Beauvoir had begun her gritty affair with Nelson Algren in Chicago, whose telephone number she got from *Partisan Review*. In London in 1945, Edmund Wilson had fallen for Mamaine Paget, and asked her to marry him a year before he was divorced from Mary McCarthy, but Mamaine Paget was about to marry Arthur Koestler, and did so before

Koestler made his first trip to New York in 1948. It was a very small world.

Ideology, however, was thicker than desire. And in this sense, Koestler was right about the importance of the New York intellectuals. Literary New York, light-years away from when it fancied itself a Bolshevik soviet, was now welcoming veterans of the wartime Office of Strategic Services, who were busy laying the groundwork for the U.S. government's postwar cultural offensive against communism. It would be two decades before the rumored facts became public, but at the end of the 1940s and the start of the 1950s, New York was where the pipeline was laid, via a handful of dummy foundations, between the CIA, offshoot of the OSS, and the intellectuals. In 1950, Sidney Hook, James Burnham, Melvin Lasky, James Farrell, *Commentary*'s editor Elliot Cohen, and the AFL-CIO's international point man, Irving Brown, joined Arthur Koestler, Raymond Aron, Hugh Trevor-Roper, and Ignazio Silone, among others, in West Berlin to present the founding manifesto of the CIA-funded Congress for Cultural Freedom, a document that owed itself primarily to the joint efforts of Koestler and Hook.

"Die Freiheit hat die offensive evgriffen . . ." ran the opening salvo in the "first major offensive against Soviet propaganda," as the Berlin conference was billed: "Freedom has seized the offensive." This jumps ahead of our story and into another one, the story of the intellectuals and the Cold War, and how they found a new direction in anticommunism; but the important alliances were forming in the late 1940s in the living rooms where Koestler, McCarthy, et al. were gathered. Mary McCarthy was not a central figure in the drama, but in the years to come she would play a provocative role in three conferences of the Congress for Cultural Freedom.

II

McCarthy's 1940s were not Koestler's. Nor were they Phillips's, Barrett's, Howe's, Abel's, Hook's, or any of the other memoirists' of her generation whose doctrinaire 1940s sound like the doctrinaire 1930s turned inside out. McCarthy's mid-1940s remind one a little of the next political generation's 1960s, seen from Haight-Ashbury. "People began once again to trust their feelings and spontaneous reactions, which are everybody's point of interaction with the world," she told a Columbia University audience in 1959; "the brutalized doctrinaire politics of the thirties were succeeded by a utopian tendency—an interest in the ideas of the anarchist philosophers, of Tolstoy and of Gandhi, in pacifism, non-resistance, free cooperatives, and communes. To this period, between the atom bomb and the hydrogen bomb," she thought, "it is possible to look back with real homesickness."

An interest in ideas, nonetheless, seems to have been the extent of the experiment with utopia, though following the war McCarthy's critical perception of modern history underwent a change. After Hiroshima, she was quick to observe how the 'human interest' conventions of liberal journalism—John Hersey's *New Yorker* interviews with Japanese survivors of the atom bomb, for example—deflected public attention from "the origin of the trouble, the question of intention and guilt. . . . [T]he bombers, the scientists, the government appear . . . to be as inadvertent as Mrs. O'Leary's cow," she wrote in a *politics* critique. Since *The New Yorker* had not, as far as she knew, "had a rupture with the government, the scientists, and the boys in the bomber," the magazine could "only assimilate the atom bomb to itself, to Westchester County, to smoked turkey, and the Hotel Carlyle," she said in 1946, biting a hand that fed her well.

When Gandhi was murdered in 1948, McCarthy was moved to expatiate on the mysterious property of goodness that leads it to provoke evil. "Was Gandhi murdered, as his assassin claimed, because of what he stood for on the Indian question," she wondered, "or rather because what he stood for in his life—simplicity, good humor, steadfastness—affronted his assassin's sense of human probability?" The same question is asked about the dead Trotsky and the murdered anarchist Carlo Tresca, and answered in a similar way; "to the murderer, the serenity of the victim comes as the last straw."

The escape from "doctrinaire politics" and the embrace of "spontaneous reactions" had introduced a distinctly otherworldly note into McCarthy's discourse on public affairs—but with varying results. Hiroshima might have provided a mature Mary McCarthy with a powerful investigative opportunity, as Vietnam did twenty years later when she stepped across the line that separates a critique of the packaging of events from a firsthand exploration, and "actually went and looked." Even her brief discussion of Hiroshima in 1946 shows a supple mind at work on an event that really did appear "as a kind of hole in human history." In *politics,* McCarthy remarks upon the pivotal moment when conventional wisdom gives way to a perception born of real emergency, when the limits of journalism are reached and the work of imagination begins. Hersey is "not Virgil or Dante—hell is not his sphere," she observes, deploying her metaphor carefully.

"Yet it is precisely in this sphere—that is, in the moral world—that the atom bomb exploded."

With McCarthy's political heroes, a different kind of otherworldliness prevailed. The goodness of Trotsky, Gandhi, later Ho Chi Minh, and briefly during Watergate, Senator Sam Ervin, seems assured in McCarthy's view by the sheer malevolence of the opposition, which by a complicated dialectic is provoked to greater mischief by the effrontery of the good. The notion that goodness—not necessarily good deeds, but good character, good karma, the karma that overruns dogma, let us say—*inspires* evil is a curious one. In politics, if it counsels anything it counsels retreat. And yet all this aside, only people and events that raised serious moral issues for McCarthy succeeded in arousing the political activist in her: the person who wrote letters to editors, and, on occasion, as in the early spring of 1948, when she organized the Europe-America Groups, called people together in a worthy cause.

III

In a 1976 biography of Albert Camus, one learns more about the Europe-America Groups than in any memoir of the American intellectuals involved. Camus stood behind a similar effort in Paris, Groupes de Liaison Internationale, which was patterned on the Europe-America Groups, and in a sense succeeded it. Both were short-lived, perhaps because both were informal networks committed to principles of internationalism and nonalignment that were defenseless in a world where the only political ideas that seemed to matter were those backed up by armies. But it was among Europeans such as Camus and Nicola Chiaromonte, as one discovers from their letters, that the need for common action among Western intellectuals who stood outside the two great postwar power blocs was felt more keenly than it was by their counterparts on the other side of the Atlantic.

Among the American members of the Europe-America Groups, which included Alfred Kazin, Dwight and Nancy Macdonald, Arthur Schlesinger, Jr., Elizabeth Hardwick, and Niccolò Tucci, in addition to Mary McCarthy, who started the organization at Chiaromonte's urging, the vision of a Third Force, an alternative to capitalism and communism, remained one of the utopian tendencies of the period. For another wing of the group, recruited in the interest of unity, which included Phillips, Rahv, Barrett, and Hook, along with Bertram Wolfe, Meyer Schapiro, Saul Steinberg, and Nicholas Nabokov, such forays into neutralism and outreach were countenanced with skepticism if not contempt. "We tended to think about Europe in terms of larger political considerations," recalls Phillips tartly, "rather than in terms of 'reaching out.' We were thinking about what Europe *meant*, rather than about how we could *relate* to Europe. We didn't get involved in Spanish Relief," he adds, referring to the Spanish Refugee Committee which was also started around this time. "We didn't get involved [in] 'helping people.' "

It was *Partisan Review* versus *politics*: the doctrinaire 1940s vs. the 1940s of 'spontaneous reactions,' when "it became possible to stick to one's contracts without incurring odium and give money to beggars on the street and even to have a good time," in McCarthy's view. In *The Oasis,* however, she was to demonstrate a valuable ability to see herself and her causes from the other side. For the "realists" in the novel (Phillips, Rahv & Co.):

> Conspicuous goodness, like the Founder's [Chiaromonte] filled them with uneasy embarrassment; they looked upon it as a form of simple-mindedness on a par with vegetarianism, and would have refused admission to Heaven on the ground that it was full of greenhorns and cranks.

Sentiments like this infiltrated the *politics* camp, as well. "I refused to belong to it," declared Lionel Abel of the Europe-America Groups in 1985. "When Mary asked me, I wrote back and said that the sign of political seriousness is the willingness to do something bad. . . . There was too much 'goodness' in this thing."

Today Europe-America is remembered as a relief group, not a political group, by veterans of both wings of the membership. Even Kazin, who is credited in Herbert Lottman's biography of Camus with having coauthored the EAG's charter with Mary McCarthy, links the organization with "Nancy Macdonald's Spanish Refugees. We sent money to French intellectuals," he says of the project, explaining that right after the war the French were without food. But in the single year the Europe-America Groups flourished, 1948, food was no longer a problem in France. The money that went to French, German, Italian, and Spanish intellectuals was raised to send the " 'Standard' Book Bundle"—Koestler's *Darkness at Noon,* Erich Fromm's *Escape from Freedom,* Robert and Helen Lynd's *Middletown,* Carlo Levi's *Christ Stopped at Eboli,* Silone's *Bread and Wine,* Bellow's *The Victim,* Faulkner's *Light in August, The Partisan Reader,* among others—and to facilitate travel and meetings among intellectuals "who were isolated not only from the great power blocs that divide the world," the EAG charter stated, "but also . . . from each other."

Chiaromonte was the courier who dispensed the funds and reconnoitered Rome and Paris for "new groups and tendencies" with which his American friends might collaborate. In July 1948, he reported to McCarthy from Paris that he had given $150 to Camus to distribute as he saw fit, $200 to Mme. Delacorte, an "ex-trotzkyist" who edited *Revolution Proletarienne,* and $60 to Andrea Caffi in Toulouse, a Russian-born Italian savant and frequent contributor to *politics,* who like Chiaromonte was fond of the Greeks and attached to an aristocratic notion of socialism as a kind of "enlightened" society. For Caffi, Chiaromonte wanted to set aside another forty dollars, partly for books and partly to get him out of Toulouse, where he lived alone in a dingy hotel room. "If I ask this for Caffi," he wrote Mary as chairman of Europe-America, "it is of course on account of my personal friendship, but also because I feel objectively entitled to say that he is quite an outstanding man, and one of the few of his generation who could give a substantial contribution to the 'formation of a new left' "—which was the kind of appeal that led McCarthy to feel "almost shame at the seriousness of the European response to our very trivial and muddling efforts," as she wrote the Macdonalds that summer from the house she and Bowden were renting in Cornwall, Connecticut.

It wasn't the Marshall Plan, which started up that same year with a $17 billion appropriation from the U. S. Congress, but in a way the Europe-America Groups was a drop in the same big bucket. ". . . [W]e believe it is a mistake . . . to conceive the struggle against world-communism too much in military terms," declared the EAG charter, which was vetted by Sidney Hook in Paris after the Chiaromontes received the first draft from Mary, "[but] we consider the political destruction of the Soviet regime (not Russia) as a precondition for peace." Which was exactly what Harry Truman and General Marshall considered, too. (Among prominent intellectuals, only Bertrand Russell privately advocated a "preventive war" against the Soviet Union in 1948.) The difference was that the EAG manifesto was aimed at "independent democrats and socialists" and espoused "principles of internationalism [and] of distributive economic justice," which tinged it with 'neutralism,' something akin to fellow-traveling. But it was precisely these vague appeals to European socialist thought that make it sound like a harbinger of the Congress for Cultural Freedom.

Some awareness of the manifesto's proximity to official thinking is undoubtedly what made it necessary for the organizers to assure their colleagues abroad that they were "acting as individuals and intellectuals, independent of the State Department or any other official agency." One doesn't expect such caveats as early as 1948, but Nicola Chiaromonte had to repeat it when he made the rounds in Europe.

The Europe-America Groups was the kind of small communal enterprise, guided by friendship, that most appealed to Mary McCarthy. Later, she would throw herself into a marathon of fundraising for another project with some of the same people—a new magazine called *Critic,* which wouldn't get off the ground partly because of the modesty of its conception. "We figured we could do it for $28,000 a year," McCarthy said of *Critic,* which was going to look into new phenomena like Levitt-towns and the impact of the Marshall Plan abroad; but as soon as she hit the fund-raising trail she discovered that nobody would give her one thousand dollars unless she spent fifty thousand dollars, a commentary on the changing times. By then, the U.S. intelligence community had groomed its first generation of private donors to advance large sums of money, backed up by government funds, for cultural endeavors that promised to shore up the body politic against the contagion of Communist ideas. This was the famous pipeline, and one of its key figures, J. M. Kaplan, who later presided over the Farfield Foundation, the CIA's most important conduit for CCF programs, was also a putative donor to *Critic* in 1953. "There were too many strings on Mr. Kaplan," McCarthy recalled of the man who had pledged to match "$100,000 with $100,000" of his own if the group could raise it. After six months of campaigning fruitlessly on behalf of a 'little' magazine nobody seemed to want, she had returned, flat broke, to her writing.

The Europe-America Groups was born of quite different circumstances. In 1947, when she inherited $23,250 from the Capital Elevator sale, McCarthy had tried to give some of it to Chiaromonte before he and Miriam returned to Paris, but Nicola, "being what he was, wouldn't accept that," she remembers, "and so I had to build this whole organization in order to slip him a little bit of money to take to Europe." By the spring of 1948, her five-hundred-dollar "nest egg" for the enterprise had been augmented by proceeds from a flurry of fund-raising events: a Provincetown art auction, a series of lectures and panel discussions at the Rand School, which she chaired, and a debate between Sidney Hook and Mark Van Doren on Henry Wallace, which she also moderated.

"I love doing organizational things like this," McCarthy told an interviewer in 1985. Organizing meant coping with the intrigue that often occurred behind the scenes, something she also loved—as when "the Sidney Hook gang tried to steal our treasury. . . ." "These birds . . . never gave us a penny, nothing!" McCarthy recalled of the night the boys packed a meeting at Philip Rahv's called to decide what to do with the latest fund-raising proceeds. Saul Bellow had been rounded up, giving Mary her first introduction to *Partisan Review*'s new star, along with Bellow's friend Harold Kaplan, whose luxurious flat on the Boulevard Montparnasse was a favorite stopover for American intellectuals in Paris after the war. "We couldn't have been more anti-Stalinist," McCarthy declares of her own faction—the "purists," she calls them in *The Oasis*—"but that wasn't the point." The point was "support of U.S. foreign policy and . . . the Cold War"; and on that score, the "Master," as even Chiaromonte's wife sometimes referred to Nicola, differed from the 'Sidney Hook gang' in a few crucial respects. Stalinism was not, in Chiaromonte's opinion, the 'main enemy' in Europe; nor did he (along with most European leftists) agree with Hook and the *PR* editors that the impetus for the next war could 'only' issue from Stalin.

The final draft of the EAG manifesto shows that Hook got the upper hand: "We regard Stalinism as the main enemy in Europe today. This does not mean the only enemy." Other enemies, however— Franco in Spain, the Christian Democrats in Italy, "authoritarian tendencies in the De Gaullist movement in France"—were either everybody's enemy or, as in the case of de Gaulle, who was a hero to most Americans in 1948, a bow to the EAG's Paris connections. The elevation of "Stalinism" as the *causus belli* was the operative plank in the program, and on that point "Professor Hook" was apparently content. After reviewing the manifesto's draft in Paris, Hook, as Miriam wrote Mary in Cornwall, had evidently decided that Chiaromonte's "metaphysical aberrations can be excused since he didn't have the benefit of an American education until too late, and it is clear that his heart is in the right place."

Two years later in West Berlin, however, Arthur Koestler wasn't so sure. When Ignazio Silone proposed Nicola Chiaromonte for membership on the executive committee of the Congress for Cultural Freedom, Koestler exercised his *"droit de veto"* to exclude him on the grounds that as late as 1949 in an article in *politics,* Chiaromonte, whom he didn't know personally, "had professed the belief that socialists should fight against their own governments, and not fight the latter's war"—in Cold War terms, the war against Soviet Russia.

As for the confrontation over the treasury, someone had tipped

Mary off about the boys' plan to shift the group's focus in a new direction. "Sidney Hook, I was told, was behind it, and I suppose they would have voted to replace me as chairman," she says, "and there would have gone our treasury. They weren't going to steal it for themselves," she adds, "it would have gone to some right-wing cause—" (then, correcting herself, for it's the 1940s not the 1980s she is describing, "Well, they weren't as right-wing as some of them are now"). McCarthy had rallied her own forces, calling in Kevin McCarthy and Montgomery Clift, both Europe-America contributors, "and so the whole thing backfired."

The showdown, in which Philip Rahv was on the wrong side, is joined in her memory with another ignominious offense committed around the same time. After the poet Alan Dowling gave *Partisan Review* a substantial sum of money in 1948, the editors had all voted themselves hefty salary increases, while extending their production manager, Bowden Broadwater, a five-dollar raise, whereupon Bowden had quit. "I think it was intended to keep me in my place," McCarthy remarks of the salary incident: " *'If she thinks she can—well, we'll show her!'* " Both incidents survive as black marks against the boys, and both helped spark *The Oasis.* "Bowden's job got in there and the five dollar raise and the attempt to steal the treasury," along with another "dirty trick" having to do with the EAG debate over the Progressive party's nomination of Henry Wallace for President.

Initially, McCarthy had been unable to persuade a single Wallaceite to confront the formidable Sidney Hook on a platform. Sarah Lawrence, where she was teaching in the spring of 1948, was full of Wallace supporters, most notably the college's president, Harold Taylor, but even before Hook had entered the debate, none of them would take the stand, perhaps because the Progressives had recently been cited for ties to the Communist party. When Mark Van Doren finally agreed, it was only after Sidney Hook had promised not to humiliate his distinguished opponent—to treat Van Doren " 'with kid gloves,' " McCarthy remembers Hook saying. "But those two hadn't been on the platform for five minutes when Hook moved in and chased Mark Van Doren across the stage and pinned him to the wall. . . . I suppose he got carried away," she adds, chuckling, "but that was a betrayal of his promise, and it left me feeling terrible about Van Doren."

'Professor Hook' makes no appearance in *The Oasis,* which takes on an easier target in Philip Rahv. Like Clement Greenberg, but with different weapons, Hook was capable of inspiring genuine fear in his opponents, and perhaps Mary was loath to take him on. Too bad, because the dapper little man with the Fuller Brush mustache was a quirky, underexposed figure on that part of the Old Left whose chief legacy seems to be to have given birth, during the Reagan era, to the New Right.

Historically, Sidney Hook, "the Hook" some of his friends called him, not Rahv, was the leader of the so-called "realist" faction. Kazin finds it "unbelievable that Sidney Hook was part of the Europe-America Groups," but as anyone studying the history of the 1930s, '40s, and '50s soon discovers, not much happened during the thirty years' war among the intellectuals in which Sidney Hook was *not* involved.

Between McCarthy and Hook, despite their almost comical differences, there was a certain camaraderie. In the late 1930s, it was Hook to whom McCarthy turned for instruction in Marxist theory. In the late 1940s, Eve Stwertka remembers Mary McCarthy reporting that Sidney Hook had praised her for something she had written: " 'You have a great mind, Mary—like a *man's!*' " he said, a guileless remark that even then, in that far-from-feminist era, made McCarthy laugh.

19

Bad Girl

"The chief fault of the creative

species is its indebtedness to life."

—MARY MCCARTHY, "MORE ON COMPTON-BURNETT"

*I*n *The Oasis,* a group of leftist, libertarian refugees from mainstream America move into an abandoned turn-of-the-century resort in the Pennsylvania foothills, ostensibly to practice what they preach: "certain notions of justice, freedom, and sociability." When the colonists find themselves using force to eject a local party of strawberry pickers who are trespassing on their new property, the experiment runs a cropper. McCarthy assembles the usual bunch: an editor, teacher, critic, Protestant minister, actor, trade unionist, girl student, magazine illustrator, novelist, middle-aged poet, and the colony's maverick, a diabetic Jewish businessman from Belmont, Massachusetts. In one guise or another, they are characters the reader meets in nearly all her fiction.

At the novel's end, a few stick to the ribs: the businessman, Joe Lockman, "a sad Jewish comedian," gray around the gills, "he lacked audience-sense to an almost fatal degree." In middle age, Lockman has taken up painting for purposes of relaxation, "only to find in art (he had gone straight to the moderns) something bigger and better than business, a gigantic step-up transformer for the communication of personal electricity which excited his salesman's vision with promises of a vast 'development.' " With such characterizations, McCarthy threw a mirror up to the culture around her—to the rise of "action painting," in this instance, and the 'actionist' criticism of Harold

Rosenberg, who worked by day as a copywriter and also had his businessman's side. (Rosenberg, whose *The Tradition of the New* McCarthy reviewed favorably in 1959, left his mark on popular culture when he invented Smokey the Bear for the Advertising Council.)

Other characters such as Macdougal Macdermott (Dwight Macdonald), the editor of a radical magazine, "tall, red-headed, gregarious, susceptible to a liver complaint, puritanical, disputatious, hard-working, monogamous, a good father and a good friend," are rooted so vividly in the soil of the real that their appearance in *The Oasis* brought an otherwise-lumpish short novel to life. At least for a few thousand followers of *Partisan Review* and *politics* was this true, and then, by the ripple effect accorded coterie literature, to others for whom the work of the principals was hardly known. " 'Do you know I once knew more about Mary McCarthy and Philip Rahv than I knew about *myself?*' " remarked a disgruntled observer of the scene. The machinery that transforms literary gossip into literature and then back into literary gossip was, in the case of the New York intellectuals, firmly set in place when the English magazine *Horizon,* where *The Oasis* first appeared, awarded the book first prize as the best short novel of 1949.

When Macdougal Macdermott pounces on his fellow colonists the night Joe Lockman's name is proposed to the "Utopian council," he sounds exactly like Dwight: "My God, aren't we going to have any standards? . . . Don't you believe in *anything*? This fellow is a Yahoo." Moving on, the reader learns something about Macdermott/Macdonald's conjugal life, as well as his relations with his children; nothing scandalous, and Macdonald, unlike Philip Rahv, never protested his portrait in *The Oasis*. ("Was Dwight intimidated by Mary?" Nancy Macdonald was asked in 1985. "Dwight was not intimidated by anybody," she replied.) But when McCarthy observes that all his life Mac suffered "from a vague sense that he was somehow crass, that he did not belong by natural endowment to that world of the spirit which his intellect told him was the highest habitation of man," she took the portrait a step closer to her subject's inner life. "Of all the enrolled Utopians," she comments astutely, "he was closest to Joe by temperament." Here was a man who would have scoffed at a poem (just as Dwight scoffed at Eliot and Pound in the 1930s), if the idea of poetry had not been explained to him. "Nevertheless, ten years before, he had made the leap into faith and sacrificed $20,000 a year and a secure career as a paid journalist for the intangible values that eluded his empirical grasp," as had Macdonald (who made "James Joyce" his

underground name when he joined the Socialist Workers party in 1939)
when he left *Fortune* in 1937 for *Partisan Review*—and, in a different
sense, as Joe Lockman does when he sets out from Belmont for Utopia.

But it is the more ambiguous portrait of Philip Rahv as Will Taub
that is interesting for the political analysis it contains of the withering
away of a dissenting culture after the war.

In *The Truants,* William Barrett recalls that Rahv, who was usually impervious to the criticism of others, was only "really crushed" by
public opinion once: "when he read Mary McCarthy's cruel caricature
in . . . *The Oasis.*" Behind this exposure was the authority of the
written word, which Rahv worshiped. Moreover, the book showed
him as ridiculous rather than evil—as when Taub is unmanned during
a stroll in the woods by a gun-toting Joe Lockman, who has presented
himself in jest to the terrified leader of the 'realist' party as "the
sheriff." Finally, the damage was done by a woman who had once been
his lover, and for whom, according to Delmore Schwartz, he had never
ceased to nurse a special attachment.

Looked at today, the scenes from *The Oasis* that show Rahv in a
state of emotional undress don't seem that significant. One is inclined
to agree with McCarthy, who insisted she meant no harm by the
portrait, that the book on the whole is "really quite tender to Rahv."
Nonsense, says Nancy Macdonald, "she was insensitive to his feelings." Rahv, in any event, did initiate a lawsuit, alleging 132 violations
of his rights, but *The Oasis*'s publisher, Random House, resisted it,
and he withdrew the charge. Dwight Macdonald himself may have
talked him out of it when he reminded Rahv that in order to win, he
would have to prove he was Will Taub. " 'Are you prepared to make
that kind of jackass out of yourself?' " he wondered.

McCarthy held to a byzantine theory that it was Rahv's "enemies"
who put him up to the suit: Greenberg, Phillips, and Schwartz. They
had lost the showdown in Peter's Restaurant, where Rahv had been
dressed down for bad-mouthing his colleagues to publishers, foundation people, and the like, "and when *The Oasis* came along they saw
their chance and put him up to suing me. . . . His feelings were
hurt, of course," she concedes; "he didn't like the part about Nathalie. . . . But these people were just goading him to sue." Why? "To
isolate him totally. . . . It was a wedge between him and me and people
who were friendly to me, like Hannah," McCarthy explained. "I think
this is the way they reasoned," she added; "at the time I don't think
I suspected it, but it was typical of somebody like Greenberg to have

such an idea, a kind of awful low cunning." It seemed strange to her that Rahv should have been so easily influenced—"he ought to have known at bottom that I was not his enemy." They had been lovers, after all, she remarked, not for the first time in this revealing narration, in which Rahv's "enemies" serve as a lightning rod for a certain cunning in McCarthy's imagination.

In the novel, Will Taub watches his fellow colonists unpack their belongings on their first day in Utopia. "The tree of life . . . is greener than the tree of thought," he muses (paraphrasing Hegel); "[h]is eye caught the girl-student sitting cross-legged in front of her cottage and ingested her long legs; Susan watched them move bulgingly down the tract of his appreciation, like a snake's dinner, to join the Jacksons' English bicycles and the breasts of the minister's wife. . . ." These little dramatizations of the mental processes of her characters show McCarthy in her element. Of Howard Furness (Dupee) in *The Groves of Academe* (1952): "His sharp, dapper mind was extremely sensitive to any disarray in the outer garment of reality."

In *The Oasis*, she delights in Taub's "materialist imagination [which] was continually at play, building on straws of report vast structures of conjecture and speculation. . . . What really interested him was information," she notes, "and the magical properties it contained for the armchair subjugation of experience." The same might be said of the author's imagination. But when McCarthy observes of Taub that "he was a politician even with thought, keeping an eye on the various developments in literature and the arts in the manner of a chief of state who has some subordinate read aloud to him the editorials in the opposition newspaper," she depicts Philip Rahv in a nutshell.

Earlier in the story, when Taub is shown at home with his wife, the portrait is darker. " 'What *fools* they'll make of themselves,' " he sneers upon hearing that a "lady purist" has pronounced him " 'salvageable' "; then abruptly he taps his wife on the shoulder: " 'We'll go,' " he declares of his last-minute decision to join the colony: " 'It will be *marvelous*,' he cried . . . rolling slightly on the sofa. The tip of his tongue fastened itself against his lower teeth, and the center broadened and protruded in a truly malignant fashion as he emitted another grating laugh, vainglorious and taunting. 'A-a-ah,' he exclaimed. . . ." Taub wasn't wholly displeased by the lady purist's remark, McCarthy observes, moving in under the skin:

Something shy and childlike in his nature felt obscurely flattered by the judgment. He and his whole party, to tell the truth, would have been glad to be redeemed or 'salvaged,' if this could only be accomplished privately, and without the loss of that ideological supremacy which had become essential to their existence.

This "ideological supremacy" is the linchpin in McCarthy's analysis of what made the *PR* intellectuals appear ridiculous in the postwar period. And it was probably this analysis that prompted Hannah Arendt to issue one of those notes with which writers open diplomatic relations with one another. "You have written a veritable little masterpiece," she said of *The Oasis* in March 1949; adding (in rusty English), "May I say without offense that it is not simply better than The Company she keeps, but on an alltogether [sic] different level." The same analytic bent, however, led Wilson's friend Dawn Powell to question whether *The Oasis* was a novel at all. Reviewing the book in *The New York Post,* she found it full of "the mothball odor of old prize essays . . . large thoughts in large words. . . ."

"The dictators of a diminishing circle of literary and political thinkers," McCarthy writes of the intellectuals she knows so well, "they maintained the habit of authority by a subservience to events," clinging to their ability to demonstrate how a significant occurrence or deed could not possibly have happened other than the way it did. In this materialist predilection—a "fixed belief in the potency of history to settle questions of value," McCarthy calls it—they flew against one of her own treasured beliefs: the "concept of transcendence," which she would describe later (in "Artists in Uniform") as "the concept that man is more than his circumstances, more even than himself."

Taub and his friends had been inactive politically for a long time, and their materialism had hardened into a "railing cynicism," McCarthy notes; "yet they still retained from their Leninist days, along with the conception of history as arbiter, a notion of themselves as a revolutionary *elite* whose correctness in political theory allowed them the wildest latitude in personal practice." It was this 'latitude' McCarthy found objectionable, not because she felt it herself—more likely because Bowden Broadwater and Eve Gassler did, the "hard-working subordinates" in the tale. At the office, "arriving late on Mondays and leaving for the weekend on Thursdays," Taub and friends "were short and harsh with the typists, rude to the telephone girls. . . ." As Eve Stwertka, who worked at *Partisan Review* after Bard, recalls: "there were these four men [Rahv, Phillips, Schwartz, and Barrett] coming into the office once a week and dictating to me; and the rest of us were women—there was one other man, but he quit after

Bowden did—so we ended up running the day-to-day operations of the magazine."

The Oasis has often been cited for the meanness of its portraits of the author's fellow intellectuals, and no one is more outspoken in making the charge that Mary McCarthy had a "wholly destructive critical mind" than Alfred Kazin. "She seemed to regard her intelligence as essentially impersonal," he states in a memoir; she was always "surprised that her victim, as he lay torn and bleeding, did not applaud her perspicacity." In conversation, however, Kazin makes a criticism of the *Partisan Review* circle that is not unlike McCarthy's in *The Oasis,* only it includes Mary McCarthy, along with the contemporary "neo-Right" (Irving Kristol, Norman Podhoretz, Daniel Bell). The political arrogance of the latter, he thinks, is rooted in the same unholy alliance of modernism in literature and politics that inspired anti-Stalinist intellectuals in the 1940s.

It is not a new theory, but Kazin, who like Mary McCarthy takes his politics personally, gives it a fresh dimension. The transformation of a self-styled revolutionary avant-garde in the United States into a reactionary one, as he relates it, becomes an episode in Jewish history, Russian Jewish history. "You have to understand that the Jews of my generation, whose parents were usually born in Russia . . . [and who] came to America because they were more or less driven out by the Czars, identified with the fact that Czarism was hell on the Jews," he reminds a younger generation.

> The Jews really thought that the Russian Revolution would give them for the first time some kind of freedom. . . . Then comes the Revolution, then comes the Depression in this country—and then one way or another people like Rahv, like Mary, people that age, Eleanor Clark, Robert Penn Warren's wife, they're all communists, but the ones who felt it most deeply were Rahv and the others [who were Jewish].

What bothers Kazin about this group is what bothers him about the neo-Right—"crooks," he calls the latter, who "still think they're giving advice to the lower orders." They're all "superior avant-garde types. . . . The whole key to the *Partisan Review* was that they were . . . Modernists about revolution," he states. "They thought of themselves the way Lenin thought of himself. Along comes Stalin who introduces real politics into the game, starts murdering people, and of course, they're intellectuals, they never murdered anybody, and they get out. But they cannot escape the fact that there were two dreams involved," he adds: "one was the dream of revolution, which is a great dream . . . and the other was [the dream of] the avant-garde." The great figure for both was Trotsky—"incredibly arrogant, incredibly sure of himself, and finally . . . knocked to death in Mexico by forces he always claimed he was superior to."

For Kazin, "Mary was in that sense a perfect example, like Philip Rahv, like Hook, of someone who had that intellectual assurance. They were avant-gard*ists*." The observation reminds him of what might have been part of the trouble between Mary and Edmund Wilson. "Wilson was not that type. Wilson was literary all the way through." (It was a distinction Reuel made as a boy when he told his mother that, unlike her, his father wasn't " 'an intellectual. He's a literary man.' ") Wilson was always friendly with Lillian Hellman, Kazin points out. He used her apartment in New York; he often saw her in Boston when she was lecturing at Harvard in the 1960s. Thinking of McCarthy's assault on Hellman's veracity as a memoirist on the Cavett show, he says: "Edmund would never have gotten mad at Lillian the way Mary did for a very simple reason—he couldn't take that [political] stuff that seriously. He had turned his back on it."

In 1985, it is the "crooks" who love to get into black tie with Reagan's people, who are "subsidized by millionaires" to give lectures at NYU's School of Economics, who edit magazines with Henry Kissinger, who sit down on "MacNeil-Lehrer" and give advice to congressmen, who stick in Alfred Kazin's craw. And his account of how a cadre of Jewish intellectuals from the 1930s and '40s managed to become the ideologues for a group of conservative business and government leaders in the '80s is an update of Mary McCarthy's analysis of how the radicals shed their spots at the end of the 1940s. Actually, McCarthy noted a link between a certain brand of youthful radicalism and a talent for making it in the mainstream as early as 1952, when she wrote Richard Rovere that she didn't want to include Daniel Bell in their new magazine venture because he gave her "the feeling that he wants to be successful and wised-up, simultaneously, an alarming combination but not untypical of a lot of the former YPSL's [Young People's Socialist League]."

When Kazin theorizes about the careers of men like Kristol, Podhoretz, and Bell in the 1980s, he points first to how "very political-minded" they have always been, and how "involved in the whole craze of journalism. . . . They care very much what [*New York Times* editor]

Abe Rosenthal thinks, what *The Village Voice* thinks." Kazin himself, a "scholar and teacher," still lives on the Upper West Side, which makes him a "Jewish intellectual—if you move to the East Side you're on your way to something else." It continues to astonish him that in his lifetime, he's "gone from this unbelievable proletarian poverty of the Depression—my father unemployed for five years, City College, trying to get jobs at department stores—up to a point now, well—"he breaks off, thinking of Podhoretz, a member of the Council for the Free World, whose son-in-law was assistant secretary of state under Reagan. "This is part of the immigrant dream," he exclaims—a dream that Kazin, of course, like Irving Howe and Norman Podhoretz, has made the subject of countless divinations in prose and public lectures.

"Podhoretz said something I understand very well, because he's from the same lousy neighborhood I am," Kazin remarks; "he said, 'the move from Brooklyn to Manhattan is the longest trip in the world.' . . . well, they're *still moving*. No, they've *moved, they made it!*" He once asked Arthur Miller: "Why did some of these people go so far under Reagan?" and Miller said, " 'They smell power.' " But Kazin's mother—"illiterate even in Yiddish"—gets the last word. " 'They're *all-rightniks*,' " she used to say of such people. " '*All-rightniks*' were people who said, 'I'm doing all right in the new country.' "

II

She was "absolutely sick" of the way she was living, Mary wrote Nancy and Dwight from the summer house in Cornwall: "the lack of accomplishment and seriousness, and one year succeeding another with nothing's being changed." 'Nothing changes,' she feared, was "practically the epitaph of our whole generation of American intellectuals."

By the time *The Oasis* was published, the Europe-America Groups were a dead letter. "When the money ran out, it ran out," McCarthy commented later; but the unraveling was more eventful than that. First, a series of bulletins which she had hoped to put together out of both Chiaromonte's reports and the letters trickling in from obscure little magazines, print shops, and bookstores in Europe had failed to win support. Maybe Dwight vetoed the proposal in the expectation that *politics* would accomplish the same task. ("If you say no, I won't go any farther with it," McCarthy had written him in July 1948; "as Nicky says, it does seem to rest between us to get anything done . . .") Mary had presented Macdonald with a " 'Yes' from three

members," Bowden, Elizabeth Hardwick, herself. "Kevin and Monty
I know I can get," she added (referring to Montgomery Clift). "I feel
sure of Isaac [Rosenfeld]; Tucci seems a pushover; you could ask Bert
Wolfe on the Cape if he is there. . . ." There even seemed to be "a basis
of support from Hook," she thought, "which ought to impress the
boys; Nabokov is surely ours, also Kazin. What is your vote?"

But the bulletins—"The Situation in France," "The Situation in
Italy," she and Elizabeth Hardwick wanted to call them—never
materialized. Nor did the "Letter to Europe" that was to be sent to
representatives abroad. McCarthy had proposed that both the Letter
and the bulletins be produced by committee; "aside from our principles of camaraderie, this seems to me the only way any of us *prosateurs*
will ever get [them] done without months of literary self-torture that
we are all too used to," but the committee was never formed.

The membership was solicited one more time on behalf of Andrea
Caffi and Mme. Delacorte. "It seems shameful that they should be so
poor," Mary lamented, "while all of us are in relative comfort (to say
the least in our case; we are having a luxuriant summer with vegetable
gardens and fresh eggs and milk and chickens and cheap heavy cream
and all the scenery thrown in)"—along with a steady procession of
guests on the weekends. And maybe that was part of the problem, too.
After the privations of a cramped railroad apartment on East Fifty-
seventh Street in the city, which Mary, Bowden, and Reuel shared for
a while with Bowden's sister, Christine—"the anthill," Reuel called
it—the enticements of the country life were irresistible.

"Nobody changes their views on vacation," Lionel Abel observes
of an earlier summer, Hiroshima summer in Truro, and the same can
probably be said of the summer of 1948. Eve Stwertka is probably right
when she suggests that "all these people had no aptitude for political
action, their own naïveté being their greatest pitfall. . . . They were all
impractical to the point of childishness, and Mary herself never saw
this clearly," she believes, a view shared by Nancy Macdonald. But for
McCarthy personally, the brief experience with organized political
activity in her thirty-sixth year seemed to stimulate a more sober way
of thinking about the world.

Initially, "some attempt at a communal program of living" had
impressed her as "the most obvious solution" to the inertia that
gripped American intellectuals, just as it impressed Chiaromonte when
he encountered communal action under way among nonconformist
Catholics and "old time syndicalists" (workplace organizers) in
France. In Paris, even Sartre's Rassemblement Démocratique et Révo-

lutionnaire seemed to be breaking away from both Stalinism and Trotskyism by creating small groups to work on local problems outside the big party machines. For Mary, however, the "communal program" soon found its natural resting place in fiction, where (in *The Oasis*) it provided her with a useful plot device, like the cruise ship in Katherine Anne Porter's *Ship of Fools,* for observing the behavior of individuals caught in the eye of a storm. When she set her mind to the problem of broadening the Europe-America Groups, however, to making "certain tentative [steps] toward a new political movement," which was the second part of her proposal to the Macdonalds, she spoke directly to a burning public issue: the rearmament of the great powers.

"Concrete aims" were needed to draw more people to the Europe-America cause and keep the organization alive, she argued; and already the EAG manifesto struck her as too confining. "Our aims *must* be radical," she wrote Dwight. In Paris, Camus had also expressed displeasure over the manifesto's vagueness and its proximity to U.S. government thinking on the question of Stalinism. And now McCarthy was convinced that a new manifesto must "raise the military question and answer it; otherwise, we might as well melt into the A.D.A. [Americans for Democratic Action]." This did not mean subscribing to a philosophy of nonviolence, which went "too far . . . at least for this group," in her opinion: "we simply have to oppose the militarization of Europe and of the United States." If this meant a "break with the boys," so be it, she argued, since "they only discredit us anyway, while feeling compromised themselves by the connection." Concretely, she proposed that a new manifesto clearly dissociate "the struggle for freedom" (Kazin's phrase) from a system of military alliances, and cite as "the *first* necessity the achievement of social gains."

Engaging in some armchair realpolitik of her own, however, she wondered what Europe-America's attitude should be toward "resistance groups that might arise in Stalinist-dominated countries—would we favor military support to them if their program was democratic?" She herself wasn't sure how she would respond to the eventuality of "England being invaded by the Stalinists with a Labor government in power. I'm not even sure what I think about the Berlin situation," she added; "should the U.S. government move out and let Stalin take over? (What do you think, by the way?)"—which was a real question for Dwight Macdonald, whose crusade against Stalinism, against 'stooges' and 'fronts,' had hardened by the late 1940s into an occupational tic.

The odd fear of England's being invaded by Stalinists links Mary and Dwight to members of the U.S. intelligence community—among whom the CIA's Cord Meyer, with his icy contempt for the ease with which the "Brits" were penetrated by the KGB, was certainly the most influential. Men like Cord Meyer and Tom Braden, who preceded Meyer as chief of the CIA's International Organizations Division in the early 1950s, made their counterattack through the programs of the Congress for Cultural Freedom. In *Facing Reality,* Meyer describes the IOD's mission thusly: "to counter with covert action the political and propaganda offensive that the Soviets launched through a battery of international front organizations." Dwight and Mary, on the other hand, contented themselves with an occasional irate letter to the editor of a liberal publication such as *The New Statesman;* as in 1951 when McCarthy vehemently protested the English paper's reference to Arthur Schlesinger, Jr., as speaking " 'the language of [Joe] McCarthy with a Harvard accent.' " In July 1948, nevertheless, she concluded that even a 'Yes' to the question of supporting anti-Stalinist resistance groups in Europe was "a far different thing from turning Europe into an armament factory. . . ." And she wanted no part of "the whole psychology of Preparedness at all costs exemplified in the P.R. editorial board."

The EAG manifesto was never revised. McCarthy's "concrete aims" ran against the current doctrine; not only the Truman Doctrine and the doctrine of 'containment' set forth by the persuasive "Mr. X" (George Kennan), but the 'realism' of American intellectuals that left them unwilling to depart from official thinking if it meant poking their heads outside the bunker of anticommunism. To Chiaromonte, Macdonald had to confess that "Mary was right—as against you and me—in her idea of splitting EAG and sloughing off the PR-Hook crowd." But finally, "no one wants to carry the ball," he wrote in December 1948, no one except Mary, and by then the group's internal squabbles left her "only halfhearted." And the organization was dissolved.

III

When Mary McCarthy went back into action, which on the weekend of March 25, 1949, she did, she found herself on more familiar turf. Teaming up with Dwight Macdonald, Bowden, Elizabeth Hardwick and Robert Lowell, who would be married before the year's end, she set out to infiltrate the Cultural and Scientific Conference for World Peace at the Waldorf-Astoria—not a difficult task, as it turned out.

The conference, sponsored by the National Council of the Arts, Sciences, and Professions, was organized to promote goodwill between the United States and the Soviet Union, and to introduce Western artists and intellectuals to their counterparts from Russia and the Eastern bloc countries. With well-known personalities such as Leonard Bernstein, Dashiell Hammett, Howard Fast, and Lillian Hellman in the American delegation (the Russian delegation was led by A. A. Fadeyev, head of the Russian Writers Union, and included the composer Shostakovich), the 1949 Waldorf conference looked like a reincarnation of the Second American Writers Congress in 1937. But storming the gates of Stalinism in New York in 1949, in the shadow of the House Committee on Un-American Activities, government loyalty oaths, and the Attorney General's subversives' list—and with nearly one thousand anti-Communist pickets, led by the Catholic War Veterans, marching outside—was not a notably radical act.

In Europe, such mammoth conferences would become increasingly common during the late 1940s and early '50s, but in the United States the Waldorf affair was a last hurrah for the idea that the ideological interests of the Soviet Union might be grafted on to progressive traditions in American society. With the outbreak of the Korean War, the level of anticommunism had risen too high for peace conferences. For the Soviet Union, which by 1949 was aggressively jockeying for position in the Cold War, allies were to be sought and enemies neutralized in Europe rather than in the United States. If, as the tireless warrior Dwight Macdonald concluded after the Waldorf conference, Communist party intellectuals and fellow-travelers seemed "humorless, ineffective and certainly no menace," there were reasons for it, though the anti-Stalinists never stopped to wonder why.

For Mary and Dwight ("the *bêtes noires* of Communist intellectuals," Joseph Lash called them in 1949), anti-Stalinism at the Waldorf served mainly to keep the 'principles of camaraderie' alive. In McCarthy's recollections of the event, it isn't the Stalinists who gave the rebels a run for their money, but the Hook crowd—a paradox that became the subject of another unfinished story, "On the Eve." When she first informed Sidney Hook about her group's plans to participate in the conference, he had laughed at her naïveté. " 'If she thinks they'll register her as a delegate, that proves how little she knows about politics,' " McCarthy recalls him saying. When the tickets duly arrived, Hook assured her that none of them would be allowed to speak. Summoning them all to a hastily organized command post at the Waldorf, "the little anti-Communist suite," William Phillips calls it in

A *Partisan View,* Hook had briefed them about how to survive a forced expulsion from the hall. They were to bring umbrellas to bang on the floor when they were not recognized, and then tie themselves to their chairs so that when they were expelled, the ushers would have to carry them out. Their mimeographed speeches would then be distributed to reporters by Hook's group, Americans for Intellectual Freedom.

As it happened, the four had brought umbrellas and did bang them on the floor, but they never tied themselves to their chairs or handed out their statements. They were each given two minutes to speak— including Robert Lowell, whose paranoid anticommunism in these years was not easily restrained. Dwight Macdonald addressed a long list of missing Russian writers to Fadeyev, who asked him at one point in the exchange "how many divisions [he] had?" McCarthy had reserved her question for the distinguished scholar F. O. Matthiessen, who described Ralph Waldo Emerson as an ancestor of American communism. Did Matthiessen think Emerson would be allowed to live and write in the Soviet Union? she asked. Matthiessen conceded he would not, and then countered that Lenin wouldn't be permitted to live in the United States.

Only one speaker punctured the ritual arguments, and this was an invited one who sat on the dais a few chairs away from Lillian Hellman. Norman Mailer, who Bowden remembered as "a preppy Frank Sinatra" at Harvard, and whose stories were then appearing alongside Saul Bellow's in *Partisan Review,* stunned everyone when he charged *both* the Soviet Union and the United States with pursuing expansionist foreign policies that subverted peace. "I have come here as a Trojan horse," he began. "I don't believe in peace conferences. They don't do any good. So long as there is capitalism, there is going to be war. Until you have a decent, equitable socialism, you can't have peace." At the risk of making himself "even more unpopular," Mailer had gone on to suggest that both systems were moving toward "state capitalism." "All a writer can do is tell the truth as he sees it, and to keep on writing," he concluded to thunderous boos.

Irving Howe, who covered the conference for *Partisan Review,* attributed Mailer's remarks to his close association with the French writer Jean Malaquais, another anti-Stalinist who had secured a ticket to the floor and, in postwar New York, a more shadowy figure than Chiaromonte, Koestler, or Camus.

Meanwhile, the Americans for Intellectual Freedom had busied themselves with intercepting mail and messages intended for the conference sponsors, and issuing false statements to the press in the peace

conference's name—tactics that "upset all but the most hardened veterans of Communist and anti-Communist organizational fights," Phillips reports. "I could understand that purists would have nothing to do
with this kind of politics, whatever the cause," he writes; "[b]ut the
alternative appeared . . . to be a complete withdrawal from politics."
The *but* is intriguing, for it reveals an inability to envision politics as
anything other than fighting communism.

Mailer's statement excepted, politics at the Waldorf-Astoria had
become a game played by Communists and anti-Communists, who
alone knew the rules. 'Peace' and 'intellectual freedom' were the
pawns. On a smaller scale, it was the game Cord Meyer replays in his
memoir without the apologetics. Whether diplomats, spies, or intellectuals, the competitors are pros who in the last analysis are really
playing for each other.

For Mary McCarthy, the Waldorf conference produced one tangible result, although she couldn't have guessed it then. It earned her the
enmity of Lillian Hellman. "She had always felt resentful of Mary,"
New York Review of Books editor Robert Silvers remarks of Hellman's interest in "giving Mary a hard time" in 1980, when she filed her
$2.25 million libel suit after "The Dick Cavett Show"; and the Waldorf
Conference, which Hellman helped organize, was one reason. The
other was a more direct confrontation that had taken place at Sarah
Lawrence the year before.

The occasion was a dinner party at President Harold Taylor's, to
which Hellman, some students, McCarthy, and the poet Stephen
Spender (who was also teaching at Sarah Lawrence that term, along
with Mary) had been invited to discuss an upcoming Writers Conference at the college. Before dinner, Mary had walked in on Hellman in
the Taylors' sun parlor, just as Hellman was telling the students how
John Dos Passos had "sold out" in the Spanish Civil War "because of
his stomach, his gluttony. . . . [When] he got to wartime Madrid he
didn't like the food," McCarthy recalls her saying. And Mary was
incensed. She had long ago parted ways with Dos Passos politically,
but she and Edmund had once been his friends, and she "couldn't bear
to hear those lies so smoothly applied to him, as if they were coming
out of a dispenser tube," she wrote her lawyer, Ben O'Sullivan, in 1980.
"[Hellman] wasn't *openly* hostile to him (which might have tipped the
girls off)," she added, referring to her antagonist's style and delivery,
so important in the determination of character, "but smiling, knowledgeable, tolerant of his weaknesses—'He did love his food.' "

Mary had interrupted to say that if the students wanted to know the true story about Dos Passos, they should read *Adventures of a Young Man*. What Miss Hellman was telling them was "just a slander." He hadn't " 'turned against the Loyalists,' " as their visitor stated, but only against the Communists who were killing Trotskyites, POUMists, and Anarchists, McCarthy declared. John Dos Passos's real turnaround hadn't come because he didn't like the food in Madrid, but because of the murder of Andrés Nin, whom he had known and liked. His position on the Loyalists was no different from George Orwell's, she added, invoking a more saintly figure.

In the several accounts McCarthy has given of the Sarah Lawrence meeting, it is Hellman's reaction to the confrontation that stands out. In the letter to her lawyer, McCarthy doesn't want to "expand upon the incident" except to note that "on her bare . . . arms [Hellman] had a great many bracelets, gold and silver, and that they all began to tremble—in her fury and surprise . . . at being caught red-handed in a brainwashing job." Hellman's arms, McCarthy reports on another occasion, "looked shriveled and fatty at the same time . . . as if she was a hundred years old, though she wasn't much older than I was." She herself was probably mistaken for a student, McCarthy suggests, which was why her presence at the door had gone unnoticed at first; then when Hellman was "taken by surprise, the bracelets shook and made a jangling noise."

When Mary McCarthy stood up and took her place in line behind the microphone on the floor of the Waldorf ballroom, the tableau was complete: Lillian Hellman seated on the stage in the place of authority; Mary, the rebellious student in the wings, about to raise her hand—only now there is an audience, a new and important wrinkle. Time will supply the spark.

In the meantime, there were new voices to be heard from Europe, and for Mary and Bowden Broadwater, a new Europe, only recently discovered.

20

The Existentialists Are Coming! The Existentialists Are Coming!

"I scarcely met any but intellectuals; but . . . what a distance from the cottage cheese salads of Vassar to the marijuana I smoked in a room at the Plaza with bohemians from Greenwich Village."

—SIMONE DE BEAUVOIR, FORCE OF CIRCUMSTANCE

". . . we were waiting to be discovered. Columbus, however, passed on. . . ."

—MARY McCARTHY, "AMERICA THE BEAUTIFUL"

The summer before they were married, Mary McCarthy and Bowden Broadwater had joined the legions of Americans who marched off to Europe after the peace. "Victors in a world war of unparalleled ferocity, heirs of imperialism and the philosophy of the enlightenment, they walked proudly on the dilapidated streets of Europe. They had not approved of the war," McCarthy noted of the young lady and her companion in "The Cicerone," the story drawn from this first trip to France and Italy in August 1946, "and were pacifist and bohemian in their sympathies, but the exchange had made them feel rich. . . . The exchange had turned them into a prince and a princess. . . ."

The exchange rate was highly favorable to Americans, who could stay in Rome's most luxurious hotel, the Grand, for one dollar a night. Even impecunious bohemians like Bowden and Mary had found it easy to fall in with a traveling American heiress such as Peggy Guggenheim.

And they were often embarrassed by the Roman "cicerone" they had befriended, a Mr. Scialanga in real life, whose own tastes had led him to steer his American charges away from the first-class hotels, expensive restaurants, and fashionable shopping districts that for the first time they were in a position to enjoy.

Paris, in particular, was swarming with ex-GIs and American businessmen, princely spenders all, who may have filled Frenchmen with the foreboding Americans feel about the Japanese in Los Angeles today. In Paris, however, culture remained in the hands of the natives; culture, in the form of haute cuisine and literature, continued to be the country's most durable export, but the reins of destiny had shifted elsewhere. While the victorious army cruised the Champs Elysées and admired Notre Dame, not to mention the French girls on bicycles and the Folies Bergère, travelers like Mary and Bowden poked their heads into courtyards in the Faubourg St. Germain, and hung around the Café Flore in the hopes of seeing the famous Jean-Paul Sartre, until they were told that Sartre no longer came there, but patronized the Pont Royal bar instead, where Bowden and Mary also went.

Saint-Germain-des-Prés was awash with rumored sightings of the "pope of existentialism" and "Notre-Dame-de-Sartre," as the French tabloids called Sartre and Simone de Beauvoir. The quarter's sudden popularity after the war owed itself in no small part to the literary renown of these two intellectuals who really did conduct their lives in the street, in a glare of publicity that would have wilted a less stalwart pair. In one of her memoirs, Simone de Beauvoir recalls a typical day in 1946 that began at the Deux Magots. She is editing manuscripts for *Les Temps Modernes* (Sartre being in America), and "making contacts." Cyril Connolly sits down to talk about some Resistance writers he is publishing in *Horizon*. They gossip about Arthur Koestler, who is living in London, and whose *Darkness at Noon* is much talked about in France, and de Beauvoir, who has not yet met the famous anti-Stalinist, professes herself "pleased to learn that Koestler enjoyed Sartre's books." Lunch turns into dinner as more friends sit down, and the group moves on to the Cheramy, and from there to the Vieux Paris, the Armagnac, and the Petit Saint-Benôit, where they greet the dawn.

"I spent my evenings at one or another of the Montana, the Méphisto or the Deux Magots," de Beauvoir continues, as if these restaurant notes are part of the history she and Sartre are making and writing at the same time. The Restaurant du Scribe, an American enclave, is given favorable mention for its breakfast of white bread, scrambled eggs, and Spam. The Flore has indeed been abandoned because "too many people knew us there . . ." and so they have set up shop in the cellar bar at the Pont Royal, "which is warm and quiet, but inconvenient. . . ."

"Around *PR,* we were all taken, more or less, with the existentialists," Mary McCarthy recalled in 1989. In 1945, after Sartre's *Les Mouches* had opened in Paris to excited reviews, and his three Resistance novels, *The Age of Reason, The Reprieve,* and *Iron in the Soul,* were published, along with Simone de Beauvoir's 'existentialist novel,' *The Blood of Others, PR*'s editors translated Sartre's "The Case for Responsible Literature" which had just come out in *Les Temps Modernes.* In a series of issues devoted to "New French Writing" in 1946, they published his "Portrait of the Anti-Semite" with de Beauvoir's "Pyrrhus and Cyneas," another discussion of the responsibility of intellectuals; and two chapters of Albert Camus's *The Myth of Sisyphus.* McCarthy remembered translating "a rather heavy piece [de Beauvoir] wrote on political revenge," which the magazine seems never to have published. She herself liked Sartre's plays more than his theoretical writing or his fiction.

At the core of existentialism's appeal to intellectuals was its focus on the experience of self—whether the physical self (Maurice Merleau-Ponty) or the volitional self (Sartre)—as the starting point for knowledge of one's *being* in the world. The heady moralizing of French existentialism, with its emphasis on responsibility and its aversion to conformism, appealed to New York intellectuals, though many would dissociate themselves from the political activism that went hand in hand with its opposition to whatever impaired individual freedom. In McCarthy's circle, being 'taken with the existentialists' seemed more a response to the persons than the ideas of the movement; there is something physical, even sexual, in the recollections of her friends, suggesting that a cinematic charisma was at work.

For Lionel Abel, Sartre possessed "the most interesting of modern faces," and had a "very special kind of virility in his style of speaking and his whole manner generally." William Phillips found Camus the more impressive one, "inordinately handsome, with a combination of sensitiveness and ruggedness, and a suggestion of boldness and adventurousness that must have been most attractive to many women." At *Vogue,* where Camus was the man of the hour, a hero of the French underground, and a cultural personality whose face was memorialized in June 1946 by Cecil Beaton, the editors were reminded of Humphrey Bogart.

"I would love to have met him," McCarthy says of Camus, "but the opportunity didn't arise. I was less interested in Sartre and least of all in Simone de Beauvoir"—who naturally was the one she did meet. Simone de Beauvoir, who McCarthy thought "quite pretty" when she was first introduced to her at a cocktail party in New York early in 1947, with "glowing cheeks and bright blue eyes, but a little too much like an athletic nun," is treated more roughly in the reminiscences of New York intellectuals. "Toward us she often came on as the school-marm or governess," William Barrett recalls; and he describes her devotion to Sartre and his doctrines as "touching" but sometimes embarrasssing. " 'If you would only read page 329 of Sartre's *Being and Nothingness,*' " she would interrupt someone in conversation, " 'you would get that clear.' " Miriam Chiaromonte remembers being interviewed by de Beauvoir on "American conditions" over lunch at the Hotel Brevoort. "It felt all so pretentious," she says; and in *America Day by Day,* "de Beauvoir got it all wrong." In Phillips's opinion, "she was politically rather weird, with the mind of a fellow-traveler. She talked endless nonsense about America."

In 1947, de Beauvoir concluded that American intellectuals as a group were "advanced paranoics" who "approved of all Truman's speeches" on the dangers of communism; a credulous generalization, but one nourished by *Partisan Review*'s editors themselves, who warned her that French intellectuals were only 'appeasing Soviet expansionism' when they gave 'qualified' support to European Communist parties. In a May 1947 *New York Times Magazine,* on the other hand, she had marveled at that "American dynamism" that transformed "mere things into instruments adapted to human purposes," by which she meant "the abundance of products displayed in drug stores and dime stores." And she praised America for having equipped a continent "in less than 200 years . . . with a history and a civilization. A humanist cannot but marvel at this magnificent triumph of man," she declared—thus inspiring the title of Mary McCarthy's 1947 essay "America the Beautiful: The Humanist in the Bathtub," which begins: "A visiting Existentialist wanted recently to be taken to dinner at a really American place. . . ."

Phillips remembers complaining to Hannah Arendt about Simone de Beauvoir's "endless nonsense," whereupon Arendt had commented, " 'The trouble with you, William, is that you don't realize that she's not very bright. Instead of arguing with her, you should flirt with her.' " The distaff note was also sounded by Janet Flanner in *The New Yorker,* when she reported seeing "[t]he Prettiest Existentialist" in New York sipping a Coke at a soda fountain, ordering whiskey at a bar, drinking an orange juice at a drugstore lunch counter. It was all public relations. "Flanner liked women, and one day she summoned me to the Scribe, where we had a drink," Simone de Beauvoir told a journalist many years later. "Thanks to her article"—which was actually written *before* de Beauvoir left Paris—"I was introduced to New York intellectual circles."

In New York, Mary McCarthy was one of Simone de Beauvoir's guides to the city. A mutual friend named Tony Bower brought them together, and on the evening McCarthy tried to find the 'really American place' de Beauvoir was looking for, they had first gathered at the Broadwaters' Fifty-Seventh Street apartment for cocktails. "A wood fire was burning in the fireplace of our semi-cold-water apartment, which appeared to displease her," McCarthy remembered in 1988; "she thought it was un-American." Eventually, they had settled on Lindy's, and then stopped at a nightclub to hear Billie Holiday sing.

There was nothing accidental about the fame the existentialists had come to enjoy. As representative figures of the French Resistance (even when, like Sartre and de Beauvoir, they had not participated in it), they were candidates for cultural missions to the United States. Camus, Sartre, and de Beauvoir each traveled under the sponsorship of the Cultural Relations Section of the French Ministry of Foreign Affairs, as did dozens of other prominent French writers and artists. Nominally, they were on state business for the provisional Government of the French Republic—just as were the American poets, painters, and novelists, Mary McCarthy included, who toured Europe in the 1950s and '60s under State Department auspices—but apart from the lecture tours that took them to dozens of universities across the country, they had few official obligations. The American junkets were a reward, a paid vacation, for service to the Republic.

Inside France, the existentialists were national heroes. There was an "amazing agreement" between what the existentialists offered and what the French public wanted after the war, Simone de Beauvoir recalls in *Force of Circumstance*. Sartre's "petit-bourgeois readers had lost their faith too, in perpetual peace, in eternal progress, in unchanging essences; they had discovered History in its most terrible form . . . and they needed an ideology which would include such revelations without forcing them to jettison their old excuses"—which is precisely what existentialism did. "In fact, it did not," de Beauvoir argues, wanting it both ways, the popularity and the ideological purity. The 'old excuses' are not identified in her memoir, but they remained, first in the idea of progress that Sartre rescued when he yoked existentialism to humanism in his famous 1945 lecture "Is Existentialism Humanism?" and later in the Marxist dialectic (Edmund Wilson's ghostly 'German Will') when Sartre assimilated Marxism.

While as a system of thought, an *anti*system, its proponents would say, existentialism never took root in American soil, its influence was felt in American fiction, in the 'dangling' men of Saul Bellow, Ralph Ellison, Norman Mailer, William Styron, and James Baldwin; and in the triumph of the color black (the color of anarchism's flag) in fashion. Unlike the cultural arbiters of a later era, Jacques Derrida, Michel Foucault, and Jacques Lacan, whose poststructuralist canons have proved more adaptable, Sartre, de Beauvoir, and Camus remained too embedded in the Cartesian solipscism to which they were heir for them to be readily accessible in the United States. As the war's victors, moreover, what need did Americans have for a philosophy that sprang from a sense of hopelessness over the 'blasting of plans and the meaninglessness of effort' (as Sartre put it after the war), even if as a personal coda, vulgar existentialism, like vulgar Marxism, did seem to affirm an inalienable American belief in the freedom of the individual to choose his own destiny?

Americans were groping for an ideology that would accommodate a quite different set of 'revelations' than the moral and material losses registered by Europeans. The revelation of American power displayed by the possession and first use of the atomic bomb was one such factor upsetting the status quo ante; another was the assumption of American responsibility for the economic reconstruction and military defense of both Europe and Japan. In intellectual circles, where the adversarial postures of the 1930s and early '40s were all but gone, the attempt to come to terms with this new behemoth with a smiling face sometimes yielded surprising results.

II

For Mary McCarthy, who had ignored the ground swell of interest on the part of writers such as Waldo Frank and Archibald MacLeish in the 'rediscovery of America' in the 1930s, and who remained largely unmoved by the belief in a 'better world' that accompanied the vast expansion of government programs inside the United States during the New Deal, the sudden proliferation of U.S. government programs abroad, via the Marshall Plan and the Point Four program, seemed to fill her with pride. "Rediscovery . . . was the characteristic mode of the

1940s," she recalled in 1959, "as though man, reemerging from a lapse into barbarism, were finding the old house he had made for himself still standing and full of fascinating furniture, bibelots, and curios." She was referring to the literary revival, the return to the classics, but the sentiment might have applied equally to the political revival—a reconsideration of the virtues of American democracy, and even of plenty—that swept the Left toward the end of the 1940s.

Of course, it had taken a "visiting Existentialist" bristling with idées fixes about America to remind McCarthy how much she "admired and liked" her country; there had to be a nay-sayer, against whom she could fortify her position. "We preferred [our country] to that imaginary America, land of the *peaux rouges* of Caldwell and Steinbeck, dumb paradise of violence and the detective story, which had excited the sensibilities of our visitor and of the up-to-date French literary world," she writes in the first of two midcentury essays, "America the Beautiful" and "Mlle. Gulliver en Amérique," which graphically express Mary McCarthy's contradictory vision of America.

"The virtue of American civilization is that it is unmaterialistic," she declares in "America the Beautiful," serene in the knowledge that the idea will strike the average reader as preposterous:

> Everybody knows . . . that America has the most materialistic civilization in the world, that Americans care only about money, they have no time or talent for living; look at radio, look at advertising, look at life insurance, look at the tired business man, at the Frigidaires and the Fords. In answer, the reader is invited first to look instead into his own heart and inquire whether he personally feels himself to be represented by these things. . . .

The sudden appeal to "feeling," so contrary to McCarthy's image as an intellectual hard hat, is characteristic of her reasoning when her affections are engaged. *Of course* the reader (like the author) doesn't feel himself to be represented by Fords and Frigidaires. Only "other people" do: the man down the street, the entire population of a certain city, the poor, the rich ("who would like nothing better, they think, than for life to be a perpetual fishing trip with the trout grilled by a native guide, [and] look patronizingly upon the whole apparatus of American civilization as a cheap Christmas present to the poor. . . ."). In 1947, the visiting Soviet critic Ilya Ehrenburg, who glorified the Check-O-Mat in American railway stations, while deploring American materialism, is another one of those 'others.' As is Simone de Beauvoir, whose fascination with American consumer goods and American neon ("I want to wrap these lights around my neck, caress and eat them"), together with her rebuke of American intellectuals, and her warnings of incipient American fascism, was aired in *America Day by Day,* and harshly reviewed in "Mlle. Gulliver en Amérique."

"Passivity and not aggressiveness is the dominant trait of the American character," McCarthy continues in "America the Beautiful," which first appeared in *Commentary* in September 1947. Another odd proposition, this one allows her to vent her deep-seated concern about the bomb: namely, that only if Americans can "differentiate" themselves from the bomb will they avoid using it; and that the habit of using things simply because they are there, or because everybody else uses them, is too deeply ingrained in the national character to provide an adequate defense:

> the movies, the radio, the super-highway have softened us up for the atom bomb; we have lived with them without pleasure, feeling them as a coercion on our natures, a coercion seemingly from nowhere and expressing nobody's will. The new coercion finds us without the habit of protest; we are dissident but apart.

Intellectuals, in particular (probably the only ones who experience such things as a "coercion"), are "dissident but inactive," McCarthy continues. "Intransigent on paper, in 'real life' we conform; yet we do not feel ourselves to be dishonest, for to us the real life is rustling paper and the mental life is flesh. And even in our mental life we are critical and rather unproductive; we leave it to the 'others,' the bestsellers, to create." "America the Beautiful," which is haunted by an existentialist's horror of the "Other"—"the murk of otherness," McCarthy calls it—is full of unexpected flashes such as this. The indictment of intellectuals is self-criticism, but a question remains. Is it "dishonest" not to act on one's principles, one wonders, pondering a certain ambiguousness in Mary McCarthy's career, or to eschew writing bestsellers?

Meanwhile, the essay's central proposition—that "possessions, when they are desired, are not wanted for their own sakes but as tokens of an ideal state of freedom, fraternity, and franchise"—is worth another look. There is something politically naïve about the argument McCarthy marshals in its defense: that "no nation with any sense of material well-being would endure the food we eat, the cramped apartments we live in, the noise, the traffic, the crowded subways and busses." Nor is there much objectivity in the assertion that only "Europeans believe that money brings happiness, witness the bought journalist, the bought politician, the bought general, the whole venality of European literary life, inconceivable in this country of the dollar." This is American chauvinism speaking.

What is most provocative about McCarthy's proposition concerning the unmaterialistic character of American life is the notion that the "republic" was founded on an "unworldly assumption, a denial of 'the facts of life.' It is manifestly untrue that all men are created equal," she declares. Interpreted in worldly terms, the doctrine results in

a pseudo-equality, that is, in standardization, in an equality of things rather than of persons. The inalienable rights to life, liberty, and the pursuit of happiness appear, in practice, to have become the inalienable right to a bathtub, a flush toilet, and a can of Spam.

It is hardly a new idea, and McCarthy notes how left-wing social critics have attributed the process to capitalism, while right-wing critics see it as democracy's logical dead end. Her own observation that "capitalism, certainly, now depends on mass production," would seem to favor the left-wing view. But on the more essential point—that the buying impulse in American society, "in its original force and purity," is motivated by *unworldly* aspirations—McCarthy articulates a conservative view, one that lay behind Daniel Bell's idea of the 'end of ideology': namely, that it is as consumers, shareholders in the national property, that Americans realize their true citizenship.

"The immigrant or the poor native American bought a bathtub, not because he wanted to take a bath," McCarthy proposes, "but because he wanted to be in a *position* to do so. . . . 'Keeping up with the Joneses' is a vulgarization of Jefferson's concept (*re* the 'pursuit of happiness'), but it too is a declaration of the rights of man, and decidedly unfeasible and visionary." What is striking about the formulation—which yields the memorable one-liner, "We are a nation of twenty million bathrooms, with a humanist in every tub," is its abrupt dismissal of the rights of man as "unfeasible and visionary."

Historically, such 'rights' are realized in society through the cumulative effects of changed economic circumstances, concerted political and legal action, all arenas in which McCarthy demonstrates little interest—even though she observes elsewhere that it is "decidedly unfeasible" to think one can substitute "the parity of the radio, the movies, and the washing machine" for that real, albeit ideal "parity of which these things were to be but emblems." Indeed, the effort to do so "has made Americans sad," she maintains. "Status" offers scant protection from the loneliness of striving, especially when the fruits of the effort are acquired too rapidly to give a man time to "live into them. . . ." The "new American [is a] nomad . . . camped out in his circumstances . . . never assimilated to them." And McCarthy is reminded of how "all along a great avenue in Minneapolis the huge stone chateaux used to be dark at night, save for a single light in each kitchen, where the family still sat, Swedish-style, about the stove"—a reverse image of the green light winking at the end of Daisy Buchanan's dock in *The Great Gatsby*.

The vaunted "rights of man," in other words, are a pipe dream, an *American dream,* which is presumably why the humanist (or the socialist) is in the bathtub. Nowadays, one might find him in a hot tub. Speaking of the socialist vision of society organized around different incentives than acquisition or consumption, McCarthy observed in 1985, with an acerbity missing in 1947 or 1952, "I would guess that idea in any large way really died with the Second War, just as the New Deal died with the Second War, and then we went into a war economy and that was that." The same fate seems to have overtaken the democratic idea after the war, the idea that for the common man, "nature's nobleman," McCarthy called him then, there was something more in store in the New World than a better mousetrap. Something more even than 'doing all right in the new country.'

In these postwar years, McCarthy was a little sad about the society she saw around her. "Homelessness" is the real theme of "America the Beautiful," "the homelessness of the American, migrant in geography and on the map of finance. . . ." The essay touches on the dark side of the postwar celebration of American power and plenty, and thus it offers a deeper perception of the times than the commentaries of less divided minds. For one impulsive moment at the end, McCarthy seems ready to throw it all up, to claim those "thousands and thousands of European peasants and poor townspeople who came here bringing their humanity and their sufferings" as her kin. "What it amounts to . . . is that we are the poor," she exclaims. "It is the absence of a stable upper class that is responsible for much of the vulgarity of the American scene." And for once she is not going to blush for the deficiency, not, at any rate, in the inquiring presence of Simone de Beauvoir, whose arrival seems to have caught her with her inferiority complex showing. The ugliness of the American scene, the ugliness of American "decoration," "entertainment," "literature," she asserts, is the "visible expression of the impoverishment of the European masses, a manifestation of all the backwardness, deprivation, and want that arrived here in boatloads from Europe. . . . Europe is the unfinished negative of which America is the proof."

To the problem of vulgarity, she has found an ingenious resolution that subtly shifts the burden of responsibility back to Europe. McCarthy gives it a psychoanalytic twist:

Given a clean slate, man, it was hoped, would write the future. Instead, he has written his past. This past, inscribed on billboards, ball parks, dance halls, is not seemly, yet its objectification is a kind of disburdenment. The past is at length outside. It does not disturb us as it does Europeans, for our relation with it is both more distant and more familiar. We cannot hate it, for to hate it would be to hate poverty, our eager ancestors, and ourselves.

In the end, McCarthy leaves us with two contradictory images of American society, and thus of her relation to it. The first is that America represents a corruption of the ideals of the Enlightenment, and indeed, that the cornucopia of goods resembles a 'cheap Christmas gift to the poor' more than any monument to ingenuity. The second is that "American civilization" marks "a beginning, even a favorable one" to the eventual triumph of a superior type; "for we have only to look around us to see what a lot of sensibility a little ease will accrue. The children surpass the fathers and Louis B. Mayer cannot be preserved intact in his descendants. . . . Unfortunately," she added in 1947, thinking of the bomb, "as things seem now, posterity is not around the corner."

By 1952, the year *Partisan Review* took its bow in the brave new world of the American Century with a starry-eyed symposium entitled "Our Country and Our Culture," Mary McCarthy seemed to have settled down with the second proposition. "The America invoked by Mlle. de Beauvoir as a country of vast inequalities and dramatic contrasts," she declared in "Mlle. Gulliver en Amérique," "is rapidly ceasing to exist." To identify the country with " 'fascism' " and " 'reaction,' " as both de Beauvoir and "much journalism of the European left" were doing, she charged, was "not to admit . . . that [the United States] has realized, to a considerable extent, the economic and social goals of President Franklin D. Roosevelt and of progressive thought in general."

In "Mlle. Gulliver en Amérique," McCarthy counters the criticism of Europeans with a decidedly upbeat vision of American society in which she seems to make her peace with the America of Coca-Cola, supermarkets, Milton Berle, and *Life* magazine. To Simone de Beauvoir's picture of a vast regimented mass of Americans lorded over by a tiny "Pullman class," a society de Beauvoir characterizes as "rigid" and "closed" despite its material abundance, McCarthy counters with an America in which mansions are being torn down and the "development" is taking their place:

> [S]erried rows of ranch-type houses painted in pastel colors, each with its picture window and its garden, each equipped with deep-freeze, oil furnace, and automatic washer, spring up in the wilderness. Class barriers disappear or become porous . . . [E]ven segregation is diminishing; consumption replaces acquisition as an incentive.

It wasn't a picture one might have expected her to extol. And in the fall of 1952, a row of pastel bungalows springing up in front of the austere white frame house that she and Bowden Broadwater had purchased in Portsmouth, Rhode Island, in 1949 (with the remainder of the Capitol Elevator sale) would lead the two of them to pull up stakes. "Crushed between the millstones of the proletariat—the proliferating little houses across the street that breed like slum-populations—and the plutocracy in Newport, we're selling our house," McCarthy wrote Dwight Macdonald in October 1952, after a "lyric" holiday at the Macdonalds' cottage in Truro led her to convince Bowden that they should buy the charming cottage they had discovered on the Pamet Point Road in Wellfleet. "I've long felt that the Cape is an impossible place to work, but I'm going in the teeth of this conviction," Mary told Dwight—going anywhere or doing anything 'in the teeth of conviction' suggesting that destiny, once again, was at work.

But for the "new America" celebrated in "Mlle. Gulliver en Amérique," McCarthy felt a deep ambivalence, one she projects onto Simone de Beauvoir at the end of the essay:

> One can guess that it is the new America, rather than the imaginary America of economic royalism, that creates in Mlle. de Beauvoir a feeling of mixed attraction and repulsion. In one half of her sensibility, she is greatly excited by the United States and precisely by its material side. . . . Yet at bottom she remains disturbed by what she has seen and felt . . . of the American problem.

The "problem," according to McCarthy, is not one of "inequity" "but of its opposite"—"the problem of equality, its consequences, and what price shall be paid for it," and "the spread of uniformity." These are the problems de Tocqueville originally framed about American democracy two hundred years ago. They are the foundations of conservative social thought; and by the early 1950s, they had become the hallmark of anti-Stalinist cultural criticism, whose real unease was neither with culture nor the system of mass production and distribution that helps shape it, but with the masses. McCarthy's question: "How create a cushion of plenty without stupefaction of the soul and senses?" was not a question calculated to impress the millions of beneficiaries of the GI Bill with its urgency.

The fear of mass culture was also a dilemma for that "upper-class minority" whose views come in for special attention in McCarthy's 1952 essay. This was the group whose "outrage . . . at the spectacle of television aerials on the shabby houses of Poverty Row . . . Frigidaires and washing machines in farmhouse and working-class kitchens, [and] above all at Truman the haberdasher, the symbol of this cocky equality," impressed McCarthy as "perhaps the most strikng phenomenon in American life today." Mlle. de Beauvoir, she complained, "remained unaware of it"—as indeed she might. A lecture tour of American campuses did not ordinarily introduce European intellectuals to the views of the American upper crust, precisely the layer of American society for whom Mary and Bowden Broadwater, for all their bohemian sympathies, shared the liveliest fascination.

III

By 1952, the lure of "the Newportians," the lure of old money and its complacent eccentricities, had begun to pale for Mary McCarthy—especially after the defeat of Adlai Stevenson, whom she had supported, was greeted by most of her Rhode Island neighbors with extravagant relief. But in the beginning of the Broadwaters' residence at Double-Axe Farm, as they called the nineteenth-century house set in thirty acres of pasture running down to St. Mary's Lake, McCarthy had assured Dwight Macdonald that after the "middle-class suburbs" of Connecticut and New York, only Newport prepared her "for the startling fact that one isn't bored outside of the *Partisan Review* circle. One feels on the edge of some exhilarating discovery. . . ."

There was no "Bohemian life whatever," she noted in another letter to Dwight, who often visited the Broadwaters in Portsmouth with Nancy over Thanksgiving weekends, when Bowden and Mary had worked for days preparing a fête champêtre and dinner. Dwight had found "more gayety and drama than happens in our secluded lives here in a month," he wrote Mary after the first Thanksgiving in 1949—when she had entertained a bandwagon of people within days of recovering from another miscarriage. "The classic fall on the stairs . . . brought about this dismal result," McCarthy wrote Dwight from the hospital, "just after, fortunately, I'd at last got my Holiday piece in the mail ['The Vassar Girl']." In the letter about the absence of "Bohemian life," she had described her neighbors as "terribly reactionary, in a most startling way," like the "nice old Scotch party" who kept a Newport boardinghouse and locked her door and hid in the parlor when a Negro convention came to town. . . ." Mary wondered "whether such a state of mind is more prevalent than we in New York could guess—a kind of hysteria anticipating social change."

McCarthy's private life had taken a turn toward the bucolic. Gone were the messy run-ins with the boys, which had included an "unfortunate experience" with Delmore Schwartz earlier in 1949, when Bowden caught him embracing Mary in the vestibule on Fifty-seventh Street after a cocktail party. Bowden had disappeared into the night, and Mary had ordered Delmore to go upstairs and wait until her husband returned so that he could tell him what had happened (which was that he had forced himself on her, McCarthy said years later). "I thought [Bowden] might throw himself in the river," she added. "He really was a very unpredictable and moody person." Bowden finally returned, Delmore made his confession, and peace was restored—until the next day Delmore "went around and told all these little boys, including Philip, that I had made a pass at him! Philip, of course, didn't believe him," she remarks, "but the others probably did."

In Portsmouth, Bowden Broadwater got a job reviewing books for Winfield Townley Scott at the *Providence Journal*. He was getting to be quite a hand with the scythe, Mary wrote Dwight; the open fields surrounding the house, where cows grazed, were alive with birds and butterflies and soft breezes, carrying the scent of hay and clover to the front door. If she and Bowden were "fascinated" with the ceremonies of society, which for the most part they were, it was because the "neighborhood, or perhaps its money," she explained, had "in some way promoted the real proliferation of character." Like the elderly New England heiress, Miss Alice Brayton, whose topiary garden full of giant birds and animals was a Newport landmark, and who served the Broadwaters as a native guide to the mysteries of Bailey's Beach, their neighbors, McCarthy concluded, had "realized themselves in a positively tropical fashion." Many years later, their Portsmouth neighbor Nicholas King would recall that Newport's old guard was "fearfully, and pleasurably, anticipating that [Mary] would sooner or later use them as easy targets of satire, but she never did. . . ."

For Mary McCarthy, the rich were a tonic, just as for a different sensibility, lowlife exercises the fatal attraction. Fifteen years later, however, when she was living in Paris and married to James West, supply tipped demand, and the attraction shifted. Then she would open her door to itinerant young writers and students traveling through Europe; and during the Vietnam War, to draft resisters and deserters whose antiwar cause became her own. In the early 1950s, however, she was as eager as Bowden to cultivate people who walked right out of a Saxon cartoon in *The New Yorker*. The string of mammoth "cottages" along Ocean Drive in Newport beckoned in quite the same way as a string of waterfront dives might have drawn Walt Whitman or Hart Crane.

The attention McCarthy gave the 'upper-class minority' in 1952 bore out a striking insight made in 1942. "Scratch a socialist and you find a snob," she writes in *The Company She Keeps*; and she points to how a person in the socialist movement can give himself "the airs of a marquis" by referring to his opponent as a "parvenu" or "upstart." A politician is always "cheap," an opportunist "vulgar." Meg Sargent recognizes that her own "proletarian sympathies constituted a sort of snub that she administered to the middle class," the class for which Mary McCarthy often felt the sharpest aversion. "If one could only be sure that one did not belong to it, that one was finer, nobler, more aristocratic," Miss Sargent reflects—sounding like a daughter of the Irish white-collar class, which Louise Bogan once described as being prone to the "dangerous . . . impulse to 'rise' and respect 'nice people.' "

In McCarthy's case, the ascent had already occurred. The truth, as Miss Sargent reflects, "was that she hated [the middle class] shakily from above, not solidly from below." One is reminded of a similar paradox in Simone de Beauvoir's well-known disdain for bourgeois society and bourgeois family life, which is despised, in memoir, fiction, and social treatise, from the shaky summit of intellect unbound. As different as these two women are, there is something they share— something they didn't like sharing—that fed their disdain.

21

Big Women (A Postscript)

What goes down, comes around.

Nearly thirty years after the 'Prettiest Existentialist' first visited New York, Simone de Beauvoir became the target of one of those character assassinations for which Mary McCarthy had become justly or unjustly (depending on your point of view) famous. The bullet was fashioned during a freewheeling interview with a visiting journalist in 1980 in the downstairs library of Mary and James West's summer house in Castine, Maine, six years before de Beauvoir's death. The charge? That the French feminist deceived herself and her public when she spoke about being "deprived because of her sex."

"How *dare* she talk about injustice to women, and how as a woman she's been deprived when she has put herself on the map solely by attaching herself to Sartre, *solely. Sartre et moi.* He *made* her," McCarthy declared. "She's not utterly stupid," she conceded acidly, "she would be a good 'B' student somewhere in the intellectual world. . . ."

The outburst occurred in the course of a discussion of modern feminism ("It just does not say hello to me at all"), but also in the shadow of the $2.25 million defamation suit that Lillian Hellman had just lodged against McCarthy for calling her a liar on "The Dick Cavett Show." When the interview took place, McCarthy, who was suffering a bout of shingles, had been ordered by her lawyers not to discuss anything related to the impending hearings—a constraint that might have opened the gates for the sudden attack on Simone de Beauvoir, another woman whom Mary McCarthy loved to hate.

Feminism, she ventured, "is bad for women. . . . [I]t induces a very bad emotional state," comprised of the loathsome emotions of self-pity, covetousness, and greed. With its indictment of female dependency and its emphasis on male privilege, feminism, McCarthy suggested, is a competitive ideology born of desperation. "I'm sort of Uncle Tom from this point of view," she admitted, having made her way in a world of men. And so presumably was Simone de Beauvoir. But de Beauvoir had taken Uncle Tom a perilous step further by adopting her mentor's philosophy ("cribbing" from Sartre, McCarthy said). And then she had the effrontery to turn around and bite the hand that fed her. Not Sartre's, of course. Her "trust" in Sartre—which de Beauvoir once described as "so complete that he supplied me with the sort of absolute unfailing security that I had once had from my parents, or from God"—remained unbroken.

"In fact, she *made* it through her sex by attaching herself to this man," McCarthy exclaimed, "and many others of us have made it through our sex," she added with a gravelly chuckle, "but it's most ungrateful in her case."

Rarely have two views of the feminine condition diverged so radically as Simone de Beauvoir's and Mary McCarthy's. "The emancipated woman wants to be active, a taker, and refuses the passivity man means to impose on her," writes de Beauvoir in *The Second Sex;* "she prides herself on thinking, taking action, working, creating on the same terms as man." And McCarthy? "I've always liked being a woman," she declares stoutly. "I like the domestic arts, cooking and gardening. I like clothes very, very much. . . . I'm so happy that I don't have to dress like a man." She also likes the "social gifts that women develop almost as a species—from their historic position of having to get their way without direct confrontation—which are the gifts of observation and analysis." And it seems to her "that one of the problems of a lot of feminists is that they don't like being women."

The venom in the attack on de Beauvoir springs from other sources than a philosophical difference over woman's estate, however. "I've only met her once but I gather she is an absolutely horrible person; she's extremely jealous," McCarthy maintains, citing the testimony of the novelist Nathalie Sarraute that de Beauvoir broke up Sarraute's friendship with Sartre.

They were friends, and he wrote an introduction to one of Sarraute's books [*Portrait d'un inconnu*, 1947]. According to her, Simone de Beauvoir permitted him to have those little girls because it didn't threaten her position, but Nathalie was her own age and a highly intelligent woman with an original mind . . . and it happened not only with her but with other intellectual women.

Sartre, McCarthy adds, was by all accounts "a very sweet and kind man, and in some way he pitied [de Beauvoir]."

Jealousy, one suspects, cut both ways. Nathalie Sarraute, an elder stateswoman of French letters, is one of a handful of French writers—François Bondy, Jean-François Revel, and Monique Wittig are others—whose friendship McCarthy made after she moved to Paris in 1962. It isn't hard to imagine the two women gossiping about Simone de Beauvoir, who had "a great cult in Paris," McCarthy commented in 1980, and who looked down on other writers outside her circle, especially American writers. "[T]o live somehow together with these characters in power and command must not be easy," Hannah Arendt wrote McCarthy of Sartre and de Beauvoir, after finishing de Beauvoir's *Force of Circumstance* in 1965—"one of the funniest books I['ve] read in years. Incredible that no one has taken [it] apart," she added. (It was typical of Arendt's respect for the mysteries of the heart, however, that she found de Beauvoir's "unwavering true love for [Sartre] the only mitigating circumstance in the 'case against her,' really quite touching.")

As for de Beauvoir's jealousy, it was a problem she herself alluded to repeatedly in her memoirs. Jealousy seems to have been the one emotion she could not admit to feeling without violating her faith in her own rationality. If she did, she might have lost her grip on the very detachment of mind that sealed her relationship with Sartre, and set her apart from other women with whom he lived out bits and pieces of his emotional and sexual life without compromising his primary commitment to her—a commitment, one gathers, to a kind of moral and intellectual pilgrimage, a marriage of minds. In fiction, nonetheless, she gave vent to her darker impulses.

In *She Came to Stay* (1943), Simone de Beauvoir's first novel (an autobiographical roman à clef that parallels Mary McCarthy's *The Company She Keeps*), in which Pierre (Sartre) and Françoise (de Beauvoir) stand "together at the center of the world which it was their compelling mission in life to explore and reveal," Françoise murders the third member of the triangle, Xavière, who is based on one of

Sartre's 'little girls.' "In this novel I exposed myself so dangerously that at times the gap between my emotions and the words to express them seemed insurmountable," de Beauvoir reflects in *Force of Circumstance,* recalling Xavière's death: "my throat constricted as if committing a real crime."

When Mary McCarthy told an interviewer at Vassar that she found it "harder to write fiction," but that "when fiction is finally done, it has more of oneself in it," she probably had similar experiences in mind. Jealousy certainly fires her characterization of Norine Schmittlapp in *The Group,* whose original, Eunice Clark, had an affair with Mary's first husband, Harold Johnsrud. And vengefulness toward Edmund Wilson steals into *A Charmed Life.* But Mary McCarthy never kills her offending characters off, only her heroines and her heroes (Kay Petersen in *The Group,* Martha Sinnott in *A Charmed Life,* Senator Carey in her last novel, *Cannibals and Missionaries*), preferring, as in the case of the slippery Professor Mulcahy in *The Groves of Academe,* to hoist a villain on his own petard.

In her attack on de Beauvoir, McCarthy's comment that Sartre pitied her "for her limitations and perhaps for her greediness and ambition" is least convincing. Only the whispered question "Don't you think some relations are maintained through pity?" compels attention, and that perhaps for the light it casts on her own relations with men, and with Edmund Wilson, in particular. Could Wilson have clung to his marriage with the wildly unpredictable Mary McCarthy through some sort of pity? ("She had a child-like side which made one feel sorry for her," he reflects in *The Thirties,* and he had "invariably wanted to rescue her.") And for Edmund, "the Minotaur," lost in his maze, had not Mary sometimes felt a certain pity, as well?

In any event, Sartre, who told an interviewer in 1965 that "I owe [Simone de Beauvoir] everything. . . . [M]y complete confidence in her has always given me complete security, a security which I wouldn't have had if I'd been alone," hardly seems to have pitied her. "When I show her a manuscript . . . as I always do," he goes on to explain, "and when she criticizes it, I get angry at first and call her all kinds of names. Then I accept her comments, always . . . because I see that they're always pertinent. They're not made from the outside, but with an absolute understanding of what I want to do," he adds, striking the same exalted note de Beauvoir does when she speaks of "the absolute unfailing security" Sartre gave her. The megalomania of the couple is a bit thick in these testimonials, and of course all sorts of renegade emotions can race back and forth under cover of such sentiments. Still,

Mary McCarthy's 'shriveled up old maid' is not history's, and one must look to her own character to understand the fury in her attack.

In *America Day by Day,* de Beauvoir undoubtedly has McCarthy in mind when she mentions "that beautiful and cold novelist who has already gone through three husbands and several lovers in the course of a cleverly laid out career." Not a reference calculated to please its original, but in the world of literary gossip, nothing much. When the 1980 interview with McCarthy in Castine was published in *The Nation* in May 1984, the writer John Gerassi, an old friend of Simone de Beauvoir's, then working on a biography of Sartre, tried to persuade her to respond to McCarthy's calumny. De Beauvoir refused, saying, " 'I never respond to things like that.' " Mary wasn't worth her time, de Beauvoir's biographer Deirdre Bair suggests. "She wasn't French, therefore she wasn't important." Gerassi took up the cudgel himself, asserting that McCarthy was only getting even for de Beauvoir's "intellectual criticism" of her "sexual and political views"; but if de Beauvoir made such criticisms, not hard to imagine, they never found their way into print.

In 1967, according to Gerassi, Mary had asked him to "arrange a get-together" with Sartre in Paris. The context (though Gerassi doesn't supply it) was McCarthy's effort to get a visa for travel to North Vietnam. As the head of the Bertrand Russell War Crimes Tribunal, Sartre might have been expected to be helpful; but Gerassi claimed that Sartre and de Beauvoir had refused to meet with her.

> As Sartre said, "She poses as a liberal, and I know that the U.S. intelligentsia considers her on the left, but the fact is that to me, and to us now, she ultimately is a reactionary who defends the American system even while she pretends to oppose the war in Vietnam—as a 'mistake' rather than imperialist policy."

It's unlikely that McCarthy was privy to this complicated analysis of her political sins. She may have interpreted Sartre's rebuff, if there was one, as the legacy of a slighting report she filed in 1964 of Sartre's and de Beauvoir's contribution to a Paris meeting on the future of literature. Its effect would have been blunted in any case when Sartre let her know later in 1967 that he liked her published reports from South Vietnam. In 1968, moreover, after her trip to Hanoi, she was invited to serve on the Russell Tribunal in Stockholm herself (she declined). Whatever her standing with Sartre, however, McCarthy's feud was not with him but with de Beauvoir.

II

Simone de Beauvoir, who occupies a more secure niche in French letters than Mary McCarthy does in American letters, and who in 1980 was the intellectual grande dame in the city McCarthy made her second home, had become one of the dreaded "other women" in Mary's life. Like "the others" in Sartre's *No Exit* who embody Hell in their infernal power to mirror what a person flees in himself, she had to be dethroned; and this not only because her image competed in the writer's hall of fame (a factor not to be discounted) but because the parallels in their lives were surprisingly close. What joins these two formidable literatae—beginning with the slippery peak they occupy in a largely masculine intellectual preserve—is just as important to understanding their animosity as what divides them.

In *Memoirs of a Dutiful Daughter* (1958), the counterpart to *Memories of a Catholic Girlhood* (1957), Simone de Beauvoir also figures as the privileged firstborn, the apple of her debonair father's eye. Her impressions of early childhood, like McCarthy's, are warm and sensuous. She delights in her father's attentions, his love of books and argument and large entertainments. Only when she is a little older does she withdraw from him when she discovers his philandering, and then judge him harshly for the dilettantism that contributes to a collapse in the family fortunes. As a little girl, she remembers the softness of her mother's body, the rich textures of hot chocolate, sweet cakes, and ices. But for de Beauvoir, unlike McCarthy, the maternal bond is fatally compromised by the ease, as she perceives it, with which her father deceived his wife. (Later, in *The Prime of Life* [1962], attributing her decision not to have children to an "absence of affinity" with her own parents, de Beauvoir repudiates these primal attachments. Any sons or daughters she might have, she explains, she "regarded in advance as strangers; from them I expected either indifference or hostility—so great had been my own aversion to family life.")

The central fact in Mary McCarthy's history—the death of her parents when she was six—is missing from de Beauvoir's, but there is an echo of it in her father's bankruptcy which transports the family from a luxurious flat on the Boulevard Raspail to a modest apartment on the Rue de Rennes (the same street McCarthy occupied in Paris). And there is more than an echo of *Memories of a Catholic Girlhood* in de Beauvoir's apprenticeship to the mesdames of the Cours Désir, in the drama of her own loss of faith, and the sense of outlawry that grows on her as she falls beyond the pale of family and religion.

In the rational life of the mind, both women looked for deliverance, and found it to a degree in a career of writing. Their differences, which are differences of voice, style, and taste, not to mention of philosophical beliefs, are expressed in a kind of autobiographical fiction that is nevertheless strikingly similar.

As with McCarthy, there is hardly a character in either Sartre's or de Beauvoir's fiction who is not a composite of the physical traits, linguistic habits, and biographical details of some member of their entourage. McCarthy's borrowings, however, often mix the inside and outside of actual people, not only to cover her tracks, but because a fresh juxtaposition (Wilson as a vulgar Irishman in *A Charmed Life*) releases unexpected streams of association. Thus, the "tall, soft-bellied, lisping" Professor Henry ("Hen") Mulcahy, whose profile is largely drawn from an actual professor at Bard in the late 1940s, Lincoln Reis, owes his paranoid psyche to the vividness of McCarthy's own imagination. ("To do that I would make the most terrible faces and grimaces," she once said, "to screw myself up into these paranoid states of mind.")

Like both de Beauvoir and Sartre, she, too, uses fiction and nonfiction to explore an ethical problem: the moral consequences of cultural relativism among the demimonde in *A Charmed Life,* the impact of the idea of progress on the class of '33 in *The Group,* the death of nature (as in Mother Nature) in *Birds of America* (1971). But it is when de Beauvoir and McCarthy objectify problems in their own lives, often replaying them in memoir in order to triumph over them, that they most resemble each other—even when their heroines arrive at very different resolutions.

In *She Came to Stay,* Françoise's conflict is experienced with other people, especially the interloper Xavière. In *The Company She Keeps,* Meg Sargent comes to see her conflict as primarily with herself, or *within* herself, between a fleshly self that hungers after false gods and a spiritual self—the soul, McCarthy would say—which sees through things and maintains what continuity is possible between ideals and behavior. "How schematically it had all been lived out," she writes in a rush of self-comprehension at the end of the book, "the war between the flesh and the spirit, between women and men, between the verminous proletariat and the disinfected *bourgeoisie.*" The concluding paragraphs of both novels—each inspired by an effort at self-transcendence—lay bare their authors' core beliefs.

In Françoise's final soliloquy after the murder of Xavière, de Beauvoir presents the existentialist's credo:

> Alone. She had acted alone: . . . no one could condemn or absolve
> her. Her act was her very own. "It is I who will it." It was her own

will which was being accomplished, now nothing at all separated her from herself. She had at last made a choice. She had chosen herself.

At the end of *The Company She Keeps,* Meg Sargent recalls a dream in which she finds herself in a cabin at a place called Eggshell College with three men, dun-colored, loutish, like the pictures of Nazi prisoners released by the Soviet press during the war. When one approaches her, she flirts with him, telling the other girls who are there ("low-class girls") that really he isn't as bad as the other two, whereupon his features change, his hair grows dark and wavy, and as he bends to kiss her, he appears almost Byronic. The kiss is brutish, and when she opens her eyes, he is of course exactly like the others. It happens again; his skin whitens, his thick, flat nose refines itself, and this time she keeps her eyes shut, knowing what she will see, "knowing that it was now too late, for now she wanted him anyway."

The dream fills Meg with shame. " 'How could I?' " she wonders. It doesn't matter that it's only a dream; one cannot disown a dream. And then she sees it: how "it was some failure in self-love that obliged her to snatch blindly at the love of others, hoping to love herself through them. . . ." At the same time, she understands: "it was she who was the Nazi prisoner, the pseudo-Byron, the equivocal personality who was not truly protean but only appeared so." A painful revelation—and yet she can still detect her own frauds. She may shut her eyes to the truth, but an inner eye remains open. Meg's summation has already been noted: " 'If the flesh must be blind, let the spirit see. Preserve me in disunity.' " McCarthy can't resist a Latin summation (as if to appease the shade of Miss Mackay at the Annie Wright Seminary):

"*O di,*" she said aloud, "*reddite me hoc pro pietate mea.*" [Oh gods, give me this in return for my devotion."]
It was certainly a very small favor she was asking, but, like Catullus, she could not be too demanding, for, unfortunately, she did not believe in God.

Against de Beauvoir's titanic assertion of will, Mary McCarthy's acceptance of the duality in her nature seems almost Zen-like. One senses the psychic struggle in the background, but the resolution is genuine. Still, one feels a lingering unease with this heroine, for whom it might be said, as de Beauvoir says of Françoise, "nothing at all separate[s] her from herself."

Simone de Beauvoir later declared herself dissatisfied with the resolution of *She Came to Stay,* and subsequent novels sought a more pacific resolution to the problem of the 'other.' But the the reification of a *self* acting alone against the world, so pronounced in this first novel, asserts itself throughout her work, most notably in *The Second Sex.* In the classic text of modern feminism, published in 1949 and translated a decade later in the United States, the road to emancipation is unmarked save for the suggestion that a woman will wake up one morning, decide to be "free," and then resolutely go about constructing the conditions for her freedom.

There is something remarkable about the succès d'estime enjoyed by *The Second Sex,* which remains innocent of any consideration of the material and historical conditions surrounding the subjugation of women. Neither Marxism nor psychoanalysis, which never penetrated what de Beauvoir called her "rationalist-voluntarist position," interested her nearly as much as they did the skeptic Mary McCarthy. Perhaps it is the singular appeal de Beauvoir makes to the individual's all-powerful ego that secures her place in the sun. And maybe this is partly why McCarthy disliked her so.

"Of course it's true, about the egotism of writers—this monstrous egotism that we seem to have," she once told Jean-François Revel in another context. "Bellow," she suggested, was "a most ghastly example of it"—"it" being the sacrifice of wives and children and dwellings to the needs of the artist (though there were certainly times when she also felt such needs, she added). Perhaps de Beauvoir was another example for McCarthy, more ghastly because closer to home. (A point made by French newspapers after Mary McCarthy's death, oddly enough, when one after another echoed *L'Humanité*'s assessment that McCarthy "had the same moral stature in her country that Simone de Beauvoir has in ours.")

"Looking at my published works, I seem to find that the only person I truly hate is Simone de Beauvoir," McCarthy wrote Doris Grumbach in 1966. "I would love to make her—them [Sartre, too]—appear grotesque and ridiculous, which, in my opinion, they are. Expose them. And this is doubtless the product of a sense of impotence toward them; I mean the violence of my feeling." A certain kind of satire would do the job, she thought, "punitive satire, the satire of disgust and horror." But McCarthy didn't think she had the talent for it, unfortunately, "or," she said, "I might be a better writer if I did."

22

That Other McCarthy

"[F]or safety's sake, I had better add that
I am . . . a McCarthyite in name only."
—MARY McCARTHY (LETTER TO THE NEW STATESMAN, 1951)

The defensive note one hears in "Mlle. Gulliver en Amérique"is not often heard in Mary McCarthy's prose, but it had become common among American intellectuals in the 1950s. Within McCarthy's own circle, the political climate had undergone one of those seismic shuffles whose reverberations would be felt far beyond a pivotal event on the Left: the much-publicized break between Sartre and Camus over Stalin's terror in 1952. Arguing that the Communist party was still the vehicle of change for the working class, Sartre refused to abandon the Soviet Union despite the latest reports of internal repression; while Camus, whose position had been solidifying over time, washed his hands of politics altogether. In France, where the popular weekly *Samedi-Soir* ran a three-column front-page extract from the debate in *Les Temps Modernes* under the headline "The Sartre-Camus Break is Consummated!", public opinion had sided with Sartre.

In New York, it was as if Paris, that "cosmopolis of artists and intellectuals," as Lionel Trilling called it, had fallen. "[T]he commanding position of Stalinism in French cultural life does not prevent our having the old affinity with certain elements of that life," Trilling declared in "Our Country and Our Culture," "but it makes the artistic and intellectual leadership of France unthinkable." Among anti-Stalinist intellectuals like Trilling, and by 1952, their silent partners in the CIA, the triumph of Stalinism in Paris appeared more threatening than the triumph of Mao Tse-tung in China. Even today, Cold War veterans of the CIA's cultural-affairs programs point to Sartre's 1952 defense of the Soviet Union, and *Les Temps Modernes'* "Stalinism," as a justification for the CIA's decision to secretly sponsor a string of European magazines more sympathetic to the American point of view. With the exception of *Der Monat,* which was set up by an American information officer working for General Lucius Clay in occupied Germany in 1946, most of the others, *Encounter, Preuves,* and *Tempo Presente,* along with journals in India, Africa, and the Middle East (most fronted by intellectuals of impeccable liberal pedigree), were launched in these years.

Inside the United States, of course, the ideological debate was dominated by Joe McCarthy. It wasn't much of a debate, for there was no political opposition to anticommunism per se. The opposition was to the violation of civil liberties by congressional investigating committees, government employers, schools, and movie companies caught up in the hunt for Communists. Even the defiance of witnesses called before the House Committee on Un-American Activities who refused to 'name names,' taking the Fifth Amendment against self-incrimination or, like Dashiell Hammett, refusing to talk at all, was rarely accompanied by a public defense of socialist ideas. When HUAC was challenged, it was on constitutional grounds rather than political grounds. Not the ends or effects of organized anticommunism—which included a mass purging of left-liberal ideas and programs from American life—but the *means,* the invasions of privacy, resorts to innuendo, the peremptory firings of professional workers, became targets for the opposition.

These were the issues that finally drew Mary McCarthy into the fray; and in 1952, she briefly considered going to law school, Harvard preferably, and becoming a crack constitutional trial lawyer. But at forty, she was ill-fitted for the long apprenticeship, she decided, after a judge she knew drove up from New Jersey to spell out what was involved. (Nor was the novelist in her likely to step aside: "My new novel [the first chapter of *The Group*] is proceeding so slowly that I'm going to have to postpone the Law till next year," she wrote Arthur Schlesinger, Jr., that same year.) And it was then that she tried to launch the magazine, *Critic,* which was conceived less as a beachhead against rampant anticommunism than as an oasis for writers looking for a way in out of "an ideologized world," as McCarthy put it, in which the established journals of opinion seemed to observe rigid if invisible rules of thought.

Referring, in 1980, to the "tinniness of New York intellectual and literary life" that made it easy for her to leave the United States in the 1960s, McCarthy pointed to this polarization of political thought in the early 1950s as a prime example. Of the two sides, McCarthyism "was worse," she said, "but the counter-hysteria was also sometimes very false and self-loving," It was a sentiment that lay behind the creation of Professor Mulcahy, who is fired for negligence on a liberal campus, and then gets his position back by masquerading as an ex-Communist who is a victim of anticommunism. There is something glib in Mary McCarthy's characterization of the 'counter-hysteria,' a willful detachment that seems grounded in either ignorance or fear. "Senator McCarthy [has] overstayed his welcome, but in a certain sense he is not important," she wrote Schlesinger early in 1953, explaining why she thought *Critic* was worthwhile, "not because it will effect anything, but because it might bring a few thousand people into contact with reality, which is good in itself, even if there is no hope in the public domain." But Senator McCarthy *was* important; and for intellectuals to give up on the 'public domain' at such a time was to consign themselves to an irrelevance that would haunt them later.

Communism, especially after it entered daytime television via the Army-McCarthy hearings in 1953, appeared largely divorced from actual events and issues in the comity of nations. In a strange kind of way that neither anti-Stalinists nor their opponents grasped at the time, anticommunism in America was in part the expression of an undeclared class war that simmered beneath the surface of domestic society following World War II. Once the U.S. government had gone international, fighting fascism, 'containing' communism, managing an intricate network of postwar regional defense associations and trading blocs, fielding a multisectoral fighting force, it took on global responsibilities that could no longer be safely shared with the folks back home. No wonder Senator McCarthy had cast his first stone at the State Department and its "Red Dean . . . the elegant and alien Acheson— Russian as to heart, British as to manner." It was in foreign affairs, which, as Truman had explained in 1947, was now "indivisible" from economic affairs, that the mass of Americans sensed they had lost the most ground.

The hunt for Communists in high places, including Hollywood, the universities, the defense laboratories, even the Army (though that would be going too far), rather than among the downtrodden and the workers, had much to do with the fact that the high offices themselves were compromised by their inflated missions following the war. How else can one account for Senator McCarthy's seemingly unlimited power to intimidate the nation's political and professional elites into silence, including President Eisenhower, while convincing millions of Americans that their country had been reduced to a "position of impotency" by the "traitorous actions" of high government officials in three successive administrations? It took more than the frustrations of a 'limited war' in Korea, which is usually cited as the reason for the madness, to fuel the vengeful spirit that he tapped. The bogey of Communist infiltration was preferable to facing the deep conflicts of interest that were unleashed by America's new imperial mission.

Most American intellectuals entered the 1950s freighted with too many entangling alliances of their own to regard HUAC and Senator McCarthy's hearings with anything but apprehension. *Partisan Review*'s editors were no exception. Their chief entanglement with the Russian Revolution had failed to pan out, and now relations with the European Left had soured, as well. With Congress in a witch-hunting mood, Jewish intellectuals, in particular, seemed to fall prey to the ancestral fear of czarism—which in mid-twentieth-century garb, McCarthyism resembled. "[J]ust when we needed most to fight," Irving Howe recalls of *Partisan Review,* "the magazine hesitated." In Howe's view, the reason was Philip Rahv, who was born in Russia and had joined the Communist party in the 1930s, and tended to see American society through categories more appropriate to Weimar Germany. As did Hannah Arendt, one might add, though she drew different conclusions. Rahv talked about McCarthyism as if it were the entering wedge of a mass fascist movement; and he "went 'underground,' " Howe declares, "not literally, but he decided that the times had become threatening and reactionary . . . it might well be the better part of Marxist sagacity to lie low for a while." In any event, the magazine had acquired new recognition as a bastion of anticommunism, a position that led the young Henry Kissinger to invite William Barrett to lead an International Seminar at Harvard in the summer of 1952, one designed to introduce teachers and journalists from abroad to a picture of American cultural life that allowed for "opposition to Communism from the Left."

For Mary McCarthy, who was unencumbered by the historical freight, the timorousness of her old comrades was disconcerting. In a letter to Hannah Arendt in March 1952, she noted that the topic of an upcoming "counter-conference" at the Waldorf-Astoria sponsored by the American Committee for Cultural Freedom (an offshoot of Sidney

Hook's Americans for Intellectual Freedom) had been changed from "The Witch Hunt" to "Who Threatens Cultural Freedom in America?" which struck her as "quite a difference." From Fred Dupee, she had learned that "the Hook group's line [was] that the goings-on of McCarthy, etc. are not within the province of a committee for *cultural freedom*."

"Cultural freedom, in the old-fashioned sense of the freedom of works of art and ideas to circulate, is still more or less intact in the United States," McCarthy conceded in her address to the 'second' Waldorf conference on March 29, 1952. It was "cultural freedom, in the sense of the genuine freedom of individuals," that was curtailed by the obsession with fighting communism; and she went on to deplore "the idea of a society, stern, resolute, dedicated, hard," which was gaining headway among American intellectuals, "particularly of the ex-fellow-traveler and ex-party member type. . . ." These are the people who "threaten cultural freedom," she told an audience full of ex-fellow-travelers and former party members, "as they make common cause with the enemy from without, with Senator McCarthy, Senator McCarran . . . and all those who demand a sterile biography."

At a schoolteachers' convention McCarthy was invited to address a few months later, she was bolder. The campaign to root Communists out of the schools and institute loyalty oaths led her to question the viability of American democracy itself. Challenging pontificating Communists in the 1930s was one thing, she told the AFT union members, but "liberals," which was how she identified herself in 1952, had to recognize that the situation had changed. "[F]ar from being indoctrinated by Communism," the student today, she maintained, stood "in danger of being stupefied by the complacent propaganda for democracy that . . . follows him through school . . . speaks to him in the movies and on television, and purrs him to sleep from the radio." In the "current indoctrination . . . pious, priggish, groupy," McCarthy detected the same tone she had objected to in the "Stalinism of the popular-front period"—which was a slippery analogy. And yet it was in this address, unpublished until 1961 when it appeared in *On the Contrary*—because, McCarthy later said, she "didn't *dare* send it out to the magazines in 1952"—that she broke through the conventional pieties of anti-Stalinism.

Pondering the " 'germ' theory" of communism, she found the idea that "Communism [was] a sort of airborne virus that could be wafted from a teacher to her pupils . . . even though the whole hygiene of school and family and civic life today was such . . . as to sterilize the child against such 'germs' " unexpectedly revealing. In the America of the 1950s, "the fear and hatred of Communism," she proposed, was "not just a revulsion from the crimes of Stalin; it [was] also a fear and hatred of the original ideals of Communism." Stalin's crimes might even be said to be "welcome news to America," McCarthy suggested, in that "they are taken as proof that socialism does not 'work' ":

> Inequality, we would like to believe, is a law of nature, and by "we" I do not mean only wealthy businessmen or blackguards like Senator McCarthy or Southern racists. As the richest nation in the world, we have developed the psychology of rich people: we are afraid of poverty, of "agitators," of any jarring notes in the national harmony.

This kind of perception stood in marked contrast to the conservative treatment of "the problem of equality . . . and what price shall be paid for it" that appears in "Mlle. Gulliver en Amérique." The ability to see her country and her culture as others less privileged might see it allowed McCarthy to transcend the circumstances of her time and class, at least for a moment; to become "more than" herself. The reasons for the 'stern, resolute' loyalty the age demanded were in this instance related to America's "guilty fear of criticism . . . this sense of being surrounded by an unappreciative world . . ." rather than to the psychology of ex-Communists.

If the schools had become the front line for "a mass vaccination against Communism," it was, McCarthy added, because "people with bad consciences always fear the judgment of children." Children, who are credited for their "detached and innocent faculty of observation," would surely "prick up their ears" if they heard American society, whose injustices they had undoubtedly already observed, criticized in the voice of a teacher. 'Children' on this occasion were also the world's poor. Americans will always fear the " 'germ' of truth," McCarthy concluded in "The Contagion of Ideas," the title of this unusual address, "as long as we try to sell the white lie of democracy abroad, to the starving nations who in fact are the 'children'—the ignorant and uneducated—whose allegiance we question, rightly, and whose judgment of us we, rightly, dread."

Speaking to teachers in the summer of 1952, McCarthy revealed a grasp of the global economic framework of American anticommunism rare among her contemporaries. When she tried to account for the hysteria afflicting intellectuals closer to home, however, as she did in the March 1952 letter to Hannah Arendt, she resorted to a more prosaic explanation, one which was "rather on the petty side, but at any rate human." Inside the American Committee for Cultural Freedom, it was generally acknowledged that "there is really no Communist menace here . . ." she wrote Hannah, but that "the great thing to be combatted was a relapse into neutralism," which might encourage Communist parties in Europe, Asia, and Africa. According to "Hook and Co.," if American intellectuals "relaxed their efforts for a moment, [S]talinism would reassert itself in government and education, culminating in appeasement abroad." Mary couldn't tell whether this was "a genuine fear (it seems so fantastic) or a rationalization"; but if the committee members didn't believe this, and they were not simply "the victims of momentum," then "what *do* they 'really' think?" she wondered. Her own impression was that the fear was genuine but localized. Anti-Communist intellectuals, she told Hannah, lived

in terror of a revival of the situation that prevailed in the Thirties, when the fellow-travelers were powerful in teaching, publishing, the theatre, etc., when [S]talinism was the gravy-train and these people were off it and became the object of social slights, small economic deprivations, gossip and backbiting. These people, who are success-minded,

she continued, "think in terms of group-advancement and cultural monopoly and were really traumatized by the brief [S]talinist apogee of the Thirties. . . . In their dreams, this period is always recurring; it is 'realer' than today."

A provocative analysis, it is characteristic of McCarthy in that it relates a question of ideology to the social dynamics of a group. Still, it fails to account for the incredible persistence of a fear that leads veterans of the period to conclude, as William Barrett does in *The Truants*, that if the liberals of *The New Republic* had had their way after the war, there would have been no Truman Doctrine and no Marshall Plan; "[t]hus Western Europe as a whole might very well have passed into the Soviet camp. . . ."

McCarthy's curiosity about the causes and effects of anticommunism in the 1950s, nevertheless, continued. "And what about anticommunism as a political movement, if it is one?" she added to a laundry list of issues she wanted *Critic* to explore at the end of 1952; "it's the biggest thing of our day and nobody stops to ask what it consists of, really. . . . Why, for instance, did nobody treat [Whit-

taker Chambers's] *Witness* as anything but another book to review,"
she wondered in a letter to Richard Rovere, written to win him over
to a vision of a magazine that "*should* have a certain historical character . . . a mix of analysis and true reportage." (Rovere and Schlesinger favored a topical political review, impersonally edited, more
along the lines of *The Nation* or *The Reporter* than of *politics,*
which remained Mary McCarthy's inspiration.

II

McCarthy's curiosity about American society generally, whose face
really was changing during these postwar years, was never again to be so
active as during the brief period in 1952 and 1953 when she lobbied hard
for the magazine that was not to be. *Critic* cut against the grain of the
times in quite the same way the Europe-America Groups had. By failing
to honor the ideological polarities central to America's political canon,
it fell into a no-man's-land between Left and Right, which Hannah
Arendt described as "between all stools." Forty years later, the list of
"totalitarian elements" in American culture that Mary McCarthy
wanted to explore still defies categorization. Not only "Henry Luce,
radio, television, Nixon, Whittaker Chambers . . ." but also "the
Catholic hierarchy, psychoanalysis, the Great Books . . . the demoraliza-
tion of the middle class, foundations, writers' conferences, municipal-
ized bathing-beaches, the psychology of the expense-account, social
work. . . . We all talk about them incessantly in private conversation,"
she noted in the long letter to Rovere, a copy of which also went to
Schlesinger, "but they're either ignored in print or treated in terms of
banalities. Strangely enough, the only phenomenon that gets any serious
attention is the movies, which are analyzed exhaustively, as though they
were cave-paintings of some dead civilization."

The fascination highbrow intellectuals had for the movies was
itself "curious and perhaps worth some thought," McCarthy proposed; she had the feeling the country had "become afraid to look at
itself, afraid to find out what it *is,* and its intellectuals only dare to
examine its shadow-projection in the movies." McCarthy, oddly
enough, wanted to find out about life in "Levitt-town and Stuyvesant
Town. The only thing you ever hear about these strange new places is
that they won't let Negroes into them. Or Lewis Mumford, theoretic,
on the architecture," she commented. What was being taught in the big
Catholic universities, like Fordham? she wondered (a "big change"
was taking place, she suspected, "perhaps an improvement . . ."). And

when was somebody going to take a close look at the formidable Bishop Sheen? Or write an intelligent article about Senator Taft, "not Taft as a symbol, but what he is?" *Time* and *Life,* she argued, furnished only "pseudo-reportage," while *The New Yorker* profiles were "simple cartoons-with-a-theme." *Critic* would cover "live history," she hoped; and in so doing the magazine would combat the "alienation" that had "advanced to the point where everybody is alienated from what happens to him every day, [and] the sense of the particular is dwindling."

Armed with a fresh interest in the mass of Americans whom Mary was beginning to regard not as a 'mass' but as a mysteriously complex society, *Critic* represented a more serious response to the upheavals of postwar America than McCarthy's previous endeavors. And somewhere along the line, after plans to take over *The Reporter* were rebuffed by its editor, Max Ascoli, she became the new magazine's designated editor "pro tem." In her search for people of talent to contribute to *Critic,* she had contacted Edmund Wilson, who "might want to join this project," she told Dick Rovere at the end of 1952— not only as a writer but as an editor, with a department of his own. The inclusion of Wilson was surprising, but for them both perhaps, *Critic* was to solve the old problem of 'where to write,' a problem that bothered McCarthy especially with *The Reporter,* which had "a sort of weird, ectoplasmic feeling, even the paper," she told Arthur Schlesinger, Jr., in 1949. "[W]ith my fatal audience-sense, I find it hard to conceive of writing there, in *vacuo,*" she said; though on five occasions in the early 1950s she did: "Mlle. Gulliver en Amérique"; "No News, or What Killed the Dog" (the March 1952 speech to the American Committee for Cultural Freedom); "My Confession"; "Recalled to Life, or, Charles Dickens at the Bar" (a book review); and "Up the Ladder from *Charm* to *Vogue.*"

"Up the Ladder from *Charm* to *Vogue,*" an entertaining survey of the women's magazines, which may well have been lost in *The Reporter*—just as "Tyranny of the Orgasm," McCarthy's review of *Modern Woman, The Lost Sex,* was surely misplaced in *The New Leader*—probably comes close to embodying the kind of journalism she envisioned for *Critic.* "[A]nalytic and satirical rather than newsy or crusading," the magazine was to be "extremist, not . . . in what it advocates, but in its power to go from the very small to the large." But *Critic* foundered on the fund-raising trail, where even a custom-made prospectus—"the Average Man's prospectus," Mary called one drawn up for rich Republicans such as Edgar Kaufmann, Sr., and J. M. "('Call

Me Jack')" Kaplan—failed to convince potential donors that the magazine was sufficiently anti-Communist. Or, as "somebody named Lou Harris" worried, that it was " 'in the mainstream of American politics.' . . ."

Thus for the rest of the decade, she had stuck with *Partisan Review, Harper's, The New Yorker,* and *Encounter* (not a favorite— "Have you seen *Encounter?*" McCarthy wrote Hannah Arendt in the fall of 1953; ". . . the most vapid thing yet, like a college magazine got out by long-dead and putrefying undergraduates"). And she had turned her attention increasingly to fiction, memoir, and a little later, with *Venice Observed* (1956) and *The Stones of Florence* (1959), to a new kind of art history, like Ruskin's *The Stones of Venice,* with the social vision of the radical Victorian Harriet Martineau.

The new magazine had been one of those 'organizational things' McCarthy loved. Jockeying for meetings with Rovere, Schlesinger, Macdonald, and Arendt in New York, where Mary and Bowden were living at the Chelsea Hotel in the winter of 1952 to 1953, in between Newport and Wellfleet, was a task she undertook with enthusiasm. Taking the train down to Washington to talk to Joe Alsop or Clayton Fritchie, with a "purse" of ten dollars made up by Dwight and Hannah; lining up prospective writers, weeding out "mediocrities and vulgarians, while giving the benefit of the doubt to well-disposed people who offer[ed] to help," such as Jim Farrell; even fund-raising, which left her "drowning in . . . bearnaise sauce," satisfied a hunger for society and an appetite for 'doing things' that the solitary life of a writer left unappeased. After six months of fund-raising, however, Mary's hunger for society was slaked, at least for a while.

The effort ended on October 28, 1953, when she wrote Schlesinger sadly: "About the magazine—I really can't go on with it." By then, the Broadwaters were "in a state of monumental brokeness," and Mary hadn't done any writing from January to June, "nothing I didn't throw away," she said. Since then, she hadn't sold anything. *Harper's* had returned "My Confession" after she refused to let them publish it with cuts that turned it into a "bloomer-joke about the thirties." And *The New Yorker* was dallying with a long story (probably "C'est le Premier Pas Qui Coûte," the third chapter of *Memories of a Catholic Girlhood*), which they had found "obscure." "Perhaps some people can combine fund-raising with writing; I evidently can't," she concluded; "[s]o perhaps I couldn't combine editing either."

The fund-raising campaign had been an adventure in itself, however, and Mary had collected some fresh intelligence on the 'upper-

class minority' of American society. "[T]he rich who become Democrats are really the defectives of their breed," she complained to Schlesinger, when one after another of the wealthy liberals he introduced her
to had fallen by the wayside; and the impression would stick for years.
The only people who had been helpful were Republicans. (Meanwhile,
she was saving the English heiress Rosemary Bull for Arthur, she said,
because "she requires male sex appeal to awaken her politically.") By
April 1953, however, McCarthy had concluded that almost all the
potential donors—except Lauren Bacall—were "intensely conformist
people. . . ."

In the heat of the campaign to launch *Critic,* Senator McCarthy
appeared all but forgotten. Perhaps McCarthyism as a period and
anticommunism as a movement would have been given a closer look
if Mary McCarthy had lived to carry her 'intellectual autobiography'
into the 1950s. Chances are the reconsideration would have been a
self-critical one. In 1953, she feared that the effort to win donors and
influence prospective contributors had left *Critic* a prey to the "strategic and politic considerations . . . that make all the other magazines so
timid and evasive. These fears and hesitations are in the air," she
warned Arthur Schlesinger, "and there's no reason to think that *we*
enjoy an immunity." The "trust-us attitude" was *not* to be trusted,
because the awful "tendencies to conformity"—both intellectual and
ideological—"exist in all of us today . . ."—something she knew
herself "from introspection." She also knew that in matters of ideology, "there's a line between courage and folly or foolishness"; and that
line was not, in this instance, one she cared to risk crossing.

Part Six

▪

Capri / New York / Venice / Florence: 1953–1959

23

Have Pen, Will Travel

"I get stupid in solitude."
—MARY MCCARTHY (1963)

*I*n February 1955, Mary McCarthy and Bowden Broadwater set sail for the volcanic cliffs of Capri. A Newport friend named Lorillard had lent them the use of his villa, and Mary hoped to finish her novel, *A Charmed Life*, which she had begun shortly after moving to Wellfleet in the fall of 1953. After side trips to Pompeii and Naples in April, the Broadwaters were going to rendezvous in Rome with Nicola and Miriam Chiaromonte, and with a former girlfriend of Bowden's, a wealthy expatriate named Carmen Angleton, who would lead them on cultural expeditions through Umbria and the Abruzzi. In May, the three friends planned to tour Greece in a borrowed jeep, but by then the plans for Mary and Bowden's third trip to Europe (they had wintered in Portugal the previous year) would start to unravel.

Mary had found herself pregnant again and at risk for a miscarriage from the very beginning. She arrived in Athens "only half-aware" of the pregnancy, "rather like [the elderly] St. Elizabeth when she got the news," she wrote Hannah Arendt a few weeks later from Rome. Sailing to Greece without the jeep, which had broken down, sleeping in the ship's hold near a manure pile, "our faces covered with flies," Mary, Bowden, and Carmen had come upon the Greek islands, shimmering "like poetic metaphors" on the Aegean Sea. For a moment, Mary was transfixed; Ithaca was "absolutely Homeric—like the virgin west of the world," she wrote Hannah, "green, with mysterious inlets and coves, swathed in faint mists and with rose-pearl clouds reflected in still waters." The classical world brought out the romantic in her; in the letter to Arendt, the line, color, the very air of the Aegean islands is penned in sensuous detail, as is the Acropolis by moonlight.

However, on the Island of Myconos, she had started to bleed, and tended by a Red Cross nurse at the hotel, she was ordered to bed for a week. Back in Athens, Mary found herself "half in, half out of bed," but once again confined to a hotel. Tests were done to see whether the fetus was still alive (it was), and a dose of the hormone corpus luteum was prescribed. "As you can imagine, this has turned our trip into a joke," she told Hannah dryly; noting, "[i]ncidentally," that she was "very pleased about having a baby, it's only the alarms and uncertainties of it that are wearing."

In Athens, Bowden took Mary to task for breaking the doctor's rules, for "crawling" up the steps to the Parthenon, for example, when she was only supposed to view it from below. A quarrel had broken out between them in Capri, whose circumstances McCarthy later forgot, and it festered throughout the pregnancy. When they got to Paris in the middle of June, they were on very poor terms, and when Mary finally miscarried in the Hôtel Métropolitain, going to a Parisian hospital for a curretage, a light seemed to go out in the nine-year-old marriage. Two years later, when she fell in love with a charming but dissipated London critic, Bowden told Mary that while they were in Greece, he and Carmen Angleton had had an affair.

In Paris, McCarthy was approached by her friend Tony Bower on behalf of Georges and Rosamond (Peggy) Bernier, the editors of a highbrow art journal, L'Oeil. The Berniers were interested in publishing a series of books about cities celebrated for their art and architecture, whose texts would be done by literary figures, and they wanted Mary McCarthy to write the first, a profile of Venice. "It was quite inspired on their part," McCarthy remarked many years later, "because before there had only been the Skira books, very dull and horribly translated." At the time, the Berniers were unknown to her, and she was an outsider in European art circles, as ignorant of the maritime history of Venice as of the careers of its Tintorettos, Bellinis, Tiepolos, and Guardis (of whom in each case there was more than one). Peggy Bernier, an American who later married the art critic John Russell, was particularly well connected, having made the acquaintance of Picasso, Miró, and Matisse in Paris. In 1983, she recalled how shy and insecure Mary McCarthy appeared when they first visited Venice together; how she worried about what to wear to lunch at a palazzo and how to address a count; while Mary herself remembered trying to maneuver conversations away from areas where her ignorance of Venetian customs and art might alarm her new patrons.

There was a big difference between writing anonymous catalogue copy for E. J. Rousuck in New York and writing about fine art for the Berniers; in this case, following in the footsteps of earlier connoisseurs of Venice such as Baudelaire and Ruskin, who had each written about the city in an unconventional fashion. McCarthy had quickly agreed to the preliminary meeting Tony Bower proposed with the Berniers in Lausanne; and while Bowden and Reuel, who had arrived a few weeks earlier, sailed home to New York on a Dutch liner, Mary proceeded to Switzerland with twenty dollars in her pocket, "my capital," she called it. The whole deal struck her as possibly a practical joke at the time, inasmuch as Tony Bower had reason to be angry with her for her articles about Simone de Beauvoir in *Commentary* and *The Reporter*. But she was game. When she accepted the Berniers' invitation in the late summer of 1955, her marriage was breaking up. "We were separating," she said later; Bowden, she added, "was glad therefore to hear that I was going off to Venice while he and Reuel went home. . . ."

Mary, one guesses, was gladder. But she was scared; and a terrible loneliness had descended on her during her last days in Paris and her first weeks in Venice. She couldn't stand the "conspicuous solitude," she wrote Carmen Angleton from the apartment she rented on the Campo San Lorenzo after the Berniers returned to Lausanne. Venice was a "subtly contrived torture for the solitary individual; everybody stares and accosts and pities and condemns," and she had taken to going without dinner to avoid the "waiters' pity when I ask for a table for *una persona*." But Venice had soon cured her; and *Venice Observed,* as it turned out, would have a great success, more than anything else McCarthy had written; first when it appeared in *The New Yorker* as "The Revel of the Earth," and then as a book that sold thirty thousand copies, twice what any previous book of hers had sold. Meanwhile, she and Bowden Broadwater made up slowly by correspondence over the next few months, but Venice opened up a corridor to Europe that in the end claimed Mary McCarthy without him.

II

By 1955, Europe had changed and so had she. Villas, writing, and the Italian connection had begun to acquire a triangular status in McCarthy's life. Nothing of the change disturbed the American legend that had gathered around her, however—one that left the paradoxes in her career largely in the shadows. The legendary Mary McCarthy, a New York figure even when she lived in Connecticut, Rhode Island, Cape Cod, or Vermont (where the Broadwaters spent several summers in the 1940s and '50s); heady, a bit austere, cold, as in "Cast a cold eye on life, on death," the epitaph from Yeats that gave McCarthy the title of her collection of memoirs and stories published in 1950, this Mary McCarthy gazed intently from dust jackets and lecterns throughout the 1950s. An intellectual woman, in shirtwaist or tweeds, her shoulder-length hair grazed a rope of pearls in a photograph introducing "the authoress" to the readers of the *New York Post* in February 1950, on the occasion of the first installment of Mary McCarthy's "Greenwich Village at Night." More often, though, her dark hair was knotted loosely at the nape of her neck, which curved gracefully over a book or typewriter; between two fingers, raised in a jaunty salute, was an ever-present Lucky Strike.

"The Lesbian in the Brooks Brothers Shirt," was how she had referred to "Greenwich Village at Night" in a note thanking Arthur Schlesinger, Jr., for his help in getting the *Post*'s editor, James Wechsler, to assign her the series on sex and vice in Greenwich Village; and the image isn't very far from the public image McCarthy cast in the 1950s. Her vision of Greenwich Village, on the other hand, showed the distance she had traveled from the freewheeling days on Gay Street. Like her letters to Hannah Arendt in the mid-1950s, which take up thorny philosophical problems such as "the shattered science of epistomology" and the "dogmatization of ignorance" among the "bohemianized people" of *A Charmed Life,* McCarthy's reflections on the Village reveal a temperament both more socially conservative and intellectually inquisitive than the public image suggested.

Greenwich Village itself had changed along with the country at large. Radical politics had been bleached out of it. "The ideologue of the late Thirties no longer lords it over Eighth Street," McCarthy had observed; though recalling "those broad-bottomed young political sages in their flapping overcoats," arguing outside The Jumble Shop was a cheap shot in the 1950s. Noting the shop windows full of berets, sandals, Mexican jewelry and pottery, the narrow streets crowded with pleasure-seekers, she was reminded of the "rialto of a foreign city, with its craftsmen and its traditional costumes and dialect. . . . a port of call, a Marseilles or Venice with a tourist industry. . . ."

Like an old fishing community that has lost its fish and ships, and slipped into the realm of the picturesque, Greenwich Village, without its original traffic in ideas, had turned into a monument of its former self. The "changeless Village girls, in their huaraches, earrings, and flowing skirts" were still there, along with an influx of homosexuals; bookstores displayed avant-garde magazines and books; but the moorings were gone, the critical relationship of an underground culture to a larger society still open to suggestion. The Village types and native artifacts, mostly imported, were props in a bazaar. It was "as a commercial proposition," finally, "a clearing-house for all those curiosities, sexual, artistic, or merely decorative, that are thought of as un-American," that Greenwich Village made sense in the 1950s, McCarthy asserted (ignoring the new jazz/drug culture and the action in literature and art that was moving east to St. Mark's Place, and beyond).

"Greenwich Village at Night" was a swan song, but the ten-part series had also provided McCarthy with a feast of new impressions. Down and out in the Village, with husband and son tucked away in Portsmouth (Mary stayed on Fifty-seventh Street for the most part, in the old apartment), she had taken in dozens of all-night restaurants and bars, savoring such sights as "a Negro prostitute in a flame dress, soul-kissing with a white-haired old daddy from uptown; his short fleshy tongue arches masterfully and strikes at hers, but for some reason the deal is not consummated—the girl drifts off alone." This kind of stuff irritated an upright friend such as Dwight Macdonald, opening a fault line that had always run through McCarthy's relations with the boys: a fear of her capacity for acting and writing impulsively. "[V]ery fond of Mary but nervous about a certain frivolity, lack of responsibility, eccentricity there, especially with Bowden around," Dwight wrote Nicola Chiaromonte in December 1950, explaining his reasons for resisting McCarthy's desire to revive *politics* under a joint editorship, a desire that had given way to *Critic*. But it was the racy *Post* series (which according to Wechsler sent the paper's circulation up considerably) that had put Mary on the map in Newport when nothing else she had written had.

The foray into popular journalism had netted her eight hundred dollars, a tidy sum in 1950. Together with one thousand dollars that *Holiday* paid for "The Vassar Girl" in 1951, and three thousand dollars each for two stories and a memoir from *The New Yorker* around the same time, along with fees from essays and reviews in *The Reporter*, *Harper's*, and *Partisan Review*, not to mention two books, *Cast a Cold Eye* and *The Groves of Academe* (with a Guggenheim grant for the second), McCarthy was beginning to make some money.

She was certainly making more money than any of the boys, and at least enough to support a household in the extravagant manner to which she and Bowden, whose free-lancer's income was always scanty, had become increasingly accustomed.

First in Portsmouth and then in Wellfleet, before throwing out new roots in Europe, Mary McCarthy had become a cosmopolitan woman of letters of a different stripe than legend supposed. She was an intellectual woman, as opposed to a woman intellectual—whose femininity (in the latter case) is more likely to be an object of scrutiny or even resistance than a source of private definition and satisfaction. An intellectual woman might write man-to-man, as McCarthy did in "Greenwich Village at Night," identifying a hotel she stayed in as the sort of place "where you could register with a girl and without baggage or be signed in with equal indifference if you asked for rooms by the week for self, wife and child." She might easily outsmart a man in debate; another woman was more likely to be her antagonist. In private life, however, she was prone to the grand gesture, and quite capable (as McCarthy proved to be with the London critic John Davenport in 1956) of willing such a gesture into a serious commitment. In close relations with both men and women, her intellectuality opened the door to the warmer emotions.

Especially in the 1950s, when Mary's relationship with Hannah Arendt began to develop, a passion for intellectual speculation went hand in hand with deep friendship. When Arendt responded to Mary's inquiry about "the shattered science of epistomology" in September 1954 with a four-page single-spaced letter tracing the "ritual of doubt" through Western philosophy, McCarthy was touched by her "act of munificence." (To Hannah, Mary's letter exploring the problem of moral relativism in contemporary society had come as "a real joy. Only when I got it, did I notice that I had been expecting it," she remarked, before plunging into the problem of "the feebleminded thoughtfulness or thoughtful feeblemindedness of intellectuals.")

Such exchanges led Arendt to define "the thinker par excellence" in a way that spoke to her peculiar faith in the life of the mind: "in the activity of thought, I am together with myself—and neither with other people nor with the world as such, as the artist is," she proposed in the long letter to Mary, noting that nowadays if a man is "alone, he is lonely, i.e. not together with himself. . . . Our friends," she added, "craving for philosophic 'information' (something which does not exist) are by no means 'thinkers' or willing to enter the dialogue of thought with themselves." They are "burlesque philosophers."

A few thousand words later she broke off—"Enough of all this." The break was characteristic of their correspondence, which like their relationship moved alternately through thickets of philosophy, confession, and gossip. She was "much amused" by Mary's report of the 1954 summer season in Wellfleet, of the huge outdoor parties that could be heard and smelled by way of the alcohol fumes half a mile away. "Our defenses have somehow been breached and we've yielded to the relentless give-and-take of invitations. . . . responding like invertebrates to the mysterious call of social duty," McCarthy had written. "One decides not to go, and then somehow . . . one finds oneself there, for fear of missing something." It was an impulse, this hunger for the society of one's peers (which starting out in the 1950s was an increasingly self-conscious literary society) that Mary McCarthy found hard to resist.

The summer was her first back on the Cape since 1945. As her letters reveal, she was in the delicate condition conveyed in *A Charmed Life* by Martha Sinnott's terror that, like her neighbors in New Leeds, she and her husband were about to fall into a trough of insobriety and moral turpitude. For Mary, it was very likely the nearness of Edmund and Elena Wilson that kicked open a hornet's nest of insecurities, although Edmund, whose house was only a short distance away from the Broadwaters, goes unmentioned in the letters to Hannah Arendt. But the fears were back. "Alfred [Kazin] was here and cutting me dead," she wrote Hannah, confiding that it upset her, "quite unjustly, since I don't like him. On the other hand, I don't dislike him so *totally*. Saul Bellow was here too, with son and dog," she added, "not very friendly, either." Even Philip Rahv, who also visited Wellfleet that summer, along with Arthur Schlesinger, Jr., (who used Mary's and Bowden's studio on the Pamet Point Road to write *The Age of Roosevelt*), had made her "horribly nervous."

McCarthy had mended her fences with Rahv in 1952, thanks to Hannah Arendt, who had urged her to apologize for the damage done their friendship by *The Oasis,* in order to involve him in *Critic.* "My wise counselor," McCarthy called her for this and other reasons; and the story of the reconciliation—a kind of trophy, fashioned from memory and desire, like the saga of 'the Sidney Hook gang'—contains the elemental drama: Crisis, and Crisis Surmounted. "I didn't feel terribly happy about swallowing my pride," McCarthy told an interviewer in 1985, given "the slanders" the boys had circulated about her; but she had agreed, and contacted Rahv, who invited her to his apartment one evening, sending Nathalie out. "I told him what was true, that I was very, very sorry that I had hurt him and that it had not been my intention to hurt him and that I was well aware by now that I had and that I felt badly about it." She didn't have to say more because Rahv was "delighted," even "jubilant." They had a drink and he invited her to lunch the next day at a *"chic"* restaurant in the Village (The Charles), "old-fashioned with white napery and silver, dignified," where they had a very good time. After lunch, they started walking up Sixth Avenue, "and who do we see coming, or who sees *us,*" McCarthy exclaims, "but Delmore!" who "turned all the colors . . . and *ran* to tell the others—and that was the end from their point of view," she finishes triumphantly. "Rahv and I had made up. Rahv had an ally. He was no longer isolated, and [referring to the old 'plot' against him, the confrontation with Greenberg, et al.] their whole strategy had fallen into pieces."

In a revealing footnote to the story, however, McCarthy points out that Rahv had just published a few pieces hostile to Joe McCarthy in *Partisan Review* and *Commentary,* while the rest of the *PR* people continued to waffle on the Wisconsin senator. "He was the only one of that group who had stuck his neck out," she states approvingly, "so he realized that . . . he was getting our friendship back in return for his wonderful behavior about Senator McCarthy." Mary's pride was not completely swallowed. Not sorrow for her own sins but forgiveness of Rahv's finally returns the princess to her favorite troll. Considering Mary McCarthy's own relatively modest efforts to discredit Senator McCarthy, the commendation prize for brave Philip falls a little flat.

Two years later, when Rahv visited her on the Cape, Mary had felt "not unfriendly; just estranged and mutually watchful." "Probably it was my fault," she conceded, but they had argued about nearly everything, "screaming at each other on the Tower of Babel." In 1954, she found Rahv's "Marxist assurance"—which seemed to resurface after Stalin's death in 1953—"antedulivian" [*sic*], and she disagreed with Hannah Arendt that he was "interesting on the subject of politics." Hannah was quick to respond. "You are probably right," she said of Rahv, "I had difficulties myself in recent months, but I sort of like him, and so do you." (Rahv may not have felt the same for Arendt, who could usually overwhelm him in argument, as Barrett recalls, "leading him into deeper waters of ideas, where, autodidact that he was, he was suddenly . . . beyond his depth." When Barrett once called Arendt a "handsome woman," Rahv snapped, " 'I think of Hannah rather as a very handsome man.' ") As for Alfred Kazin "cutting [her] dead," Kazin's second wife, Ann Birstein, was jealous of his friendship with

Arendt and McCarthy, and Hannah wrote Mary that he was "acting on orders. I am rather sad and also surprised. Wouldn't have thought it possible."

Mary had also passed along a "funny picture" Bowden had drawn of Sidney Hook deserting to the Soviet camp and issuing a pamphlet entitled *Conspiracy, Yes; Heresy, No* (after Hook's 1953 *Heresy, Yes, Conspiracy, No*). Hannah thought the quip possibly prophetic: "You will see Sidney in three years, publishing another book, repenting on this one . . . etc." She didn't trust American anti-Communists such as Irving Kristol, Elliot Cohen, and Sidney Hook, who played a "disagreeable role" in society, she thought, and reminded her during the years when Senator McCarthy was gunning down the Voice of America and the State Department's overseas information libraries, of the Weimar intellectual "elites" in the 1920s and '30s who allied themselves with "the mob" in Germany. The fact that most of the vociferous anti-Communists had "more or less well-known Communist pasts, and thus [had] some reason to fear," she proposed, "[didn't] make it any better." Indeed, judging from the controversial essay Arendt published in 1953, "The Ex-Communists," this fact made it worse in her mind. Communists "turned upside down," she argued, had become "prominent on the strength of their past alone. Communism [had] remained the chief issue in their lives." Anticommunism, "as a theory, as an ism," she wrote, was "the invention of the ex-communists," those who "had lost a god," as they themselves said, and then gone in search of a new one. And nothing dismayed her more than the tendency she observed among American intellectuals in the 1950s to make a "cause" of democracy; democracy, Arendt insisted, "cannot be fabricated," much less imposed, on other societies.

In the summer of 1954, thanks to Nixon's perseverance, the government ruled that J. Robert Oppenheimer, one of the inventors of the atom bomb, who opposed the development of the hydrogen bomb in 1949, had passed secrets to the Russians. Mary, who found Oppenheimer personally "eerie" but no security risk, had noted that "Danny Bell, amazingly, sent a telegram to the [American] Committee for Cultural Freedom nominating Oppenheimer for Chairman." Others from the committee—like Martin Greenberg, who held that Oppenheimer, then head of the Institute for Advanced Study in Princeton, should be jailed, and "beefy, middle-aged sultans" like Herbert Solow and Allen Stroock of the American Jewish Committee, who condemned Oppenheimer for "political 'immaturity' "—impressed Mary as being "sententious pigs. I wish you would write something about it," she implored Hannah, adding that she had to set the idea aside herself, since her "ideas weren't clear enough." In 1954, McCarthy had fallen back on a psychosexual perception of politics first advanced in "Portrait of the Intellectual as a Yale Man"; the fury of Oppenheimer's critics, she proposed, boiled down to "a sort of puritan envy. Old hacks like [Martin] Greenberg and Solow grudge Oppenheimer his lunch in Paris with [Haakon] Chevalier [a Communist in the 1930s] as if they were faithful husbands watching a colleague have an affair with an actress."

Hannah had responded that Daniel Bell was "generally behaving better than those around him; he is the only one who has got a conscience that bothers him once in a while. He is also a bit more intelligent than the others," she noted, slipping easily with Mary into a tone that had earned her the sobriquet "Hannah Arrogance" around *Partisan Review*. Rahv, Mary reported, had concluded "the case proved that intellectuals should not work for the government," a judgment with which McCarthy was inclined to agree. Hannah Arendt agreed, too, with the proviso that physical scientists not "wise up to this wisdom" and refuse government contracts; for in ten years, she feared, "America will have fallen behind in science and that can be a catastrophe in our age" ("America," for this refugee from the Third Reich, representing an island in the storm of mutating nation-states).

To the paranoia that had overcome Mary during the summer of 1954 (at Bowden's insistence, the Wellfleet house was sold the following year), Hannah Arendt made no direct reply. The worst thing about places like this, Mary had complained, was that "your value is continually being called into question and you shiver at social slights. . . . And all your friends are eager to tell you, on the beach, about parties you aren't invited to. You can't avoid knowing just what your current status is," she added dismally, "unless you stay in the house with the door locked. Even then you meet Mrs. Kazin, Mrs. Levin, Mrs. Bellow, Mrs. Weschler, etc."—a punishing situation that made her long for the curmudgeonly Dwight, who was away from the Cape that summer. Mary had begged Hannah to come to Wellfleet for a visit after Labor Day, when Cape Cod would become "golden and peaceful again." And Arendt, who was more comfortable with Heinrich Blücher in the Catskills or on Morningside Drive in New York than in any artistic community, replied delicately: "Don't you think you would rather like to come to NY and stay with us??" If Mary could leave sooner, Hannah proposed she come immediately to Palenville, New York. Heinrich was returning to the city shortly, she would be alone, "and we could have a wonderful time. Think that over," she wrote.

Though the Wellfleet house was unheated, Mary stayed there until October, when she and Bowden took a winter's lease on another house in Newport, called Paradise Farm, a rambling eighteenth-century affair with seven fireplaces and a carriage house called Paradise Farm. She couldn't have gone to Palenville or New York, she explained in a subsequent letter, because Reuel was with her (Reuel now divided his summers between his parents), and Mary had to get him outfitted for boarding school. In the teeth of adversity—"hurricanes, illness, streams of visitors, and the house at sixes and sevens because Bowden is painting the dining-room"—she was determined, moreover, to get in a block of work on her novel before leaving the Cape. She wanted to finish it by the first of the year, and only "a regular work schedule of five to eight hours a day, without days off," would see her through.

III

The novel, A Charmed Life, had grown out of a short story that McCarthy had written in the fall of 1953 and published in The New Yorker. From the very first page, an air of impending doom had clung to the account of the Sinnotts' return to the scene of Martha's former marriage, and soon Mary had found herself in the midst of a novel she had not planned. The novel she had planned, and begun the year before, The Group, had been set aside after three chapters for two reasons: The Vassar girls didn't seem to be going anywhere, not just as characters in fiction but as people capable of holding their author's interest; and now life had thrown up a new problem, or an old one, that fiction might resolve. Having fled Newport—"the Last Resort," Bowden and others called it—for the familiar shores of the outer Cape, the problem for McCarthy was not only how to lay the ghost of Edmund-past to rest but strangely, for a woman of such apparent sophistication, how to rejoin bohemia without becoming bohemian: a specter that followed her all the way to Capri.

Capri "is just another bohemian place with an overlay of tourists," McCarthy wrote Hannah Arendt from Rome in June 1955; and to Dwight, she sent news of the "inevitable Bennington-type girls who come and marry fishermen or boat guides." With its "terrific quota of alcoholics and as many crutches and casts among the expatriates as there are at Lourdes," Capri reminded McCarthy of Provincetown, prompting the fear that "the whole world . . . will soon be like Provincetown." It was in Capri, however, that she had finished *A Charmed Life;* killing her heroine off on the last page in an automobile collision with a drunken lady poet, a New Leedsian driving on the *wrong* side of the road. And it was after that—after disposing of the anxiety-ridden Martha Sinnott—that the charmed life of Mary McCarthy may be said to have begun.

"I really think there is such a thing as catharsis in writing," McCarthy wrote Arthur Schlesinger in November 1955 when the novel was already in the bookstores; and she was settled in a colorful apartment near the Grand Canal and working on a brand-new project. By then, she had found herself "utterly dauntless before the prospect of becoming a New Leedsian, which seems to me, now that I've faced it, a child's bugaboo; whatever I have to fear, it is not that. . . ." Which of course it wasn't. But there was more to McCarthy's aversion to Cape Cod's bohemia than a fear of falling afoul of its alcohol fumes or moral vagrancies. There was the more fundamental question of identity that Martha Sinnott wrestles with in the novel as the ex-wife of a domineering man whose continuing influence over her emotional life provides her with her most intense sensation of self. As Martha's obsessive relationship with Miles Murphy suggests, the *ex*-Mrs. Edmund Wilson may have felt less like Mrs. Bowden Broadwater in Wellfleet in 1954 than like Mrs. Edmund Wilson turned upside down.

With Schlesinger, who was frankly disturbed by the autobiographical implications of *A Charmed Life,* she had agreed that Martha "has to die, as you say, in the book, because a story like that could not have a happy ending [Martha had become pregnant after sleeping with Miles, and is killed after secretly borrowing money for an abortion], but whether this means that I thought I had to die, I don't know myself," she said. More likely the book's ending was "a kind of distress-signal," McCarthy thought, "a cry for someone or something to rescue me or at least to *pay attention* to my situation. . . ."

In the fall of 1954, nevertheless, the 'catharsis' had not yet taken place. McCarthy was still struggling with the novel whose " 'personal' note," she confided to Hannah Arendt, troubled her greatly. "I have misgivings about the taste of this novel, which localize around your anticipated or feared reaction," she said, referring in particular to the sex scenes. "You are tugging at my elbow saying 'Stop' during a seduction scene I've just been writing," she explained, noting that Arendt's "imagined remonstrances" had led her to rewrite the scene from the man's point of view—"[b]ut you still won't like it," she feared. Many great novelists betrayed such a 'personal' note, she had tried to assure herself; Tolstoy in the character of Levin, Dostoevsky hiding behind Stavrogin, and George Eliot's heroines, who bear "an ungainly, almost mawkish likeness to the author." But precedent was a poor rallying point for works of art, she suspected. Then why did she follow this piper? Why did she write from memory that was tainted by anger and a certain shame? " 'Why do you do it if you don't want to?' " another character asks Martha Sinnott about something else in *A Charmed Life*. And the answer, Mary McCarthy noted heavily in the letter to Arendt, was " 'I don't know.' "

Like 1945, 1954 was a turning point. Many things were over: *Critic* had come to naught, and with it another search for community. What camaraderie remained between Mary and the boys seemed to have finally collapsed. Enough had ended to invite a new beginning, but the middle 1950s were not a time for new beginnings within the United States. And Mary had begun to travel. In the late 1930s and '40s, her years were divided between Stamford, Truro, Wellfleet, New York, Cornwall, Connecticut, Pawlet, Vermont, and Portsmouth, Rhode Island, and then, in 1953 to 1954, Wellfleet again, in tandem with Newport, Montpelier, Vermont, Portugal, Capri, and Rome, jumping-off point for the grand tour, whose fabled shrines in Greece, Italy, North Africa, and the South of France Mary McCarthy would visit and revisit the rest of her life.

For the remainder of the 1950s, she would sail back and forth between New York, Venice, and Florence. Even at the very end of her life, at seventy-seven, crippled by an arthritic condition of the spine, weakened by a persistent bronchial condition, a faltering heart, and recurrent cancer, Mary McCarthy was still shuttling back and forth between homes in Paris, Castine, and Annandale, New York, unable or unwilling to come to rest. In 1989, Reuel Wilson was struck by the persistence of the pattern. The constant travel was prompted by his mother's need to "treat herself" after a stint of hard work on a book, he suggested; and it was also some kind of compensation for the "deprivation" in her childhood, the loss of home and family. Standing outside New York Hospital, where he was born on Christmas Day in 1938, and where, on October 7, 1989, his mother lay dying, Reuel reflected that the bouts with bronchitis, pleurisy, and grippe that plagued the latter half of Mary's life, had often occurred during these strenuous trips abroad. She couldn't slow down; unless she was working, she couldn't stay home.

Before leaving for Capri in 1955, McCarthy had finally managed to make several visits to Hannah Arendt in New York, having a "wonderful time, staying with you, as always," she wrote back afterwards. The apartment in Morningside Heights acted on her "like a magnet," in part because it offered her a pied-à-terre in a city that was a "port of call" in her commerce with editors, agents, and publishers, but also because of Hannah, who was more than Mary McCarthy's closest friend. According to Reuel, who remembers Arendt as a kind of "aunt," she was his mother's "intellectual conscience," an estimate shared by mutual friends—though Arthur Schlesinger found "Mary's exalted view of Hannah Arendt" a "mystery," in that "Mary's mind was so concrete . . . and Hannah's is sort of windy, full of Hegelian abstraction." Still it was Hannah who "made Mary put her marvelous brain to work," in Schlesinger's view. Without her friendship, Reuel suggests, his mother might not have developed the interests in European history, politics, art, and architecture that sustained her after *A Charmed Life*.

Like McCarthy's mentors at Vassar, Anna Kitchel and Helen Sandison, Arendt also had a mother's touch. "Hannah always thought she knew what was important to Mary, what she was feeling," says Robert Silvers, who knew them both. She seemed to dote on Mary out of pride in the younger woman's ability to confirm her seniority, to draw on her richly complex experience, her classical learning and knowledge of what she and Blücher called "World-History," a kind of titanic invisible poltergeist at large in the world.

It was primarily as a thinker that Arendt impressed McCarthy in the 1950s; a woman one could *watch* think, she recalled at the memorial service after Hannah Arendt's death in 1975. "When she talked, it was like seeing the motion of the mind exteriorized in action and gesture as she would flex her lips, frown, pensively cup her chin," she told the mourners who filled Riverside Church. As a thinker of consequence who was also "a beautiful woman" in Mary's judgment, "alluring, seductive; most speakingly the eyes, which were brilliant, sparkling, as though rays of intelligence leaped out of them . . ." Arendt seemed to commend herself to Mary McCarthy in middle life as a kind of feminine Virgil. Together they moved comfortably among the immortals, taking positions with Socrates or St. Augustine, sharing the travails of Tolstoy, Dostoevsky or Flaubert; querying Kant, Kierkegaard, Pascal, Nietzsche, and Hobbes. With each other, like true lovers, they found their grandest dreams confirmed.

24

Venice Unbound

"Venice, as a city, was a foundling,

floating upon the waters like Moses in his basket. . . . It was

therefore obliged to be inventive, to steal and improvise."

—MARY McCARTHY, *VENICE OBSERVED*

When Mary McCarthy began her love affair with the early Renaissance in September 1955, living alone for a change in the master suite of a rococo town house in the Cathedral Quarter of Venice, she followed an English tradition as paradoxical as the love-hate relations that visitors from Gibbon, Byron, Browning, Ruskin, and Herbert Spencer maintained with the watery city. Burrowing in libraries, consulting with scholars and experts, loitering in a piazza to observe the sidelong light of the afternoon sun on the wall of a church, she might have been an English don, like the young eighteenth-century scholar she met in the library of the Correr Museum, Francis Haskell, who became a lifelong friend; or the Cambridge art historian William Mostyn-Owen, secretary to Bernard Berenson, who squired her around Venice and took her to Mantua, Modena, and Bologna, later driving her all the way to Paris in the black Chevrolet she had brought to Venice. But she had the heart of a desperado—English, too, in a way—and an insatiable curiosity.

Armed with letters of introduction from Ignazio Silone, whom Mary had met in Rome with the Chiaromontes, she looked up the head of the gondoliers' cooperative, an old antifascist fighter jailed under Mussolini, who invited her to a reception given by the Chinese Opera Company for the Venetian citizenry. There she met respectable ladies in lacy blouses, pillars of the community, many of whom had also been in jail under Mussolini. She lunched with more than one count and contessa in their palazzi, and met the famous Berenson himself, "a regular old Volpone of ninety summers," she wrote Hannah Arendt, "with a glistening gold smile, more like a puma, really, than a fox," whose hand had traveled up and down her arm as they talked in the privacy of his rooms at the Hotel Europa. Berenson, surprisingly, was familiar with McCarthy's work, and shocked her when they first met by asking after her "pessary" (a reference to the diaphragm in "Dottie Makes an Honest Woman of Herself," which had appeared in *Partisan Review,* and later became Chapter Three of *The Group*).

She had met "at least seven new elderly English homosexuals, all 'living quietly' here," she wrote Hannah, and one night in the Piazza San Marco she had seen Mr. Scialanga, the "cicerone" who had guided Mary and Bowden through Italy in the summer of 1946, in the company of a very good-looking young woman; nothing had changed. She had begun to wander about the city, discovering out-of-the-way churches, and one afternoon, a synagogue where a service was underway—it being Yom Kippur—which she observed from the women's gallery. Many of the people she met gave her books and leads on Venice, including Peggy Guggenheim, who was inclined to forget the ungainly portrait McCarthy had drawn of her in bed with Mr. Scialanga in "The Cicerone." In 1956, Peggy Guggenheim insisted on driving Mary McCarthy from Venice to Padua. " 'I couldn't let you go alone, especially after I remembered the ending of *A Charmed Life,*' " McCarthy recalled her saying; after which she wrote Bowden: "I will never hear another word against her."

In Venice, McCarthy turned to the everyday life of the streets for the key to a city whose literary image as a citadel of illusion irked her because it was so predictable. "*Nothing can be said here* (including this statement) *that has not been said before,*" she remarks in *Venice Observed,* remembering herself proclaiming in the summer of 1946 "that St. Mark's at night looks like a painted stage flat," a fact "which everybody notices and everybody thinks he has discovered for himself." "No stones are so trite as those of Venice," she goes on, punning Ruskin, who came to dislike Venice for its "false fronts," but whose own feet of clay (he was impotent, "a worshipper of the pragmatic fact," McCarthy claims, "who was always flying in the face of the facts of life") perfectly equip him to play the foil in her joust with Venice.

She herself concluded that it was too easy to dismiss Venice for its "parvenu art, more like painting than architecture," which nonetheless "worked." Among Venice's "spells," she decided, was its "power to awaken the philistine dozing in the skeptic's breast. People of this kind—dry, prose people of superior intelligence—object to feeling what they are supposed to feel in the presence of marvels. They wish to feel something else. The extreme of this position is to feel nothing." And she rummages through the archive to make her point. Stendahl: "Venice left him cold." Herbert Spencer, exasperated by the Doge's Palace, deplored the " 'dumpy arches of the lower tier . . . the meaningless diaper pattern covering this wall, which suggests something woven rather than built. . . .'" D. H. Lawrence, like Ruskin, a debunker: " 'Abhorrent green, slippery city, Whose Doges were old and had ancient eyes. . . .' " And Gibbon, who " 'was afforded some hours of astonishment and some days of disgust by the spectacle of Venice.' "

McCarthy takes a contrary stand. But if she ends by affirming a popular perception of Venice as a city of marvels, which at first she herself had decried ("what intelligent iconoclast could fail to experience a destructive impulse in her presence?"), she does it with an originality of expression suggesting heresy. "[T]hat modern kind of sophistication that begs to differ, to be paradoxical, to invert," she writes, "is not a possible attitude in Venice. In time, this becomes the beauty of the place. One gives up the struggle and submits to a classic experience."

Surrendering to what McCarthy depicts as "the spirit of enchantment under which Venice lies, pearly and roseate, like the Sleeping Beauty," was also a classic experience for a different kind of prose person, whose heart (like McCarthy's) hankered after a golden age. In an earlier generation, it was Henry James who found " 'nothing left to discover or describe' " in the city he loved, where " 'originality of attitude is utterly impossible,' " though after a few weeks in the " 'vast museum' " that was Venice, he began to feel restless, as on board a ship, finding the Piazza San Marco " 'an enormous saloon. . . .' "

Something of this restlessness got to Mary, as well; and a few weeks after her arrival—after the miscarriage in Paris, the marital crisis with Broadwater, and the uncertainties of the new assignment—Hannah Arendt had joined her ("to hold me up," McCarthy recalled), and the two of them had gone to Milan for a long weekend. There, a Congress for Cultural Freedom conference was under way, which they were invited to attend as auditors. Arendt, who never went to another Congress event, and publicly deplored the CCF's covert alliance with the CIA when it was exposed in 1967, found the debates in Milan "deadly boring." McCarthy, not unlike Henry James before her, was reconnoitering international literary society, which by 1955 was steaming with intrigue; asked about the Milan conference in 1986—"The Future of Freedom," it was called—she could no longer remember what it was about ("Oh, they're always the same," she said), but she remembered the people. Silone and Nicola Chiaromonte were there, and also Czeslaw Milosz, whom she met for the first time in Milan.

After Hannah returned to New York, Mary was still brimming over with gossip about "the overflow of people from the Congress" in Venice: Nicholas Nabokov, Vladimir Nabokov's cousin, and a conference convener, Melvin Lasky, codirector, with the CIA's Michael Josselson, of the Congress magazines, though neither Mary nor Hannah knew about the CIA connection then, John K. Fleischmann, who helped finance *The New Yorker,* and whose Fleischmann Foundation was a conduit for CIA funding of CCF conferences. Melvin Lasky, Mary pronounced "appallingly vulgar, but with curious convictions. He hates all of us," she thought, "and yet he has become in the last months very heatedly anti-anti-Communist." By "us," she meant anti-Stalinists like herself, Hannah Arendt, and Dwight Macdonald, who remained critical of organized anti-Communism.

McCarthy didn't know it then, but by 1955 the Congress for Cultural Freedom had begun to downpeddle anti-Stalinism in Europe in order to enlist wider support from non-Communist writers, artists, and composers. By 1963, at a CCF conference McCarthy addressed in Madrid, with Franco still in power, even Communists, along with the usual complement of socialists and Social Democrats, would be enlisted in the cause of 'cultural freedom.' A CIA version of the united front, perhaps. But the turnaround—for so it appeared to zealots like Sidney Hook and Max Eastman in New York—was condemned by the American Committee for Cultural Freedom, which severed relations with the international body for being insufficiently anti-Communist. The CIA, of course, in its capacity as "a refuge for liberals and foreign policy freethinkers in government," as Arthur Schlesinger (also in Milan in 1955) recalls, was actively engaged in subsidizing the non-Communist left in Europe. Just as in South Vietnam a decade later, when the liberal wing of the CIA secretly promoted a 'Third Force' of disaffected military men, Buddhists, and religious minorities, the pursuit of an apparently benign foreign-policy interest via covert action led eventually to misunderstanding and mayhem all along the line.

In Mary McCarthy's surrender to Venice, there is a touch of Isabel Archer in *The Portrait of a Lady,* another American abroad, also an orphan though an heiress, whose travels induct her into aesthetic experiences unavailable in the United States. Like James's heroine, McCarthy drew the interest and admiration of a great many people who in one way or another busied themselves with her welfare. Berenson, Mostyn-Owen, Guggenheim, not to mention Tony Bower and the Berniers, together with the Italian critic Roberto Papi, and, in Milan, Isaiah Berlin and his wife, who introduced her to the resourceful Countess Anna Maria Cicogna in Venice. (Back home in New York, Bowden Broadwater, not unlike Caspar Goodwood in James's novel, would come to see his lady as a stranger.)

The benediction McCarthy bestows on Venice is a celebration of sheer aestheticism: "the marble veneers of St. Mark's sides, especially when washed by the rain so that they look like oiled silk, are among the most beautiful things in Venice," she writes, noting that "it is their very thinness, the sense they give of being a mere lustrous coating, a film, that makes them beautiful." Venice is the "world's unconscious," she plunges on, "a miser's glittering hoard, guarded by a Beast . . . and by a saint who is really a prince who has just slain a dragon." Alongside such gossamer surfaces, a "palace of solid marble, rainwashed," she observes, anticipating manly Florence, looks "bedraggled."

In *Venice Observed,* which was widely perceived in the cultural community as "anti-Venetian" when it first came out, thanks in part to a hostile review by the influential London critic Sacheverell Sitwell, McCarthy honors a city whose fairy-tale themes—the medieval conquest of Byzantium, the confrontations with the papal Curia, the Venetian romance with reliquaries—mirror certain strands in her own persona. She revels in the city's historic accumulation of goods: wine from Apulia, jewels and drugs from the Orient, silks and cloth of gold from Byzantium. "These are the gifts of the Magi," she exclaims, intoning an English hymn: " 'Pearls from the ocean and gems from the mountain; myrrh from the forest and gold from the mine.' " It is a litany whose wealth of fleshly detail evokes the booty in Augusta Morganstern Preston's closets thirty years before.

McCarthy's portrait of her Jewish grandmother, who had died in 1954 while the Broadwaters were in Portugal, was written around the same time as *Venice Observed,* and traces of the memoir, "Ask Me No Questions," can be found in the book's preoccupation with Jewish history. Historically, the Venetian trader was the quintessential Jew, McCarthy declares. She concurs in a theory that anti-Semitism can be traced to a medieval hatred of capitalism. "To the medieval mind, the Jew was the capitalist par excellence. But this could also be said of the Venetian," she points out, "whose palace was his emporium and his warehouse." It is no accident that popular opinion still confuses Shakespeare's Merchant of Venice with Shylock, the Jewish money-lender of the play, she adds; for the Venetians had a name for sharp dealing, for " 'sticking together,' artful diplomacy, business 'push,' and godless secularism—traits familiarly ascribed to the Jews." The Venetians, however, were never sharper than when dealing with their own Jews, who enjoyed "*specific* rights, the rights [they] paid to enjoy." Jews could set up loan banks, trade with the East, practice medicine, sell old clothes, but for a price. "The Venetians were toler-ant, but the Ghetto [built on a Venetian island in the sixteenth century] was a Venetian invention," McCarthy observes, "a typical piece of Venetian machinery, designed to 'contain' the Jews while profiting from them. . . ."

"A commercial people who lived solely for gain," both she and Ruskin say of the Venetians; but McCarthy, unlike Ruskin (who blames the " 'degenerate' " Venetians of the Renaissance for the cor-ruption of the city's architecture), traces the origins of "Venetian rapacity" to the Crusades. It was in the twelfth century that Venetian merchants began to extract booty and trade concessions from Chris-tian and heathen alike, she notes; an "impartiality," which "caused them to be hated, as sometimes the Jews were hated, for being 'outside' the compact." Venice served the Crusaders primarily as a shipping agent, she continues, relishing a foray into medieval history that ap-pears to her as a child's pageant, and an occasion for following the money interest behind the eternal cavalcade of war, religion, and art. Except for the Fourth Crusade, when the Venetian armada led the sack of Trieste and Byzantium, the city treated the Crusades as a business operation. The Fourth Crusade, however, had been fatal to Christen-dom, and the overextended Latin Empire, including Byzantium, fell prey to the Turks. With the fall of Constantinople, Venetian involve-ment in the Crusades ended; St. Mark's merchants withdrew to the sidelines, content with their acquisition of " 'half and a quarter' " of the empire, until later in the thirteenth century when they signed a treaty with the Turks, and began trading in forbidden goods: slaves, arms, and wood for shipbuilding. The only serious fighting the Vene-tians ever did in the Holy Land was against the Genoese, who were rival traders, McCarthy comments.

It was the *business* of looting foreign shores that had outfitted Venice with its dazzling facades: its colored marble veneers and col-umns, precious mosaics, gold encrustations, statuary; the Byzantine Madonna in front of the Doge's Palace, the painted crucifix within,

stolen from Constantinople, along with the verd-antique gravestones
of the Byzantine emperors. From the outside, St. Mark's has the look
of an "Oriental pavillion, half pleasure-house, half war-tent,"
McCarthy remarks in *Venice Observed,* while inside it looks like "a
robber's den." It all depends on the light and time of day—and one's
mood—but Venice, McCarthy suggests (borrowing from James), takes
you unawares, looking beautiful one moment and ugly the next, as
changeable as a nervous woman.

As "a place of enchantment," the city confronts the modern visitor
with a paradox. "A commercial people who lived solely for gain—how
could they create a city of fantasy, lovely as a dream or a fairy-tale?"
But there is no contradiction once you stop to think that images of
beauty in fairy tales invariably arise from images of money:

> Gold, caskets of gold, caskets of silver, the miller's daughter spin-
> ning gold all night long, thanks to Rumpelstiltskin, the cave of Ali
> Baba stored with stolen gold and silver, the underground garden in
> which Aladdin found jewels growing on trees . . . treasure guarded
> by dogs with eyes as big as carbuncles, treasure guarded by a
> Beast. . . .

Venice was the same: "A wholly materialist city," McCarthy concludes, "is nothing but a dream incarnate."

II

Venice, of course, was also Mary McCarthy's unconscious: "a
miser's glittering hoard" of fantasies from a Catholic girlhood. "The
Venetian mind, interested only in the immediate and the solid"—not
unlike her own—"leaves behind it . . . clear, dawn-fresh images out of
fairy tales." A fortuitous marriage of mind and matter, *Venice Observed,* more than anything McCarthy had written before, caught the
eye of the influential Janet Flanner in France. "I feel I dined with her
in order to gobble up her praises," Mary wrote Bowden irritably when
she met with the *New Yorker*'s Paris correspondent in September 1956,
after Broadwater had returned to New York. "I acted like a modest
school girl being lauded for a recitation, and I couldn't seem to extract
myself from this ludicrous role," she said. But experts on Venetian
painting didn't like the book, and, more important for Mary, neither
did Bernard Berenson.

It was the lavish illustrations that displeased Berenson: a garish mix of color plates with black and white photos, which gives the Bernier edition the look of a coffee-table book. "The text is simply buried in chic and folderols," McCarthy wrote Berenson apologetically, adding that she now felt "rather sorry that I lent myself to what seems mainly a fashion enterprise," which sounds rather harsh under the circumstances. But by 1956, relations between Mary and her Lausanne-based patrons had begun to cool. *Venice Observed*, nevertheless, was the best-selling art book in 1956 and 1957, and still stands as a memorial to Venice's resurgent charms.

Berenson may have objected to more than the book's appearance. From McCarthy's defense of the text—"It seems to me original; I don't know of anything like it"—one guesses it was the mix of art history and commercial history, social observation and memoir that rubbed him the wrong way. For the Lithuanian-born art connoisseur whose visa was stamped on most of the fine art transported from Italy to the United States during the first half of the century (the booty of *American* merchants), McCarthy's peregrinations on Venetian history, which include a portrait of her Venetian landlady, a canny figure who comes to personify Venice, weren't about *art*.

For Sacheverell Sitwell, the book's iconoclasm was positively unnerving. "She's been everywhere in Venice and seen everything and read everything," Sitwell conceded in a *New York Times* review, but *Venice Observed* "leaves a sour taste in the morning." Why drag Herbert Spencer in, for example, when Spencer was no more to be trusted on Venice than on any other subject concerning the arts? In the end, Sitwell found the book "one long denigration." Citing a reference to Tintoretto as " 'the literary amateur's painter' "—and missing the evidence of Mary McCarthy's unabashed affection for Venetian painting, a painting she relishes for its "enhanced reality, [its] reverence for the concrete world"—he wondered, "Is there forever to be gall in her ink-pot?"

Sitwell had reason to dip his own pen in gall, as the chivying tone of his review suggests. When Mary McCarthy met the brother of Dame Edith Sitwell at the Countess Cicogna's Venetian palazzo later in 1956, it wasn't for the first time. They had met on a train in Italy in the summer of 1946, when Mary and Bowden were touring postwar Europe. At Anna Maria Cicogna's, she learned that for years Sitwell had thought that he was the butt of "The Cicerone," whose "bounder"—"tall, straw-colored . . . like an English cigarette"—he was sure had been modeled after him.

Both Berenson's and Sacheverell Sitwell's disapproval is echoed thirty years later by Rosamond Bernier Russell, who maintains that McCarthy's treatment of art " 'was not the strongest part of the book. . . .' " Georges Bernier found the discussion of Venetian painting " 'not up to his standards,' " she states, and he had accepted it only because McCarthy was " 'the kind of independent, strong-minded writer who would say, "Take it or leave it". . . .' " They had not asked McCarthy " 'for a book on Venetian painting, but a book on Venice,' " she adds, suggesting why the Sorbonne art professor and expert on Venetian painting André Chastel was called in at the last moment to supply notes on the plates and comments on Venetian civilization; a move that irritated McCarthy not only because it represented a lack of confidence in her but because she first learned of it from an ad for the book.

McCarthy's critics are not very explicit about where *Venice Observed* goes wrong, but Chastel's notes in the back of the book indicate the kind of prose with which art historians are more comfortable. "Veronese painted several well-known canvases on the theme of Feasts or the Last Supper which he adapted brilliantly to his taste for monumental compositions . . ." Chastel writes; "The Banquet in the House of Levi" (1573) portrays "the agitation of servants about the tables and the play of dogs, all framed within the large frontal architectural elements that sustain the compositions." McCarthy devotes two pages to this extraordinary painting, in which Veronese "celebrated Christ's communion as a glittering debauch." The painting was a center of controversy during the Inquisition, she reports, when the Holy Office demanded that Veronese show why " 'it was fitting that at our Lord's last supper you should paint buffoons, drunkards, Germans, dwarfs, and similar indecencies?' " And Veronese, who had been ordered to alter it at his own expense, had hit on a simple expedient: "a true son of the Veneto," McCarthy relates, he merely changed the title from *The Last Supper* to *The Banquet in the House of Levi*.

Looking closely at what actually happens in the painting—McCarthy's real forte as a critic—she makes a small but telling discovery. Veronese's work, like so much of Venetian art, "a riot of dress goods," is indeed sacrilegious; not because of dwarfs and Germans but because of Christ. "It is He, conventionally represented, with a sickly halo, who strikes a false note—a note of insincere feeling—in the brilliant Renaissance tableau." Veronese's false Christ reminds McCarthy of how a false note is often struck in Venetian painting whenever the figure of Christ appears, except in Tintoretto, a large exception; and except when the Christ figure is dead or dying. "The real trouble with Veronese's picture," she proposes, "is that Christ, its center, is hollow," which in a certain sense (though McCarthy doesn't say it) is the trouble with much late Renaissance art.

Not many critics writing about art today can turn a painting into the mirror of an age the way Mary McCarthy does in *Venice Observed,* without at the same time losing sight of the painting. Despite her own fascination with Venetian mercantile culture, McCarthy never leaves her subject, which remains the character and art of Venice.

After moving on to Florence in 1957 and 1958, she became more enamored of early Renaissance architecture and sculpture, which is where the action lies in Dante's city. "Painting has a thin and flimsy quality by comparison. It has this element of witchcraft," she said many years later, recalling that she and Hannah Arendt discussed these issues when they traveled to Princeton in the middle 1950s to attend the Gauss lectures—W. H. Auden, V. S. Pritchett, Rosalind True, and Arendt herself (in 1953) being the featured speakers—much as two old grads might descend on the Sugar Bowl. Arendt had led Mary to look on painting as "a painted image," a kind of "necromancy," McCarthy remembered; while sculpture she came to see as "civic."

In *Venice Observed,* however, McCarthy is clearly enamored of oil painting, which conjures up "the feel of stuffs. . . . Florentine madonnas wear transparent veils and genteel 'old stuffs,'" she comments, scanning Venetian art like a seasoned shopper at I. Magnin's: "—faded blues and old roses with dulled gold trim—that have been handed down for generations in a miserly Tuscan family. This will not do for the Venetians. *Their* madonnas and St. Lucys and St. Catherines are dressed in brand-new materials fresh from the bolt," she exclaims. "No Venetian saint or secular figure is permitted to dress drably"—a proviso she would increasingly apply to herself.

In Europe, McCarthy had begun to take special pains with her wardrobe, which was purged of what remained of the bohemian look. Now the names of favored designers took their place alongside favorite architects, sculptors, and painters. Writing Bowden in the fall of 1956 from the Hotel Montalembert, she wanted to make sure Bergdorf's had fixed a jacket mentioned in a previous letter. "Only the Pirovana really suits these 'little' dinners," she said, referring to a designer dress in her wardrobe that saw repeated service in evenings with the Berniers, trips to Longchamps with Tony Bower, and one afternoon at the races with her brother Kevin, who was passing through Paris, "very moody and Call-Me-Ishmael in brogue," she noted. "I hope you got some nice suits," Mary wrote her husband from Paris the following fall, after he had returned to New York once again from the sojourn abroad, to report to work at the St. Bernard's school. "I am in favor of nice suits, flowers, and furniture," she said. "Why not? That is what all the quattrocento painters were in favor of, after all."

For Mary McCarthy, of course, it was precisely the tie between art and society so evident in Venetian painting that invigorated her criticism. "The absence of fanaticism in Venetian life, the prevalence of mundane motives in politics," she suggests, "were reflected in the concreteness, the burnished order and sanity of Venetian painting." It was the kind of connection she and Hannah were fond of making when they toured museums, castles, and monasteries in Europe, which beginning in Venice and Milan in 1955 they did more and more frequently. *Venice Observed* is full of these aperçus, to wit: "If there is some mystery in the fact of a business civilization's producing generation after generation of incomparable artists, it lies perhaps in this 'eye,' greedy for materials, for a bargain, but true as a jeweler's lens."

Venice leaves Mary McCarthy "more amused than inspired," one of her biographers maintains, reasoning that it would be "temperamentally difficult for such a truth-seeker to derive inspiration from a trompe-l'oeil city like Venice." But this is not so. Venice fascinates McCarthy with its revelations concerning the tie between medieval piracy and Renaissance art; and such insights gathered in the line of critical duty never failed to inspire her. Besides, she was half in love with Venice, or with her new independence there; in *The Stones of Florence,* she only bows down to the greater city.

Venice's trompe l'oeil facades ring a bell for Mary McCarthy. She doesn't share the repulsion of the "architectural purists" and "American puritan housewives" who deplore the "slummy rear views of the palazzi. . . . Venice is not made to be seen in the round," she declares. The city lacks a foundation in the geometric plains of Lombardy or the stony hills and vineyards of Tuscany; hence both the spaciousness and volume of classical Florentine architecture is missing, and in Venice there is only the "thin snake of a Canal to mirror decorated facades." An odd and revealing observation follows: "The perennial wonder of Venice is to peer at herself in her canals and find that she exists— incredible as it seems. It is the same reassurance that a looking-glass offers us: the guarantee that we are real." Around and around McCarthy circles the mystery of her "foundling," prodding the runic city to reveal its secret name. *"You cannot make a silk purse out of a sow's ear,"* she declares, but "Venice," she concludes with satisfaction, "seems to exist to confound such universal maxims."

25

Scoundrel Time

"Dear Bowden, I think of you alone in the apartment

very sadly. Or did you burst into tears of laughter on the dock?

Perhaps you and old Rahv laughed and laughed.

I hope not, for I'm really desolate without you, reduced to

a single dimension, like a bare line."

—MARY MCCARTHY, LETTER TO BOWDEN BROADWATER, 5/5/57

Crossing the Atlantic on the *Cristoforo Colombo*, the *Queen Mary*, *Île de France,* or the *Liberté* in the late 1950s, as Mary McCarthy did each May and October, betting on the ships, not for speed but for fun, was one of those period excursions, like crossing the United States by Pullman in an earlier era. In May 1956, she took the *Cristoforo Colombo* to Naples, where she met Carmen Angleton, who accompanied her to I Tatti, Berenson's villa in Settignano outside Florence— but not before Mary drove her black Chevrolet off the ramp and into a crowd of bystanders (harming no one seriously). She had "had a rather difficult time" with Paul Tillich on the way over, and Tillich's advances had thrown her into a state of "psychic shock" that took days to wear off, she wrote Hannah Arendt later, speaking delicately, for Hannah and the esteemed German theologian were friends. "I'm not so naïve as to be surprised at a religious man's having what Dr. T. calls 'pagan moments,' " McCarthy said, "but he takes it too much for granted in himself somehow, as though it were an effusion of godhead in him." She had never met a man "with so much egoism and so little confidence in himself," she remarked.

Paul Tillich had made a pass at Mary McCarthy once before at a New Year's Eve party at Hannah Arendt's. Now he called her a "puritan." In the ship's card room, he had moved rapidly from hand-holding and talk about how she had the "bump of philosophy on her knuckles" to a squeeze and stolen kiss on the cheek, and then—"I can't say it," Mary had written Bowden in the breathless voice one encountersin*The Group;* but it was "all to the tune of pseudo-scientific conversation about sadism, beatings, and biting and Greek Gods. . . ." Tillich had a foot fetish, she reported many years later. He had chased her into her cabin to see her feet. He was always trying to argue the virtues of pluralism in sex, she added; he thought that was how to seduce a woman.

In May 1956, as on all her crossings, McCarthy had probed the mysteries of the classes. Everywhere on the *Cristoforo Colombo* was a smell of vomit, she reported to Bowden, except in first class; when she had gone up there for a while, she felt as if she had brought the smell with her. Cabin class, her own, was "the prosperity-version of steerage," and steerage, with its "peasant chatter" and slumped-over bodies, screwed "like built-in furniture" to the floor, was "like looking in at a dog pound." The passengers in the lower lounge were Sicilians and Neapolitans returning home on an Italian liner. To McCarthy, nevertheless, they were "foreigners"—"grizzled foreigners with moustaches, old women in shawls and black oxfords. . . ." It was "pure Stieglitz," she said, noting primly that the Italians ordered Coca-Cola with meals instead of wine, and that many ate with their knives.

The May 1957 crossing on the *Île de France* was eventful in a different way. "[A]n awful trip—almost the worst yet," Mary wrote Broadwater. The swimming pool was full of tattooed men with powerful crawl strokes who cut her with their toenails. Some of her fellow passengers in cabin class were traveling to an international Rotary convention; and only a Philadelphia social worker and his wife, both avid *Nation* readers, provided her with conversation. It wasn't long before McCarthy had consulted the first-class passenger list for relief and discovered the name of the screenwriter S. N. Behrman, a *New Yorker* contributor soon known to her as Sam. "I immediately dispatched him a note and he invited me to dinner," she wrote Bowden:

The food is not good in first class either, heavy on the caviar, asparagus, and bearnaise sauce, but poorly cooked. The Queen Mary was better. Behrman is a funny man—bald, heavy, black-eyed, white-faced yet somehow mottled. . . . His two favorite people . . . are [William] Shawn and Isaiah [Berlin]. He thinks Isaiah a terrific brain, which made me suddenly realize that I didn't. . . . We talked about Berenson, Edmund [Wilson] (they're friends), Johnnie Walker, my grandmother, Max Beerbohm (not

Jewish), on whom he's doing a piece . . . Danny Kaye, that ventriloquist from the Palladium who told him a story out of Unamuno—
what is his name, Señor Wences?

Like the letters Bowden Broadwater wrote Mary McCarthy from
New York when she was holed up at Bard College in 1945 and 1946,
Mary's letters to Broadwater in the late 1950s, datelined the *Cristoforo
Colombo*, the *Île de France*, I Tatti, the Hotel Montalembert, the
Albergo della Signoria in Florence, buzz with nourishing gossip. After
dinner, Sam Behrman had introduced her to the Hollywood writer
Nunnally Johnson (*The Gunfighter*) and his wife, who were soon
joined by the divorced wife of Edward G. Robinson, an ex-chorus girl
named Gladys who had reportedly cleared $2 million from the sale of
Robinson's art collection and house. Gladys, who was buying a farm
in France and looking for a husband, was "bitter, as the phrase goes,
about the break-up of her marriage," Mary reported, "and talks viper-
ously about Robinson, who is a Rumanian. . . . 'If you have a
Rumanian for a friend, you don't need an enemy,' etc." After Mary
had offended Nunnally Johnson by praising *The Gunfighter* as parody—"very *delicate* parody," she had hastened to add—Johnson had
introduced her to Mrs. Robinson as "Miss McColl."

When Behrman asked Mary to read a new J. D. Salinger story, a
"letter-writing bee" had commenced. Mary had submitted her opinion—it was "a Document of our Times, the most extreme case yet of
'Louis Quatorze, c'est Moi' among Jewish writers. Just wait till you
see it," she wrote Bowden—and Behrman had agreed, adding that the
story reminded him of Marlon Brando, whom he found "a horror."
Behrman told her he was troubled by the fact that Edmund Wilson had
taken an earlier story of Salinger's seriously, the one where Franny
vomits because she's having a mystical experience, and Mary wrote
back "that Contemp. Lit. was never Edmund's strong point." Behrman, she told Bowden, "is better on his typewriter than in person; in
person, he's a pure Hollywood style vulgarian." A type for which
McCarthy harbored a stealthy affection, and she had dinner with him
again. ("I wore the new navy blue dress the first time and for tonight
I can't decide between the new white, the Dior, or simply the
Pirovano," she fussed before her second visit to first class.)

S. N. Behrman had the table next to the Jewish philosopher Martin
Buber: "a very old, spade-shaped man, with a soft, blue-grey beard and
a pink complexion. Saintly looking. I had thought of dispatching *him*
a note," Mary told Bowden, until she saw him, and then she no longer

had the "temerity," because she couldn't imagine what they would talk about. "Also, I felt slightly cheapened by my other acquaintances in first class," she added. As for the rest of the trip, she had done "nothing but read . . . until my eyes hurt." And she had only had a "single champagne cocktail, alone, in the bar before dinner," she assured Bowden; for she was trying to cut down on her drinking and cut down on another hard-to-control urge: falling in love.

"As for Him," the May 5, 1957, letter continued, "I'm not looking ahead much, hardly at all. Whatever lies ahead—I mean, whether I see him or not—is in God's hands." The deified 'Him' was John Davenport, the London critic with whom McCarthy had begun a spirited affair after meeting him in Rome in June 1956, where she had gone following her first visit to I Tatti. Within days she had been transported from the muffled serenity of Berenson's Tuscan villa, where an elderly one-eyed maid brought her breakfast on a tray with a pink rose, to the raucous Roman streets and tangled sheets of the Hotel d'Inghilterra, where John Davenport, too, was on an Italian holiday.

Davenport, an ex-prizefighter, petty thief, and alcoholic, though McCarthy would only learn the full story later (and it wouldn't make much difference), was as strange a man as she would ever take up with. He had a fast tongue, and the kind of sharp, punishing humor that hurts; he was also extremely well-read, and both wit and erudition shone in his fiction reviews for the London *Observer*. In Rome, he had easily swept Mary McCarthy off her feet with the force of a personality that seemed to fatten on dangerous liaisons. And throughout the summer of 1956, after Broadwater arrived at the end of June, and Mary, Carmen, and Bowden, the odd trio, began touring again, McCarthy's and Davenport's letters flew back and forth across Europe like sparks kindling the bonfire to come.

" 'I've wanted all day to answer by letter, but it's been an *awful* day, proofs and other things,' " McCarthy had written him from Milan, where she was struggling with the fact checkers' queries on the *New Yorker* proofs for the Venice essays, " 'so this monk [on the front of the postcard] will have to speak for me in his dejected way, looking forever out his window, forever hangdog, the outsider. . . . Or is the monk more like you?' " And later from Lake Garda: " 'This is a pretty, rustic place . . . with wonderful icy swimming, but my inner agitation gives me the keenest sensation of imprisonment.' "

The Broadwaters' marriage was again under siege, and Carmen Angleton, no longer able to offer much consolation to either side, had abruptly left them in Milan. A few weeks later when the Broadwaters rented the entire floor of a palazzo overlooking the Grand Canal in Venice (for not much more than the rent of a Cape Cod shack), Mary would beg Carmen "to come and share the apartment and fun," adding that "our domestic life is more peaceful than when you last witnessed it, though J.D. is still a thorn." Venice was swarming with old acquaintances: Nancy Macdonald, now divorced from Dwight, visited with her two sons, Mike and Nicky, followed by Dwight Macdonald and his new wife, Gloria, and the art dealer John Myers. Reuel Wilson popped in and out from Paris, where he was studying at the Sorbonne.

In 1955, Dwight had visited Mary in Venice after the Milan conference, as had Arthur Schlesinger and his wife, Marian; Venice, and to a lesser extent Florence, was on the Cape Cod–Capri circuit in these years, along with Paris—not only for Mary McCarthy's group but for the up-and-coming writers of the Beat generation, such as Gregory Corso and William Burroughs. Burroughs, who first caught McCarthy's attention with a funny story about hunting for the cannabis plant in South America in a Chicago magazine called *The Big Table,* would catch it again with *Naked Lunch* in 1962. In August 1956, he was traveling in the company of Auden's secretary, Allen Anson, who introduced him to Mary and Bowden in Venice.

Writing Carmen from the midst of the excitement, Mary had assured her that the distracting romance with Davenport was soon going to "resolve itself; if not, I shall have to resolve it . . . somehow; I don't quite know how." But when she met Davenport again, which she did during a secret trip to England not long after Bowden went back to New York in September, she no longer saw an end to it. "This has all gone very deep, on both sides," she wrote Hannah Arendt from the safe house he secured for them in London in October 1956, an apartment over a green square, where Mary remained inside most of the time, "like a captive canary." One day they had ventured out to Hampstead, where Davenport visited a daughter in the hospital while Mary waited in a pub. All four of his children and his ex-wife had been in and out of hospitals since June, while John, although he clearly drank too much, and couldn't stay out of brawls, was never sick. At the end of the month, McCarthy had returned to Paris and eventually New York (traveling first class on the *Queen Elizabeth*). Back in the United States, it had looked as if the affair would take to the mails again. Mary began writing Davenport immediately. He wrote back once. She wrote again. And then there was silence. She kept writing, but there was no more word from him; and then suddenly, with the impending marriage of McCarthy's good friend Sonia Orwell to Michael

Pitt-Rivers in the winter of 1956, she found herself in London again. She had no idea, she said many years later, whether she would see Davenport or not, but they had met, and it was then she learned that his ex-wife had committed suicide, and that there had been yet another wife and other children.

They had gone to a pub in London, and then proceeded to Cambridge, where Davenport had just installed himself and his motherless children—who were "darling," McCarthy recalled in 1989, a few months before her death, reliving the strange interlude as if it had never stopped happening, which in a sense (for she never repudiated this affair, or the satisfaction it brought her) it never had. Davenport had prepared a delicious joint of roast beef for supper. In the living room, books were piled from floor to ceiling, not yet on the shelves. Davenport's four children seemed to be frightened of him, McCarthy recalled. Everything appeared a little threadbare, and she had lent him five hundred dollars.

After flying back to New York, she had written him, just as before, and Davenport had written back once. She wrote him again, and perhaps one more time. He never wrote her again. (Later, McCarthy learned that a bookseller on the West Coast had acquired her letters to John Davenport; how, she never knew. "It would have been like him to sell them," she said, "but I prefer to believe that the children sold the letters after his death.") At the end of the winter of 1956, Mary McCarthy, then forty-four, of sound mind and body, suffered an angina attack, starting with a telltale pain in the upper arm, the outward manifestation of a "broken heart," she said in 1989.

On May 5, 1957, meanwhile, she was approaching England on the *Île de France* with no more idea than she had had in London the winter before of whether she would meet Davenport. "I think I shall do nothing until I've seen Dwight [who was working for *Encounter* that year], who will be certain to tell me if there have been any new hair-raising developments in that quarter," she wrote Bowden, indicating that the question of seeing "Him" was not entirely in God's hands, others were involved—and also that Broadwater had been drawn into the vortex of an affair whose luster was deepened by the pretense of secrecy. John Davenport had bragged about his liaison with Mary McCarthy all over London, and the only "fortunate thing," as a friend of John's, a lawyer living in Belgravia, told McCarthy when she sought his help in finding Davenport as soon as she got off the boat, "was that he was known to be such a liar that in this instance no one believed him."

In London in 1957, McCarthy was presented with "the case for the

Crown" against Davenport, as the lawyer, Mr. Hughes, called the unsavory facts he felt he had to present to her, but her attachment to the affair had only deepened, as if the rude awakening quickened those 'keener sensations' to which persons of McCarthy's type are addicted. Byronism, Miss Kitchel might have said, citing the bard: "It is this 'craving void' which drives us to . . . intemperate, but keenly felt pursuits. . . ." *Memories of a Catholic Girlhood* had just been published before Mary embarked for England; perhaps she was more than usually attuned to the drama inherent in the London affair, not as 'material' for fiction or memoir, which it never became, but as a manifestation of the wayward impulse in her nature so much the theme of the book. One of the *PR* boys might have said she was simply bored with Bowden; Davenport was a more 'interesting figure.' ("Dinah wants to get married again so that she can once again have someone to whom to be unfaithful," Delmore Schwartz wrote about his Mary McCarthy character in his notes for "The World Is a Wedding.") But Davenport didn't play the other side in this drama; nor did Mary behave in a way she had before.

A "bad blow," she called the meeting with Mr. Hughes in a postmortem to Hannah Arendt, which reads like a Restoration comedy or a drawing-room scene out of Ivy Compton-Burnett, but also reveals the hidden door in Mary McCarthy's satirical talent, which is her inexaustible credulity. "At a quarter of six, I was ushered by the old housekeeper into a very elegant Belgravia flat," the narration begins; "Mr. Hughes, a tall dark man in white tie and tails, stood up to greet me. There was no one else there. (Somehow I had foreseen this)." The lawyer, who turns out not to be Davenport's cousin, as John had claimed—another lie, like his "gentle birth" (he was the son of a songwriter and an actress who played charwomen)—had promised to round him up by telegram; and that failing, to send his housekeeper after him. (Davenport's phone had been shut off for lack of payment.) They both look at their watches; in a half hour, Mary's host will have to leave for an official dinner with the Duke of Edinburgh. They chat about Edmund Wilson, whom Hughes knows, and also about Reuel, who has just finished his freshman year at Harvard. "Then we plucked our courage," Mary wrote Hannah, "and moved closer to the subject of our meeting: John. How can I tell you?"—and off she goes, breathless with horror and delight.

" 'What distinguishes [McCarthy] from other writers,' " Hannah Arendt said in 1959, putting her finger on the source of Mary McCarthy's talent for satire—which in the Davenport saga is unintentional—" 'is that she reports her findings from the viewpoint and with the amazement of a child who [has] discovered that the Emperor [has] no clothes.' " So it was in life: this capacity for 'amazement' actually increasing as the years wore on. " 'She always begins by believing quite literally what everybody says and thus prepares herself for the finest, most wonderful clothes. Whereupon the Emperor enters—stark naked. This inner tension between expectation and reality,' " Arendt thought, gave McCarthy's novels " 'a rare dramatic quality.' " There is a third element in the drama, which Arendt overlooks: the resolution, so obvious as to be easily missed. As in the Davenport affair, McCarthy nearly always comes home again, like a pigeon with a message tucked safely under her wing. When all is said and done, a Mary McCarthy character, like the author herself, ends up not very far from where she began, or from where convention places her.

Davenport never showed up, giving Mr. Hughes time to supply the particulars. He had stolen books from *The Observer* and sold them, which is nothing for an itinerant reviewer, but he had also stolen silver from Hughes. During this sad recitation, with McCarthy "nearly fainting," the housekeeper rushed in shaking because Davenport, who either could not be found or refused to come, had frightened her. And finally Mary "drew a breath and said: 'Perhaps I'd better not try to see him.' " Hughes said to think it over; if she still wanted to see John he'd try to arrange it. But the next day Mary told him she had given up the idea, for what was the use? "We couldn't make love, thanks to the publicity he, John, has given the affair," she wrote Hannah, "and if we talked simply, I wouldn't be able to dissemble the knowledge I now had. . . . It also struck me that *he* would probably rather not see *me*."

Even after all this, she assured Arendt, " I still care about him, just as much as ever," though "this caring," she conceded, "is really hopeless now." Even Hughes's acknowledgment of Davenport's good qualities confirmed the hopelessness; for they were all wasted: "the love of books, generosity, loyalty, even a weird kind of integrity." He started to write too late, Hughes said, and lacked discipline and good work habits, so he kept making "these massive escapes into lies and drinking." In 1989, Mary McCarthy tried to account for Davenport's attraction. "He looked like a prizefighter, he was very ugly," she said. "He was charming. He had a wonderful sense of humor," and brightening, "the real attraction was sex."

During the tortuous week in London McCarthy caught a bad cold that turned into bronchial pneumonia by the time she reached Florence—no doubt a result of her "undeception . . . regarding J. D.," she wrote Bowden. At the Albergo della Signoria, as in Greece in 1955, a retinue of caretakers bustled about her person: "an excellent, very cautious, young German-Swiss doctor," together with the hotel's padrone who darted in and out with flowers and specially prepared meals, broths, and slivers of white sole. After another week's convalescence, she limped off to I Tatti. Berenson was feebler, deafer; one eye was hemorrhaging. "He lives only on gossip," McCarthy wrote Hannah. "What a rich feast I could give him, if I would, but I won't. Not even as a sort of blood transfusion."

In a postscript to the letter about the London meeting with Hughes, she told Arendt (in case Hannah saw Bowden) that "he knows all the above, except about my feelings. Naturally, *he* is feeling vindicated and delighted that I did not see John. And loyalty to him (Bowden) under the circumstances was a motive that sustained me in not seeing John." (Whether it would have "sustained" her if John had wanted to see her is another question.) The note about "feelings" may have rubbed Arendt the wrong way. In her response, which was swift and sympathetic and bristling with theory on the phenomenology of love, she was careful to distinguish between people who lie about facts (Davenport), "which will come out and show them to be liars no matter what they do," and people who lie about feelings: "if one lies about his 'feelings,' he is really safe; who can find out?"

Mary, she thought, had come too close to the English version of the " 'lost generation'—which apart from being a cliché is a reality. They are always the best and the worst. . ." she proposed; though for Arendt, the 'best,' their supreme defiance ("what one falls for is . . . this defiance"), clearly outweighed the 'worst.' "The lying is *pseudologia phantastica,* the emphasis on the phantastic," she declared, "and to lie about one's origin and to play the aristocrat in England is . . . as much satire on the English . . . as it perhaps is also the attempt to lie yourself into something you are not." But Mary was right not to see Davenport again. The real problem was the bottle, but apart from that there were two things that could " 'save' " him, Arendt maintained: "either a woman, but then saved for what? Evidently for some form of respectability. Or . . . genius . . . a talent so compelling that it will overrule everything else. (This," she added, "is of course the case of people like Brecht or Heidegger.)"

Mary in her wildest imaginings had not suggested that Davenport had 'genius,' but Hannah had her own point to make when she noted that "if this 'Who they are' is not matched by qualities and gifts, what can there remain to do?" Life became "a very long and rather boring business; for the Who as such is nowhere recognized in our society, there is no place for it. Under such circumstances, to destroy one-self . . . can be a time-consuming and rather honorable job," she suggested. "More honorable and probably less boring than to save oneself." An interesting thesis, right out of Kafka, and typical of the abstraction Hannah Arendt slipped into when she contemplated the fate of the exceptional man or woman.

The idea that a 'bad man,' a destructive or self-destructive person might be 'saved' by genius or the possession of great talent is another interesting thesis, one that fit nicely with McCarthy's youthful idealiza-tion of those 'great atheists and sinners,' Marlowe, Baudelaire, Vol-taire, Byron. " 'Here you have someone upon whom you can*not* rely,' " Arendt quoted Brecht on himself in her letter to Mary, speaking of the "lost generation"; with Goethe, she tended to agree that poets do not shoulder such a heavy burden of guilt when they misbehave. In her essay on Bertolt Brecht in *Men in Dark Times,* which is a kind of grappling on Arendt's part with her respect and affection for a man whose personal and political behavior made him hard to take, she concludes: "one shouldn't take [such poets'] sins altogether seriously." The chronic misdeeds of artists have been a political and moral prob-lem since antiquity, but the final determination of whether their "sins" are grave, she concludes, must arise from listening to their poetry. Brecht, who wrote, "Alas, we who wanted to prepare the ground for kindness could not be kind./ . . . Remember us with forbearance," is, of course, saved.

The German philosopher Martin Heidegger is another story. Hei-degger was Arendt's Davenport, in a way. And her soliloquy on love in the letter to Mary McCarthy surely owes something of its intensity to the affair she had had with him many years before. "Certainly, there is a great deal of cruelty in all this," Arendt said of Davenport's disappearance (ascribing it nonetheless to a sixth sense on the doomed man's part that he must never "drag other people into [his] own amusements"), "but then you can't expect somebody who loves you to treat you less cruelly than he would treat himself. The equality of love is always pretty awful," she reflected. "Compassion (not pity) can be a great thing but love knows nothing of it."

Arendt's love for Heidegger had developed when she was a gradu-ate student at Freiburg University in the late 1920s. In 1971 when she published a tribute, "Martin Heidegger at Eighty," in *The New York Review of Books,* it was her romance with Heidegger as a teacher, and with his thought—with the idea of "passionate thinking," a thinking that dissolves the opposites of reason and passion, spirit and life—which she honored. But her love for the man was sufficiently strong that even after she broke contact with him in 1932 when Heidegger entered the Nazi party, it was still alive in 1949 when professional obligations took her back to Freiburg. Then she had sent him a one-sentence note (unsigned) and he had come directly to her hotel, where they spent the night together. To a woman friend, she later said the reunion had confirmed "the level of passionateness and honesty on which one lives." And to an old comrade from student days, Arendt wrote: "As always, I received through him the German language, uniquely beautiful, Poetry really. Man tut was man kann, one does what one can."

Arendt was forty-four in 1949, not yet the author of *The Origins of Totalitarianism* or *The Human Condition,* but a respected political thinker and writer; and Heidegger was reportedly startled to find her reputation such that she was invited to address the German Book Trade in Freiburg. When some years later she sent him the German translation of *The Human Condition,* there was an outburst of hostility from Heidegger and his followers. To Karl Jaspers, another mentor from Arendt's student years, who found Heidegger's reaction "unbelievable," she wrote that she knew

> it is intolerable for [Heidegger] that my name appears in public, that I write books, etc. I have really fibbed to him about myself all the while, behaving as though none of this existed and as if I . . . could not count to three, except when it came to giving an interpretation of his own things; in that case it was always gratifying to him when it turned out that I could count to three and sometimes even to four.

When the fib had finally became "quite boring" to her, she had sent Heidegger her magnum opus, and she had paid for her change of mind, she noted dryly, "with a knock on the nose. . . ." For the man, however, she never had a change of heart.

"Grand passions are as rare as masterpieces," Balzac said, and Arendt used the maxim as an epigraph for an essay she wrote on Isak Dinesen in 1960, which also appears in *Men in Dark Times.* It was an observation with which she concurred. Twenty years after the 1949 reunion with Heidegger, she ventured a footnote on the theme: "Wisdom is a virtue of old age," she reflected, "and it seems to come only to those who, when young, were neither wise nor prudent."

II

Reading the chameleon-like correspondence that McCarthy maintained with Bowden Broadwater and Hannah Arendt in these years, the glittering prose of *Venice Observed,* the searching memoir of Augusta Morganstern Preston, "Ask Me No Questions," finished in the summer of 1956, and with it *Memories of a Catholic Girlhood,* one is struck by the multiplicity of voices at Mary McCarthy's disposal. During an especially busy week in October 1956, Mary had written Broadwater ostensibly from Paris about sight-seeing in Holland with Hannah Arendt and seeing a Rembrandt exhibition, when she was actually in the London flat with John Davenport. "I see you gallantly alone in the apartment [in New York] and my heart is stabbed. Possibly you miss Tucci?" the letter ended. In Paris, McCarthy had told the Hotel Montalembert that she had gone to the country to visit friends, and then when she decided to stay over with Davenport another week, she had written Hannah (who had returned to Paris from Amsterdam) to fix things up with the hotel and also to mail the enclosed letter to Bowden, who might worry if he didn't hear from her, McCarthy said, noting that "obviously I can't send a letter from here."

Something more complex than deception is at work in the contrasts one discerns between the letters to Bowden Broadwater and those to nearly everyone else, Arendt included. In the midst of I Tatti's splendor in May 1956, of dinners with Italian men of letters and English notables such as Harold Acton, Laurence Olivier, and John Walker, director of the National Gallery, Mary could suddenly sink into a slough of despond with her husband:

> I feel very much alone, frightened and helpless, as though everything were going to fly apart. It's almost as if the nervous breakdown I kept prophesying to Ruth Jencks [a Wellfleet neighbor and model for Jane Coe in *A Charmed Life*] had finally come about. . . . Meanwhile, the air feels laden with presagements and I must nerve myself for the smallest actions, such as dressing for dinner or going out into the hall to look at the pictures. I feel I shall *never* be able to get myself out of here and into a hotel, unaided. And yet of course I shall.

As soon enough she did, checking herself into the Hotel d'Inghilterra, although it was Carmen Angleton who made her reservations in Rome. In the very next paragraph, the depression is brushed aside. Bowden is not to worry. "It's doubtless the old European *angst* again." Her Italian is improving, and so on.

And yet the moments of disorientation recur. Arriving in Paris at the end of September 1956 with Tony Bower, who had driven the Chevrolet from Padua (after Peggy Guggenheim had chauffeured McCarthy from Venice to Padua), Mary wrote Bowden that she had "immediately slipped into my usual state of Parisian depression and agoraphobia." She felt "a horror of going out into the street, a horror of making a telephone call," which may have had something to do with the "cool meeting" she had just had with Peggy and Georges Bernier over the allegedly "anti-Venetian" tone of the *New Yorker* essays. The same letter was full of news about the Titians and Veroneses at the Louvre, and instructed Bowden to see whether Mannie Rousuck could organize an exhibit of Venetian painting at Wildenstein's in concert with the upcoming publication of *Venice Observed*. "I'm sorry you're so much St. Bernard's captive this year," it closed. "We must try to have a good winter, nevertheless, and to make some splendid plan for next summer. . . ." (Next year, same time: "Dear B., I'm sorry for all that work you have. We must get you out of that job next year.")

The next day, she received her first letter from Bowden since his return to New York, and the "morbid condition"—whatever it was, real or feigned, or both, dramatization being a way to relieve real tension—was "somewhat abated." Already she had embarked on a series of lunches and dinners and excursions to Longchamps. Parisians seemed "extraordinarily good-looking after the Italians," and she was looking forward to returning to the city after the upcoming trip to Holland with Hannah, who adored Paris and might introduce her "at long last" to some French intellectuals. (As it happened, Arendt, who was surprised at McCarthy's ignorance of the city, mainly introduced her to dead intellectuals, taking her to St. Étienne du Mont, where Pascal is buried, and the Place des Vosges, where Victor Hugo lived, the Bastille, and the Closerie des Lilas, her favorite café.)

McCarthy's anxiety overtook her when she was alone in a new place and when Bowden hadn't written, a condition that seemed to stir up a terror of abandonment from childhood, but it was rarely allowed to persist. Writing Bowden from I Tatti in the spring of 1956, she longed for his coming later in the summer, "but feel I ought not to, since I must, *must* learn to endure solitude without feeling it as degradation." Climbing out of her sickbed in Florence toward the end of May 1957, McCarthy's prayers for company were answered when she discovered that her old Wellfleet neighbors Charlie and Adelaide

Walker, and also Edna and William Phillips, were staying "*here,* at this hotel" (which prompted her to remind Bowden to bring the Broadwaters' calling cards when he came that summer). Her disorientation took strange forms, as when she would drift off to a troubled sleep and wake up terrified, not knowing where she was or even who she was; once making out that she was in Florence, accurately enough, but that she was George Weidenfeld, the English publisher.

In later years, McCarthy managed to beat these outbreaks of anxiety back into the corners of private life, or at least to forego dramatizing them in letters. Only twice, once in 1962 and again in the early 1970s, would she confide to close friends that she felt on the edge of a nervous breakdown. By the 1980s, this sort of thing seemed to have been purged from memory. "I can't remember any particular depression connected with Paris," McCarthy reported in 1988, when the letters from the 1950s were brought to her attention. Even the summer of 1955, when she underwent the protracted miscarriage and relations with Bowden were so poor, is remembered as a "positive" one because it ended with her going off to Venice to start the Venice book.

"The truth is . . . I wasn't depressed in September of '56," she states flatly; "I must have been pretending to be for Bowden's benefit. In fact I am rarely depressed," she insists. But McCarthy protests too much. Depression, one senses, is dangerous, like the cardinal sins she attributes to feminism: self-pity, shrillness, covetousness, greed. Repudiating depression is a point of honor. "I distinguish between depression and being sad about something," she explains owlishly. "The sadness has a reason and depressions, I believe, from the little I know of them, feel causeless." The battle with such emotions remains an underground task, as mastering the loneliness of domestic routines, or the abrasions of professional life might be for someone else; over her long life, it was something McCarthy attended to alone, knowing that up in the open air where armies clash, real victories depended on it.

26

"Chase Away Care"

"The apple was more human there than here, but it took

a long time for the blinding golden rind to mellow."

—ROBERT LOWELL, "FLORENCE"

"Whenever you're near discovery, you're near Florence."

—MARY MCCARTHY (*PARIS REVIEW* INTERVIEW, 1962)

Not until the fall of 1957, when she returned home from Europe on the *Liberté* did Mary McCarthy finally resolve the question of "What Next?" that had perplexed her since *Venice Observed*. She was going to write a series of essays on the art and architecture of Florence for *The New Yorker*—"A City of Stone," it would be called—which might turn into another book for Georges and Peggy Bernier, though their sponsorship was uncertain. She had begun to think about Florence while working in the Correr Library in Venice in the fall of 1955. "You could see that all the trails led to Florence," McCarthy said later. Venice had only "a very tiny history" about which "very little is known," while the history of Florence, densely intertwined with the rest of Italy, "is so extraordinarily complex and rich." But then she had worried the question for a year, like a cat teasing a mouse it has not yet declared a meal.

With Bowden in the summer of 1956, she had traveled to Turin, Bergamo, Amalfi, Parma, Verona, Mantua, Treviso, Bassano, Rimini, Urbino, and Bologna, looking for a theme that might inspire a book with the force of the fairy-tale history of Venice; and acquiring in the process "a multiplied sense of recognition," she wrote Hannah Arendt in New York, so that Italian painters she had never heard of six months before "now nod to me from the walls of galleries like old friends." Florence, initially, had been set aside as too imposing. " 'But, my dear, what do you *know* about Florence?' " Bernard Berenson had demanded of Mary during one of her visits to I Tatti. And as much as she had learned from Berenson about the city of *his* dreams, it was hard to overcome his resistance to the idea that she might have something valuable to say about Florence that hadn't already been said with more authority before.

Besides, Berenson had begun to interpose himself as a subject between Mary McCarthy and her next assignment. "B.B., greedy appreciator," she sometimes thought of the esteemed consultant to millionaire collectors, whose "little light [was] slowly extinguishing itself" by the late 1950s. In 1957, McCarthy saw him as a "deteriorating fresco" that some people wanted to restore and others wanted to leave alone; and in the last years of his life, when she got to know him well, he had prompted some interesting speculations about the meaning of monuments, himself included. What a wonderful "tale" it would all make, she thought, if "one could understand the relation of . . . B. B. to Art, to the art-book, to tourism and the preservation of monuments. . . ." Henry James's *The Death of the Lion* and *The Spoils of Poynton* came to mind. But there was another side to Berenson, "that roughness and briny independence," McCarthy called it, which gave the old courtier a "queer charm," and opened up a hidden chamber in his personality; one that probably led back to his apprenticeship to the fabulous Isabella Gardner—Mrs. Jack—in turn-of-the-century Boston, though it was a connection McCarthy left unexplored.

Another "Rogue's Gallery" might have sprung from such ruminations. There was only an extraordinary difference of degree between the subject of McCarthy's 1939 story, Mannie Rousuck, one-time bootlegger, fence, and dealer in 'antiquities,' turned director for the great art emporium Wildenstein's, and Bernard Berenson, the Lithuanian-born son of Jewish aristocracy and self-exiled Bostonian, who stood watch over the Renaissance treasure at Settignano like the mythical beast of legend. In the late 1950s, McCarthy still wrote exhibition copy for Rousuck on occasion, and supplied him with tasteful quotations for his Christmas cards. With *Venice Observed* and *The Stones of Florence,* in a more roundabout way, she was writing for Bernard Berenson.

"Took Mary McCarthy to Gricigliano back by the Sieci and along the Arno," Berenson reported after one of their excursions in the late 1950s. "Tuscany at its most enchanting moment, a wonder and joy for my eye. But Mary scarcely opened her eyes to all this beauty," he noted in his diary. "Yet she will write about it, and be evocative and give readers the longing to come and experience for themselves, as I never, never could. Such is the power of a gift for words, and the technique for using them."

Berenson and I Tatti would have made a superb subject for Mary McCarthy, especially if her own peculiar relationship to the "delicate little *élégant,*" as Alfred Kazin recalls him, were brought into the picture. One sees the two of them winding through the Tuscan countryside in Berenson's touring car, a gauzy wool lap robe thrown over their knees, walking sticks propped by their sides; Beauty and the Beast, discoursing on the fragility of the past, the flight of the Tuscan peasants, the money-hunger of the gentry, the tragic dismemberment of the old farms and villas. Berenson, with his wispy Shiite beard and beautiful clothes, listens carefully while his companion makes some response, turning toward him a profile of classic regularity. Oddly, when they get out to walk, her graceful carriage will be accompanied by an almost jerky gait—a peculiarity of Mary's that some of her friends were just beginning to notice.

Berenson himself, a baptized Catholic though an unbeliever, was an interesting match for Mary McCarthy. (" 'Oh, dear,' " he exclaimed after having "Ask Me No Questions" read to him, " 'is *everybody* Jewish?' ") He was not an intellectual, not even an art critic, but something more important to McCarthy in these years, a messenger from the past. He knew things she wanted to know. For him, Mary McCarthy was a woman he might have wanted to possess, a thing Berenson suggested more than once to friends. At the very end of his life, half-blind and restricted to quarters, "like some specimen preserved in a bottle," Mary wrote Hannah, Berenson had all of *Memories of a Catholic Girlhood* read aloud to him. "[I]f I survived that, I can survive anything," she recalled him telling her.

Berenson had quizzed McCarthy closely about Hannah Arendt, not because he was interested in *The Origins of Totalitarianism,* as Mary supposed, but because he was fascinated by Mary and curious about the company she kept. "I wish my admirers weren't all quite so old," McCarthy wrote Broadwater from the *Liberté* in October 1957, when it was Igor Stravinsky who was pursuing her. " 'Vous avez un grand talent, mon enfant; très beau, et très mechant [You have a great talent, my child, very beautiful and very naughty],' " Stravinsky said, for he, too, was reading *Memories of a Catholic Girlhood*; and Mary had replied, "Mais vous aussi êtes mechant [But you too are naughty]." The advanced age of such figures reminded her of the need for "a well-planned reforestation program" among men.

*   *   *

Berenson's interest and his influence had its darker side. Conversations at Villa I Tatti took "a consistently sighing tone," McCarthy said of a 1956 visit, which left her dazed by the enormity of the losses the old man mourned in contemporary culture. She wanted Reuel to see the Tuscan monuments before they disappeared forever, she wrote Bowden, then wondered, "[W]hat is the good of seeing [the past] if it's going to disappear, irrevocably, like some sunken Atlantis? . . . [I]f one is facing a deteriorating perspective, wouldn't it be better to forget about the past, abolish it . . . so that there would be no reminders, nothing to sigh over?" There is a petulance to the question that hints at McCarthy's temerity in the face of personal losses, but the despair is also an emanation of the period, which was full of angst. "Abolish museums and shrines of every description," she exclaims, working herself into a lather of renunciation that gives way to a new idea. Museums, she proposes, are "dependent, indispensably, on some hidden notion of progress: how could they be tolerable otherwise?" The first museums and collections began in the Renaissance when people felt reborn and able to look ahead—"as though tomorrow *was* another day." This was not how she felt in 1956.

At I Tatti, McCarthy told herself that "these are old people and old people naturally detest change and exaggerate former virtues. And yet I feel they are right," she worried. If they are, "how are we all going to survive? If the future becomes, not something to live for, but something to live *against*, how can . . . 'tomorrow be another day,' or the morning be wiser than the evening?" she wondered, reiterating those "comforting maxims" (which Bowden had heard before) that served her as "shock-absorbers."

Reflections like these, nourished in the Marienbad-like atmosphere of Casa Berenson, had also played their part in keeping McCarthy off the road to Florence. "Florentine history . . . stopped such a long time ago," she suggested to Hannah, "while the city continued developing along normal, modern lines. Just the opposite of Venice, which keeps reenacting its story in a sort of frozen form." The old papal city of Bologna, on the other hand, "Red Bologna" in modern times, a hotbed of Marxism, seemed "to have a mysterious life of its own that bears some relation, even if an inverse one, to its past," and briefly she had contemplated writing a book about three cities: Bologna, Mantua, and Florence, each considered according to its problematical relation to the past. Florence, "patroness of the lovely tyrannicides" (as Robert Lowell depicted it), was approachable, if at all, obliquely, by way of comparison and contrast.

Not only did the vision of Florence's great sculptor-builders of the quattrocentro seem buried in the mists of time, there was something disturbing about the boundless audacity of the Renaissance itself. "More willful than beautiful," McCarthy said of San Lorenzo the first time she visited Brunelleschi's church; and gazing at the Pitti Palace or the Strozzi, she could never completely overcome the suspicion that this "bristling prepotent stone" was the site of some "terrible mistake . . . a mistake that had to do with power and megalomania, or gigantism of the human ego." And if these apprehensions were not enough to make her hesitate, there was the brute fact of contemporary Florence, swarming with Vespas, Lambrettas, bicycles, Fiats, Chevrolets, Cadillacs, and tour buses.

"Dull, dry, provincial," a city whose buff-colored buildings and classical statuary recalled the schoolroom and the customs-house, this Florence discouraged the kind of intimate examination that had proved so rewarding in Venice. The "virile" aspect of the Florentine Renaissance, which had introduced a certain dynamism in all the arts, now seemed to express itself in a preponderance of banks, loan agencies, and insurance companies, along with the manufacturers of umbrellas, luggage, shoes, table linens, and optical equipment, whose names—Ferragamo, Gucci, Buccellati, Bellini—reminded McCarthy of the old banking firms: Bardi, Peruzzi, Pazzi. This Florence had long ago been abandoned by the "selective tourist" and overtaken by the masses, who swept barelegged, smelling of sweat and suntan oil, across the marble floors of the Uffizi, led by their polyglot guides to the Medici Tombs, the Baptistery doors, and the Pitti Palace, craning their necks to see Botticelli's "Venus on the Half-Shell." " 'Nobody comes here any more,' " Berenson said, and it was true, there was no contradiction: " 'Nobody comes here any more,' " McCarthy observed, was "simply the other side, the corollary, of the phenomenon of mass tourism—the universal deluge."

By the summer of 1957, however, this perspective on Florence was giving way to a more inquisitive one. When she recovered from the bronchial pneumonia that had overtaken her in London after the end of the Davenport affair, Mary had rented an apartment on the Via Romana, which set her in the very heart of the city. The old Roman 'way,' the Via Romana was still the main route from Siena and Rome; and beneath her window flowed a stream of cars, trailers, motorcycles and scooters, donkey carts delivering sacks of laundry, baby carriages, bands of workmen carrying bureaus and credenzas (for this was the artisan's district), utility workers jackhammering the sidewalk, American tourists peering into guidebooks, clerks, artists, priests, housemaids with shopping baskets, trucks of crated lettuces, live chickens, olive oil, tripe vendors with glassed-in carts packed with smoking entrails, telegraph boys on bicycles, and overhead a plane—which seemed to recapitulate the entire history of Western locomotion, minus the Roman litter, McCarthy remarked in the first essay of "A City of Stone," an introduction to contemporary Florence that irked the ninety-two-year-old Berenson for its "*New Yorker* touch." Mary exaggerates, Berenson maintained, a charge that reportedly brought tears to her eyes when she heard it from Berenson's lips a year before his death.

"Horns howl, blare, shriek; gears rasp; brakes squeal; Vespas sputter and fart; tyres sing"—rarely would the *sounds* of a place figure so prominently in McCarthy's descriptive writing. But noisy Florence, the Florence that offends the cultivated sensibility, sets the stage in the larger portrait for the contemplation of the simplicity and balance that she would ultimately find in the architecture of the quattrocentro; just as 'parvenu' Venice serves as the foil in *Venice Observed* for her discovery of the mythic city, whose art and architecture exist as an etherealization of commerce. Bernard Berenson died before the publication of *The Stones of Florence,* whose stark black and white design owed itself in part to his influence, but it is unlikely he would have been sufficiently mollified by the book's celebration of the "sabbath stillness" of Brunelleschi's smaller churches to reconcile himself to her runaway penchant for polarizing a subject.

"There is too much Renaissance in Florence," McCarthy announces on the first page of *The Stones of Florence,* "too much 'David.' . . . Historic Florence is an incubus on its current population," she states, noting that most Florentines are too busy to pay attention to the antique statuary jutting up out of the city squares, or the treasure trove of sculpture and painting buried in museums. Almost immediately, the screw turns, however. The 'bad' Florence that offends the "selective tourist"—the Florence that "makes no concession to the pleasure principle," but "stands four-square and direct, with no air of mystery, no blandishments, no furbelows"—becomes, on closer inspection, the 'good' Florence. In it, McCarthy discovers something of that "simplicity of life which classical Florence shared with Athens," another hill city, also hewn from stone, whose "barefoot philosopher," Socrates, reminds her of the simple, down-to-earth Filippo Brunelleschi. And the architecture of Brunelleschi, who built the gravely classical little churches of Santi Apostoli and Santo Spirito, but also the great dome of the Duomo, reminds her of "Socratic . . . philosophy, in which forms are realized in their absolute integrity. . . ." A window cut out by Brunelleschi is "a Platonic *idea* of a window," quite different from the "so-called 'ideal forms' " of Michelangelo's sculptures, which she doesn't like (too many furbelows), where " 'ideal' means 'mental,' 'imaginary,' 'not true to life' . . . in other words, 'idealized.' . . ."

"Florence is a manly town, and the cities of art that appeal to the current sensibility are feminine, like Venice and Siena," she concludes, fickle in her newfound love. (Berenson didn't like this sex typing, either—"sentimental twaddle," he called it.) When McCarthy returned to Venice briefly in 1958 to look at some buildings designed by the Florentine Sansovino, Venetian architecture appeared "scrappy and nondescript," the very opposite of Florentine 'order' and 'solidity.'

From her beachhead on the Via Romana, McCarthy had gradually begun to explore the larger city. "Being alone in Florence is even worse than in Venice," she wrote Bowden early in June 1957, mourning the punishing solitude of the one meal a day she allowed herself to eat out in a restaurant, because she didn't want to be seen eating alone twice. The men on the street are "shameless," she added, and she hated to think what it would be like if she was "young." She was forty-five, a handsome woman who was rarely alone, except when she was working in the library at I Tatti or the German Institute in Florence, where she read the Renaissance critic L. B. Alberti on oil painting and John Pope-Hennessy on Uccello and the problem of perspective.

Florentine history had begun to click into place, but the art was still a problem, especially sculpture, which was "to Florence what oil painting is to Venice," she suggested, but she didn't "have nearly as much natural feeling for it." Stalking the sculpture galleries of the Bargello, she couldn't tell one San Georgio or San Giovanni from another. Visiting the Florentine frescoes, "Chase Away Care," in the Palazzo Schifonoia in Ferrara, she was impressed by their "almost sinister beauty," but couldn't decipher their allegories of the seasons and signs of the zodiac. And yet she was on the trail of a story in Florence that couldn't be forced; and the pattern in the stone would soon reveal itself, though not without the intercession of a Florentine friend who showed McCarthy a side of the city that Berenson never had. This was the good-looking Roberto Papi, critic, poet, and member of B.B.'s inner circle, whose reservations about the master's tastes in Florentine art were a poorly kept secret.

McCarthy's good fortune in a companion would help break the ice in Florence; but it was the timely publication of *Memories of a Catholic Girlhood* that allowed her to conceive a study as ambitious as the one she eventually undertook. In 1957, she had two new books to her credit—three, counting *Sights and Spectacles* (1956), a collection of theatre pieces from *Partisan Review*. The much-acclaimed *Venice Observed*, six months in the making, had opened the way to *The Stones of Florence,* which would take McCarthy two and a half years to research and write, and was published by Harcourt, Brace and Company. But it was *Memories of a Catholic Girlhood,* stitched together in the harum-scarum fall and winter of 1956, and published in May 1957, that marked a breakthrough—not only in a larger public's recognition of Mary McCarthy's capabilities as a writer, but in her own. After this, she would undertake more far-reaching projects, no longer bound by the concerns of a narrow band of intellectuals.

II

"Miss McCarthy, who writes better than most people, here writes better than herself," announced an early notice of *Memories of a Catholic Girlhood;* while Charles Poore's appreciative review in *The New York Times* of McCarthy's struggle to separate fact from fiction in the reconstruction of a harrowing childhood had sent the author "up like a helium-filled balloon," Mary confided to Bowden. Of all her books, *Memories of a Catholic Girlhood* was "most as you are yourself," Hannah Arendt had declared (which was "not a 'value-judgment,' " she added enigmatically). Arendt was impressed by the "absence of self-pity and self-idolotry . . . most writers apparently being quite incapable of even mentioning their childhood without bursting into tears. . . ." Still, it was the free play of feeling in McCarthy's portraits from childhood, so different from her other writing, which was too often "ultrasmart" in the opinion of many, that struck some readers with the force of revelation. Here was a writer whose romance with the past, traumatic as that past was, unleashed a flood of associations in the reader—hundreds of whom now wrote McCarthy about their own childhoods, Catholic and otherwise, the deaths of parents, the tyrannies of guardians.

It was Dwight Macdonald, more perceptive than most friends gave him credit for, who understood the real importance of *Memories of a Catholic Girlhood* for McCarthy personally. Praising the memoirs for being "*felt* for once, and direct and simple and moving," he suggested to Nicola Chiaromonte: "Maybe she can only love herself as a fictional character!" He didn't mean that she was lying. Rather, that in reconstructing a wrenching past without rancor, she had recreated a Mary McCarthy she could live with. In everyday life, as Dwight and Nicola well knew, Mary was far from the self-righteous Solomon she often appeared in print or conversation. She was often racked by self-doubt, not about her critical or aesthetic judgments, even less about what she felt about somebody or something; the question was, *Who was she?* Where did *she* stand in the swarm of desires and inhibitions, fears and aspirations, assertions and counterassertions that made up her inheritance?

It was after *Memories of a Catholic Girlhood* that McCarthy could say that she was "not interested in the quest for the self any more" (as she was, most self-consciously, in *The Company She Keeps*). "It's absolutely useless to look for it, you won't find it," she told Elisabeth Niebuhr in 1961, "but it's possible in some sense to make [the self]. I don't mean in the sense of making a mask . . ." she added. "But you finally begin in some sense to make and to choose the self you want." And Niebuhr, interviewing Mary McCarthy for *The Paris Review,* wondered, "Can you write novels about that?" Which in fact she never did. "I've never even thought of it," McCarthy said. "That is, I've never thought of writing a developmental novel in which a self of some kind is discovered or is made, is forged, as they say." And so, she supposed, she didn't know any more about her "identity" then than she did in 1941. But of course she did. She was somebody in 1961; the "developmental novel in which a self . . . is forged" was her memoirs.

If McCarthy stopped looking for a personal 'identity' with the arrival of the 1960s, she had become someone who believed in "the solidity of truth," where before she had not. "Yes. I believe there is a truth," she declares emphatically, "and that it's knowable." Upon that benediction, the interview ends. The quest for the "self," in effect, had been turned inside out into a search for an objective "truth" that is grounded, experientially, in something *out there*. History, architecture, sculpture, feats of engineering, even the "irreducible facts" of geography in *The Stones of Florence*—stone, sky, water, the material counterparts of Plato's "eternal essences," love, justice, beauty—all these things loom reassuringly behind McCarthy's final appraisal of Florence. Discovering them, she sets forth what she believes in, what she is for, and says it "very affirmatively," even though the golden age of Florence ended long before Shakespeare.

Memories of a Catholic Girlhood marked a breakthrough for McCarthy because it was through the medium of writing about her wayward years that she managed to reach certain 'truths' about herself that heretofore had lain beyond her grasp—her "*candore* and *spirito generoso*," for example, as Roberto Papi remarked of her character after reading the memoirs in October 1957. Papi praised McCarthy for her "patent truthfulness" and " 'courage,' " and also for the "test" she was making of herself in "this solitary European venture," at a time when she was poised at a moment of vulnerability and promise. " 'Courage' " was the last thing she felt in Florence after Bowden had returned to St. Bernard's in September 1957, and she found herself "terrified by the solitude and by the alternative—a false sociality." Papi had reassured her by saying, "of course, you want to scream aloud, but there's nothing to be afraid of; you will get through it." And so she had. But it helped that now her early fears were inscribed and surmounted in the pages of a book that even her detractors were praising.

With the publication of *Memories of a Catholic Girlhood*, McCarthy was relieved of some of the burden of personality, one might say; of that peculiar fragmentation of personality that was her lot. She had been changed by the assimilation of one lesson from her orphaned childhood, in particular: that after great losses she always got another chance; no matter how hard she fell, she picked herself up again, if sometimes with the intercession of a redeemer: her Grandfather Preston and, in the fall of 1957, Roberto Papi.

When McCarthy dedicated *The Stones of Florence* to Papi in 1959, she acknowledged a debt that went beyond a gift of expertise, but Papi's contribution was matched by an influence from a more remote corner. The spirit of Harold Preston, "just, laconic, severe," like Caesar, presides over McCarthy's celebration of the "wise ruling of space" in Florence—while the ghost of Augusta Morganstern Preston, with her fondness for costume and Turkish Delights, hovers over *Venice Observed*. Even the praiseworthy aspects of the "republican tradition of lucidity, order, and plainness" that McCarthy came to appreciate in Florentine architecture appear interchangeable with the qualities she celebrates in Harold Preston's character in *Memories of a Catholic Girlhood*.

"The injustices my brothers and I had suffered in our childhood had made me a rebel against authority," McCarthy writes in her memoir, *"but they had also prepared me to fall in love with justice, the first time I encountered it,"* which had been in the person of her grandfather when he rescued her from the Minneapolis McCarthys in

1923. 'Justice' henceforth would be associated with a certain rank and position. But for the mature McCarthy, years had passed since she had felt the pinch of the ideal, of 'justice,' in her own life. When it appeared unexpectedly in Florentine architecture and sculpture, thanks to the intercession of her Florentine Virgil, she embraced it.

Toward the end of the 1950s, with the arrival of the Beat generation, the literary world had succumbed to a sensation-seeking vulgarity, in McCarthy's opinion; while politics, not since the late 1940s an arena for independent action among intellectuals, had, for the moment, passed her by altogether. She was "revolted by the hipsters in the Kerouac and Ginsberg novels [*sic*]," she wrote Broadwater in September 1957, finding them not so different from the rock-throwing "hoodlums" who appeared in the latest photographs from the anti-integration riots in Little Rock, Arkansas. For the "life we keep being pulled into," she felt only "loathing," she added, referring to the dizzying social round abroad that seemed to substitute for any concerted literary or political activity. "What can one do? . . . How can one live without being degraded and degrading a dozen times a day?" she wondered, noting that "a clean break doesn't seem to be possible. The places people escape to really seem to be worse (i.e. Venice) than the places they are escaping from."

Even the Venice and Florence pieces appeared to McCarthy momentarily as "an irrelevancy, a bore even (for others), too much of an artifice or a manufactured product." And she felt "a strong urge to write something—that is, to speak out again." About what, she doesn't say. Nor does she say when she last 'spoke out,' though it would be interesting to know when she marked that occasion. Naturally, she would get on with Florence. "It will be more amusing to write here than to do anything else, anything social," she suggests, as if Florence is her cloister and she is embarked on a retreat, a perception designed to propitiate Broadwater perhaps. Her social calendar over the next few weeks wouldn't bear her out, any more than the two years that remained in the writing of *The Stones of Florence* bore out the notion that if she was "lucky" she "might be finished by Christmas."

When McCarthy finally got hold of the story that set her feet on 'pietra dura,' 'pietra forte,' 'pietra serena'—the Italian words themselves retaining a stony power in McCarthy's prose, like counters in a game—her fear of falling afoul the tawdriness of the times abated, at least for a while. It was Papi who rescued her from lonely restaurants and cocktails with the 'friends of friends' whose invitations she had anxiously collected from Tony Bower, Niccolò Tucci, Carmen Angleton, the Countess Cicogna, and Elizabeth Hardwick and Robert Lowell, who had visited Florence in 1950. Tours of the city with Papi invariably began with a presentation of gifts over an exquisite lunch where the day's program was discussed—in Italian, Papi speaking little or no English—and ended, very often, with a drive into the surrounding hills.

"A strange, amusing, gifted man," McCarthy said of Roberto Papi many years later. And of course speculation was rife that the good-looking Papi, who was clearly attracted to Mary, was something more than a first-class cicerone. But it is unlikely the attraction was carried to the couch—not because Papi was married, and the family villa at Groppoli the scene of frequent entertainments for Mary, Bowden, and later Carmen Angleton when she joined Mary in Florence, for such conditions would not impede a 'European' affair. Rather, the cultivated Papi seems to have played a different role in McCarthy's life.

Writing Broadwater after a sculpture tour with Roberto early in October, which ended with a drive to a remote basilical church near Mount Morello, Mary assured him that Papi "did not make an advance, not the slightest, at the same time that everything was on terms of the warmest intimacy. I think he is a very *good* man, very emotional, as you know," she added, striking an exalted note that recalls the platonic tie with Nicola Chiaromonte—which had itself borne fruit in recent years in a mutual admiration society of two. ("I consider you and myself the best theatre critics now extant," Chiaromonte wrote McCarthy in November 1959; the main reason being "that I don't see who else attributes the importance you and I attribute to the intellectual structure of a play." In letters to Macdonald, however, Chiaromonte sounded a different note. After reviewing *The Stones of Florence* positively for *Partisan Review* that same year, he told Dwight he found "many questionable ideas or cracks, as usual. But that is Mary, an overly intelligent woman, with a streak of foolishness.")

In 1957, Roberto Papi's appreciation of McCarthy's charms, not least the intensity with which she threw herself into a new venture, was in the bloom of discovery. She couldn't know it then, but in time she would look back and see her forty-five-year-old self as "an insect that had shed its carapace," Papi assured her, evoking from his "Merlin deeps" the shimmering image of a genuine savant, or at least a woman who was attempting the paradoxical task of establishing a fresh relation with history (Mary's own history and Florence's mysteriously converging). The image of the molting insect startled her for its likeness to the image of the water wings floating out of reach at the end of "C'est Le Premier Pas Qui Coûte," which marks an earlier turning point. Papi saw through her to the person she imagined herself to be in her better moments. When he talked about her "truthfulness," she couldn't help but think of all the lies she told; nor could she stem the tide of "ironic, amused reflections" that ran through her mind as he spoke. "The trouble with being taken on the highest terms is that one always feels such a crook, or slightly a crook," she confided to Bowden; but perhaps Papi knew about these thoughts, too, and forgave her.

What Mary McCarthy got right about Florence she got from Papi, some of her Florentine friends later asserted; but what's "right" about *The Stones of Florence* is not necessarily the accuracy of its reporting, nor its interpretation of the "republican traditions" manifest in Florentine architecture, much of which McCarthy did get from Papi. What's 'right' about the book, and places it alongside the best that has been written about Florence, is the vigor of its characterizations of both the artists and the art of the Italian Renaissance. For this, McCarthy brought a novelist's eye to bear on the materials at hand—to more dramatic effect, one might argue, than in many of her novels. But to establish an intimate relationship with the artists and their work, she had Papi to guide her: a poor writer in his own right, but a good talker; and a gentleman, who had married into the famous art-collecting family, the Pontini-Bonacossi.

It was Roberto Papi's intense involvement with the *whole* of historic Florence, not just the buildings, statues, and murals, but the materials out of which the city sprang: the iron gray stone and black and white marble of the Tuscan hills, as well as the historic strife between Pope and Emperor, Guelph and Ghibelline, described by Dante and Machiavelli, that gave McCarthy the broad vision she needed to attempt a panoramic canvas. Roman Florence was founded by the veterans of Caesar's legions, who had defeated the rebel Catiline in the battle of Pistoia in 62 B.C.—a confrontation born of an ancient schism already close to Mary's heart, and one, she suggests, that inspired the medieval feuds, "as though the witches' brood of Catiline took an ancestral revenge on the city that arose from the Roman camp on the river."

In *The Stones of Florence*, McCarthy takes to the Manichaean streak in Tuscan history like a duck to water. Brunelleschi and Donatello (Donatello's friezes and balconies) are pitted against Leonardo da Vinci, Michelangelo, and Arnolfo di Cambio (who built the tribune of the Duomo; the great dome was completed by Brunelleschi). In the balanced forms of the first two, she finds a resolution of the historic extremism in Florentine politics, while in the careers of master builders such as Leonardo, Michelangelo, and Arnolfo, she sees evidence of the "tyranny of genius," a dangerous obsession with the power of man *over* nature, which explains the affinity of these artists for popes and princes. What seals her judgment are the unsavory personal traits of these giants, especially Michelangelo, whose jealousy and suspiciousness offend McCarthy more than a penchant for grandiose gestures in art, but less than certain hygienic violations: "He must have smelled horribly," she writes of his goatskin gaiters and boots, and habit of never washing.

It's hard to forget McCarthy's Michelangelo, who when he dickers with the Pope's agents resembles Benjamin Franklin at the French court. And it is interesting to be reminded of his bad luck with patrons, who put britches on the nudes in the *Last Judgment* and attached a gilded fig leaf to his *David.* Nor will one see Donatello's famous statue of David wearing nothing but polished boots and a girlish bonnet in the same way after reading McCarthy's reflections on homosexuality in Renaissance culture. "Homosexuality or bisexuality has always been very common in Florence," she notes, having run "like the gout" through the Medicis, whose "effeminancy" and "uncontrollable aversion to women" nearly caused their extinction.

Michelangelo's dimpled *St. John the Baptist,* the curving smiles of Leonardo's Madonnas, the enigmatic *Mona Lisa,* and Donatello's *David,* a "transvestite's . . . dream," all remind McCarthy of that " 'sin' " to which the intellectual Florentines appear nearly as prone as the Athenians. " '*Michelangelo non avrebbe potuto peccare di piu col cesello* [Michelangelo could not have sinned more with the chisel],' " Papi remarked when he contemplated the soft white curves of Michelangelo's *Bacchus* in the Bargello. Looking at the art of the quattrocentro through these eyes, one becomes aware of a profusion of stately, well-turned male legs; buttocks encased in tight hose, toes pointed slightly outward to reveal the beauty of the calf; standing, idling, striding across a piazza, these boyish pairs of legs are a hallmark of Florentine painting, she observes, with a nod to Botticelli's Mercury in the *Primavera,* the god of travel and business. Legs are the male principle of action. But these are legs of fashion. They aren't going anywhere.

The resident humanists who tutored the Medici children represent a different type. "The humanists of this generation, talented, envious, easily wounded, had something in them of the modern interior decorator," McCarthy remarks; "taste was their special province, and they were bent on doing over the whole house of Italian civilization from top to bottom in a uniform classic style." There is no more suggestive figure in the Renaissance pantheon, however, than the Grand Duke Cosimo, the first of the Medici to rule after the fall of the republic in 1434. "A tame, cruel house-mouser," McCarthy calls him; and Cosimo I, who promulgated drastic laws against sodomy and bestiality, while patronizing the suggestive sculpture of Cellini, appears the perfect puritan-sadist type. In a mordant scene drawn from Vasari's diary, she shows the grand duke violating his sleeping daughter on a sticky August afternoon in the Pitti Palace (while Vasari lies concealed on his painting scaffold high above the bed).

This is the "cat-like" Cosimo who constructed a vast network of aerial passageways to connect the ducal offices in the Uffizi, via the Ponte Vecchio, to the Pitti Palace, so he would never have to set foot in the street. He conveys the streak of madness and eccentricity that runs through the legend and the reality of the Italian Renaissance. McCarthy draws him well, as she does the whole cast of characters who are absorbed with "Nature's oddities and 'mistakes.'" Leonardo, an alchemist and inveterate tinkerer, is an "Enchanter," and the enigmatically smiling Mona Lisa is a witch, naturally, which is why people are tempted to slash her and draw mustaches on her. Uccello, with his vanishing points and optic insurrections, typifies the Florentine obsession with mathematical puzzles. McCarthy's sensitivity to the wild side of Renaissance culture is part of her own perceptual apparatus; a counterweight to her enchantment with *republican* Florence, citadel of virtue and civic peace.

One often gets something off-color in Mary McCarthy—like the sudden rumination on the size of male genitalia in "A Divorcée on Gay Street"—alongside a tonic of analysis. *The Stones of Florence* is permeated with the familiar dualism. Far from contradicting each other, the opposing points of view, or voices, shore each other up by proximity; they are born of the same resurgent, Janus-faced will.

Just before sailing back to New York in the fall of 1957, Mary McCarthy wrote Broadwater to see whether he thought the two of them could design *The Stones of Florence* for Harcourt, Brace in case the Berniers' sponsorship fell through, which by then it already had. Later, McCarthy maintained that Georges Bernier was using her as "bait" in a come-on with American publishers to get all their art books published in the United States, and that when she learned this, relations went bad. Relations had already soured by 1957, however. Mary kept hearing that Peggy and Georges found her temperamental, while the Berniers had surely caught wind that Berenson disapproved of *Venice Observed* and had counseled McCarthy to get rid of " 'those awful people.' " After *Memories of a Catholic Girlhood*, however, the interest of her own publisher intensified with the involvement of William Jovanovich.

Bowden Broadwater did become more closely involved in the production of the book, as he had in others. When the photographer Evelyn Hofer was taken on, he accompanied her on her rounds through Florence and the surrounding countryside, acting as grip, chauffeur, gofer, and general hand-holder, as he often did with Mary. He is due some credit for the superb portrait of Renaissance architecture that Hofer, with her reputation for finicky perfectionism, finally produced ("a handful," McCarthy called her, "with the temperament of twenty divas"). Working Saturdays in the fall and winter of 1958, Bowden, Hofer, Mary, the designer Janet Halberson, and Bill Jovanovich, who at thirty-eight was already president of the company, got down on their knees in a boardroom in the Harcourt, Brace building and laid out the book. The interlude provided McCarthy, in a 1986 interview, with one of her cherished stories.

The drama opens in the empty offices, already decimated by "one of the early disturbed times at Harcourt, Brace, when all sorts of people had been fired or quit. It was like going into a hospital where all the patients had died," she remembers. The tableau of the happy comrades busily working together on a common project dissolves to a showdown that had happened a few weeks before in the Broadwaters' apartment (a new and larger one, on East Ninety-fourth Street). Jovanovich and another editor, Gerry Gross, "small, blond, somewhat insinuating" (the *villain*), have arrived to persuade Mary to sign a four-book contract with Harcourt, Brace. Gross, it seems, had already told Mary that HB would drop the Florence book if she refused, which, indignantly, she had, and Jovanovich presumably had come to patch things up, without conceding the critical demand. Something like the FBI's good guy/bad guy arm-twisting technique had ensued, for Jovanovich had sent Gross home, and then pressed the point himself: " 'No contract, no Florence.' "

For Mary, who was opposed to such contracts on principle, there was also a question of loyalty to a former editor. Denver Lindley, "a sweet and sensitive man" (the *victim*), who saw *Memories of a Catholic Girlhood* through production, had crossed swords with Jovanovich and recently left HB; and Mary had assured him that if he needed to use her as an "asset" in his discussions with other publishers, she would promise him her next book after Florence. The lines were thus drawn between Jovanovich and Lindley—who both once leapt to their feet during a board meeting to defend their "highland blood," Lindley boasting of his forbearers from the Scottish Highlands, and Jovanovich defending his "Montenegrin blood." And Mary was, in this context, a pawn. In her account, however, it is Gerry Gross who is "playing a double game," who "hated Denver Lindley (I didn't know this then)"; and Gross is blamed for attempting "some sort of coup for Jovanovich and turning the knife in Denver at the same time"; if she had signed even a two-book contract, "it would be on the publishing grapevine at once, and would certainly not do Denver any good." And so she held firm. "We might lose I don't know how many books," she recalls, "but I was not going to betray this friend" (who, as Arendt's editor, was also close to Hannah).

Finally Jovanovich had agreed, and Mary, "like somebody dealing with a near-Eastern rug merchant," went to the kitchen and made some coffee. They toasted an agreement that would remain in effect until her death; for McCarthy never did sign such a contract, it being understood that if she liked what her publisher did, she would continue the relationship. The following morning, Mary received either two dozen red Bacarat roses or two dozen American Beauty, probably the latter "(That's much more Jovanovich). And so," she concludes, "that was the beginning of this friendship."

" 'You have made a city sit for its portrait,' " Hannah Arendt declared of *The Stones of Florence*, which she liked without reservation, agreeing even with McCarthy's treatment of Michelangelo— "you are much more careful than I expected, by the way," she added. Fourteenth-century Florence, with its evocation of Plato's ideal Republic, which even if it "never existed as a political fact, but only as a longing, a poignant nostalgia for good government that broke out in poems and histories, architecture, painting, and sculpture," McCarthy writes, was close to one of Hannah Arendt's dreams, a dream of perfectibility not of men but of institutions. The Constitution of "scrappy" Venice actually came closer to enacting 'the art of the good and the fair,' as embodied in Roman law, than anything in Florentine life; but by the end of the 1950s, sermons in stone, not the "costume parade" of history (as Roberto Papi called it), seemed to speak more eloquently to Arendt's and now McCarthy's imagination.

Florence was "a far cry from Venice, the difference between a dream [Venice] and a complicated discourse," McCarthy told Katharine White at *The New Yorker,* but *The Stones of Florence* also embodies a dream. In form, it is the dream of 'wise rule' that was ignited in Goethe's breast when he visited Florence in 1786. Surveying the orderly plan of the city, Goethe saw " 'proof of the prosperity of the generations that built it' "; and the conviction was borne in on him " 'that they must have enjoyed a long succession of wise rulers.'. . . Hearing that assured German pronouncement, the angels could have wept," McCarthy remarks. "Still, the poet's perception, if not his inference, was right." Anyone taking a bird's-eye view of the city, "drawn up for inspection in parallel ranks on either side of its green river," would come to the same conclusion. Moving in closer to examine the bas-reliefs on the Campanile, depicting Agriculture, Metallurgy, Weaving, Law, Mechanics, all suggesting "an incised, exemplary system of political economy," she concludes that "[e]very aspect of Florence, from the largest to the most minute, affirms the immanence of law."

Perhaps there is a law of compensation in the quantum mechanics of personality that leads an individual on the brink of change to identify herself with an imagined rule of law in the external world precisely when the orderly arrangements governing personal life are about to break down. Within a few months of the publication of *The Stones of Florence,* on December 29, 1959, when Mary McCarthy first met James West in Poland, a pattern of allegiances near the core of her identity would suddenly end: marriage to Bowden Broadwater, long by Mary's standards, and not noticeably unhappy, along with residency in the United States. By another rule of paradox, Mary McCarthy would become a best-selling American novelist only after she became an expatriate.

Part Seven

■

New York/Vermont/Warsaw/
Bocca di Magra/Paris: 1959–1967

27

Jumping Ship

"'You know, probably, that I'm going
to Poland and Jugoslavia, which will be a decided
change. I may embrace Communism."
—MARY McCARTHY TO HANNAH ARENDT, 11/11/59

One way or another, throughout the 1950s, Mary McCarthy always came back to the neighborhood, to the squabbling fraternity that was her piece of the action in New York. Her camp had moved uptown over the years; sector by sector, until a good many of "the boys from over the Bridges," as Hannah Arendt called New York's Brooklyn-born intellectuals, had seized the commanding heights of the Upper West Side. By the late 1970s, of course, a few like Norman Podhoretz("one of those bright youngsters with bright hopes for a nice career," Hannah wrote Mary in 1957) had jumped both the Williamsburg Bridge and Central Park for the more fashionable Upper East Side.

Mary McCarthy remained a star attraction at the Ninety-second Street Y, along with Randall Jarrell, Robert Lowell, and John Berryman, whose reputations had grown hard and gemlike in the abstract 1950s. It was at the Ninety-second Street Y's Poetry Center in February 1959 that McCarthy read the first chapter of *The Group* (written in the summer of 1952) to bursts of laughter and applause from the audience. But toward the end of the 1950s, her appearances in New York had become less frequent. Joining Broadwater in their East Ninety-fourth Street apartment after a sojourn in Venice or Florence, it was as if she was visiting from abroad. The once-stateless citizen of the world, Hannah Arendt, had become the real New Yorker.

The city was still swarming with Europeans, who were entertained in typical fashion at private parties of thirty to fifty guests, each having a little 'name,' as Mary would say, all shouting at once. Only the names had changed with the times, which now favored English intellectuals over French, and men and women of fashion—Cecil Beaton, Laurence Olivier, Stephen Spender, Sonia Orwell (whose marriage to Michael Pitt-Rivers ended a few months after it began), Kenneth Tynan and his wife, Elaine Dundy, Isak Dinesen, Kingsley Amis, Christopher Isherwood—over ideologues of any persuasion.

When McCarthy gave a party for her Venetian acquaintance Anna Maria Cicogna in March 1958, she wrote Berenson that she hoped the countess would treat the noisome event as a tourist might regard "a national pastime, like a bull fight . . ." for it was bound to be a brawl. Like literary parties in Rome, New York parties were rough on a newcomer, who might find herself dropped after an introduction like a stray piece of luggage left standing on the station floor. At home in New York, McCarthy made sure that her guests were wined and dined in style, often enlisting her brother Kevin's services as bartender, and borrowing Mannie Rousuck's Park Avenue maid. For the party in honor of the Countess Cicogna, Rousuck had also sent a shipment of smoked salmon and sturgeon, which Mary and Bowden augmented with caviar and foie gras.

She had moved up in the world; and it was no longer necessary to borrow paintings from her art-dealer friend to impress her guests, as she and Bowden had done when they lived in the East Fifty-seventh Street walk-up in the mid-1940s; once borrowing some original nineteenth-century French oil paintings to "fix up" the apartment for Lionel and Diana Trilling, who were coming to dinner. Then the Broadwaters had been poor and their guests grand, or so they thought, until Lionel Trilling, "all eyes," had peered at one of the paintings whose impasto was especially thick, exclaiming, " 'Well, I've never seen that reproduction.' " In 1947, the food had turned bad on the Trillings, too, McCarthy remembered many years later; they couldn't tell what anything was, not the sherry, "a Manzanilla with an exquisite little Spanish olive," or the pasta, *"gnocchi a la romano,"* or the dessert, a meringue with strawberries (egg yolks having been used in the *gnocchi*). " 'Oh, these are wonderful! Where did you buy them?' " Diana Trilling had said of the latter, unable to conceive of "a pastry that didn't come from a bakery."

The party for the Countess Cicogna was one of those rewards to which Mary treated herself at the end of an arduous task, like a trip to Settignano or Rome after working hard in Florence. In February 1958, when she finished the first of the Florence essays for *The New Yorker,* she had collapsed and been sent to bed for 'a complete rest'; afterwards she had returned to the party circuit, started the next chapter of "A City of Stone," and somehow written a précis of Hannah Arendt's long and difficult treatise on the life of action, *The Human Condition,* for *The New Yorker.*

McCarthy's piece, "The *Vita Activa,*" might have provided the poet and critic Louise Bogan with an instance of that cronyism Bogan detested in the literary world. The practice of people reviewing their friends and exchanging favors in print was almost as common at *The New Yorker* as it was at *Partisan Review,* where an attack on an acquaintance's book, by the same token, might generate an equal amount of attention—a practice that would be taken to new lengths by *The New York Review of Books* in the 1960s. Reading "The *Vita Activa*" in October 1958, the unsuspecting reader would never guess that "Miss Arendt," "a graduate of Heidelberg and a pupil of the existential philosophers Jaspers and Heidegger," was also the reviewer's best friend. How was a reader to know that when McCarthy praised the author's "combination of tremendous intellectual power with great common sense," she was celebrating a combination that she and Hannah privately extolled in themselves? ("We both had a lot of common sense," Mary told an interviewer in 1985, "which is against the grain of what most people like to think, because strangely enough it's very unconventional. Conventional people actually have absolutely zero common sense.")

But the *New Yorker* review sparkled with ideas that the average reader might find harder to follow in Arendt's schematic prose. In McCarthy's hands, the ancient categories of labor, work, and action through which Arendt threads her analysis of the human condition become a "memory-jogger and a measure" of the "bewildering transformation" of modern life. 'Labor,' repetitive, routinized, is traditionally concerned with maintenance, she explains, while 'work'— that which defines a man as human, "as *homo faber,* man the maker and creator"—creates a product; in a work of art, the product may rework the material world itself. Through automation, the supplanting of man and his tools by machinery, 'work' is reduced to the labor required to maintain the machines; and the products, mass-produced, disposable, become "consumer products," made to be used up as quickly as possible in order to fuel 'demand.' "Labor and consumption, as Miss Arendt points out, are only two stages of the same thing, and a laboring society such as our own is a pure consumer society," McCarthy concludes, "in which everything is done to 'make a living.'"

The human condition is the *vita activa,* as opposed to the *vita contemplativa* of the philosophers; and in the original triad of labor, work, and action, 'action' denotes politics, those words and deeds that take place in the public realm, where men "inter*act* with each other," presumably to reshape their condition. Politics, however, together with the strategic distinction between private and public, "Household" and "*Polis,*" so basic to Hannah Arendt's thought, is given shorter shrift in McCarthy's *New Yorker* review than in *The Human Condition;* as is Arendt's complex formulation of "that curiously hybrid realm where private interests assume public significance that we call society." The omission is surprising. What is original in Arendt's book, which was reviewed favorably by another crony in England, W. H. Auden, and hailed by *The New Statesman* in 1958 as "the first important revaluation of the human condition since Marx," is precisely this vision of post-industrial society in which "behavior" substitutes for "action"; and bureaucracy, "rule by . . . nobody," Arendt calls it, supplants both representative government and "personal rulership."

'Society' devours both private and political spheres, in Arendt's view, first by injecting "household activities into the public realm" via mass production, and also by mass-conditioning the public to interpret personal experience in *socially* acceptable categories (that is, through the mass production of ideas). Put another way, social and economic affairs traditionally conducted by families and communities are usurped by national bureaucracies, over which no one exercises control. Hannah Arendt doesn't name the system, but the world she describes in *The Human Condition* is the infantilized world governed by multinational corporations. Her overextended, all-conquering 'society' is popularly known as the Global Village, whose myriad inhabitants, tethered to their appliances, wired for silence, await their redeemers.

McCarthy's quirky review of Harold Rosenberg's *The Tradition of the New* for *Partisan Review* a few months later was a more palpable instance of cronyism. Rosenberg, who coined the golden phrase 'action painting,' was Hannah Arendt's close friend and very likely her lover. In her review, "An Academy of Risk," McCarthy celebrates "the bold figure of Harold Rosenberg," rather more than the book itself, a collection of essays on art, politics, and literature, not unlike McCarthy's *On the Contrary* (1961) but with an angle. Rosenberg views the twentieth century as a kind of mad scientist's laboratory for the invention of the new: new technologies, new men, new ideas, whose obsolescence is guaranteed by their being perpetually turned into commodities.

Rosenberg impressed McCarthy in the late 1950s primarily for his ability to embrace the new himself, without falling afoul of its evanescence. Willem de Kooning, for example, was a cause of his that did pan out; but finally she applauded him for his detachment, not his commitments. She was drawn to his quick mind and gift for gab, which is reviewed as a performance in an article certainly calculated to annoy Philip Rahv, who deeply distrusted Rosenberg. To Rahv, the daytime Harold who sold his wit to the Advertising Council was a little like the Party member in the 1930s whose public persona invariably concealed its negative. For Dwight Macdonald, he would always be "the formidable and mysterious Harold Rosenberg." He was not an intellectual in the familiar Menshevik style, an organization man, but like Clement Greenberg, whom even Hannah thought Harold sounded like sometimes, as when he "talked for hours with great assurance an astounding amount of nonsense about art," he was half dialectitian, half magician. Ultimately, McCarthy praises him for being interesting at a time when ideas of any weight were rare as hen's teeth.

She admires his graphic images and gleeful phrasing (" 'it would be just as well to bump the old mob off the raft' "). "This plain talk nearly persuades you that he is right," she observes, referring to Rosenberg's central argument that "by being an act, an experiment," 'action painting' renounces the aesthetic as a category of judgment. It is hard to resist his theories, hard to step back from "this blast of vitality," but at the eleventh hour, that is what she does; asking "whether the theory of action painting is not just a new costuming of the old Marxist myth, in which the proletariat [now the alienated artist], having so long been acted on by history, decides to act into [sic] history and abolish it."

McCarthy herself had begun to prove susceptible to the sweeping statement when the time and place were right; as at a Congress for Cultural Freedom festival in West Berlin in June 1960, when *Time* quoted her as saying, "culture is just the writing on the ceiling of the whorehouse." (That wasn't what she said, McCarthy insisted later, but all she could remember was what she was quoted as saying.) Seen from the "Cultural Freedom sideshow in Berlin," as she described the occasion to Hannah, the old Marxist saw about 'culture' being the 'superstructure' of class society made sense. Confronted with Harold

Rosenberg's nihilism in 1959, on the other hand, McCarthy had rushed to the defense of the aesthetic principle, insisting that even a high-wire act with the brush had to yield a product which either satisfies the viewer's sense of form and color or not. You can't hang "an act" on the living room wall, only a picture, "which may be found to be beautiful or ugly, depending, alas, on your taste." And this applied to a Cimabue crucifixion as much as to a Pollock, a de Kooning, or an African mask—her own tastes running to Cimabue.

With contemporary theatre, McCarthy found herself on firmer ground. And throughout the years when she was immersed in the Italian Renaissance, theatre, especially the theatre of John Osborne, one of London's Angry Young Men, allowed her to keep a finger on the modern pulse. She had often treated Broadway plays as commodities, as valuable for what they revealed about the dreams and hungers of their audiences as about the strengths and weaknesses of their creators. Thus, the accumulated reviews of *Sights and Spectacles* and the updated collection, *Mary McCarthy's Theatre Chronicles: 1937–1962*, offer their readers an informal social history of American culture that lies beyond the purview of most drama critics. In the late 1950s, when McCarthy turned to the English theatre, whose writing and acting generally pleased her more than the American, this regard for the stage as society's bellwether yielded interesting results.

In *Look Back in Anger*, Osborne's antihero, Jimmy Porter, bored, petulant, histrionic, reminds her of Hamlet, whose tirades and asides, plainly calculated to disturb the court, indicate that he, too, has declared war on a rotten society. Osborne/Porter probably reminded McCarthy of John Davenport, as well, with his vigorous contempt for the status quo. Such sensibilities were unfitted by class or education to accept their lot in life. Each learned to substitute a nagging, wagging tongue for action; to make talk action, as Harold Rosenberg did.

"Those who want to be told what is biting the playwright have only to look around them, at the general fatuity and emptiness which is so much taken for granted that it appears as normal," McCarthy declares of the wider world behind *Look Back in Anger* and Osborne's *The Entertainer*, performed in Boston in 1958 with Laurence Olivier. In the winter of 1959, she reviewed the brief New York run of Osborne's play, written in collaboration with Anthony Creighton, *Epitaph for George Dillon*. With Osborne, a leftist who excoriated the Welfare State, McCarthy found herself on common ground, especially with his devilish portrayal of the "artist," George Dillon.

"You would know he was some sort of actor or writer . . . because of his long rather greasy hair . . . hungry, ferret face, sleepy gait, selfishness, and mooching habits," she remarks of the character Dillon onstage; "added to this, he is a vegetarian, speaks in an educated voice, and tells lies. No ordinary person could be as awful as George. . . ." When the play Dillon has been writing unexpectedly gets produced, and improbably wins fame and fortune for its author, the ultimate ignominy is reached: success, "the vulgarity of making good. . . ." Dillon moves "like a clown, from the cliché of failure to the platitude of success"—which is a trajectory McCarthy herself would soon trace (if "failure" is understood in market terms) with the huge success of *The Group*. With a blockbuster novel making its way toward Hollywood on the heels of a carefully orchestrated advertising campaign and red-hot reviews, she would feel something of the same pinch as George Dillon, who had "thought he was that mysterious, ridiculous being called an artist," and instead finds himself "written into a script of his own creation. . . ." But this jumps ahead of our story, which in the case of Mary McCarthy, nonetheless, is frequently anticipated in just this fashion, in fiction and reviews, all along the way.

II

By the spring of 1959, McCarthy was itching to get on the road again, or at least to get out of New York, where the smog of intrigue and gossip lay heavy over her quarter of the city. "*Another vicious attack,* as Philip Rahv used to say on opening his copy of the *Hudson Review* [which had taken to sniffing about the 'Jewish Establishment']. Now it is *Commentary*," she wrote Hannah Arendt in a state of high agitation in June, shortly after she and Bowden had taken the house in Pawlet, Vermont, which they had rented in the summer of 1947. She wanted to know whether Hannah realized that her "attacker," the man who reviewed *The Human Condition* for *Commentary*, Lincoln Reis, was "the man of *The Groves of Academe*"—the Bard professor who had inspired Henry Mulcahy? "The review has the characteristic mark, a kind of glistening malignancy," and the "resurrection" struck her as "strange and creepy" after Reis "had dropped out of sight for so many years. . . ." Bowden thought Sidney Hook may have put him up to it, she said, adding that Bowden also thought that Reis was attacking both Mary and Hannah when he referred to a certain "*précieuses ridicules*" in Arendt's work. It all seemed "quite wicked," and she was sure the review was "commissioned, the way you commission a murder from a gangster."

"I had not the slightest notion of who the gentleman was (his name again escapes me)," Hannah replied, coolly enough for someone who had twice been asked to write pieces for *Commentary,* which were then rejected as too controversial; most recently, "Reflections on Little Rock," which ended up in *Dissent.* But she, too, had noticed "a tone of real hatred," which surprised her. Now the reason was clear. Obviously, *Commentary*'s editors, Clement and Martin Greenberg, "identify us and preach the gospel. They could do much worse."

The whole issue of *Commentary,* traditionally a bastion of hard-line anticommunism, had a new and peculiar undertone, McCarthy went on, "a sort of jacobinism," and in a review by Harold Rosenberg, of all people, "a kind of righteousness quite unlike the old *Commentary* cynicism"; and she wondered where the " 'leftist' note" was coming from. Perhaps it was a reflection of something happening in Israel, she speculated, alluding to the magazine's parent organization, the American Jewish Committee. *Commentary,* in fact, was about to be taken over by the thirty-year-old Norman Podhoretz ("the Pod," Bowden called him), who would indeed give it a 'leftist' tinge, throwing open the windows of its expanded East Fifty-sixth Street offices in 1960 to the fresh gust of liberalism rising from the Potomac. In the summer of 1959, Podhoretz was already meeting AJC board members privately with his proposals for ousting the old editors and turning the magazine around, for making it less Jewish and less anti-Communist—a process Podhoretz later claimed only began under his stewardship, but one that was already under way.

Mary McCarthy, meanwhile, was embroiled in a battle of a different order with *The New Yorker,* one that shook her confidence in herself more than any political or literary challenge. From the *New Yorker*'s editor, William Shawn, she had nothing but praise for both the Venice and Florence essays; and Shawn was just then dangling an offer of a new assignment, a profile of Jerusalem, which left her sorely tempted, she confided to Arendt, "partly by the money . . . and partly by a kind of glamour, a purple-gold glamour, that the name Jerusalem has for me." Her problem was not with him or with the fiction editor Katharine White but with the magazine's fact checkers, who, in discovering dozens of mistakes in the final installment of "A City of Stone," inadvertently stepped on the tiger's tail.

"I hate to be wrong about dates, facts, etc., for I trust to my memory the way one trusts to one's eyes," McCarthy lamented. But memory, "poor fallible thing," had been challenged. The effort to substantiate disputed facts had kept her running back and forth to the nearest library, whose reference books were out of date and themselves extremely inaccurate; and yet she couldn't give up "the quest for certainty. I found myself nearly going wild and unable to sleep over details like the placing of an accent," she exclaimed in a letter to Hannah. "A normal person cooperates with the checkers or uses them as a convenience," she noted, "but I cannot help competing with them." In the last stages of reviewing the galley proofs of her manuscript, she was on the phone to New York three or four times a day, arguing over the spelling of a word or the placement of a date. The *New Yorker*'s special institution, the "Checking Department," was her very own "third degree . . . invented by some personal Prosecutor of mine to shatter . . . morale."

Hannah Arendt was sympathetic; the "phony scientificality" of the research department was "one of the many forms in which the would-be writers persecute the writer," she said. "And since this is nicely combined with job-holding and job-justification this kind of torture has become an institution." As for whether Mary should accept Shawn's proposal to take on Jerusalem, Hannah agreed with Bowden that studying the history of pre-Diaspora Judaism might be a more sterile occupation for her than learning about the Italian Renaissance. On the other hand, there was no book on Jerusalem and the market possibilities were sure to be high. Jerusalem, moreover, was the only city Arendt knew that gave one an idea of what a city in antiquity was really like. "It has been frozen through religion," she observed, and while she didn't know what to do with that, she had "always been impressed by the enormous quiet significance that is present in every stone."

Bowden had argued that Mary should not even consider the Jerusalem proposal, even though it was understood that she wouldn't start until she had finished *The Group*. "He says these years, the next ten, are the best years of a novelist's creative activity," McCarthy had written Hannah, "and that it would be wicked to squander them on journalism, even very high-class journalism"—an opinion Mary seconded by citing George Eliot, who began writing fiction in her late thirties and reached her peak in her early fifties. But she hated "judicious pondering about the Career, though as one grows older [she was forty-seven] and there is less time left to pronounce the word that is in one (if it *is* there), one has, I suppose, to look to the ant instead of the grasshopper. But, oh dear," she added, "I still feel more like a grasshopper."

"[D]on't think of precedents," Arendt shot back, "they are always wrong." And she advised Mary to leave the ant and grasshopper considerations out of the decision making: "You have plenty of time to become an ant if ever you want to be one, which I doubt." Years later, McCarthy would remember Hannah Arendt urging her on to Jerusalem; Hannah and Heinrich had sent her some photographs of the city to whet her appetite. In 1959, her own imagination was fired with images not of the ancient Jewish city but of Jerusalem during the Crusades. With an historical novelist's vision that went back to a childhood interest in Richard Coeur de Lion and St. Louis, McCarthy briefly contemplated another plunge into history.

Bowden Broadwater had his hands full keeping Mary at her desk when she finally did return to *The Group*. Dwight Macdonald remembered him guarding the gate against intruders like Cerberus. A second Guggenheim she had applied for to complete the "compendious history of that faith in progress of the nineteen-thirties and -forties, as reflected in the behavior and notions of [eight] young women—college graduates of the year 1933," as she wrote in her grant application, had been accepted (the first application, in 1952, was rejected); now it was time to get down to work. "It is a crazy quilt of *clichés,* platitudes, and *idées reçues.* Yet the book is not meant to be a joke or even a satire, exactly," she told the Guggenheim committee, "but a 'true history' of the times despite the angle or angles of distortion."

Meanwhile, Kevin McCarthy had arrived with a maid and two children (his actress wife, Augusta, was away on a tour). And he was followed by a couple of Bowden's fellow teachers from St. Bernard's. The summer was a wet one, and the hills around Pawlet, draped in a soft gray mist, rumbled with thunder week after week. In the beginning, Mary liked the sound of the needle like rain on the blue slate roof of the house. There were toads in the cellar and snakes under the studio, and an effect of "something strange and folkish about [the] country . . . [a]n odd *underlying* feeling that one doesn't get anywhere else in New England."

For weeks, the Broadwaters saw no one but "two domesticated pansies," as Mary called some neighbors, "who have a little hand printing press and talk about wild flowers and cooking." Bowden Broadwater's own latent homosexuality was known to at least some of their friends, such as their Wellfleet neighbor Mary Meigs, who remembers feeling "bound together by a common secret" with Bowden "which both of us took great pains to conceal. It was obvious to me that he was a homosexual, and obvious, no doubt, to Bowden that I was a Lesbian who was still in the closet," she states in her memoir, *Lily Briscoe: A Self-Portrait.* "Homosexuals, as we know from Proust, have extrasensory means of recognizing each other. But Bowden, in the triumph of his marriage to Mary, extolled the wonders of heterosexual life while I listened, silently rebellious. . . ."

After thirteen years of marriage, the sheen of heterosexual life for the Broadwaters appeared relatively unruffled by anything other than a few extramarital affairs, mostly Mary's. Bowden and Mary had long ago perfected the public roles they chose to play as husband and wife, host and hostess, page and queen, roles that sustained them after the marriages of more skeptical friends, such as Macdonald's and Rahv's, had collapsed. Mary would confide to Hannah Arendt later that her marriage to Bowden was just two people playing house, like congenial children. And this was certainly an image that impressed itself on the painter Mary Meigs, who recalls the Broadwaters in their red house on the hill in Wellfleet, presiding over a dinner party, sometimes dressed in matching black and white like characters out of Henry James. They "made a work of art of their life," she thought—an impulse that began in Newport, in her opinion.

But it was only after Mary McCarthy met Jim West that she called all her love affairs and marriages "snug, sheltered little games." In Pawlet, her problems with Bowden seemed to center mainly on his chronic search for a literary project of his own. He was unhappy teaching at St. Bernard's, and had taken an administrative position there instead; but he was employed. What was missing was some creative work. And it was the sudden arrival of a French translation assignment, and its equally sudden disappearance when William Jovanovich learned that another translation was under way, which left Bowden once again empty-handed. Stunned, he had gone right on translating for several days like a chicken with its head cut off, Mary wrote Hannah, noting dryly, "So far no substitute has been thought of."

Long after their divorce, an old friend of Broadwater's, Daphne Hellman, remembered Bowden giggling over how Mary had never known a thing about his homosexual interests, which struck her as dubious. "I would think she would have known; Mary was pretty sharp. It might have been a relief to be married to a homosexual," she suggests. Like some others who knew them both, Hellman was struck by how "very deferential" McCarthy behaved toward this lanky young man, still in his thirties, with the strange half smile and dinosaur eyes, magnified by thick lenses, which reminded Mary of a pterodactyl. " 'What do you think, Bowden?' " McCarthy was forever saying. It was a "courteous and nice arrangement," Hellman reflected, "surprising in a way."

In 1959, Broadwater was eager for Mary to get back to work on a novel whose wealth of social trivia concerning the affairs of eight young women from Vassar reflected some collaboration. It was exactly the kind of challenge to which he rose, acting as "an extra pair of eyes and ears for Mary," as Mary Meigs puts it, recalling how Bowden Broadwater used to roam through Wellfleet in 1953 gathering stories about people, usually damaging, which ended up in *A Charmed Life*. Meigs's account of her own pain and confusion upon seeing herself "swallowed and reconstituted" in the character of Dolly Lamb was a cry of protest that would be heard from others after publication of *The Group*. "When I first read Mary's book, it was as though I were nibbling imprudently at a mushroom, like Alice, and shrinking so suddenly that my chin knocked against my feet," Meigs relates. McCarthy had mocked not only the outward person: Meigs's preference for instant coffee, her collections of shells and bones, " 'her neat dish face,' " and body, " 'curiously flattened out, like a cloth doll that had been dressed and redressed by many imperious mistresses' " (*A Charmed Life*). By describing her painting as " 'cramped with preciosity and mannerisms,' " she had also activated "the dormant seeds of doubt that made me so ready to hate myself and my work," Meigs recounted. McCarthy, "with her unerring accuracy, had hit everything that was vulnerable in me, the indecisiveness of my life, the tightness of my work, my prudish habits."

Mary Meigs had told Bowden about a youthful rendezvous with a sailor that had left her not knowing whether or not she was a virgin, and this story had turned up as " 'the truth about Dolly Lamb,' " which was at least better than to have been a lesbian in McCarthy's book—and in her "craven way," Meigs was "grateful to her for staying her hand." And then, in her memoirs, Meigs took her small revenge by relating how Bowden had once put her to the "ritual test," proposing himself as a "mentor" one night when his wife was out of town. They were having dinner together next door at Meigs's cottage, "prepared with two dry martinis," and "it was over in seconds," she reports, noting that she had proved to herself, at any rate, that she wasn't "frigid." This first proof meant nothing, however, if it was followed by failure; and sure enough, the next morning she woke up to see Bowden "stealing toward my bed." She had "a headache and a sense of disgust" with herself, and cried, " 'No, no, no!' " as if he had come to rape her, and she was thankful to him for returning to his own room and for his "subsequent delicacy and forbearance." But she had given him "rich material for an enlarged portrait of me as a non-woman, afraid of sex," she feared; "perhaps this was fed discreetly to Mary (without going into detail) and was useful to her when she made me into Dolly Lamb. . . ."

Bowden was no amateur player. "He was always quite priapic," Elizabeth Hardwick remarks (she, for one, believes that Mary never knew about his homosexuality). In 1959, nonetheless, he no longer knew how to make himself indispensable, although *The Group* certainly engaged his talents for a while. It was at Bowden's urging that McCarthy went back to it in the first place; and, when "the air went out of the tires again," she persisted. It was probably his faith in this novel that allowed him to acquiesce so readily in the staged withdrawal she was already making from their marriage. Looking for a sheltered place to work in the fall, she had shipped out to North Africa in October to spend six weeks at the Countess Cicogna's luxurious villa in Tripoli, where she would carry *The Group* over the halfway mark, and then run aground again. Before going to the Villa Volpi in Libya, McCarthy had accepted a State Department invitation to join the "Experts and Specialists" program with Saul Bellow for a three-month lecture tour of Poland, Yugoslavia, England, and Scotland, starting January 1. Arthur Schlesinger, Jr., had put her name forward and urged her to go. "[A] decided change," she said happily, when she joked with Arendt about embracing communism. Road fever had set in again.

The Broadwaters would regroup over the 1959 Christmas holiday for a whirlwind tour of Vienna and Prague—where Bowden, Reuel, and Mary spent "a sepulchral Christmas, gloomy beyond belief in that worker's hell"—and Warsaw, which Mary hoped would be a treat for Reuel, who was studying Slavic languages at Harvard, and had just begun Polish. On December 28, 1959, the planes were grounded in Prague—"I think one of the engines just defected to the West," Reuel said—and a great many conveyances had to be used before the little party reached Warsaw the next day. The first night, a man from the American embassy came to take them to dinner at a place called the Diplomat's Club. "The Old Pretender" Broadwater would shortly come to call James Raymond West. Bowden was the Young Pretender.

Writing Arendt of the whirlwind romance three months later from Rome, where McCarthy was briefly encamped with Carmen Angleton, after having flown in and out of New York in April 1960 to pack her belongings, and say good-bye to Bowden, Mary exclaimed, "And that all this should happen with a U.S. government official seems utterly bizarre." But it wasn't really.

28

Love, Mary

"Loving life is easy when you are abroad. When no
one knows you and you hold your life in your hands . . . you
are more master of yourself than at any other time."

—HANNAH ARENDT, *RAHEL VARNHAGEN*

"It was reported that during this period an employee of the American
Embassy in Warsaw, James West, was having an affair with Miss
McCarthy. . . . West, whose family lived in Warsaw, frequently
stayed overnight in Mary McCarthy's hotel room."

—USIA REPORT, 4/23/62, FBI FILES

On March 30, 1961, in the Hotel Chambiges in Paris, two weeks before her marriage to James Raymond West, Mary McCarthy sat down to write a long letter to Edmund Wilson. Reuel Wilson was now in Cracow on a fellowship; and despite her incessant mobility over the past few years, or because of it, she had seen more of him than his father had. "The report on Reuel is very favorable," she said, adding that he was very much "in" with the younger bohemians in Cracow, "where he is celebrated for his 'anti-Communism.' " When he went up to Warsaw, he stayed with Jim West (whom he had taken to immediately, Mary had assured Hannah Arendt, adding that Reuel, in her view, "feels the lack of a virile and straightforward man in his family," Bowden being "a child, and Edmund . . . an old woman"); and soon he was coming to Paris for the wedding which would take place at the *mairie* (the town hall) in the 8th arrondissement on April 15.

Jim West, she wanted Edmund to know, "is a very nice man, different from all my other husbands, though he seems to feel a certain kinship with you." Though he was not Irish, he reminded Mary of the McCarthy men, "not any one of them but all of them; that is with a certain wild solitary streak combined with an engaging air, combined with a kind of solidity. But maybe it's only that like my father and my grandfather and Uncle Harry," she added, "he has prematurely grey hair." He was an only child born in 1914 in Old Town, Maine— "where there are Indians who make canoes," Mary added, knowing of Wilson's current interest in the Mohawk. His parents were divorced when he was two, and like herself, he had been raised mainly by his grandparents. His mother, who had been a nurse and telephone operator in a Bangor hotel, married the local rich man. Jim had gone to Bowdoin College in Maine, and afterward worked for several newspapers in Washington and Boston. He had lived in Greenwich Village and in Europe, and in the summer of 1941 (the year Mary and Edmund moved into their house in Wellfleet), he ran a theater in Provincetown.

"I give you all these biographical details because I know you like that kind of thing," McCarthy wrote Wilson, noting that in the war, Jim West had been a flier, a navigator, and had taught celestial navigation to cadets. He flew bombing missions out of Italy, and left the air force a major. After knocking about for a couple of years, he landed his first 'diplomatic post' as a guard [actually, a clerical worker] at the American embassy in Paris, and then went to work for the Foreign Operations Administration. In 1954, he took a job with the United States Information Agency in Washington, which is when he learned some Polish. During the Joe McCarthy years, he realized that in the late 1930s he had been on the fringes of the "Harry Dexter White circle," a group of young fellow-traveling liberals in the Commerce Department ["Commie *voyageurs,*" West called them many years later], which included Alger Hiss. "He is a direct actionist," Mary told Wilson, "very honest (unlike the McCarthy men), very intense, likes danger. Very strong-willed."

These qualities had played their part in West's attraction to Mary McCarthy, which was sudden and profound but not without a certain foreshadowing. Years before, he had read something of hers in *The New Republic,* and as if seized by premonition, had underlined her name and written his own at the top of the page, drawing a line between. The second night when he had taken Miss McCarthy, Broadwater, and Reuel out on the town in Warsaw, he had asked Mary to dance—it was in an underground jazz club called The Crocodile—and told her point-blank he intended to marry her. She had stared at him as if he was mad (he was after all married), and then smiled broadly. During their first weeks together, Jim West kept saying she reminded him of the 1930s. He had read some of her books, most recently

Memories of a Catholic Girlhood, but he wasn't one of those people who followed her career as if she were a wayward comet. He was a serious reader, and a side of West's personality is suggested by the cartons of books he kept stored in the basement of his apartment in Warsaw—philosophy, ethics, and the novels of Henry James.

In Warsaw, and two years later in Paris, when James West became Director of Information for the Organization of Economic Cooperation and Development, it was not this romantic streak, but his reserve—an air of unflappable good sense, that 'solidity' perhaps—that made him indispensable to his employers and his friends. An ability to read people and to interpret the *portent* of information, whether for an ambassador, a secretary-general at the OECD, or for Mary McCarthy later, set him apart from the typical intellectual of the day, who was often too busy listening to himself to notice what was happening around him. "Bellow is right in a way about Jim West—he is worth more than 10 PR contributors put together. Morally," Dwight Macdonald conceded in a letter to Fred Dupee, grumbling: "But there's more to be said. Decency isn't All." "When Mary met Jim she met the ideal American man," Carmen Angleton related many years later. "A husband-type husband," Elizabeth Hardwick called him.

As for the wild streak, it had been activated by an attractive woman before, not long after West graduated from Bowdoin, when he fell in love with the divorced wife of the composer Roger Sessions, nine years his senior (they never married). Older women seemed to attract him, but an exception to the pattern was West's second marriage (his first was a short-lived affair) to a much younger woman, which had resulted in three children, aged eight, seven, and five, who lived in Warsaw, and of whom he was extremely fond, though he had grown estranged from his pretty young wife, Margaret. The qualities Mary McCarthy extolled in Jim West in her letter to Edmund had been sorely tested in his dealings with Margaret West since he had met Mary; for Margaret had thrown up much the greater resistance to a divorce than would Bowden Broadwater. For the second Mrs. West ("*that* woman," Mary called her, unmercifully), divorce meant the inevitable eviction of herself and her children from Poland, as well as the surrender of the valued rank of embassy wife to a usurper; though until May 1960, Jim had tried hard to keep the 'other woman' out of the picture, not very successfully. With Margaret, he had insisted that irreconcilable differences made the continuation of their marriage impossible. But his wife wasn't having it; and for nearly a year, he pressed for one settlement plan after another.

When the embassy finally took official notice of the breakup early in November 1960, by inviting Jim and Margaret West to " 'keep up appearances' " until their divorce was settled, to appear at certain public functions together, and give a luncheon, Margaret had agreed; 'keeping up appearances' was a lifeline in a disintegrating marriage. And Jim had complied. Nothing had been said about Mary McCarthy, who was then living incognito in Warsaw in a "remote traveling salesman's hotel," named, with delicious irony, the Grand Hotel, where Jim had recently installed her and himself across the hall for the two successive three-week visits permitted on a tourist visa. For them both, "the hideous room with flowered bedspreads and curtains decorated with Red stars and the listening device in the lighting fixture" had come to be regarded, especially after this latest imposition of embassy protocol, "as a tenderly loved home and refuge." It was "[a]s though we were living a peculiar modern idyll: intense love in extreme conditions, to be transcribed by the Secret Police," McCarthy wrote Hannah Arendt—alive, as always, to the melodrama in her life. But for Jim West the strain of the double life had become insupportable, and he had decided to take action.

In mid-November he had gone to the American ambassador, Jacob Beam, to announce that his marriage was over and that he hoped to marry Mary McCarthy as soon as possible. Indeed, the two of them had already picked out their furniture in Copenhagen for the new house that the embassy had assigned West pending his divorce from Margaret. ("The house is going to be very pretty, and in a different vein from the other houses I've had," Mary had written Hannah from the Grand Hotel on October 26, happy as a new bride. She had picked out "every item down to the last toilet-paper holder and soap dish. . . . You can't imagine how difficult it is in Denmark to find chairs and sofas to sit down on that don't look like manifestoes . . . and lighting fixtures that don't resemble sculpture. But it was fun," she exclaimed, and all on the embassy tab.) Mrs. West, meanwhile, would neither proceed with the divorce nor leave Warsaw.

Twice Jim and Margaret had reached agreement on the settlement terms and an Alabama divorce, with the concurrence of Margaret's parents, who had come to Poland, and twice she had reversed herself at the last minute. In one instance, she had gone to Paris to meet with her lawyer about the divorce, and taken an apartment for which Jim paid the first month's rent, and then suddenly returned, declaring that she would not leave Poland until the following spring. In another twist worthy of Noel Coward, Mary McCarthy would briefly take the same

Paris apartment in December, when her Polish visa ran out. (When Mary turned up with Jim in October to take measurements in the new Warsaw house, the Polish contractor had scratched his head in wonder; he had just finished repainting West's apartment with Margaret in it.) Under the circumstances, West told Ambassador Beam, he was ready to resign from the foreign service or ask for a transfer, whatever was needed to detach himself from his wife.

This time, the ambassador was sympathetic to Jim, and he ordered both West and Margaret to return to his office to hear an ultimatum. The Wests' marital troubles had become " 'an embarrassment to the Embassy,' " Beam said, and if Margaret West could not offer tangible proof in a few days that she was going to leave Poland by the end of December, he would have to order Jim West's immediate transfer. The next day, she had agreed (though her actual departure was delayed until the end of January 1961). A transfer would have undoubtedly taken her husband to Western Europe and cost him the four-thousand-dollar "hardship pay" the government tacked on to the annual salary of a foreign service officer serving behind the Iron Curtain, thus reducing the alimony and maintenance payments he could make to her. In a Western country, moreover, he might live openly with Mary McCarthy without a separation agreement and divorce, and not cause the scandal that their affair had already unleashed in Poland—where thanks to Margaret West's talk, in Mary's opinion, a rumor abounded that the Polish government was going to declare the philandering James West *persona non grata.* Privately, West doubted that the U.S. foreign service would tolerate such an arrangement anywhere, and if Margaret remained obdurate about the divorce, he would have to resign from government service altogether, a conclusion that, when he had discussed it with Jake Beam, had made him feel agreeably " 'small and light.' "

At forty-six, however, and with a career spent mainly in military and government service, the prospects for finding new employment appeared uncertain, or so McCarthy had worried privately in conversations with Hannah Arendt—who never could fathom what all the rush about getting divorced and remarried was all about. " 'Why do you have to marry him? Why can't you just live together?' " she demanded. But "I was always the marrying type, especially in this case, because of the children and the character of his ex-wife," McCarthy commented many years later. Hannah would be persuaded, but then faced with West's continuing struggle with his wife, she would announce gruffly, " 'You go to Europe and you establish yourself in Paris or Rome, or wherever you want; and then he will visit you and you'll be his mistress.' " Mary would have secured a divorce from Bowden, in this scenario, something that wouldn't have happened as quickly as it did without Hannah Arendt's patient intercession with Broadwater, who felt, understandably, that he had become overnight a *"quantité négligeable."* But there was no reason in Arendt's mind for Jim West to jeopardize the welfare of his children and his career for the sake of another marriage—his third, Mary's fourth. And until Mary and Jim were actually married in Paris in April 1961, and Hannah Arendt, who missed all of Mary McCarthy's weddings, was on her way to Jerusalem to report on the trial of Adolf Eichmann for *The New Yorker,* she never abandoned this scenario.

Mary's own career was nearing a takeoff, something that Bill Jovanovich, for one, was well aware of—not only because of handsome returns from both *Venice Observed* and *The Stones of Florence* but because of the commercial promise he discerned in the early chapters of *The Group.* And even while Mary McCarthy was shuttling from one hotel room and borrowed apartment to another throughout 1960, meeting Jim West for furloughs in London, Paris, Vienna, Rome, Zurich, and Copenhagen, separated from her books and typewriter, she had managed to edit fifteen years of essays and reviews for *On the Contrary,* which was published by Farrar, Straus and Cudahy in early 1961 to immediate critical acclaim.

Dwight Macdonald had been particularly impressed with this collection of criticism. Thanking Mary for some kind words about one of his fall 1961 movie columns in *The New Yorker,* he said he was glad she liked his stuff because he had, "as you must know by now, a great (and a healthy) respect for your opinion. Have been rereading On the Contrary. It seems even better than it did the first time." Robert Lowell was also appreciative. "It's odd," he wrote in a letter accompanying three plays he wanted Mary to critique, "some things can be said in print that can't be said in conversation . . . very important things that are dear to us. . . ." In *On the Contrary,* "it was as though you were talking, and the voice rose and surprises came."

What was new in *On the Contrary* were three essays at the end, "The Fact in Fiction," "Characters in Fiction," and "The American Realist Playwrights," each written up from the lectures McCarthy had given to audiences in Eastern Europe and the British Isles over the first three months of 1960. These audiences had sometimes included schoolchildren or retired workers, but usually Mary had addressed Writers

Union functionaries and their counterparts in English-speaking countries clustered around universities. With them, she set out what she had learned about literature—not from writing, for she didn't always practice what she preached, she admitted, but from reading.

"The staple ingredient present in all novels . . . is fact," because the novel really is, or was, a bearer of news, with many of the same functions of a newspaper, McCarthy argues in the first essay. "The Fact in Fiction" is studded with inviting references to Boccaccio, Defoe, Hugo, Balzac, Austen, Tolstoy and Dostoevsky, Henry James, Dickens, and Joyce. Dos Passos, D. H. Lawrence, Camus, Joyce Cary, and John Updike are treated in "Characters in Fiction." Both essays explore one of McCarthy's controlling ideas: that contemporary fiction has lost interest in the social, and thus suffers a nearly fatal depletion (e.g., 'the novel is dead'). Certain realities of modern life are 'stranger' than fiction, she points out—the use of nuclear weapons as tools of diplomacy, the actuality of Auschwitz—and thus somehow displace it, render it obsolete. "[T]he novel, with its common sense, is of all forms the least adapted to encompass the modern world, whose leading characteristic is irreality. . . . The souped-up novels that are being written today, with injections of myth and symbols to heighten or 'deepen' the material," she suggests (without naming them), "are simply evasions and forms of self-flattery."

Several versions of this idea—that reality has somehow displaced fiction—were bruited about during the mid-1960s, when frustrated novelists such as Norman Mailer, William Burroughs, and Truman Capote turned to public spectacle for inspiration. But it was Mary McCarthy who first drew attention to the failure of the modern novel to entertain the fantasies inherent in the daily news, even though her own fiction seemed to represent a regression to earlier forms. In "The Fact in Fiction," first published in the Summer 1960 *Partisan Review,* she might have been plugging *The Group* when she wrote: "if the breath of scandal has not touched it, the book is not a novel. That is the trouble with the art-novel (most of Virginia Woolf, for instance); it does not stoop to gossip." In this essay, McCarthy also got off some memorable one-liners: "The worst thing . . . that can happen to a writer today is to become a writer." And: "We know that the real world exists, but we can no longer imagine it."

Hannah Arendt was particularly pleased with the fact-in-fiction essay when she first read it in *Partisan Review.* "It is such a relief to read some sense on this matter instead of the more or less sophisticated nonsense to which we usually are treated," and to have it written "[v]ery carefully, precisely, often beautifully," she wrote Mary. Writing Hannah back at the end of August 1960 from Bocca di Magra, a small fishing village on the border of Liguria and Tuscany, popular with French and Italian intellectuals, Mary was grateful for the praise. The only other person who had read the essay, not counting *PR*'s editor William Phillips, "who niggled rather," was Jim West, who liked it, she said, "but he is not literary, besides being in love." She was always honored to have a fan letter from Hannah, starting with the first in 1949 about *The Oasis*. "The sensation of being honored," she assured her, "doesn't diminish with familiarity."

II

Bocca di Magra was to become one of Mary McCarthy's sacred groves over the next seven years, and for a few weeks at the end of the summer of 1960, the town, which stands at the mouth of the Magra River and faces the gleaming Apuan Alps, had given her some time out from love. After a strenuous "vacation" together in an embassy car that broke down all the way across Czechoslovakia, Germany, France, and back again, Mary and Jim had " 'got to know each other' (the car too)," she wrote Arendt in New York; though most of their time had been spent in garages (nineteen), or standing by the side of the road, or being pushed, or towed. It was a real test, and love had passed it.

In Bocca di Magra, meanwhile, "a very affectionate place," McCarthy had regrouped with some familiar faces: Miriam and Nicola Chiaromonte, Mario and Angélique Levi ("Anjou," later McCarthy's French translator and close friend), and Carmen Angleton, who arrived after her summer in Venice, full of gossip about Bowden Broadwater—who had also summered in Venice, and lived with Gregory Corso. Mary was all ears, and not so caught up in her new life as to be untroubled by the loss of the old.

Broadwater, who had taken Mary McCarthy's sudden departure very hard, doggedly resisting the finality of it at first and then anguishing openly over the loss ("It was a terrible shock to Bowden, he was desperately hurt," Daphne Hellman states), had spent a runaway summer with the poets of the Beat generation. With Corso ("not a homosexual," Mary wrote Hannah, but Hannah corrected her), Bowden had been very active socially, "very malicious," according to Carmen, who felt that he "had acquired the confidence of having 'established himself' . . . though not in high society." Hannah had nurtured "a little fond hope for him and Carmen," and after Carmen's visit, Mary wrote: "I can't convince myself that there's any possibility of her marrying Bowden, especially since she reports such details about him as that he's started lying about his age," which was forty—while his new friends were in their late twenties.

Not Carmen but Bowden's apparent turnabout now invaded Mary's happiness, and began to fester, like the pea underneath the princess's mattress, working its way to semiconsciousness in the form of anger that this husband of thirteen years seemed to have forgotten her so quickly. Carmen had also suggested that Bowden had begun to sleep with "casual women," but that he would try to keep it a secret because it contradicted his line about not giving Mary a divorce because he believed in "monogamy." And Mary was doubly incensed, pronouncing Bowden's behavior "unprincipled."

Arendt urged her to discount "Carmen's gossip," something she seemed as incapable of doing as she had been unable to resist Bowden Broadwater's gossip; and then Hannah noted that if she had any suspicion about Bowden's sexual inclinations, it would not lie in " 'the casual woman' " direction; nor, of course, was Carmen a possibility. "The sad truth of the matter is that he loves you and that he has discovered this in a sense only après coup, after you left him," she said. It wasn't very likely that this was going to change very fast, no matter whom Bowden slept with; and it also had nothing to do with principles, Arendt added, "such as 'belief in monogamy.' " She hoped Bowden's true feeling wouldn't come as a shock to Mary—"it really should not. And God knows I don't like this role of having to report what he tells me, etc.," she exclaimed; but she was afraid Mary might "make mistakes" unless she knew exactly what she was up against.

Mary couldn't hear it. Maybe it was the wear and tear of the life she was leading, or maybe it was Carmen Angleton's influence— " 'Sorry, the Mrs. has run off with the silver,' " was another tale she told on Bowden, reportedly said to dinner guests in the Ninety-fourth Street apartment, which made McCarthy furious—but she couldn't shake off the unreasonable idea that it was Bowden who had somehow abandoned *her*. "I do not agree with you that he loves me," she wrote Arendt from Rome, where she had gone to stay with Carmen after Bocca di Magra, before pushing on to Warsaw and the rendezvous with Jim West at the Grand Hotel. "If he did he would not have sat in Venice all summer making spiteful remarks about me and drinking cocktails and leading a bravura social life; he would have tried . . . to see me, which would not have been hard. Or written me in a friendly way. At least to find out how I was." Naturally, he had been hurt, McCarthy conceded, and his behavior reflected that. But "he finds it less painful and more dignified . . . to say that he loves me than to say that he has been hurt. He has entered the love-competition," she asserted, "and is playing a solo part in it—the man who loves . . . all alone on the stage." Even Jim West had been certain that Bowden would try to see her, and she thought so, too, and knew she would have to say yes, even if Jim didn't like it. "And I thought my heart would be wrung if I saw him in Rome, where we'd been together so many years ago," she said. But this scene was not to be enacted. She was spared. "But he did not spare me out of kindness," McCarthy snapped.

For the first few months, the affair with Jim West and the move to Europe had actually shaken Bowden and Mary out of their customary roles, and they had confided in each other as they never had before, as if the 'new man' was an episode in their own relationship, a growing pain. At first, Bowden "had no great opinion of Jim as a possible rival," seeing him as "a very ordinary-seeming diplomat," Carmen Angleton recalls. Bowden had reminded Mary that love for her was more intense than durable—"enchantment and disenchantment *is* you and the spring of your talent and energy." It was so much a part of her, he observed shrewdly, that in *The Stones of Florence,* she was "compelled to present the facsimile of disenchantment to allow the real love to follow." Most of their friends were unwilling to accept the reality of her new affair, except philistines like Mannie Rousuck, he wrote, or Becket-like characters such as Carmen Angleton. (This was true—the new alliance shocked everyone, including brother Kevin.)

Still, Bowden thought about Mary every waking moment and dreamed of her every night. "You are here and I am in Rome," he said of the dreams, whose wish-fulfillment quotient was high—except in one revealing episode, dreamed in a fever when he had caught the mumps at the end of May. In this dream, Bowden saw himself helping Mary into a steely blue-gray plane. She wore a cowled version of her brown Dior dress. "We were in the clouds; I seemed to be an angel . . ." he wrote her. "In the second scene, the plane was ascending over New York," and he was "peacefully floating away in the left fore-corner of the picture, with my fingertips inserted in some sort of exhaust vents in the wing tip. I noted that if I kept my fingers far enough inside to secure myself, I both burnt my fingers and made the engines cough." In the dream, he had looked around for another hold but couldn't find one. "The plane went higher; the city was a paler blue and green; the air was getting colder; I thought, not worrying, I will have to do something eventually." And then he woke up.

Shortly before that, he had tried to console himself by relishing the scene of Mary in love, seeing her eyes on Jim, "drawing out his thread and weaving it into glowing tapestry"; enjoying it because it made her so "very fresh and dewy and really quite without compare." He would almost let her go in peace, Bowden wrote, but for a stubborn grasping at the person he loved, and also because while he liked to " 'see' " her in love, he knew that she would always tell herself stories, "like a child in bed. . . ." She was at "a classic moment when women will themselves into love," he commented, something she would surely see in another woman; and the opportunities for self-deception were high. Broadwater was curious to know whether Jim West thought he was the man Mary believed he was. He had his own doubts about the judgment of someone who had fathered three children with a woman he professed never to have loved; "he might be a *very good* man," he conceded, "but it truly seems unlikely that he is the same one. And since you're either to have the next twenty-five years with him, or a short and awkward interval," he wondered if she knew what she was doing.

It was a serious question, and Mary promised to ask Jim, "in all honesty, if he feels the discrepancy between him as he is and my image." And then she was impelled to say that her image of Bowden hadn't changed very much from when they had first met. "It's true that I took your faults (e.g., your passion for society and habit of cold disparagement) more lightly then, but I wasn't blind to them," she said. There were two Bowdens, she thought, one an "attitudinizing" self and the other, the "primary self, very fine, brave, gentle, intelligent," which resembled a "concealed drawer which opens only to certain touches." In the last few years, that drawer had been shut tight, and she had been left with the "social self, whose company (I'll be truthful) has been a little wearying. This is the explanation . . . of my friendship with Roberto [Papi] and my affair with J.D.," she added: "a sense of being shriveled, prematurely, by prolonged contact with a dry and withering element."

She didn't want to speak of Bowden's faults, however; for six weeks after she and Carmen had packed her trunk in New York, she could think only of her fondness for Bowden, which seemed to grow more tender as he receded into the distance. To Hannah Arendt, she had written about how Bowden had said "he never knew he wanted or loved anything before. But now he knows there is just one thing: me." McCarthy was aware of an "element of dramatization," but the "picture of a morally reeducated . . . Bowden makes me smile as one would at a dear child," and she had chosen to believe it.

"Meanwhile and as a strange soaring trumpet-music to this growing tenderness I feel for Bowden," she wrote Hannah, "my love for Jim is increasing till I am quite dizzy." She felt herself changing, "or perhaps that is not the right word, coming to life in a new way, like somebody who has been partly paralyzed." And this appeared to make her more sensitive to the feelings of others—if those feelings concerned her. "You will not believe how painfully sorry I am that I have done this to you," she wrote Bowden by the end of May. "Can't you, *can't* you fall in love with someone else and remember me as I remember you?" To which a sadder and wiser husband replied, "There's no chance of my falling in love for I already am, and, well, I am what I am."

Around the same time, McCarthy was moved to tell Bowden Broadwater all about Jim West, whose identity she had concealed at first (to hide the affair from the embassy and Mrs. West); about how he reminded her of the McCarthy men, and Kevin McCarthy, in particular. She had gone further with Bowden than with Edmund Wilson, noting how Jim West had also been farmed out to relatives who were "crooked, like ours, and spent the money that was supposed to go for his upkeep on themselves. One difference was that he was not beaten," Mary noted. His chief punishment had been his grandfather's disapproval; and his grandfather had been the only one he admired, which prompted her to reflect that "[t]here always seems to be one good man in these stories too." The effect of Jim's experience was "a kind of solitariness, behind a convivial bonhomie," she said, "and this solitariness" was what she fell in love with. And then she added, apropos of Jim's losing his own children when he left Margaret: "He sees of course that he's about to repeat his own orphaning."

By the summer of 1960, Mary was still confiding in Bowden , and still mulling over the old problem of "identity." During the weeks when she was "totally alone, far from finding my identity," she said, "I lose it and become simply a collection of small actions and motor responses." Writing Hannah in January 1961, after Broadwater had finally broken off contact—calling Mary's "chatty letters with their show of false concern, confused thought, and appeals to 'sentiment' . . . extremely disillusioning"—she wondered, briefly, whether she had unwittingly become the sort of person Bowden's accusations fit. "My 'I'—[not] my ego but the self I thought I was familiar with—has become rather battered in the past few months, so that I hardly recognize it when it talks," she said. It was partly the fault of the moving about from one uncongenial spot to another, but also the result of love, she thought, "which does seem to have the faculty of taking your identity away from you and not always in the way the poets mention." She was doing her best to steady herself, "to work and resist nightmare fugues," she told Arendt ('work' being the last essay in *On the Contrary,* "The American Realist Playwrights"); and this, of course, was how the question of identity was usually resolved.

In the nightmare fugue to Hannah Arendt, McCarthy revealed another stratagem she had perfected in the battle for salvation: martyrdom. "Whenever I cry and afterwards reproach myself for weakness, I say to myself sharply, 'You never would have been able to stand a concentration camp.' . . . Perhaps it is always martyrdom, in one form or another, that one childishly feels one must ready one's soul for." A concentration camp, of course, was the last thing McCarthy had to fear; nor would she ever be thrown to the lions for her faith in a higher power. Imagining her own extinction, more than the loss or pain of someone else, even a husband, seemed to pinch where it hurt, and restore her to herself. If she didn't crack under the fear of death, how could she bow under criticism?

Back in the summer of 1960, when the letters between Mary and Bowden still flew back and forth, McCarthy had filed her stories from abroad as if nothing had changed. Zurich was a civic paradise that "made Rome look like Gimbel's basement"; and she told Broadwater about a Swiss convention on terrorism that Ignazio Silone recalled from the 1920s when he was engaged in clandestine activities in Zurich, which treated terrorism as an occupation, like carpentry or shoemaking. From Bocca di Magra in September, she wrote that during an earlier visit she and Bowden had missed the " 'right part,' the marble rocks and pebbled deserted beaches where one goes . . . to swim." In this tireless reporting, she resembled a popular turn-of-the-century Seattle novelist, Elizabeth Champney, who wrote some forty books about the adventures of three Vassar girls abroad: *Three Vassar Girls in England, Three Vassar Girls in France, . . . at Home, . . . on the Rhine, . . . in Russia and Turkey,* in which the history and political problems of the countries involved are carefully set out, alongside tales of international intrigue and run-ins with spies. All of which also entered Mary McCarthy's adventures in 1960.

III

Before the correspondence with Bowden ended, McCarthy had written him about getting an invitation, fare and expenses paid, to the Congress for Cultural Freedom conference in West Berlin in the middle of June. The 1960 conference (dubbed "Progress in Freedom," with 230 participants from fifty countries), marked the ten-year anniversary of the Congress's founding, and getting asked hadn't been easy. Only after Nicola Chiaromonte intervened had Mary received her invitation from Nicholas Nabokov, the CCF director whose tall, craggy figure dominated the six-day affair.

The Berlin conference was just the kind of "gathering-in of old friends and new ones," as McCarthy described it in a letter to Hannah Arendt, "which had a sort of millenial character, including the separation of the sheep from the goats," that Mary most enjoyed. West Berlin seemed very unreal, "like Coney Island transported into East Germany," she remarked, "and in its unreality, precisely fitted for such Congresses," which took place in the mammoth Kongresshalle. Her favorite moment was a noisy showdown in a panel on "Modernity and Tradition" over the question of mass culture between the sociologist Edward Shils and William Phillips, in which Shils, who was the chair, defended mass-mediated culture as a showcase for American democracy, and Phillips, along with John Kenneth Galbraith, attacked it for its flimflam and conformism. This one time, McCarthy had found herself in Phillips's corner, and when he was ejected from the hall, she had stalked out with him, after denouncing Shils as a Dr. Pangloss (*Candide*'s Dr. Feelgood) without his innocence.

Arendt was piqued with Mary's cavalier references to the city: "West Berlin is unreal though not quite like Coney Island," she wrote back, "but it is not unreal to me, and should not be. I would have been ashamed to be in Berlin in a crowd of celebrities." She had "half promised" someone in the Willy Brandt government to come to Berlin to discuss "actual political topics" with students and young trade union members from both East and West Berlin, she informed McCarthy crisply. "I may do it this winter," she said (and did). Hannah had a healthy distaste for the grandstanding common at Congress affairs, but she seemed to relish Mary's reports, which in June 1960 included an account of CBS's Frank Stanton's avowal that "Shakespeare, if he were living now, would be writing for television," together with a description of an unnerving encounter with the nuclear physicist Robert Oppenheimer, who had called the Congress "sinful."

Oppenheimer, who was welcomed to the fold in the middle 1950s, along with another Establishment renegade, George F. Kennan (who also spoke in West Berlin), told Mary that he had sent a "message" to the Chinese people in his opening address, specifically in a sentence about how in a nuclear war, no country would have enough living to bury their dead. "Paranoid megalomania and a sense of divine mission," she had diagnosed. ("If he actually believes the Chinese need his cryptogram to know what every scientific and non-scientific magazine can tell them, he must be insane," Arendt replied.) "Communism," *Time* magazine would say of the Berlin conference afterwards, "was scarcely mentioned at all."

Warsaw, where Mary went to stay a few weeks with Jim after Berlin, had seemed "real, pretty, and almost pastoral, shimmering in a deep summer green of thick vines, with pots of red and white geraniums lining the streets . . . and a gold Bellotto light in the churches." It was love that brought the color streaming back into McCarthy's letters. She was in the kind of love that "doesn't appear to be an emotion you feel but an element you've been submerged in. A fixed element like time or space. Do *not* worry," she told Hannah: "all is well." She just felt so "comfortable, strangely, as if I belonged here. . . ."

Tucked away in a hotel (not yet the Grand), she had awaited Jim's arrival every day at noon and again at 5:15, when, "very domestically," he brought the day's magazines and papers, the office gossip, and sometimes a parcel of raspberries stashed in his briefcase. Domesticity—Jim's, not hers—had worked on her like an aphrodisiac. Driving out to see the West children early one evening, where they were encamped with their nurse in a summer cabin on a bluff by a broad river, she was enthralled when Jim sat down on a stool to cut their toenails and the hair around the youngest one's ears, "very competent, concentrated and yet laughing." Jim and Mary had brought provisions from Warsaw and presents from Vienna, and everyone was gay and buoyant, including the driver and the nurse, who had presented Mary with a pink rose and a dish of fresh cherries. When they went back to Jim's place for dinner (Margaret was in Paris), it was the same; "the cook was in a transport of smiles and she was humming in the kitchen," the first time Jim had heard her do this. "All this, of course, is a tribute to him and the reverse of a tribute to Madame. But (perhaps I'm being sentimental) it seems also more than that," she suggested to Hannah, "and as felt by the children too—a recognition of something good."

She was not so exalted by love as to miss the irony in the fact that while everyone was rejoicing, "as if only good could come out of this occasion, which of course is not true," she and Jim were tightening the bonds that would take him away from his children. ("The mother in a case like this . . . has the right to the custody of the children," she reminded Hannah earlier, when Arendt, upon hearing of Margaret West's plan to send the two older children to separate boarding schools, had wondered whether perhaps they shouldn't all remain with their father.) But finally Mary had found it impossible to see the problem in "any traditional way, as a conflict between love and duty . . . the very idea of a conflict appears implausible," she observed, "and the fact that the children will undoubtedly suffer does not appear as a fact."

In the end, she and Jim West had both gotten Alabama divorces with surprising rapidity. But when it had appeared as if Jim was about to get his divorce, and Bowden was holding out, Mary had momentarily lost her balance. The situation had become "harrowing," she wrote Hannah. Love apart, there was the impossibility of making plans for the future, the lack of a place to live, the separation from books and papers. And then there was the prospect of Jim, having gotten his divorce, and sent his children away, living alone in Warsaw. "And I will be where?" she wondered; not with him, for she could only get a three-week visitor's visa to enter Poland; and Jim, stripped of his income by alimony payments, would be unable to travel.

It was then that she had 'made mistakes,' and the histrionic note that sometimes appears in McCarthy's letters from abroad had leapt to the fore. With Bowden, who had seized on McCarthy's imperious demands for an immediate divorce in the fall of 1960 as a chance to interject his own forlorn interests, and threatened to withhold his consent for a year, Mary was "tremulous with anger, disappointment, and incredulity. Yes, incredulity," she exclaimed to Arendt. She couldn't see how Bowden could possibly justify "this refusal" to himself, much less to someone else, someone like Hannah, for instance— "(and I may as well say this)," she tumbled on: "It strikes me . . . that he has somehow persuaded you that he is right."

This was indeed the side of love the poets didn't mention. "I am more deeply in love with Jim than ever and vice versa, and it is simply too ridiculous for us to be the passive foils of other people," McCarthy had written Arendt a few weeks later from the Grand Hotel in Warsaw (after the shopping spree in Copenhagen). But Bowden Broadwater had already agreed to the divorce, thanks to Hannah Arendt's efforts as a mediator. And now, patiently, with her own exasperation sternly held in check, Hannah addressed herself to Mary's charge that she had somehow "condoned" Bowden—"which to me does not make sense one way or another," she declared, but there were things she did not understand. "As I see it," she began, in a letter which is a masterstroke of personal diplomacy:

> Bowden has not delayed . . . your marriage or anything you wanted to do by one week or by one day or even by one hour. This could happen only if he would refuse the divorce after Jim West has received his divorce. This was the reason why I never understood that you wanted to press this point. Obviously, he is not only not omnipotent but utterly powerless, and you know as well as I do that under such circumstances it is only natural for people to dream up some possibilities of power. . . .
>
> Since I wanted to persuade him, I have seen quite a bit of him during the last few weeks. I could do this only my way and I am sadly aware of the fact that it was not the way you would have wanted me to do it. The alternative was to let things well enough alone, and this I did not dare to do because it seemed as though I had some influence. Hence, I talked to him without any threats. . . . I talked to him as a friend and I did not lie. For to me the fact is that you brought him into my life, that without you he never would have become—not a personal friend which, of course, he is not—but a friend of the house, so to speak. But once you placed him there, you cannot simply take him away. . . .

So long as Bowden didn't do something truly "outrageous" or really turn against Mary, Arendt continued, she wasn't going to sit in judgment. "That his life is in ruins is quite obvious to anybody who's willing to have a look at him and his situation," she said, adding that if he were to commit suicide, which she thought was "not probable but not altogether impossible either," she would be the first to tell Mary that she was not to blame. But it wasn't exactly a time "when one feels like adding insult to injury." Whatever Bowden may have said in his most recent letters to Mary, Arendt had counseled her to begin divorce proceedings through her lawyer. And then she let fly another arrow, which, if it ever hit the mark, McCarthy's correspondence doesn't say. "You say you cannot trust him," Arendt said, referring to Mary's suggestion that Bowden might agree to play his part in the divorce, and then back out at the last minute:

Perhaps you are right, perhaps you are wrong. . . . But it strikes me that you can forget so easily that you trusted him enough to be married to him for fifteen years. Or to put it another way: You write that it is just "too ridiculous" for the two of you (Jim West and you) to be "the passive foils of other people." If you want to look at the matter in these terms . . . then it seems to me rather obvious that you both are the victims of your own, self-chosen past. This may be inconvenient but it is not ridiculous, unless you wish to say that your whole past was not only a mistake, but a ridiculous one.

"Thank you for your intervention with Bowden," McCarthy replied from the Grand Hotel in Warsaw. "I didn't know what had persuaded him to change . . . and was inclined to think that perhaps Reuel's letters to him had had some influence." Period. "As for me," she went on, "my love has become boundless or, rather, very definitely bounded and contained by these four walls."

In January 1961, Bowden Broadwater agreed to sign the separation papers before Margaret West went to Alabama; and at the last minute, he proposed going to Montgomery himself. There would be less publicity for Mary if he got the divorce, and it would only cost her his fare and legal expenses, he suggested. But the real reason was that he couldn't stomach the charge of cruelty that McCarthy (with the help of her Paris lawyer) had lodged against him. He would charge her with desertion, he said, which would be both true and innocuous. As it turned out, McCarthy made the trip a week after Margaret West did.

In the fall of 1960, meanwhile, her love may have been bounded by four walls in the Grand Hotel, but she was not. In Warsaw, McCarthy had already begun to throw out new shoots; to discover a fresh image of herself in yet another city and, remarkably, to pick up the unfinished manuscript of *The Group*. Stepping out of the cramped little room with the bug in the light, she had mingled in the afternoons with the "colorless crowds, milling along the grey streets"; her own anonymity, the chrysalis of a new chapter unfolding in her life, corresponding somehow to the anonymous character of the modern socialist state.

She had begun to think about the years she hoped to spend in Poland with Jim after they got their divorces (two years remained to his assignment). "I would have these dreams where we're living there in Warsaw and . . . we hardly see anybody," she said years later, "and I'm reading Hegel. I'm just sitting there reading Hegel." It would be a period of reflection, she thought, a quiet time, when she would study philosophy. In the mornings, McCarthy had busied herself with the novel begun in the icy dawn of the Eisenhower administration eight years before, and revived in the summer of 1959. Briefly, in Bocca di Magra, she had pulled out the chapter where Harald Petersen loses his job, and reworked it. "It's rather like a certain kind of embroidery stitch where you go back with your needle each time before advancing," she had observed then. Now she began to draw in the net. "From then on it really didn't stop," she said later. "That was it. In the Grand Hotel."

29

On the Road

*"All of us reason about and understand what
people necessarily must be; we dream about, are bewitched
by, what they accidentally and incomprehensibly are."*

—RANDALL JARRELL, PICTURES FROM AN INSTITUTION

*L*ife didn't settle down with marriage to Jim West, which took place on April 15, 1961, as planned, in a Paris "leafy and light, like spring millinery." Far from it. The ceremony was preceded by weeks of upheaval, while Mary McCarthy, self-professed "perpetual motion machine," shuttled from the divorce court in Montgomery, Alabama, early in February, to Dobbs Ferry, New York, to see Kevin and his family and old friends. From there, she had gone to meet Jim in Copenhagen to order the last of the furnishings for the new house in Warsaw; after which she returned to Paris to deliver a lecture before pushing on to Rome to pack up the books and clothes she had stored with Carmen Angleton.

It was during a second reunion with her brother in Dobbs Ferry in February 1962, when the Wests and the McCarthys gave a party for Sonia Orwell, that Mary cooked up a cassoulet Toulouse much talked about at the time, requiring three geese, fifteen pounds of beans, and three days to prepare. Dinner was followed by a program of theatricals, presented by such amateurs as Robert Lowell, Arthur Miller, Niccolò Tucci, Kevin McCarthy, and Zero Mostel. In February 1961, as in 1962, Kevin's house served as a base camp for Mary's forays into Manhattan, which was full of "a kind of parrot-talk about politics, sex, Norman Mailer," she reported to Hannah Arendt, then lecturing at Northwestern University. Only Robert

Lowell, Cal to friends, who was in between breakdowns, and Philip Rahv, who everyone else said had become a "gloomy monster," had made McCarthy feel rich in personal connections. Philip had brought her up-to-date on the latest gossip ("a sub-literary genre," he wrote her once, "in which fancy is . . . a small ingredient garnishing a piece of truth"). After attending one of Lillian Hellman's parties, which he rarely missed, he told her how he had suddenly realized there was no young "cadre of writers to replace people in our generation."

Somehow, in the midst of all the visiting, in a household with three children and four telephones constantly ringing, Mary had managed to get out a review of Camus's collected work for the London *Observer*. She had taken the assignment, she suggested to Elisabeth Niebuhr a few weeks later in Paris, because she had run into another snag with *The Group;* one that made her wonder whether what she was writing wasn't something other than a novel-satire maybe. Reviewing Camus's fiction gave her a chance to reflect on "the question of the novel in general," as well as a break from fiction writing, which was always harder to do than criticism. Reading all of Camus would allow her to decide "what I think about him finally," McCarthy told Niebuhr, noting that she had wound up as baffled as ever by Sartre's old rival— who had been killed the year before in an automobile accident at the age of forty-seven.

The critical piece had prompted a candid reflection on her own fiction: "I'm not sure any of my books are novels. Maybe none of them are," McCarthy states in the *Paris Review* interview. "Something happens in my writing," something she doesn't intend, "—a sort of distortion, a sort of writing on the bias, seeing things with a . . . swerve and swoop." It was the kind of slant that led Mary Meigs to see "a writer's witchcraft" at work in the construction of Dolly Lamb. In the beginning of *A Charmed Life,* McCarthy had tried simply to introduce the characters and set the scene for an old-fashioned New England town, she told Niebuhr, but immediately the writing had been colored by a jaundiced eye.

A similar distortion had entered *The Group.* If the eight Vassar girls appeared frozen in time, which to Mary they did in the spring of 1961, when she still hoped to bring them from Roosevelt's inauguration to Eisenhower's inauguration (a plan abandoned in the novel), perhaps it was because they were "all essentially comic figures," she reflects, "and it's awfully hard to make anything happen to them." Comic characters, including villains, are always "*fige, are immortal.*" Heroes and heroines exist and develop in time because they are equipped with purpose; comic characters, on the other hand, appear eternally yoked to fate, which unfolds not in time but in the social sphere, in behavior. When drawing her own characters, McCarthy tried to be "as exact as possible about the essence of a person," she assured Niebuhr, "to find the key that works the person both in real life and in the fiction." Thus she could hardly object when people played "the *roman à clef* game with [her] novels. . . ." But this was part of the problem, though McCarthy doesn't say it. The hunt for a single "key," an "essence," almost always leads to caricature.

The Camus review had met the second and third of three requirements that Mary McCarthy set for undertaking a critical essay: that it "be some sort of thing that I want very much to take sides on, or something I'd like to study a bit. . . . Or where there may, in the case of study, be some reference—very indirect—back to my own work." A review of Kenneth Tynan's *Curtains*, "Drapes," she titled it, written for *The Observer* the following year, met the first requirement. As England's leading drama critic, the young Tynan presented a tempting morsel for McCarthy's appetite for controversy; and she chided him for his tendency "to write advertising copy" instead of criticism: to promote his favorite people and pet ideas, much as a salesman pumps his product and spikes the competition.

"Rational discourse is not Tynan's strong point," McCarthy proposed; though she couldn't help but enjoy his parodies when they took off on Graham Greene or William Faulkner's overheated prose in *Requiem for a Nun* (Tynan: " 'Down behind the morgue a few of the young people are roastin' a nigger over an open fire, but I guess every town has its night owls' "). It was his " 'quotable' " praise of Tennessee Williams and Arthur Miller—" 'the finest two playwrights at present writing in English' "—that prompted a sharp rap on the knuckles, and a plug for one of her own friends. Kenneth Tynan might belong to "the school of wits" that included Beerbohm, Benchley, George Jean Nathan, and Wolcott Gibbs, McCarthy declared, and he was much better than the average drama critic, but he would not bear comparison "with, today, Nicola Chiaromonte in Italy. . . ."

" 'Isn't it *awful* to be in your forties and still find yourself attacking people?' " Elizabeth Hardwick remarked to McCarthy around this time, thinking as much of herself. " 'Wouldn't you rather just write nice things about people you enjoy reading?' " And Mary reportedly replied, " 'Oh Lord yes, I know just what you mean. I don't want to do it. It's something for young people to do. *But they don't do it!*' " This ignored some lively criticism in *The Observer*, *The Nation*, and

Esquire during these years, but there were no new Mary McCarthys or Elizabeth Hardwicks grappling up the garden wall, and really never would be. McCarthy, in any case, had a reputation to protect: one memorialized by Randall Jarrell in *Pictures from an Institution*, in which the character everyone took for Mary, Gertrude Johnson, "whose bark *was* her bite," is admired by many of her readers "in the tones of butchers from Gopher prairie admiring the Murderer of Düsseldorf; they could not mention [her] style without using the vocabulary of a salesman of kitchen knives." McCarthy might not 'want' to attack, but when her 'fatal audience-sense' smelled fresh controversy, she went for the jugular.

"Who would've thought the young man had so much blood in him?" Brock Brower asked in a July 1962 *Esquire* article entitled "Mary McCarthyism," referring to Tynan's naked corpse, "left for dead in the blood-stained alley behind *Partisan Review*," after Mary had "pinked him mortally. . . ." Jarrell was right about the kitchen-knife vocabulary (though Gertrude was only "the same general type as Mary McCarthy," he wrote Philip Rahv; "readers who knew Jean Stafford best think she's Gertrude . . ."). In *Esquire*'s special issue on "The American Woman," whose "Three Interesting Ladies" featured Jacqueline Kennedy, Brenda Lee, and Mary McCarthy, even Mary's famous smile is depicted as a "subtle emanation of the mind: the poised cutting edge on one of the most knifelike female intelligences. . . ."

Kenneth Tynan, however, with his profiles of Bea Lillie, Gordon Craig, and Tennessee Williams, on the one hand, and didactic "crotchets" ("the drama should show 'respect for ordinary people' "), on the other, represented a wave of the future in the early 1960s. As did Norman Mailer, another contemporary whose literary reviews, collected in *Cannibals and Christians,* like many of Tynan's theater reviews ("excited performances," McCarthy called the latter), were not critical exercises so much as displays of temperament—and none so tempestuous as "The Mary McCarthy Case," Mailer's review of *The Group* in *The New York Review of Books* in October 1963. ("These pissass characters with their cultivated banalities, their lack of variety or ambition, perversion, simple greed or depth of feeling . . . Yes, our Mary's a sneak.")

It was Elizabeth Hardwick who would give her old friend the Tynan treatment with a parody of *The Group,* entitled "The Gang," and signed Xavier Prynne; a more 'awful' attack than McCarthy's Tynan review, because, as McCarthy herself observed of *Curtains:* "No author can be parodied successfully who has not already commit-

PRECEDING PAGE: *Mary McCarthy, caught in a candid moment by her new husband, James West, summer 1961.*
ABOVE: *McCarthy leaves the scene of her fourth marriage, with West, in Paris, April 15, 1961.*
LEFT: *At the wedding party in Orgeval, the guests included (left to right) James Jones, Janet Flanner, Rosamund Bernier, and Peter Harnden.*

*Waiting for the wedding couple to emerge from town hall: K. A. (Kot) Jelenski,
Mario and Angélique Levi, Georges Bernier, Janet Flanner, Rosamond Bernier,
and unidentified woman.*

Mary McCarthy and Carmen Angleton, an American friend living in Rome, picnicking during a summer 1960 excursion in the Italian Alps.

Jim and Mary West take the West children, Alison, Daniel, and Jonathan, with their nurse, Maria, for a carriage ride in Paris, around 1962.

Peggy Guggenheim, the subject of a wicked portrait in McCarthy's story "The Cicerone," welcomes Mary to her palazzo on the Grand Canal in Venice, 1965.

ABOVE: *McCarthy joins forces with Nicola Chiaromonte, gesturing, at a left-wing CIA-backed literary conference in Madrid, 1963.*
RIGHT: *Mary McCarthy and Stephen Spender talk at the Wests' weekend house outside Paris in the mid-1960s.*

LEFT: *W. H. Auden and Mary McCarthy address a cultural convention in Vienna, 1967.*
BELOW: *Mary and Miriam Chiaromonte at the beach in Bocca di Magra, where the Wests spent their summer vacations in the mid-1960s.*

ABOVE: *Nathalie Sarraute and Mary McCarthy meeting at the Cafe Flore in the summer of 1966.*
BELOW: *Janet Flanner and McCarthy in Paris around the same time.*

Mary McCarthy visited Vietnam in 1967 and 1968 to write about the war.
In North Vietnam, ABOVE, she is helped across a stream.
BELOW: *With another American, Franz Schurman, she meets Prime Minister*
Pham Van Dong.

ABOVE: *Journalist Bernard Fall with Mary McCarthy in Danang, South Vietnam.*
Fall was killed by a land mine shortly after this photo was taken, in February 1967.
BELOW: *McCarthy surveys a bombed neighborhood outside Hanoi, March 1968.*

ABOVE: *McCarthy at the 1973 Watergate Hearings in Washington, D.C.*
BELOW: *With Dutch friends at a meeting of Parliament in the Hague, 1975:*
Liesbeth List, Cees Nooteboom, Mary, Hans van Mierlo, Harry Mulisch.

ABOVE: *The political philosopher Hannah Arendt, Mary's confidante and intellectual mentor for twenty-five years. When Arendt died in 1975, McCarthy dropped her own work to edit Arendt's final lectures for* The Life of the Mind.

TOP: *McCarthy with some of her roses in Castine, Maine.*
ABOVE: *Robert Silvers, Robert Lowell, Elizabeth Hardwick, and Mary McCarthy, picnicking on Penobscot Bay, 1969.*

ROLLIE MCKENNA

ABOVE: *At dinner in the Wests' house in Castine (pictured* BELOW RIGHT, *with the 1963 Mercedes in the driveway) are (clockwise) Lillah McCarthy (Kevin McCarthy's daughter), Hannah Arendt, Mary, and Kevin.*
BELOW LEFT: *Lillah, Kate McCarthy (Kevin's second wife), Jim West, Alison West (Jim's daughter), Flip McCarthy (Kevin's son), and Mary, 1979.*

ABOVE: *Mary with Elizabeth Hardwick in Peterborough, N.H., where Hardwick presented McCarthy with the 1984 McDowell Medal "for her outstanding contribution to literature."* LEFT: *Castine visitors Sandra and George Weidenfeld, Mary, and Kot Jelenski, in the summer of 1970.*

Philip Rahv, fond of berating the "rural idiocy" of country life, out for a sail on Jim West's boat.

ABOVE: *Kevin and Mary, on the porch of the house Bard College made available to her when she held the Charles Stevenson Chair of Literature (1986 to 1989).*
LEFT: *Mary and Jim, tying up in Castine's harbor.*

ABOVE: *Mary McCarthy, a few years before her death on October 25, 1989.* RIGHT: *At the New York Public Library in 1984, McCarthy was awarded the National Medal for Literature. Top to bottom: With presenter, Brooke Astor; with former Vassar president, Virginia Smith, and assistant, Robert Pounder; with old friends, Arthur Schlesinger, Jr., and Stephen Spender.*

ted self-parody." (Words failed Hardwick when she wrote Mary McCarthy after first reading *The Group* in August 1963. Casting about for an acceptably 'critical' expression of her dismay, which leaks through the lines, she suggests: "The technical problem of *The Group* is not so much who is speaking, but who is being addressed." And concludes, lamely, "What I want to say is congratulations," but she cannot say it.)

With reviews and parodies such as these, a new chapter in American literary life had begun, one in which the prominent reviewer wielded more power than the author, not because of the priestly functions of criticism but because fewer people took reading and writing seriously, and thus reviewers got the last word—especially when they were also famous authors, blocked, for the moment, from the 'creative stuff.' Dealing in reputations rather than texts put them in the cockpit in a world where reputation, meaning celebrity, was the common coin of realm.

When Mary McCarthy finally returned to Paris in March 1961 to get married, a mountain of paperwork still stood between her and the wedding. Sworn documents, secured from the American embassy and consulate, had to be presented to the French Ministry of Foreign Affairs, and then taken, together with blood tests and X rays, to the prefecture and the town hall where the marriage would occur. A new diplomatic passport was applied for, along with a Polish visa. And then there was the "wedding shopping. I'm still undecided between an olive-green suede belt and a tree-green velvet ribbon," McCarthy wrote Carmen Angleton, "so I bought both. And a green chiffon (in two tones—pale and olive) bonnet from Elizabeth Arden that . . . looks rather like the boudoir caps my mother used to wear in the nursery. . . . And some pale pink shoes from Perugia. . . ." All of these made her worry that she might appear in the red and gold splendor of the *mairie* "looking like something in a high school pageant."

With its massive chandeliers and towering statues of the three Graces, the 8th arrondissement *mairie* did look like the setting for a pageant. And the mayor's reading of the marriage vows, exhorting the bride to fulfill her conjugal duties, bear children, and so on, added to the unreality of the scene. (Two years later, when the new Mr. and Mrs. West, gray and graying, having been tossed out of Poland, presented themselves to a London fine furniture dealer to outfit their new apartment in Paris, the salesman looked them over wonderingly and said, "What happened? Did a fire wipe you out?")

On April 15, Carmen Angleton gave Mary and Jim a wedding supper, and Georges and Peggy Bernier produced a garden party. Hannah Arendt was tied up in Jerusalem, and Nicola Chiaromonte was recovering from a heart attack in Rome, but Dwight Macdonald and his second wife, Gloria, attended the ceremony, along with Evelyn Hofer, Janet Flanner, the novelist James Jones and his wife, Gloria, and a handsome expatriate couple, Eileen and Stanley Geist, whom Jim knew in Paris. Together with a tiny band of Europeans, Mario and Anjou Levi, and J. K. (Kot) Jelenski, a Polish friend of Mary's from the Paris office of the Congress of Cultural Freedom, these were the people who would comprise the nucleus of McCarthy's group in France.

After the wedding, there was a " 'fête champêtre' typical of Mary," Dwight wrote Nicola, who had followed McCarthy's turbulent "engagement" with a certain disbelief, finding it odd but characteristic that with her fourth husband, this forty-eight-year-old veteran of three marriages would behave like a girl in love for the first time. "She is going to be the Queen again—and he the Prince Consort," Chiaromonte predicted darkly, and this would sometimes seem to be the case. "James" McCarthy addressed her husband in later years, in a resonant baritone, as in "Jeeves!" and he would reply with alacrity, "Yes, my dear?" But the twinkle in their eyes hinted at another scenario: life imitating art perhaps, or dallying with it.

The wedding had been followed by a honeymoon in Switzerland; and then the carefully laid plans had unraveled. Telephoning the American embassy in Poland from Interlaken, Jim West learned to his horror that his ex-wife had suddenly returned to Warsaw, and, pleading a set of personal emergencies, was occupying their old apartment. Under the circumstances—Margaret West was still traveling on a diplomatic passport—the ambassador ordered the new Mrs. West to stay away until her predecessor left. At first, Jim had stayed away, too, remaining with Mary in Vienna to wait Margaret out, but embassy business had drawn him back. Mary later slipped across the southern border, planning to hide out with Reuel in Cracow, but when Reuel couldn't be found, she was forced to return to Vienna, which is when she suffered a painful slipped disk and entered an Austrian clinic for nearly three weeks of excruciating therapy. When she finally crossed back into Poland at the end of May, it was in a wheelchair, with her neck in a brace.

By then, Ambassador Beam had finally tired of Jim West's marital dramas. By then, too, someone had raised the question of Mary McCarthy's political views, and the Honorable Beam had found himself in receipt of a letter from Arthur Schlesinger, Jr., now Special Assistant to President Kennedy, assuring him that despite "a brief flirtation with the Trotskyites" in the 1930s, "there has never been the slightest question of her deep and abiding loyalty to the United States." In any event, in the midst of a major security scandal involving the sale of classified information by an embassy employee to a Polish spy, Jim's second tour of duty was abruptly canceled, and he was sent to Washington for reassignment. So much for the house furnished in Danish Modern, and McCarthy's dream of reading Hegel in the sun and snow of Central Europe. Initially, West had been reassigned to Vienna, an unwelcome post that he refused mainly because neither he nor Mary spoke German. Then after months of zigzagging across the United States—camping out in borrowed houses and apartments in Washington, New York, and Stonington, Connecticut, where the poet James Merrill gave Jim and Mary his room in the former Elks Hall; flying to San Francisco to see Reuel, who was enrolled at the University of California, Berkeley, and seemed "sad and orphaned" (also "desperately poor," McCarthy wrote Edmund Wilson); and visiting Mary's uncle Frank Preston in Seattle, who was grieving for his dead wife, Isabel—the Organization for Economic Cooperation and Development job had opened up.

Jim had flown to Paris to meet with the OECD's secretary-general, Thorkild Christiansen, "The Belt," as he was known in Denmark for the austerity programs he sponsored as finance minister. They had got on well despite West's lack of formal training in economics, a requisite for the job of directing the vast information services of a Common Market organization; and Jim was hired, though with the understanding that it might be only a two-year assignment (it lasted until West's retirement in 1979). When the State Department agreed to 'second' him to the OECD—"at a very high rank," Mary wrote Hannah, "just below that of minister, imagine, and $3300 a year for housing"—it was, in effect, a promotion. It was also a stroke of luck, since rumor had it that a responsible post in the USIA had been denied West in Washington because of his wife's controversial career.

II

"Gertrude, unlike many writers, really did have a private life, one that she never wrote a word about," Randall Jarrell observed in his satirical novel, *Pictures from an Institution*. Never was the point more applicable to Mary McCarthy than during the years 1960 to 1962, when she put an ocean between herself and the hard-driving desperado she had been. "That's why I married Jim," McCarthy once remarked, "to get away from New York." This left out love; but getting away from New York, and from the part of herself that fed on the city's giddy energy and torrent of gossip and controversy, was a private matter of some importance. And little of it ever found its way into fiction or even memoir.

Living closer to the pulse of desire than at any other time in her life, McCarthy would be hard-pressed to transfer the events and emotions of this period to prose; except when writing about a new place she had come to love, such as Bocca di Magra in "The Hounds of Summer" (1963). Then her affections flowed freely, though not to the benefit of her fiction. About falling in love at a 'classic' age, leaving the United States, shipping out and starting over, she would write hardly a word. Her critical sense forbade it. ("I think it would be indecent to write about happy sex," McCarthy once told a reporter who wondered about *The Group*'s saturnine approach to love; whether because it was an invasion of privacy, or because the experience wouldn't stand up to the printed word, she didn't say.) But what is written up is never again of use in the same way as what one leaves to the regenerative power of memory, something Mary knew well.

With Hannah Arendt, McCarthy had shared her view of Jim West: "the most true-hearted and complete and honest man I've ever known. . . . [i]rritable occasionally, impatient with nonsense, occasionally ruthless, but not tough or hard." Camped out in a Polish hotel in January 1961, awaiting his divorce, while Mary waited for hers in Paris, "seeing nobody except the people at the office and his children, and in a strange way . . . happy and satisfied," he had reminded her of a "trapper in the Maine woods. . . ." Such a figure would never have been drawn or believed in fiction. "Sensibility writers are very good at creating dream men," like Rhett Butler, McCarthy told Peter Duvall Smith in a 1963 interview in *Vogue,* the note of disparagement clear in her voice. She much preferred writers of "sense" like Jane Austen to writers of "sensibility" like Virginia Woolf. But "Sense and Sensibility," oddly enough, was a title McCarthy proposed for her biography ("Portrait of the Intellectual as a Vassar Girl" was another), only half in jest, because, of course, both ways of seeing and feeling vied for dominance in her nature.

By 1962, when the career of diplomat's wife and American author in Paris began, the gap between social life and intellectual life, already striking, grew greater, though not necessarily to the deficit of

McCarthy's critical faculties. It was in her fiction that a deficit appears: a mannered monotone in the narrator's voice in stories such as "The Hounds of Summer," a tale of confrontation between intellectuals and mass society not unlike McCarthy's "The Appalachian Revolution" (1954). In the later story, the narrator's point of view seems to merge with a stable of jet-setting characters whose summer retreats are always under siege from philistines of one sort or another. In their collective indifference to a larger world, they make one pause—like the taxi driver in *The Group* who turns at a stoplight to gaze at the New York society girl, Pokey Prothero, "fat and fair" and wreathed in sables, who has been carrying on about the silliness of weddings, fittings, coming-out parties, all the way downtown to the church where Kay and Harald Petersen are to be married.

Here is McCarthy on Porto Quaglia (Bocca di Magra) in "The Hounds of Summer":

> It was a fishing village, *un petit hameau de pêcheurs, un piccolo villaggio di pescatori*. That was how those who went there for their vacations found themselves describing it to their hairdressers, manicurists, pedicurists, concierges, postmen, train and air companions en route from London, Rome, Paris, Milan. True or false?

The rhetorical question allows the narrator to distinguish between appearances—there is no picturesque fishing fleet in Porto Quaglia—and reality: The inhabitants do fish for a local mullet. And to make the point that Porto Quaglia's great virtue is precisely its indeterminate quality: "if your concierge or your hairdresser already knew about Porto Quaglia, so that the mere name produced a ready-made description like a pop-up toaster, then the reason for going there would have vanished."

The story is 'placed' by the references to hairdressers, etc., which invite McCarthy's readers to settle themselves comfortably in a well-worn social niche, one commonly found in *The New Yorker,* where the story was published. When Porto Quaglia is threatened by the arrival of *"les vacances payées"* ("The vacations of the masses were necessarily mass-produced," explains Arturo, a character based on Mario Levi), the summer people rally to defend their turf from the incursions of commercial development. An organization for the defense of Bocca di Magra was actually formed in 1961, with Mary McCarthy named "vice-presidentessa," and Nicola Chiaromonte, Italo Calvino, and Dwight Macdonald, numbered among its members.

A similar conflict arises in "The Appalachian Revolution," which is set in East Calais, Vermont, when the outsiders—refugee psychiatrists, in this instance—gradually take over the " 'old' summer people's" swimming hole. No more than a moment's anguish accompanies the exclusionism to which the incumbents resort. Gone are the days when McCarthy's protagonists debate the prospect of a turf fight with the natives, as they do in *The Oasis* before the strawberry pickers are chased out of camp at gunpoint. In "The Appalachian Revolution," Pickman ("Pickles") Callaway, a "get things done" type and a Republican, buys an old beaver pond to assure a private beach for the vacationing mothers and children who have been driven away by the newcomers at Poor Farm Pond, where they themselves have long been squatters. Callaway, one of those Babbitt-like men for whom McCarthy nurtures a furtive affection, then traps and transports the beavers back to the original pond in revenge, not against the psychiatrists, who have disappeared, but "for those others," the reluctant mothers, "who couldn't take the obvious bourgeois step of securing pleasure through ownership." The story is an acerbic look at the personal politics of a counter cultural middle-class in the mid-1950s.

In "The Hounds of Summer," the irony in the intelligentsia's position, or in the author's perception, has all but dissolved, and a rank nostalgia overtakes the familiar tale of encroachment. There is no escaping "the 'Germans,' " as the newly enfranchised European working class (not all German) are called, except for the very rich; and Arturo wonders teasingly what his wife will tell her coiffeur when he asks where they will now go for their holidays. "*Il faut avoir une résponse, Hélène. C'est une question très importante* . . . [One must have an answer, Hélène. It's a very important question . . .]." What will she say? "An undiscovered Greek island? A wood-cutters' hamlet in the Alps? A hotel in Turkey?" But little Hélène, a translator like the diminutive Anjou Levi, doesn't respond to her husband's levity. "There were Germans everywhere . . . '*Bon, donc. Au travail* [So be it].' She leaned her head against his chest. '*Mais comme j'aimais Porto Quaglia!* [But how I've loved Porto Quaglia!]' To which Arturo responds, " '*Oui, c'était beau* . . . [Yes, it was beautiful . . .].' " The Italian and French go untranslated in the story, whose readers, presumably, are fluent in the languages the narrator and characters speak. They're all one happy family.

"The Hounds of Summer" was written to pay for renovating the spacious sixth-floor apartment on the Rue de Rennes that Mary and Jim West acquired in the summer of 1962; and when he learned of this,

William Jovanovich, who was already priming the publicity pumps for *The Group,* promptly dispatched a new advance on royalties to his most promising author, imploring her, not for the first time, to refrain from writing anything else until the novel was finished. McCarthy wouldn't write another story, but three major reviews were sandwiched into the last months before *The Group* was finally completed.

The first, "General Macbeth," a contemporary interpretation of Shakespeare's murderer as a kind of organization man, an "expert buck-passer," struck an immediate chord with Hannah Arendt, who was writing her report on the trial of Adolf Eichmann for *The New Yorker* when McCarthy's piece appeared in *Harper's.* "When did you write it and why did you not let me know?" she demanded, having been duly informed of the other pieces: a celebratory review of Nabokov's *Pale Fire* in *The New Republic,* and a shorter notice of Salinger's *Franny and Zooey* in *The Observer* (which was "very viperish and mean and gave me no pleasure," Mary said), neither of which had impressed Arendt as much. Confronted in Jerusalem with the unexpectedly ordinary figure of the Nazi administrator who had dispatched the trains that carried millions of Jews to their deaths during the war, Hannah Arendt had been moved by the contrast "between the unspeakable horror of the deeds and the undeniable ludicrousness of the man who perpetrated them . . ." as she writes in *Eichmann in Jerusalem* (1963). Something of the awful paradox is suggested in McCarthy's commentary on *Macbeth*:

> Macbeth is not a monster, like Richard III or Iago or Iachimo, though in the catalogue he might go for one because of the blackness of his deeds. But at the outset his deeds are only the wishes and fears of the average, undistinguished man translated into halfhearted action. Pure evil is a kind of transcendence that he does not aspire to.

McCarthy's review of *Pale Fire,* "A Bolt from the Blue," might have alarmed Jovanovich more had he known what went into it. Treating Nabokov's 999-line poem as a "terrific puzzle . . . [requiring] several players to work it out . . . fantastically appropriate to this age of groupiness," Mary had gone all over Paris to unravel its mysteries. She had visited libraries, museums, friends who spoke Russian and German, and others who knew something about rare birds and butterflies, the movements of stars, and chess, or who could help her decode the passages from Pope, Shakespeare, Plato, Aristotle, and Goethe with which Nabokov's tome was peppered, much to Mary's delight, for she reveled in such pedantry.

"*Pale Fire* is a Jack-in-the-box, a Fabergé gem, a clockwork toy, a chess problem, an infernal machine, a trap to catch reviewers, a cat-and-mouse game, a do-it-yourself kit," the review begins; the metaphors tumbling over each other in deliberate profusion, like the multiple "levels" in Nabokov's narrative, which turn out to have false bottoms and fold one into the other. "[T]hese 'levels' are not the customary 'levels of meaning' of modernist criticism but planes in a fictive space," McCarthy explains, "rather like those houses of memory in medieval mnemonic science, where words, facts, and numbers were stored till wanted in various rooms and attics, or like the Houses of astrology into which the heavens are divided." What made the job of unraveling the messages such a joy, she wrote Hannah, was that unlike *Finnegans Wake,* whose references simply led you back to the text, with Nabokov's book "everything you're led to is beautiful in itself. . . ."

The framing tale, set in Wordsmith College in New Wye, Appalachia, was "terribly funny . . . and terribly sad too." And the whole book seemed to her "to have more of America . . . in it than anything I've ever read . . . it's the first book I know to turn this weird new civilization into a work of art. . . ." It was an odd characterization for a vision as expressive of old Europe as Nabokov's; and it suggests how far McCarthy had traveled from the workaday world of the United States by 1962. When Elisabeth Niebuhr asked her whether the old problem of "the American in Europe" interested her as a novelist, McCarthy said no. She no longer saw "that Jamesian distinction" which was alive for her when she and Broadwater traveled to Europe in the summer of 1946. "I don't know whether I cease to feel so much like an American or what; New York is, after all, so Europeanized," she remarked, "and so many of one's friends are European, that the distinction between you as an American and the European blurs. Also Europe has become so much more Americanized." Mary McCarthy's New York, of course, was not America.

Nabokov was a crush Hannah Arendt did not share. "There is something in N. which I greatly dislike," she wrote Mary: "As though he wanted to show you all the time how intelligent he is. . . . There is something vulgar in his refinement," she thought, noting that she was "a bit allergic against this kind of vulgarity," because (old-world refugee that she was) she knew "so many people cursed with it." Dwight Macdonald, who "couldn't have been more surprised by

[Mary's] lengthy fanfare," was even more outspoken in his distaste for *Pale Fire,* which he reviewed for *Partisan Review.*

Nor could Hannah Arendt muster much interest in another book that attracted Mary McCarthy at the time, Günter Grass's *The Tin Drum.* The novel's "epic sweep" might be an "error of vanity," McCarthy thought, but the "grotesque posturing" of the dwarf who is the book's antihero, like the "arrogant acrobatics" of Nabokov and Niccolò Tucci (whose first novel, *Before My Time,* had just appeared), impressed her as "a new genre—the genre of the displaced person." When Hannah had read *The Tin Drum* in German a few years before, she found it "an artificial *tour de force*"; Grass, she thought, wrote "as though he had read all of modern literature and had then decided to borrow and to do something of his own." A film such as the New Wave director Alain Resnais's *Last Year at Marienbad,* which Mary reported was all the rage in Paris, Arendt found "a bore." But she listened sympathetically when McCarthy complained of missing "a 'circle' in Paris," a group of friends who all knew each other as Mary had in Rome and they all had in New York.

In Paris, the Wests' friends seemed to come in isolated pairs, as on the Ark. There was also "an American semi-Bohemian circle," among whom was Larry Rivers, then struggling with a pencil sketch of Mary McCarthy, but this circle, usually found at art openings, struck Mary as "of rather low quality, frankly. . . ." The only French person she really wanted to meet was Nathalie Sarraute, a desire Hannah seconded, proposing her childhood friend Anne Mendelssohn Weil as an intermediary.

Nineteen sixty-two was another year when McCarthy and Arendt didn't always see eye-to-eye. "They hanged Eichmann yesterday; my reaction was curious, rather shrugging, 'Well, one more life—what difference does it make?' " Mary wrote Hannah on June 1, 1962. Short of rejoicing at his death, or being angry over it, what can an ordinary person feel? she wondered; and that was the problem. "To execute a man and excite a reaction of indifference is to bring people too close to the way the Nazis felt about human life— 'One more gone.' " Arendt's response was less complicated. "I am glad they hanged Eichmann," she stated. The Israelis "would have made themselves utterly ridiculous . . . if they hadn't pushed the thing to its only logical conclusion." Strangely enough, given the outrage that *Eichmann in Jerusalem* soon provoked among prominent Jews—as much for its criticism of Israeli showmanship in the courtroom as for its much-publicized allusion to the aid the Jewish coun-

cils rendered the Nazis in their identification of European Jewry—
Arendt's reaction was not always shared by Jewish leaders. One Re-
form rabbi who came out for "mercy" had actually criticized the
Israeli execution as " 'unimaginative.' "

These were turbulent years in both women's lives. In the fall of
1961, after McCarthy had come to the United States with her new
husband for an obligatory home leave required of foreign service
personnel, and to see about West's next post, Arendt's husband, Heinrich Blücher, had suffered a ruptured aneurism from which he was
given a 50 percent chance of recovery. He and Hannah had recently
returned from a long-anticipated trip to Europe, Heinrich's first since
coming to the United States in 1941. He had met Hannah in Zurich in
June after the conclusion of the Eichmann trial, and she had taken him
to Basel to meet her old friend and teacher Karl Jaspers and his wife,
after which the two of them had toured classical sites in Italy. Back
home, Blücher, a self-taught scholar who never went to college, had
returned to teaching the Common Course at Bard, an introduction to
western philosophy; and Hannah Arendt had gone back to work on
the manuscript of *On Revolution,* and returned to a fall semester post
at Wesleyan University's Center for Advanced Studies. When Arendt's
husband collapsed, Mary McCarthy stepped in to teach her Machiavelli seminar at Wesleyan.

By November, Blücher was on the mend, and Arendt was able to
split her time between long weekends with him in their new Riverside
Drive apartment and three days a week teaching at Wesleyan. *On
Revolution* was picked up and finished, not without help from Mary,
who proposed some clarifications in terminology, corrected a few
historical references, and provided alternate translations for several
French quotations. After lecturing at the University of Chicago in
January 1962, Arendt had succumbed to one of those deep respiratory
infections to which Mary was prone. Then, when she was back on her
feet in New York, and clearing her desk for the mountain of documents she had asssembled for the Eichmann report, she received another blow when a taxi she was riding in was hit by a truck crossing
Central Park, leaving her, at fifty-six, with a concussion, hemorrhages
of both eyes, broken teeth, abrasions and lacerations of the face and
scalp, fractured ribs (nine), and, more serious for later life, heart-
muscle damage related to shock.

Only Hannah Arendt would exercise the critical faculties of thinking, judging, and willing, to determine, on the spot, her chances for

survival. When she awoke in the car that rushed her to the hospital "and became conscious of what had happened," she remembered later:

> I tried out my limbs, saw that I was not paralyzed and could see with both eyes; then tried out my memory—very carefully, decade by decade, poetry, Greek and German and English; then telephone numbers. Everything all right. The point was that for a fleeting moment I had the feeling that it was up to me whether I wanted to live or die. And though I did not think that death was terrible, I also thought that life was quite beautiful and that I rather like it.

It would be nearly two months before she was fully recovered and back at work. The 'fleeting moment,' meanwhile, was regarded as a gift snatched from misfortune; an empirical proof of the soul's existence, perhaps, not unlike the momentary suspension between life and death which Jung describes in *Memories, Dreams, and Reflections*.

McCarthy, then in Washington with Jim, had flown to New York to find Hannah covered with bandages but in good spirits. "You should not have come when you came, but now, if you were here, it would make such a difference!" Arendt wrote her a few weeks later when she was back on Riverside Drive, and Mary and Jim had returned to Paris. Hannah still had two bruises on her face, which she covered with powder, and the dentist had fixed her teeth, but a scar over one eye led her to wear a patch in public (temporarily). "I don't think I'll buy a whig [sic] until the hair is grown back" she remarked, preferring to wear scarves "turbanwise" to cover a bald spot where stitches had been taken. A month later, still "no whig. . . ."

Mary had returned to Europe "in great luxe" on the S.S. *United States,* and regaled Hannah with a report of a shipboard encounter with Dame Rebecca West, who was a brilliant conversationalist but "cracked . . . she imagines that various authors are alluding to her and all her relations under disguises in their books." Back in Paris, she had begun to settle into some new routines, including the role of diplomat's wife, which behooved her to make "a slight effort on the social side. . . ." This sort of entertaining largely ceased after publication of *The Group,* when McCarthy became an international figure. After that, "the attention was always directed to her and not to Jim," a frequent guest recalls, "and the entertaining was literary" (except for later, in the mid-1970s, when she embarked on a conscious campaign to promote her husband's career in the Common Market).

Early in May, it was Mary who was sent to bed with the grippe, followed by a sinking depression, "like a heavy poison in one's veins," which left her "in a mood to hide myself, like a dirty bundle, in a hotel room," she confided to Hannah, "so that no one I love can see me. . . ." It could have been a characteristic of the germ, or something else—road fever, one imagines—"or perhaps it's change of life," McCarthy proposed. In a few weeks she would turn fifty, a milestone, curiously enough, which goes unmentioned in her correspondence.

For a while, nothing went right, though it would only be a month before McCarthy sprang back into action with the Nabokov review. The French struck her as more "hysterical and chauvinistic" than usual—a condition no doubt inflamed in the presence of an American by the unraveling of French power in Algeria. One couldn't criticize a piece of fruit in the market without a vendor screaming at you about *"La France, 'vous êtes en France, vous savez.' "* Mary complained. Elisabeth Niebuhr had actually been slapped by a shopkeeper for picking up a peach. Paris and its environs appeared ravaged by industrialization, whose excesses were to be measured not by sprawling petrochemical plants but by the "cute weekend bungalows"—" 'coquettes,' " the real estate ads called them—lining the banks of the Seine as far away as Normandy.

For Arendt, Paris remained "the only place entirely fit to live in." The city was like a house with many, many rooms, she wrote Mary in the summer of 1962, "where you feel never exposed. . . ." But for McCarthy, even after she and Jim had found the sunny seven-room apartment on the top floor of a balconied Victorian building on the Rue de Rennes, where they would live for the next twenty-nine years, not far from the Gare Montparnasse and with a view of a convent—"a gay apartment," McCarthy thought, and a bargain at $31,000—Paris left her feeling uneasy. If she had finally put New York behind her, she still had a foot planted in Rome, whose intellectuals, "so much more *intimate* with the Italian political and social scene than the French" were with theirs, pleased her more.

Listening to Nicola Chiaromonte's friends trading stories about the Church, the Demo-Christians, censorship, criminal trials, the uglification of Rome, all with "a kind of exasperation that suggests a family situation," McCarthy was keenly aware of the political powerlessness of Italian intellectuals. "[T]hey must be the most disenfranchised intellectuals in any Western country," she thought. There was no Mendès-France to " 'represent' " them, and someone like Jean-Paul Sartre was unthinkable. Italian intellectuals were "spectators, connoisseurs of the national idiocy"; but she couldn't "help loving the Italians and not loving the French."

Paris felt cold and inhospitable, as it had in the middle 1950s and would again, a city whose intellectuals never really found a place for Mary McCarthy in their pantheon; nor would McCarthy ever stop 'not loving' them—with notable exceptions made later for Nathalie Sarraute and Jean-François Revel. In August 1962, she and Jim West left the city for Bocca di Magra, taking the West children with them. Later, McCarthy would stay by herself for two weeks in September to work in tranquillity on the final chapters of *The Group*. But she was still on the move. Like an old trouper barnstorming the hinterlands—"old George in *The Entertainer*," she once described herself—she could not stay off the road or out of the limelight for very long. When an invitation had arrived earlier in the summer from Sonia Orwell to address the annual Edinburgh Festival's International Writers' Conference in the middle of August in Scotland, she accepted happily.

30

Beauty and the *Priest:* *The Burroughs Connection*

". . . [W]hen It happened, it was not at all what the
group or even Mother would have imagined, not a bit
sordid or messy, in spite of Dick's being tight."

—MARY MCCARTHY, THE GROUP

" 'So I guess he come to some kinda awful climax.' "

—WILLIAM BURROUGHS, NAKED LUNCH

*E*dinburgh was a watershed for me," McCarthy said many years later of one of the more bizarre literary events of the decade. Alongside Edinburgh's 1962 festival, with its parade of panelists rising to confess to being homosexuals or heterosexuals, or to announce religious conversions, or report communications with the dead, the Congress for Cultural Freedom's monster rallies looked like Shriners' conventions. Given the insurrection of homosexuals and drug users at Edinburgh—the latter represented by novelists Alex Trocchi and William Burroughs, along with a "Registered Heroin Addict" who led the Scottish opposition to the doughty Hugh Macdiarmid, Scotland's leading poet—one might have expected to find Mary McCarthy aligned with the conservative faction grouped around her good friend Stephen Spender. But Spender was the chair, and Mary never could resist a pit fight.

Besides, there was something oddly familiar in the far-out William Burroughs that she liked—the humor in *Naked Lunch* for one thing: "peculiarly American, at once broad and sly," she wrote a few months later in an enthusiastic review of Burroughs controversial second novel in the maiden issue of *The New York Review of Books;* like the humor of a "vaudeville performer playing . . . in front of the asbestos curtain of some Keith Circuit or Pantages house long since converted to movies." In Burroughs, the same jokes are trotted out again and again, refurbished to suit the changing scene, the way a vaudevillian in the 1920s changed Yonkers to Renton when he was playing Seattle. McCarthy, who *likes* these old jokes, can't resist repeating them. " 'Stop me if you've heard this atomic secret' "; and " 'A simopath . . . is a citizen convinced he is an ape or other simian. It is a disorder peculiar to the army and discharge cures it.' " A few are full-fledged vaudevillian numbers, as when the novel's two hoofers, Clem and Jody, hired by the Russians to give Americans a bad name abroad, "appear in Liberia wearing black Stetsons . . . and talking loudly about burning niggers back home."

The surreal side of Burroughs' imagination reminds McCarthy of a Marx Brothers movie or a Jimmy Durante act, a "Hellzapoppin effect of orgies and riots" and metamorphoses, like the Mixmaster in *Naked Lunch* that tries to climb up the puzzled housewife's skirt; or the aggrieved citizens who turn into carnivores and crabs, or appear equipped with interchangeable parts; or the freaks who escape from a circus to mingle with the controlled population of "Freeland" (which is reminiscent of Elizabeth Bishop's "And Then Came the Poor" in 1933). "Passages of dialogue and description keep recurring in different contexts with slight variations," McCarthy observes with a fascination that hints at an unexpected correspondence between Burroughs's apocalyptic vision of the modern scene and her own.

The novel's galloping odyssey from Chicago, St. Louis, New Orleans, Mexico City, Malmo—"a circus [which] travels but is always the same," she calls the narrative technique—mirrors her own travels (though McCarthy doesn't say it) from Tunis, Prague, Warsaw, London, Paris, Vienna, Copenhagen, Rome, Bocca di Magra . . . and back and forth across the Atlantic. The soured utopianism she detects in Burroughs' parodies of the American heartland is echoed in a dry recognition that came upon her at this time that the almighty Common Market, umbrella organization to the OECD, was "really capitalism's five-year-plan. . . ." William Burroughs' mirror is the fun-house type and McCarthy's personal identification is probably largely unconscious. But the remarkable drive and energy in the 1963 review, written partly to correct the misconception that at Edinburgh she had called the book 'one of the great novels of the century,' suggests that in Burroughs' ferocious underworld, McCarthy has found a black-comic metaphor for a fugitive side of her own experience—and not for her experience alone, but for the times.

The most striking fact about Edinburgh "was the number of lunatics both on the platform and in the public," she wrote Hannah Arendt when the festival was over, noting that one young woman novelist had been released temporarily from a mental hospital to attend. Niccolò Tucci had arrived looking like "an exiled prime minister," wearing a black suit with his arm in an ermine sling. When Tucci stood up in a public session to read a long letter to the 'Statesmen of the World' concerning atomic warfare, he had made an awful spectacle of himself, in Mary's opinion.

Norman Mailer, another conference participant who spoke out in Burroughs' defense, had proved more entertaining, though Mailer kept losing center stage to the sideshows that erupted from drunken Scots speaking Gaelic and angry delegates from Eastern Europe threatening to boycott the festival. "I confess I enjoyed it enormously," McCarthy remarked in 1962; and nearly twenty-five years later, grinning over the memory of the bearded Sikh with hair down to his waist who argued that homosexuals were incapable of love, just as hermaphrodites were incapable of orgasm, to which Stephen Spender retorted that he should have thought " 'they could have *two*,' " she was still amused. Edinburgh was where she had made several new friendships that would last a lifetime, including one with a twenty-nine-year-old Dutch writer named Cees Nooteboom, who would be McCarthy's guide to Holland fifteen years later when she went there to research her last novel.

The lunacy was part of a deeper madness that was underscored in September 1962 when Mary learned from Nicholas Nabokov that Cal Lowell was in a mental ward in Buenos Aires and that Marilyn Monroe had committed suicide because she had been having an affair with Bobby Kennedy, and the White House had intervened (via Kennedy's brother-in-law Peter Lawford). "Our age begins to sound like some awful colossal movie about the late Roman Emperors and their Messalinas and Poppaeas," she ventured at the time; "[t]he Bobby Kennedy swimming pool being the bath with asses' milk."

Elizabeth Hardwick and Robert Lowell had gone to South America on a CCF junket arranged shortly before the Lowells attended a White House dinner for intellectuals in May 1962. (" 'Who pays for the Congress for Cultural Freedom, anyway?' " wondered Elizabeth Bishop when she heard that Cal was coming to visit her in Brazil.) Lowell's duties were nebulous. As "our side's emissary," the CCF representative, Keith Botsford, recalled in 1981, he was picked as "an outstanding American to counteract . . . Communist people like [the Chilean poet] Neruda," a condition that seems to have inspired Lowell to manic heights. In Buenos Aires, he had pronounced himself "Caesar of Argentina" and Keith Botsford his "lieutenant." After a string of double martinis at the presidential palace, he had insulted the general who was about to become president, and then called the U.S. cultural attaché, who had never heard of Robert Lowell, "illiterate." When he later dragged his "lieutenant" on a tour of equestrian statues, undressing and scrambling up their sides to sit next to the riders, Lowell finally had to be physically overpowered and taken to a hospital, where Botsford recalls he was put in a straitjacket and given 20,000 milligrams of Thorazine four times a day.

If Burroughs, with his Swiftian savagery, drenched in paranoia, was what the age demanded, in McCarthy's estimation, it was in part because his vision seemed to encompass the kind of world in which writers in her circle increasingly moved. These included Delmore Schwartz, that "hero of wretchedness," as Saul Bellow called him, whose crack-up a few years earlier was a study in paranoid delusion, but whose seedy world, when he hit bottom in the 1960s, was the reverse of Robert Lowell's. In *Humboldt's Gift,* Bellow draws an unforgettable picture of Delmore's last days on the skids in New York. Citrine, the dapper, well-dressed Bellow character, is on his way to Brentano's to check something Keats says about how a luxurious imagination deadens in exposure to things that are attainable, when he is stopped short by the terrible sight of his old friend Humboldt: "His head was all gray webbing, like an infested bush. His eyes were red and his big body was floundering in the gray suit. He looked like an old bull bison on his last legs, and I beat it." (Which he had; "East River gray," was how Bellow described Delmore's pallor when he saw him for the last time. He died at the age of fifty-two in 1966 in a transients' hotel off Times Square.)

Lowell's world was a mad vindication of the dream that had tormented Delmore, the dream of winning power and glory through the medium of great poetry; even when he was certifiably schizophrenic, Delmore had hoped his 'madness' would pay off in celebrity and hard cash. Lowell's breakdowns brought misery to the people close to him, but they didn't keep him from being invited to the White House evenings for intellectuals during the Kennedy administration. The May 1962 dinner had been preceded by a glamorous reception for André Malraux, which Mary might have been invited to had she been in the States at the time, Lionel Trilling told Nicola Chiaromonte.

"If Lenin were alive today he'd probably be writing for *Esquire* and having dinner at the White House, or maybe just lunch," quipped William Phillips (which showed what he thought of Lenin). But the collapse in political morality among the cognoscenti was real enough. In Phillips's opinion, it was a period for Dwight Macdonald, "who thinks everything is wonderful as long as he can write articles saying it stinks." McCarthy stood by Burroughs; and at Edinburgh she also praised *Naked Lunch,* along with Nabokov's *Pale Fire* and *Lolita,* as an example of a new kind of novel based on statelessness. Burroughs may not have been a political exile, she argued over Spender's violent objection to the comparison with Nabokov, but the drug addicts he described, living outside the law, were continually on the run; as was the confirmed homosexual: "a chronic refugee, ordered to move on by the Venetian police, the Capri police, the mayor of Provincetown, the mayor of Nantucket." The uninflected reference to homosexuals was unusual; McCarthy often struck a meaner note. But in the great hall of the Scottish Presbyterian university, in the company of Messrs. Burroughs, Trocchi, and Mailer, anything was possible—or almost anything.

When the BBC, spotting a good story, offered Norman Mailer one thousand dollars if he would appear on TV in Edinburgh and "fight it out with Mary McCarthy"—who would also get one thousand dollars, Mailer assured her, leaving the subject of their debate up to her—she refused. Probably it was too soon after *Esquire*'s "Mary McCarthyism" for her to risk another public display of temperament. In September, she had apologized to Hannah for having suggested that Arendt be an informant for the article's author, Brock Brower, who had promised Mary that the cover story "wouldn't be a 'personality piece.'" As a result of his deception, or her own self-deception, she had "resolved never under any circumstances to give another interview . . ."—a vow that was broken a few months later with Peter Duvall Smith for *Vogue;* but at Edinburgh, she had stood firm, and the journalists who were already beginning to swarm around Mary McCarthy a year before *The Group* were kept at bay.

Norman Mailer had been sorely disappointed. " 'You're the regent of American writers, but you're a weak regent,' " McCarthy remembered him saying, when she declined the BBC invitation. After the poor showing of both *The Deer Park* (1955) and *An American Dream* (1965), Mailer may have found himself at one of those moments, recorded in *Advertisements for Myself,* when he felt "like an actor looking for a rare role." At heart, he wanted "a war"—which is what he declared in "The Mary McCarthy Case" the following fall, when, in the midst of the media storm surrounding *The Group,* he charged "our lit arbiter, our broadsword, our Barrymore (Ethel), our Dame (dowager), our Mistress (Head), our Joan of Arc . . . her sword breathing fire . . ." with having brought forth a "lady-book."

After Malcolm Muggeridge flashed the news of Mary McCarthy's praise for *Naked Lunch* in *The New Statesman* ("a shot heard round the world," McCarthy remarked later, judging from the reverberations in Paris and New York), she reflected that Burroughs must have "felt more and more like the groom in a shotgun literary wedding. . . . And the monstrousness of the union, doubtless, was what kept the story hot." But the overture to William Burroughs was more than another adventure in defiance.

In "Burroughs' *Naked Lunch,*" McCarthy revels in the speech of the novel's so-called "ordinary men and women, going about their ordinary everyday tasks": the "whine of the put-upon boy hustler," talking about " 'All kinda awful sex acts.' " The junkie: " 'You think I am innarested to hear about your horrible old condition? I am not innarested at all.' " The aggrieved housewife: " 'I got the most awful cold, and my intestines is all constipated.' " In the review, the trip across the literary tracks strips a certain patina of class from McCarthy's own prose, which comes, one sometimes feels, from an overexposure to issues of taste. Mailer would strike home when he charged that "Mary's vice is her terror of being ridiculous"; and McCarthy herself once acknowledged that she was too easily "taken with a highly finished young writer, such as Alison Lurie or John Updike," when experience had shown her they were the ones most likely to "abort. I don't see the gold in rough ore," she remarked.

The savagery of Burroughs' repulsion for all those people who talk about their diseases and " 'horrible' discharges" was sometimes a bit much for McCarthy; and to justify him she was moved to invoke Swift, a literary ancestor with his own scatalogical obsessions, but whose chief concern, like Burroughs', is a fierce repugnance for the hypocrisy of the body politic. "The 'factual' appearance of [Burroughs's] narrative, with its battery of notes and citations, some straight, some loaded, its extracts from a diary, like a ship's log, its pharmacopoeia, has the flavor of eighteenth-century satire," she argues; noting, approvingly, that Burroughs calls himself a " 'Factualist.' " But the book's aerial sex acts and flights of popular jargon—" '. . . so long as you got a legitimate condition and an RX from a certified bona feedy M.D., I'm honored to serve you' "—are what engage her fancy.

It was in fiction reviews that Mary McCarthy often explored a theme that lay beyond the reach of her own novels. Later in the 1960s, her reviews of Ivy Compton-Burnett treated the dance of opposites in everyday language, as well as in the human personality, with epigrammatic subtlety, viz. " 'Patience contains more impatience than anything else' "; and, "Only a villain would dare to be true to himself." Similarly, "Burroughs' *Naked Lunch*," with its vicarious immersion via abundant quotation in a world where the addiction to platitudes and commonplaces is just as deadly as the addiction to drugs and sadomasochistic sex, shows McCarthy in an experimental mood.

In *The Group,* whose white-gloved young women couldn't be more remote from Burroughs' junkies and hustlers, a similar linguistic experiment was under way, a mimicry of that bird chorus of voices from McCarthy's Vassar dormitory thirty years before. " 'Yes, Dick,' [Dottie] whispered, her hand twisting the doorknob, while she let her eyes tell him softly what a deep, reverent moment this was, a sort of pledge between them"—which is Miss Renfrew when she realizes that Dick has just ordered her to get a "pessary," not a "peccary" ("a coarse piglike mammal"). And Priss Hartshorn, indulging in group-think: "Great wealth was a frightful handicap; it insulated you from living."

Or Kay Strong Petersen, closest to Mary McCarthy, a "legend in Salt Lake City: 'The girl who went east and made good.' . . . By marrying Harald. The theatre. It all sounds so glamorous to . . . the girls I went to school with. You see, I wanted to be a director myself. Or an actress. But I really have no talent. That's my tragedy.' " McCarthy, of course, partly believed this of herself, without viewing her dramatic failure tragically, since she always had a pen up her sleeve. Parodies of her own life serve a different kind of mimicry, one with definite curative powers. The resuscitation of the class of '33, with its troubling legacy of uncertain friendships, was a kind of exorcism for the author, as well as a grand in memorium to a bygone era.

McCarthy's mimicry of the distaff side of upper-class American life would achieve an almost mythic status in a society where novels really do 'carry the news'; and where novels about society, high and low, but especially high, serve as passkeys to realms of experience off-limits to ordinary mortals. As "coterie literature," *Naked Lunch* never was intended for the general public, but for the downtown literati; and it was mainly intellectuals who busied themselves with William Burroughs: McCarthy, Mailer, the critic Leslie Fiedler, and others, such as Philip Rahv, who chastised the former for promoting "a non-novel full of sadistic homosexual extravagance. . . ." It was nearly everyone else in the reading public who snapped up *The Group*.

31

The Book That Roared

". . .[Y]ou've passed through the raised clubs. What a
roar, what a forest fire, of praise and abuse!"

—ROBERT LOWELL TO MARY McCARTHY, 2/20/64

"I awoke one morning and found myself famous."

—LORD BYRON

W omen's secrets again," Louise Bogan said of *The Group* when it first burst on the scene; and in a letter to her friend Ruth Limmer, she singled out the seduction of Dottie Renfrew, "told as though by slides in a microscope," as "the best." The various involvements of "high-minded girls with low-minded men" were all "wittily put forth," in Bogan's opinion, and McCarthy's style had become "v. sharp and economical, too. But the semi-Mary protagonist gets killed again (suicide?)," she noted of Kay's fall from the Vassar Club window at the end of the book, while Mary's "*other* half (rich, soignée, onto everything) turns out to have been a corrupt and corrupting *lesbian*, all along. V. strange!"

The "*other* half" is Elinor Eastlake, "Lakey," whose looks and fine-arts studies were modeled on McCarthy's old *Con Spirito* comrade Margaret Miller, and personality—"a kind of hauteur or . . . fathomless scorn"—on Nathalie Swan. Kay's appearance is borrowed from a member of the original South Tower group, Kay McLean, while her personal experiences are essentially McCarthy's own (excluding the Macy's job in New York). Scenes from two marriages—with Johnsrud and Wilson—are mixed to create life with Harald Petersen. As for Lakey's lesbianism, a resentful Elizabeth Bishop came to believe that Mary had drawn on Bishop's affair with a woman in Brazil, an assumption McCarthy tried to refute in a letter that was returned unopened in November 1979, for it reached Bishop the day she died.

Identifying the bodies in the 'blood-stained alley' behind *The Group* quickly became a favorite pastime for McCarthy's acquaintances. A handful of alumnae from the class of '33 spotted Helen Kellogg's butler, Finch, in Pokey Prothero's butler, Hatton. Dick Rovere recognized the "real Elizabeth McAusland" behind Libby MacAusland, a Smith graduate who was the *New Masses* art critic in 1938 and later wrote for *The Springfield Republican*. Others spotted bits and pieces of Nancy Macdonald's brother, Selden Rodman—who edited *Common Sense*—in the character of Norine Schmittlapp's husband, Putnam. Speculations like this were rarely silenced by denials, any more than gossip about the originals of *Madame Bovary* were silenced a century before, as Mary McCarthy noted ruefully in a 1964 essay on Flaubert's sensational novel. "[A]s an author, [Flaubert] must have resented the cheapening efforts of real life to claim for itself material he had transmuted with such pain in his study," she mused, remarking that "[t]his endless conjecturing on the part of the public is the price paid by the realistic novelist for 'writing about what he knows.' "

The journalist Sheila Tobias, meanwhile, canvassed the disgruntled members of the original South Tower group for their recollections of the author: " 'She stood out as being from nowhere. . . .' " " 'She was a homeless urban operator. . . .' " " 'For her, everything, and especially Vassar, had to be all or nothing.' " Their memories had grown sour. But another classmate, who saw herself writ large in the androgynous Helena Davison, Frani Blough Muser, found the group portrait "hilarious." Writing Mary from Liège after having fallen out of contact for years, Frani even forgave her old friend "that bit about [calling the character based on her] a mule. It's such a pleasure to find (one's self?) laughing out loud when reading . . ." she said, that "I find it difficult to wrench myself thirty years back to the present." Mary McCarthy herself was still uncovering fresh deposits of her checkered past in the novel twenty-five years after publication. At a memorial reading in Vassar's Main Hall in 1988, she suddenly paused to marvel at the justice of having given the "awful Harald to Kay," when it was Kay McLean who had wounded her senior year by saying that Mary was " 'just another feather in Johnsrud's cap.' "

Louise Bogan was one of the few readers in 1963 who saw Mary McCarthy in Elinor Eastlake, a resemblance borne out less by appearances than by aspiration, by the telltale juxtaposition of wealth, beauty, and intelligence in the Lake Forest girl's vitae. (Of all the young women in the group, the "rich arrogant green-eyed beauty," who is played by Candice Bergen in the movie version of *The Group*, was the only one Norman Mailer said he wouldn't flee at a cocktail party.) But it is Lakey's lesbianism, established at the end of the book ("corrupt and corrupting" principally to Harald), that lifts her above the crowd and makes her a vehicle for McCarthy's more detached commentary on the group's relationships with men. Lakey's heightened sensitivity to women, especially to Kay, gives her critical judgments a cutting edge.

Lakey, who sails for Europe soon after Kay's wedding, returning for the funeral that closes *The Group*, "is a kind of value center," McCarthy once said; "she is what's not in the book." In effect, the "Madonna from Lake Forest," whose "fine white Renaissance nostril" is forever "dinted with a mark of pain," is the alter ego of an author whose own inner eye never sleeps. In *How I Grew*, McCarthy sounds exactly like Elinor Eastlake when she recalls how during her wedding night with Johnsrud she knew she "had *done the wrong thing*. To marry a man without loving him . . . was a wicked action." The twenty-one-year-old McCarthy hadn't done anything about it. Her realization was just another nocturnal truth emission; but out of such chasms between insight and action, both memoir and fiction came.

In her remarks on the economy of McCarthy's style, Bogan was also one of the few writers to understand what the novelist was doing with the patois of privilege that engulfs the book. Robert Lowell was another who saw in the novel's "cloistered, pastoral souls breaking on the real rocks of the time" a portrait he would have liked to have drawn; although Lowell, alone among friends who spoke up for *The Group*, actually identified with the larger cast of McCarthy's characters. What was troubling about the story, he wrote Mary, was realizing how in the late 1930s "we were ignorant, dependable little machines made to mow the lawn, then suddenly turned out to clear the wilderness."

Among serious reviewers, only a few such as Robert Kiely in *The Nation* recognized that McCarthy was engaged in a virtuoso display of "narrative mimicry." Reviews in *The New Republic* and *The Reporter* ridiculed her for succumbing to the clichés of her characters, as did Norman Podhoretz in *Show* and Norman Mailer in *The New York Review of Books*. The dragon lady had fallen afoul the "profound materiality of women," Mailer declared, "until the Eggs Benedict and the dress with the white fichu, the pessary and the whatnot, sit on the line of the narrative like commas and periods, semi-colons, italics, and accents. The real interplay of the novel exists between the characters and the objects which surround them," Mailer observed, veering from reason to madness in a single sentence, "until the faces are swimming in a cold lava of anality, which becomes the truest part of her group, her glop, her impacted mass." Out of the obsession with *things,* he argued, Mary had failed to write anything more than "the best novel the editors of the women's magazines ever conceived in *their* secret ambitions." She was condemned for writing a novel of manners from a woman's point of view. It was an intention McCarthy had set forth herself in 1959, without disparagement or special pleading, in her Guggenheim application: "No male consciousness is present in the book; through these eight points of view, all feminine . . . are re- fracted . . . all the novel ideas of the period concerning sex, politics, economics, architecture, city-planning, house-keeping, child-bearing, interior decoration, and art."

She was charged as well with the heresy of maligning the 1930s, which had become precious to younger intellectuals like Mailer and Podhoretz in the 1960s. Podhoretz only briefly: "the sixties was Nor- man's period, when he more or less came into his own," Podhoretz told one of Mailer's biographers, Peter Manso, in 1984. "In the end I was repelled by the sixties." Writing in *Show* in October 1963, never- theless, in a review ballyhooed in advance in *Newsweek*'s four- page spread on *The Group* (Podhoretz was going "to slice [the book] to tatters . . ."), *Commentary*'s editor struck a leftist note. By seeing mainly "foolishness and insincerity [in the 1930s] dream of self- transcendence," he argued, "despite the fact that she herself was . . . beautified once by the dream," McCarthy had committed a *"trahi- son";* and the Muses had rewarded her "with a flatly written and incoherently structured book, a trivial lady-writer's novel."

The 'lady-book' epithet stuck like a burr to negative reviews of *The Group,* including a few written by women. Eleanor Widmer called McCarthy's "major triumph—a 'ladies' novel,' " and went on to agree with Mailer that McCarthy had " 'failed out of vanity, the ac- cumulated vanity of being overpraised for too little, and so being pleased with herself for too little. . . .' The assertiveness, the knowl- edgeability, the sophistication," Widmer concluded, "[had] finally turn[ed] quaint. . . ." The vindictive note in these rebukes referred to McCarthy's mercurial career as much as to her book. Not just a novel but the character and life of a difficult woman—one, moreover, who had defected to Europe—was finally being put on the dock.

II

Fat and sassy and hugely successful, *The Group* offered McCarthy's critics the one weapon against which a serious intellectual lacked defense: popularity, 'the vulgarity of making good.' Not even Saul Bellow, who alone among the old *Partisan Review* crowd was breasting a wave of commercial success (with *Henderson the Rain King* and *Herzog*), could match the high voltage of publicity set off by McCarthy's book in 1963. And even if he had, he wouldn't have been treated to the roar of praise and abuse that greeted her 'triumph.'

The mythmaking had begun as early as 1959 in Philip Roth's best-selling novella, *Goodbye, Columbus*. When Neil Klugman encourages Brenda Patimkin to get herself "fitted," Brenda pounces on him for knowing about the Margaret Sanger clinic:

> "You've done this before?"
> "No," I said. "I just know. I read Mary McCarthy."
> "That's exactly right. That's just what I'd feel like, somebody out of her."

Philip Roth had read "Dottie Makes an Honest Woman of Herself" in *Partisan Review* in 1954. Together with chapter readings like the one McCarthy delivered at the YMHA in February 1959, the richly embroidered tale of Dottie's medical instruction created a climate of excitement about *The Group* long before William Jovanovich began to court mainstream reviewers in the spring of 1963.

What no one anticipated was the speed with which *The Group* would make it to the nation's bedside tables, not just the tables of people who read *Goodbye, Columbus* and *Herzog* but their mothers', uncles', sisters', doctors', and neighbors'. Immediately upon publication in August 1963, the book shot to the top of the best-seller lists, where it would remain for nearly two years. After a first printing of seventy thousand, nearly three hundred thousand copies were sold by the end of 1964 in the United States and Europe—where the chronicle of eight Vassar girls, swashbuckling through the Depression, soon acquired a half-life of its own.

In England, *The Group* also became a best-seller, but it was in Germany, where sales of over a quarter of a million copies of *Die Clique* ("*Der Gruppen*" having been tainted by the Nazis) supplied Mary and Jim West with a steady infusion of income until 1987, that the novel found its home away from home. The German success was attributed by McCarthy to curiosity about a period Germany had been cut off from by the war. The same might have been said for Italy, but in Italy, as in Ireland and Australia, *The Group* was initially banned as an offense to public morals—thanks largely to the chapters about Dottie Renfrew. (Even in the United States, as Jovanovich, who was in receipt of hundreds of outraged letters knew well, *The Group* came close to rousing the dragons of decency. Letters to McCarthy were particularly threatening: "What kind of filthy perverted mind do you have to write a novel like 'The Group'?" And: "I believe you have a son in college. How could you look him in the face after he had read that book?") Jovanovich and George Weidenfeld, McCarthy's English publisher, managed to stem the foreign lawsuits before either publisher or author was ordered to stand trial. In the end, the scandals fueled publicity, especially in Australia; but McCarthy, a principled foe of censorship of any kind, and rarely one to avoid a confrontation, confessed herself "disappointed that the publishers seem finally to have decided not to fight the [censorship] case in court. . . ."

Ultimately, Jovanovich would sell the foreign rights to publishers in twenty-three countries, including Japan, Iceland, Hungary, and Bulgaria. After Charles Feldman bought the movie rights for $162,500 in the fall of 1963, and ploughed $50,000 into additional advertising for the book, the novel's fortunes were enhanced. The movie, whose Vassar scenes were shot at Connecticut College because of Vassar's disapproval, never matched the success of the novel. " 'The Group' reminds me of a tracing made of the general outlines of a continent by a retarded student and called, say 'Europe,' " Kevin McCarthy wrote his sister, after seeing it in 1966. "Trust *Time* to find it 'sharply written by [dull, old] Sidney Buchman, and directed with lively Roosevelt period flavor by [deadly, painful] Sidney Lumet' . . ." (Kevin's brackets.) Mary kept her distance from the production, forgoing public comment, but when she saw the movie in Paris with some friends who included Nicholas King, she quite enjoyed it. In the United States, the actual number of *The Group*'s readers would always exceed the sales; for the book, one of the most passed-around novels of recent times, soon enjoyed an underground notoriety as persistent as the publicized one. As of 1991, more than 5.2 million copies had been sold worldwide.

Mary McCarthy had written a "whopper, not necessarily a masterpiece—but a real novel," wrote the *Chicago Daily News*' Hayden Carruth in a typical review from the daily press; typical in that it hailed the author of *The Group* as a prodigal daughter who had finally come to her senses. Now it seemed there were two Mary McCarthys: the critic, whose "earliest reviews and essays, written when she was still a schoolgirl [were] famous for their hardness and wit," and whose previous novels were scorned for their "sneering attitude toward everyone and everything," and the born-again author of a dazzling social panorama, "one of the best novels of the decade." No wonder some of Mary's fellow writers in New York had fallen to plotting and gnashing their teeth. It was as if Sacheverell Sitwell had sat down to tea with the vampire of Venice, and fallen blissfully in love.

Norman Mailer set the tone for the New York crowd's attack on *The Group* when he opened "The Mary McCarthy Case" by marveling, "It had to happen. It was in the command of all the ironies that there would come a day when our First Lady of Letters would write a book and lo! the lovers would stand." Arthur Mizener, Granville Hicks, Clifton Fadiman, Gilbert Highet, Edmund Fuller, Virgilia Peterson, all saluted McCarthy for her success. These were some of the 'literary salesmen' McCarthy had belittled nearly thirty years before in "Our Critics, Right or Wrong," including "Kip" Fadiman, who now maintained that "men resent the fact that she has a harder head than they have (she makes a so-called tough kid like Norman Mailer sound like an Eagle Scout)."

The amazement Norman Mailer expressed over the popular reception of *The Group* was widely felt. Among intellectuals whose audiences, increasingly, were to be found in the marketplace or not at all, such attention paid to one of their 'purer' members—"the highbrow's highbrow," Granville Hicks called McCarthy—stirred up mixed emotions. (" 'Say, listen, I knew the country was headed for trouble as soon as there began to be big money in art,' " one of Bellow's characters says in *Humboldt's Gift* in a slightly different context. " 'To make capitalists out of artists was a humorous idea of some depth. America decided to test the pretensions of the esthetic by applying the dollar measure.' ") Even the loyal Lowell wrote Mary in October 1963 that, "bad" as was Mailer's front-page piece in the *New York Review*—and at its worst: "She is simply not a good enough woman to write a major novel; not yet . . ." it was pretty awful—the review hadn't irritated him half as much as the blockbuster spread in *Newsweek,* "with that mixture of flattery and venom. . . ."

Mailer, Lowell suggested, had simply "taken up the boxing fight he had proposed in person with you in Edinborough(?), and taken a swipe at you when your head was turned. . . . He rather lays himself open," Lowell added, wondering if it would be "impertinent [to suggest] that you should, at your leisure, write a reply—not a reply but a serious consideration of Mailler's [*sic*] own work?" It was impertinent. Nothing had persuaded McCarthy of the "treachery of the New York Book Review [*sic*] people" more than that they had "kept pestering" her to write for them both before and after soliciting the review from an "announced enemy" (Mailer). Lowell, meanwhile, wanted Mary to know he remained her "loyal friend and I hope a formidable one."

Today, it is Robert Lowell who is credited by Robert Silvers with having supplied the rationale for getting Norman Mailer to review *The Group*. Lowell, Silvers remembers, reported that Mary had once surprised him by speaking favorably of Mailer's comments on the contemporary novel in *Advertisements for Myself*. "I don't believe that she said he was 'wonderful' on this subject, but that he was interesting in what he did," Silvers recalls. Mailer, who was the highbrow's lowbrow (e.g. Diana Trilling's "The Moral Radicalism of Norman Mailer"), was apparently already under consideration as McCarthy's reviewer. But there must have been doubts, if not about how Mary would take the Mailer treatment, then about his penchant for grandstanding. Silvers himself insists he knew nothing about the go-round between Mary and Norman in Edinburgh the year before. "I had no idea they knew each other," he says, "or had even met for that matter," only that "somewhere in the world they would have met."

How was Silvers to know that Mailer would charge "Lady M." with having "deposited a load" on the "grand premise of the novel"? ("I can't understand how or why they printed it," Hannah Arendt exclaimed of this review, which she found "so full of personal and stupid invectives. . . .") Looking back on it now, Silvers finds that "it was an unhappy business because Mary was so upset. But we were pleased when Norman took on the book," he adds, "and if he had made a case for it, of course we would have been glad to publish it." But Mailer didn't. McCarthy herself remembered Bob Silvers telling her in 1963 that "he couldn't get anybody to write a favorable review of *The Group*," which "may have been true," she thought, though she was "highly *offended* at the time"; while Mailer, who calls the review today "one of the nervier things I ever did," remembers being put up to the job ("some people were pulling my feathers") because nobody else dared to say anything bad about Mary McCarthy. "I felt like I was attacking the King," he says (not the Queen, the 'King').

Hannah Arendt, meanwhile, believed "that Elizabeth [Hardwick] had the bright idea to ask [Mailer]—just as she had the brilliant idea to ask [Lionel] Abel to do the PR piece [on *Eichmann in Jerusalem*]." She had admitted it to Hannah, she told Mary, "[b]ut she probably would not have done either if there had not been fertile ground for precisely this kind of stab-in-the-back." Hardwick had already published "The Gang" anonymously in *The New York Review of Books* a few weeks before. ("Maisie had always, rather demurely, thought of the great event as a 'defloration,' for the Late Latin, *defloratio*," which was a tribute to passages in *The Group* such as: "Tonight was midsummer's night, the summer solstice, when maids had given up their treasure to fructify the crops; [Dottie] had that in background reading for *A Midsummer Night's Dream*.") When Mary wrote Hannah about the magazine's "treachery" in October, she noted that the editors had never even mentioned the parody, "perhaps hoping that I would not notice it." And that wasn't all. A Levine drawing, a biting caricature, had also been planned, she learned afterwards, but Lowell ("at least as he told me") had insisted he would resign if the editors ran it, and so they hadn't.

Elizabeth Hardwick later wrote McCarthy in Paris to apologize for the parody, which "was meant simply as a little trick," she insisted. She hoped Mary would forgive it, for she valued her friendship and "utterly exceptional company," and didn't know how to express the "sense of desperation" she would feel if it couldn't be put aside. Alluding to the train of abuses that had come McCarthy's way, she echoed Arendt's view that it was "chaos and individual destructiveness rather than any sort of plot" that was at fault. Hardwick herself was "desolated by the glimpses one got of the country, by the grossness of the appetite for publicity, the lack of moral and political standards. . . . And then it is simply horrible that Kennedy is dead," she finished, referring to Kennedy's assassination in Dallas a few months before, adding: "You don't have to answer this." McCarthy didn't.

"I think it's easier to forgive your enemies than to forgive your friends," she commented to Lowell in a 1964 New Year's Eve letter. "With your enemies you don't feel a sense of betrayal, and what is at the bottom of a sense of betrayal but bewilderment—a loss of your bearings?" The usual self-defense was "to revise your opinion of the friend, in a downward direction," but she didn't want to do that with Elizabeth, she said. It would be inconsistent with her sense of truth perhaps—loyalty looming larger in her legend than it would, in the end, for some of her closest friends. Or maybe she decided that Hardwick had merely given *The Group* the 'Mary McCarthy' treatment. When Elizabeth liked Mary's work, she was extravagant in its praise, as when she said of the ideas in "Characters in Fiction" and "Fact in Fiction," in a 1961 review of *On the Contrary* in *Harper's*: "they are the only new things said about the art of the novel in many years."

The fall of 1963 was an "autumn of crackling controversy," when "the entire PR world seems to be throwing bricks at one another," Lowell remarked. Arendt, who was being stormed by a Jewish "mob"—her term, Mary didn't like it—over *Eichmann in Jerusalem,* was particularly stung by the way the *PR* crowd had turned on her. It was one thing for the Anti-Defamation League to instruct rabbis to preach against her on New Year's Day, and quite another for Jewish intellectuals like Lionel Abel, William Phillips, and Saul Bellow to excoriate her for making the trial of Adolf Eichmann an occasion for exploring 'the banality of evil' in a totalitarian state, or for bringing up the culpability of the Jewish councils in the context of Eichmann's crimes against the Jewish people. (In Paris, the *Nouvel Observateur* published extracts from Arendt's book, with commentary entitled *"Est Elle Nazie?"*)

"If I am upset, I can imagine what you must be," Mary had remarked of the Eichmann furor, which had preceded the attack on *The Group,* but also anticipated it, in McCarthy's opinion, as if she and Hannah were tied to the same stake. (Her own defense of *Eichmann in Jerusalem* in *Partisan Review,* "The Hue and Cry," January 1964, would fan the flames of controversy.) The slander against Hannah was the more serious—Abel accused her of making Eichmann "aesthetically palatable, and his victims . . . aesthetically repulsive"— both because the slander was so pervasive, and because it was patently aimed at destroying Arendt's reputation. But the "treachery" of *The New York Review of Books* counted for something, too, McCarthy lamented, all the more because it lacked "even the hypocritical justification that Jewish piety . . . provided."

III

The 1960s had arrived on hissing cats' feet. Everything was in dispute; anything that wasn't, wasn't worth talking about. Younger writers arrayed themselves against older writers, younger critics against older critics. At a much-debated panel entitled "Literary Criticism Today" in the fall of 1963, Dwight Macdonald argued that no American writing of any importance had happened since Faulkner. Susan Sontag, who had recently made her debut with "Notes on Camp," an esssay celebrating the higher aesthetics of kitsch, and taken over Mary McCarthy's theatre column at *Partisan Review,* shot back that Macdonald didn't understand the work of younger writers not of his generation. People like Lionel Trilling and Edmund Wilson— "over-rated," Sontag called Wilson—were through; which moved the fifty-seven-year-old Macdonald to say that "Wilson has more life, is sharper, and has more to say than any of you kids."

Rahv would later sum up the mid-1960s cultural insurrection with his usual pith: "Middleclassicism à la Trilling is out; perversion is in." Privately, to Mary, he fumed: "Susan Sontag. Who is she? . . . Above the girdle, the girl is a square." Norman Mailer, he ventured, was a "psychopath," a "favorite of the literary establishment," who had no ideas. In 1973, with Mailer still a star attraction at *The New York Review of Books,* Rahv complained that he had nothing to sell but his personality. If there was anything that modern criticism had taught writers *not* to do, it was this "substitution of personality for the work itself. . . . If one does possess personality," he wrote Mary, "it will come through."

There was something oxygenating about the breakup of the literary camp, which was hardly breaking up for the first time or the last. In her letters to Hannah, McCarthy sounded genuinely distressed by the "desire to make a sensation" that seemed to have overtaken the intellectual world; certainly it was bewildering and disorienting to find oneself the butt of a scandal that one's own friends were fueling. The last thing she wanted to do was reply to Mailer in *The New York Review of Books,* whose "editors have become showmen," she complained, while the reader is a mere "spectator in a circus ring." But when McCarthy left Paris to keep an appointment at the Ninety-second Street Y in New York, on November 10, 1963, then, on home ground, introduced by the faithful Dwight, she entered the ring.

She wasn't going to defend *The Group* against its attackers, she insisted at first, stepping out on the YMHA's stage on a brisk Sunday afternoon to thunderous applause, looking elegant in a white dress and with graying hair. "Dwight [had] taken care of *that*" in his introductory remarks, which indeed he had, speaking excitedly in his high-pitched, halting voice about how long he had known Mary and how much he admired her work, including *The Group,* which hadn't been understood by its critics. To Chiaromonte, privately, however, Macdonald had confided his doubts: "Mary tried for something very big, a collective novel, but didn't have the creative force to weld it all together. . . ." The YMHA appearance, however, was no time for criticism, especially since Mary McCarthy had just defended him in *The New Statesman* against an attack in *Encounter.* ("It was loyal, trustworthy, brave, honorable, etc. of you to write the letter," Dwight had written Mary in Paris, noting that "friendship, this one at least, is something to be counted on in the flux.") And then, on the tail of

Macdonald's send-off, McCarthy launched her defense of *The Group*.

It was the same case she had presented to the Guggenheim Foundation, the intellectual's brief. *The Group,* she argued from a stage jammed with overflow chairs from the audience, was two things her critics failed to understand: a novel of ideas (a purview of the 'idea of progress'), and also an experiment in marrying style with content, language with concept. Hence the clichés, the trivia, the group-speak mistakenly taken by her detractors as the author's own. As a novelist, she was also interested in showing how everyday functions become technologized. People don't think about sex, they think about contraceptives; women don't think about babies but about breast-feeding versus bottle-feeding. Brand names are used throughout the novel not for snobbish reasons, she stated, but to demonstrate how what is primary—the product—is superceded by what is secondary, the brand. "A lot of the provincial critics got it," McCarthy noted of this deliberate immersion into the mind of the feminine consumer, "while most of the big-city critics did not." The two Normans, for example, saw in her mastery of a vernacular that one reviewer called " 'educated banal' " only a "deteriorated prose style."

The argument left untouched the more serious charge that Mailer had leveled against McCarthy's characters; namely, that they were tiresome: "premature suburbanites," who make no journeys to other classes, who neither participate in the historic events of their time, nor become "victim[s] of [an] outsize passion." Mailer's judgment was not entertained by the vast majority of *The Group*'s readers, who neither shared his premises nor his private vendetta with the author. As criticism, this part of the review was an expression of his vision of what a 'major novel,' a work of realism by a modern Zola, should be doing in the middle of the twentieth century; and exactly what that was remained cloudy. But in his own perverse way, while deliberately diverting "judgment away from [McCarthy's] technique and over to her character," he took both novel and novelist more seriously than many of McCarthy's more satisfied customers.

"Finally she suffers from a lack of reach," he concluded, after paying homage to her "sense of detail . . . her single most impressive achievement." "She chooses to be not close enough to the horror in the closet." Her "nice girls" live on the "thin juiceless crust of the horror beneath . . . the buried diabolisms of the grand and the would-be-grand"—which was Mailer tapping into his own dark closet. (It was shortly before this that he stabbed his second wife, Adele.) But the charge strikes a psychic reef that is indeed missing from Mary

McCarthy's still water of society. In *The Group,* as in most of her fiction, McCarthy's characters rarely cast a shadow longer than the personality index the author gives them. Trouble in McCarthyland is what's just around the corner, not what lies buried in the past, or in the future, or remains otherwise hidden from conventional wisdom. Big events and small, like Kay's incarceration in Payne Whitney, or Dottie, with her never-to-be-used diaphragm, being stood up in Washington Square, are pivots on which fate revolves to make its triumphs known; they rarely admit the unbidden elements of experience into the drama. "One does not have to have that [horror] in one's novel," Mailer said of the underground reality, "but one has to have a sense of that madness if the book is to be resonant, and Mary," he maintained, "is too weak to push through the crust and so cannot achieve a view of the world which has root."

In 1963, Mailer was in thrall to his own glamour-dream of romantic domination; his 'First Lady of Letters' is a female nemesis, whose snowy brow must be 'struck through.' Madness aside, however, he was onto something; something that McCarthy's former student at Bard, Eve Stwertka, also refers to when she wonders why the women in *The Group* never fully come alive for her. It is the problem Mary has with emotions, Stwertka suggests: "She steers away from emotion and doesn't let herself handle emotion, and she is really quite repelled by certain kinds of emotions." A novelist who shrinks from emotion, who fears becoming "physical or even sentimental," she says, risks becoming a caricaturist; so it is with *The Group*; "it comes too close to satire to really work on all the levels a novel should." (The same shortcomings may clear a path to first-rate criticism. "She was our most brilliant literary critic," Gore Vidal said upon Mary McCarthy's death in 1989, because she was "uncorrupted by compassion.")

Madness, of course, *was* a horror in McCarthy's closet. As a teenager in Seattle, the fear of madness took the form of a recurrent anxiety that certain friends and relations (Uncle Frank's wife, Isabel, for one) found her ridiculous. With Edmund Wilson, the fear became a mania. In later years, nothing could be further from the spirit of McCarthy's literary imagination than Mailer's "existential premise" that the writer's task is to break on through to the other side of reason's world. Common sense forbade it. Literature owed its heavenly status to its palpable ability to elevate the unruly experiences of daily life—via the sacraments of character, action, the dramatization of ideas—away from a domain where entropy rules to one of eternal forms. For McCarthy and Edmund Wilson both, literature was a foil against madness, as well as a hedge against death. A devil's bargain, it meant that something was subtracted from the victory, "some scent/some kernel of hot endeavor," in Louise Bogan's words, that distinguishes the living work of art from the merely brilliant, well-crafted one.

The Group is a case in point. Into its carefully lighted scenes, its supple characterizations, its antic situations, McCarthy pours the paradoxical adventures of her youth; of that part of the 1930s that is an extension of her 1920s—although something of the materialist 1950s, when most of the book was written, forms the consciousness of her characters. As social history, *The Group* is a hybrid, a fantasy, which would *not* be "enormously successful as sociology," as Mailer predicted, but would survive instead as a literary confection from a by-gone era, a ventriloquist's tour de force. At Vassar in the early 1990s, the novel is still read by students for whom the old school, the female academy, exercises a mysterious attraction. But there is something missing at the core.

Only rarely does McCarthy falter in her discipline, *Partisan Review*'s reviewer commented shrewdly: "then the *author* enters, and one hears—'Her eyes, which were a light golden brown, were habitually narrowed, and her handsome blowzy face had a plethoric look, as though darkened by clots of thought.' At such moments, one is forcibly reminded of what has been sacrificed to obtain the virtuoso style-that-is-no-style of *The Group*." This 'sacrifice' was something to which McCarthy herself often returned; fretting, in *Ideas and the Novel*, over the constraints of the ventriloquist's box: a Jamesian invention that prevented her from appealing directly to the reader's imagination and intelligence. It was only when she stepped on stage to read aloud from *The Group*, to play its many parts, as she did at the Y in 1963, that her doubts went by the board. Then literature slipped into theater, and Mary McCarthy became star and dramatist both.

Most of McCarthy's readings were good theatre, memorable for the gusto with which she portrayed her more reprehensible characters especially. November 10 was no exception. Reading a passage from Chapter Six, the 'You were Sandison. We were Lockwood' chapter, in which the 'blowzy' Norine Schmittlapp tells Helena about how her husband Put's impotence led her to sleep with Harald, McCarthy's delight in Norine's chicanery was uncontainable. A stray reference to Bloomingdale's in the account of Norine's buying black chiffon underwear to stimulate her husband made her grin; while the line "that should get his pecker up," delivered hand on hip, head thrown back, sent her into gales of laughter.

One thinks of similar accounts of Edmund Wilson, "outrageous but articulate," a contemporary recalls, reading from *Memoirs of Hecate County* at the Ninety-second Street Y in the late 1940s. Wilson, too, is remembered for the lustiness of his rendition of the ranker scenes, and for the satisfaction he took in his creation. In the end, maybe that's what it's all about. "To make something, to give oneself and others pleasure," McCarthy told a CBS interviewer in 1985, who wondered why she had written *The Group* if it wasn't "for fame and fortune," motives McCarthy publicly deplored. "To put something in the world that wasn't there before."

32

Funny Money

"A novelist is an elephant,
but an elephant who must claim to forget."
—MARY MCCARTHY, "ON *MADAME BOVARY*"

Meanwhile, there's the usual picture of Mary, looking just the same as always—neat, clear-featured and pulled together—gazing out over a Parisian suburb, this time," Louise Bogan remarked to Ruth Limmer in her September 1963 letter about *The Group*. The flesh and blood Mary McCarthy, however, had begun to show her seams. Other photographs of the period, unposed, are less flattering. Time has opened the gaps between her front teeth, which are unevenly capped. The sight of her neat little bun, endlessly reproduced in newspapers and magazines, had led McCarthy to chop it off, but the new style, a page boy, hasn't come into focus. She is still slim, but her body has begun to thicken, and the bow in her legs appears more pronounced. " 'Maturity' has definitely set in," remarked an admirer, after getting a close look at McCarthy at the YMHA reading in New York, though Mary looked better than her recent photographs, he thought.

She had reached one of those intervals in a woman's life when the parts don't quite fit together. From her brother Kevin's point of view, Mary had never been very agile. She had never skated or played tennis; she hadn't learned to ride a bicycle until she was a grown woman, and after the late 1950s, she no longer drove a car. Kevin McCarthy was always aware of his sister "*seeming*, when she walked, slightly awkward. With all her grace and beauty and intelligence and wit," he reflects, "she was not graceful physically." In a few years, she would be looking better; the teeth fixed, the hair more gray than not; the tense, eager "yeoman loveliness" that Robert Lowell saw in his Castine neighbor in 1967, evident in the snapshots her husband took. But the year of fame and fortune had taken its toll.

After finishing *The Group* in the spring, Mary and Jim West had treated themselves to a trip to Rome, where she had collapsed. This time, a flu attack turned into viral pneumonia and hepatitis, which lingered throughout the summer of 1963, sapping McCarthy's strength for the month and a half the three West children joined them in Bocca di Magra. On October 8, nonetheless, she had left for a six-day conference on the novel in Madrid; "surreptitiously backed by the Congress for Cultural Freedom and under the semi-protection of the French Cultural Institute," she wrote Hannah Arendt, "it was mainly peopled by Communists and their sympathizers."

The 1963 Madrid conference was an "exhilarating respite"—not only because of the political high jinks but also because news of *The Group* had not yet penetrated the pure mountain air of Madrid. In Paris, McCarthy was besieged by clippings, many hostile, and by endless requests for photographs and interviews. "Success seems to take so much of your time; you are devoured by it," she wrote Hannah. "Yes, fame is very tiresome and very tiring," Arendt replied, after telling her how glad she was to see her on the best-seller list, and happy, too, "that you get so much money. That is the right thing for you, dear," she said, "enjoy it and be happy!"

In Spain, McCarthy was like a child on holiday, touring the countryside in an open-air bus with comrades from many nations and a Franco policeman who accompanied them wherever they went. When she opened her conference address by saying, *"Je ne suis pas Communiste. Je suis même anti-Communiste,"* a lone member of the audience had burst into applause. "That was the cop," she recalled. She had gone on "to turn this around and come out on the other side of the fence," to make a radical critique of the Communists, and the applause was not repeated. The conference itself had turned into a joust between proponents of the *nouveau roman* and social realists, with the Marxist critic George Lukacs serving the young Communists as their Aquinas. Speeches from both sides took a scholastic turn; and Mary spent considerable time outside official sessions with Nathalie Sarraute, and the son-in-law with whom Sarraute was always feuding, " '*mon chou-chou*,' " she called him, Jean-François Revel.

McCarthy was first introduced to Sarraute at a party in Paris shortly before Mary and Jim were married. It was not long after the appearance of *The Planetarium,* a book McCarthy liked, and she had been eager to meet France's leading experimental novelist. But it wasn't until after the Madrid conference that the friendship deepened, and Mary and Nathalie began to lunch together nearly every week at the Coupole or the Ministère. Twelve years McCarthy's senior, Jewish, an intellectual woman, Sarraute, at first, would play the role of female elder in Mary McCarthy's life, not unlike Hannah Arendt. Over lunch, they discovered a striking similarity between Mary's Morganstern grandmother and Sarraute's mother, which even included the botched face-lift. And Sarraute professed herself "smitten" with Arendt, an attraction that did not seem to arouse Mary's jealousy, as would Susan Sontag's overtures to Hannah Arendt in 1967. It was a strange and emblematic relationship, more an alliance than a friendship, and its rupture in 1973 revealed much about the intricacies of French-American literary relations.

The Madrid affair doesn't appear on the official list of conferences sponsored by the Congress for Cultural Freedom. Perhaps the CCF hand was gloved to ensure the presence of all those Party members among the Spanish and Portuguese delegations—most of whom had been in prison under Franco or Salazar. "Nobody on the Left . . . could have believed that the CIA was backing 90 Communists to stay at, you know, not at the Ritz, but—" McCarthy said in 1985, by which she meant "the New Left—the Old Left maybe could have [believed it]." Perhaps subterfuge had been necessary to disarm them; or maybe the gathering was too controversial for Washington to give the meeting open billing.

By the 1960s, the CCF's executive director, Michael Josselson, was struggling to counter the idea that the Congress was a U.S. tool in the Cold War; and it wasn't only left-wing political opponents outside the organization he was up against but anti-Communist intellectuals within it, who could see no other reason for the Congress for Cultural Freedom to exist than to combat Soviet influence in the arts and sciences. For Josselson, the multinational interest transcended the sectarian one; nothing suited his agenda better than an international conference on the novel with Mary McCarthy and Nathalie Sarraute as featured speakers. Meetings like this were like an "Elks convention for the poor Slavs from outer Slobobia to meet George Kennan and Mary McCarthy," says a retired Columbia professor who serviced the CIA pipeline in the 1950s and '60s. Such meetings cast the East/West debate in literary terms; in Madrid, the Western interest in 'pure literature' was advanced another notch (so it was hoped) against the challenge of socialist realism—or 'committed literature,' as the variant was called in Paris.

"Whoever was backing Madrid was doing a very sensible thing, during Franco's lifetime, imagine!" McCarthy reflected in later years. Most of the Communists were young—who knew where they would be positioned twenty years down the road? The CIA's involvement in Madrid, like its support of François Bondy's *Preuves* in Paris and Chiaromonte's and Silone's *Tempo Presente* in Rome, the two CCF magazines McCarthy felt closest to, "obviously was a left-wing activity from the CIA's point of view," and so, from her own point of view, presumably harmless. "I've never had a CIA phobia," McCarthy added, noting that she "never had a Stalinist phobia either." The CIA, "like every organization has a left and a right and a middle . . ." and it was the right wing that was "very, very bad in the CIA, while the left wing had people like [Daniel] Ellsberg in it." (Ellsberg, a Defense Department employee when he liberated the documents that went into *The Pentagon Papers,* was symbolic of a breed of renegade analysts serving the intelligence community who became whistle-blowers in the 1960s and '70s.)

In 1963, of course, Mary McCarthy, like other anti-Stalinists on the conference circuit, wasn't supposed to know that the Congress for Cultural Freedom got its money from the CIA. And for the most part she upheld conventional orthodoxy among liberals—conservatives like Sidney Hook and Diana Trilling were more candid—on the question of whether Western intellectuals knew who was providing all those per diems in Paris, Milan, Berlin, Venice, Rome, Tokyo, and Madrid. They did not know, McCarthy maintained; or at least she didn't, and others, well, they had to be taken one by one.

Nicolas Nabokov had once told Stephen Spender, *Encounter*'s literary editor from 1953 to 1967, about the CIA connection while riding in a taxicab, and then he had jumped out of the cab and disappeared, Spender told Mary in Bocca di Magra in 1966; though in his memoirs, Spender claims he was misled to the bitter end by his American colleagues. As secretary-general of the Congress, Nabokov would have surely known to which government agency he owed the extraordinary flexibility the secretariat enjoyed in Paris. The State Department, which was sometimes said to be the power behind the Congress, couldn't possibly have involved itself in such ideologically slippery enterprises as the Madrid conference or even with a magazine like *Encounter.* Smaller sums were sometimes slipped to itinerant intellectuals such as William Phillips, who got some money from the State Department in 1950, when he traveled on a Rockefeller Foundation grant to Europe, and then again in 1962 when he made the "big jump—what was called a world tour . . ." Mary McCarthy was one of Phillips's references for that trip, which was sponsored by "a combination of State Department and the branch of the Cia [*sic*] Dwight is interested in," he wrote her in May 1962. "It's the Congress and State."

State Department programs were subject to congressional review, as the CIA's chief of International Organizations in the early 1950s, Thomas W. Braden, pointedly reminded the American public in May 1967. "Does anyone really think that congressmen would foster a foreign tour by an artist who has or has had left-wing connections? . . . [W]hen the cold war was really hot, the idea that [the U.S.] Congress would have approved many of our projects was about as likely as the John Birch Society's approving Medicare." Jim West, as a State Department employee himself, had cleared the question up for Mary as early as 1961: CCF programs simply did not appear on State Department dockets. Somebody else was paying the bills. In any event, Phillips's 1962 letter suggests that insiders already knew the score.

And yet officially even Nabokov 'knew nothing.' When Paul Goodman took a stab at publishing the truth in the Winter 1962 *Dissent,* burying his explosive words—"Cultural Freedom and the Encounter of ideas are instruments of the CIA . . ."—inside parentheses in a rambling essay on Kennedy-style 'democracy,' it was Nabokov who wrote back to "deny the implication," and assert that the Congress supported the same "experimental self-improving units" that Paul Goodman did. Even unofficially, "Nicky always claimed that he had not been told it was the CIA," one of Nabokov's friends recalls today.

In Italy, Ignazio Silone must have known, McCarthy thought, "since he was a very wise old political bird. Kot [Jelenski] always thought Silone knew," she added, "because he [Silone] was that kind of experienced political man." Nicola Chiaromonte, however, "was an innocent person," McCarthy insisted, citing Nicola's astonishment, after the CIA's relation to the Congress magazines was officially conceded in 1967, that the CIA would have allowed *Tempo Presente* to publish so many articles critical of American foreign policy. But if Silone knew, wouldn't information of this caliber have found its way to his partner? Italian intellectuals never stop talking among themselves about the intrigues of politics and money. Nor do they commonly display the same shock over CIA revelations as do French and English intellectuals. In 1967, when the cover was blown from *Tempo Presente,* Italians had been accusing everybody of being in the pay of the United States for so long that they were not surprised.

McCarthy herself attributed the smattering of anti-American articles in *Tempo Presente* to the fact that the agency people involved couldn't read Italian. "It was like Bocca di Magra," she said of the magazine, "so far off down the peninsula that nobody paid much attention to what they were doing." That Chiaromonte himself saw things quite differently is indicated by his private assessment of why the CIA suddenly pulled the plug on his magazine. Not the exposé, but "the general policy . . . of appeasement of Russia" explained the "panicky cowardice" of the Congress, he thought; "since we have annoyed Soviet intellectual bureaucracy much more than *Preuves* has. . . ."

The absence of anti-American articles in *Encounter* and the half-dozen English-language journals published throughout the Third World was a telltale fact of another order. *Encounter,* "the most distinguished" of the Congress magazines, in Bob Silvers's opinion, "had a peculiar blind spot—it hardly ever contained any critical articles about the United States, as if this was forbidden territory." When Dwight Macdonald submitted an article in 1958 relating his 'culture shock' at the violence and ugliness of American life, after coming home from a year's sojourn in London as an *Encounter* editor himself, the magazine had accepted the piece, with cuts, then rejected it, then accepted it, with further revisions, and then, after an interminable go-round, summarily rejected it. ("America! America!" ended up in *Dissent,* and sure enough, *Tempo Presente* in Italy.) Stephen Spender had liked it, but his coeditor Irving Kristol found the article " 'almost John Osborne-ish' in its 'unhealthy self-lacerating.' " Nabokov, however, not an editor at all but one of the "front-office Metternichs"—in Macdonald's words—had gotten the last word when he declared that Dwight's essay would make "fundraising" for the Congress harder.

The allusion to fund-raising reflected the CCF's official line that its programs relied upon private philanthropy—not just small fry like Julius Fleischmann and J. M. Kaplan (who presided over the Farfield Foundation), but major foundations like Ford and Rockefeller. But too many writers involved in Congress affairs also served as consultants to the big foundations not to notice that Congress enterprises hardly ever applied for their support. As for *Tempo Presente*'s occasional anti-Americanism, the CIA's International Organization Division itself offers the most convincing rationale for the show of independence. It appears in the last of the division's four-point procedure for infiltrating international bodies: " 'Limit the money to amounts private organizations can credibly spend. . . . Use legitimate, existing organizations; disguise the extent of American interest; protect the integrity of the organization by not requiring it to support every aspect of official American policy.' "

Irving Kristol was another link in the chain of innocents. After Tom Braden dropped his bombshell in the May 1967 *Saturday Evening Post* ("I'm Glad the CIA Is 'Immoral' "), noting, in particular, that an American "agent became an editor of *Encounter*," Irving Kristol declared that it couldn't have been him because he had never been told, and that he would sue anyone who claimed otherwise. Kristol was telling the truth, says a former Farfield official under contract to the CIA, who found Kristol "understanding" when he told him later that he had been "lied to" about the origins of *Encounter*'s funding. When Stephen Spender was finally undeceived, he wondered publicly whether "the individual . . . at the receiving end of an organization which is deceiving him [should] have recourse to the law." But most other Europeans involved knew where the money was coming from, according to the Farfield official, though that didn't necessarily mean they surrendered editorial control, he adds, noting how hard it was to imagine someone "telling Silone or Nick Chiaromonte what to do."

The agent-editor at *Encounter* has never been definitively identified, though the likely candidate is the putative founder of the Congress for Cultural Freedom, Melvin Lasky, who replaced Kristol in 1958 as coeditor of *Encounter*. Like Kristol and Daniel Bell, a veteran of City College faction fights in the late 1930s, Lasky also proclaimed his innocence after the Braden revelation, blaming the CIA's main man in the Congress, Michael Josselson, for deceiving them all; but Stephen Spender is not alone in remembering Josselson and Lasky as "a team who spoke to us as a joint authority . . . on many occasions," and Lasky remains a plausible suspect. In Mary McCarthy's recollection of Macdonald's brief tenure at the magazine, Irving Kristol appears as "the 'other one' " in the proverbial hit team: "there's a front man, a gull, and another one," she says, "and of course Kristol was the 'other one,' and Dwight was the innocent." (Stephen Spender was "equally with Macdonald 'a gull,' " he insists today.) Kristol, at least, was frank with Macdonald about telling him where Dwight's opposition was coming from in 1958, McCarthy maintained, adding that others "were giving him some very false story."

And McCarthy herself, for whom knowingness was next to godliness, how could she not have known who was running the gravy train in the 1950s and '60s? Knowledge in this case wasn't power, though it could save one from being gulled. It might even be an embarrassment for oneself and one's friends—as it was for Paul Goodman, who, together with Alfred Kazin, Philip Rahv, and Meyer Schapiro, remained one of a handful of New York intellectuals who stayed off the train. For an on-and-off-again passenger like Mary McCarthy, the knowledge that a "shrewd, realistic, Jewish semi-intellectual" such as Mike Josselson was working for the CIA might have been muted by her affection for the man—friendship in her case mattering more than politics—as well as by the fact that within the Congress spectrum, the Estonian-born Josselson (who served General Patton as cultural affairs officer during the war), together with Kot Jelenski and François Bondy, also friends, seemed to occupy the Paris secretariat's 'left wing.'

Whatever knowledge McCarthy had did not, in any event, carry with it a responsibility to deceive, as it might for a magazine editor or conference organizer. Only from time to time, it seemed, would she deceive herself—as when Josselson intercepted a letter she had drafted to *The New York Times* around 1964 asserting the independence of CCF magazines, "because he knew it wouldn't be true," she recalled. "He said, 'Just lay off, dear. Forget it.' " On this occasion, she may have been protesting her own innocence as well—but innocence, one suspects, could be chosen at such times, as the West was 'chosen,' for political reasons.

Twenty years later, Mary McCarthy pronounced the CIA's patronage "catastrophic for all the magazines because of the psychological effect of its having been covered [up]. . . . One was either a dupe or a deceiver." In the summer of 1967, however, her name was missing from "A Statement on the CIA" that appeared in *Partisan Review*. Signed by Paul Goodman, Hannah Arendt, Dwight Macdonald, Norman Mailer, William Phillips, Philip Rahv, and Lillian Hellman, among others, the carefully worded protest against the CIA's "regular subsidization" of so-called "independent" publications—as distinguished from its "occasional grants to individuals" for travel and meetings—seemed calculated to clear the names of the American signees and pass the buck to the European magazines, which may explain why McCarthy demurred when Phillips solicited her signature. The Europeans were her friends. Had she made her suspicions public, she might have been regarded as a betrayer—something worse than a deceiver or a dupe, until the Vietnam War turned the CIA connection into the greater liability. But even in 1967, loyalty to Jelenski, Bondy, Chiaromonte, and Spender led Mary McCarthy to keep quiet.

What is noteworthy about her ultimate judgment, which is more emphatic than that of many of her peers but still conventional wisdom on the subject, is that the ax falls on the cover-up and not on the sweetheart deal that Western intellectuals enjoyed with the dark angel of American government for nearly two decades. The latter issue, by far the more interesting, has never received the attention it deserves, perhaps because it still strikes custodians of the period as natural, a nonissue. Just as the possibility that CIA-financed writers in Europe reached the editorial decisions that satisfied their sponsors *all by themselves* somehow proves their independence. An unquestioning anti-communism still blocks the way to reason. Or maybe the rationale is more basic, as plain as the nose on your face, which cannot be seen without seeing yourself as others see you. After World War II, only the CIA endowed a program of politics and culture on any large scale with which Western intellectuals could live. "Since the 'brand' of radicalism we preferred had no appeal for the masses (only the CIA, as it turned out, was interested)," McCarthy reflects in the last chapter of *Hanoi,* "we had no clear alternative but to be 'believing' socialists and practicing members of capitalist society."

II

For intellectuals, the Cold War consensus was born with the CIA's historic perception that "socialists who called themselves 'left'—people whom many Americans thought were no better than Communists—were the only people who gave a damn about fighting Communism." And this sudden and unprecedented appreciation had provided a measure of satisfaction to obscure scribblers: "The fact that the CIA knew about them was itself a measure of how far, for better or worse, they had already traveled . . ." Norman Podhoretz observes. From the socialists' point of view, the CIA "was the only way to get money from the U.S. government that didn't have to be accounted for to Congress." Thus the relationship was sealed by circumstances that allowed it to slip unnoticed into well-worn grooves. It was touched by a higher mission, an anticommunism too esoteric for the masses to understand; it was secret; and it bore strange fruit: Oppenheimer in Berlin, Lowell in Buenos Aires, the ninety Communists in Madrid—who could believe it!

That so many distinguished poets, novelists, artists, critics, sociologists, philosophers, and physicists involved in cultural exchange programs in the 1950s and '60s would find themselves beholden not to a representative arm of government or to the marketplace but to a U.S.

counterintelligence team remains one of the Congress for Cultural Freedom's most provocative legacies. It gives new substance to the much-talked-about 'alienation' of intellectuals after the war. All this is not to deny that the CIA's black operation was itself riddled with contending forces; or that its operators were not occasionally lit by a steely idealism. CIA 'cut-outs' straddled an ideological spectrum, as Mary McCarthy suggests, at least as wide as that which existed among intellectuals outside the agency. But as in Alice's world behind the looking glass, the meaning of a political position—the meaning of a 'left-wing' position on Vietnam, for example—was not what it appeared. Its content was one thing, its effect quite another.

With the waning of the Cold War in the 1960s, what mattered to a responsible political organizer like Michael Josselson was to hang on to his constituency. Older intellectuals whom he respected, such as Chiaromonte, Spender, and Mary McCarthy, were lining up against the widening Vietnam War, while a younger generation was openly making contacts with Communist-led movements of national liberation throughout the Third World. Josselson's own antiwar position in the mid-1960s, no simple matter of expediency, put him in sharp conflict with the Indian and Australian branches of the Congress for Cultural Freedom. He "agree[d] with [George] McGovern," he wrote the prowar Australian chapter in May 1967, "that our deepening military involvement in Vietnam is the most regrettable diplomatic, political, and moral failure in our national history." When a CIA specialist openly applied to attend a seminar organized by *China Quarterly* (a Congress magazine), he objected strenuously. Michael Josselson's antiwar stand may have even tripped the wire that sent an order cascading out of Lyndon Johnson's Oval Office in 1967 to blow the Congress for Cultural Freedom out of the water. But its immediate effect, intentional or not, was to hold down the fort; to assure the continuity of CIA programs in the field of culture by securing the allegiance of influential intellectuals around the world, who had begun to speak out against U.S. intervention in Southeast Asia with a fervor not heard since the 1930s.

Had Josselson been a free agent, he might have turned state's evidence against his superiors, and cut himself and his clients loose from a sinking ship. In her own way, it was what McCarthy did when she temporarily jettisoned her next novel, *Birds of America*, along with her "detachment and novelistic powers of objectivity," to go to Vietnam "looking for material damaging to the American interest. . . ." To break from the CIA, however, would have asked too much of such a man, who was not so different from dozens of State Department and Pentagon bureaucrats—even Secretary of Defense Robert McNamara was said to be 'secretly against the war'—who gnawed their knuckles for the duration of the bloodshed. Instead, Josselson quietly resigned from both the Congress and the CIA in the fall of 1967, and the ship sailed on, minus its cultural-affairs program—which found a new, albeit less imaginative benefactor in the Ford Foundation.

The likelihood that Braden's revelation was originally calculated by an embattled President Johnson to deliver the deathblow to the Congress for Cultural Freedom has been suggested by a veteran of the period. Asked why Braden spilled the beans, a former Farfield official speculates that Johnson had become furious when he discovered that some of the anti-American sentiments from Europe were coming from CIA-supported magazines and conferences. " 'To hell with them!' he probably said. 'We'll destroy them!' " A year and a half before, American intellectuals had turned a White House Festival of the Arts—originally conceived as a tool to quiet opposition to the war—into an angry platform on Vietnam. Robert Lowell had refused his invitation (as had Edmund Wilson, with a "brusqueness" that stunned the festival's organizer, Eric Goldman); and Dwight Macdonald had arrived with a petition supporting Lowell and denouncing American policy, which was signed by Hannah Arendt, Lillian Hellman, Alfred Kazin, Larry Rivers, Philip Roth, Mark Rothko, William Styron, and Mary McCarthy (among the uninvited). At dinner, Macdonald had collected nine more signatures, almost coming to blows with Charlton Heston and reportedly leaving the President with the feeling afterward that the White House had been taken over by a gang of traitors. The idea that Lyndon Johnson might have subsequently interested himself in the mid-1960s dissolution of both the National Student Association—another CIA front organization lobbying against the war—and the Congress for Cultural Freedom is not hard to imagine.

Why the CIA itself didn't end its subsidy in the early 1960s, after Cold War confrontations involving students and intellectuals had subsided, and the U.S. Congress had mellowed on questions of cultural exchange, is another question. "You can't call in a fleet of battleships after they are once dispatched," the ex-Farfield official remarks, which is part of the answer; government programs invariably perpetuate themselves as sinecures for the interest groups involved. But for the CIA's first generation of spooks, whose radical 'Thirties' remain their clandestine service in the 1940s and '50s, there is another factor: a curious nostalgia for the life of the mind that inclined 'semi-intellectuals' like Josselson to regard the secret manipulation of magazines, seminars, and conferences dedicated to the 'free flow of ideas' as more than a Cold War necessity. There was something redemptive in it, something selfless.

After American-Soviet tensions relaxed, new revolutionary movements in the Third World had "stolen the great words . . . 'Peace' and 'Freedom' and 'Justice,' " as Braden put it, together with the twin promises that the Russian Revolution had unleashed of a classless society and a transformed mankind. For the agency's dreamers, the OSS men who had flirted with a sanitized leftism after the war, it was more important than ever to demonstrate that culture behind the golden arches was preferable to culture on the barricades. After 1969, of course the CIA's covert operations in the field of politics and propaganda turned dirty. Under the agency's COINTELPRO program, student antiwar organizations, coalitions, and newspapers were targeted not for manipulation but for immobilization. Alongside COINTELPRO's Operation Chaos, the Congress for Cultural Freedom was a tea party.

And what of the intellectuals themselves? In the end, an attraction to powerful patrons proved stronger than the "peculiar spell" (Braden again) that a socialist vision of society had once cast over their imaginations. They had been flattered and fed for too long to break the tie themselves. Cut loose from the ship, cast adrift on society's open seas, what would they have done with their freedom? Without the CIA subsidy, in Mary McCarthy's opinion, the Congress magazines would have failed, period. For her, the tie was worth it; at least in the case of *Preuves* and *Tempo Presente*, both of which filled a void that in *Preuves*' case, she believed, was never again filled in France.

The void, nonetheless, leaves one wondering about the vitality of the intellectual life behind it. "The CIA's most important impact was that it made us unafraid to go ahead and do what we thought was right," Gloria Steinem declared in 1967, when her own cover in the CIA-funded Independent Research Service was blown. "It increased, not diminished, our freedom of action." But what kind of 'freedom' is it that requires the secret services of government to protect it from its competitors?

That American writers should and could have gone it alone is a possibility that Bob Silvers still entertains. Had there been no CIA support, perhaps "other kinds of magazines that were not tied to that secret source of ultimate control would have emerged. . . . They wouldn't have been as elaborate or there wouldn't have been as much travel money," he suggests, "but people like Mary or Dwight were used to collaborating on small magazines. . . ." For Silvers, the "perfectly obvious thing is that the relations between intellectuals, people doing serious work, should not require the persons in charge to lie." For him, the cover-up poisons the well; but Silvers, too, leaves unexamined that curious harmony of interests that allowed intellectuals to work so compatibly with the propaganda wing of government.

By the 1960s, Mary McCarthy and Dwight Macdonald were used to bigger magazines and extended travel, with first-class accommodations in Mary's case. "Like you I preferred the less grand more grand Grand," Kevin McCarthy wrote his sister in 1966 of a fashionable hotel in Venice; though Mary remembered her brother staying at the more expensive Gritti, and at the Ritz in London, where she wouldn't "dream of daring to pay the room rentals there, [though] Kevin felt his image required it." They had both inherited their parents' appetite for luxury, Kevin proposed. Mary, however, began to watch her expenses once she began to make real money, if only because her expenditures had increased: a white Mercedes convertible for Jim's November 1963 birthday, periodic loans to Kevin, who was divorced in 1964 and paying alimony, and, from 1965 to 1966, six hundred dollars a month to Reuel and his new wife, Marcia.

After Vietnam heated up, she and Dwight Macdonald would confer on several schemes to mobilize public opinion for American withdrawal from Southeast Asia, beginning with tax refusal. During the Christmas 1972 saturation bombing of North Vietnam, McCarthy enlisted Macdonald and others in her plan to send a group of prominent citizens to Hanoi to stave off a possibly genocidal raid by American B-52s on the Red River dikes. But few of these proposals materialized—and none included an attempt to start a new magazine; that impulse was exhausted in the early 1950s with the death of *politics* and the stillbirth of *Critic*.

When these two old friends made the moves that cut their ties to the past, which both Dwight and Mary did in the late 1960s with a flair for the dramatic that sets them apart from most of their generation, they acted individually and impulsively—after the CIA bridge was burned. Far from fashioning themselves into a new intellectual elite, one endowed with "an historical privilege," as Diana Trilling saw it in 1967, "to propose and even direct the positive operations of government," they joined the young rebels of the 1960s in the back of the class—the 'vermin' that Edward Shils referred to when he cried, in December 1968, "The WASPS have abdicated. What has taken their place? Ants! Fleas!"

Part Eight

▪

Paris/Hanoi/Castine/New York: 1964–1989

33

Princess in Paris

"I think I've been longing to get

into a fight with someone—France or Sartre and Simone.

It is the same thing."

—MARY MCCARTHY TO HANNAH ARENDT, 12/22/64

*P*aris has always been a gateway to fantasy for American writers, as it was during the eighteenth century for American Revolutionaries. Franklin and Jefferson mingled with philosophers, artists, and physiocrats in the salons of the Faubourg Saint-Honoré after the American Revolution. Paris was their intellectual capital; London was business, banking, and law; America was the offspring, the synthesis, the Grand Experiment. American writers have often been drawn to one feuding parent or another when the experiment ran thin, or to their nemesis, the 'scarlet woman of the steppes.'

For the men of the Enlightenment, there was nothing otherworldly about the lure of Paris. The life of minds like Franklin's, Jefferson's, and John Adams's (who also lingered in the city after negotiating the Treaty of Paris in 1783) ranged freely over philosophy, government, architecture, education, science, agriculture, and mechanics; and in the broad esplanades opening to the Seine, the new public buildings constructed under Louis XVI, the Place de La Concorde, the Théâtre Français, the Palais de Justice, these veterans of the Revolution found a concrete embodiment of Reason's dream of mastering the physical universe. Paris, Jefferson noted approvingly, was the only city in the world with a municipal regulation relating the height of its buildings to the width of the streets on which they stood.

In one form or another, the French capital would always offer a reconciliation of the rational life with the classical ideal. So it was for Mary McCarthy. And for another American writer closer to McCarthy in time and style, Edith Wharton. "[T]he whirling princess, the great and glorious pendulum, the gyrator, the devil-dancer, the golden eagle, the Fire Bird, the Shining One, the angel of desolation . . . the historic ravager": The striking phrases are Henry James's speaking of Edith Wharton, who settled in Europe after her divorce in 1913 and maintained a beautifully appointed house in Paris. Any one of the images might fit Mary McCarthy, who was, at the end of 1964, in one of her 'angel of desolation' phases.

When McCarthy was seized with the urge to scrap with Sartre and Simone de Beauvoir, along with a France that was 'aussi Sartre,' to paraphrase de Gaulle, she had just emerged from a seven-week bout with the French translators of The Group. The original translation had proved a disaster when the translator, "Coco" Gentien, gave the second half of the book to his cousin, a businessman known as "Fifi" Fenwick, who then rewrote his part, upgrading the characters in the Social Register and downgrading the others. After presenting Mary with a white cyclamen from his greenhouse, Fifi Fenwick vanished. The new translators were another team. "Both fairies," Mary wrote Hannah, albeit "sweet ones." Translations, for a writer fluent in the second language, not to mention a writer as careful with words as McCarthy, were a bane no more easily borne than ignored.

At the end of 1964, McCarthy had also taken a potshot at Sartre and his "life companion," which, while it produced a "cause célèbre" in Paris, had left her feeling uncomfortable. The occasion was a debate organized by Young Communist leaders at the Mutualité, a Left Bank hall used for political meetings that reminded Mary of the old Webster Hall in lower Manhattan, although the likelihood of four thousand young people assembling to consider the question "What Can Literature Do?" in the United States is hard to imagine.

At the meeting, Sartre and de Beauvoir had been uneasily pitted against the novelist Jorge Semprun, a freethinking member of the Communist party sympathetic to the Young Communists, and Jean Ricardou, a partisan of the nouveau roman, among others. Semprun had offered "a plain, blunt answer" to the literature question when he said, citing Solzhenitsyn's A Day in the Life of Ivan Denisovich, that what literature can do is tell the truth. "To vow to tell the truth, whether pleasing to the authorities or to your readers, is genuine literary commitment," McCarthy observed, adding that she herself knew of no other kind.

Jean Ricardou's response was more mischievous, but it won her admiration, as well. What literature can do is interrogate the world by submitting it to the test of language, Ricardou suggested. "Language, for the maker of fictions, is not a vehicle for conveying messages to the public; it secretes . . . a message or messages in its own structures." To weigh literature in the balance with hunger was the "Art-for-Art's-sake formula turned inside out." An aesthete might say, " 'Art is more important than a child's dying from hunger,' while Sartre says 'A child's dying from hunger is more important than art.' " It was like choosing between pears and yellow. "Language," McCarthy paraphrased Ricardou, speaking also for herself, "cannot be opposed in a scale of values to man, since language *is* man. In a world without language, *i.e.* without literature, a child's dying from hunger could have no meaning."

In her write-up for the *Nouvel Observateur,* McCarthy had noted Sartre's discomfort at finding himself stuck in the position of defender of the faith in " 'committed literature,' " though what that meant was never clearly explained, least of all by Simone de Beauvoir, who spoke "with an air of nervous bravery" about literature as a " 'vision of life' " and a "remedy for solitude," while Sartre expressed his bromides with "dogmatic intransigence," as though the two of them were "facing lions. But *they* were the lions. . . ." McCarthy exclaimed. Youth is always attracted to the minority position, something Sartre knew well; hence "the current dilemma of Sartre and Simone de Beauvoir throning in France," she wrote; they "cannot be a minority and in the majority simultaneously. . . ." In McCarthy's "Crushing a Butterfly," youth got the last word: " '*Ce sont les écrivains réactionnaires de gauche*' " ("Those are the reactionary writers of the Left"), a young man is overheard telling a friend as the meeting ends.

The *Nouvel Observateur* was not pleased; and when McCarthy refused to 'soften' the story, it was rejected. The leading French leftist weekly could not afford to offend Sartre; but then neither could the mainstream *Figaro Littéraire,* which also returned the story when McCarthy offered it to them. And so she had given it to François Bondy at *Preuves,* who routed it on to *Der Monat* and *Encounter.* "The sad thing is that it is not even very good," she commented at the time. Because it had become a "document," she wasn't allowed to change it. Sartre-bashing, of course, was a mainstay of the Congress for Cultural Freedom. Chiaromonte had just debunked Sartre's refusal of the 1964 Nobel Prize. Bondy would take apart de Beauvoir's *Force of Circumstance* the following fall. For Mary, there could not be the same satisfaction in baiting Sartre and de Beauvoir under Congress auspices as there might have been in their own camp.

In December 1964, McCarthy was midway through a documentary film on Paris for the BBC, "a little study of *bien pensant* France," done for the money, which then came late, as such checks often do, when she no longer needed it. The film, her first, had also left her with mixed feelings. She had tried to communicate what she liked about Paris, the city of gray stone with its narrow, winding streets, its medieval cathedrals and tiny *épiceries*. It was harder to photograph a negative statement, such as " 'there are hardly any clocks in Paris,' " and the experience had revealed the essentially static nature of her visual imagination. Most of the ideas she tried to communicate cinematically were about things that stand still; she thought in photographs, not in moving pictures. But the actual filming, which was "grueling," was redeemed by the heady experience of working collectively with a French film crew—"a queer kind of democracy, pro tem," she found.

McCarthy's relations with the French literary world were less satisfactory—though years later she would tell friends that she liked Paris as a place to work because she didn't know anybody, which was not to be taken literally; a guest at the Wests' annual Thanksgiving or Valentine's party might be forgiven for concluding that Mary McCarthy knew everybody. (*Dans son salon, elle reçoit les plus grands noms de la littérature* [In her salon, she received the greatest names in literature]," a French newspaper said at her death.) But her twenty-eight-year sojourn in France (even after buying the house in Maine in 1967, and after Jim West retired from the OECD in 1980, Mary and her husband spent most of each year in Paris) was lived outside the main currents of French cultural life.

"She was isolated in Paris," as was Edith Wharton, says Nicholas King, Mary and Bowden Broadwater's old Newport friend, who was press attaché at the U.S. Embassy in the 1960s, and a cousin of Wharton's on his grandmother's side. Just as Edith Wharton's Parisian friends stood on the fringes of French culture (her real intimates in Paris were Henry James and J. M. Barrie), so did Mary's friends, with the exception of Nathalie Sarraute. Like Mario and Anjou Levi, Kot Jelenski, François Bondy, Georges Bernier, Claude and Jean-François Revel, they were not "standard people." "I just don't belong to any French social or literary milieu," McCarthy told an interviewer in 1985. "I have friends—that's much better." Kot Jelenski confirmed this. "In Paris everything is governed by cliques," while Mary's "sociability," he explained, was "anti-clique." French literary people see each other much more rarely than Americans, McCarthy went on to say. "Each one has a set that revolves around him that can contain a doctor, an artist, a city planner and a writer, but not two writers." Unlike New York, one might add, where writers camp with other writers, painters with painters and maybe a musician or two. In France, writers get together during political emergencies, like the Algerian War or the May revolt in 1968.

New York would have been Mary McCarthy's undoing had she not left it when she did. When the cultural bandwagon began to roll in the early 1960s, she might have been hard-pressed to steer clear of it. Had she become a regular at the Theatre of Ideas, spoken on panels, talk shows, hobnobbed at Elaine's on the Upper East Side, or slipped into social orbit alongside a "swinging soothsayer" such as Arthur Schlesinger, Jr. (the phrase is *Time*'s), her reputation might have sagged with the weight of publicity. ("New York is both quiet and very tiring," Elizabeth Hardwick wrote Mary early in 1970, referring to the inertia that lay behind the bustle. "The phone rings all day with meetings one could attend, plays one is urged to go to . . . [There are] malignant growths of mail, bills, anxiety about the cost of things, the look of things, clothes, weight, hair, hems. . . . You feel as if you'd been in a play running for years and then it closed and you went uptown and no one called." Washington, meanwhile, was overrun with "these strange, old-fashioned people . . . putty-faced creatures, policing the veldt. . . .")

Living in Paris, Mary could fly to Hungary to attend a PEN Congress, or join Jim West on an OECD trip to Bonn, Cologne, and Trier, both of which she did in the winter of 1964. She could accept jury invitations to festivals, which were "a way of seeing friends and occasionally making a new one." She could always go to London, where everybody she knew gave parties, to review a new John Osborne play and appear on the BBC; or fly to Rome, which she and Jim usually did around Christmas (in later years staying at the American Academy) to visit with the Chiaromontes and Carmen Angleton. "In London she would have been lionized beyond belief," another American friend in Paris, Eileen Geist Finletter, suggests. "In Paris she was safe. . . . She could work."

Particularly during the Vietnam War, Paris impressed McCarthy as "a very healthy place to be . . . I was able to do so much more," she said; 'much more' including raising money for draft resisters and American soldiers AWOL in France. In New York, she would have spent all her time going to cocktail parties, which is what many of her friends were doing. In 1985, she felt the same way: "there's something very unserious about politics in New York," she thought. "Basically it's sort of a dinner party, cocktail party, look-at-your-watch life."

McCarthy, unlike Wharton, kept herself up-to-date on French culture, but she didn't know a great many French people, and she didn't like them very much. Among writers, she disliked Marguerite Duras, whom she saw several times with Sonia Orwell, almost as much as Simone de Beauvoir; the dislike was mutual. French people generally she found self-righteous and opinionated, and they, in turn, rarely responded to the peculiar intensity of her personality; they admired her as a figure, but they didn't 'get' her. When she died, French Minister of Culture Jack Lang, sent Jim West a "sickening telegram" (in Nicholas King's opinion) about how " 'this great spirit . . . led every movement, was in every debate' . . . very French. And they certainly thought that in the end," King states. But it wasn't Mary. ("*L'une des pionnieres du feminisme. . . . on disait d'elle qu'elle était la 'Simone de Beauvoir américaine'* [One of feminism's pioneers . . . one might say she was the 'American Simone de Beauvoir']," declared *Le Quotidien de Paris* on October 27, 1989, which showed how much they knew.)

What the French missed in Mary McCarthy, King suggests, is what they missed in Edith Wharton: a "personal authority . . . impossible to convey." She was hard to fathom precisely because she didn't find a school or an 'idea'; she was not associated with an ism, but rather sowed seeds of dissension whenever one appeared. The *nouveau roman,* McCarthy once called a "hoax," imposed on the French public "by a mixture of incessant theorizing, astute publicity, and terror." Any notion of "program" in the arts struck her as "senseless," she said in 1971, at the height of the *nouveau nouveau roman,* "nowhere more so than in literature."

Eileen Finletter is also reminded of Edith Wharton when she considers McCarthy's relative estrangement from the French literary scene. The French didn't cotton to Wharton, she thinks, "because she was an overpowering woman and they didn't understand her, and what they don't understand bothers them." Something about the Anglo-Saxon temperament—in Mary's case her Irish hotheadedness—remains impenetrable to the French. "You have to be very '*légère,*' no matter how serious you are," Finletter explains. "Some people are born with it. Mary was not. And at times she would come down like an elephant, which she [wasn't]," but in French she sounded heavier. Her French was grammatically perfect, though her accent was "appalling," another friend recalls (hailing a waiter, Mary sometimes sounded like Jean Seberg in *Breathless*). It was almost as if her refusal to master the rhythms of French speech, much less the body language, was a form of resistance to the culture itself. Perhaps it was because "she [didn't] have a French turn of mind," as Finletter suggests; and also because "it was extremely frustrating not to be able to be witty in another language." Language meant too much to her to risk being anything less than perfect in its expression. Whatever the reasons, there was a restraint on Mary McCarthy in French-speaking company that wasn't there with her English-speaking friends.

None of these restraints inhibited McCarthy's social impulses, however, which were in their own way political impulses. As usual, alliances were struck and broken at parties, especially parties at 141 Rue de Rennes, whose sixth-floor seven-room apartment had acquired, by Christmas 1964, both an elevator and a sleep-in maid, the Polish housekeeper who had looked after the West children in Warsaw and would look after Mary and Jim on both sides of the Atlantic until 1987. At least in the beginning, parties at the Wests' sometimes resembled the 'Turkish bazaars' described in *The Truants,* with the international set distributed on chintz-covered sofas and chairs instead of the Bauhaus modern favored by Philip and Nathalie Rahv. Only later, when Mary was comfortably settled with her own group, which included the literati of three continents, as well as a handful of American journalists in Paris—Jonathan Randal, Flora Lewis, Tom Curtiss, Jane Kramer, along with Gloria and Jim Jones and Jessie and Clement Wood— would she come into her own as a mistress of ceremonies. In the 1970s and '80s, an evening at the Wests for a hundred friends served her visiting American friends as a salon in the grand style; Mary McCarthy had become, as Kramer recalls, "their most celebrated American-in-Paris." The parties themselves grew more relaxed, as was the hostess, who threw herself into preparations, pounding the veal, stringing the beans, hand-whipping the mayonnaise, peeling dozens of oranges for an exotic Middle Eastern dessert—alongside her maid and sometimes her secretary, who frequently stayed late the afternoon of a party— with the air of an excited Cinderella anticipating the ball. In her own way, and on a scale undreamed of fifty years before, she had become the 'fabled Czerna Wilson' of Seattle's Queen Anne Hill—though with her beribboned gifts at Valentine's parties, she reminded Jessie Wood of "a lady giving a party for her garden club."

At a party for Nicola and Miriam Chiaromonte in January 1965, however, "full of widows, like *Richard III*"—Sonia Orwell, Francine

Camus, and the widow of the writer Georges Bataille—the hostess was disturbed by an impression of "the second-rate or also-rans" that France, perhaps, imposed on the "slightly marginal people" who comprised her circle. Even Nathalie Sarraute had made a disagreeable impression that night when she talked about Simone de Beauvoir's Chicago affair with Nelson Algren (then featured in a *Newsweek* review of *Force of Circumstance*) with a "malice in her sharp face [that] was like a kind of voracious greed." Sarraute had arrived with two "sycophantic" young men who circled around her like satellites, and the whole evening had made McCarthy feel as if "a disappointed minority was assembled. . . . What used to be called the anti-Communist Left—that is, the minority of a minority" (an interesting allusion, suggesting that the critical function of the antis in society, when inverted into the anti-antis, turns to spite).

Nathalie Sarraute's 'sharp face' appears again and again in McCarthy's recollections. "There is something of a little forest animal in that face, the look of the alerted eyes," she said in Paris in 1986, picturing a recent evening on the Rue de Rennes when Nathalie asked her host to pour her a stiff bourbon before dinner. "She got completely plastered," McCarthy remembered. "She was sitting at the dining room table next to Jim, a rather small person, and she slid under the table and the next minute she reappeared, and this little head came up, with the eyes. . . ."

Speaking of their friendship, which never fully recovered from a break in 1973 over a negative review of one of Sarraute's novels in *The New York Review of Books*, which Sarraute blamed on Mary even though she didn't write it, McCarthy says: "I liked her as a person, I still do, except she's mad, and of course it's really obvious in the books, too. . . . But she has a very pleasing voice and a marvelous face." To convince Sarraute that she could not have dictated editorial policy at *The New York Review of Books*, she had showed her Mailer's "The Mary McCarthy Case," which "shook her for a moment" but didn't dissuade her. Elizabeth Hardwick and Hannah Arendt had also been blamed; although Arendt, McCarthy suggests, like herself, the author of a glowing review of Nathalie Sarraute's work in a previous issue, was more likely blamed for the "awful crime" of falling asleep in the front row during a lecture Sarraute gave at Princeton in 1972. Hardwick had been accused of snubbing Nathalie at a Christmas party at the Wests in 1972, when Lizzie had "turned away" because her French was poor. "The whole thing was seen as a 'conspiracy,' " McCarthy recalls; Sarraute would be "unpersuaded" for a time, then return to the obsession, "because for some reason she wanted to believe it."

One reason was near at hand. In Paris, where writers have traditionally had more power than in New York, a respected author may overrule an editor's decision to assign the book of a friend to a potentially hostile reviewer. McCarthy herself had pulled rank when she refused an invitation to write for the *Nouvel Observateur* in 1968, because of *"Hannah Arendt: Est Elle Nazie?"* When the editor, Jean Daniel, wondered how he could make amends—*"Vous avez parfaitement raison. C'était honteux* [You are perfectly right, it was shameful]," he said—she suggested that he allude to Arendt in another context, "and attach words of praise and, if possible, regret." A writer like Sarraute, who with *Tropisms* (1938) and *Portrait of a Man Unknown* (1947) pioneered what Sartre called the French *"anti-roman,"* might be said to stand 'above criticism' in France. Like Samuel Beckett, Alberto Giacometti, Marguerite Yourcenar, and Marguerite Duras, "solitary people," Kot Jelenski explains, who inhabit "peculiar niches of their own," she is one of the *"santone,"* the "untouchables," of the pantheon, "about whom nobody in Paris writes a bad word."

When Bob Silvers learned that Sarraute was still blaming McCarthy for the review nearly ten years later, he, too, had tried to set her straight. When Sarraute wrote him to say that it wasn't the review but something else Mary had done that led to the break (something about treating her in a "rough way and contradicting her," McCarthy suggested), Silvers, always the peacemaker, wrote back to say that whatever had happened, "it was surely a case where generosity of spirit was what was really called for." Sarraute then sent him a note saying, " 'I appreciated your reply' "; and Mary, Silvers claims, told him things were "smoothed over." But Sarraute, who would always see Mary, Hannah, and Lizzie as members of the *New York Review* clique, never again invited the Wests to her country house on weekends; nor did she resume her lunches with Mary at the *Coupole,* though they saw each other on ceremonial occasions.

"She wanted to break with me," McCarthy concluded simply. "I think that she perhaps just got sick of me, of our friendship and those weekly lunches. . . . Maybe this is true of many of her friendships; a moment comes when she wants to break, and with a paranoid psychology it's not hard to find a reason." Jelenski concurs in the reference to Sarraute's paranoia. "One could spend hours with Nathalie," he recalled in 1986, "saundering about like kids [goats] in green pastures, and three days later the suspicion would overtake her that she had confided too much." As in *Tropisms*, "what happens *under* a conversation is what matters—so that one is always under suspicion." But Sarraute, he thinks, may have stopped seeing Mary for a simpler reason. She was "shocked by Mary McCarthy's bourgeois style," he says, referring to the "formal conventions" McCarthy adopted at dinner parties, seating people according to importance. "The French are conventional," he explains; "they are conventionally unconventional," while Mary was too "unconventionally conventional" for Sarraute's taste. (McCarthy's formalities never bothered him. "Ritual made things easier for her"; her character depended on it—all the more important in her case, Jelenski suggested while she was still alive, since "Mary's work is really herself.")

Other differences may have also doomed the relationship with Sarraute: Israel, for example, which Nathalie visited during the Arab-Israeli conflict in 1969, returning to Paris in a state of "passionate partisanship for the Israelis." McCarthy was eager to discuss the problems inherent in the "*voluntary* communism" Sarraute had discovered in the kibbutzim. Didn't it amount to "rule by your neighbors," which could have very unpleasant features? "[I]t might be preferable to be ruled by the state," Mary suggested, "which at least would leave you with the psychic freedom of disagreement." But Nathalie had shut off any discussion by taking the familiar line that improvements must await the coming of peace, which became "an alibi for everything," in McCarthy's opinion.

Sarraute was "obsessed by the *survival* of Israel, as though it were a beloved person in danger," McCarthy wrote Hannah Arendt. She herself didn't see how, "short of a miracle," Israel could survive in the long run "*qua* Israel, i.e., as an artificial willed circumstance; though if the Soviet Union deported its Jews there, that would at least give the nation a 'demographic boost.'" Her own view could not help but irritate Nathalie Sarraute: "if there were no anti-semitism [sic], there would be no pressing need for Israel," Mary reasoned, "but Israel, in turn, placed where it is in history and geography, excites anti-semitism or . . . offers a pretext for it." She saw no way out: "If the Israelis make concessions to the Palestinians (which they ought to do anyway), then they are . . . in danger of losing their national identity, of becoming once again a minority which could anticipate persecution." Yet somewhere along that road, it seemed to her, was the point where a "miracle" might occur.

After reminding McCarthy, apropos the kibbutzim, that "if one honestly believes in equality, Israel is very impressive," Arendt had been moved to expatiate on the argument that "you needed Israel in case another catastrophe happens in the Diaspora or/and because antisemitism [sic] is eternal. . . ." The argument is "specious," she declared. "The Jews actually are as afraid of complete assimilation as they are of extermination," she said, recalling a remark Ben-Gurion once made to the effect that he hoped his sons would die in Israel but that he had little hope his grandsons would. One might wonder, then, why Israel pressed "this nearly hopeless business," Arendt continued; and the answer, "the really Jewish answer," she said, was that a second catastrophe in the Holy Land (after the destruction of the Temple in A.D. 70) "will do for the coming centuries or perhaps millenia what the first did in the past. The memory will keep the people together; the people will survive." This was all that mattered. "Jews think: Empires, governments, nations come and go; the Jewish people remains. There is something grand and something ignoble in this passion," Arendt reflected, adding that she thought she didn't share it. "But even I know that any real catastrophe in Israel would affect me more deeply than almost anything else," she told Mary. Nathalie's partisanship struck Hannah as "naive and childish, she talks like any unreflected Jew"; and she noted, testily, that it was "quite characteristic that she has reflected upon herself almost excessively and still it never occurred to her to examine herself qua Jewess"—something Hannah Arendt did in the little-known biography of the Weimar figure she once described as her "closest friend, though she has been dead for some 100 years": *Rahel Varnhagen: The Life of a Jewess* (1959/1974).

The real tension in Nathalie Sarraute's and Mary McCarthy's relationship very likely grew out of the dissonance between their respective talents: McCarthy's, essentially critical; Sarraute's, inventive. In this difference certainly lay the original attraction, which is set forth, on McCarthy's side, in two of the most admiring appraisals of contemporary fiction she ever wrote, both about Nathalie Sarraute: a review of *The Golden Fruits* for *The New Statesman* (1964) and of *Between Life and Death* for *The New York Review of Books* (1969).

Both novels plumb the shallows of the literary life with an ear tuned to the successful author's cant: " 'I always write on the typewriter. Never in long-hand' " (which might have been Mary, who usually composed directly on a typewriter, a manual). And the interviewer's " 'Where do you find your ideas?' 'How did you get your start?' . . . 'You have a "thing" about fountain pens? How interesting.' " "Such interrogatories," McCarthy notes in her review of *Between Life and Death,* "are the modern index to fame, above all in

Europe, where the publication of a book is the signal alerting a mass of professional questioners with pencils and notebooks, tape recorders, microphones, cameras." It was a phenomenon—this moment when "a factory whistle [blows] in the communications industry"—that McCarthy knew firsthand after *The Group,* and found hard to resist (her protests to the contrary). In criticism, however, she made her amends:

> Insofar as we are famous, we are fools, and fame is something we cannot exactly help but which is done to us with or without our eager co-operation. . . . [I]f a writer has the folly to complain of his fame, he is smiled at, like a rich person talking about the "curse" of having money. The writer wanted it, did he not? He worked for it. Probably what he really wanted was glory, which, unlike fame, is not a market commodity.

For Sarraute, McCarthy's reviews were the attraction. "She was very, very enthusiastic, oh yes, *deeply, really* [enthusiastic]" about the 1969 review, McCarthy recalled. She was less happy when Mary remarked of the controversial 1973 novel, *Vous les entendez,* that "it was her most finished, perfect little work . . . in form," but that she didn't like it as much as *Between Life and Death.* "To a writer those are just fatal words, to say that you don't like the last one as much as the one before"; and even though Sarraute had agreed with her, saying, " 'That's just what I feel myself,' " McCarthy speculated later that she had overstepped herself with even a gently implied criticism.

On the subject of Mary's fiction, Sarraute had nothing much to say, except to declare of *Birds of America* that the hero, Peter Levi, was based on her. "I don't think she had any interest in anybody else's writing," McCarthy states; at least she never heard her express it. An exception was the young French novelist Monique Wittig, whose technical innovations in narrative form both women championed; McCarthy, in another glowing tribute: "Everybody's Childhood," a 1966 review of Wittig's *The Opoponax.*

Returning to their differences, McCarthy thinks: "Maybe it's too nerve-wracking if you're someone like Nathalie, to be praised by someone [for whom] you feign respect, because how long can it go on?" Perhaps McCarthy's own shortcomings as a fiction writer were the irritant. It is a striking conjecture for a writer who thought of herself as a novelist rather than a critic, and who rated fiction higher than criticism, because only with a novel can one 'put something new in the world.' To see herself as wanting in the eyes of a master, however, or in her own eyes, was another way of keeping faith with the craft.

II

In Paris, it was easier to live the part of the writer, harder to write, especially when one's métier was the traditional novel. "The traditional novel . . . is so undermined that one feels as if one were working in a house marked for demolition," McCarthy said of an early stab at *Birds of America,* the story of an American student coming of age in Europe that she started and stopped a dozen times after *The Group.* The problem was also social, however; not just in the obvious sense that social obligations got in the way, though increasingly they did.

During the 1965 May–June 'American landings' in Paris, McCarthy was visited by her brother Kevin, Carmen Angleton, Niccolò Tucci, Nancy Macdonald and her son Nick, the Rahvs, Max Lerner, the art dealer John Myers, two old friends from the Annie Wright Seminary, and Mary's uncle Louis McCarthy. In a typical week, she had lunch with a young friend from Senegal, tea with a Portuguese acquaintance wanting help in publicizing the cause of Portuguese writers, dinner with a Dutch woman who had written admiringly of *Eichmann in Jerusalem.* Among the dozens of incoming calls was one from Lanvin informing Mrs. West that she had been sent the wrong dress.

No matter what else was going on, McCarthy usually sat alone at her desk in the mornings from around nine until two, every day but Sunday. Then she might face one of those "horrible blanks" that sometimes occurred in the middle of a lecture, when the next point she was about to make slipped away. "It struck me that there was *nothing* I wanted to say," McCarthy said of the blank page that stared up at her the morning she first sat down to *Birds of America* in the summer of 1964. "Or, more accurately, that I could not remember the person (me) who had been wanting to say something. That is, in the form of a novel or even a story. . . ." The 'person' was scattered in a dozen *relations* with people, plans, schedules for fittings, interviews. The problem was to collect 'her' and drive 'her' in the desired direction— which was uphill. There were no end of articles and reviews McCarthy wanted to write; the difficulty was in creating something new. Article writing, after *The Group,* felt like "an evasion or distraction, like loud chatter to cover up a social silence."

It was times like this when McCarthy turned to Hannah Arendt in long letters that began or ended with fierce expressions of longing: "Dear Hannah, when *will* we see each other? I miss you so much. In Paris, I have no real friends. . . ." Arendt felt this way, too: "Dearest, you write soon! I miss you in countless ways. . . . *je t'embrasse*—" Packed with news, the letters apologized for being too short, or too late, or too gloomy; a "no-letter," Arendt called one of her own in October 1965 that carried the news of Paul Tillich's death and the fear that Jaspers and Heidegger would soon follow. For McCarthy, writing Hannah during a 'blank' was like rubbing the magic lamp in the fairy tale; sooner or later a genie would appear, as it had on June 9, 1964, in the form of an Idea having to do with equality. And she felt she had something to work with.

The "spectre of equality," which has haunted the world since the eighteenth century, McCarthy proposed, had haunted her all her life. It had, of course, although its earliest manifestations went unmentioned this time: the envy Mary felt as an orphan for her well-dressed cousins in Minneapolis; the envy her brothers must have felt for her pampered life in Seattle, though what McCarthy felt about that was never aired. Philosophy, the sublimation of untenable feeling, came to the rescue. "Once this notion [of equality] was introduced into the human mind, existence became unbearable, and yet once there it can never be banished," the letter continued. Only people at opposite extremes of the social scale, "benighted squires" and "benighted peasants" accept inequality as a "mystery of Fate" or "disposition of [God's] favors." Everyone else is prey to guilt and envy. " 'Why should I have this and not he?' or 'Why should he have this and not I?' "

Mary herself had become obsessed by these questions as a result of "recent success," measured by "an increasing number of dresses in my closet, car, trips. Basking in the air of privilege," she said, was all right "if it's impermanent—a treat. But not as one's private air-conditioning." She wanted to probe the problem in fiction, and perhaps exorcise her fear (a profoundly conservative one) that "the worm of equality was not only eating away at the old social and economic foundations but at the very structure of consciousness, demolishing the 'class distinctions' between the sane and the insane, the beautiful and the ugly, the good and the bad."

The situation had come to a pass where Mary felt "guilty and awkward in the presence of a psychotic person, as though I ought to conceal my sanity in the interests of equality with him." It was the same with a "stupid person," she told Arendt. She was "mortified in conversation with him, afraid of saying something that will disclose his stupidity to him." This fear of exposing someone else's ignorance or chicanery *to his face* would bear strange fruit a few years later in Vietnam, when McCarthy disdained interviews with U.S. and South Vietnamese officials on the grounds that she hated embarrassing anyone to whom she was talking. Arguing was another matter. "But to sit across a desk, deferential notebook in hand, from some powerful personality you disapprove of, who would start lighting your cigarettes, beaming at you, seeking your sympathy for his difficult position . . . no!" she exclaimed; "I would almost rather assassinate such a man, if put to the choice, than fell him with an awkward question."

She was only happy in conversations with her equals or superiors, she wrote Hannah in 1964, though of course her "superiors" might feel "mortified" for her. (Not by her, *for* her.) The equality problem, in any event, was to be laid out in a novel whose hero was a nineteen-year-old boy studying abroad, "from an old-fashioned 'humanist' moderate left background," whose father was a refugee intellectual teaching in the United States (and mother a beautiful and talented harpsichordist of old New England stock, though this character crystallized later). The boy, Peter Levi, was initially called Peter Bonfante after a young reporter named Jordan Bonfante, who had just done a lavish spread on "Mary McCarthy in Paris" for *Life*.

The fictional Peter is "three-quarters Americanized," she told Hannah; "a nice kid, very mature for his age intellectually (his family goes to Cape Cod for the summer, and he knows the Dupees, Dwight, Arthur Schlesinger, etc.), shy, scrupulous, very logical, and lonely but brave away from home." A bore, in the novel, one feels, because he is so very nice, so very well connected (though the Dupees, etc., never make an appearance)—a frail reed for bearing the burdensome inquiry into equality. *Birds of America* would be a favorite of many of McCarthy's close friends, like Nicky King, who saw it as "a catalogue of her tastes: If you wanted to know what Mary thought about history, buildings, birds, cooking, it was all there." Or Cees Nooteboom, the young Dutch novelist McCarthy befriended in Edinburgh, who admired the "old American virtues" celebrated in the novel—intellectual honesty, perseverance, hatred of waste—which were the virtues he saw in Mary. But for somewhat the same reason the book was derided by critics, such as Helen Vendler, who disliked its "bright topicality" and right-thinking, and found it "ruthlessly circumscribed by [McCarthy's] own lived experience."

Writing Arendt in 1964, McCarthy had enumerated the models she had assembled for Peter, which included the sons of Czeslaw Milosz, Niccolò Tucci, and the literary historian Daniel Aaron, whose son, Jonathan, inspired a scene where Peter takes his plant for a walk in Paris; other models were Jordan Bonfante and, of course, Reuel Wilson (but not Nathalie Sarraute). In the laboratory of McCarthy's fiction, the specimens are often laid out on the ice for inspection in advance of an operation; thus the author becomes familiar with her materials before putting them to the knife. Afterwards, feeling a special tenderness toward these flesh and blood donors, who have offered up their little stories, tics, and mannerisms to the greater glory of fiction, she might draw them into her social orbit.

Birds of America opens in a New England shore town, Rocky Port, a transplant of Stonington, Connecticut (where the Wests spent a two-month home leave in 1964), with touches of Portsmouth, Rhode Island. The American interlude allows McCarthy to ventilate a Marie Antoinettish disdain for the loss of the "pastoral" conditions of the war years in the United States, when you had to do things yourself and rationing made you economize. Now (the mid-1960s, when "Students for Civil Rights" is in Mississippi), mixes and frozen foods have crowded out fresh produce; only the gulls feed on whole fish. Peter's divorced mother, "the fair Rosamund," is cooking 'early American' during their brief idyll together (before Peter leaves for the Sorbonne), after cooking Tafelspitz and Austrian desserts for her second ex-husband, Hans, and *lasagne al forno* for Peter's father, known as "the *babbo*."

The bulk of the novel's action, which is serendipitous, a series of encounters designed to test Peter's faith in equality and the Kantian ethic (" 'The Other is always an End: thy Maxim,' " announces a card in his wallet), takes place in Paris, with side trips to Rome (friendlier, cheaper than Paris) and to the Sistine Chapel where a dissertation on mass tourism takes place. The point of view is the student's, whose self-conscious theorizing rings true to his age but also permits the grown-up author, who is crouched inside a glass-walled ventriloquist's box, to indulge in some top-heavy theorizing of her own.

The 'catalogue of tastes' in *Birds of America* frequently touches on questions of personal morality couched in references to a Great Thinker. "Maybe the categorical imperative is not the best guide for Americans abroad," Peter speculates in a chapter-long letter to "Ma." "When you think of it, the rule of thumb about tipping is just the opposite of Kant: watch what everybody else does and do the same," which would seem to exhaust the question of whether to tip or not to tip—but it doesn't. "Maybe any action becomes cowardly once you stop to reason about it," Peter continues, after asking himself if tipping or not tipping is the more cowardly. "Conscience doth make cowards of us all, eh, *mamma mia*? If you start an argument with yourself, that makes two people at least, and when you have two people, one of them starts appeasing the other." Elizabeth Hardwick might have had a field day with Peter Levi, as she did with Dottie Renfrew: "now that she was here in the cold-water flat, she was determined to go through with it, like Kierkegaard through clerical ordination."

Birds of America is full of these effusions from McCarthy's later period, when she had begun to 'mellow,' people said—little guessing, or not reading, what issued from her typewriter during the same years after she went to Vietnam. Peter remembers his mother saying that you can divide travelers into those who like churches and those who like *châteaux*. The latter are "social climbers" who are bored by churches unless they are full of loot. The former, well . . . the author never really says what lies behind Peter's, and her own, dogged attraction to churches, especially Gothic churches, whose soaring pinnacles McCarthy tracked across the whole of Europe, without ever getting her lifelong romance with them into the pages of a book.

It is in Rome that Peter Levi's commitment to equality is tested and found wanting. Like his creator he is at bottom an aesthete, or a utopian, which is the same thing in the social realm, who concludes that "the rules of democracy work better when there isn't too much cash around. The way it used to be in Athens." Even if the Athenians (like Jefferson) did have slaves. In Rome, Peter hatches an image of "mobs of tourists [who] are just garbage dumped here by planes and sightseeing buses, with the guides and storekeepers diving for them like scavenger gulls!" which is shocking; just as Edmund Wilson's vision of the fragility of human habitations, of palaces, railway stations, and cathedrals during World War Two is shocking, when he views them from a plane as "wasp-cells stuck in the slit of a blind, . . . mere shells which men have knocked together in order to crawl inside . . . and which a bomb dropped casually from above can shatter in a moment."

Peter Levi decides that the only solution to the desecration of the temples of art is to make tourists pass an entrance exam to see the Sistine Chapel or the Mona Lisa, a dubious notion which is easily taken apart by the squirrely academic whose research into mass tourism sets the stage in the novel for the discussion of art values versus political values. Mr. Small, a fervent apologist for capitalism—"the most subtle force for progress the world has ever known. . . . Boring from within the old structures, leveling, creating new dreams, new desires, and having the technical know-how and the dynamism to satisfy them"—is a brilliant foil *intellectually* for Peter Levi, but lumpish as a character.

When *Birds of America,* more a '*conte philosophique*' like *The Oasis* than a traditional novel, appeared in 1971, the house of culture, especially in France, was awash with new waves. The *nouveau roman* had been pushed to the sidelines, not only because its doyens—Claude Simon, Alain Robbe-Grillet, Michel Butor—had quieted down "but because they had been covertly trafficking with meaning," McCarthy suggested at the time. Now that the *nouveau nouveau roman* was ascendant (Ricardou, McCarthy reported, was plotting to launch the "*nouveau nouveau nouveau roman*"), fiction had proclaimed its independence of anything outside pure linguistic structure. It was not an auspicious moment for Mary McCarthy's fifth novel, which met with less than rave reviews.

"Here nobody but a philistine or somebody who does not mind being called one admits to any retrograde tastes in art, music, books, film, theatre," McCarthy told *Partisan Review*'s readers in the summer of 1972, in a symposium on "The New Cultural Conservatism"; "there were no signs of [the phenomenon] in Paris," she wrote, adding that "if there were, I think I might rejoice." France, after all, was "a country of fashion, and the fashion-makers [were] still the intransigents of *Tel Quel* [a deconstructionist literary magazine] and the splinter groups from it. . . ." The *nouveau nouveau roman* was perceived as an "event, like the discovery of the double helix (which people were also impressed by without understanding the formula)."

Apart from the rightward political shift of Saul Bellow, and the patenting of terms like *radical chic* by Tom Wolfe, McCarthy didn't see much evidence of a nascent conservatism in the United States either, not in the cultural sphere. Someone like Tom Wolfe was more interesting "[a]s a social mutant," she proposed; and she grouped him with "other pod-people like William Buckley, Spiro Agnew, Joe Alsop. The invasion of the body-snatchers," she called the tendency, alluding to the popular movie in which Kevin McCarthy starred; "[t]hey may be multiplying."

The poor critical reception given a *vieux vieux roman* like *Birds of America* might not have surprised McCarthy, had she been the critic and not the author. As Hannah Arendt observed, "no one ever expected you to write this kind of book" (which was what William Phillips said of *The Group*). But surprise her it did. She believed in the novel, naturally—in fiction one didn't hedge one's bets—even though this one had caused her no end of trouble; it was her favorite, in fact. She couldn't help but take the rejection personally, because the sneering reviews in *The New York Times, Time, Life,* and *The Saturday Review* were so "weirdly personal," leading her to wonder if "the book reviewing profession is made up of personal enemies." "MARY MCCARTHY AGAIN HER OWN HEROINE—FROZEN FOODS A NEW VILLAIN," ran a typical headline in *The New York Times.*

"[T]he amount of malice that is floating around here in literary circles is enormous," Hannah reported from New York; "you are an ideal object to crystallize it and this is an old story." It was; but with *Birds of America* there was a new twist. McCarthy wasn't criticized for having produced a 'lady-book' or for stooping to conquer the middle classes, but for a lapse in literary taste in drawing on a personal belief system for the mise-en-scène of a novel. "The discrepancy between public image and actual person is greater in your case than in any other I know of," Hannah Arendt had gone on to say, casting the problem in a sympathetic light; "in this book it is your whole person that speaks as the author." This was the reason why the criticism hurt so much more than it did with *The Group*; it *was* personal. But it may have also been why the book failed to stand on its own.

By the summer of 1971, however, Mary McCarthy was packing her bags for Fort McPherson, Georgia, to cover the trial of Captain Ernest Medina for his role in the My Lai massacre in South Vietnam. In June 1973, she would travel to Washington, D.C., to report on the Watergate hearings for the London *Observer* and *The New York Review of Books.* In times of political emergency, fiction was put aside for nonfiction, first in 1967, when she flew to South Vietnam, and again in 1968, when she went to Hanoi. Long before *Birds of America* was finished, in fact, McCarthy would break new ground as an investigative journalist and political commentator; but this novel, for all its faults—notably, its almost childish faith in the spirit world of ideas—reveals a side of McCarthy's 'actual person' that really was hidden from public view.

The revelation is sharpest in the closing scene of the book when Kant himself appears at the foot of Peter Levi's bed: "a small man, scarcely five feet high, in an unbuttoned twill jacket with a white stock. . . . His hair was curled in sausages and powdered . . . and fastened behind with a gray bow. He was in the prime of life"—exactly as in an old print Hannah Arendt had unearthed. Peter lies in a delirium in the American Hospital in Paris after having been bitten by a black swan at the zoo; an allergy to penicillin has thrown him into shock, during which he has had several imaginary visitors, "helpers and hinderers," McCarthy calls them, including Kant:

> "Excuse me, sir, you have something to tell me, don't you?" The tiny man moved forward on the counterpane and looked Peter keenly in the eyes, as though anxious as to how we would receive the message he had to deliver. He spoke in a low thin voice. "God is dead," Peter understood him to say. Peter sat up. "I *know* that," he protested. "And you didn't say that anyway. Nietzsche did." He felt put upon, as though by an impostor. Kant smiled. "Yes, Nietzsche said that. And even when Nietzsche said it, the news was not new, and maybe not so tragic after all. Mankind can live without God." "I agree," said Peter. "I've always lived without Him." "No, what *I* say to you is something important. You did not hear me correctly." . . . Again he looked Peter steadily and searchingly in the eyes. "Perhaps you have guessed it. Nature is dead, *mein kind.*"

On that note, one that struck McCarthy's usual detractor, Alfred Kazin, as something worth thinking about, *Birds of America* ends. Hannah Arendt wanted to quarrel with the implied "opposition of culture and nature. Culture is always cultivated nature—" she said, "nature being tended and being taken care of by one of nature's products called man. If nature is dead culture will die too, together with all the artifacts of our civilization." But maybe that is the point. The 'tending' has long since gone the way of the family farm, and it is only a matter of time before our *faith* in nature, McCarthy suggests, like our original belief in God, goes, too.

In Peter Levi and his mother, nevertheless, McCarthy has invested her own irrepressible longing for beauty, wisdom, love, justice; and it is in culture—not society, not politics, not even nature, for none of her characters ever encounters nature outside a zoo or a park—that these ideals are kept alive. "Nature," in both Arendt's and McCarthy's formulations—Kant's, too—remains the heavenly amphitheatre, with earth, and 'man' spinning his multiform webs, anchored at the core.

What is striking about the dream sequence is what it reveals about the dream life of Mary McCarthy. Looked at one way, Kant's appearance is a classic deus ex machina: the ultimate authority invoked to deliver the novel's punch line. One almost hears the wheels and pulleys whirring in the wings. But if Peter's hallucination rings truer than that—and with the "shivery sadness" that overtakes him as he recalls it, it does—the reason lies in McCarthy's own rapport with the spirit world of dreams. Especially in times of crisis, as when Arendt's husband, Heinrich Blücher, died of a massive coronary in November 1970, dreams came to the rescue.

"Last night I had a vivid dream about Heinrich," Mary wrote Hannah in April 1971:

> literally a resurrection. He came out of his grave very merrily, dressed in outdoor clothes and wearing a little checked cap. It turned out that, though he'd been buried, he'd been alive all the time, just playing possum; it was a little joke he'd played on us. I was very much surprised and noticed that you weren't and said to myself, "Hannah has known all along." Yet I didn't dare ask you about this, as if it were a secret. Instead, I asked Heinrich how he had managed, underground, to keep breathing, and he explained that it was easy. . . . It was a gay, lively dream, naturally.

And it consoled her. Heinrich had come back for a visit, offering McCarthy an answer to the inconsolable question: Where does a friend go when she/he dies? He had become a 'helper,' like Kant—whose message is bleak but whose readiness to deliver it in person is not—and like Kant, he is dressed exactly right (that "little checked cap"), so that nobody could ever ever mistake him for an illusion.

34

Hanoi Gothic

"I am concerned with my own comfort,
being able to 'live with myself,' as people used
to say. And that, in a nutshell,
was why I had come to North Vietnam."

—MARY MCCARTHY, *HANOI*

Getting to Vietnam in February 1967 was a little like getting married in Paris in the spring of 1961—logistically speaking, the kind of nightmare from which Mary McCarthy invariably awoke refreshed. The paper chase for visas, vaccinations—securing a new 'Mary McCarthy passport' to use in place of the diplomatic one made out in her husband's name; even drawing up a new will—brought out the gaming instinct in a woman who, until the end of her life, actually relished the week in June when she sat down to do her taxes.

" 'If you go to Hanoi with that, they'll think you're a spy,' " Ambassador Charles Bohlen said of the passport issued to Mrs. James West when McCarthy reported to his office on the Avenue Gabriel, after having informed the ambassador, as a courtesy, of her impending trip. " 'It could even get you into some trouble in Saigon,' " Bohlen added, but then she had been issued the regular blue passport the very next day, along with State Department clearance for travel to North Vietnam as a journalist. Bohlen had given her a "rather hard-line talk on Vietnam" that reminded McCarthy of school, "when you have to listen respectfully to the principal as she carries out her duty, which is to point out to you the errors of your thinking, even though she knows you will do what you have determined to do anyway." Her decision to go to North and South Vietnam had clearly pained Ambassador Bohlen, who had been received at the Wests' home, as Mary and Jim had been at his, but he had responded "gallantly."

Getting a visa from Hanoi proved more challenging. When McCarthy went to the North Vietnamese embassy around the corner from the Closerie des Lilas, she was told to write a letter stating the reasons for her trip, and that she could expect to hear nothing before she arrived in Phnom Penh, Cambodia, a jumping-off point for both Saigon and Hanoi. Her initial request for a Cambodian visa had gone unanswered. But even with it, she was assured by two recent visitors to North Vietnam, journalists Jacques Decornoy and John Gerassi, that she wouldn't be able to go to Hanoi if she went to Saigon first. With permission to enter South Vietnam stamped on her passport, she would never be allowed to enter North Vietnam. And if she arrived in Phnom Penh with her U.S. passport stamped "Cleared for North Vietnam," John Gerassi added, the North Vietnamese would turn her back anyway, because they only wanted people who would lose their passports by going there, as he had.

"I wonder if any of that is true. Or invariably true," McCarthy had written Bob Silvers in New York, but for safety's sake she delayed having either clearance stamped on the 'Mary McCarthy passport.' Bob Silvers had first asked her to go to South Vietnam for *The New York Review of Books* in March 1966, when she had refused, for fear her husband would have to resign from government service. Nine months later, when Silvers asked her again, there were four hundred thousand American troops in South Vietnam, and *The New York Review of Books* was playing an active role in domestic opposition to the war. Then she had agreed, accepting a commission of $1,000 an article, plus travel and expenses, for what turned out to be a six-part series on Vietnam, a hefty sum.

Like a good many journalists, photographers, professors, and antiwar activists passing through Paris on their way to and from Hanoi at the end of the 1960s, Gerassi and McCarthy both seemed to slip into a web of intrigue in their dealings with each other. Gerassi, a former *Newsweek* reporter who visited Hanoi in December 1966 as a representative of the Bertrand Russell War Crimes Tribunal, told McCarthy he was writing about his trip for the *New Yorker*'s "Reporter at Large," which turned out not to be true. "A rather mole-like character," McCarthy thought; "[i]mpossible . . . to get the geography of his tunnels." But when she was asked whether *The New York Review of Books* was going to publish an article Gerassi had submitted on Santo Domingo, she had evaded his question, not wanting him to know she didn't keep up with the magazine, "for fear he would think I was an impostor and tell Sartre, who would tell Hanoi. . . ." Sartre and Simone de Beauvoir, both friends of

Gerassi's parents, headed up the Russell Tribunal, in which Hanoi placed considerable faith.

The fact that McCarthy had written against Sartre in *Encounter* ("Crushing a Butterfly," the account of the literary debate at the Mutualité), Gerassi told her in 1967, would surely cook her goose. Apparently nothing was said of the old postwar feud with 'Mlle. Gulliver en Amérique.' If Hanoi found out that McCarthy was married to an American diplomat, however, she would be suspected of being a CIA agent, Gerassi said; and he "was quite suspicious, at first, himself," McCarthy wrote Silvers, adding, apropos her efforts to get herself crossed into Communist Vietnam, "It almost looks as if the only way I could get there would be to defect."

Dealing with the North Vietnamese, McCarthy's instinct had been to play it straight; to tell them she was going to Saigon and wanted to visit Hanoi afterwards. "This would give them time, at least, to investigate me and work on the visa," she suggested to Silvers, who was exhorted to do what he could from New York "to move Hanoi." Then, she hoped, she could get her visa at the end of February on her way *out* of South Vietnam. Nor was she averse to suggesting to the North Vietnamese, "modestly," that she was "a quite important person," and that it would be desirable if she could be given "a word of encouragement or discouragement" before she left Paris for Saigon— neither of which arrived before Mary McCarthy boarded the 11 A.M. Air France flight to Saigon on February 2.

A few weeks earlier, she and Jim had met at the Deux Magots to celebrate the "great moment" when they agreed she should go to Vietnam, a "moment" that brings out the schoolgirl in McCarthy—"I cried for happiness. We held hands. My eyes were still wet when we saw Henry Moore, the sculptor, come up the street . . . gray and numinous . . . an omen." Opposition to the war had broken out inside the diplomatic community itself. At OECD headquarters on the Rue André Pascal, Secretary-General Christiansen was an outspoken critic of American policy. At the American embassy, Nicky King, who was press attaché, was besieged with "protesters," including Eileen Geist (later Finletter) and James Jones's wife, Gloria, who appeared one afternoon wrapped in their mothers' mink coats to present an antiwar petition from the expatriate community to the consul general.

When Mary asked Jim whether acceptance of her trip meant he would still have to resign, he had said, " 'Hell, no. They'll have to fire me.' " Naturally they hadn't—even after McCarthy concluded the last of her articles from Hanoi the following year by reflecting that while no peace candidate in the United States could admit that "peace" in Vietnam entailed an American surrender, because "surrender is a confession of failure," Americans "will be lucky . . . if failure, finally, is the only crime we are made to confess to."

Ambassador Bohlen had been outraged by the opening salvo in McCarthy's first dispatch from Saigon:

> I confess that when I went to [South] Vietnam early last February I was looking for material damaging to the American interest and that I found it, though often by accident or in the process of being briefed by an official.

" 'How dare you go to Vietnam with the intention of blackening the name of the United States!' " Bohlen demanded when they confronted each other at a party hosted by the number-two man in the embassy, Robert McBride, shortly after the article first appeared in *The Observer*. Nicky King, who was there, recalls how Bohlen had made all sorts of special arrangements to ease McCarthy's passage through South Vietnam, and that while "he wasn't hoping for an endorsement of the Vietnam War . . . still he thought that was rubbing it in. [It was] a little stiff." That Mary had already told the ambassador and American officials in Saigon exactly what she thought didn't blunt the fact that opinions look different in print. "The shock treatment," King calls the direct line she took in the Vietnam essays, "that was Mary's way."

Ambassador Bohlen's anger passed without serious repercussion. McCarthy had been ready for it when she went to the party alone (Jim was away), thinking she had to "show" herself and "stand behind" what she wrote. American officials in South Vietnam, like the Agency for International Development man McCarthy quotes in the first article—who says of the " 'refugees' " forcibly herded into camps, after their villages have been burned to the ground: " 'We're teaching them free enterprise' "—had been generous in providing her with 'material.' Her profiles of U.S. civic action and Revolutionary Development programs, in particular, handed the government a damning indictment of America's 'other' war. Nor had she ignored the military side of the conflict.

A short trip by helicopter from Saigon in any direction had afforded her a ringside view of the small aircraft traveling in pairs ("like FBI agents") that dropped their bombs during an average of 460 sorties a day in support of ground action. And she had written feelingly of the ravaged countryside, dotted with bonfires from the bombing and seared by purplish brown tracts from the defoliation program. As had Edmund Wilson, oddly enough, writing in *The Cold War and the Income Tax,* after reading Homer Bigart's early reports of herbicide use in South Vietnam in *The New York Times.* In 1963, Wilson was one of the first to publicly challenge the Pentagon's claim that the defoliating agent, later known as Agent Orange, was " 'no more harmful than the gardener's weed-killer.' " News of both Operation Ranch Hand, as the defoliation campaign was called, and the army's Strategic Hamlet program in 1962, prompted him to reflect that "Sherman did this in the South, and many people think he was justified, but why should we be doing it to the Vietnamese, who live not next to us but next door to China, for the purpose of convincing these uninstructed peasants that the American Way of Life is freer and more desirable than that imposed by the Communist ideology?"

The military side of the war, nevertheless, interested Mary McCarthy less than the social side. The truth she was after "would not be found on the battlefront," she believed, "which would be no different from battlefronts in any other war, but among the people, theirs and ours, in hamlets, hospitals, and refugee camps. . . ." When the French-born war correspondent, Bernard Fall urged her to go up on a bombing mission, she refused. She had already promised Jim she would try to stay out of combat situations—though the promise had later made her squirm (" 'No, thank you, Major, I can't go along with you to see what that shooting is about. I told my husband . . .' "—which reminded her of when she had had to tell a boy her grandparents wouldn't allow her to go out on dates). Jim West, interestingly enough, was more anxious about his wife's safety in South Vietnam than he was later when she visited North Vietnam. (Mary felt the reverse.)

When Bernard Fall pressed her, however, McCarthy felt it would be "wicked" to go into combat. Knowing herself, she was sure that if the plane was shot at, she would start empathizing with the pilot, the bombardier, and the door gunners; if it wasn't, she "would passionately hate them, as they strewed their bombs and napalm around, and hate myself for my complicity. . . ." Fall had argued that she should train herself to go up and feel nothing, as he had; maintaining one's detachment made one strong and proud. She would rather "be weak and humble. Or, rather, I *was* weak and humble," McCarthy decided. For a "natural civilian" such as herself, "insentience" would have been the last thing to seek, while for Bernard Fall, "who loved war and its implements, it was the opposite; he responded to the thrill of danger, and it was this he had taught himself to curb."

A few days after Fall and McCarthy met for the last time at the Danang airport—the swashbuckling correspondent bristling with canteens and field gear, the lady novelist wearing an army jacket and cap loaned to her by a reporter from the *Baltimore Sun*—Bernard Fall was killed. He stepped on a land mine in Hue, the site of his moving account of the first Indochina war, *Street Without Joy*. At home, Jim West had quaked when he picked up the newspaper and saw the headline: "AMERICAN WRITER KILLED IN VIETNAM." (McCarthy's brief sketch of this interesting man, like her Goyaesque portraits of Major Be and Mr. Chau, the Vietnamese counterparts of the American social scientists who used South Vietnam as a laboratory for a vast experiment in 'revolutionary' behavioral modification, sets her Vietnam articles apart from other contemporary accounts as, at bottom, character studies of the noncombatant men of war.)

At Bob McBride's party, meanwhile, McCarthy had easily held her ground with Bohlen, despite the fact that her position had been rendered "shaky" by a graveled terrace into which her heels sank, pitching her forward and back with each new thrust in the argument. After Ambassador Bohlen left in a huff, a handful of embassy people had come forward to say they agreed with her, and to proffer their congratulations. News of the scene had quickly made the rounds in Paris; McCarthy's reputation for swordsmanship, subject to tarnish after *The Group,* was reaffirmed.

Times had changed since April 1965, when Mary had found herself at a dinner party at Ambassador Bohlen's, in setting not unlike the party in "The Genial Host" where Meg Sargent surfaces as a Trotskyist in a sea of Stalinists. In 1965, she had sensed that everyone was waiting for someone else to speak up; she felt "anxious and hamstrung." "The old Red-Dead jingle is coming true in a ghastly way," she confided to Hannah Arendt; for Mary, there was "no doubt that in Indochina it would be better for the vast majority to be Red." But then she had curbed her tongue "because of Jim and his job."

Two years later, when McCarthy stood up in Paris to defend her dispatches from South Vietnam, it was no surprise that it was the American ambassador with whom she squared off. Vietnam was that kind of war: for its opponents, a war fought with authority first. One took one's convictions into the lions' den. The effort to reach out and mobilize popular opinion was always harder, as Mary McCarthy would discover later, to her chagrin, when *The New York Review of*

Books series, published by Harcourt, Brace and World as *Vietnam* and *Hanoi,* sank like a stone.

II

It was in 1966, in an interview with Edwin Newman in Paris, that McCarthy first spoke out publicly against the Vietnam War. If Americans didn't actively oppose it, she argued, they would resemble the " 'good' Germans" under Hitler. She was nearly halfway through *Birds of America,* and for a time the rigors of fiction had confined her antiwar activity to cocktail lobbying and a vigorous campaign of letter writing. Johnson's speechwriter, Richard Goodwin, was the recipient of one of her letters protesting the bombing of North Vietnam.

McCarthy's fifth novel had the exuberant support of her publisher, William Jovanovich, who no doubt hoped for a second best-seller after *The Group.* "There isn't another writer in English . . . who make[s] the novel . . . do what it is supposed to, which is to recreate events and circumstances in such a way that one sees them for the first time . . ." Jovanovich had written McCarthy excitedly after reading the first chapter. "Everything fits in this story, and everything makes a difference to it," he added, pointing to the "counterpoint of outside and inside, the natural setting and the household" as especially "brilliant." He *liked* the nineteen-year-old Peter Levi and his mother, and found himself "wanting *them* to like *me,* a rare reaction. . . ." The idea of a " 'good' character" creating action had recently presented itself to him in the person of Georges Simenon's heroine in *The Little Saint;* and now he found himself experiencing the same "dramatic appreciation of [Peter and his mother]," which did not "depend on any forced attention to flaws . . . in their characters."

When McCarthy wrote Jovanovich at the end of January 1967 to say she was dropping everything to go to Vietnam, he was not pleased. It would be "a betrayal of Peter Levi unless I put him in uniform and send him to Vietnam too," she had explained, thereby using her young hero as a kind of alter ego to ride into battle—even if 'he' stayed home (which in *Birds of America* Peter Levi does, joining only arguments against the war). "It would be too false to be close to the hero," McCarthy reflected later, "and just be writing a novel."

Jovanovich's displeasure had precipitated a temporary rift in their relationship. When it came time to publish the South Vietnam essays as a booklet, McCarthy confessed to "a sort of *malaise*" about letting Jovanovich do it rather than Roger Straus (of Farrar, Straus & Giroux). "Since Roger is enthusiastic about the articles, why not give him the pleasure of publishing them?" she wrote Jovanovich (who was not an outspoken critic of the war), adding that it was as if she was giving "a party" she was keen on, "and you came . . . reluctantly but out of a sense of duty, continuity, friendship, a little vanity." She didn't like to see people "doing things without pleasure and unnecessarily, unless there's some very strong reason, involving conscience"—which certainly wasn't the case here. It wasn't "as if nobody would publish the articles unless you did . . ." she reminded him.

Jovanovich's loyalty was being tested once again, and he had passed—but not before Mary assured him, teasingly, that she was "deeply fond" of him and wasn't going "to hurt [his] feelings" by "an infidelity," but that still she wanted him "to think it over. . . ." It was true she was having "a sort of publishing flirtation with Roger," but she wanted Jovanovich to know that there had "never been any thought . . . of giving [Roger Straus] a work of fiction, which would be the equivalent . . . of the 'final favor.' " Jovanovich, in reply, had taken the high road. He was not "annoyed" by McCarthy's letter, "and could not be," he wrote back immediately, "even were I in a selfish spoiling mood, for I am too much committed to you as a friend to *use* you in any way. I want to publish the Vietnam book," he declared. He was "pleased to publish it," and he came to Mary's "party" (to use her word) because he wanted to be there. As for another publisher's "pleasure," he counted his own before that, he said, "which is natural enough."

There were other chips on the board. McCarthy had sent Bill Jovanovich a list of essays she wished to include in a new nonfiction collection, *The Writing on the Wall,* which had come up for discussion during a conversation the two of them had recently had about her publishing future. "They will make an impressive book," Jovanovich assured her; and on her side, Mary had promised him that she would "take out little Peter Levi from the drawer and try to get on terms with him again"—which she did, but only after traveling to North Vietnam the following year.

The decision to set a promising novel aside for a stint as a war correspondent involved a certain sacrifice; and Nicola Chiaromonte was another voice warning Mary in 1967 that she risked her " 'position' " as a writer, as well as her personal safety. But sacrifice in one form or another was essential to McCarthy's motivation—as, indeed, it was for the antiwar movement itself, whose messianic strain in the 1960s, a reliance on confrontation, on direct and risky action generally, seemed calculated to ensure the protester's personal salvation.

* * *

An attraction to action demanding extreme sacrifice was never more critical to Mary McCarthy's motivation than it was in February 1968, when she set off for Hanoi via Phnom Penh and Vientiane, Laos, in an old four-engine Convair left over from the last Indochina War. The same impulse would guide her in 1972 during the Christmas bombing of Hanoi, when she tried to organize a group of prominent citizens to "live under the bombs as witnesses—in the Biblical . . . sense of the term." In 1968 and 1972, the need to act in direct accord with her beliefs had prevailed, along with a remnant of Catholic training: "the idea that it was necessary to be the same person at all times and places." This notion surfaced in Hanoi in March 1968 when, as McCarthy warmed to her North Vietnamese hosts, she grew ashamed of writing "little observations about them" in her notebook, like a novelist, "for you ought not to be two people, one downstairs, listening and nodding, and the other scribbling in your room."

The supreme sacrifice, death at the hand of American bombs, she noted with half-playful pragmatism, "might at least convince a few Americans that civilian targets were being aimed at. I was not a military objective. On the other hand, other Americans over their fresh-frozen orange juice would be saying 'It served her right.' " In *Hanoi,* common sense reminds her that she has gone to Vietnam and risked her life "chiefly for [her] own peace of mind." She is "working at [her] own salvation," and since she has "no belief in a future life," her "salvation" must be achieved in the here and now. The result, a curious reconciliation of old-time religion with a hyperactive sense of self, finds McCarthy poised on a deeply bended knee.

The "private tumults and crises" she undergoes in North Vietnam, "trivial as was their occasion"—who *cared* whether she wore the ring made from a shot-down plane (she didn't wear it), or said " 'puppet' " when referring to the South Vietnamese (she couldn't), or " 'Viet Cong' " for the National Liberation Front (she did)—"involved the omnipresence, the ubiquity of God. *He* cared," writes McCarthy. "Being an unbeliever made no difference. I had swallowed Him too many times as a child at the communion rail, so that He had come to live inside me like a cherry stone growing or like Socrates' unshakable companion and insistent interlocutor: oneself." The corollary is unmistakable: When I am true to myself, I am true to God.

The passage, from the last chapter of *Hanoi,* hammers together a medieval theory of transubstantiation with the ethics of Plato and the philosophy of Kant which might have taken Hannah Arendt's breath away. Only Arendt, with her youthful romance with St. Augustine, could have followed the complex train of associations (unless it was an orthodox Episcopalian such as Nicholas King, who was always impressed by the "religious freight" in McCarthy's writing, and frequently conversed with her on biblical points). Yet Hannah Arendt, significantly, found little to her liking in the book's remarkable concluding essay, "First Principles."

Twenty-five years later, *Hanoi* still irritates some of McCarthy's contemporaries. "I was against the war too but I was *not* for the North Vietnamese," snaps Alfred Kazin; and William Phillips concurs: "Mary just had gone too far politically. . . ." For Arendt, whose unease with a friend's writing was conveyed by silence (in *Hanoi,* only the chatty portrait of rural life, "North Vietnamese Bucolic," drew her praise), there was something unseemly in Mary's exercise of public breast-beating; as if the penitent, bowing under the weight of privilege (she had "only to look in the mirror," McCarthy writes, to see evidence of her complicity with American imperialism), wanted it both ways, cake in the morning, humble pie in the afternoon.

"[L]ike most of the non-Communist Left, I was moving effortlessly into a higher and higher income bracket," McCarthy reflects in *Hanoi,* and she admits that the "slight discomfort" caused by success "was outweighed by the freedom from any financial stringencies and the freedom to write exactly what I wished. That freedom (cf. Norman Mailer) is a perquisite of successful U.S. authors." The bullish literary market had kicked in for American writers, in fact, just as their government patrons had bowed out. Mailer, McCarthy proposed in 1968, was a walking advertisement for the liberties permitted the successful novelist: " 'Watch me, young man, and learn how to do it. In our country, you do not have to sell out to sell.' " Success had spoiled something in her own achievement, too; her vaunted "objectivity" had turned into "a trade mark or shingle advertising a genuine Mary McCarthy product ('Trust Her to Speak Her Mind')." In the shadow of American bombs, she had even wearied of her "excess mental baggage . . . of allusion and quotation, the 'acquirements' of college, study, travel, acquaintance with prominent figures."

"My dear, I arrived in Hanoi wearing a Chanel suit, and carrying many suitcases!" McCarthy reminded a journalist in 1985 who assumed that her trip to North Vietnam in 1968, like the journalist's own in 1967, deposited the famous novelist in the trenches. But McCarthy's visit was a relatively sheltered one, taken up with endless meetings with dignitaries, and it became an occasion for pondering the political experience of her own generation as much as that of the North Vietnamese. In Hanoi, the vaunted 'freedoms' of Western writers, along with the material rewards, the travel, the clothes, no longer appeared so enviable. She had made new connections.

Seated across a low lacquered table in the Presidential Palace from the ascetic figure of North Vietnam's Prime Minister Pham Van Dong, "a man of magnetic allure, thin, with deep-set brilliant eyes, crisp short electric gray hair, full rueful lips drawn tight over the teeth," she glimpsed another way of life at once more orderly and passionate than her own. Vietnamese culture, McCarthy notes approvingly in *Hanoi,* is suffused with images of lightness and swift pliability: bamboo bending to the wind instead of snapping like oak; the sturdy bicycle, sandals, straw. In the company of the "fastidious" Pham Van Dong, for whom "bombs were a low-grade intrusion into the political scene, which he conceived, like the ancients, as a vast proscenium," her own "automobile-TV culture" seems "gross and heavy." Pham Van Dong's contempt for the idea of a socialist consumer society, like the contempt he showed for danger at the sound of a bombing alert when he invited Mary to remain seated with him in the palace, prompts "a feeling of happy agreement."

She has found a Communist after her own heart; one whose fluent French reminds her of those "old revolutionaries pentecostally blessed, like the Apostles, with the gift of tongues—Lenin, Trotsky, Ho Chi Minh, and behind them Rosa Luxemburg, Marx, Bakunin, and our own Benjamin Franklin, who sits like a funny antique in the garden of the American Embassy in Paris." Colonel Ha Van Lau, who headed up North Vietnam's War Crimes Commission, is another: "a delicate-featured, slender, refined officer from Hue, of mandarin ancestry," he reminds McCarthy of Prince Andrei in *War and Peace.* These are fatal attractions; reverse images of the fatuous French-speaking Major Be, who trains anti-Communist cadres in the South, and his assistant, Mr. Chau, who wrote his doctoral thesis at the Sorbonne on Virginia Woolf. Catching Colonel Lau lingering outside the Thong Nhat Hotel with the small, simply dressed chief justice of the Supreme Court, the Minister of Health, and his daughter, McCarthy suddenly sees Hanoi, like Florence, as one "large village, where the notables take the air in the evening on the main street."

Touring the countryside with her guide and interpreter, Mr. Phan, she observes "the tenderness of the intelligentsia for the peasantry and for what the Florentines call the *popolo minuto* (barbers, tailors, small craftsmen). . . ." Later she ponders the wariness in the prime minister's response to her eager questions about the political implications, "*après*

guerre," of the decentralization of authority forced on North Vietnamese society by the war. Was it perhaps a fear of human nature (not
unlike her own) that sees modern man as " 'naturally' a capitalist
accumulator . . . ceaselessly beset by marketing temptations," that
leads Pham Van Dong to reserve judgment as to the benefits of local
autonomy after the war? Wishful thinking leads McCarthy to imagine
otherwise. The example of consumer society in South Vietnam will
surely provide the deterrent, "like some dreadful emetic mixed with
alcohol to cure forever a taste for drinking. The samples of U.S.
technology that had been showered on the North were mainly in bomb
form," she reflects, "yet the simplest Vietnamese could perhaps see a
connection that eludes many American intellectuals between the spray
of pellets from the 'mother' bomb and the candy hurled at children in
the South by friendly G.I.'s. . . ."

In her own opinion, "the whole Saran-wrapped output of American industrial society" could no longer be separated into "beneficial
and deleterious, 'good' and 'bad.' . . ." Politics, like culture, had
become homogenized,

> so that "good"—free elections, say—is high-speed blended with
> commercial TV, opinion-testing, buttons, streamers, stickers,
> canned speech-writing, instant campaign biographies, till no is-
> sues are finally discernible, having been broken down and dis-
> tributed in tiny particles throughout the suspended solution, and
> you wonder whether the purpose of having elections is not sim-
> ply to market TV time, convention-hall space, hotel suites, cam-
> paign buttons. . . .

The infamous 'free elections' of 1968, which Mailer memorialized
in *Miami and the Siege of Chicago,* prompt these baleful reflections,
but so does a revolutionary vision of change that for a brief moment
in middle age led McCarthy to believe that "somehow this experience
in Vietnam was going to change my life. I didn't go there with that
purpose," she recalled later, "but while I was there I thought it
would." It didn't. The experience "sharpened some perceptions for a
while and then they wore off." After a flare-up during the 1972 bombing, the possibility that human nature was subject to regeneration,
conveyed to McCarthy via "the idea of forgiveness and rehabilitation"
that Hanoi's leaders extended to government functionaries in the
South, finally vanished; and she returned to a tour of English cathedrals. In 1980, referring to the remark in *Hanoi* about how the anti-

Stalinists of her generation "had no clear alternative but to be 'believing' socialists and practicing members of capitalist society," she pronounced herself "perhaps a little bit less 'believing,' and more 'practicing.' "

While the vision of change remained, however, McCarthy had sharpened several perceptions; to wit, that the great theme of nineteenth-century fiction and early movies—"[c]onversion, from bad to good, or vice versa"—had dropped out of Western culture. It was as if "the West had agreed that people were incapable of change. You do not see Bonnie and Clyde *decide* to become mass murderers," she observes; "no choice seems to be offered them. In the Free World, to judge by its artifacts, nobody is free to make a decision to be different from what he is. But in the un-Free World, the opposite is assumed. . . ." President Johnson, for example, was pursuing a mistaken policy; even the stock market told him so. Why *not* correct it? the North Vietnamese wondered. They assumed the President was free to change his course, while the opposite was pretended and possibly believed by Johnson, who acted as if he was locked into a bombing policy that bore the name of the " 'first step in unilateral de-escalation.' "

The double-talk about American bombing reminded McCarthy of the vocabulary she detested in the Stalinist era, when " 'volunteers' " meant conscripts, " 'democracy,' " tyranny, and so on. Beginning with the word " 'advisers,' " the U.S. government had adopted the "slippery Aesopian language" itself, while the North Vietnamese, with stiff formulations such as " 'the American imperialist aggressors,' which, like it or not, expressed the current truth," spoke more plainly. "Although we complain of the monotony, the truth," she concluded, "renamed by us 'propaganda,' has shifted to the other side."

But it was the North Vietnamese approach to human behavior, "at once categorical and in a strange way indulgent," that led her to see something new beneath the rhetoric about 'puppets' and 'bandits.' "Unlike Western liberals, they do not accept difference," she perceives, "but they accept change axiomatically . . . which Western liberals do not; that is why liberals have to be tolerant of difference, resigned to it." The critique of liberalism prompts a heretical criticism of liberalism's celebrated faith in dissent, a faith that in Hannah Arendt's galaxy burned with special brightness: "Freedom always implies the freedom of dissent," Arendt maintained. In 1968, once again the dissenters' dissenter, McCarthy called the "license to criticize . . . just another capitalist luxury, a waste product of the system." What was the point of reading both sides on the war, or seeing the horror on television, she reasoned, if in the end one couldn't do anything about it?

35

Crime and Perdition

*"Ever since my mind and emotions became centered on Vietnam, I
have been thinking about the problem of purgation and atonement."*

—MARY MCCARTHY, *THE MASK OF STATE*

*I*n Hanoi, the men with whom McCarthy found herself most at home
came from the central section of Vietnam once known as Annam. The
Annamites, who are not well liked by other Vietnamese, she considers
the "Tuscans" of the country: "difficult, self-sufficient, proud, provin
cial, obstinately 'local,' frugal, tradition-bound, vain of [their] past"—
the very qualities that North Vietnam appeared to be mobilizing for
the task of socialist reconstruction after the war. With certain notable
exceptions (frugality, for instance), they are also qualities one finds in
the ideological reconstruction of Mary McCarthy in the late 1960s.

"A virtuous tyranny," McCarthy called North Vietnam's socialism in a letter to Dwight Macdonald in 1969, adding, "I have enough
tyranny in me to respond to the appeal." North Vietnam was the only
" 'people's democracy' " she had ever seen that was "run on aristocratic principles and largely by aristocratic persons with a traditional
code of manners and morals." It was the kind of socialism Chiaromonte theoretically favored, though he never came to the defense of
North Vietnam (and never cared for *Hanoi*, finding it "too far to the
left"). "This doesn't mean I think North Vietnam is a *model*,"
McCarthy wrote Dwight; "aside from the shortage of freedom and the
awful art, it is a peculiar country, impossible to imitate—certainly by
the West. . . . And yet," she concluded, "it was very attractive, even
alluring. . . ."

"North Vietnam is still pioneer country," she observes in *Hanoi*, "where streams have to be forded," and the ethnic minorities remind her of American Indians. The appeal to her Western origins is unexpected. The old-fashioned desks in the evacuated schools, the kerosene lamps in the villages, the two-seater toilets, with a water buffalo ruminating outside, bring back "buried fragments" of McCarthy's history: motoring trips through northern Minnesota with her Grandmother McCarthy; Medicine Springs, Montana in the 1920s. "I was aware of a psychic upheaval, a sort of identity crisis," McCarthy writes in a vivid passage, "as when a bomb lays bare the medieval foundations of a house thought to be modern." Mary's attraction to North Vietnam's 'virtuous tyranny,' made Dwight Macdonald uneasy. "I'm for elitism in culture," he wrote back, "but not in politics."

For a while, after the Vietnam trips, during the escalation of protests in the United States—of draft-card burnings and university shutdowns, moratoriums, mobilizations, and the Weatherman's Days of Rage—Mary McCarthy had been less haunted by the war. Her "soul" had been "appeased," she told Dwight, explaining her refusal to join him in a tax-refusal campaign inspired by the MIT linguist Noam Chomsky. Macdonald, who felt he "must DO something [about the war], must stick my neck out some way," even if it risked landing him in jail, was clearly acting " 'for his soul,' " McCarthy surmised, and not "to be effective politically. . . ." She knew the feeling, but she urged him to think about his dependents and "future earning power."

By 1971, however, the wave of protests had subsided. The 'peace' candidates were gone. Bobby Kennedy was dead; Eugene McCarthy had disappeared in a puff of smoke, and with him the Children's Crusade that had formed in the wake of his 1968 presidential campaign. The killing of four students by National Guardsmen during a demonstration at Kent State University in May 1970 sent a chill through an antiwar movement already foundering in frustration. "You could not just go on marching up and down," McCarthy reflected. It was hard to believe that a policy so openly and widely opposed could be followed to the bitter end, but that was what was happening. Under Nixon, the "Vietnamization" of the war had diverted American attention, if not American men and matériel, away from Southeast Asia, and yet the aerial bombardment of North and South Vietnam continued.

Once again, McCarthy found herself lying awake nights plotting "solutions." She couldn't write anything, she believed, without a fresh point of contact with the subject. With the trial of Lt. William Calley in the fall of 1970 for his part in the massacre of noncombatants at My

Lai, she thought she saw an entry point, but then she was busy correcting page proofs for *Birds of America*. When Calley was convicted, however, and the great debate began over who was guilty, Calley or the Army (*"They were both guilty,"* McCarthy thought), she was drawn to take a second look. The Swedish economist Gunnar Myrdal, whom she met in Paris in the spring of 1971, suggested that by juggling the blame back and forth between an individual and an institution, Americans were absolving themselves of responsibility. " 'You should write about this,' " he said; and when the next opportunity presented itself, in the form of the Army's trial of Calley's company commander, Captain Medina, she did.

The Medina assignment, solicited from *The New Yorker* in the hopes of reaching a larger audience than *The New York Review of Books,* gave McCarthy a shot at a drama to which she was drawn by blood and temperament: a trial by jury, where the shadow play of good and evil could be observed in more concrete fashion than in everyday life. After Calley's conviction, however, the trial of Ernest Medina, while it laid out a larger canvas, from air and ground, was popularly regarded as an also-ran. "[B]ox-office turkey," McCarthy reported from Fort McPherson, Georgia, in August 1971, where Homer Bigart had already concluded, " 'The once lurid testimony seemed stale.' " (Checking into an Atlanta hotel to cover the Medina trial "was not the flashy thing to do," McCarthy's secretary at the time, Margo Viscusi, recalls; as perhaps the trips to Saigon and Hanoi might have been construed—wrongly, in Viscusi's opinion. Mary was "truly anguished" over the Vietnam War, she states; in 1972, when Nixon sent B-52s against Hanoi, and she started telephoning people about going to North Vietnam, "she almost lost it.")

McCarthy would pry a number of revelations from the frozen wastes of testimony, not only about what actually happened at My Lai on the fateful morning of March 16, 1968, but also about what was going on behind the scenes at Fort McPherson and in the country at large, which lent an air of unreality to a trial whose outcome—acquittal—seemed already to have been decided in the court of public opinion. On this point, McCarthy parted company with much of the New Left, including the GI movement, which saw both Calley and Medina as scapegoats for the crimes of the brass (a 'scapegoat' is innocent, she fumed) and My Lai itself as but the tip of an atrocity that was the war itself.

"Leaving out the part played by President Nixon in reducing the

Calley conviction and the part played by [Governor George] Wallace and the extreme right in heating mass fury," McCarthy argued, "the determination of the left not to consider *anybody* a war criminal short of a three-star general has meant that no three-star general will ever sit on the accused bench. Medina," in her view, "was a transition figure between the war-makers and the 'animals' (as the airmen in Vietnam called the infantry), and his acquittal halted a process that might have gone up the ladder of responsibility." If Medina had been sent to jail, it would have been harder to acquit Colonel Henderson, another My Lai officer from the 20th Infantry, Americal Division, then being tried at Fort Benning. Had public pressure been maintained, "it might not have been left to the Army to decide when enough was enough. If there was a conspiracy," McCarthy concluded, "it was a great nationwide breathing together of left, right, and much of the middle to frustrate punishment of the guilty."

The *New Yorker*'s readers, meanwhile, were treated to some vintage character sketches in McCarthy's 25,000-word report from Fort McPherson. The defendant and his counsel "yawned, stretched, doodled, slumped, whispered, rolled martyrs' eyes skyward, nudged neighboring ribs, cupped mouths to pass sardonic asides, like a pewful of restless schoolboys during a particularly dull and long-drawn-out chapel service." The chief defense counsel, F. Lee Bailey, "rose, shaking off his ennui and settling his collar, to make one of his 'innocent' interventions, like the school bad boy, plump and feigning stupidity, who rises to ask a loaded and deferential question: 'Sir!' " These glimpses of courthouse drama, reminiscent of old Spy cartoons in *Punch,* show Mary McCarthy engaged in a favorite pastime: uncovering the child in the man.

The Army's prosecution team presented an equally tempting spectacle. Bumbling, poorly prepared, a classic "forcible-feeble pair," the two officers assigned to try Medina remind McCarthy of players stuck at "the lower end of the batting order with two strikes on them and making blustering motions in the box." The jury itself is straight out of central casting: Lt. Col. Bobby Berryhill, Jr., of Decatur, Georgia, "double-chinned, pendulous, with large soft brown eyes and a long nose"; he naps but then asks the only serious questions of the defendant. Maj. Dudley L. Budrich, an airborne ranger from Chicago, "blond, with bangs and weakly drawn cowboy features," sucks his cheek or chews his gum, "his jaws opening and shutting on their hinges, like a machine beating time." The foreman, from Dunwoody, Georgia, wears a "ferocious glare of command behind accusatory glasses, as though compelling the evidence to present arms and salute him." A black officer from Enterprise, Alabama, leans back in his chair and looks "indulgent, an adult overseeing a child's game."

Originally, some young lawyers in the judge advocate general's office had wanted to try all the My Lai suspects together in a mass trial along Nuremberg lines. Had the idea not been vetoed by the Army in favor of multiple separate trials, with separate juries, and administrative decisions absolving certain parties without trial, both the tedium at Fort McPherson and the pervasive sense of unfairness, in McCarthy's opinion, would have been avoided. "My Lai was a single big crime, committed by many parties . . ." which should have been treated as such, she maintained.

The view gave credence to the idea that My Lai was an aberration in a war that, brutal as it was, nonetheless observed the limits of 'policy,' if mainly in the breach. "In Vietnam, murder of non-combatants and assaults on prisoners, however often they occurred, were not 'policy,' " McCarthy concluded, after listening carefully to the testimony of witnesses who regarded the deliberate creation of 'refugees' through the destruction of villages, rice fields, and livestock as normal, but fumbled for excuses when confronted with the shooting of unarmed peasants. At Fort McPherson, the "tranquil acceptance of organized brutality by the Army" shocked McCarthy, but it did not lead her to reconstruct a larger, darker picture of what the United States was doing in South Vietnam; or to imagine that there might not have been a courtroom in the world big enough to contain the suspects that a full accounting of My Lai would summon to the dock.

The massacre in Quang Ngai province was only a more advanced expression of the policy of " 'forced urbanization' " she had observed in central Vietnam in 1967. That she didn't see the link between the aerial bombardment of suspected Vietcong territory, the relocation of hundreds of thousands of peasants to heavily fortified camps, whose intolerable conditions were apparent to her in 1967, and Captain Medina's order on the night of March 15, 1968, to " ' "destroy everything that moved," ' " is surprising. But McCarthy herself had fallen into a trap posed by the legal system, which is that the charges are tailored to fit the conscience of the court.

It was the bombing of North Vietnam that first aroused her conscience, moreover; nothing that happened in the South would ever match the moment in the spring of 1965 when she passed a Left Bank kiosk on her way to a bakery and saw the headline announcing the first raids north of the 17th parallel. "We had done it," she remembered thinking; and she was reminded of another morning, twenty years before, when she saw the Hiroshima headline while buying a loaf of Portuguese bread in Truro. "I was unable to believe that we would actually attack from the air a small poor country that had not attacked us—" McCarthy reasoned at a time when the United States had already hurled more bombs against South Vietnam than throughout all of Korea. The bombing of the North seemed different, like a Chinese water torture calibrated to break the victim's will. If, as a result of the raids, Johnson succeeded in forcing North Vietnam to negotiate on U.S. terms, that was almost worse than if he failed, she feared; for then there would be no restraining him. If he didn't, he was likely to escalate still further. If Johnson attacked Hanoi, that was the end as far as she was concerned: "I would not find it acceptable to be an American any more," she told Hannah Arendt—for whom Vietnam, far from Europe, Israel, and North America, her own centers of interest, was never the moment of truth it was for Mary.

Arendt, at least in 1965, took a position closer to Diana Trilling's; "one of our real problems is how to get out," Hannah wrote Mary; "we cannot simply let all people down and without protection who ever were on our side; they would simply be massacred." The alternative was "to cease bombing and start negotiating." McCarthy, however, was for unilateral withdrawal. When Diana Trilling had warned her of a "Communist bloodbath," she reached for her typewriter. "Let us drop the crocodile concern and talk about reality," she said in a controversial exchange published in *The New York Review of Books.* Hundreds of thousands of South Vietnamese had been compromised by working for the Americans, she acknowledged; 140,000 were on the military payroll alone. If Vietnam went to the Communists, the most "crooked" collaborators would probably be " 'saved' " by their U.S. sponsors, while the " 'little people' " would be left to face the music. One could only hope they were secretly working for the Vietcong, McCarthy ventured, but if not, "that [was] the tough lot of being a camp follower." (Jim West was disgusted when he found Mary hammering out this reply to Diana Trilling. It was a waste of time better spent on *Birds of America,* he said.)

McCarthy wasn't alone in responding to the onset of the Pentagon's Operation Rolling Thunder as Armageddon. The bombing of the North had also taken Robert Lowell over the edge from peaceable petition signing to civil disobedience at the Pentagon march in October 1967. But when Nixon actually ordered the bombing of Hanoi and Haiphong in December 1972, and Mary McCarthy contemplated going to the North again, this time with a delegation of notables (Ramsey Clark and Stephen Spender had agreed to go), she would come closer than anyone in her circle to 'dropping everything,' including, for one perilous moment, her marriage; for Jim West had little sympathy for the 1972 trip. It was too "death-centered" for his taste, as it was for the North Vietnamese, who suggested, kindly, when Mary took her proposal to the embassy in Paris, that if she wished to die under American bombs, she ought to do it in front of the White House.

The Medina trial might have taught McCarthy a truth that her own tours of 'New Life' hamlets and model hospitals in South Vietnam had concealed from her; namely, that South Vietnam's battleground was not like the battlegrounds of other wars. The chance to play amateur advocate at Fort McPherson was hard to resist, however, and in the end she was too committed to the logic of the evidence, which argued overwhelmingly for Medina's conviction, to let the villain get away. In a conclusion that Hannah Arendt advised her to cut, she argued the missing case for the prosecution, as well as her own case for the moral responsibility of the individual—curiously enough, by donning the enemy's robes.

"Were the North Vietnamese and the NLF to win the war," McCarthy proposed, "they would undoubtedly try the immediate authors of the massacre, as well as Johnson, Westmoreland . . . and any other higher-ups they could catch. . . . but if they could not catch Johnson and Westmoreland, they would still try and condemn all the guilty smaller fry they could lay their hands on. To act otherwise," she said, "would be to imply that because Hitler eluded justice by committing suicide in his bunker and Bormann and Eichmann escaped it would be *unfair* to pick on the smaller Nazis such as Ilse Koch and the lieutenants and executioners at Auschwitz." McCarthy was thankful that Lieutenant Calley was convicted, and angry at America's " 'counter-culture' " for snatching the "plum" (conviction) away before it could be tasted. The result was a bitter pill, sharper than *New Yorker* readers were accustomed to swallow: Medina and Henderson off the hook, Calley's sentence reduced, and

several identified and unidentified mass murderers welcomed back into the population. Now any member of the armed forces in Indochina can, if he so desires, slaughter a reasonable number of babies, confident that the public will acquit him, a) because they support the war and the Army or b) because they don't.

II

Reviewing David Halberstam's *The Best and the Brightest* for *The New York Review of Books* in 1973 was a mopping-up exercise after the long essay in *The New Yorker,* which was promptly repackaged by Jovanovich as *Medina* in 1972. Unlike *Vietnam* and *Hanoi,* Medina was reviewed here and there, but without enthusiasm. Halberstam's huge 'backgrounder' on America's Vietnam involvement—"studded, like a ham, with anecdotes and gossip about historic decisions and high-status personalities, syrupy with compassionate insights into the gamesmanship of power"—permitted Mary McCarthy to return to an earlier chapter of the war. It also let her settle an old score with the Kennedy administration, one rooted in an aversion to the Kennedys' Irish Catholic clannishness, which reminded her of the Minneapolis McCarthys, but which also hints at pique over never having been invited to the White House 'evenings' in the early 1960s.

"[N]ot brains and birth but packaged ideology" came to Washington with the Kennedys, McCarthy writes; the myth to the contrary, to which David Halberstam subscribes, is simply "Kennedy advertising." That anyone should refer to the " 'honed-down intelligence' " of a "stick like McGeorge Bundy" strikes her as preposterous. Unlike Roosevelt's academic advisers (Felix Frankfurter, A. A. Berle, Rexford Tugwell), the men in the " 'glittering constellation' " Halberstam cites impress McCarthy as "pale fish out of university think tanks." Many of them, she observes, moving on to the more important issue of their infatuation with counterinsurgency doctrines, are "adepts of political science—a pseudo discipline of 'ruthless' thinking about political 'realities' " that flourished under Cold War auspices, and that, in McCarthy's view, is only slightly more pernicious than sociology.

"The gross stupidities and overconfidence of the Kennedy-Johnson advisers, not to mention their moral insensitivity, issued from a sectarian faith in the factuality of the social sciences, which is not by any means the religion of an elite," McCarthy proposes. The "sectarian faith" that lay behind the glorification of counterinsurgency is blasphemy; a "crass body of beliefs," propped up by computers and fed by "input" from " 'scientists.' " The jab at the social sciences—a common theme in discussions with Hannah Arendt, who regarded sociology, along with psychology, as folk disciplines at best and social control systems at worst—was also a New Left perception. The Kennedy administration, the argument ran, first sold Vietnam to liberals as a giant experiment in 'nation-building.'

More than anything else McCarthy wrote about Vietnam, "Sons of the Morning," as the Halberstam review was called, was inspired by a New Left sensitivity to the power of a revolutionary movement to put American foreign policy on its most savage footing. To answer the thorny question of Why Vietnam? it wasn't enough to cite the Cold War and the 'loss' of China, as Halberstam did, along with the collapse of the French and British empires, which left the United States holding the bully stick after World War II. The Cold War argument was moot, since nobody in power believed anymore in a " 'world Communist threat.' " Something more basic was at stake.

Disposing of the traditional notion of imperialism's search for raw materials and cheap labor—neither of which would survive the whole-sale destruction of Vietnam's rice fields and rubber plantations—McCarthy argued that in a larger sense American investments and markets *were* at stake in Southeast Asia. Vietnam had become a "symbol of the right of U.S. capital to flow freely throughout the globe and return home," not because of any capital that might someday flow from South Vietnam's offshore oil fields, even less because of the lure of real estate development at Cam Ranh Bay, but because the "revolutionary challenge represented by the Viet Cong" had turned Vietnam into a neoimperialist proving ground.

The defiance of American will on the part of a " 'backward' nation" was nothing less than "[t]he shot heard round the world"; and a "Viet Cong 'take over,' " once allowed, McCarthy writes,

> will deal a blow to the American way of life and free-enterprise mystique, not only because the revolutionary spirit is contagious and may be carried like Asian flu to the Philippines, South America, Africa, but because the very concept of a self-elected alternative to the Americn pattern is injurious.

Such perceptions, of course, rested on the assumption that the Vietnam War was unavoidable; and, indeed, McCarthy took issue with Halberstam's suggestion that there might have once been an " 'honorable' " exit from " 'America's tragedy.' " In 1972, the *Pentagon Papers* had taught her to discount the influence of the 'loyal opposition' inside government, at least when national security interests were perceived. The terror of revolution ran too deep in the national psyche to brook any interference with America's destiny, which was to stamp out change. Besides, there was the ineradicable myth of superior technology (American " 'muscle' "), which supplied another reason for staying in Vietnam. Even "peace," if it should finally come, McCarthy concluded grimly, "will only be an intermission in a series of confrontations. . . ."

She was wrong, at least in the short term. At home and abroad, the revolutionary spirit of the 1960s was not contagious. Peace, when it finally came to Vietnam in the spring of 1975, ushered in a collapse of will inside that tiny battered nation from which it still has not recovered. Back home, the 'American way' was hollowed out by the moral and material costs of the war, but the edifice stood; propped up, McCarthy suggested later, by the symbolic cleansing of past sins provided by the Watergate hearings. Meanwhile, it was left to the bloc countries of Eastern Europe in the late 1980s and to the Russian people in 1991 to reaffirm the 'free enterprise mystique.' "Actually, what we are doing in Vietnam is a mystery," McCarthy remarked in a candid moment of uncertainty in 1973. When all is said and done, it remains a mystery.

McCarthy's own attraction to the mandarin revolutionaries of North Vietnam never found an audience, either among the Old Left or the New—whose ideas reached her after they had lost their grip on the young. She had figured that people put more trust in the perceptions of writers they know as novelists than they give to the "press's 'objective' reporting or political scientists' documented . . . analyses." Another miscalculation. She had an "asset" other reporters lacked: her readers—if not "the millions" who read *The Group,* she thought, at least some of them. But the "asset" wasn't convertible; *The Group*'s readers weren't interested. Even when Harcourt Brace Jovanovich reissued all McCarthy's Vietnam writing under a single cover, *The Seventeenth Degree,* prefaced by a new memoir, "How It Went," in 1974, the collection passed largely unnoticed.

An exception was an omnibus review of McCarthy's wartime reporting, "The Blinders She Wears," by James Fallows in the May 1974 *Washington Monthly,* which took the "star political correspondent for *The New York Review of Books*" to task for a "lack of objectivity so profound as to make even sympathizers wary." McCarthy, of course, never claimed to be 'objective' in her Vietnam reporting; Fallows was attacking her outspoken criticism of the American position, and her sympathetic portraits of Hanoi's leaders, though the punches are hidden behind a swipe at the 'star' reporter's professionalism ("she has not fully comprehended that journalism is a serious business"). She was chided for writing about "a land she had never seen," and "people she knew nothing about" instead of staying in Paris—oddly enough—"to tell her husband's story," the story of how a U.S. foreign service officer turned sour on the war. The criticism is an argument for the journalist as insider, a variation of Diana Trilling's view of the intellectual as handmaiden to power. "[O]nly by trying to understand people as they understand themselves can a writer ever really hope to reach them," Fallows argues, assuming, as Mary McCarthy does not, that the journalist's job is to help the policymaker clean up his act. Thanks in part to critical attention such as this, *The Seventeenth Degree* is still one of the least known of McCarthy's books.

"Publish in hard covers if you want to be sure of reviews? Or don't publish first in *The New York Review of Books*?" Mary herself couldn't explain the poor showing of the original books, whose sluggish sales did not, in any case, put much of a dent in an account with her publisher that had already reached $270,000 by October 1968, thus yielding a nine-year reservoir of $30,000 a year (independent of future sales). *The Writing on the Wall* (1970), the collection that includes "General Macbeth" and "Burroughs' *Naked Lunch*," along with McCarthy's criticism of contemporary French literature, was reviewed, mostly favorably, all over the country. (At Jim West's suggestion, *The Writing on the Wall* was sent giftwrapped with a set of the books treated in the collection to one hundred reviewers, which may have accounted for some of its success.) "So it could not be just me that nobody wanted to hear from," McCarthy thought. "Perhaps me on Vietnam—the combination."

No doubt the Vietnam series followed too hard on too many books about the war—around two hundred, William Jovanovich calculated at the time. (When Hannah Arendt received Susan Sontag's *Trip to Hanoi* in December 1968, she didn't read it, remarking, "[t]he whole thing seems too obvious." Rahv, on the other hand, did, and praised it in a letter to Mary.) McCarthy's reporting was different: her ear for bureaucratese, for the killing power of cliché, is faultless; her novelist's eye for telling detail is as alert as ever. The efflorescence of language in time of combat is treated with a wit and thoroughness in *Vietnam* and *Hanoi* that recalls Orwell's "Politics and the English Language." But her personal crusade in Vietnam, in part, a search for a lost innocence—her own and her country's—has relegated McCarthy's wartime writing, unfairly, to a limbo in American letters.

36

The Duchess of Castine

"Five nations: Dutch, French, Englishmen, Indians,

and we, who held Castine, rise from their graves in combat gear—

world-losers elsewhere, conquerors here!"

—ROBERT LOWELL, "FOURTH OF JULY IN MAINE"

"To use the Bloomsbury language: 'Oh, my dear,

I cannot not wait to see you and the blessed Jim, amongst

the peonies, threading the baby sweet peas.' "

—ELIZABETH HARDWICK TO MARY MCCARTHY, 6/11/71

Vietnam brought Mary McCarthy home again. "Bit by bit, Vietnam had altered the pattern of our lives," she reflected in 1974—first by turning her into a roving correspondent, and then, as early as her return from Saigon in 1967, by making her homesick, as Jim West was, for the United States. When Jim proposed that they buy the Gillette house in Castine that Cal Lowell had told them about that spring, instead of spending another compulsory home leave in a rented house in Stonington, Connecticut, Mary was ready. "[I]f I was going to take a stand against U.S. policy, I ought to have a piece of U.S. ground under my feet," she reasoned. Hannah Arendt called it an "Archimedean lever" (a standpoint from which to move the world), though Hannah and Heinrich Blücher had contemplated an opposite move the following year: exile in Switzerland, where they planned to sit out the revolution in American streets, and the counterrevolution Arendt was sure would follow under Nixon. ("Here goes everything from bad to worse," she wrote Mary around this time. "It looks like the end of the Republic, though not necessarily of the country.")

The Blüchers stayed on Riverside Drive; but on July 4, 1967, Jim and Mary had disembarked in Castine, "a real Fourth-of-July New

England village," Mary said of the town that she had never seen before, but that Jim could almost call home (and does today), having been born outside Bangor, sixty miles away. Castine was the site of two hundred years of struggle for dominion over northern Maine between France, England, and the United States. With its Revolutionary-era fortifications still intact, its classical lyceum and myriad historic markers, it was more in the Rocky Port tradition than Wellfleet, Truro, or Provincetown. Except for its location at the end of a long spur of land, well off the road to more famous places—Bar Harbor and Mount Desert—it was nothing like Bocca di Magra, where the Wests used to spend their Augusts, which had itself changed in recent years, sprouting filling stations and fast-food *ristorantes* where public fountains once stood, and gradually shedding its literati.

Castine's harbor remains home to the Maine Maritime Academy's training vessel, a converted cruise ship whose gunmetal prow looms over the waterfront village. Around it dance the sundry yachts of the townsfolk, many retired military men, including General Edward Gillette, the widower who sold the Wests his handsome Federal-style house for $32,000 in 1967 and then ran off with the local innkeeper's wife. Dwarfed by the Maritime ship, Castine's sailboats and a handful of fishing boats look like toys. And the village itself, with its triangular white churches and elm-shaded greens, its big boxy sea captains' houses with tall, thin chimneys, marching down Main Street to Penobscot Bay, appears toylike, too, like a red, white, green, and blue diorama where the acid rain never falls.

Castine lacked an artists' community such as one found on the Ligurian coast or the outer Cape, but it didn't take Mary long to re-create the society she craved in the summers. "Come to Castine," she wrote Dwight Macdonald early in August, telling him about the Cercle Français she had started on Saturday nights that read Pascal and Montaigne—not unlike the evenings of Shakespeare she had organized in Truro in the summer of 1945. "America is a shock," she told Dwight, sounding a theme that tolls through *Birds of America*: the problem of "reverse technology," the disappearance of farms, local fishing fleets, and handicrafts from the countryside, and the substitution of tasteless facsimiles, or nothing at all. It was "all very pathetic," she said of her first encounter with this side of Maine life—which twenty years later would be brimming with homegrown produce and local crafts. "People drive for miles to attend cake sales," she complained, while she and Jim had to import a paperhanger all the way from Bar Harbor, "practically like colonial times."

Dwight Macdonald dropped in on his return from Expo '67 in

Montreal, along with two more cronies from the old *Partisan Review* gang, Philip Rahv and Fred Dupee, who visited at different times. Other houseguests that first summer included the nature writer Eleanor Perényi and her mother, the novelist Grace Stone; the poet James Merrill; and the faithful Bill Jovanovich. In later years, Jovanovich flew down from his summer home in Murray Bay, Canada, in the company jet, sometimes drawing up at Mary's front door on Main Street in a white limousine whose driver, a retired New Jersey cop who wore ruffled shirts, and served as Jovanovich's personal chauffeur, would later remind neighbors of the man who drove the getaway limo in a famous 1980s bank robbery in nearby Blue Hill.

In September, McCarthy had also begged Hannah Arendt to come. The white sea captain's house, built in 1804, was being repainted a lemon yellow (much to the consternation of the neighbors), while the library was stripped of its dark green draperies and papered in grass print; and a freestanding stairway, positioned fore and aft in the central hallway, was reinforced and covered with a canvas duck tread. Jim had thrown himself into reclaiming the gardens, and soon Mary would be planting antique roses. The house was full of workmen, but the bedrooms were peaceful, she assured Hannah, and there was a separate apartment over the garage where Hannah could be by herself and get some work done. If she came before the eighteenth, Maria, the Polish maid, would bring her breakfast on a tray, which was "one of her pleasures," Mary said. After that, Maria would be going to Expo '67 herself, and Hannah could help Mary with the dishes.

"[W]e're living very simply, owing to the presence of the workmen, and . . . there is *no social life* whatever. That ended with the departure of the Lowells," McCarthy declared, somewhat disingenuously, because the Wests brought more visitors to town than Elizabeth Hardwick and Robert Lowell, who had been coming to Castine since the 1950s. "The Wests are here," Lowell reported grumpily to Elizabeth Bishop the following August; he found "Mary a bit hard . . . to get at. The beautiful big house, the beautiful big meals, the beautiful big guests. . . . [N]othing seems addressed to me, and nothing I say is heard," he fussed, adding that she reminded him of Randall Jarrell in his off moods, though Mary was never discourteous. Speaking as a poet, Lowell drew a gentler picture: "Your eight-inch, star-blue, softwood floorboard, your house / sawn for some deadport Revolutionary squire. . . ." And Mary: "Dark Age luminary and Irish hothead, / the weathered yeoman loveliness of a duchess. . . ."

McCarthy failed to overcome Hannah Arendt's distaste for summertime frolics, for she didn't come until after Blücher's death in 1970; in the summer of 1971, she took the garage apartment for six weeks to write a controversial and widely read essay, "Lying in Politics: Reflections on the *Pentagon Papers*." As for Robert Lowell, in 1970 he left Castine—"defected," Mary said—leaving Lizzie for a new girl in London, the very attractive Lady Caroline Blackwood, a member of the Guinness family and once a lady-in-waiting to Princess Margaret. Jim West allowed that Lowell had left the "temple standing"—the town's summer life would carry on without him; but Mary saw Cal "as a wild Samson leaving us to the rubble and the Philistines, of whom Castine contains quite a few."

By September 1967, the West children had come and gone, never to return to Maine again together. The year before, Jim's ex-wife had suddenly left Paris for New York, taking Danny, Alison, and Jonathan out of school in France and sending them to boarding schools in England, thus ending the weekends they regularly spent with their father and stepmother in the country house Jim and Mary rented outside Paris. Now the children got together with the Wests only at Christmas and over the Easter holiday, which was often spent traveling in Italy or the "imaginary country" Mary McCarthy fell in love with in the 1970s, Holland. After 1967, Margaret West, whose jealousy of Mary increased by leaps and bounds following *The Group,* refused to allow Alison to go to Castine at all, and the boys' visits grew shorter and less frequent.

Jim West was upset by these disruptions in the routines he had established with his children, disruptions that themselves became routine as the years wore on. Meanwhile, Mary's relations with Reuel Wilson, now a Ph.D. candidate in Comparative Literature at Berkeley, and soon to be a father himself, were strained for more obscure reasons. In the weeks preceding his visit to Castine in September 1967, her uneasiness over what she called Reuel's "recent outbreaks of hatefulness" spilled over into letters to Hannah. Reuel, she said, had been turning into "an extremely hostile parasite." It was impossible to find out anything from him about the progress of his work, or whether he had passed his orals. Some of the problems she traced to Marcia Wilson's pregnancy. "It's clear that the coming baby means increased support from me—with increased resentment on their part. Classic," she said; "they are both beaming fondly on Edmund, who ceased his contributions several years ago." (Wilson's fortunes, always scanty, were tied up in litigation with the IRS, whose tax collectors he battled throughout the 1960s as if they were agents of the Czar.)

Two days before Reuel and Marcia were due to arrive, and the day after Maria left, Mary suddenly developed a paralyzing pain in her left arm, which she attributed to holding the mainsail in Jim's new sailboat. The doctor diagnosed "tendonitis" and gave her a large injection of cortisone and a prescription for Demerol. There was nothing unusual in the mishap, but crises like this, including a recurrent slipped cervical disk that immobilized her right arm and fingers, often accompanied unwelcome news, as if the victim had made a pact to deposit her anguish over certain issues in a medical emergency.

After Lillian Hellman sued McCarthy in 1980, and Mary fell victim to a series of Job-like afflictions, beginning with shingles and followed by a loss of equilibrium first diagnosed as ataxia and then hydrocephalus, or water on the brain, her studied aplomb in the face of three brain operations and endless CAT scans managed to convince a good many people, most importantly, perhaps, herself, that nothing was seriously amiss. After a recurrence of breast cancer in 1987, first treated in the middle 1970s, and a grueling regime of radiation therapy, which in turn precipitated a respiratory crisis and a series of cardiac episodes in the spring of 1988, Bill Jovanovich, no stranger to intensive-care units, was moved to chide Mary for understating the severity of her case. " 'A bit of health trouble,' " indeed. "I believe there is such a thing as too much stoicism," he exclaimed. "You need to give yourself a break—I wish I knew what *that* could be."

As for McCarthy's conflict with her son, it broke out again in the summer of 1978, when Reuel Wilson executed a wordless departure from Castine after declining to participate in a series of excursions his mother had organized for her houseguests, Margo and Anthony Viscusi: a sailing picnic to Smith's Cove, dinner in nearby Blue Hill. Reuel's tennis partner remembers how upset he was that summer over the breakdown of relations with Marcia, from whom he was about to get a divorce. He wanted some private time with Mary "to get some motherly advice," but Mary had gone right on entertaining her guests.

McCarthy was still helping Reuel defray his expenses, which probably didn't help matters. In January 1978, he had thanked her for covering the cost of a trip to Cuba that he and Marcia had taken in 1977. Before the trip, Marcia had written to enlist her mother-in-law's help in sorting out their marital problems; and McCarthy, who always blamed Marcia for having given Edmund Wilson's only grandson her own family name rather than Wilson's, as custom proposed, must have been helpful; for in June 1977, Marcia thanked her for her concern, adding that she had come to see Mary and Jim West almost as parental figures. One way or another, McCarthy was involved in the fate of this marriage, which makes it odd that when it ended she demonstrated far more concern with Reuel's behavior in front of her guests than with his feelings about the divorce.

After 1978, Reuel chose to stay at a nearby inn when he stopped in Castine on his way to Talcottville or Wellfleet, rather than submit to the rigid formalities that prevailed in his mother's house. Breakfast at eight, lunch at one, cocktails at seven; it was "pretty vigorous," Kevin McCarthy admits, especially when one arrived with a toddler, as Reuel had after Jay Hilary Wilson was born—and as Kevin and his new wife, Kate, did in the 1980s, bringing two young children when they visited the Wests, usually in August.

Kate McCarthy experienced these formalities as a power struggle between women, in which she, as the much younger one, the interloper, could never win. Kevin's second wife was twenty-eight, wearing short shorts and a French T-shirt with no bra when Kevin first introduced her to his illustrious sister in 1979; "she thought of me as a little bimbo," Kate remembers, shuddering at the indignity of being handed the candle-snuffer after meals, because it was the " 'tradition of the house' " for the youngest to snuff out the candles. "I kept making little mistakes," she recalls, as when Mary "spilled some coffee and I handed her my napkin, and she said, 'Oh no, I don't want to use *that*! . . . Kevin hadn't really prepared her for me," she recalls; nor had Kate been prepared for Mary.

Kevin, then sixty-five, had driven all the way up from New York with his young wife in her old Volvo on a hot day in August to introduce her to Mary and Jim, and Kate had just assumed that Mary "was going to be . . . like Kevin. I had no idea that she was going to be this *proper* person," she said. From the moment Mary first looked her up and down at the door, it was "like *ice*." No doubt this was the jealous reaction of an older sister, "though as an intellectual, Mary would never have admitted to that," she suggested. For Kate McCarthy, a law school graduate whose career was put on hold when she married Kevin, relations with Mary McCarthy never got much easier. "You [came] to Mary's house and it's *à table* at 8 A.M. . . . It's charming for about a day, and then it became this imposition of will," she said in 1987. "You [couldn't] come into her house and say, 'Oh, don't worry about me, I'll find something to eat.' "

Kevin ascribes this rigidity to his sister's growing unsteadiness after 1980, and to the fact that nobody really knew what was wrong with her. "If everything holds steady and I know what's going on,

[then] I can think, I can use my brain," he imagines her feeling. The rituals were a controlling device; she could maintain her dizzying schedule—which, beginning in 1986, included teaching at Bard College—if she could "have things in a certain order, in a certain hierarchy."

II

It was not always like that in Castine. The early summers Mary McCarthy spent in Maine were an extension of the year's political and literary commitments. Thus, in 1968, a watershed election year like 1948, she had involved herself in electoral politics. "If it is a choice between Humphrey and Nixon, I agree with the French student slogan: ELECTIONS TRAHISON," she declared. But before it came to that, she had campaigned for Eugene McCarthy, which in Castine meant hosting and attending dozens of picnics and cookouts, with reporters and television crews gathered in the wings, along with Secret Service personnel when Senator McCarthy himself came to town—which he did, playing tennis with Robert Lowell, then going out for a sail.

The following summer, Mary McCarthy had redecorated the house, which was now "exquisitely beautiful," she reported to Hannah Arendt, with "Dutch interior light effects that make me hold my breath with pleasure." The garden was full of wild strawberries that she and Jim had transplanted from adjacent fields. "When you come, if you come," she said, "it will be jelly-making time." Writing from Paris six weeks before, McCarthy had echoed Arendt's anxiety about the increasing polarization of American society caused by the unending war. "From here too, it looks as if it may be the end of the Republic, and I'm desolate and also puzzled. . . . [A]ll utterances on the subject of student violence, black power, etc., fill me with nausea," she ventured. The "moderates" were almost the worst: " 'There is a proper way to express dissent: through the spoken and written word' " (this in *Time*, from the parent of a "militant"). "On the part of older people there is a sudden enormous production of clichés, which is how you know that what's being said is false," she continued. "As for the language of the young, it resembles incantation," McCarthy added. "But the incantation may work, as incantations probably did quite often in the days of 'superstition.' "

Still, if Nixon didn't extricate himself from Vietnam very soon, McCarthy was afraid he would "bring the whole structure down on his head. . . ." Maybe he would perish with it like Johnson, but it looked like Nixon had no intention of ending the war. Nor did the North Vietnamese seem hopeful of an early resolution, as they had in 1968. "The only non-nauseous contribution to this whole subject that I know is your 'Reflections on Violence,' " Mary wrote Hannah from Paris. "Write more." Meanwhile, her own reaction to the escalation of rhetoric on the Left, and killing power on the Right, was "to go and order a lot of dresses made, as though they would be my last. The reverse of a hope chest. And I have visions of Castine burning," she added, "just as soon as we get it fixed up."

By November 1969, however, the political atmosphere was once again charged with hope, because the young had acted. McCarthy was in New York for emergency dental work, which together with meetings with her publisher now constituted her primary business in the city. While she was marshaling signatures for a new antiwar proclamation, Dwight Macdonald and Robert Lowell were on their way to Washington for a week of demonstrations. Hannah Arendt had pronounced the October Moratorium "a splendid thing. . . . One feels once more the hopes one had during the McCarthy campaign. But this is better," she thought, "because it bypassed the whole party system altogether and rested solely on the constitutional right of the people to assemble and petition."

It was amazing what a few hundred thousand protesters voting with their feet in the nation's capital, or demonstrating "on campus, in church or in Wall Street" could do for the older generation's battered faith in democracy: "No ideologies, no *weltanschauungen*," Arendt exulted; and she was equally optimistic for the November Mobilization, which indicated that "the new generation . . . [would now] really come into their own, lose the 'extremists' with their hollow rhetoric, and perhaps rediscover the republic, the public thing."

Throughout 1970, McCarthy had wrestled with the final recalcitrant chapters of *Birds of America;* the "horrible novel . . . [was] drowning in verbiage," she complained to Hannah in the spring. There wasn't much time for politics, though there was always time for travel: London in March, Holland and Japan in April (on OECD business with Jim), New York in May, Switzerland in June, where she visited Arendt in Tegna; Castine in July, August, and September. In Castine, McCarthy worked ten to twelve hours a day on the novel that Arendt thought she would feel "closest" to because it was the least "society-minded." The summer was a relatively quiet one; none of the West children came, Lowell was gone, and apart from Jim and Mary's annual lawn party, a visit from Philip Rahv (his last), and a delegation from abroad that included George Weidenfeld and his wife, and Kot Jelenski looking like Pham Van Dong in a khaki tunic, social life, with its rounds of tennis and sailing, rumbled along like that of any other well-heeled New England town on vacation. The political euphoria of the previous year had evaporated after Nixon invaded Cambodia in April and the Ohio National Guard shot four protesting students at Kent State University in May.

In July 1971, Elizabeth Hardwick met Mary and Maria at the airport in Bangor—Jim West always came later. Lizzie had a new button to propose for "Women's Lib," she wrote McCarthy earlier, after reading an article by Edmund Wilson in *The New Yorker* that was "very critical of poor old Elena [Wilson's fourth wife] and . . . filled with descriptions of the pleasant services and accommodations offered by the young Hungarian girl" Edmund knew in Talcottville: "Good wives finish last!" McCarthy, meanwhile, was troubled by the poor showing of *Birds of America,* which had made the best-seller list in May (thanks to a massive pre-publication publicity campaign) and then abruptly fallen off. It was knocked off, McCarthy believed, by influential reviews like Helen Vendler's in *The New York Times Book Review,* which found "no creature more devoid of existential-ist reality . . . than this so-carefully documented Peter Levi. . . . [H]e has no insides," Vendler declared; "Mary McCarthy, for all her cold eye and fine prose, is an essayist, not a novelist." It was a judgment that echoed Miss Kitchel at Vassar; and after working for years to disprove it, Mary was discouraged.

Politics had come to the rescue. Perhaps in a way it always had. In August 1971, after waiting to spend a few days of Jim's vacation with him in Castine, McCarthy had flown to Atlanta to cover the Medina trial. ("She missed the first week of the Medina testimony because of her husband's vacation plans," snapped James Fallows in his *Washing-ton Monthly* review; he would also blame her for dropping out of the Watergate hearings early, "because it was time to return to Paris.") After Fort MacPherson, McCarthy was swamped with testimony, ex-hibits, maps—not unlike Hannah Arendt after the Eichmann trial, only in McCarthy's case, ploughing through the quagmire of documen-tary material on My Lai had not brought a surcease of tension.

In December 1971, she was "still slogging away on Medina," she wrote Lizzie Hardwick, shortly before she and Jim left for a Christmas tour of English cathedrals (the Gothic, one suspects, was McCarthy's respite from politics). She hoped Lizzie wouldn't be hurt by their plan to spend Christmas Eve with Cal and Caroline, now married, and their new baby in Kent. The "Medina syndrome," she noted glumly, was her first experience of writer's block, "and God knows what exactly is the reason," she added, meaning the cliché literally perhaps: 'God knows.' When the following summer, *Medina,* too, was largely panned, McCarthy succumbed to a moment of genuine despair. "[P]erhaps I won't write any more—what's the use?" she wrote Hannah Arendt after the "depressing reviews. . . . There's a limit to how much one can take of that. Especially if one feels, as I do, that the act of writing has something to do with communication."

By the summer of 1972, the act of despairing may have had something to do with the death of Nicola Chiaromonte, who collapsed of a heart attack in an elevator in Rome on January 18, 1972, after delivering a broadcast on Jean-François Revel's *Without Marx or Jesus.* Nicola's death, at sixty-seven, hit Mary McCarthy very hard. She didn't feel anything at first, she told Arendt the day after Anjou Levi called to tell her the news, because Nicola was still *"there."* She had gotten used to his *"not* dying" for so long, ever since his first coronary in 1961, that she believed him "eternal." Anjou was broken up, sayng she couldn't go on, sobbing distractedly; "I think of it as antique Jewish mourning, remembering my grandmother when she screamed at Aunt Rosie's death," McCarthy observed. But Mary had screamed, too. "She let out an animal-like shriek such as I have never heard again," Margo Viscusi remembers. Almost immediately she had composed herself to relate the circumstances of Chiaromonte's death to Margo, then working as McCarthy's secretary in Paris; there were "no tears. But it was clear that someone more important probably than a parent had just been taken away."

Nicola's death was "hateful," Mary wrote Hannah—a disturbing notion that had almost caused Arendt to reach for the transatlantic phone to debate the point. "Mary, look, I think I know how sad you are and how serious this loss is," she wrote instead. She found herself going through New York and looking at all the houses "which Death has emptied. . . . And God knows I have some experience in the presence of absence," she added, referring to Heinrich's death the year before. But if you say such things are " 'hateful' you will have to say hateful to many more things. . . . One could look upon one's whole life as a being-given and being-taken away; that starts already with life itself, given at birth, taken away with death; and the whole time in-between could easily be looked at as standing under the same law." If that was too abstract, there was the inscription on Jewish funeral homes: "The Lord hath given, the Lord hath taken away, blessed be the Lord. Or: Don't complain if something is taken away that was given you but which you did not necessarily *own*. . . . If you believed you owned, if you forgot that it was given, that is just too bad for you." Not that Anjou Levi's behavior wasn't also "quite Jewish," Arendt commented; as a Mediterranean people, Jews are demonstrative and know how to lament—"And lamentations (of which I am perhaps no longer capable)," she added, "are what we owe the dead ones precisely because we go on living."

When the Wests returned to Paris from Chiaromonte's funeral in Rome, Mary had noticed a black speck in her right eye. Ignoring Jim West's advice to see a doctor, she had continued working on the Medina piece for the next two weeks, going to the hospital only after she mailed the 25,000 word article to *The New Yorker* early in February. A torn retina was diagnosed, and McCarthy had checked into the American Hospital at Neuilly for laser surgery. Recovering at home, her eyes bandaged, unable to move her head for weeks, she slipped into a kind of time warp, whose medical circumstances were clear enough but whose closeness to Chiaromonte's death gives the interlude a symbolic character.

"I have the strange feeling of having had almost a blackout in my experience during those nearly two months, which seem dim and hard to recall now, as if they'd dropped out of my calendar," McCarthy wrote Arendt when she came up for air in April. Even before Nicola's death, the 'Medina syndrome' and also Jim West's troubles with his ex-wife, who was suing him for more child support, had left Mary "feeling wrapped in a dark heavy cloud, which may be just the world. I keep thinking about Dante. But we're past the middle of life's journey," she had written Lizzie in December. Whatever the circumstances, the actual darkness appeared to transport her to never-never land. "I suddenly knew what she looked like as a small child—" Jim wrote some friends in Castine at the time, "in a neat bed in a darkened room, her arms lying straight down along the covers and the sweetest expression of attention, watching something intently—with covered eyes."

As soon as she was up and about, McCarthy had gone to Rome to help Miriam Chiaromonte raise money for the publication of Nicola's uncollected writings and letters, staying with Carmen Angleton, who had visited Mary and read to her during her convalescence. Then she and Jim had traveled to Strasbourg with some American friends, for the Easter holiday. It was during this tour of Rhenish cathedrals that McCarthy formulated an opening for the long-dreamed-of book about the Gothic: a meditation on the figures of Ecclesia and Sinagoga that she saw in German churches. The Synagogue figure reflected the presence of a large colony of Jews along the Rhine in the Middle Ages, which reminded her of the Jews of medieval Venice. "I find the Synagogue figure very poetic; she is almost always more beautiful in her melancholy than the Church, her sister," she wrote Hannah Arendt—adding, enigmatically, that "as Peter Levi said, he was fond of hymns and carols that had Jews in them."

The 1972 presidential campaign was not the event 1968 had been, though for Democrats, the convention (reformed after the 1968 melee in Chicago) afforded some risible moments: as when George Meany, observing the representatives from New York, exclaimed, "What kind of delegation is this? They've got six open fags and only three AFL/CIO people . . . !" Nixon was at the peak of his power, thanks to his midnight rides to Peking and Moscow, and to the illusion, assiduously fostered by Henry Kissinger, that a settlement with the North Vietnamese was just around the corner in Paris. This time next year, Nixon's slide downhill would be swift; the five 'plumbers' had just been arrested in June 1972 for breaking into Democratic headquarters.

Nineteen seventy-two's dark-horse liberal, George McGovern, was never popular in Left literary circles. For Mary McCarthy, the question of whom to vote for, always approached solemnly, was merely toyed with in 1972. Especially after McGovern's midsummer retreat on both defense cuts and withdrawal (no longer 'immediate'), along with his redefinition of amnesty for draft resisters and AWOL soldiers, now excluding the latter, McCarthy's "civic conscience" told her she "*couldn't* vote for him, out of sheer self-respect." But the available protest votes—Dr. Spock? the Black Panther party candidate (if there was one)?—weren't very promising. "The fact is there is *nobody* to vote for, even as a gesture," she concluded; and she half-jokingly considered telegraphing Pham Van Dong in Hanoi to ask him what *he*'d like her to do, a prospect not as absurd as it sounds, since they exchanged greetings well into the 1970s.

In a July 1972 guest column in *Newsweek,* McCarthy displayed a flash of visionary thinking on the 'race issue' not usually ventilated in the mass media. Racism was at bottom an economic issue, she argued; and she proposed as an alternative to "bussing," which wasn't working, "a separate-but-equal effort to bring slum schools up to the level of non-slum schools. . . ." Such a program would unmask the underlying problem of poverty, which bussing sought to circumvent, she contended, and thus lead to more fundamental changes: school breakfasts, child-care units, expropriation of slum landlords, creation of cooperatives based on light industry. Of course it wouldn't fly. "One has only to conceive of something down-to-earth and faintly practical to watch it dissolve into a utopian dream," she reflected wistfully. "Better to stick with the 'debate' on the pseudonymous issue of bussing"—but the column, "Imagination, Anyone?" offered *Newsweek* readers something to think about during the lackluster election summer of 1972.

When the Watergate revelations broke in April 1973, Mary McCarthy was traveling across the United States, picking up honorary degrees, lecturing, and visiting relatives. She had jumped at the chance to cover the hearings in the old marble-pillared Senate Caucus Room, whose revolving armies of spectators reminded her of the Sistine Chapel. Setting up camp at the Watergate Hotel early in June, she had telexed her weekly stories, six in all, to *The Observer* every Friday night; three more, written for *The New York Review of Books*, rounded out *The Mask of State: Watergate Portraits*, published in 1974.

Working alone, writing under deadlines, hadn't come easily for her, and when McCarthy saw Norman Mailer at the hearings with a twenty-two-year-old blond "assistant," she had phoned Margo Viscusi in Paris, exclaiming, "If Norman can get that *girl* in I can get *you* in"; and Margo had flown to Washington to join her. Together they went to Capitol Hill early in the mornings, returning frequently to a Spartan supper cooked in their kitchenette. On Fridays, Margo Viscusi proofed McCarthy's final copy for "typos and awkwardnesses" as it came out of the typewriter. ("I just adored having Margo as a secretary," McCarthy said in 1986. It was a companionable arrangement, as were most of her relationships with secretaries. Margo, who later became one of her literary executors, had been preceded by Mary Brady, the wife of a counselor at the U.S. embassy in Paris, who helped McCarthy pack for Saigon and Hanoi, and was remembered fondly for saying "Throw it!" while revising her files. After Brady and Viscusi, came Patsy Leo, whose husband, Jim, was the dean of the Episcopal Cathedral in Paris. The Duchess of Windsor was one of his parishioners, and when she died in April 1986, Jim Leo was summoned to Windsor Castle to bury her. Patsy had gone, too, after Queen Elizabeth herself had reportedly said, " 'Let her come.' Imagine, the *Queen*!" McCarthy marveled at the time, relishing the drama.)

*   *   *

No one caught the spirit and the letter of the Watergate cover-up better than Mary McCarthy when she described the wagons drawn up around the White House:

> Inside are Nixon, General Haig, and the spirits of Haldeman and Ehrlichman; Colson is up in a tree picking off the enemy; Magruder is trying to infiltrate back. Dean has been smoked out, Mitchell has been smoked out, but that feral old dog [Mitchell] . . . may stay faithful, circling around the perimeter, despite the savage mistreatment given him in the last few days, and trying to scare away the senators with his bark.

McCarthy's Watergate portraits, like the character sketches in *Medina,* are laced with allusion. Maurice Stans, "[w]ith his white fluffy celebrity sideburns, small, well-cut features, smart suit accessorized with tie clasp and cuff-links, bearing the presidential seal, resembled . . . Claude Rains in *Caesar and Cleopatra.* . . ." Jeb Stuart Magruder's "zeal to be fair . . . was perhaps a genuine part of the cliché around which he was building a fresh, contrite personality." Senator Sam Ervin, a figure from "the 'old' parental America," and a McCarthy favorite—until the final hearings, when he pulled back from the fray, and she remembered he was a "hawk"—reminds her of one of Shakespeare's "honest common-sense rustics."

At the time, she was criticized for the hyperbole in the portraits. Fallows pounced on her hypersensitivity to grammatical indiscretion, and to a one-dimensionality in her critiques of character. Anthony Howard wondered, in *The New Statesman,* whether there weren't more important things to learn about Nixon's attorney general than that there was "something turnipy about Mitchell" or that he has "small lifeless eyes like those of a wintering potato." But Howard was impressed by the reasoning in McCarthy's concluding argument that the real instigator of the break-in could only have been the President.

As entertainment, the "Ervin show," as Mary called it, was a tremendous success, even in Castine, where tradesmen kept the hearings running all day in the shops. When Watergate first broke, McCarthy had been surprised by the quantity and quality of the coverage in regional newspapers, and by the grasp ordinary people had of the intricate web of associations connecting the White House to the various scandals. "What a treat to find Americans who are not professional intellectuals engrossed in what is a decidedly intellectual study, requiring feats of memory, concentration, orderly procedure," she remarked in the expanded first chapter of *The Mask of State*. Watergate, then, was a vindication of print over television, and of the truism: "Printer's ink and domestic liberty have an old association. Whereas television, being a mass medium, can be controlled and manipulated."

But it was television, not print, that had become the medium for the public's education over the summer. If Watergate was "a great equalizer," cutting across class and party lines in its ability to turn everybody into an expert, television was largely responsible. When she returned to Castine from Washington early in August, the wife of the local plumber had pointed out that housewives made a natural jury for the Watergate hearings because "their soap operas . . . had trained them to tell the good characters from the bad characters." An interesting observation, it offered her a key to understanding why Watergate's moral issues ultimately proved so transient (if she wondered), and why Nixon was pardoned in 1974.

Castine was full of tranquilizing distractions. Jim West was rebuilding a low brick wall around an abandoned windmill at the back of the property, where they had also put up a fence. Mary planted hollyhocks, Canterbury bells, foxglove, and columbine. "The contrast between Castine and the rest of the world gets more striking every year," she wrote a friend. The people stayed the same, barring divorce and death: The village kept its usual quota of retired military officers, lawyers, and Episcopal ministers; there was always a martini and lobster salad lunch for out-of-town guests, with pot de crème au chocolat for dessert. Elizabeth Hardwick had sold the Lowell house on the green and was making over the barn (where Cal used to work, overlooking the bay). Mary's Cercle Français, down to four members, was reading Chateaubriand. Eileen and Tom Finletter, summering in Bar Harbor, had entertained Bowden Broadwater. That was news; but Bowden and Mary had not met, nor would they ever meet again, though once or twice their eyes met across crowded rooms.

In 1974, Alison West had visited Castine, along with McCarthy's eighty-year-old uncle Frank Preston, who brought his second wife and stepson from Seattle. Hannah Arendt arrived for a few days in September. The house and garden, with its resident hummingbirds and goldfinches, had never seemed so idyllic; as it also did the following summer, leading Mary to conclude that she might well sink into " 'rural idiocy,' " as Philip Rahv called it—"But only for four months of a year." She was spending more time in Castine, whose local politics had begun to fascinate her almost as much as Watergate had.

In the midst of a terrible heat wave in August 1975, a village political storm erupted over a new property tax voted by the state legislature for the purpose of equalizing public funding of Maine's schools. When Castine, "fired with the Spirit of '76 and acting like a bunch of minute-men," in McCarthy's opinion, refused to either collect or pay the tax, a superior court judge in Portland had ordered town officials to pay or be held in contempt; and on August 4 a town meeting was called to decide what action to take. "*Everyone* attended, some virtually in wheelchairs, with Bangor reporters and TV cameras watching," McCarthy wrote Hannah Arendt in Switzerland. The legislation was designed to penalize "the 'rich coastal towns' with high property assessments to favor the poor parts of the state which don't raise enough money in property taxes to pay for their local schools," she explained. "The coastal towns, naturally, are indignant and some have banded together to declare the law unconstitutional and fight it in the courts. On that point almost everybody here is in agreement," she stated. Opinion was divided on how to correct the inequity.

The coastal towns that had joined the legal battle had either paid the tax over provisionally to the state or were holding it in escrow until the state supreme court handed down a decision. Castine stood alone in its mutinous attitude, and the five selectmen risked going to jail or paying a substantial fine if they persisted; hence the town meeting. "The moderate or law-abiding party includes most of our friends and us . . ." McCarthy reported, "[w]hereas the immoderates included most of the natives and some transplants like the local retired military. . . ." The Wests' next-door neighbor, the poet Philip Booth, had emerged as the leader of the moderate party. The situation was "paradoxical," McCarthy continued, "with the richer, i.e., more educated residents—those who stand to suffer most from the new law—urging compliance, while the poorer—the bulk of the population—are up in arms."

The moderates were also mostly summer people, and therefore couldn't vote (the Booths and Wests were exceptions), though they were allowed to speak at the meeting. At the same time, they paid a high share of the property taxes. Thus the confrontation was a microcosm of "Vacationland" politics—though McCarthy had left out the radical party, those who had supported the property tax in the first place, presumably a majority of the state's voters, but only a handful in Castine.

The showdown confirmed the liberal's traditional despair over "village democracy." The town meeting had been "comical, also depressing," Mary wrote Hannah; the atmosphere "so inflamed that anybody who didn't want to see the town officials go to jail was treated as a public enemy, and this morning it was being said—by extreme elements—that Phil Booth was . . . a 'communist.' " "Russia" was identified with Augusta, the state capital. "Of course the natives have good reason . . . to be angrier than we are," McCarthy observed, "because they can't afford, many of them, to pay the additional tax, while we can. So that there *is* a class division, though the leadership elements of the locals are, naturally, the illiberal rich and propertied." Looking at the tense, excited faces, it was all too easy to see

> the fascists in embryo . . . who are carrying the more conservative and frightened innocents along with them. . . . And where "Russia" was much invoked by the minute-men, Watergate, though not mentioned by name, played an obvious part in swaying those natives who moved over to the moderate position, mentioning the necessity for "respect for the law" on the part of public officials. . . .

As it turned out, the liberals did better than expected, losing by 65 to 125. McCarthy predicted that all was not over; there would be another town meeting when people noticed the heavy fines and legal fees they were going to pay, "as well as—probably—the jacked-up property tax in the long run." She was wrong about the property tax, which was overturned by the court; the 'rich coastal towns' carried the day.

Ten years later, the Spirit of '76 broke out again in a town meeting called to debate the Navy's planned installation of an early-warning radar tower in Castine; and this time, Jim West joined an insurgent 'action committee' organized to challenge the safety and legality of the tower. In August 1985, the Wests and their houseguests, including Alison and Danny West, had filled an entire pew in Emerson Hall. Afterwards, just as in 1975, they and their friends retired to the house on Main Street for refreshments and postmortems.

The tower, part of the huge GWEN network of antisubmarine stations stretching along the Atlantic coast, was eventually built somewhere else. Once again, a wealthy coastal community prevailed, only this time it was because members of the moderate persuasion—up in arms over the Pentagon's infringement of local sovereignty—had behaved like minutemen.

* * *

When Jim West retired from the OECD in 1980, the path was cleared for full-time residence in Maine, something he might have welcomed, but Mary wouldn't hear of it. "The social life, there's too much of it," she claimed. A single Christmas in Castine in 1972 had introduced her to the winter round of cocktail parties, which were harder to avoid, she explained, "because you're visible: all the leaves have fallen off the trees—socially as well as literally." Living there year-round, she would either become "universally hated, or be going out and holding inane conversations."

By 1980, Mary had 'broken' with more than one old Castine friend. She had begun to refer to some of her neighbors as "morons." Shingles had given her an excuse to stay away from most of that summer's parties; and with the September 30, 1980, referendum to shut down the Maine Yankee Nuclear Power Plant in Wiscasset she had seized upon "a successor idea," which was to "refuse to see anybody socially who voted 'no' in the referendum." Jim said she couldn't do that, she said, laughing at the time; but she would do something very much like it a few years later. Early in November 1984, at her husband's seventieth birthday party, an old friend of his from Paris after the war, Elizabeth Vondaris had taken it upon herself to remove a large Mondale button Jim was wearing. When Mrs. Vondaris, a wealthy Republican, went on to say insulting things about Geraldine Ferraro, Mary had wheeled on her: "I'm going to ostracize you!" she announced, stampeding the startled woman to the door. The next day, Mrs. Vondaris telephoned Anthony Viscusi—the party was at the Viscusis' apartment in Manhattan—to find out what *ostracize* meant. McCarthy was serious; the only thing one could do with such people was not talk to them, she maintained, and she never spoke to Elizabeth Vondaris again.

In the 1980s, Castine was top-heavy with Reaganites. Mary McCarthy wasn't betting on any dark horses, or thinking about consulting with Pham Van Dong, but lacking alternatives made it no easier to consort with the 'enemy.' For this and other reasons, the red-walled, book-lined study in Paris remained her center of operations until she died.

Beginning in 1981, when she finally took up the 'intellectual autobiography' Bill Jovanovich first proposed in 1973, she had started to explore the "American tincture" in her experience—not least the way she "first became conscious of the fact that there was such a thing as an intellectual," which was not the same as an artist or someone who wrote books, she told an interviewer, but a "class of person . . .

different from other people." It had happened when she was a freshman at Garfield High School, through contact with one of her young uncle Harold Preston's friends, a "campus intellectual" who edited the humor magazine at the University of Washington. But Mary McCarthy had long ago fallen under the intellectual sway of Europe, the Europe of Tolstoy, Brunelleschi, and Kant.

The Europeanization of Mary McCarthy began with Nicola Chiaromonte on the beach in Truro in 1945, and intensified during her long and intimate friendship with Hannah Arendt. Marrying Jim West, settling down in Paris, gave it an address. Castine could never hold her; and the six-month intervals spent in Maine from 1980 to 1985, before McCarthy started going down to Bard to teach in the fall, were hard times. The shadow of Lillian Hellman hung over these years, along with poor health, and Castine itself, without the company of old friends to maintain the vital connection to her American past, began to wear thin.

37

How They Go

"I came home very depressed. . . . I have been surrounded here for
weeks by old people who suddenly got very old."
—HANNAH ARENDT TO MARY MCCARTHY, 8/22/75

"The present can try to bury the past, an operation that is most
atrocious when it is most successful."
—MARY MCCARTHY, "THE INVENTIONS OF I. COMPTON-BURNETT"

One more thing," the letter from E. Jay Rousuck said: "I have a
yearling. His sire (owned by Paul Mellon) is 'Crack Pot' who was sired
by 'Tom Fool.' My yearling's damn [*sic*] is 'None Fairer.' Please
furnish a name." Mary McCarthy's answer is unrecorded, as are the
inscriptions she regularly wrote for Mannie Rousuck's Christmas
cards, except for the line that went with a Degas he used in 1965: "*A
prancing, dancing Christmas.*" Rousuck had often passed her his gold
pencil and memo pad during lunch at Lüchow's or Lutèce: " 'Just give
me a few lines on Cooper-Henderson,' " he would say, referring to an
artist in an upcoming exhibition.

Over the years he had paid her handsomely for writing his business
letters and brochures. In *Cannibals and Missionaries* (1979),
McCarthy draws liberally on Mannie Rousuck's social connections
and his intimate knowledge of sporting art. Rousuck himself, however,
is usually missing from the family tree when McCarthy's life is drawn.

" 'Mannie is a very good getter,' " Reuel used to say of this old
friend—whose death in 1970 was the first in a series that "brought
down the pillars of my life," McCarthy reflects in *How I Grew*. Rousuck was always picking up things she needed, like the divorce lawyer
in 1945, or something Reuel needed, such as an old station wagon in
1966 that Mannie procured from one of his society friends. He was
devoted to Mary, and had her books bound in red leather bindings for

his private collection long before the Franklin Library produced their deluxe editions. For him, Mary McCarthy was an uptown girl who had a knack for keeping him out of trouble; who knows but that he felt a certain pride in having been her first employer.

"He trusted me (which was not the same as being willing to do what I told him) and depended on me," McCarthy declares in her memoir. "If he represented an outlaw stripe in my nature [as Edmund Wilson maintained], I may have represented for him a 'moral' streak in himself." They were an odd couple, a product of the New York theatre world of the 1930s and '40s—for the theatre was an interest they shared, along with an interest in 'society.' "We never had a love affair, not even what he called 'an affair,' " McCarthy maintained; and this must have been part of the uniqueness of the relationship for a woman who once told an acquaintance that she had slept with over one hundred men. Nor could she and Mannie be "intimate friends," McCarthy continues, "thanks to my intellectual pursuits. . . ."

Mannie Rousuck, not a man of ideas, wrote as he spoke: "I had to call Phillip Rhav [sic] the other day—he acted as if he were dying—his voice is like a jackass braying, made no sense. . . ." But the rough edge matched a rough side of McCarthy's sensibility, a side Elizabeth Hardwick may have had in mind when she referred (in her presentation speech at the MacDowell Colony in 1984) to "the deflating slyness of Mark Twain" that one sometimes hears in her literary voice, along with the "cranky, idealistic American genius" of loftier minds: William James, Ralph Waldo Emerson, Margaret Fuller. In conversation, as Hardwick knew well, Mary could put H. L. Mencken to shame.

"Dear Mannie, who died charmingly, while being shaved in his Park Avenue apartment," McCarthy wrote in 1987 in Paris. But she was shaken by the loss and felt sorry that she hadn't gone to the funeral. Mannie Rousuck had been followed a few months later by Heinrich Blücher, then Chiaromonte, then Edmund Wilson, whose death on June 12, 1972, in Talcottville did not appear to shake any pillars, unlike the passing of Philip Rahv on December 23, 1973, in Cambridge, whose death at sixty-five provoked a sudden eruption of feeling from the past.

Philip Rahv (1908–1973), aka Ivan Greenberg, did not die 'charmingly,' though reports of his condition at the end diverge. According to Elizabeth Hardwick, he had spent a miserable last year, because of the breakdown of his brief and unhappy fourth marriage and because of poor health, which Rahv's chronic secretiveness kept from his friends. Early in December 1973, he had telephoned Lizzie from Boston, where he had been teaching literature at Brandeis on and off since the late 1950s and living in a rancorous state of exile, to ask her to spend New Year's Eve with him in New York City. "I can't say I looked forward to it because there was plenty of his harshness and bullying on the phone . . ." Lizzie wrote Mary afterwards, but she had agreed. Then a student friend of Rahv's had called with the shocking news that he had been found dead in his apartment. Because the newspaper said the death was being investigated, Hardwick believed that a fatal combination of alcohol and pills had been the cause, as it had been in Auden's recent death; but suicide was never established.

Hardwick and Bob Silvers had flown up to Boston for the funeral on Christmas Eve, and the burial that took place afterwards in the Jewish Cemetery at Brandeis. She was glad to have agreed to say a few words, she wrote Mary, "because it was a dismal occasion"—only around thirty people showed up, including Philip Rahv's brother, who looked just like him only slighter; Philip's mother, Lizzie noted, was still living in Palestine. On the return trip to Logan Airport, the same student had told her that Elizabeth Bishop was lying "in a ghastly state" in her studio in Boston, apparently the victim of a similar cycle of alcohol and depression. Bishop died in 1979, two years after Robert Lowell died—of a heart attack in a New York taxi outside Hardwick's apartment. It was September 1977; his marriage to Caroline Blackwood had run aground; and he had come home again.

The Palestine connection turned out to be another side of Rahv's secret life. At his death, he was worth nearly a million dollars, thanks to an estate inherited from his third wife, Theo Stillman, whom he had married in 1956 after divorcing Nathalie Swan. Theo Stillman Rahv, also an heiress and a descendant of John Jay, died in a house fire in 1968. Rahv had no children, and after his death he had ordered the money given to Brandeis and Israel, with the lion's share going to Israel—"astounding news," Hardwick reported; and all the more so when it backfired. Rahv, some of his friends theorized, had done what he did to keep the money from going to his fourth wife, who he claimed had made substantial financial demands on him after the collapse of a stormy eighteen-month union. But the separation agreement had not been signed at the time of his death, and the bulk of the estate went to her anyway.

Other friends, more sympathetic to Philip's last wife, a professor of French at the University of Massachusetts who was often the target of his verbal abuse in public, saw the bequest to Israel as "a strange atavistic regression. . . . He never talked about Israel, *never*," unless it was to criticize Israeli foreign policy, the writer Frances (Frankie) FitzGerald recalls—though McCarthy remembered differently: "one of Philip's charms was the tenderness of his feeling for the Jewish state," she wrote in one of her 'intellectual memoirs.' Behind his deep alienation from the country at large, and from the society of intellectuals he had once dominated, the underground tie to Israel had apparently tightened.

Elizabeth Hardwick's report of Rahv's "utter *'isolation,'* heavy drinking, sleeping drugs, total disintegration" impressed Mary McCarthy as involving "a good deal of projection . . . of [Lizzie's] own assessment of her position on to him." Frankie FitzGerald and Alan Lelchuk, Rahv's colleague at Brandeis and the managing editor of *Modern Occasions,* the magazine Rahv started in 1970, had spent an evening with him the night before he died. From Frankie's account of the conversation, which included some "scandalous stories about a certain lady playwright [Hellman]" that Rahv related apropos his projected memoirs, it sounded to Mary "as if he was very much the old Philip in his benign and confidential aspect." What she didn't know was that Rahv, who really was on the physical downslide, had confided to Alan and Frankie that he had written Lillian Hellman in New York to see whether she could help him return to the city. Hellman had responded with a chatty letter, full of affection. Had Mary known this, the farewell she paid Philip Rahv, published on the front page of the Sunday *Times Book Review,* might not have been so fond.

"So he's gone, that dear phenomenon," the reminiscence begins. "If no two people are alike, he was less like anybody else than anybody. A powerful intellect, a massive, overpowering personality and yet shy, curious, susceptible, confiding." At a memorial service later organized for Rahv in Cambridge, Frankie FitzGerald read McCarthy's tribute aloud; "the best thing I'd ever seen written on him, *ever,*" she later said. It accorded with the memory of one of Rahv's students who remembered him at Brandeis as "the real McCoy—a man of the people who called his students 'Mr.' and 'Miss.' . . . and brought a deep sense of class to the interpretation of literature, without mixing it with politics." As a character study, McCarthy's portrait of an unreconstructed Marxist who remained a resolute modernist, and a lover of Henry James and Tolstoy, is considerably more inviting in its complexity than many of her fictional characterizations. It makes amends for Will Taub in *The Oasis*—just as Mary McCarthy's obituary for F. W. Dupee in 1979 rescues another one of the boys ("Jaunty, wry, rueful. Flash of kingfisher blue eyes. . . . A person of courage and irony") from parody in *The Groves of Academe*. The death notice became a new genre for McCarthy before the decade was out, acknowledged in her last critical collection, *Occasional Prose* (1985), which opens with four valedictories: to Rahv, Chiaromonte, Dupee, and Hannah Arendt, who died of heart failure on December 4, 1975, in the living room of her Riverside Drive apartment, after serving dinner to friends. ("There's a way in which, as long as some of us live, the dead live through us," Mary wrote Frani Muser after mourning Helen Sandison's suicide in 1979. "It's a funny kind of immortality.")

At the February memorial service for Rahv in Cambridge, a corrective to the dismal Christmas Eve funeral, the New York group was represented by Clement Greenberg, Roger Straus, Robert Brustein, and their wives, along with Nathalie Swan and Rose Styron, among others. But not William Phillips or Will Barrett—both of whom would make Philip Rahv the devil in their ego theories of New York literary politics a decade later. The breakup of the *Partisan Review* camp was too deep for death to mend, a fact that is driven home in Hardwick's account of trying to reach Phillips with the news of his old comrade's death. She had called him first to get family information for the funeral, and then, after repeated busy signals, just to tell him the news. When the next morning the operator said the phone was off the hook, she asked a friend who lived nearby to go to Phillips's apartment. It was four in the afternoon when the young woman rang the bell and announced herself through the speaker, saying she had a message from Elizabeth Hardwick. Phillips

> did not buzz her in, but through the door she finally saw this strange pale figure coming down the stairs carrying in his hand a huge club. She stood there in the vestibule; William looked through the glass and did not open the door, apparently imagining accomplices hidden behind the back of this beautiful young girl. She finally yelled at the glass between them. "Your phone is broken. Elizabeth wanted to tell you that Philip Rahv is dead."

"I find I miss him disproportionately," McCarthy wrote Hannah Arendt in March 1973; "I can't bear to take his picture (in color) off my desk or file away his last two letters, which alas I never answered— he wanted me to write something for his magazine and I felt I couldn't." After running a banner interview with Mary McCarthy in the first issue of *Modern Occasions*, Rahv had continued to propose "possible themes": an essay on "Writers and Snobbery" in which

Mary was to look into the snobbism of "idealists manqués" such as Proust, James, Fitzgerald; another on the Jewish American literary scene ("You know almost everything there is to know about Jews," he assured her); a review of Juliet Mitchell's *Woman's Estate,* which McCarthy thought not worth writing about "unless one is deep in the Women's Lib movement. [The book is] so sterile and abstract. . . ."

"It's strange, but his death has hit me harder than anybody's, even Nicola's, though I was much closer to Nicola and saw him all the time. . . ." McCarthy continued in the letter to Arendt. "Maybe love, even such a long-ago one, gets at your vital center more than friendship and admiration." And she realized that she "*must* have loved him when we lived together and continued to do so, though unaware of it." Otherwise why did Rahv's death leave her feeling so sad? Jim West thought it was because she felt Philip had lived "an incomplete, tentative sort of life," unlike Heinrich or Nicola. And it was true that while she was interested in the "survival and persistence of their thought," she couldn't work up much enthusiasm for the projected publication of Philip Rahv's uncollected works. "Philip's 'ideas' weren't interesting, except as an expression of his personality," McCarthy suggested. "Though he certainly wasn't stupid and had a mental life, it didn't achieve independence, of the temporal, of *him.*"

"I long to see you," Rahv had abruptly ended his last letter to Mary in May 1973. "Do you realize that they're legends around about my relation to you that have no foundation in fact? Astounding," he exclaimed. If Philip's death was the only thing that had really moved Mary in 1973—and everything else, books, politics, social life, she said, was "rather blah"—her feeling for the 'long-ago' love would also be one the last things McCarthy wrote about before her death. It was only because she had been "drunk" that she had first slept with Edmund Wilson, she claims in the third chapter of her *Intellectual Memoirs*; it was Philip she loved, not Wilson.

Hannah Arendt had been deeply moved by the death of Auden, who came close to persuading her to violate her basic motto: *"Kein Mitleid"* ("no pity"). Shortly after Heinrich Blücher's death, Auden had asked Arendt to marry him; and the two circumstances— Auden's shocking disintegration, which had prompted Arendt's doorman to escort him from the lobby to her apartment the afternoon of the proposal, on the assumption he was a bum, and the proposal itself, heartfelt, tearful—were intertwined. Hannah Arendt had also slaked her anguish in a reminiscence, both tender and stern, published in *The New York Review of Books*. But her recognition of the extremity of Auden's pain, unlike McCarthy's deflection of Rahv's, was unblinkered.

Three years later when he died, she was "still thinking of Wystan, naturally, and of the misery of his life, and that I refused to take care of him when he came and asked for shelter." For that was what the proposal, which was not without its homely precedent of shopping trips to Saks Fifth Avenue to buy Auden clothes, actually represented. Auden wanted Hannah Arendt to look after him, in part, she speculated, because Oxford had turned him down earlier when he appealed for an academic chair. Arendt got at least one more proposal—from the political scientist Hans Morganthau, a former colleague at the University of Chicago, and after the death of their respective spouses, a frequent escort. Auden's visit haunted her for years. Stephen Spender, with whom Auden often stayed in London, recalls being "sympathetic to Hannah's feeling that it was tragic," when she later told him about the proposal, "but concerned that she should not burden herself with regrets for not having been heroic beyond the reasonable line of duty."

When Auden died on September 28, 1973, Arendt had turned not to the Old Testament for solace but to the Greeks: "Homer said that the gods spin ruin to men that there might be song and remembrance. (Helen said in the Iliad: Zeus brought evil on her and Paris 'so that in days to come we shall be a song for men yet to be.' ") Sentiments more consoling to noble heroes than to ordinary folk, perhaps. In Arendt's view, Auden, the poet, "was both the singer and the tale. But God knows," she wrote Mary, "the price is too high, and no one in his right mind could be willing to pay it knowingly"; the "worst," she thought, had been his proud boast at the end to have been " 'lucky.' "

II

When Hannah Arendt died, Mary McCarthy was a year into *Cannibals and Missionaries,* which owes one of its major themes to Arendt's suggestion, after hearing McCarthy lecture on "Art Values and the Value of Art," that Mary explore the politics of art ownership in a novel. Upon Hannah's death, however, McCarthy had set the novel aside to take up Arendt's unfinished inquiry into "The Life of the Mind." She didn't return to her own writing until 1977, when she had finished editing and annotating the manuscripts of Arendt's University of Aberdeen lectures on "Thinking" and "Willing" and piecing together extracts of her New School lectures on Kant's political philosophy to show where Hannah might have gone with the third faculty of the *vita contemplativa,* Judging. *The Life of the Mind* was Arendt's "pendant" to *The Human Condition,* whose working title was "The *Vita Activa,*" and whose meditations on labor, work, and action posit a parallel trilogy.

Hannah Arendt's death, at sixty-nine, had followed a period of unprecedented activity, beginning a year after her husband's death, and only intensified, it seemed, with the onset of angina in December 1971. Brushing aside "the usual talk—slow down, stop smoking, etc," after the angina attack, Arendt had reiterated a principle largely shared with Mary McCarthy: "Since I am certainly not going to live for my health, I'll do what I think is right . . ." which was to avoid "what might put me in an unpleasant situation . . . in which I am forced to make a fuss." She would cut out smoking if it didn't keep her from writing—"If that is not possible, *tant pis.*"

She did not stop smoking, or cancel engagements, which now included speaking out on political issues at public forums, collecting honorary degrees from Yale, Dartmouth, Fordham, and Princeton, and participating in international conferences on such windy topics as "Institutions for a Post-Technological Society" and "Terrors of the Year 2000," which recall the Congress for Cultural Freedom in its heyday. Nor did she stop teaching. "The History of the Will," given at the New School for Social Research in New York in the fall of 1972, became the occasion for drafting the first Gifford Lecture on "Willing," which was delivered at the University of Aberdeen in May 1974.

In the middle of the 'Willing' lecture, Arendt had a heart attack that could have been fatal had Bill Jovanovich, who sat in the audience, as he did for many of Arendt's and McCarthy's lectures, not rushed to her aid with the nitroglycerine he carried for his own heart condition. After the attack, as soon as the oxygen tent was removed from the hospital room, she had reached for her cigarettes. Strangely, one month after Arendt returned to the Casa Barbete in Tegna, Switzerland, to recuperate, she set off for Freiburg to see Martin Heidegger, then eighty-four, whom she had also visited in 1973, and would again in 1975—when he seemed "suddenly very old, very changed . . . very deaf and remote, unapproachable as I never saw him before." Perhaps she was reacting to the 'deforestation process' of old age and wanted to see this old trunk one more time before it fell: alone, if possible, something Heidegger's jealous wife had always tried to prevent, until the last visit in 1975, when the two women finally declared a truce. But there was another reason, or another effect of these visits, which was to confirm in Hannah Arendt the recognition that it would be all right to incorporate a critique of Heidegger's theories concerning the will in *The Life of the Mind*. He would not live to read and be offended by the reservations of his most precocious student.

After the heart attack in Scotland, Mary McCarthy felt the stab of Hannah Arendt's irritability, not unusual in cardiac patients, but she didn't see it that way. Being in a delicate condition for her own reasons—the *Washington Monthly* had just launched its attack on her political journalism, without anyone coming to her defense—Mary had assumed that Hannah's short temper, both in Aberdeen and London (where she had accompanied Arendt on her way to Switzerland), and later in Castine, reflected an unspoken judgment on the part of McCarthy's friends that she was "peculiar, in some way . . . *indefensible*." It was her fate to be perpetually incapable of " 'getting through' to [her] imagined listeners," Mary lamented. The "punishment," for thus she saw her friend's silence, "was somehow mysteriously, arcanely, related to [her] eternal self: the bars of the cell [were], so to speak, [her] own ribs."

It was a lacerating perception, not unlike the time in 1964 when McCarthy confessed to a stranger, in an unmailed letter, that if none of her Vassar roommates in the South Tower had asked her to spend the holidays at their houses in 1932, it was because there was something wrong with *her*, and they were punishing her for it. Reason, of course, rescued Arendt from the charge in 1974; not only was she in a hospital in Scotland recovering from a heart attack when the attacks on McCarthy's wartime writing occurred but Hannah was a "tainted witness"; she couldn't have protested, since people would have said she was repaying the "Eichmann debt," or that they had dedicated books to each other. Mary had expected "help to come from somewhere in the middle distance—not from my nearest and dearest," she wrote, noting, nonetheless, "that if *Jim* had picked up his pen" she would have rejoiced. "Or my brother Kevin," which showed she was "no feminist." (Arendt herself was left "speechless" by the suggestion that Mary had gotten on her nerves. "You may be right or wrong in being suspicious of your friends, but you could not very well be suspicious of *me*," she exclaimed, begging her, to "stop it, *please*.")

Soon after she filed her complaint, McCarthy withdrew from the edge, thanks in part to a whirlwind tour of Norman fortresses and cathedrals in southern Italy, organized by Carmen Angleton in September. By November 1974, she was back in the novel-writing business. To Arendt, she confided the hope that this one, her seventh, and, as it turned out, her last, was going to be different. With *Cannibals and Missionaries,* the story of the hijacking of a Boeing 747 bound for Iran, carrying a group of millionaire art collectors and a delegation of liberals bent on investigating torture under the Shah, she wanted to establish "the tone . . . of the omniscient author"—the "old" tone, though new to McCarthy, which might liberate her from the ventriloquist's box. This kind of fiction would be harder to do than the autobiography Jovanovich was pressing on her, "and, being a perverse creature," she had been "seduced by the temptation of difficulty. If it is a moral temptation, then I am making a mistake," she said, "but if it's an aesthetic one, maybe I am not."

It was the 'moral' challenge McCarthy had risen to, the need to triumph over despair, by no means a mistake; but the aesthetic difficulty remained unsolved. A few weeks into the novel—which begins with an Episcopal minister, a member of the liberals' investigating team, saying grace in the rectory dining room of his Gracie Square church—she was already aware of a telltale feeling of confinement. "I am staring down a channel with some very familiar landscape on either side," she wrote Arendt of the opening scene, in which the Reverend Frank Barber's wife and children are gathered around the candlelit table on the morning of his departure; six boiled eggs sit nestled in little felt hats on a Lazy Susan, "dark blue for medium, yellow for soft." After breakfast, the Reverend Barber (whose "happy protruding ears and twisted bow-tie," his goshes and darns, recall McCarthy's Castine neighbor, the retired Reverend Ed Miller) blows the candles out, "not waiting for Matthew, who as the youngest had the right, to go around with the snuffer."

She was trying to do something new, McCarthy told Hannah Arendt, but the Episcopal minister kept sounding like either the girls in *The Group* or Peter Levi, her "Scylla and Charybdis. It is sad to realize that one's fictions, i.e., one's 'creative' side, cannot learn anything," she reflected. "*I* have learned, I think, but they, or it, haven't." The confining boundaries, she supposed, were set by a "life-experience which lies in vaguely upper-middle class territory lying between those girls and Peter. My mental experience is broader, but that doesn't seem to count for the imagination." It all led "to the awful recognition that one *is* one's life; God is not mocked"—which was some consolation, 'God' embodying Mary McCarthy's eternal faith in the objective existence of truth.

She never did resolve the problem of tone, which is the old question of voice. Her own voice, McCarthy suggested toward the end of her life—her 'real' voice—is not to be heard in any of her novels. She didn't mean her autobiographical voice, the one deployed in criticism, journalism, and memoirs, but something closer to Tolstoy's omniscient narrator—the voice a writer earns when the ego is disengaged from the contemplation of reality. This voice McCarthy could sometimes turn on herself, dissolving her ego's defenses with startling results. But she could barely extend it to the world around her, neither to people nor to places, not even to flowers, which she loved, but which are rendered anthropomorphically in her writing, in their aspect of service to an ideal of the good life.

The 'awful recognition' stopped short of a larger truth; for what about a *bourgeois gentilhomme* like Flaubert, or a rich landowner such as Tolstoy, who are quite capable of imagining men and women whose lives resemble theirs not at all? McCarthy doesn't manage it. In the end, her limitation as a novelist is a failure of imagination—not nerve, as Mailer charged—to let *herself* go when she writes, which is different than surrendering to one's demons.

With *Cannibals and Missionaries*, McCarthy couldn't imagine creating anyone (or thing) she had not herself experienced, if only by projection. Thus, when she contemplated a Jewish character in the novel, a 'New Journalist' attached to the liberals' delegation, Sophie Weil, she felt a "temptation to make her *half*-Jewish, in the belief that I cannot fully imagine, from the *inside*, the outlook of a Jewish girl." Projection, of course, is the novelist's stock in trade. One imagines how a character *feels* in order to understand his or her seemingly magical power to move the action one way or another. The difference between a great novelist and a merely competent one lies in whether the writer can reach beyond personal experience into the impersonal realm of the imagination, where the experience of ancestors, perhaps, resides, or descendants—or strangers, complete unknowns.

For McCarthy, the habit of seeing herself in the round is too ingrained to allow the necessary range. She is always on stage, even when alone; a brilliant, multifaceted subjectivity overflows into every character she creates—which is why the models for her fictional characterizations often feel violated. They are violated, though not necessarily by the pictures she draws of them. The invasion of privacy is perpetrated literally when she slips into character wearing *their* clothes, adopting *their* mannerisms, stealing *their* lines.

In *Cannibals and Missionaries,* the art collector, "Mr. Charles," an ancient sybarite of subversive views, whose "high piercing voice" rings through the novel, is a case in point. "My occupational hazard is that I can't help plagiarizing from real life," McCarthy wrote the eighty-eight-year-old Rowland Burdon-Mueller, the original for Charles Tennant, when the book came out, "but as I 'mellow,' " she said, "it's done, as you'll see, with smiling affection, in fact with thanks for the marvel of your existing—a gift to life and to the artist." Poor Burdon-Mueller seems not to have known what to make of the mincing dandy who masquerades as himself. A Berenson-era figure who shared McCarthy's horror of the Vietnam War, together with her fondness for 'beautiful things,' he "felt completely lost in an unknown world" when he took up the novel, which is dedicated to him. "I have never been in an aeroplane and the various characters were such as I have never encountered in my quiet life," he wrote McCarthy sadly. He had known very few collectors apart from "dear old Mrs. Havemeyer"; the "Rothschild friends" of his generation didn't collect anymore. "I am old and my world was very different," he said, adding that perhaps he would "understand the book better" when he read it two more times. One wonders whether maybe Mary McCarthy got it wrong, and the way things are with this old man and his 'quiet' corner of the world of art and money is not more interesting than her gaudy impersonation.

In the final year before Hannah Arendt's death, both Mary and Hannah logged more than their usual number of trips. In April 1975, Arendt, who had retired from the New School, flew to Copenhagen to accept the Sonning Prize for "meritorious work for European civilization," becoming the first U.S. citizen and first woman to receive the award (and $35,000 gift), previously given to Winston Churchill, Albert Schweitzer, Bertrand Russell, Niels Bohr, and Laurence Olivier, among others. Mary McCarthy, who saw to it that Hannah bought a new dress for the occasion, was there, too, escorted by Bill Jovanovich. On May 20, Arendt accepted Mayor Kevin White's invitation to address America's bicentennial celebration at the Boston Forum, an event that exposed her to a sudden outpouring of public attention. Citing the recent "years of aberration" that included Vietnam, Watergate, Nixon's resignation, Ford's pardon, and the final rout of American forces in Saigon, Arendt concluded that the power of the 'Republic' had sunk to its lowest ebb since World War II. It was not a 'happy birthday' speech, but it caught the country's mood, and was broadcast on public radio, quoted in magazines, and lauded by Tom Wicker in *The New York Times*.

For Mary McCarthy, the writing of *Cannibals and Missionaries* was full of perks that eased the tensions associated with the start-up of a new novel. When she finished the first chapter, Jim had declared a holiday, and they descended on the center of France to explore churches and "gastronomic points." Far from cutting her off from society, this book became a vigorous communal enterprise of a sort that would be activated only one more time—when McCarthy defended herself against Lillian Hellman in the early 1980s. Jim West had supplied diagrams of 747s and transport helicopters, along with his own expertise as a World War II navigator to help Mary get the flying scenes right. Both Rousuck and Nicky King guided her in the use of New York and Newport society names. Tom Curtiss supplied his personal experience of being hijacked. And Carmen Angleton's brother, the tall, donnish James Jesus Angleton, who was the CIA's chief of counterintelligence until he was dismissed by William Colby in 1974, helped with technical matters—getting down on his hands and knees at Carmen's house in Rome to show Mary how the Dutch farmhouse the commandos use for a hideaway would have been wired for demolition.

McCarthy's research trips to Holland, whose politics, customs, and landscape figure prominently in the novel, were the real payoff. In Holland she was feted as nowhere else, partly because the OECD's secretary-general at the time, Emile van Lennep, gave her entrée to Dutch officialdom; and partly because her old Edinburgh cronies, the Dutch novelists Cees Nooteboom and Harry Mulisch, saw to it that she went everywhere and met everyone. Cees Nooteboom, in his capacity of admiring companion and faithful guide to all things Dutch, played a role not unlike the one Roberto Papi had performed for his glamorous guest in Florence twenty years before.

McCarthy's diplomatic connections included the Left liberal deputy, Hans van Mierlo, who, together with Nooteboom, inspires the novel's most attractive character, the "handsome, strong-jawed, hazel-eyed, high-colored" Henk Van Vliet de Jonge—another member of the liberals' team, along with the "actorish" Senator Jim Carey, a look-alike for Eugene McCarthy. Hans van Mierlo took Mary to Parliament and introduced her to the Dutch prime minister, Joop den Uyl, who then invited the Wests to dinner. "He [the prime minister] and the Secretary of Defense gave me very pertinent advice about some of the technical problems of my novel," Mary wrote Hannah afterwards. "Very amusing and very nice people," she remarked, adding, "The only fear is that, Holland being such a small country, everybody will soon know the plot of my story." As if the plot—which turns on whether the hijackers can convert the incalculable art values of a Vermeer, El Greco, Titian, Degas, Dufy, and several Cézannes into the political value, in revolutionary terms, of forcing the Hague out of NATO—is a national secret. It is a hurried letter, this last communiqué, dictated, shortly before Arendt's death, mainly to reassure Hannah about some blood tests Mary had taken to identify a lingering "malaise"; still, the absence of irony in the cozy social note from the Hague is revealing. Mary McCarthy had arrived, if not at fiction's sacred grove, then at a rock-ribbed literary celebrity that came in second.

At her late-summer residence in Tegna, Hannah Arendt went to work on the critique of Heidegger for the final Gifford Lecture on "Willing," which she had postponed. After an exhausting month in Marbach, Switzerland, where she had fulfilled her duty as one of Karl Jaspers's executors after his death the year before, by organizing his unpublished manuscripts and correspondence for future publication, Arendt had turned to "good old Kant" to prepare herself for the Judging section of *The Life of the Mind*. The posthumous fragments of Kant's *Critique of Judgement* had struck her as particularly moving; for instance, the notion that "speculations about an afterlife could be likened to a caterpillar who knows that his true destiny is to become a butterfly."

After participating in an international symposium outside Paris in September, she returned to New York, whose deteriorated streets, soaring crime rate, and collapsing public services—the city's 1975 to 1976 fiscal crisis was in full swing—quickly persuaded her to accept an offer to teach at Smith College the following fall. The day after Thanksgiving, she tripped on the edge of a pothole and fell not far from the entrance to her door on Riverside Drive. Surrounded by onlookers, she lay there for a few minutes, checking her vital signs, and then picked herself up before the police or ambulance arrived, and walked into her building.

When Hannah Arendt died four days later, the typewriter was loaded with the first page of the Judging manuscript. After dinner she had settled into her chair to serve coffee to guests, two old friends with whom she had worked on the Commission for Jewish Cultural Reconstruction after the war. A spirited discussion was under way when she suddenly started coughing, then sank back in her chair and lost consciousness. Her friends called her doctor, who came at once, but within an hour she was dead.

As deaths go, it was a lucky one: no fuss. Surrounded by those "impatient propitiatory offerings" that Mary McCarthy remembered from countless evenings in Morningside Heights and Riverside Drive—the after-dinner coffee, cheese and fruit, perhaps a liqueur, a dish of chocolates; good conversation with close friends—Hannah Arendt couldn't have arranged a more graceful exit. The week before, she had completed her treatise on the Will; Judgement beckoned from the desk.

Hannah Arendt was fond of quoting an ancient joke she had found in St. Augustine when she was writing her dissertation on "Augustine's Concept of Love" in Heidelberg in the 1920s. "To the question: What did God do before he created Heaven and earth? The answer is: He prepared Hell for those who ask such questions." Given her own lifelong questioning of the foundations of rational thought—the same impertinence, in secular terms—it was a punishment from which Arendt would have exempted herself. Hell, if it was anything at all, was the sleep of the mind.

At the funeral service in Riverside Memorial Chapel, Mary McCarthy surprised many of the more than three hundred mourners by evoking "the dark times [Hannah Arendt] had borne witness to, as a Jewess and a displaced person, the long-drawn-out miscarriage of a socialist revolution, the present perils of the American Republic. . . ." There was a "religious" side to Hannah, she suggested, as if she "had heard a voice such as spoke to the prophets. . . . One can look on this more secularly," she added,

> and think that she felt herself indentured, bound as though under contract by her particular endowments, given her by Nature, developed in her by her teachers . . . and tragically enriched by History. It was not a matter of self-fulfillment (the idea would have been laughable or else detestable to Hannah) but of an injunction laid on all of us, not just the talented, to follow the trajectory chance and fate have launched us on, like a poet keeping faith with his muse.

Arendt's task had been

> to apply thought systematically to each and every characteristic experience of her time—*anomie,* terror, advanced warfare, concentration camps, Auschwitz, inflation, revolution, school integration, the Pentagon Papers, space, Watergate, Pope John, violence,

civil disobedience—and, having finally achieved this, to direct thought inward, upon itself, and its own characteristic processes.

Then she tried to evoke her dear friend's "physical being." "Above all, her eyes, so brilliant and sparkling, but also deep, dark, remote, pools of inwardness." Watching the public Hannah pacing the platform during a lecture, hands shoved in her pockets, or, fire laws permitting, a cigarette jabbing the air as she inhaled deeply, tossing her head abruptly, "as if arrested by a new, unexpected idea," McCarthy was reminded of a "magnificent stage diva."

This is not the Hannah Arendt that stares out of photographs from the 1960s and '70s, the long, weathered face, aquiline nose, soulful eyes, and thin set lips resembling George Washington more than "Bernhardt or Proust's Berma." Mary McCarthy, of course, is evoking a love object; her "magnificent stage diva . . . implies a goddess." But Arendt's physical charms—her "small, fine hands, charming ankles, elegant feet"—could be equally real to others. Carmen Angleton, who thought there was "a bit of Marlene Dietrich inside Hannah," admired her "smart suits . . . and sexy legs"; the gentlemen who circled around her after she delivered her Gauss lectures at Princeton, Angleton relates, "admired her not always for what she was saying."

Kot Jelenski called this mutual admiration "feminist patriotism: the love of beautiful women for each other." Hannah Arendt admired Mary McCarthy's "elegance and beauty," and the way it was set off by a "sense of intellectual superiority," he said. Mary was primarily attracted to Hannah's intellectuality; she thought Hannah was "pure," Elizabeth Hardwick offers, "purer than herself, because she lived simply." Still, it was a charisma of gesture, a "power of being seized and worked upon" by an idea or emotion, "whose instrument her body became, like an actor," as McCarthy put it in her remembrance, that excited Mary's senses. Jelenski himself portrays Hannah Arendt as an "elegant woman," though he can't say he read her books with pleasure, finding her "too abstract and arrogant," unlike Nicola Chiaromonte, who shared Arendt's high intellectual and ethical standards, in his view, but was more modest and possessed of some humor.

"I am sure Chiaromonte was in love with Mary," Jelenski adds. Hannah Arendt was probably in love with Mary, too, one guesses; but Arendt's affections were not qualified behind her back, as were Chiaromonte's in his letters to Dwight Macdonald. When Hannah was confronted with some personal habit of Mary's that drove Elizabeth

Hardwick mad—a "privileged conceit" about food, for example, a hankering for expensive restaurants, lavish entertainments—she said nothing. She would think such matters were Mary's private business, and her loyalty would keep her from criticizing or prying into personal affairs, Hardwick explains, admitting that she herself would sometimes sputter, " 'Well, Mary, don't you think—' Their relationship [Hannah's and Mary's] had a *moral* quality," she says.

In her relations with Hannah Arendt's friends, especially her female acquaintances, Mary herself was sometimes prey to a corrosive jealousy. When the harpsichordist Sylvia Marlowe told her she was " 'crazy' " about an essay Hannah Arendt had written on Rosa Luxemburg, finding it " 'Hannah's most personal work,' " because Hannah had " 'identified' " with Rosa Luxemburg, and seen Luxemburg's quarrel with the German Socialists as similar to Arendt's quarrel with organized Jews, Mary told Marlowe angrily that she saw nothing of the sort. "It was as if this identification theory were a big keyhole through which she could look into your hidden emotions," she wrote Hannah afterwards, calling Sylvia "a gruesome *voyeur*." In 1967, after watching Susan Sontag corner Hannah Arendt at a party in New York, McCarthy had written Hannah testily to find out what happened: "it was clear that she was going to seek to conquer you. Or that she had fallen in love with you—the same thing. Anyway, did she?"

When Lillian Hellman asked Arendt out to dinner in the late 1960s, it was as if Lucifer had proffered the apple of friendship. "She wanted to become Hannah's intimate," McCarthy claimed after both were dead; Hellman, she said, "was a tremendous lion-hunter and literary social climber, and she always wanted to be accepted by people in the anti-Stalinist world—it was like a perversion, a sexual perversion," she added, grinning happily over a slur for which she could no longer be sued. The same urge had made Hellman go after Edmund Wilson, whom she had "captured . . . more or less," McCarthy continued. Hannah, meanwhile, "might have easily fallen for this except that Hellman said some bitchy things about me"—which had included an angry reference to an old review—"and that was very ill-judged on her part," McCarthy commented; for afterwards Hannah had marveled that anyone could "treasure up a bad review for twenty years," concluding, " 'that's not for me.' "

III

In December 1977, Mary McCarthy returned to *Cannibals and Missionaries,* both exhausted and renewed by the work of bringing *The Life of the Mind* to public view. In abbreviated form, "Thinking" appeared in *The New Yorker* early in 1978; the two-volume book, with its modest "Editor's Postface," arrived a few months later. The long labor of love helped McCarthy keep her grief at bay and Arendt's spirit close at hand. When she plunged back into her fiction, it was with some sense of fulfillment.

Cannibals and Missionaries, however, despite its proximity to the immersion in philosophy, is the least reflective of McCarthy's novels. Ideas bob on its intricately plotted surface like bright decoys, inviting comparison with the natural world but not quite making the cut. A character's journal entry, torn from context at the end of the book, addresses a lifelong question: "Art merely the medium, the element, by which the sacred, i.e., the extraordinary, is conveyed." The politics of terrorism are treated aphoristically: "Today's arch-revolutionaries had no faith in a future life for their ideas; it was gone, like the Christian faith in God's design." In extremis, when the terrorist aims at moral instruction, or *de*-instruction, as McCarthy's pet terrorist, Jeroen, the former Dutch art student who commands the hijackers, does, terrorism becomes "art for art's sake in the political realm."

Jeroen regards the notion that terrorism will usher in a new society, still believed by his partner, Greet, an ex-KLM hostess, as "an impurity," a dream that "had been dreamed too often." He thinks Trotsky's notion of "permanent revolution" was right but insincere—Trotsky's suppression of the Russian sailors at Kronstadt showed his real attitude. The modern revolutionary must expose the hypocrisy behind the West's appropriation of humane values: liberalism and art, in particular. Behind this black dandy, nonetheless, lurks an idealist, who speaks in the high German style:

> There was a potential in man for rising above . . . gross material concerns that the revolutionary by his act and example sought to bring to full life in every human creature, while the bourgeois and the bourgeois revisionists sought to strangle it at birth, above all in the working masses but finally, perforce, in themselves.

In form, *Cannibals and Missionaries* is a series of character sketches, harvested from the friendships and associations of the last quarter of McCarthy's life. The model for the old-fashioned liberal who is above reproach, Bishop Gus Hurlbut, is another Episcopal prelate, the retired Bishop of St. Louis, Will Scarlett. The "Red Bishop," as this close friend of Eleanor Roosevelt was known in Castine, where he also spent his summers, died in 1973. Elizabeth Hardwick can be heard in the talky Arkansas-born college president, Aileen Simmons, whose

> fault was only an unusual degree of mental activity. The curse of intelligence. Stupid people were unconscious of their slow-moving thought processes. But take Charles's plain gold ring: a mind like hers could not fail to perceive immediately that it was on the "wrong" hand and be aware of what conclusions to draw. Though he must be nearly eighty and queer in every sense, there he was, a man and unmarried. With a fair share of worldly goods.

As in much of McCarthy's fiction, the weakest characterizations are of people who stand at opposite poles of the social spectrum. " 'Henry says a gentleman leaves his financial page to his broker,' " prattles a female collector; while the Palestinian militants, "bewitched by the kulacks' living space" in the farmhouse they are occupying, giggle and splash each other in the shower like the Three Stooges. But the novel's serious failure is one of credibility.

When Jeroen learns that the Dutch government will not meet his political demands, he is left surrounded by his masterpieces (which he has exchanged for their owners), impregnable but powerless, an explosive combination. And so he self-destructs, as McCarthy's heroes often do when excited scruple collides with convention. Even Jeroen's suicide backfires—" 'He had planned to die alone with the "Girl" he had fallen in love with [Vermeer's *Girl in a Blue Cap with Guitar*],' " a wounded Arab commando explains tearfully after the death of his leader—and through a breakdown in the chain of command, Jeroen takes the other commandos and several hostages with him when the Dutch farmhouse (wired for demolition) goes up in smoke.

Dramatically, there is something incongruous about the mayhem in the final pages of what is essentially a novel of manners, a study of how captors and captives react to conditions of confinement and confrontation. The explosion of theories, bodies, and masterpieces comes as a red flag, signaling thin ice in the realm of probability. If "plausibility is the morality of fiction," as the novelist A. B. Guthrie remarks, *Cannibals and Missionaries* is a slightly immoral novel, afflicted with several credibility gaps, beginning with the premise that a government would ever surrender its vital interests to save a work of art.

When the most important characters are blown up at the end, the reader is left empty-handed. One doesn't care. "You're not meant to," McCarthy insists; "the emotional depth of the book is extremely shallow . . . in terms of the characters," she concedes, because the "method, by mimicking each character's interior voice, precludes identification." When Miriam Chiaromonte telephoned her in anguish over the death of Senator Carey, who Miriam thought was Jim West, McCarthy was "absolutely astonished," less with the identification than with the intensity of Miriam's involvement with the fate of a character—"because they're not meant to be real in that sense."

"If there is anything to get close to here," McCarthy suggested in 1981, "it's not people but something like a place-spirit, Holland being understood as 'an imaginary country' inhabited by a funny kind of democratic demiurge." That, at any rate, was her "provisional defense" after the book came out—to lukewarm reviews and moderate sales, which at least surpassed the poor response to *Birds of America* eight years before. Notably, the one rave review, by Mary Gordon, occupied the same prime spot in the Sunday *Times Book Review* in 1979 that Helen Vendler's cold dismissal of McCarthy's skills as a novelist had in 1971.

If Holland was a 'place-spirit' for Mary McCarthy, it doesn't come alive in the story, whose settings are too contrived, too obviously researched, to ring true. Two old newspaper friends from Vietnam, Jonathan Randal and Gavin Young, had briefed her on Iranian politics, including the Shah's persecution of dissidents which sets the stage for the liberals' fact-finding mission; and no doubt they were caught by surprise when Iranian militants stormed the U.S. embassy in Teheran in November 1979, taking fifty-four Americans hostage, and Riza Pahlevi sought refuge in the United States. The turnaround in Iran added to the book's credibility problems. Nor was its fragile topicality reinforced by further upsets that year: the Russian invasion of Afghanistan, the Sandinista triumph in Nicaragua, the establishment of diplomatic relations between the United States and China.

"Today people see terrorists differently," Anjou Levi suggests, apropos the novel's alternately romantic and condescending treatment of the hijackers. The truth is that by the mid-1970s Mary McCarthy's grasp of the underlying political conflicts in the world arena was increasingly circumscribed, not only by a class-bound view of the world *"de haut en bas,"* but by a mental life deriving its ideas from books and newspapers more than from direct experience. On the sociology of art collecting in *Cannibals and Missionaries*, the reader gets a quick course in the theories of Max Horkheimer, T. W. Adorno, and Walter Benjamin, rather than a fresh meditation on the practical experience of a Mannie Rousuck, Rowland Burdon-Mueller, or Clement Greenberg. McCarthy's political ideas show the mark of Adorno, too, with a dash of Herbert Marcuse.

"Actually, what I put in that novel was a real experience of trying to get a delegation to go to Iran," McCarthy states, in defense of the fact-finding team. The project came up in the early 1970s, when reports were rife of SAVAK's torture campaign against opponents of the Shah. "There was this character who came to see me in Paris and stayed on my sofa for about six weeks with his folders," she recalls, "and I was writing all these people like Ramsey Clark and Bishop Paul Moore. All that was true, including the fact that the committee that he talked to me about turned out not to exist, like the disappearing rabbi in the novel. One's life does tend to repeat, *yes*."

The character on the sofa was preceded, in November 1971, by a handsome young freedom fighter from Bangladesh who had been sentenced to death for possessing explosives to blow up the Karachi airport and who came to see McCarthy on behalf of another cause. In the fall of 1973, after the socialist regime of Salvador Allende was toppled in a bloody coup in Chile, McCarthy had been approached by an American woman in Paris and her French boyfriend, who were organizing an "underground railroad" to help former members of the Allende government flee the country. Having assured herself that the United States under Nixon wasn't going to "put some pressure on the junta to tone down the slaughter," Mary had contributed $750 (Jim another $250), and agreed to raise more money from friends, especially after she learned that the chief agent in the operation was an old friend of Trotsky's.

Politically, she was not out of circulation. Transposed to fiction, however, these experiences tended to yield unreal situations, not only because McCarthy's relation to actual political events was remote (Vietnam was an exception), but also because her borrowings reproduce an essentially static vision of public life, in which the leverage for action usually lies with the junta; or, as in *Cannibals and Missionaries*, with a junta of convention ("Den Uyl . . . would not take Holland out of NATO . . . at the beck of a terrorist's will"). Revolutionary and liberal alike can only toss a monkey wrench into the wheels of history, or launch a rescue operation when the 'slaughter' gets out of hand.

Both as fiction and political commentary, *Cannibals and Missionaries* brought Mary McCarthy to a dead end. It was like one of those "streams of experience" in her senior year at Vassar that felt like a "torrent" but then dried up; and afterwards she resolved never to write another novel. After sixty-five, neither memory nor social perception can be counted on to produce the primary materials for fiction, she maintained. And yet in a roundabout way, *Cannibals and Missionaries* was a breakthrough. Like the "placid stream" that was Miss Peebles Contemporary Prose Fiction in 1932 to 1933, "which led to Sacco and Vanzetti and thence to *The New Republic*"—and so helped launch Mary McCarthy in New York—her last novel landed her on the Cavett show, where, thanks to her interviewer's nose for trouble, she was rescued from oblivion.

38

With Malice Toward One

"Who steals my purse steals trash; . . . But he

that filches from me my good name Robs me of that

which not enriches him And makes me poor indeed."

—IAGO, SHAKESPEARE'S *OTHELLO*

"Anger was her essence."

—JOHN HERSEY, EULOGY FOR LILLIAN HELLMAN, 1984

"There's no satisfaction in having an enemy die—

you have to beat them."

—MARY MCCARTHY, CBS INTERVIEW, 1985

On October 18, 1979, when Mary McCarthy sat down in the WNET-TV studio to talk with Dick Cavett, her gray page boy appearing blond under the studio lights, the audience was full of friends: Anthony and Margo Viscusi, Kevin McCarthy, Frani and Curt Muser, whose East Eighty-sixth Street apartment the Wests were using for their fall stopover in New York. Watching at home when the program was aired three months later, on January 24 and 25, were other friends, such as Eileen Simpson, who with her second husband in Paris had often witnessed Jim West's efforts "to change the subject" when Mary started ripping into someone in conversation, to get her "to think of herself as a 'personality,' especially on television." For them all, "The Dick Cavett Show" was followed with a certain excitement, not unmixed with apprehension.

American television was not a medium McCarthy was very familiar with; nor had Americans heard much from her during the years she was editing Hannah Arendt's lectures for *The Life of the Mind* and writing *Cannibals and Missionaries,* whose publication was the occasion for her appearance on the show. Compared to Lillian Hellman, whose hugely successful career as a dramatist had faltered in the 1950s and '60s, but whose second career as a memoirist had catapulted her to the top of the best-seller lists, Mary McCarthy was almost a has-been, known to a wider public, if she was known at all, as the author of a sexy novel from the 1960s. It was among a shrinking circle of literary people that she commanded a respectful following at the end of the 1970s, and that mainly as a critic of theater, literature, and the arts in the 1940s, '50s, and '60s. In more recent years, her critical eye had pulled back from its familiar haunts, partly because the reign of the overinflated American playwrights and novelists of midcentury seemed to be over, and her own largely adversarial talent had nowhere to go, and partly because, like many younger intellectuals, her critical faculties had been riveted on Vietnam and Watergate.

When McCarthy appeared on the Cavett show, she had slipped into the obscurity that Edmund Wilson observed in Edith Wharton's career at the end of her life. In "Justice to Edith Wharton," Wilson notes how "the more commonplace work of her later years had the effect of dulling the reputation of her earlier and more serious work," *The House of Mirth* and *The Age of Innocence.* By 1979, something like this had happened to Mary McCarthy, whose own pioneer work, like Wharton's, had also been partly stimulated by 'a pressure of maladjustments.' In McCarthy's case, the first moment of high productivity had been touched off by a marriage, to Wilson, that recapitulated the central drama of childhood, with its attendant themes of enslavement and helplessness, at a time when she was secure enough no longer to deny the past. Thus had memory reasserted itself, gratefully, in fiction and memoir; and marrying Edmund Wilson, for a brief moment of literary clairvoyance—erased at the end of McCarthy's life, when he was once again assigned the role of jailer—appeared " 'the most dangerous action [she] had ever performed as an adult.' "

Edmund Wilson related Edith Wharton's decline as an artist to the happiness she realized after she emerged from the constrictions of marriage and 'society' and settled down to a more congenial life in Paris. There is something moldy and self-serving about the limitation he assigns a woman's "genius [which] may be stimulated by some exceptional emotional strain, but will disappear when the stimulus has passed," while "[w]ith a man, his professional, his artisan's life is likely to persist and evolve as a partially independent organism through the vicissitudes of his emotional experience." Thus Mrs. Wharton, unlike her mentor, Henry James, whose *"métier"* developed "in a virtual vacuum" (emotionally speaking) to the end of his days, had no *"métier* in this sense." But the trade-off Wilson discerns in Mrs. Wharton's career bears an uncanny resemblance to the bargain that Mrs. West struck with her angel of mercy.

In Paris, Edith Wharton

> seems at last to become comfortably adjusted; and with her ad-justment, the real intellectual force which she has exerted through a decade and a half evaporates almost completely. She no longer maims or massacres her characters. Her grimness melts rapidly into benignity. . . . She even loses the style she has mas-tered. . . . a prose of flexible steel, bright as electric light and striking out sparks of wit and color, which has the quality and pace of New York. . . .

"[A] prose of flexible steel" comes closer to describing *The Company She Keeps,* and especially a story like "The Man in the Brooks Brothers Shirt," in which Meg Sargent wonders whether she really belongs to the "fraternity of cripples" she has consorted with in New York—"or was she not a sound and normal woman who had been spending her life in self-imposed exile, a princess among the trolls?"

The Mary McCarthy who bantered with Dick Cavett about *Cannibals and Missionaries* in the fall of 1979 had long ago moved from 'princess' to 'regent.' In Margo Viscusi's view, she had already evolved into the "grand old lady . . . persona we all saw toward the end, amusing but not really mean-spirited, somewhat above it all." Cavett "remembered the other person, and he wanted some of that"; and as he plied her with questions, like a hostess plying a shy performer with drinks, it was "quite clear" to Viscusi that he was "goading her."

To Eileen Simpson at home, it appeared that Mary "was on her very best behavior. . . ." Everything seemed to be just right: "her dress, her hair, her gestures. . . ." When Cavett (who was well briefed on McCarthy's aversions) questioned her about the Kennedys, and she aired her dislike for the 'U.S. style Catholicism' of the Kennedy clan, she interrupted herself to make "sure there [was] nothing libelous here." "It was a bad remark, but it was still in the homestretch," Simpson recalls; Cavett replied, " 'no, no problem about libel,' and she relaxed, and then he asked her about Hellman."

Actually, Cavett had asked McCarthy what contemporary writers she thought were "overrated, and we could do without, given a limited amount of time"; a loaded question and a standby in tired interviews, and Mary parried it by suggesting that overrating writers was not exactly a contemporary problem. "We don't have the overpraised writer anymore?" Cavett persisted. "At least I'm not aware of it," she said, and then proceeded to name a few 'holdovers,' including John Steinbeck and Lillian Hellman—"who I think is tremendously over-rated, a bad writer, and *dishonest writer,* but she really belongs to the past," which of course she didn't. And Cavett pounced: "What is dishonest about Lillian Hellman?" *"Everything,"* McCarthy answered; "I said once in some interview that *every word she writes is a lie,* including 'and' and 'the.'" When "it all spilled out—the old Mary," Simpson, a psychologist, was reminded of what sometimes happens in therapy. "You're finishing with a patient, you take them to the door, and at the door they tell you. . . ." In the studio, Cavett's head dropped in amazement, a finger flying involuntarily to his lips. "I'm sure she would write you to correct that," he said weakly, through the outburst of laughter that followed McCarthy's remark; and he wondered, "Have you ever run into Miss Hellman lately?" Two weeks later, when Cavett was named a codefendant along with Channel 13 in Hellman's $2.25 million suit—$1.75 million for "mental pain and anguish" and for being "injured in her profession," and $500,000 in punitive damages—he would say he questioned her inclusion on the 'overrated' list simply because of his great admiration for her. (Of the three defendants, McCarthy, Cavett, and the Educational Broadcasting Corporation, Cavett was ultimately exempted from the action on the grounds that he was not involved in the preparation or editing of the program.)

At home, Eileen Simpson was sure that "Jim must have *died*"; but at Channel 13, the mood was lighthearted. Saying 'every word she writes is a lie' was an outrageous remark—"pure hyperbole"—that no one could possibly take literally; nobody, including Mary, as far as Margo Viscusi knew, "had any second thoughts about the propriety of having said such a thing." When Herbert Mitgang of *The New York Times* first reached McCarthy in London on February 15 with the news of Hellman's suit, she had trouble taking it seriously. Mitgang reported that Mary McCarthy "made no effort to modify what she said about Miss Hellman in the broadcast." "Please write. I am laughing but slightly scared," she wrote her attorney on the twentieth. Only when she and Jim returned to Paris ten days later, after Mary had delivered

the Northcliffe Lectures at the University of London (published as
Ideas and the Novel), did she learn what was alleged in the complaint—that her statement was "false, made with ill-will, with malice,
with knowledge of its falsity, with careless disregard of its truth, and
with the intent to injure the plaintiff personally and professionally."
And only then did she learn from the newsclips in a deskful of back
mail "what in fact I'd *said* on the Cavett Show (so many months ago),"
along with the fact that "the sum demanded was two and a quarter
million dollars—I'd understood that it was two, not that, from my
perspective of $63,000 in savings, the difference is perceptible." On
April 21, 1980, McCarthy opened the door to a man who inquired,
"Mary McCarthy?" "*Oui,*" she said; and he handed her the summons.

Later, Frani Muser couldn't help pondering "the question of
whether 'and' and 'the' can be a lie or not." It would have been great
fun, she thought, if the lawyers had waded into that semantic swamp.
She never could understand how the defense team had allowed itself to
be outwitted by Hellman's attorneys. "Any good lawyer could have
whacked [the defamation suit] down right away," she suggests, both
on technical grounds: that McCarthy was quoting a statement of
opinion already in the public domain (the 'every word . . .' remark first
appeared in an interview with the *Paris Metro* in 1978), and on the
grounds of free speech.

"The fact is Mary's a critic with a right to make judgments, and
Lillian Hellman's a public figure," Dwight Macdonald observed, anticipating the pretrial argument the defense lawyers would file in June
1983 for a summary judgment for dismissal. The argument was that
McCarthy's comments were "literary criticism, which is pure opinion
protected by the First Amendment"; and that as "a public figure"—a
pivotal contention—Hellman could recover damages only if she
proved "by clear and convincing evidence that the comments were
made with actual malice. There is no such evidence," McCarthy's
attorneys maintained. As a 'public figure,' moreover, plaintiff had
ample recourse to the media to defend herself.

Both the commonsense reasoning and the legalese ignored a crucial
aspect of the case, however, which was that McCarthy made her
judgment not in the pages of *Partisan Review* or *The New York
Review of Books* but on a television talk show. One of McCarthy's
later pretrial depositions developed the literary argument: that Hellman's memoirs "distort events which are part of the history of the
plaintiff's time, distort and aggrandize her relationship to those events,
and are harshly unfair to many individuals . . . most of whom are dead

and unable to defend themselves." It didn't matter whether there was a conscious intent to lie; "it may well be that plaintiff has persuaded herself of her version of the truth and is deaf to any other," McCarthy speculated, a possibility she entertained only after the Cavett show, when with the help of friends and strangers who came forth with evidence of Hellman's distortions, or volunteered their research time, she discovered the astonishing range and variety of the fabrications. Deliberate or not, the result was, in her opinion, "pervasive falsity." But nothing of this context was offered with the televised remark.

In cold print, McCarthy's quip might be instantly recognized as "rhetorical hyperbole," as her attorneys argued, as well as an "expression of opinion," as Mary grudgingly conceded in the deposition she filed on August 12, 1981, with Hellman's chief attorney, Ephraim London:

> I don't mean *literally* nothing when I say "nothing in her writings rings true." . . . I mean the general tone of unconvincingness and falseness.
> Q: And that was your intent in making the statement?
> A: To point to this trait in her work.
> Q: The trait in the work, or your opinion of the trait in her work?
> A: It is the same. When I give it as my opinion, I am pointing to this trait in her work, that is, to what I see as this trait in her work.

On television, however, such a statement *sounds* defamatory—"a terrific slam," Kevin McCarthy called it—whether it 'reads' as opinion or fact. Sights and sounds are what matter, as Lillian Hellman, who was also watching on the night of January 24, alone in her New York town house, recognized instantly.

American television is not a critical medium but an organ of mass entertainment and propaganda. Educational television may transmit 'live' events of genuine import; only rarely, except sometimes in election years, does it open a channel for controversial discussion and substantive debate. Even McCarthy's one-liner about Hellman's honesty has a made-for-television ring, in that it traffics in reputation, not issues. No wonder Hellman scorned Cavett's invitation afterwards to appear on the show to rebut the charge—she would have looked silly defending her honesty on national television, and "looking silly" for such a "judgmental person," who always "saw herself as a moral arbiter," Norman Mailer comments was insupportable.

In May 1984, Judge Harold Baer, Jr., denied McCarthy's motion for acquittal, surprising a great many observers who, like Mailer, deplored McCarthy's words but feared Hellman's legal action more. Baer's ruling reflected a sensitivity to how the medium shapes the message, missing in the calculations of many intellectuals: "to call someone dishonest, to say to a national television audience that every word she writes is a lie, seems to fall on the actionable side of the line, outside what has come to be known as the 'marketplace of ideas,' " he reasoned. Had Lillian Hellman not died a few months later, and McCarthy and the PBS affiliate appealed the decision, as they planned to do, then the historically significant question of whether First Amendment rights extend to television might have been confronted. It was to argue this issue, among others, before a New York State appeals court, that the constitutional lawyer Floyd Abrams—who successfully defended *The New York Times* against the government in the *Pentagon Papers* case—joined McCarthy's team in June 1984.

What was unexpected about Judge Baer's ruling, given Lillian Hellman's celebrity and her continuing involvement in political issues through the Committee for Public Justice—an organization of prominent literary figures, lawyers, and scholars that she founded in 1970—was that Baer accepted Ephraim London's argument that she was not a public figure. In addition to "general notoriety," a public figure must be a person who is involved in a "public issue, question or controversy," he stated. Lillian Hellman's image may have been sufficiently well known for her to appear unidentified in a Blackglama mink ad (in 1976) under the line "What Becomes a Legend Most?" but she was not, by 1980, presumably, actively engaged in influencing public events. (The Committee for Public Justice, founded to safeguard civil liberties, was dissolved at this time, purportedly because of Hellman's rough handling of staff people, but also on the advice of her co-chairman, Ephraim London.)

II

Mary McCarthy's dislike for Lillian Hellman sprang, like hope eternal, from the very center of her being. It was only partly based on politics, on the anti-Stalinist's traditional mistrust of those whose support of the Soviet interest or the Communist Party's interest in a given historical dispute appeared to override all other considerations, especially when such support masqueraded as something else—which, given the depth of anticommunism in American life, it usually did. Of course, it was more complicated than that; and anti-Stalinism among the intellectuals, particularly during the Cold War, was sometimes a Trojan horse for a vested interest in Pax Americana; while after the great purge of 1936 to 1937, Stalinism, or 'anti-Fascism' as Malcolm Cowley preferred, was often a force for accommodation between insurgent political movements and the federal government.

The political part of the showdown with Lillian Hellman, which went all the way back to the Spanish Civil War, and the night McCarthy tangled with the famous playwright at a dinner party at Bob Misch's, was provoked by *Scoundrel Time* (1976). More than *An Unfinished Woman* (1969) and *Pentimento* (1973)—whose flagship story "Julia" was made into a popular motion picture starring Vanessa Redgrave as the heroic antifascist, Julia, and Jane Fonda as her chain-smoking, tough-talking companion, Lillian Hellman—*Scoundrel Time* triggered McCarthy's ire for its lopsided reconstruction of a period in American history which she, like many other veterans of the anti-Stalinist movement, generally preferred to forget. When McCarthy called Hellman a "dishonest writer," it was this memoir, with its winsome self-portrait of the author standing up to the House Committee on Un-American Activities while most American intellectuals ran behind the barn, that she had in mind. ("I mean you'd read this god-damned *Scoundrel Time,* and you'd think she went to *jail* almost!" McCarthy fumed.)

In her depositions, McCarthy documented the distortions that gave readers the impression that Lillian Hellman alone had defied HUAC in the early 1950s, when in fact she had pleaded the Fifth Amendment to questions she didn't want to answer, just as previous witnesses had. These were questions about other people's politics, but also those relating to her own association with the Communist party during the years 1937 to 1946, a pattern later spotted by one of Hellman's biographers, William Wright. Arthur Miller took the more courageous stand, in McCarthy's view, when he pleaded the First Amendment and refused to answer any questions, an opinion shared by Hellman's lawyer Joseph Rauh, who also represented Miller. Arthur Miller was cited for contempt, like the Hollywood Ten, something Hellman didn't want to risk, but he was later exonerated on appeal.

Then there was the voice Hellman describes shouting from the press gallery: " 'Thank God somebody finally had the guts to do it!' " that no one reported at the time, or remembered later, including Rauh. The voice is pure invention, McCarthy argued, calculated to dramatize the author's view of herself, but also to distract the reader at a critical juncture when Hellman appears ready to explain why she shifted back and forth from answering some questions to pleading the Fifth. Nor is it clear, given the Fifth Amendment pleas, what someone 'finally had the guts to do.' Even the famous challenge Hellman directed to the House Committee—"I cannot and will not cut my conscience to fit this year's fashions . . ."—struck McCarthy as a distorting gloss on the letter from which it came:

I do not like subversion or disloyalty in any form and if I had ever seen any I would have considered it my duty to have reported it to the proper authorities. But to hurt innocent people whom I knew many years ago in order to save myself is, to me, inhuman and indecent and dishonorable. I cannot and will not cut my conscience to fit this year's fashions, even though I long ago came to the conclusion that I was not a political person and could have no comfortable place in any political group. . . .

The letter, addressed to HUAC's chairman, and entered into the *Congressional Record* by a committee member, was written to explain why Hellman was going to plead the Fifth Amendment if forced to testify against other people. When Rauh passed out copies to the press, it was this letter, with its subtly defiant sentence excised by the press from the surrounding tissue, that made headlines.

After *Scoundrel Time,* reading *the letter* became the climax of Eric Bentley's Off-Broadway play *Are You Now or Have You Ever Been,* and Colleen Dewhurst, Tammy Grimes, Peggy Cass, and Liza Minnelli lined up to enact the scene. "Each had a turn in refusing to cut her conscience, generally one week per actress," William Wright reports; and the house went wild. But a strange thing happened to Hellman on the way to immortality. Wright reports that after a few weeks of rave reviews, she phoned her agent in a fury to find out whether the actresses had the right to read the letter without paying her. A deal was cut, presumably with the playwright, and the show went on; but Lillian Hellman, Wright notes, "stood ready to close down a play that anyone else with the slightest interest in self-glorification would have paid to have produced."

What Mary McCarthy didn't know at the time of her own research was that in the original draft of the HUAC letter, Hellman had actually admitted to being a member of the Communist party from 1938 to 1940. Discovered by a later biographer, Carl Rollyson, in Joseph Rauh's papers at the Library of Congress, the draft letter contradicts

Hellman's claim in *Scoundrel Time* that she never joined the Party. The 1988 revelation by Rollyson puts a new twist on the celebrated sentence. Instead of defying the anti-Communist fashions of the period by affirming her political allegiances, Hellman had followed convention by pretending she was not then, or ever, a Communist. The admission of Party membership during the years of the Hitler-Stalin pact would have cost her liberal support, not only in 1952 but in 1976, even if it could be shown that hers was a 'customized' membership, the kind that allowed for considerable latitude in political and artistic expression, which it obviously was.

Hellman herself no doubt saw the question of membership as irrelevant, if not malicious, in a period of galloping anticommunism. No one, not even Dashiell Hammett, who went to jail for refusing to cooperate with a grand jury investigation of Communist bail funds in 1951, publicly argued the right to belong to the Communist party in the 1950s; though why ex-Communists rarely if ever defended their earlier affiliations was a more debatable question, especially for anti-Stalinists. Like William Phillips, many of them attributed their own failure to support Hellman and others when they were under fire to the fact that "[s]ome *were* communists and what one was being asked to do was to defend their right to lie about it. . . ."

Hellman, in any event, never strayed from the spirit of her own truth. Neither in the 1950s nor the 1970s did she indulge in mea culpas for her left-wing past. Far from it. Referring in 1980 to her "virtually unreconstructed Stalinism," Mary McCarthy professed herself "surprised . . . that she has stuck to it so faithfully," for it seemed to her to be "a surface manifestation." Hellman, she came to believe, really wasn't a political person; loyalty to the past, she decided, "may be her idea of 'integrity.' "

Loyalty to Hammett perhaps, or Stalin himself, whom she met in Moscow in 1944, may have supplied the inner spring to an elastic political conscience. McCarthy doesn't suggest it but Norman Mailer does, when he says, "Lillian was a celebrity-fucker. . . . She was one of those people taken with high political figures. She could be very critical of Communists in private, but never criticize them publicly"; not only because of loyalty but because "it was fashionable to be anti-Stalinist," as she saw it. "The ways in which [the anti-Stalinists] were awful were worse than the ways in which the Communists were awful, . . . and she just wasn't about to give satisfaction." Pride inflamed Hellman's political loyalties, in Mailer's view, as it did her dramatic work (cf. Regina in *The Little Foxes*). What was important in politics—perceived as a contest between good guys and bad guys—was that in throwing your influence in a certain direction, you didn't give aid to the other side. Thus, in 1952, Hellman wouldn't let Rauh use evidence of Communist party criticism of her 1941 play, *Watch on the Rhine,* in her HUAC defense, because it "would amount to my attacking them at a time when they were being persecuted, and I would . . . be playing the enemy's game." In *Scoundrel Time,* a glancing reference to "the sins of Stalin Communism . . . that for a long time I mistakenly denied" is tucked inside the more emphatic statement that many American intellectuals found in these sins of Stalin "the excuse to join those who should have been their hereditary enemies."

The coy allusion to "Stalin Communism" enraged Sidney Hook, who noted in 1976 that such " 'sins' " included the Moscow purge trials, the Nazi-Soviet pact, the invasion of Poland and the subjugation of the Baltic States, the invasion of Finland, the mass execution of returning Russian prisoners of war, the Berlin blockade, the crushing of the Hungarian Revolution, and the incarceration of dissenters in insane asylums inside the Soviet Union. "Who would guess reading the soigné prose of *Scoundrel Time,* that Miss Hellman was once one of the most vigorous public defenders of those 'sins' which even Khrushchev did not hesitate to call crimes?" he exclaimed. But it was the spiteful charge that intellectuals who never "raised a finger when [Joe] McCarthy and the boys appeared" had joined "their hereditary enemies" that infuriated the anti-Stalinists, and led Alfred Kazin to depict Hellman's third memoir as "historically a fraud, artistically a put-up job and emotionally packed with meanness."

"The children of timid immigrants are often remarkable people: energetic, intelligent, hardworking," Hellman writes in *Scoundrel Time,* "and often they make it so good that they are determined to keep it at any cost." It was a nasty reference to her own hereditary enemies among the New York intelligentsia, which extended to Hollywood producers and studio heads who cooperated with HUAC to save their necks. "I don't think [they] had ever before thought of themselves as American citizens with inherited rights and obligations," she says of the latter:

> Many of them had been born in foreign lands and inherited foreign fears. It would not have been possible in Russia or Poland, but it was possible here to offer the Cossacks a bowl of chicken soup. And the Cossacks in Washington were now riding so fast and hard

that the soup had to have double strength and be handed up by
running millionaire waiters.

The crude reference to Cossacks—more common in a fund-raising
drive for Israel than in political argument—was Hellman, a German
Jew, at her meanest. It was the flip side of the rosy self-portrait she
presented to HUAC of someone "raised in an old-fashioned American
tradition" to uphold "ideals of Christian honor. . . ."

Twenty-five years after HUAC, however, in the wake of Vietnam,
Americans were ready to atone for the sins of McCarthyism; and
Hellman's controversial contention that most American intellectuals,
"either by what they did or did not do, contributed to McCarthyism,"
because they wouldn't "fight for anything if doing so would injure
them . . ." was warmly received, partly because it appealed to the
common perception that self-interest and perfidy lie behind actions one
doesn't approve of (while only good intentions inspire one's own), and
partly because it was true. At least there was enough truth in it to leave
Mary McCarthy, who was uncomfortable with the timidity of anti-
Stalinists in the 1950s, as she was with the unreconstructed anticommunism of Sidney Hook and Diana Trilling in the 1970s and '80s,
notably silent on this point. It was probably Hellman's edge in the
debate over what had happened in the McCarthy period that made
Mary uneasy with commentators who portrayed the Hellman-
McCarthy confrontation as a "long-standing political feud." "It's
strictly personal as far as I'm concerned," she wrote her attorney, Ben
O'Sullivan, early in 1980, "and can hardly be called a feud since she's
not much present to my consciousness. I don't know what brought her
to mind on the Cavett Show," she added, somewhat disingenuously,
for Lillian Hellman had been much on Mary's mind in October 1979.

The reason was both personal and political, as tempests among the
literati often are; and began, oddly enough, with Mary McCarthy's
effort to halt an anti-Hellman vendetta that had erupted inside the
Spanish Refugee Aid Committee, the organization started by Nancy
Macdonald in 1953, which McCarthy chaired in the late 1950s. When
an influential board member, a Ukrainian fur importer named Gabriel
Javsicas, who fancied himself an anarchist and contributed a great deal
of money, had suddenly spotted Lillian Hellman's name among the list
of sponsors, he had exploded. It had been there for five years, and he
himself was present at the meeting when Dwight Macdonald had
lobbied for Hellman's election on the grounds that "she had gone

straight," as McCarthy recounted it, "and she was going to give us a lot of money" (she didn't), but Javsicas didn't have his hearing aid on, and never noticed it. Afterwards, he had persuaded Jim Farrell and Mary McCarthy (who claimed not to have noticed it either) to resign; but Dwight had convinced Mary to reconsider before the resignations became public, and when she had landed in New York, she was bent on making amends to Nancy for her rashness.

Javsicas had sued Spanish Refugee Aid for eighteen dollars in the Court of Petty Claims for taking his money on false pretenses (the group was supposed to be "strictly non-Communist"), and now he was busy recruiting further resignations. McCarthy had tried to calm him down: " 'You don't do that in the radical movement, you don't sue your own people,' " she argued; " 'it's just like calling a policeman.' . . . And so that was all on my mind," she told an interviewer later, "and I'm sure that when [Cavett] asked me for an example of an overrated writer, Hellman swam into my consciousness." Gabriel Javsicas, meanwhile, had suddenly died; he would have gone mad, McCarthy thought, had he lived to see Hellman sue her.

Why Lillian Hellman wanted her name on such a list was no mystery to Mary McCarthy: "it made her respectable. That was what she was looking for—to be respectable, to be admitted into all kinds of society." A corollary to the theory was frequently heard in McCarthy's camp; namely, that "jealousy" prompted Hellman's suit. "Maybe she still thinks of Mary as being a rival," the art historian Meyer Schapiro speculated, noting that *Partisan Review* had always " 'stood for perhaps a more accomplished style of writing and a more knowing audience than she achieved.' " "She's an incredible phoney, it's a difference in quality," Simpson maintained. While Lillian Hellman was better known, she wasn't in the *New Yorker* crowd or the *New York Review* crowd, despite her friendship with Bob Silvers and Jason Epstein. "Here was Mary, who didn't publish very much, and was always flitting around," Margo Viscusi comments, "but for some reason she was *in*, she was accepted as a serious member of literary society, whereas Hellman was not."

Hellman's defenders mounted the same argument from the other side. Her "elitest" critics were answered by "public opinion," which obviously preferred Hellman's work to McCarthy's. " 'Missionaries and Cannibals" [sic] is an absolute disaster," Ephraim London told *The New York Times*; "[i]t must be a bitter pill to swallow to see someone who you think is a less good writer than you are to be so much more successful."

As for the question of 'overrated writers,' McCarthy was already mulling it over when she arrived at Channel 13, for Cavett's researcher had raised it the night before the taping, and while McCarthy insisted she had rebuffed it vehemently, the researcher testified that she had responded with great enthusiasm. "I think she mistook *vehemence* for enthusiasm," McCarthy later explained, adding that it was on the phone and she hadn't given it another thought before "it popped up" on the show. But Frani Muser remembers talking about Hellman and the 'question' that morning. "She knew it was coming," Muser says, adding that the "bon mot" about " 'and' and 'the' " was bandied about then, too: "It was fun at the breakfast table, of course."

Of course. Without fun, nothing serious ever happened in Mary McCarthy's life. For better or worse, it lay behind her creative impulse, leading sometimes to the caricatures in fiction that others saw as malicious. "If something is going to be fun, she'll do it," Eve Stwertka observes; "the fun of saying that witticism [on the Cavett show] was just too great," Stwertka thought, "and Mary was betrayed by it." (Something similar may apply to Lillian Hellman's famous temper, which often appeared out of control toward the end of her life: " 'Don't rule out idiocy. With Lillian it was fifty years of *schtick,* ' " says an old friend.) Hellman, Eve Stwertka suggests, was not *the enemy,* but it occurs to her that originally McCarthy had planned a career in the theatre—while Hellman, it should be noted, aspired to be a novelist. McCarthy had failed as an actress, and her single attempt at playwriting at Vassar came to nought. She lacked a feeling for dialogue—a judgment she questioned later when it was too late to experiment—and tended to pack her characters' spoken words into long prosy paragraphs. She had a sharp eye for context, for the dramatic setting of speech, but not an open ear for the rhythms of ordinary conversation—except in the Theatre Chronicles, when her own conversational style is most pungent.

Stwertka wonders whether Hellman's early success as a playwright "may have caused Mary a great deal of bitterness, maybe not even consciously." Lillian Hellman had reached "center stage" with her plays, while McCarthy stood outside the profession as a critic, looking on. "Perhaps there was a bit of irony there for her," she suggests, "because Mary thought that she would have liked to do that, and perhaps would have done it better, more to her taste." By 1979, meanwhile, Hellman had made her mark in a genre much closer to home. And when McCarthy called her a "dishonest writer," it wasn't only politics she had in mind but something basic to memoir writing.

To Ben O'Sullivan, she noted that it was Lillian who invariably presented the conflict in political terms—as indeed she did. Writing Stephen Spender in 1983, Hellman wondered whether he "remember[ed] the evening when you invited me to your house for a meeting with your students, three of whom told me that I had been invited there so that you and McCarthy could Red-Bait me? It was long ago," she said of this second encounter with Mary McCarthy, at Sarah Lawrence in 1948 (one that Mary and Spender recalled somewhat differently), "but the seeds of malice grow more fertile through the years." The gray-haired novelist who called her a liar on "The Dick Cavett Show" was the impudent young Trotskyite grown old; and this never-ending story, for Hellman more than for McCarthy, was driven by a strange animus that went beyond politics.

III

It was no secret that, as Norman Mailer declares, "Lillian wanted to wreck [Mary McCarthy] with this lawsuit"; a likely prospect, in that by the time a libel action comes to trial, the legal expenses are so great that the defendant has already lost, even if a motion to dismiss is won on appeal. McCarthy, who wasn't a wealthy woman (unlike Hellman, a very rich woman, who was not charged by her attorneys), might easily have been broken by the costs of her defense had it not been for the "angelic intervention" at the last minute of the *Paris Review* publisher, Deborah Pease, with a check for $25,000. Had McCarthy ultimately lost the case, which a few of her friends, among them her HBJ editor, Julian Muller, feared she might, she would have been ruined. It was a real prospect, and one of the first things McCarthy did in April 1980 was transfer her bank accounts, including Hannah Arendt's, for which she was trustee, from New York to Maine. "She was afraid of losing all of her assets," including the Castine house, Margo Viscusi relates. "She was afraid of losing her whole way of life. She wasn't afraid of losing her reputation," she adds, but her fear of Hellman's power to "drain all of her money away . . . was a distraction"—whose reality, given Hellman's influence in the interlocking worlds of publishing, journalism, and theatre, only a member of McCarthy's generation might appreciate.

"The power of L. H.—a puzzlement, even when one knows how concentrated she has been in its service," Elizabeth Hardwick wrote McCarthy in Paris in 1977. Hardwick's wonderment was triggered by the decision of Hellman's publisher, Little, Brown, to cancel publication of Diana Trilling's *We Must March, My Darlings* because it contained critical references to *Scoundrel Time*. Diana Trilling, no slouch as a literary infighter, remembers "Lillian [as] the most powerful woman I've ever known, maybe the most powerful *person* I've ever known.' " When Trilling solicited an enthusiastic blurb for her book from Mailer, Hellman summoned him for a talk, after which he had telephoned Trilling's new publisher to alter his comments in a way that rendered them useless. All this, however, was before Mary McCarthy's $2.25 million remark began to be bruited about in newspapers, magazines, and books; and the reliability of Hellman's memoirs, as reportage and autobiography, was systematically examined and found wanting; then the extraordinary legend of Lillian Hellman began to slide into the limbo where it resides today. At the time of the suit, however, Hellman's disfavor was not something one wanted to encounter in the dark alley of American letters.

Even before the Cavett show, Hellman had given evidence of the depth of her grudge against Mary McCarthy, one wildly out of proportion to the handful of criticisms she had sustained from McCarthy's pen and person over the years. In her 1967 review of a *Little Foxes* revival, Elizabeth Hardwick had issued a more crushing indictment of Hellman's dramatic work than all McCarthy's notices put together. McCarthy had made only a few passes: the 1946 reference to "the oily virtuosity of George Kaufman, George Abbott, Lillian Hellman, Odets, Saroyan . . ."; a 1947 opinion that "[e]xcept in the neighborhood of Moss Hart and Lillian Hellman, there is everywhere in the theatre this season a sense of restored dignity." She had admired *The Children's Hour* when she saw it with Harold Johnsrud in 1935, but professed never to have seen the other plays—"I couldn't be bothered," she claimed. Hellman let it out that McCarthy had panned all her plays, but the only one she ever reviewed was the operetta *Candide,* which Hellman had adapted to the stage; and then she had merely taken the playwright and her collaborators to task for playing it safe. "Anything in the original that could give offense to anyone—Jews, Arabs, or Holy Church—has been removed. . . . A bowdlerized *Candide,* a *Candide* that cannot afford to be candid," McCarthy asserted, "is a contradiction in terms." It was an opinion Hellman partially shared. And it was the last notice McCarthy paid her work. But Hellman's grudge seemed to feed on itself.

At a dinner party in New York in the early 1970s, Eileen Simpson remembers getting a tongue-lashing from Lillian Hellman simply for mentioning McCarthy's name. Her host, Roger Straus, had asked how

Mary was doing in Paris, where Simpson had just been. Fine, every-thing's fine, she had replied, whereupon Hellman had pointed a finger at her and snapped, " 'You! You were old enough, why didn't you talk to Mary? Why weren't you candid with her, why didn't you get her to see that her attitude was befuddled?' " Simpson, astonished, had turned to see who Hellman was shouting at. "She went on and on, and the table was paralyzed. . . . I couldn't say, 'I really don't know what you're talking about' "; but finally Roger Straus said, " 'Oh, Lillian, cut the crap, come off it,' and that was the end of it." The event Hellman was fuming over was the Waldorf conference, nearly twenty-five years before, where she had been a sponsor and McCarthy an insurgent. Eileen Simpson knew nothing about it, but she did learn how "really *enraged* at Mary" Lillian was.

Mary McCarthy's own efforts to keep the legal conflict separate from the 'political feud' made her initially cool to the proposals of friends like Jonathan Randal in Paris and Bob Silvers and Elizabeth Hardwick in New York to start a defense fund on her behalf. She had "a reluctance to posing as a Scottsboro Boy," but mainly she was afraid a defense fund would further polarize the conflict along ideolog-ical lines. When Diana Trilling contacted Bill Jovanovich to explore the possibility of starting a defense committee " 'to extrude Lillian from the intellectual community,' " McCarthy found the idea "appall-ing." "That Cold-War Bellona," McCarthy maintained, was more interested in pursuing her own vendetta than in helping her in a practical sense. It was as the daughter and granddaughter of lawyers, who believed in the law, that she pronounced herself against "trying a case in the court of public opinion"—until May 1984, when she lost the motion for acquittal. Then, Judge Baer's ruling that Lillian Hell-man was not a public figure led McCarthy to consider "confronting [Hellman's] political persona," by citing "the appeals she signed or initiated, the mass meetings she addressed and sometimes organized, her 'Committee for Public Justice.' . . . Perhaps the time has come when I need help," she told her attorney, "or when the voice of opinion should be heard."

By 1984, opinion had already shifted if not in Mary McCarthy's direction, then away from her opponent, thanks in part to the decon-struction of the Hellman legend by a small band of critics who were undeterred by the lawsuit's preemptive intent. "Hellman was cer-tain . . . McCarthy's brutal attack would be followed up by others," Carl Rollyson was told by Ephraim London, "and she wanted to punish anyone who went so far as to call her a liar"—an effort at intimidation that backfired, to say the least. Like Samuel McCracken, whose " 'Julia' and Other Fictions by Lillian Hellman" appeared in *Commentary,* and one of her biographers, commentators now drew on Mary McCarthy's defense files, which were bulging with incriminating evidence that McCarthy herself was foresworn from using publicly for the duration of the suit.

One who worked alone was Martha Gellhorn, whose "Guerre de Plume" in *Paris Review* first documented the fabrications in Hellman's Spanish Civil War accounts, including Hellman's 'apocryphal' meetings with Hemingway, who was accompanied by Gellhorn (his third wife) in Spain. "Her incomprehension of that war is near idiocy," Gellhorn concluded; and the article leveled a charge that reappeared in subsequent challenges: that Hellman told self-serving tales about the famous, now dead, which made herself more famous. But it was the dismantling of "Julia" from its moorings in fantasy—a fantasy so deep-seated that the lines between fact and fancy were all but erased—that opened the breach in Hellman's reputation.

The melodramatic account of Hellman's secret mission to Berlin in 1937 to deliver money concealed in a hat to her childhood friend Julia, an American heiress and medical student active in the Austrian Resistance, was compromised by inconsistencies both external and internal to the narrative, including a stray reference to the teenage Julia, who is remembered joking that John Donne wrote his poem "Julia" for her, while the name Julia, Hellman explains elsewhere, is fictitious. Why the identity of an American who rescued dozens of Austrian Jews in the 1930s had to be concealed forty years later was never satisfactorily explained. If "Julia" was a true story, Mary McCarthy argued, friends of this brave woman, purportedly killed by the Nazis, would surely have stepped forth with information establishing her identity. None did. "The only hero or heroine the plaintiff allows posterity to honor," she observed, "is plaintiff herself."

The most embarrassing moment for Hellman had arrived in 1983, when Dr. Muriel Gardiner, a medical student in Vienna in the mid-1930s, published a memoir of her activities in the Austrian Resistance entitled *Code Name Mary,* which left little doubt that Lillian Hellman had helped herself to large portions of the author's life. In 1978, Dr. Gardiner, who was always being asked whether she was Julia, had written Hellman to inquire about the resemblance, noting that they had never met, and that she hadn't known of another American woman in Germany at that time doing underground work. Later, at

McCarthy's request, Gardiner had checked this last point with the director of the Archives of the Austrian Resistance, Dr. Herbert Steiner, who confirmed that she was the only one. Hellman never wrote back.

In August 1983, in another letter to Stephen Spender, who had known Muriel Gardiner in Vienna and spotted her as Julia, Hellman claimed she had never heard from her. "... Miss Hellman will reveal the name of Julia when the time comes," she added huffily, after chastising Spender for belonging to the "anti-Hellman group," whose headquarters she placed on West Sixty-seventh Street (where Elizabeth Hardwick lived). Spender had been mistakenly cited in *The Times Literary Supplement* as an intermediary who had originally solicited McCarthy's apology as a condition for Hellman's not filing suit, when what he actually had done was telephone Leonard Bernstein on his own initiative *after* the litigation began to see whether Bernstein, as Hellman's friend, could persuade her to drop the suit. Bernstein reported a failed mission. " 'She's a very angry lady,' " he told Spender.

There remained the question of how Hellman had acquired her intimate knowledge of Muriel Gardiner's exploits in Austria; and the answer almost certainly lay in an overlapping relationship she and Gardiner had in the 1930s with a man named Wolf Schwabacher. A sociable bachelor in the years he knew Lillian Hellman, and shared a summer house in Pennington, New Jersey, with Muriel Gardiner, Schwabacher also served as each woman's attorney, representing Hellman in her efforts to lift the Boston ban of *The Children's Hour* in 1935, and Gardiner in her marriage to the former leader of the Austrian Left-Socialists, Joseph Buttinger, in Paris in 1939. Schwabacher may well have entertained his New York friends with tales of Gardiner's and Buttinger's clandestine work during a period when Hellman's imagination was afire with the antifascist cause. After *Code Name Mary* appeared, his son Christopher Schwabacher reported that the characters Kurt and Sara Muller in *Watch on the Rhine* were based on Muriel and Joseph Buttinger.

Muriel Gardiner, it seems, had been a touchstone for Lillian Hellman, a brave and fearless alter ego with whom it was not hard to fall in love—as Hellman (Fonda) does with Julia (Redgrave) in the movie. In *Pentimento,* meaning "the painter 'repented,' changed his mind," Hellman writes that she found in "the old conception" (in the case of "Julia," perhaps the initial attraction to Gardiner's tale) "a way of seeing and then seeing again." With this story certainly she satisfied a yearning to picture herself as a heroic figure on the world's stage.

Gardiner's vita contained several attributes to which Lillian Hellman was drawn: old wealth, adventure, intellectual stature (as a psychoanalyst), not to mention 'good politics.' By having Julia lose her leg, and then her life to the Nazis, moreover, Hellman satisfied another condition of her nature, noted by Carl Rollyson, which was to feel personally injured or threatened by the forces she opposed politically.

"It's no news that each of us has our own reasons for pretending, denying, affirming what was there and never there," Hellman acknowledges in her fourth and final memoir, *Maybe* (1980). "What I have written is the truth as I saw it," she reflects, "but the truth as I saw it, of course, doesn't have much to do with truth." Such runic utterances were the only accommodation she would ever make to the damaging disclosures circulating through the media. To publicly acknowledge her debt to Muriel Gardiner, to a reality not her own, and to the folly of the dramatization, was a prospect Hellman regarded with the same stiff-necked resistance Mary McCarthy displayed toward the idea of apologizing.

Looking back at the injuries Lillian Hellman sustained personally and professionally in the last years of her life, as the reported incongruities in the memoirs massed themselves against the totemic power of reputation, one senses an almost tragic reversal. Rauh had been right to warn her against a suit that could lead the defense to " 'bring up every word you ever wrote or said and examine it for its truthfulness. Do you really want that?' " he had asked, and Hellman had slammed down the phone. It was as if the rage that fueled the multimillion-dollar suit, being incommensurate with the cause, swamped the ship sent out against the accuser and, sweeping back over the plaintiff, dragged her under waves of criticism that now hammered at her work and person.

In the early months of the suit, opinion had leaned toward Hellman, who had been transformed overnight into a victim. Malcolm Cowley spoke for more than the 'anti-Fascist' side of the debate when he complained that "Mary's the one who's dragging up the past. I would like to shove it aside." Among McCarthy's close friends were also voices wishing she had let sleeping dogs lie; who worried over the high price she paid for her provocative remark, financially, emotionally, and physically. But there were others who had been cut by her tongue or pen and who saw her as a "hatchet woman," who welcomed Hellman's suit with a stealthy satisfaction and "felt that Mary deserves this. . . ."

It was writers who still believed in a free 'marketplace of ideas,' for whom artists are always public figures, who spoke out against the libel action; as Norman Mailer did, stepping into the ring as 'peacemaker' in May 1980 to warn that "[i]f Lillian wins, then every American writer will have to feel that much more tongue-tied at daring to criticize another American writer without qualification." But even Mailer had beat the drum on Hellman's behalf when he added that he wished she would drop the case but doubted if she could, because "the insult has been too personal. . . . To say what Mary McCarthy said, knowing with her critical sense that her words had to be deadly to Lillian's honor, was a barbarity and a brutality."

Not that McCarthy's charge was false. "There was a good deal of truth in the accusation," Mailer observes today. "Lillian Hellman didn't know the boundary between fact and fiction"; if she relied on "lies" to create the character of the "noble woman . . . passionate, complex, a woman of affairs," it was because "she was afraid of the truth"—which was that she could be the "most fearful of women," timid physically (especially in an automobile, which, like McCarthy, she didn't drive). Mary McCarthy, on the other hand, "insisted on the truth because she was lacking in imagination," Mailer suggests; her "stubborn insistence on 'fact' kept imagination at bay." A double paradox. They both created their personas in memoirs, he adds, "only Mary was closer to the person she created." None of these fine distinctions appeared in Mailer's original "Appeal to Lillian Hellman and Mary McCarthy," however, which reinforced the popular assumption that there is no more 'truth' in literature than there is in politics—that McCarthy's charge was therefore "blarney."

Mary McCarthy could "detest" Hellman's work, but not "issue the one accusation against which no writer can defend himself or herself," Mailer maintained. "No writer worthy of serious consideration is ever honest except for those rare moments—for which we keep writing—when we become, bless us, not dishonest for an instant. Of course, Lillian Hellman is dishonest," he stated. "So is Mary McCarthy, Norman Mailer, Saul Bellow, John Updike, John Cheever, Cynthia Ozick—name 500 of us, Willa Cather, Edith Wharton, Henry James—we are all dishonest, we exaggerate, we distort, we use our tricks, we invent." (It was "absolutely appropriate and right" that Norman should lecture these "cranky women," George Plimpton remarked at the time, in a perfect expression of literary groupthink: "It could only be done by somebody who sits at the top of the heap.") What is interesting about this fanfare, however, is the blessed exception, when a writer becomes "not dishonest for an instant"; further on, Mailer notes that "it's almost impossible even writing at one's very best to come near the truth." The 'truth,' it seems, exists, like an angry Jewish God peering out from behind His thunderhead of bad news. One can never please Him, but if one stops trying one is no longer doing one's 'very best.' (McCarthy, of course, went further: "About truth I have always been monotheistic," she once wrote.)

"We do the best we can," Mailer reflects today, referring in his own way to a lifelong effort to fashion a self out of the literary project. In a memoir he will think he has finally "created a character that reflects my true nature, and then later it appears like only a small part of me," which is why "all memoirs are fiction," he concludes. And one wonders: Maybe this 'self' is fiction; and the myriad selves that bloom on the ego's stalk must devour each other to attain their fleeting moments in the sun. The memorialization of the 'self' in literature, in any event, a peculiarly American enterprise, is what links writers as dissimilar in other ways as Norman Mailer, Mary McCarthy, and Lillian Hellman. But there is a big difference between the psychological relativism Mailer argues and lifting facts from another person's life to reinvent one's own.

As for the alleged "brutality" of McCarthy's words—which were "intentionally extravagant," Hellman's attorneys charged, "an exaggeration," thereby seeming to concede the essential point— Norman Mailer's objection, then and now, rests on the contention that McCarthy broke a cardinal rule of combat by hitting another writer when she was down. "A much-damaged warrior," he called the seventy-three-year-old Hellman in 1980, who suffered from emphysema and glaucoma, and "could not raise a pistol since she can no longer see." The language of war is deadly serious. After ridiculing Mailer for his "maudlin appeals" to " 'make nice,' " and for being the "Bob Arum of the literary ratings," Richard Poirier lectured him from Justice Holmes to the effect that people should be allowed to speak freely in public, but not falsely. To which Mailer responded, with a carbon copy to Hellman, McCarthy, Silvers, Phillips, Harvey Shapiro, and Christopher Lehmann-Haupt of *The New York Times:*

> . . . I have to hand it to you. There was the need only to attack my letter, but you also had to attack me—on a small scale, but still— precisely what McCarthy did to Hellman. It makes me want to be wealthy enough to sue you. I would lose the case of course, but have the pleasure of seeing you broke after paying your lawyers. Then we would see if you still quoted Holmes.

When Lillian Hellman replied to Mailer ("Normie," she used to call him, much to his consternation), noting that "There could not be any answer to your letter to Richard Poirier," and concluding, after a brief answer, that she was "sorry about you and me, genuinely sorry," carbon copies went to the same list, minus Mary McCarthy. Such epistolary wars used to amuse Philip Rahv, who once told Jules Feiffer that he planned to write a satire of the letters columns of various literary magazines. It was all "jockeying for position," he thought; and behind the cool, reasoned rebuttals were murderous fantasies: "They're supposedly arguing about something, but they're really saying, 'I disagree with you. Therefore there's only one thing left for me to do and that's kill you.' "

With Lillian Hellman, Mary McCarthy really was arguing about something, which isn't to say she wasn't also inspired by a murderous fantasy as well as by fun when she made her remark. To many, of course, the McCarthy-Hellman fight was "a coupla women . . . hauling off, with their nails out," only briefly diverting. For the intellectuals who were summoned to their old shooting positions, the chance to articulate again "one's attitude toward communism," what the indefatigable Irving Howe called "the central political-cultural-intellectual problem of the 20th century," was a family reunion that offered the literary press some titillating copy. But for a larger public this drama fell on deaf ears.

In her depositions, McCarthy made it clear that when she called Hellman dishonest she wasn't talking about aiming at the truth and missing, nor about politics, but about an impulse to assimilate historical events and persons to one's own life, as well as to the lives of one's family: Uncle Willy, for example, in *Pentimento,* whose character and house, she demonstrated, were borrowed from a prominent New Orleans figure connected with the United Fruit Company. But it was the subtler instances of invention, such as an interlude with Dashiell Hammett and some turtles at Hardscrabble Farm (also in *Pentimento*), that disturbed her more. They violated a critical premise in McCarthy's autobiographical writing, which is that it should reverse the drift of life away from fact, even if, especially if, fact hurts.

"You knew that not one word that was spoken in that story [about Hammett and the turtles] was ever spoken by human lips. It was all somehow inflated or conflated in the interests of a narcissistic portrayal of a couple that wasn't a couple," McCarthy said after Hellman's death, when she was midway through her own late memoirs. The Hammett interlude, she thought, was "a kind of awful way of giving yourself loveability"—something she was far from doing in *How I Grew,* or its unlovable sequel, *Intellectual Memoirs: New York, 1936–1938.*

IV

"Lillian Hellman knew how to *write* a terrific person," William Wright concludes. "What is regrettable is that the real Hellman, although not as admirable, is, with her mixture of strengths and failings, far more interesting." Reading McCarthy's last memoir, "Edmund Wilson," one comes to the opposite conclusion. Mary McCarthy, in her aspect of penitent for a life (with Wilson) that she persisted in not comprehending, is more interesting than the 'real' McCarthy who took what she needed from a dangerous liaison, and went on to settle the questions of love and marriage later in life.

Fifty-two years after she first made love to Edmund Wilson on the couch in his study at Trees, McCarthy was still fretting over the fact that he misunderstood her, and that she "only wanted to talk to him." Martha Sinnott is given the line in *A Charmed Life,* and now, finally, McCarthy wonders whether "[m]aybe . . . I was fooling myself about Martha's motives and am still fooling myself today, when I should be old enough [at seventy-seven] to know better, about what drove me into Wilson's study on that long-ago night." Perhaps it was only "the unwillingness to end an evening that gets hold of people who have been drinking—*anything,* sex included, to avoid retiring."

Wilson, McCarthy reports, "was hell-bent on my marrying him," but during their clandestine courtship, she had "no premonition" of it. When she finally agreed, it was because she saw it as

> my punishment for having gone to bed with him. . . . The logic of having slept with Wilson compelled the sequence of marriage if that was what he wanted. Otherwise my action would have no consistency . . . no meaning. I could not accept the fact that I had slept with this fat, puffing man for no reason, simply because I was drunk. No. It had to make sense. Marrying him, though against my inclinations, *made* it make sense. There is something faintly Kantian here.

There is something preposterous about this 'logic,' which is less Kantian than Catholic—the idea of marriage as absolution for sin. Kant, however, with his central thesis that men deserve to be judged for the reasons behind their actions rather than for the consequences of their actions, seems to have taken up the spiritual slack for McCarthy when she outgrew religion. If she had married a fraction of the men she had slept with by 1938, she would have put the Wife of Bath to shame, but Wilson, of course, was different.

There were "other reasons" for marrying him, some previously alluded to in interviews and now offered as tokens of an undying faith in the redemptive power of memoir. After the death of her Presbyterian grandfather, Wilson, from the same Anglo-Saxon stock, gave her a "feeling of coming home." Besides the inducements of a "classical education" (reading Juvenal, and so on), and the lure of horseback riding, fishing for trout ("all of which were beyond Philip [Rahv]"), there was Wilson's promise that marrying him would " 'do something' for me, that is, for my literary gift," McCarthy states. " 'Rahv doesn't *do* anything for you,' he argued, meaning Rahv was slothfully content to have me do those theatre columns. . . . It was Wilson's belief that I ought not to be writing criticism—I had a talent, he thought, for imaginative writing . . ."

Wilson was right about Philip, McCarthy writes: "If it had been left to Rahv, I never would have written a single 'creative' word. And I do not hold it against him," she rushes on, when one wants to say, *Stop! What do you mean? Who's running this show?* Philip Rahv must be given his due: "His love, unlike Wilson's, was from the heart. He cared for what I was, not for what I might evolve into," because this love, which Mary McCarthy feels "vividly, as I write these words," matters more than the literary stuff. To say that may seem "ungrateful" to Wilson, she worries, "for what he did, in the first months of our marriage, to push me into 'creativity.' If he had not shut the door firmly on the little room [at Trees] . . . I would not be the 'Mary McCarthy' you are now reading. Yet, awful to say," she concludes wistfully, "I am not particularly grateful."

Written in the final year of her life, and lost for a while at *The New Yorker,* whose new editors weren't interested (*Paris Review* published it in the summer of 1991 before it appeared in the book), this remarkable document presents Mary McCarthy in solitary confinement with a conscience that has become, over the years, the true repository of her imagination. What is one to make of the obsessive flogging, not so much of Wilson as of McCarthy herself, as she presents herself in these memoirs, lurching drunkenly from one man to the next? Is her shame so great for what is presented, at last, as the real reason for yielding to Wilson? This is "the Marxist explanation": "Wilson, relatively

speaking, was upper class. That was all there was to it . . . he commanded a higher word rate [than Philip]. . . ."

Or is she satisfying an ironic convention as old as the passionate
confessions of the famous seventeenth-century penitent Moll Flanders?
Also an orphan, "Born in Newgate, and during a Life of continu'd
Variety for Threescore Years, besides her Childhood, was Twelve Year
a *Whore,* five times a *Wife* . . . Twelve Year a *Thief,* Eight Year a
Transported *Felon* in *Virginia,* at last grew *Rich,* liv'd *Honest,* and
died a *Penitent.*" In McCarthy's memoirs, the curious insistence that
life, much less sex, "make sense," and that she herself, having not
always acted nobly, be exonerated by the 'fact' that she was driven by
forces beyond her control, places her confessions in the same tradition.
The fond hope that life make sense sets the stage for one pratfall after
another; and a picaresque life of pratfalls, as readers of *Memories of
a Catholic Girlhood, How I Grew,* and *Intellectual Memoirs,* have
surely noticed, is how Mary McCarthy ultimately reads her life.

It is a reading that contributes to the peculiar sense one gets from
McCarthy's character, as well as from her prose and politics, that she
stands somehow above the fray, outside the consequences that attend
other people's participation in the banquet of just deserts. It is not that
she doesn't take large bites of life, but that when she comes up with
gristle, she doesn't suffer for it. In this, McCarthy really does resemble
Moll Flanders, who speaks with abhorrence of her former life, and
engages in frequent self-reproach, but invariably distinguishes her 'sinful' behavior from her essential self, which remains untainted by the
influences around her. Like Moll (the London street name for Mary),
McCarthy was generally well served by men, including Edmund Wilson, despite his boorishness as a husband and his cruelty when drinking. She flatters them and they assist her, and thus she is a product of
that earlier generation's world, where women gave and got more than
either men or women do today. But she remains untouched by experience, a free spirit, spotless, like the "slab of white lamb on an altar,"
that Meg Sargent envisions herself to be in "The Man in the Brooks
Brothers Shirt." And this, perhaps, is her 'fatal flaw.' She leads a
charmed life.

Epilogue

"So we'll go no more a-roving

So late into the night."

—LORD BYRON

Mary McCarthy died on October 25, 1989. Her death caught me by surprise, as it did many people who knew her well. "She was seventy-seven and did not want to die and, indeed, had no intention of dying," her Paris neighbor Jane Kramer wrote in her obituary. "She considered illness an intrusion into her life-in-progress and into the gallant householding of her old age," which was why it was hard for Mary's friends, Kramer noted, "to summon the appropriate platitudes about a long full life or a life achieved or a life completed."

It was true, Mary McCarthy wore her age and infirmities—water on the brain, an arthritic condition of the spine, breast cancer, heart problems, emphysema—lightly; until the lung cancer that killed her six weeks after it was diagnosed left her hooked to a respirator for a month in New York Hospital, unable to speak or eat. And even then, embedded in her nest of wires and tubes, with a breathing tube sutured to her larynx jutting out from between dry lips, her eyes stood at attention, all the life in her concentrated in their gray-green depths.

There were two halves to the face one saw in the elevated hospital bed in the fall of 1989: the bottom, gagged, while the upper, with its smooth brow and expressive gaze, suggested a triumph of mind over mutating matter. When I first visited Mary on October 6 in the intensive care unit, which was not the "blinking, beeping technological" wasteland Jane Kramer imagined, but more prosaic, her eyes appeared translucent, as if rinsed of their pigment. "It's like Grand Central Station out there in the nurse's station," I told her after standing awhile by her bed, holding her hand, carrying on an unaccustomed one-way conversation that was answered by her eyes, which crinkled with warmth, welled up with tears when I couldn't hold back mine, shut, opened wide, like the eyes of a child, bravely swallowing her medicine. One of the nurses was reading the *National Enquirer,* another the *Star,* I reported; there was a constant bustle of doctors, visitors, orderlies pushing trays of medication in and out of the ante-room, separated by a glass partition from McCarthy's bed. "I thought it would be worse, more alienating," I said, searching for the saving grace in the nightmare scene.

It was a big-city hospital with big-city ways. One could get lost in the catacomb of tunnels and elevators connecting the Baker Pavillion, where McCarthy lay, with the other wings and buildings, and during the first of several visits, I did. So this is New York Hospital, I thought, where Mary had her appendix out in 1935, her nervous breakdown in June 1938, and her baby on Christmas Day in 1938. In the spring of 1986, she had come for a nuclear magnetic resonance test after returning from a reading in Denver, Colorado, which had left her "a bit tired and [maybe] affected by the altitude," she wrote me then. The test had come out "alarmingly well," she said—impressed, as always, with the technological side of medicine, which allowed her to measure her sense of her condition against the vaunted objectivity of the machine— "[t]hat is, there's something . . . the matter with me subjectively but no sign of it in this supposedly ultra-accurate test."

When a series of tests undertaken at the end of McCarthy's fall 1988 semester at Bard disclosed an obstructed artery in her hip, which her doctors suggested might be contributing to her unsteadiness, she had checked into New York Hospital for surgery that, for a brief period, seemed to signal a turnaround. "She much enjoyed the operation; she found it very educational," Margo Viscusi told me at the time. She liked the young Italian physician, who was very attractive, Mary said afterwards; and she had regretted the curtain that prevented her from watching what he was doing and merely allowed her to follow his commentary to the attending resident. There were ten people who had come in and out of the operating room, and she had watched them all, noting their different shades of skin color and contrasting uniforms. A few days later, before the stitches were removed, she had walked a mile through Central Park on the arm of her old friend Niccolò Tucci.

If McCarthy's health problems had been restricted to the hydrocephalic condition and the chronic unsteadiness she suffered as a result of stenosis of the spine, or even the emphysema that led her to finally lay down her Lucky Strikes, she might have threaded her way through the shoals of old age to the plateau of eightysomething, but the problems included cancer. In the fall of 1987, she had had a small cancerous lump removed from her breast, the second such occurrence (the first had been ten years before); and back in France, she had commuted to a clinic outside Paris for radiation treatments, five days a week for six weeks. Medical events of this sort were reported laconically. In February 1988, she wrote me that the radiotherapy, whose progress was monitored by X rays and blood counts, was going well. The cancer was very small in the first place, she pointed out, adding that when the lymph nodes were examined, the report was "a hundred percent perfect. So that is all right." Outside the French clinic, two pink camellia bushes had started to bloom, making her nostalgic, she said, for the Pacific Northwest.

But everything wasn't all right. In April 1988, McCarthy had experienced the telltale symptoms of oxygen depletion, and the doctors had administered cortisone. When shortly afterwards she was hospitalized for a chest infection, and drip-fed antibiotics, she had three cardiac episodes in succession and was sent to intensive care. "With a little treatment, that seems to be all right now," she assured me in May 1988, noting simply that henceforth she would be on nitroglycerine. On her way back to the United States and Castine, after stopping in New York to see her American physician, she had gone to Smith College to receive an honorary degree. The cancer in the lung had not been spotted, though emphysema had; but she was slowing down—not in her travel commitments ("The more precarious life became," Jane Kramer rightly observed, "the more adventurous she became") but in the degree of concentration she mustered for a task, whether it was being interviewed or preparing a meal.

The pattern of moving from hospital bed to airplane, lecture hall, and desk was repeated the following year when, after having been operated on for the obstructed artery, McCarthy flew back to Paris and threw herself into a schedule of full-time writing. Returning to the United States in the spring of 1989, she traveled to two more colleges to accept honorary degrees, Colby College and Tulane, and then to Yale to deliver a lecture. The spring writing stint on her memoirs brought her up to 1938 and marriage to Edmund Wilson, and also yielded a reminiscence of Niccolò Tucci, whose collection of short stories, *The Rain Came Last,* was published in 1990 with an introduction by Mary McCarthy.

The essay on Tucci was a familiar exercise, one Mary had performed for Nicola Chiaromonte in the preface to his *The Worm of Consciousness*: the attempted rescue of a minor writer, who was a major friend, from relative obscurity. Half-Florentine, half-Russian, related to Tolstoy's wife on his mother's side, and since the mid-1940s an American citizen, Tucci is "an international man," McCarthy suggests, who as a writer of English (a second language) reminds her of Conrad and Nabokov. The reminiscence allowed her to include a personal memoir of "Hiroshima summer" in 1945, when she first got to know Tucci, whose importance to McCarthy's intellectual development came from having introduced her to Simone Weil in the reading room of the New York Public Library early in 1945.

The summer is recalled in loving detail: Dwight living in "the fish house" in North Truro, Chiaromonte in a blue ruffled apron, sweeping out the cottage above Dyer's Hollow beach that he shared with his wife, Miriam, where Tucci stayed; Jim Agee and Philip Rahv joining in the beach picnics at night around the fire to talk about (among other things) Tolstoy and Dostoevsky. One is reminded, perversely, of Eliot's couplet in "The Love Song of J. Alfred Prufrock": "In the room the women come and go / talking of Michelangelo." But the passage perfectly illustrates the premise behind the intellectual autobiography that occupied McCarthy's last eight years, which is that the life of the mind, like the acquisition of new ideas, is a distillation of personal encounters, usually with people, sometimes with books, more often with both. *Place* is as important as the encounter; thus, to summon up a stage in the formation of one's sensibility—which is intellect in the broadest sense, with feeling—one reconstructs the scene: One tells the story.

In the introduction to Tucci's book, McCarthy recounts how she came to suspend, at least for a while, her habit of polarizing everything into good and bad after reading Simone Weil's *"L'Iliade, ou le poème de la force"* in 1945. Homer's *Iliad* serves as an allegory for the fall of France in 1940, yet the correspondences are not exact. Hatred of the victors and grief for the defeated are palpable in Weil's text, but "Greeks" didn't translate into "Nazis" or "Trojans" into "anti-Nazis." In Weil's thinking, "there was no place for equal signs," McCarthy recalls. "Her subject was force . . . always fearsome, always at fault, whoever wielded it, Hector or Achilles. One of the most beautiful moments in the essay," McCarthy notes, "is the account of the quiet meeting between Priam and Achilles—Hector's father and Hector's killer. I was used to thinking in opposites," she reflects, "and

I can date a radical change in my mental life from the meeting with Tucci in the reading-room, which led to my translating the essay for Dwight's magazine [*politics*]. That was on Cape Cod, in Truro, during the Hiroshima summer; I took my typewriter to the beach and got sand in it."

In May 1989, McCarthy had gone down to New York to be inducted into the American Academy and Institute of Arts and Letters, the highest honor she received after winning both the National Medal for Literature and the MacDowell Medal in 1984. In New York, someone gave a party for her where Jane Kramer remembers her sitting "on a pale sofa in a new silk pleated suit, receiving friends, nodding her acknowledgements like a materfamilias of New York literary life, loving the congratulations and the compliments." Jim West watched her from across the room; all the traveling and talking were wearing her down, but he couldn't stop her, and she wouldn't stop herself. It made him angry, Kramer relates, but then Mary "caught his eye and shot him a dry, complicated, complicitous look, and he shrugged and said, 'What the hell. Why not?' . . . He knew as well as anyone that she needed that last high roll. It was a kind of remission for her."

When I went up to Castine to see Mary McCarthy in the summer of 1989, as I had every summer since 1985, though this time it was no longer to interview her for this biography but to discuss another project, I could see she was slipping. Not intellectually—she still welcomed the opportunity our talks presented for sifting through an old debate, though even more than usual it was the personal intrigues among the literati that interested her as much as the issues involved. Her curiosity about people who played no role in her personal life, or people who were not artists, writers, historic figures, remained distressingly slight; but she herself had developed an acute sense of her own insignificance in the larger scheme of things.

"We all live our lives more or less in vain," she had said in her acceptance speech for the MacDowell award. It was "the normal common fate, and the fact of having a small *name* should not make us hope to be exceptions, to count for something or other." Reviewing her career had convinced McCarthy that as a person and a writer she had "had little effect, in the sense of improving the world I came into or even of maintaining a previous standard." Looking around her, she could see "deterioration in nearly every department of life. The very belief in progress which animated my youth," she said, "has left us," except in the proliferation of labor-saving devices: Cuisinarts, word processors, etc., which she steadfastly opposed.

"I like labor-intensive implements and practices . . ." she declared. "In word production, housekeeping, gardening, reading, I actually believe that the amount of labor that goes into a human manufacture determines the success of the enterprise." Nor would she surrender principle to convenience and use a credit card, which she opposed on political grounds, because she was "against the forced registration of citizens," and because she thought you should pay as you go. (Jim West went along with this, and the two of them often traveled with enormous wads of cash.) Only on a big issue could she have "the slightest influence," McCarthy told the MacDowell audience, and yet it was her conviction, "learned from literature, in particular from Shakespeare . . . that the small issues, the seemingly unimportant, why-bother issues, are the nub and pith of experience. . . . Where, beyond the practice of ordinary daily life," she wondered, "will principle get any training for an emergency?"

This swan song for failing to leave the world a better place was a reflection, I think, of the doubt McCarthy harbored about the lasting value of her literary work. "At best," she concluded, "we writers, artists in general, give pleasure to some, and the pleasure we have offered our readers comes to seem a sort of bribe that will persuade them to listen to us when no pleasure is involved"—as when she went to Vietnam and wrote about the war "to turn around some of the readers of The Group" (when, indeed, few noticed). But is this why writers, novelists, in particular, write? Along with giving pleasure, isn't there also the challenge of foraging on the frontiers of human experience, possibly modifying the common culture via an unforgettable character or an innovation in language? While the writer turned pundit or reformer is common in American letters, the development usually signals a failure of creative nerve.

When I visited McCarthy in July 1989, it was in the kitchen, where her hands no longer kneaded a piece of dough with the same dexterity, and on the living room couch, where we discussed her twenty-five-year correspondence with Hannah Arendt, that I noticed gaps in her attention. The summer before she had baked beans for Jessie and Clement Wood when they visited Castine, leaving them, as always, with the impression of a woman who "felt very well in her skin." But this summer she appeared distracted. Jim West, whose caustic humor was more abrasive than usual, seemed to be struggling with a kind of moral exhaustion, if not a physical one. There weren't as many guests, but Kevin McCarthy later brought his family, and Reuel and his second wife and child had visited. To her husband, Mary had occasionally complained of respiratory pains, but when he urged her to see the doctor in Bangor, she declined. Toward the end of August, she had assembled her books and papers for the fourth teaching semester at Bard; Jim had tended the gardens, looked after the house, and packed the 1963 Mercedes for the long drive south to Red Hook.

A few weeks into her classes—two, one on D. H. Lawrence, another on modern criticism—McCarthy experienced extreme difficulty breathing and was rushed to Dutchess County Hospital, where cancer cells were found in her lungs. Just before leaving, she had telephoned her Allandale Road neighbor, Fred Dupee's widow, Andy, to say they wouldn't be having dinner together at Vassar that weekend, as planned, with Robert Pounder, a classics professor and assistant to Vassar's president, and Vincent Giroux, the French translator of *How I Grew,* two new friends Mary had made in recent years. When Eve Stwertka reached her at the hospital, she said she had never felt worse, she had " 'never been so sick before.' Coming from her that really meant something," Stwertka reflected later. Her lungs were rapidly filling with fluid, and three days later she was transported by ambulance to New York Hospital, where emergency drainage procedures were begun. There her lungs had collapsed while she lay on a stretcher awaiting a CAT scan, in the company of Elizabeth Hardwick, who would sit beside Mary nearly every night after the other visitors had left, until the end.

"I would long ago come to New York to see a lover, then to see a psychoanalyst, then an editor or publisher, then a lawyer, and finally the dentist," McCarthy wrote some friends in 1969; "I can't quite make this work out to the Seven Ages of Man." Now, with her arrival at New York Hospital in September 1989, she had come back to die.

The second weekend I went down to the city from Maine to visit Mary in the intensive care unit, I knew where to go. The Grand Central feeling had slipped into the room itself, which was fully occupied. Standing beside McCarthy's bed, I overheard someone ask the patient behind me, a dark-skinned man, whether he had tried to kill himself. Did he have sex with someone who might have AIDS? the voice asked. Was he seeing a psychiatrist? Had he tried to kill himself before? Mary was dozing through the effects of a morphine injection; her hand felt light in mine; a white rose from the garden in Maine was taped to the bed rail, an offering from a neighbor visiting from Castine; periodically her face screwed up in pain, but it was a pain from inside, not outside the body's defenses; I don't think she heard what I had overheard (though the dying are said to hear everything), and of course I never mentioned it. Nor did I say that the blue corrogated tube hooked up to the respirator, which was now supplying 80 to 100 percent of her oxygen, looked like one of the giant ducts jutting out of the manholes outside on East End Avenue—though it was the kind of detail she would have noticed.

I wondered whether during the hours she lay awake in her bed, in between the visits of friends and family, doctors, nurses, and social workers, including a 'gray lady' who glided between the beds dispensing spiritual consolation, she followed the death dramas unfolding around her. Did she know it when the man in the next bed died the following night? Or was she already preparing for her own death? Death must be gotten through just as life is gotten through; chances are she would no more muddle through hers than she had muddled through life. When her friends were gone, and her son, brothers, and husband had left, and the 'famous doctor,' John Murray, a San Francisco lung specialist and the husband of novelist Diane Johnson, who flew in from California at the eleventh hour, had done what he could, would the patient be left to do it alone? A paradox, the noun *patient*: "one that is acted upon," from the Latin *pati*: "to suffer"; and yet all the resources of the adjective, "bearing pains or trials calmly . . . manifesting forbearance under provocation or strain," are needed to die.

On October 13, standing in the nurses' station, I watched Jim West lean over Mary's bed to show her something. She looked up but gave no sign of recognition. He bent closer and spoke; there was a small response. Afterwards, he showed me what he had brought her: a calling card, yellowed with age, with the word *love* written inside a heart stamped at the center, and the initials *M* and *J* inscribed at opposite ends of an invisible arrow. Jim told me the card had always stood for something between them, but that then, even though her eyes were open, only when he told Mary what it was, did she smile in recognition.

There was still talk of removing the breathing tube, if only for a short time, so that Mary could speak, although when it had been done two weeks before, she had lasted only three minutes before gasping for breath. Jim carried a little tape recorder for when the moment might arrive. I fell into the false dawn of hope myself that weekend, when Mary's dying was still unthinkable. When I went in to see her, I told her what she had no doubt heard herself, that the small tubes then draining her lungs were to be removed from her chest, and that after a new drug was administered to make the pleural lining "stick" to the chest wall, hopefully by Monday (*hopefully,* a word McCarthy detested), she might be unhooked from the respirator.

Her eyes widened with excitement, and anticipation and pleasure were plain on her face. It pains me to think of it, for even then I felt I was deceiving her. But Mary, I understand now, was still in the grip of life. "People can be so mighty bad and get better," muses the old woman in Dorothy Richardson's story "Death." "While there's life there's hope." Mary, I think, was seesawing between her indomitable will to live, to surmount difficulties, and the unfamiliar challenge of letting go, of entering a dark night of the soul that lies beyond the flicker of consciousness—a state of nature that never had aroused much interest in her, possibly because it makes no appeal to the intellect or the senses. ("I cannot bear the thought of that accumulation of so many beautiful things seen and heard, books read and written, and then bang, it's gone, destroyed!" Jim West remembered her exclaiming on a rare occasion when they had talked about death.)

The breathing tube was never removed; "a touch of peritonitis" had already set in, and the cancer was "ferocious," the size of a grapefruit, a nurse reported. One lung was permanently collapsed, the other failing. The next day, Saturday, I spoke 'hopefully' again. Standing beside her bed, holding her hand in both of mine, feeling for her weak pulse, I told her I would try to see her the following night, something I already knew was going to be impossible. It was the last time I saw her. Her eyes were closed and I concentrated on sending a message through my hands. Jim West, who was standing on the opposite side of the bed, said, "We're going to leave now," but Mary didn't respond. Then he asked her whether it was all right to go, and she nodded and gave my hand the faintest squeeze. Her eyes opened and focused on mine. There was recognition.

I have copied the last five sentences from a notebook I kept, changing only the tense. I still can't duck beneath the protective cover of the record to say what I felt, and feel, about the terrible death of this valiant woman. Knowing her, I fear she wondered what she had done to deserve it. For Mary McCarthy, speech was golden, an instrument of conquest as well as a medium for the refinement of perception. More than for most, the lively narration was an affirmation of self. After her death, it is her conversation one remembers, husky, imperious, full of swoops and swerves and invisible italics. Very little in her ever seemed to grow old, but especially was this true of her voice, the seat of expression for the endless delight she took in the oddities of life. To have been deprived of it—to stare out at old friends and family from her deathbed and not be able to speak—was a punishing cruelty.

Unlike Hannah Arendt, Mary McCarthy did not go peacefully into her last good night. During the final week she had gestured violently to remove the breathing tube; Jim West had persuaded her to leave it in place, but she had made her wishes known, and the legal ground was established for terminating the life-support system. Unlike Philip Rahv, however, Mary McCarthy did not die 'alone' or 'forgotten.' Upon her death, one would not think to "Sing of human unsuccess / In a rapture of distress," as Arendt had done at Auden's funeral. The memorial service that Harcourt Brace Jovanovich organized for her at the Morgan Library on November 11 overflowed into the halls and lobby. The October 31 funeral in Castine, in the triangular white Unitarian Church only a short walk from the cemetery overlooking Penobscot Bay where she is buried, might have pleased her.

"Insofar as I, a believing atheist, have a foot in any religion," she wrote toward the end of her life, "I am a Protestant . . . and when I die I hope that some kindly Protestant pastor will say last rites over me even though I am outside his church"—which he had. The retired Reverend Ed Miller conducted the simple service, which drew on McCarthy's love for the Easter ceremony, with its allusion to suffering, death, and rebirth. "I wish I believed in redemption, but I can't," she lamented in a short memoir written for *Boston College Magazine,* which the Jesuits didn't publish, reportedly because it arrived too late for the issue devoted to writing and religious training, but also perhaps because it came down so hard on Catholicism ("a stale, sour canting mixture of prejudice and ignorance, totally devoid of brotherly love"). And yet it shook her, she said, to hear the *Qui tollis peccata mundi* ('Who takes away the sins of the world') of the Agnus Dei. And that, together with the "Alleluliah" and the Easter hymn, with its correspondence to spring, McCarthy's favorite—"Forth He came at Easter, like the risen grain"—were sung by the congregation and performed by the trio of musicians at the service. The church, too, was filled to overflowing, this time with the inner circle of McCarthy's American friends, her brother Preston (Kevin, whose plane was delayed, came bounding up the cemetery hill afterwards, just as the casket was being lowered into the ground), nieces, a nephew, and neighbors in Castine.

Mary McCarthy knew she was loved, but there *was* something uncompleted about her life, which even more than her awful death made it hard for her friends 'to summon the appropriate platitudes about a long full life.' She felt it herself, I think, and expressed it when she said—apropos the attempt to establish her consciousness of the world, her true 'voice,' in fiction—"I still haven't *succeeded!*" Her frustration is conveyed in *How I Grew,* which doubles back over the familiar ground of *Memories of a Catholic Girlhood* instead of moving on through the 1930s, '40s, and '50s, as one might expect the autobiography of one of America's foremost intellectuals to do. It was as if she needed to return to childhood, to the high contrasts of Seattle and Minneapolis, to awaken the sense of an embattled self that lay behind her most vivid prose. And then she found the childhood gone.

"You can't put together a memoir without cannibalizing your own life for parts," Annie Dillard has observed. "The work battens on your memories. And it replaces them. . . . The work is a sort of changeling on the doorstep—not your baby but someone else's baby rather like it, different in some way you can't pinpoint, and yours has vanished." Or as McCarthy wrote Frani Muser in 1979, worrying over the loss of her memory of "the thirties" and Harold Johnsrud to images already in print: "Once you've written about something, all you can recall is what you wrote."

There is a missing person in *How I Grew*; or the person who is there is burdened with a literary self overripe with emotions already 'tried out' in previous memoirs, stories, novels, interviews. In the successor chapters, McCarthy's *Intellectual Memoirs,* on the other hand, candor about the author's promiscuity and infidelities seems calculated to drum up new business for the conscience—though it ends by leaving the reader with a perplexing impression of sexual alienation.

There is something odd about the protestations of grief in McCarthy's final memoir. Perhaps she owed the longevity of her spirit to the fact that she was an incorrigible optimist, even when she suffered. "Being the person I was, in the midst of my grief for Philip, I was excited by the momentousness of it all," McCarthy writes in "Edmund Wilson" of the dark day of reckoning in January 1938, when she finally told Rahv about Edmund. This last memoir is the only one in which a note of sadness enters. Maybe she was incapable of real suffering. She had schooled herself to resist it at an early age when she was left alone to confront the deaths of her parents.

McCarthy's blind spots did seem to issue from a hardening of the emotional artery that connects the wounds we sustain, and the wounds we inflict, to the brain. She still wondered in 1989, "whether I 'really' wanted to marry Wilson or prayed to be spared it." How could she not know such a thing? What obstructed her vision? Of course Edmund Wilson made her feel foolish, even crazy, a troubling experience; but McCarthy's refusal to admit that she often behaved foolishly, and maybe wasn't crazy enough, remained a roadblock to knowing herself.

Her ability to hurt a friend through the medium of fiction was legendary. In later life, McCarthy sometimes tried to make amends for this, as she did after reading Mary Meigs's account of the pain the portrait of Dolly Lamb in *A Charmed Life* caused her when she read it in the 1950s. "She didn't understand that this was fiction, and that these criticisms of her work are expressions of another character," McCarthy insisted; but in 1982 she wrote Meigs: "It pains me awfully to think of you suffering all those years over these passages. Misread by you or not, they are still my doing," and she apologized for having "grossly invaded your privacy . . . even though I don't know how to rectify and never did. I *cannot* stop using real people in my fiction."

It was the old problem of the novelist's 'indebtedness to life.' To Mary Meigs, McCarthy quoted Hannah Arendt in her defense: "You are a critic, and so you must quote." But Mary McCarthy was indebted to "the ridiculous side of people," her French translator and friend Anjou Levi rightly observes; it was "her inspiration, the core of her humor, and her vision of things." It was this angle of vision, "a sort of distortion, a sort of writing on the bias," as McCarthy herself perceived, that sometimes hurt those friends who were not unaware of their ridiculous sides themselves but regretted the immortality McCarthy granted them.

The same angle of vision kept most of her fiction—though not necessarily her criticism—from reaching the first rank. Too often she wrote from the spoils of experience rather than out of a respect for its mysteries. "Freedom (the subjective) is in the fiction, and necessity is in the fact," she remarks sagely in "The Fact in Fiction," but her own fictional worlds are driven by necessity; her characters are usually not free to talk back to the author. Ultimately, her importance as a writer lies less in her ability to prize great secrets from the relatively narrow bands of experience she traverses than in her extraordinary sensitivity to the emotive power of language. It is her respect for words and their mysteries that makes her literary example worth pondering.

The peculiar intensity of McCarthy's prose, the authority one feels behind its observations and judgments, comes in part from a scrupulous commitment to accurate expression. "The McCarthy 'style' depends for its power on two things," the Maine poet Constance Hunting comments: "absolute precision of vocabulary and the pressing of literary substance to yield utmost immediacy of perception and clarity of emotion." No slackness, no vagueness, no "voluminous drapery," no waste. Perception, emotion, are 'felt' through the medium of language. McCarthy's commitment 'to the word' is something akin to a religious dedication. When all else fails, when the flesh weakens, the spirit falters, it is as if words, with their ancient moorings in deeds, are signal fires guiding the mind's eye to far horizons. Not only in literature but in life, a word tumbling out of a potential character's mouth 'sets' that person on a certain stage. What McCarthy calls, in an essay from the 1950s, "the natural symbolism of reality" is matched for her in the linguistic realm by a kind of natural symbolism in language, sometimes overheard, sometimes created.

Finding the right metaphor to illuminate something murky in the psychic drama is her forte; certainly it produced some of her most arresting images. "Surrounded by friends, she rode like a solitary passenger on her train of thought," she writes of Hannah Arendt after the death of Arendt's husband. Of Hannah herself: "thought, for her, was a kind of husbandry, a humanizing of the wilderness of experience . . ."—which writing was for Mary McCarthy. In a 1947 story, "The Cicerone," Mr. Sciarappa's suspicions have a flickering quality: "the light in him went on and off, as he touched one theory or another, cruising in his shaft like an elevator."

A talent for marrying words from one arena to events in another keeps the best of her memoirs, fiction, and criticism fresh. The images remain, shored up against the wear and tear of reputation. American writers, whose native culture is of relatively recent origin, have often exhibited the keenest sensitivity as to whether their books will achieve immortality. Time is needed to answer this question, usually a couple of generations, certainly more than a lifetime, but sometimes a writer can't wait—as Sinclair Lewis couldn't when he and the English novelist Evelyn Waugh argued in the 1940s over who was the greater writer. " 'Waugh,' " snapped Lewis, " 'have you written any books that have passed into the language? *I* wrote *Babbitt*. *I* wrote *Main Street*.' "

And Mary McCarthy? What has 'passed into the language' from her pen? "The Man in the Brooks Brothers Shirt," *Memories of a Catholic Girlhood*, a half-dozen social and cultural commentaries from *On the Contrary*, some pithy criticsm in *Theatre Chronicles* ("Streetcar Called Success," "The Will and Testament of Ibsen," "General Macbeth"), *The Group*, by popular acclaim. I would add *Venice Observed* and *The Stones of Florence* for the sheer love of finding oneself in a beautiful city that the reader discovers in each. And for personal reasons, because I was there in 1967, and can vouch for a good many of McCarthy's perceptions, *Hanoi*.

But perhaps it was for "swimming against a current," as she said of herself in 1984, that one finally appreciates Mary McCarthy. "The world only goes forward because of those who oppose it," Goethe believed; and McCarthy, the dissenters' dissenter, who played no small part in the forward motion of the intellectual world she embraced—partly, I think, because her roots remained in another, more traditional world—never broke for shore.

Biographical Glossary

By Gilbert Grail

Lionel Abel (1910–   ), longtime writer for *Partisan Review, Dissent,* and *Commentary,* summed up his years with the New York and Paris literati in *The Intellectual Follies* (1984).

Theodor W. Adorno (1903–1969), German writer on philosophy and the social sciences, was associated with Max Horkheimer at the Frankfurt Institute for Social Research. He wrote *Prisms* and *Against Epistomology.*

James Agee (1909–1955) had a varied literary career, beginning with a book of poems in 1934. In 1941, while working at *Fortune,* he published *Let Us Now Praise Famous Men,* about Alabama sharecroppers. Years of film criticism followed, for *Time* and *The Nation.* Then he went to Hollywood and wrote the scripts for *The African Queen* and other films. His novel *A Death in the Family* won the Pulitzer Prize in 1958.

Salvador Allende (1908–1973) was the first democratically elected Marxist head of government when he became president of Chile in 1970. Reelected in 1972, he was murdered in an army coup, possibly with CIA connivance.

Maxwell Anderson (1888–1959), a prolific playwright from the 1920s to 1950s, scored his first success with *What Price Glory?* in 1924. Other major plays are *Both Your Houses* and *Mary of Scotland* (both 1933), *Winterset* (1935), *Key Largo* (1939), and *The Bad Seed* (1955).

William Barrett (1913–   ) has been professor of philosophy at the University of Illinois, University of California, Brown, and New York University. A champion of existentialism, he coauthored, with Henry Aiken, the four-volume *Philosophy in the 20th Century.*

Daniel Bell (1919–   ) has combined teaching and journalism at Columbia and Harvard, and in *Partisan Review, Harper's,* and the *American Journal of Sociology.* His *The End of Ideology* was an influential book in the early 1960s.

Saul Bellow (1915–   ), Canadian-born American writer, is probably best known for his novel *The Adventures of Augie March.* For his urban antiheroes (*Dangling Man, The Victim, Humboldt's Gift, Herzog*), alienated from society but not from themselves, he won the Nobel Prize for literature in 1976.

Walter Benjamin (1892–1940) is sometimes considered the foremost Marxist literary critic of the first half of the twentieth century. Berlin-born, he left Germany in 1933 when the Nazis took power, and lived in Paris, Moscow, and Naples, taking his life on the Franco-Spanish border in 1940 in order to escape the gestapo.

Bernard Berenson (1865–1959), U.S. (Lithuanian-born) art critic who advised the international art dealer Lord Duveen, lived in Italy most his life. His monumental *Italian Painters of the Renaissance* was published in 1952. I Tatti, Berenson's much-visited villa and library in Settignano, was bequeathed to Harvard.

Isaiah Berlin (1909–   ), a British intellectual historian who emigrated to England from the Soviet Union in 1920, he taught at Oxford for many decades. His *The Hedgehog and the Fox,* a meditation on Tolstoy, is considered a masterpiece of literary criticism, but he is better known for his works of political philosophy, including a biography of Karl Marx.

John Peale Bishop (1892–1944), American poet and novelist, was born in West Virginia and lived in New York, Paris, and Cape Cod. His *Collected Poems* was published in 1948.

Louise Bogan (1897–1970) turned out elegant lyrics until 1940, when her efforts went into criticism, teaching, and translation. Her *Collected Poems, 1923–53* appeared in 1954, and *Selected Criticism* in 1955. Bogan was poetry critic for *The New Yorker* for thirty-eight years.

Bertolt Brecht (1889–1956) used the stage to propound his Marxist beliefs. Leaving Germany in 1933, he eventually settled in the United States, returning to East Berlin after the war. Kurt Weill provided the music for many of his plays, most notably *The Threepenny Opera* (1928).

Rupert Brooke (1887–1915), an English poet whose promise was cut short by his death in World War I, was immensely popular in the 1920s when Mary McCarthy was a teenager.

Van Wyck Brooks (1886–1963) exerted a strong influence on American letters from the publication of *America's Coming-of-Age* in 1915 until his death more than half a century later. His *The Flowering of New England* won the Pulitzer Prize in 1936.

Earl Browder (1891–1973), the presidential candidate of the Communist party in 1936 and 1940, devoted twenty-five years of his life to the party, and was expelled in 1945 as a "revisionist."

Andrea Caffi (1887–1955) was born in St. Petersburg (Leningrad) of Italian parents. A lifelong socialist, he led a peripatetic existence in Europe, writing for magazines and newspapers. His work is collected in *A Critique of Violence* (1966).

Albert Camus (1913–1960) was associated with Sartre in the existentialist movement that flourished in Paris after World War II. His early novel *The Stranger* was concerned with life without God. Later he broke with Sartre and went his own way, writing the novels *The Plague* (1947) and *The Fall* (1956), the play *Caligula,* and the philosophical essays gathered under the title *The Myth of Sisyphus.*

Robert Cantwell (1908–1986) had published two proletarian novels, *Laugh and Lie Down* and *The Land of Plenty,* when McCarthy met him in the 1930s. Later he worked for the Luce magazines and achieved some prominence for his original treatment of Nathanial Hawthorne's counterintelligence career as U. S. consul in Liverpool, in *Nathanial Hawthorne: The American Years.*

John Chamberlain (1903–   ) was associated with *The New York Times* for many years, writing daily book reviews, before moving to *Fortune* as an editor. He remained in Henry Luce's employ for much of his life, moving from the left to extreme right, as reflected in his 1963 book *The Enterprising Americans.*

Ramsey Clark (1927–   ), the son of a Supreme Court justice, was Lyndon Johnson's attorney general during the most tumultuous period of the Vietnam War. A lifelong peace activist, he wrote the book *Crime in America.*

Ivy Compton-Burnett (1884–1970) wrote novels that, though not widely read, were highly praised by writers such as Joyce Cary, W. H.

Auden, Nathalie Sarraute, and McCarthy. *Pastors and Masters* (1925) was the first to gain attention; and she continued writing her singular works every few years, while living a quiet life in London.

Cyril Connolly (1903–1974), an English writer, edited the influential London magazine *Horizon* from 1939 to 1950, publishing Bertrand Russell, Stephen Spender, and Dylan Thomas, among other British and French writers of the time. His novel *The Rock Pool* came out in 1935, and among his collected essays are *The Unquiet Grave* (1944) and *The Evening Colonnade* (1975).

Macolm Cowley (1898–1989) was a member of the "Lost Generation" in Paris in the 1920s. In his many years as an editor for Viking Press, he was a major influence on American letters, promoting Faulkner, Fitzgerald, Cheever, and Kerouac. Cowley wrote the literary histories *Exile's Return, Think Back on Us,* and *The Dream of the Golden Mountain: Remembering the 1930s.*

Eugene Debs (1855–1926) ran for President on the Socialist ticket four times. Originally a union leader, he achieved national prominence for his support of the railway workers in the Pullman strike of 1894. He was jailed for his vigorous opposition to U.S. entry into World War I.

John Dewey (1859–1952), foremost American philosopher and educator, taught at the University of Chicago and Columbia University. A founder of the progressive movement in education, he wrote *Child and the Curriculum* (1902) and *Experience and Nature* (1925), among other influential works.

John Dos Passos (1896–1970), the American novelist who was one of Edmund Wilson's close friends on the Cape, wrote the *U.S.A.* trilogy, a national epic that opened Mary McCarthy's eyes to the promise of modern American literature and American radicalism.

Theodore Dreiser (1871–1945) wrote novels seminal to the naturalistic movement in American literature. *Sister Carrie* (1900) and *An American Tragedy* (1925), in particular, advanced his thesis that misfits and criminals are created by society itself.

Frederick Wilcox Dupee (1904–1979), literary critic, editor, and teacher, was long associated with the 'new' *Partisan Review,* and before that *The New Masses.* F. W. (Fred) Dupee, a classmate of Dwight Macdonald's at Yale, chaired the English Department at Bard College and hired McCarthy to teach there in

1945. Later he taught at Columbia, and wrote for *The New York Review of Books.*

Sam Ervin (1896–1985) was a U.S. senator from North Carolina and chairman of the Senate committee that investigated Watergate and precipitated the resignation of President Richard Nixon in 1974.

James T. Farrell (1904–1979) moved to the forefront of American novelists in the early 1930s with his *Studs Lonigan* trilogy. He and his wife befriended McCarthy when she was a struggling young writer in New York and encouraged her to become active in left-wing politics.

Howard Fast (1914–   ), an American historical novelist, was in the opposing camp to McCarthy in the Stalinist/Trotskyist dispute but held her respect. Fast, who later left the Communist party, served a year in jail for refusing to cooperate with the House Committee on Un-American Activities in the 1950s.

Otis Ferguson (1907–1943) joined the staff of *The New Republic* in 1934 and achieved a wide following with his weekly film criticism, greatly influencing James Agee and subsequent film critics. Ferguson joined the merchant marine during World War II and was killed by German bombs in Sicily in 1943.

Janet Flanner (1892–1978), signing herself Genêt, was the *New Yorker*'s Paris (and, occasionally, London) correspondent for a half century. Her essays are collected in *Paris Journal 1944–65* and *Paris Journal 1965–71.*

Waldo Frank (1889–1967), an important American writer in the decades between the two world wars, was a leading radical who went to Harlan County, Kentucky, to support the coal miners in one of their bitter strikes (as did Edmund Wilson and Mary Heaton Vorse).

Christian Gauss (1878–1951) had a distinguished career at Princeton for forty years, first as Professor of Romance Languages and then as Dean of Students. Among his students were Edmund Wilson, F. Scott Fitzgerald, and John Peale Bishop.

Paul Goodman (1911–1972) lectured on architecture, city planning, and psychology at various American universities. He published several works of fiction and an acclaimed book on juvenile problems in twentieth-century America, *Growing Up Absurd.*

Peggy Guggenheim (1898–1979), one of this century's most famous patrons and collectors of modern art, spent much of her life abroad. She was made an honorary citizen of Venice, where

she first met Mary McCarthy during the latter's 1946 trip to Europe.

Elizabeth Hardwick (1916–   ), after graduating from the University of Kentucky and Columbia, began her literary career with *The Ghostly Lover,* a novel, and then established herself as a critic. Her essays are collected in *A View of My Own, Seduction and Betrayal,* and *Bartleby in Manhattan.* Of all her books, Hardwick's third novel, *Sleepless Nights,* was McCarthy's favorite.

Ben Hecht (1894–1964), a Chicago newspaperman and novelist, won fame and fortune in Hollywood writing the screenplays for such disparate films as *Scarface* (the 1932 version) and *Wuthering Heights* (with Charles MacArthur), among many others.

Martin Heidegger (1889–1976), a German philosopher usually classed with the existentialists (though he declined the label), explored the phenomenology of *being.* He was Hannah Arendt's teacher and mentor at the University of Freiburg in the 1920s, and published his seminal book, *Being and Time,* in 1927. In the mid-1930s, when he was Freiburg's rector, he joined the Nazi party.

John Hersey (1914–   ) is an American novelist whose major works are concerned with World War II: *A Bell for Adano* (1944), *Hiroshima* (1946), and *The Wall* (1950).

Granville Hicks (1901–1982), author and critic, was for many years with the *Saturday Review.* Like many of his generation, he turned from radical politics to literary criticism after the Depression years.

Sidney Hook (1902–1989), Marxist scholar, and after 1936 an indefatigable critic of the Soviet Union, wrote and edited more than thirty-five books. A student of John Dewey and exponent of pragmatic thought, Hook's celebration of liberal democracy hardened into ideological canon.

Irving Howe (1920–   ) has written volumes of literary and political history, and is the editor of the magazine *Dissent.* In 1976, he published the widely read *World of Our Fathers,* a portrait of Jewish immigration to the U.S. Howe's intellectual autobiography, *A Margin of Hope* (1982), surveys the world of New York intellectuals with which McCarthy was long associated.

Randall Jarrell (1914–1965), an American poet, critic, and novelist, influenced Robert Lowell and other postwar poets. Jarrell taught for many years at the North Carolina College for

Women at Greensboro, and wrote the satirical novel *Pictures from an Institution* (1954).

Karl Jaspers (1883–1969) taught philosophy at Heidelberg until he was dismissed by the Nazis in 1938. He then moved to the University of Basel, where he taught for twenty years. His three-volume *Philosophy* is regarded by many as a major existentialist work.

K. A. (Kot) Jelenski (1918–1987), Polish-born intellectual, active in the Resistance, edited the *Anthologie de la poesie polonaise* in Paris in 1963, where he worked for the Congress for Cultural Freedom.

Alfred Kazin (1915–   ), one of the 'new writers' McCarthy met in the 1930s, recorded this and subsequent periods in New York intellectual life in *Starting Out in the Thirties* and *New York Jew*.

George Kennan (1904–   ) was a major advocate of the U.S. policy of containment during the Truman and Eisenhower years. He wrote *Russia Leaves the War* (1956) and two volumes of memoirs, in 1967 and 1989. Appointed ambassador to the Soviet Union in 1952, he was recalled at that country's request.

Anna Theresa Kitchel (1882–1959) was a professor of English at Vassar during McCarthy's years there. Her *George Lewes and George Eliot* (1933) was the first biography to approach the famous couple from Lewes's side.

Arthur Koestler (1905–1983), born in Hungary, fought for the Loyalists in Spain, and with the French Resistance and the British Army, becoming a British citizen after the war. An essayist and novelist, Koestler's masterpiece is *Darkness at Noon* (1940). His concern with questions of political morality shifted in later years to a preoccupation with the psychic processes underlying creativity, e.g., *The Act of Creation* (1964) and *The Ghost in the Machine* (1967).

Irving Kristol (1920–   ) was coeditor, with Stephen Spender, of *Encounter* in the 1950s. Since the 1960s, he has been on the NYU faculty and is coeditor of the magazine *The Public Interest*.

Louis Kronenberger (1904–1980), critic and editor, published books on dozens of literary greats from Alexander Pope and Samuel Johnson to Bernard Shaw and W. H. Auden, and was drama critic for *Time* from 1938 to 1961.

D. H. Lawrence (1885–1930), described as a "debunker" by McCarthy, took a jaundiced view of twentieth-century life in his dozen novels, beginning with *The White Peacock* in 1911, and in his poetry, essays, and travel books.

Sinclair Lewis (1885–1951) was the first American to win the Nobel Prize for literature, thirty years after its inception. In 1945, a poll of American critics named his novel *Arrowsmith* as the greatest American novel of the twentieth century.

Henry Luce (1898–1967) founded the trail-blazing newsmagazine *Time* in 1923, and later *Fortune, Life,* and *Sports Illustrated.* When McCarthy endeavored to start her own magazine in the 1950s, Henry Luce was one of the "totalitarian elements" she wished to explore.

Rosa Luxemburg (1870–1919), German Marxist writer and activist, spent years in prison for opposing World War I. Imprisoned again after the war for her Communist activities, she was murdered on government orders.

Archibald MacLeish (1892–1982), poet, playwright, and public servant, was Librarian of Congress from 1939 to 1944 and an assistant secretary of state who was active in the launching of the United Nations in 1945. His play *J.B.* received the Pulitzer Prize in 1958.

André Malraux (1901–1976), French writer and statesman, served in the Loyalist army in the Spanish Civil War and was a Resistance hero in World War II. Later he was Minister of Information and of Cultural Affairs in the de Gaulle government. *Man's Hope* was his celebrated novel of the Spanish Civil War.

Herbert Marcuse (1898–1979), Berlin-born author of *Eros and Civilization* (1955) and *One-Dimensional Man* (1964), taught in American universities from 1934 to 1976. His synthesis of Marxist and Freudian tools of social analysis was immensely popular with student radicals in Europe and the United States in the 1960s.

Harriet Martineau (1802–1876), an English intellectual and writer on women's rights, theology, and economics, was much admired by Charlotte Brontë. She visited the United States in 1834 to aid the abolitionist cause, and wrote *Society in America.*

F. O. Matthiesen (1902–1950) taught English at Harvard while writing books on Henry James, Theodore Dreiser, and T. S. Eliot, and involving himself in labor disputes such as the Minneapolis truckers' strike in the 1930s.

Joseph R. McCarthy (1908–1957) was the junior senator from Wisconsin who added the word *McCarthyism* to the dictionary with his televised accusations of disloyalty in the 1950s, none of which was ever proven.

H. L. Mencken (1880–1956), an influential American critic and editor of the 1920s and '30s, is probably best remembered for his study *The American Language*. He was a longtime pen pal of Theodore Dreiser and an early champion of Sinclair Lewis.

Arthur Miller (1915–   ) is an American playwright whose *Death of a Salesman* won the Pulitzer Prize in 1949. *The Crucible* was produced in 1953 during the McCarthy era and pointed out similarities between that period and the witch-hunts of seventeenth-century New England.

Tom Mooney (1882–1942), socialist agitator and labor activist, could be called the American Dreyfus. Wrongfully imprisoned for twenty years in San Quentin, he was the most famous convict in the world, until pardoned in 1939.

Alberto Moravia (1907–   ), whose realistic novels of lower-class Italian life enjoyed considerable popularity after World War II, is known today for *The Woman of Rome* (1949) and *Two Women* (1958).

Lewis Mumford (1895–1989) was a distinguished American social critic, historian, and city planner. His many books include *The Culture of Cities* (1938), *The Pentagon of Power* (1970), and an early biography of Herman Melville.

Anaïs Nin (1903–1977), novelist and memoirist, grew up in New York and Cuba, and kept a remarkable diary of her life in the literary circles of New York and Europe.

Cees Nooteboom (1933–   ) is a Dutch novelist, poet, and dramatist. Two of his novels, *Rituals* and *In the Dutch Mountains*, have been translated into English.

Clifford Odets (1906–1963) established himself as a major playwright with *Waiting for Lefty* in 1935. Other successes followed before he answered the call of Hollywood to write screenplays and direct films such as *None But the Lonely Heart* in 1944.

Robert Oppenheimer (1904–1967) was in charge of the American team that developed the first atomic bomb. He then campaigned for international control of atomic energy and opposed the development of the hydrogen bomb. This, and his left-wing political views, brought about his suspension by the Atomic Energy Commission in 1953.

John Osborne (1929–   ), the first of England's Angry Young Men, started a new movement of social protest in the theatre of the 1950s. *Look Back in Anger* (1956), *The Entertainer* (1957), and *A Patriot for Me* (1965) are his most notable plays.

Walter Hines Page (1855–1918), whose collected letters provided McCarthy's grandfather with his favorite reading, was Woodrow Wilson's ambassador to England throughout World War I.

Dorothy Parker (1893–1967) was considered the wittiest member of the literary group that frequented the Algonquin Hotel in New York in the 1920s and '30s. She also wrote short stories for magazines and screenplays for Hollywood.

Maxwell Perkins (1884–1947), celebrated New York editor, for many years with the publishing house of Charles Scribner's Sons, edited the manuscripts of F. Scott Fitzgerald, Thomas Wolfe, Ring Lardner, Ernest Hemingway, and Edmund Wilson, among others.

William Phillips (1907–   ) was a founder-editor of *Partisan Review* and stayed with the magazine through a half century of change. Born in New York of Russian Jewish immigrant parents, he tells his story in *A Partisan View* (1983).

Norman Podhoretz (1929–   ), longtime editor of *Commentary* and author of a 1967 exposé of the New York literary racket, *Making It,* castigated Left liberal opinion for the failures in American life, in *Breaking Ranks* (1979).

Burton Rascoe (1892–1957) was literary critic of the *New York Sun* in the early 1930s and drama critic for the *New York World-Telegram* in the 1940s. He also wrote for *The American Mercury, Esquire,* and *Newsweek,* and published books on Theodore Dreiser and on the nineteenth-century French novel.

John Reed (1887–1920) observed the Russian Revolution firsthand and wrote about it in *Ten Days That Shook the World.* A Harvard graduate who became a Marxist activist, Reed returned to Russia in 1919 and died there the following year.

Edwin Arlington Robinson (1869–1935), creator of Miniver Cheevy and Richard Cory, was one of the leading American poets of the first decades of the twentieth century.

Isaac Rosenfeld (1918–1956), after graduating from the University of Chicago, moved to New

York and briefly became a member of the Trotskyist community and a magazine reviewer. He taught at New York University and wrote a novel, *Passage from Home*. Returning to the Midwest, Rosenfeld taught at the University of Minnesota and his Chicago alma mater.

Richard Rovere (1915–1979) was the Washington correspondent for *The New Yorker* for many years. His books include *The Eisenhower Years, Senator Joe McCarthy*, and *The Goldwater Caper*.

John Ruskin (1819–1900), English writer on social and economic problems, and influential art critic, was a towering figure in the Victorian world. His three-volume *The Stones of Venice* preceeded Mary McCarthy's book on Venice by a century.

Bertrand Russell (1872–1970), English man of letters, philosopher, and mathematician, received the Nobel Prize for literature in 1950. An anti-Communist after World War II, he chaired the Congress for Cultural Freedom in the mid-1950s but was accused by some of its American members of kowtowing to Russian peace proposals. His antiwar position during the Vietnam conflict led to the formation of the Bertrand Russell War Crimes Tribunal in Stockholm in the late 1960s.

Helen   Sandison (1884–1978),   Elizabethan scholar and chairman of the Vassar English Department during McCarthy's residence, was a Bryn Mawr graduate and later taught there. She edited the work of Sir Arthur Gorges, Walter Raleigh's friend and the translator of the Roman poet Lucan's *Pharsalia*.

William   Saroyan (1908–1981),   a California writer of Armenian descent, was admired by McCarthy for his vivid characterizations of certain perennial American types in the far West. Saroyan's *The Time of Your Life* (1939) and *The Human Comedy* (1943) are his best-remembered works.

Meyer Schapiro (1916–   ), scholar-critic, whom William Phillips describes as standing "at the outer edge of the inner circle" of New York intellectuals, was known for his extraordinary erudition in all fields of culture and political theory, and his dramatic abilities as a lecturer, both on and off the podium.

Delmore Schwartz (1913–1966), whose tragic fall from literary grace is memorialized by Saul Bellow in *Humboldt's Gift*, was a promising arrival on the literary scene—as poet, short-story writer, and brilliant conversationalist—when he joined *Partisan Review* in 1937.

Max Shachtman (1903–1972) cofounded, with James Cannon, the Socialist Workers party in 1938. This was the leading Trotskyist group in the United States, with moral support from Trotsky himself. Following Trotsky's death in 1940, Shachtman became the administrator of his literary estate.

Ignazio Silone (1900–1978), Italian writer and radical reformer, was an opponent of Mussolini's fascist state who went into exile in Switzerland in 1930, returning to Italy only after World War II. His novels, especially *Bread and Wine* in 1937, deal largely with the downtrodden under fascist rule. The magazine he coedited with Nicola Chiaromonte in the 1950s and '60s, *Tempo Presente*, was secretly financed by the CIA.

Upton Sinclair (1878–1968), prolific novelist and dedicated social reformer, used his creative powers to expose the social injustices he observed in American life. Published in 1906, Sinclair's *The Jungle* attacked conditions in the Chicago meat-packing industry, and made its author a household name.

Sacheverell Sitwell (1897–1988), the younger brother of Dame Edith and Sir Osbert, commenced his critical career in the 1920s with *Southern Baroque Art*, and then turned to poetry, biography, and essays.

Susan Sontag (1933–   ), critic, novelist, and scriptwriter, who followed McCarthy's footsteps when she became theatre critic for *Partisan Review* in 1963, has collected her most significant work in *A Susan Sontag Reader* (1982).

Herbert Spencer (1820–1903), an influential Victorian philosopher and social theorist, was supposed to have popularized the term *sociology*. He spent some time in Venice in the years between the visits of Ruskin and McCarthy, and was less impressed with it than either of them.

Stephen Spender (1909–   ), an English poet who made his reputation in the 1930s with a conscience-stricken poetry of protest, became better known in later years as an editor of the magazines *Horizon* and *Encounter*, and as a critic. The author of many collections of poems, stories, literary criticism, and memoirs, Spender was knighted in 1983.

Allen Tate (1899–1979), born in Kentucky, was one of a group of poets known as the Fugitives, who sought to preserve southern traditions in the twentieth century. His *Ode to the Confederate Dead* has been much anthologized.

Norman Thomas (1884–1968) was the dominant figure in the Socialist party after the death of Eugene Debs. He ran for president on the Socialist ticket six times, from 1928 to 1948.

Paul Tillich (1886–1965), a German-born theologian, taught at several German universities before emigrating to the United States in 1933. In *The Courage to Be* (1952) and other widely read books, he attempted to relate traditional Christianity to the complex problems facing modern society.

Diana Trilling (1905–   ), critic, journalist, and frequent contributor to *Partisan Review*, often served Mary McCarthy as a whipping post in the latter's skirmishes with the rigid anticommunism of her contemporaries.

Lionel Trilling (1905–1975), a noted critic and teacher at Columbia, entered the literary scene in 1939 with his widely acclaimed book on Matthew Arnold. He is the author of *The Liberal Imagination* (1950) and *Freud and the Crisis of Our Culture* (1955).

Leon Trotsky (1879–1940) was, next to Lenin, the most important figure in the Russian Revolution. He was Soviet minister of war from 1918 to 1925. The loser in a power struggle with Stalin after Lenin's death, he was exiled to France and then to Mexico, where he was murdered, apparently on Stalin's orders.

Mark Van Doren (1894–1972) was professor of English at Columbia University from 1920 to 1959, writing poetry, novels, short stories, and critical studies. His *Collected Poems* won a Pulitzer Prize in 1940.

Mary Heaton Vorse (1874–1966) was a labor activist and reporter whose career spanned a half century, from the Lawrence, Massachusetts, textile strike of 1912 to the Hendersonville, North Carolina, textile strike in 1959. She also covered World War I and its aftermath for U.S. newspapers, and wrote popular magazine stories.

Charles Walker (1893–1974), labor writer and translator of Sophocles and Aeschylus, was McCarthy's neighbor on Cape Cod. His books include *Steeltown* (1950) and *Toward the Automatic Factory* (1957).

Robert Penn Warren (1905–1989), an editor of *The Southern Review* in the 1930s and '40s, won Pulitzer Prizes for fiction, *All the King's Men* (1946), and poetry, *Promises, Poems 1954–1956* (1957). He was professor of English at Yale University for many years.

Simone Weil (1909–1943), French social philosopher, was praised by such diverse contemporaries as T. S. Eliot, Albert Camus, and Dorothy Day. She was a schoolmistress and labor activist who joined the Loyalists in the Spanish Civil War and the Free French in World War II. Of Jewish parentage, she acquired a deep Christian faith, expressed in her posthumously published manuscripts and letters.

Rebecca West (1892–1983), Anglo-Irish novelist and journalist, published a book on Henry James when she was twenty-four and, two years later, the first of her many novels, *The Return of the Soldier*. Her reputation as a political analyst rose after World War II with her coverage of the Nuremberg Trials and the publication in 1949 of *The Meaning of Treason*.

Edith Wharton (1862–1937) brilliantly pictured New York/Newport society at the turn of the century, most notably in *The House of Mirth* and *The Age of Innocence*. Mrs. Hazeldean, mentioned in connection with McCarthy's "The Man in the Brooks Brothers Shirt," is the heroine of Wharton's novella *New Year's Day*.

William Carlos Williams (1883–1963), whose literary work has much influenced modern American poetry, practiced medicine most of his life in Rutherford, New Jersey. His verse collection *Pictures from Brueghel* was awarded the Pulitzer Prize in 1963.

Wendell Willkie (1892–1944) was a corporation lawyer who received the Republican nomination to run against President Franklin Roosevelt in 1940. After his defeat, he served as Roosevelt's special envoy to England in 1941.

Bertram Wolfe (1896–1977) lectured on modern Russian history at several U.S. colleges and at Oxford. A frequent visitor to the Soviet Union, he met Kerensky, Trotsky, Stalin, Molotov, and other leaders. He coauthored, with American Communist Jay Lovestone, *Our Heritage from 1776: A Working-Class View of the First American Revolution* (1926).

Notes on the Notes

The principal manuscript collections consulted in the text are abbreviated as follows:

Mary McCarthy Papers, Special Collections, Vassar College Libraries: MPVC
Edmund Wilson Collection, Beinecke Rare Book and Manuscript Library, Yale University: WCYU
Dwight Macdonald Papers, Manuscript and Archives, Yale University Library: MPYU
F. W. Dupee Papers, Columbia University Libraries: DPCU

Frequently cited periodicals are also abbreviated:

The New York Times: NYT
The New York Times Book Review: NYTBR
The New York Herald Tribune: NYHT
The New York Herald Tribune Book Review: NYHTBR
The New York Review of Books: NYRB
Partisan Review: PR
The New Yorker: NY
The New Republic: NR

The titles of most of McCarthy's books are abbreviated after their first appearance in the notes. The editions used, in the order of their *original* publication, are as follows.

FICTION
The Company She Keeps. New York: Harcourt, Brace & World, 1970. CSK
The Oasis. New York: Random House, 1949. Oasis
Cast a Cold Eye. New York: New American Library/Signet, 1950. CCE
The Groves of Academe. New York: Harcourt, Brace and Company, 1952. GA
A Charmed Life. New York: New American Library, 1955. ACL
The Group. New York: New American Library/Signet, 1964. Group
Birds of America. New York: Harcourt Brace Jovanovich, 1971. BA
Cannibals and Missionaries. New York: Harcourt Brace Jovanovich, 1979. CM
The Hounds of Summer and Other Stories. New York: Avon/Bard, 1981. HS

NONFICTION
Venice Observed. New York: G. & R. Bernier, 1956. VO

Memories of a Catholic Girlhood. New York: Harvest/Harcourt Brace Jovanovich, 1974. MCG
The Stones of Florence. New York: Harcourt, Brace and Company, 1959. SF
On the Contrary. New York: Farrar, Straus and Cudahy, 1961. OC
Mary McCarthy's Theatre Chronicles, 1937–1962. New York: Farrar, Straus & Giroux, 1963. MMTC
The Writing on the Wall. New York: Harcourt, Brace & World, 1970. WW
The Seventeenth Degree (includes "How it Went," *Vietnam, Hanoi, Medina,* and "Sons of the Morning"). New York: Harcourt Brace Jovanovich, 1974. SD
The Mask of State: Watergate Portraits. New York. Harvest/Harcourt Brace Jovanovich, 1974. MS
Ideas and the Novel. New York: Harcourt Brace Jovanovich, 1980.
Occasional Prose. New York: Harcourt Brace Jovanovich, 1985. OP
How I Grew. New York: Harcourt Brace Jovanovich, 1987. HIG
Intellectual Memoirs: New York 1936–1938. New York: Harcourt Brace Jovanovich, 1992.

I have used Mary McCarthy's initials when citing my interviews with her. Interviews I conducted with others are identified by full name and date of the interview when first cited, and then by last name and year in subsequent notes, unless more than one interview was held.

McCarthy's most frequent correspondents are identified by initials when letters to and from them appear in sequence; thus, Edmund Wilson: EW; Bowden Broadwater: BB; Arthur Schlesinger, Jr.: AS; Hannah Arendt: HA; Dwight Macdonald: DM.

References to McCarthy's work are cited in the notes, except in the case of fiction and memoir, when the title from which a quotation is taken is given in the text. On the assumption that Mary McCarthy's published work is available to interested readers, specific page references, in such instances, have not been added.

Secondary sources are fully cited on first mention, and thereafter listed by author and title, or title alone when the author is previously identified in a chapter.

The reader will find a working bibliography by consulting frequently used titles in the Notes.

However, some books proved more useful than others to my own interest in reconstructing the historical setting and intellectual tone of the period when Mary McCarthy came of age. They are:

Arendt, Hannah. *Men in Dark Times.* New York: Harcourt, Brace & World, 1968.

Atlas, James. *Delmore Schwartz:* The Life of an American Poet. New York: Harvest/Harcourt Brace Jovanovich, 1977.

Barrett, William. *The Truants.* New York: Doubleday, 1982.

Cowley, Malcolm. *And I Worked at the Writers Trade, 1918–1978.* New York: Viking, 1978.

Dvosin, Andrew James. "Literature in a Political World: The Career and Writings of Philip Rahv." Ph.D. dissertation, New York University, 1977.

Howe, Irving. *A Margin of Hope.* New York: Harcourt Brace Jovanovich, 1982.

Kazin, Alfred. *Starting Out in the Thirties.* Boston: Atlantic Monthly Press/Little, Brown, 1965.

Macdonald, Dwight. *Memoirs of a Revolutionist.* New York: Farrar, Straus and Cudahy, 1957.

Meigs, Mary. *Lily Briscoe: A Self-Portrait.* Vancouver: Talonbooks, 1981.

Pells, Richard H. *Radical Visions and American Dreams.* New York: Harper & Row, 1985.

Schwartz, Delmore. *The Letters of Delmore Schwartz,* ed. Robert Phillips. Princeton: Ontario Review Press, 1984.

Wilson, Edmund. *Letters on Literature and Politics,* ed. Elena Wilson. New York: Farrar, Straus & Giroux, 1977.

Young-Bruehl, Elizabeth. *Hannah Arendt, For Love of the World.* New Haven: Yale University Press, 1982.

Notes

INTRODUCTION

xiii "red-hot gossip": interview with Eileen Simpson, 11/21/87.

xiii–xiv "step . . . counter": Mary McCarthy, *A Charmed Life* (New York: New American Library, 1955), 205.

xiv "radical. . . . tendency": Elizabeth Hardwick, "Mary McCarthy," *A View of My Own* (New York: The Ecco Press, 1962), 34, 38; "lost . . . America": Hardwick, "Presentation Address," Edward MacDowell Medal Award Ceremony, 8/26/84, [MacDowell] *Colony Newsletter* (Summer 1984), 3.

xiv "the attractive" to "her whips": William Barrett, *The Truants* (New York: Doubleday, 1982), 67.

xiv "express[es] . . . life": Elizabeth Hardwick, foreword to *Intellectual Memoirs, New York 1936–1938* (New York: Harcourt Brace Jovanovich, 1992), xxii.

xiv "stinging whip" to "any time": Barrett, *Truants*, 67.

xv Alfred Kazin quoted in *Newsweek* (11/6/89), 91.

xv "one of" to "William Phillips' ' ": interview with Ann Birstein, 3/10/86.

xv "younger Mary" to "those years": interview with Simpson, 1987.

xv "friendly" to "of approval": William Jovanovich to MM, 4/20/70, Mary McCarthy Papers, Special Collections, Vassar College (MPVC).

xvi "real plums" to "imaginary cake": "Mary McCarthy," interview by Elisabeth Niebuhr, *Writers at Work*, The *Paris Review* Interviews, Second Series (New York: Viking Press, 1963), 291.

xvi "neoclassicist . . . romantics": Irvin Stock, *Mary McCarthy* (Minneapolis: University of Minnesota Press, 1968), 5.

xvii "as a . . . perhaps": author to MM, 10/16/79.

xviii "let [me]" to "about [myself]": biography panel, Society of American Archivists convention, Hyatt Regency Hotel, New York, 9/5/87.

xviii "legitimacy" to "evil one": MM to author, 11/4/87.

xviii "self-pity . . . greed": Carol Brightman, "Mary, Still Contrary," interview, *The Nation* (5/19/84), 616.

xix "Human beings" to "contradictious": Lytton Strachey, *Eminent Victorians* (New York: Garden City Publishing Co., n.d.), vi, 350; "attack his" to "careful curiosity": ibid., v.

PROLOGUE

5 "a veritable . . . Rush": Mary McCarthy, "Names," *Memories of a Catholic Girlhood* (New York: Harvest/Harcourt Brace Jovanovich, 1974), 128.

1. A CHILD OF PARTS

6 Roy McCarthy's calendar log, MPVC.

7–8 Seattle history drawn from *Washington, A Guide to the Evergreen State*, the original WPA guide to Washington (Portland: American Guide Series, 1941); Robert Cantwell, *The Hidden Northwest* (New York: J. P. Lippincott, 1972); and interview with Jess Rosenberg, 4/14/87.

8 "The Seattle" to "or two": interview with MM, 8/29/85.

8 "fairy-tale . . . bulges"; "Ask Me No Questions," *MCG*, 201.

9 "working stiffs," "Coon Hollow": interview with MM, 8/29/85.

9–10 Seattle's Jewish history: interview with Rosenberg, 1987.

9–10 "Jewish quarter" to "prejudiced alternately": Mary McCarthy, *How I Grew* (New York: Harcourt Brace Jovanovich, 1987), 102–03.

10 "immaculately groomed" to "Francisco convent": Mrs. James T. Guilford to MM, 6/30/65, MPVC.

11 Simon Manly Preston's lively journals, with their offbeat slant on Reconstruction-era politics, identify this old gentleman as Mary McCarthy's literary ancestor.

11 "the most . . . Seattle": "Ask Me No Questions," 203.

12 For background on Roy McCarthy's drinking history, I am indebted to Carol Gelderman's reporting in *Mary McCarthy: A Life* (New York: St. Martin's, 1988), 10–12.

13–14 "a record" to "'Oh, Roy'": "To the Reader," *MCG*, 11, 14–15.

14 "strange lady": "Ask Me No Questions," 200.

14 " 'How did . . . it' ": ibid., 199.

15 *"everything . . . prayers":* "To the Reader," 13.

16 bonfire and pistol episodes: interview with Kevin McCarthy, 4/18/87.

16 *"that . . . moment":* "To the Reader," 9; "the mayor" to "March 14": calendar log.

17–19 Unless otherwise noted, McCarthy's recollections from "Yonder Peasant, Who Is He?" *MCG,* 35–37, 48.

19 "Come now" to "was dead": "Ask Me No Questions," 202.

20 "waiting" to "this loss' ": "Yonder Peasant ," 38.

20 " 'Poor . . . [them]": ibid., 29.

2. FALL FROM GRACE

21 "beautiful when" to "wasn't there": "Lady with a Switchblade," *Life* (10/13/63), 62.

22 "a Puget . . . college": *HIG,* 29; "jaundice-colored house": ibid., 15.

22 " 'mountain of blubber' ": "A Tin Butterfly," *MCG,* 81.

22 stipend of $8200: "Yonder Peasant, Who Is He," *MCG,* 51; *"one of"* to *"in correctness":* "To the Reader," *MCG,* 17.

22–23 "to roam" to "greater consideration": "Yonder Peasant," 38.

23 References to early memoirs: ibid., 30–31.

24 Memories of Lizzie McCarthy: ibid., 50; and *HIG,* 14.

24 " 'She doesn't' " to *"say* anything' ": "Yonder Peasant," 44.

25 "Laughter . . . compensation": *HIG,* 17.

25 "Surely she" to "of attractive": interview with Kevin McCarthy, 1987.

26–27 "mortuary reminiscence" to "practical results": "Yonder Peasant," 45.

27 "We thought" to "its course": ibid., 46.

28 "his blue . . . his chest": "Tin Butterfly," 56.

28 "consigned to" to "of taste": *HIG,* 15.

30 *"it was"* to *"mystery plays":* "To the Reader," 18.

30 " 'My father . . . you're not' ": "Tin Butterfly," 57.

30 "what the hell" to "on fire": interview with Kevin McCarthy, 1987.

31 " 'Say you" to "a saint's": "Tin Butterfly," 77–78.

32 "and found" to "his hand": ibid., 80; " 'Your uncle" to *"two memories":* ibid., 82–83.

32 *"But who . . . opportunity":* ibid., 83; "You know" to "did it": Telephone interview with Kevin McCarthy, 5/2/87; "the very . . . brothers": "Tin Butterfly," 77.

3. COMING OF AGE IN SEATTLE

34 "A true . . . travel": interview with MM, 9/25/80.

34 "escape," "revenge": *HIG,* 16.

35 "the underbred" to "Protestant father": Mary McCarthy, "Ghostly Father, I Confess," *The Company She Keeps* (New York: Harcourt, Brace & World, 1970), 265.

36 "How could" to "be saved": "The Blackguard," *MCG,* 89. "Sufficient knowledge" to " 'want to' ": ibid., 91.

44 "There is" to "of art": Mary McCarthy, "The Inventions of I. Compton-Burnett," *The Writing on the Wall* (New York: Harcourt, Brace & World, 1970), 138–39.

4. CUTTING LOOSE

47 "the Hebrews": "Ask Me No Questions," *MCG,* 211; "neither . . . society": interview with MM, 8/29/85.

47 "Preston mansion,": Gertrude Rigdon to MM, 11/18/63, MPVC.

47 the "Goose": interview with Rosenberg, 1987.

49 "Catilinian poses" to "but 'Caesar' ": "The Figures in the Clock," *MCG,* 153–54.

50 Information on John McCarthy from Gelderman, *Mary McCarthy,* 50.

49–50 *"The injustices"* to *"above suspicion' ":* "Figures in the Clock," 167.

50 *"L'Illustration . . . Century":* HIG, 93; "I am . . . Life": ibid., 99.

51 Mrs. Preston's family history and character, "Ask me No Questions," 203–04.

51–52 "The soul" to "wicked queen": Rigdon to MM, 11/18/63.

52 "It was" to "passed muster": "The Man in the Brooks Brothers Shirt," *CSK,* 112; "stage . . . beauty": *HIG,* 22; "This body" to "her perspiration": "Ask Me No Questions," 225.

53 "Did she" to *"She succeeded!":* interview with MM, 8/29/85.

53 "[P]roceeding at" to "always good humored": "Ask Me No Questions," 218–20.

55 "medium short . . . pipe": *HIG,* 65.

55 "the things . . . afterwards": ibid., 156.

55–56 "She was" to "be hidden": telephone interview with Barbara Dole Lawrence, 4/13/87.

56 "disciplined habits" to "about it": interview with Rosenberg, 1987.

57 "one-way traffic" to "literary art": *HIG,* 54–56.

58–59 "I was" to "look away": *HIG,* 77–78.

59 "My love" to "born then": ibid., 83, 81.

60 "You might . . . mind": from "For Mary McCarthy," in Robert Lowell, *Notebook 1967–1968* (New York: Farrar, Straus & Giroux, 1970), 12.

5. "TOUCHSTONE AMBITIONS"

63 Vassar joke: Ruth Mathewson, "The Vassar Joke," *Columbia University Forum* (Fall 1963), 10.

64 "and . . . Miss A—": Mary McCarthy, "The Vassar Girl," *On the Contrary* (New York: Farrar, Straus and Cudahy, 1961), 196.

65 "coupled . . . ice": ibid., 195.

65 "The acquirement" to "to women": "Proper Studies," Vassar College commencement address, 1976, MPVC.

66 "It was" to "his beer": "Proper Studies."

66 Another 'highly Vassar remark' is the comment of a Vassar male, interviewed in the Spring 1991 *Vassar Quarterly,* that "people might see us as being elitest just because we're not."

66 "pride and" to "store combined": "Vassar Girl," 197; "Vassar . . . excellence": ibid., 198.

67 "practicing tolerance" to "from them": MM to *NYHT* editor, 2/6/64, MPVC. This draft, identified in McCarthy's handwriting as "other version Belle Rosenbaum letter—not sent," was never mailed.

67 "nice little" to "and angles": MM to Ted Rosenberg, 10/5/29, MPVC.

68 " 'Cum-cum' " to "else did": *HIG,* 197.

69 "charisma" to "us all": interview with Frani Blough Muser, 1/16/86.

69 "We considered" to "says so' ": Eunice Clark Jessup, "Memories of Literatae and Socialists, 1929–1933," *Vassar Quarterly* (Winter 1979), 32.

70 "life [had]" to "understand her": Adelaide B. Preston evaluation, 6/12/29, MPVC.

70 " 'I thought" to "Johnsrud voice": ibid., 198–99.

70–71 "job anxieties" to "hearty breakfast": "Proper Studies"; "for fun": ibid.

71 Vassar curriculum: *Miscellany News,* 1931–1933, especially 11/5/32; Eunice Fuller Barnard, "The College Girl: 1932–a33," *Scribner's* (January 1933), 51–54, Vassar Collection.

72 "Do . . . means": interview with Muser, 1986.

73 "Ladies . . . primitive": quoted in *HIG,* 227.

74 " 'Oh, he . . . bird' ": ibid., 209.

74 " 'Michael,' " "boring": Frani Blough to her mother, 12/6/31, courtesy of Frani Blough Muser.

75 "debonair and disabused": *HIG,* 134; "less . . . alter ego": ibid., 136.

75 "Robert Greene" to "family name": Senior thesis, "Robert Greene: An Omnigatherum," MPVC.

75 "was delighted" to "their butlers": MM to *NYHT,* 2/6/64 (unsent draft).

75–76 "sententious novels" to "as well": Senior thesis.

76 "an almost . . . nerve": Jessup, *Vassar Quarterly,* 32.

76–77 " 'The road' " to "of infants": *Con Spirito* (February 1933).

77 "Nothing . . . wishy-washy": Frani Blough to her mother, 10/25/31, courtesy of Frani Muser.

77 *"con granus salus"*: interview with Helen Ratnoff Plotz, 10/9/85.

78 MM's contributions: "Two Crystal-Gazing Novelists," *Con Spirito* (February 1933); *"In Pace Requiescanes"*: *Con Spirito* (April 1933).

78 "cerebral whoredom" to "seventh row": quoted in *HIG,* 259.

79–80 "She was" to "had before": interview with Plotz, 1985.

80 Helen "Intimidation" Lockwood: interview with Elizabeth Daniels, 10/26/88.

80 "when the" to "best order' ": *HIG,* 206; "Amusing," "squelched in" to "and myself": Frani Blough to her mother, 3/16/32, courtesy of Frani Muser.

6. PORTRAIT OF THE INTELLECTUAL AS A VASSAR GIRL

82 "rejoice . . . being": Goethe, *Faust, Part Two,* trans. by Philip Wayne (Middlesex, England: Penguin Books, 1973), 78.

83 "unusual weaving" to "from Dos Passos": Mary McCarthy, "Politics and the Novel," *Occasional Prose* (New York: Harcourt Brace Jovanovich, 1985), 202.

84 "the worst" to "with me": *HIG,* 249–50.

84 "whole . . . history": "Ghostly Father, I Confess," *CSK,* 292.

85 "[W]hatever he" to "Johnsrud cap": *HIG,* 253, 251.

85 " 'There's a . . . Unbelievable": MM to Blough, 7/22/32, courtesy of Frani Muser.

86 "frivolously deciding . . . say": "Proper Studies," Vassar College commencement address, 1976.

86–87 1929 Freshman *Sampler,* Vassar Collection.

87 "The daily . . . jar": Mary McCarthy, "Living with Beautiful Things," *OP,* 110.

88 "stale . . . ignorance": Mary McCarthy, untitled *ms* submitted to *Boston College Magazine* in the summer of 1989, in response to an inquiry into the significance of religion for Catholic-educated writers, courtesy of Mary McCarthy Literary Trust.

88 *"arresting . . . art"*: "Vassar Girl," *OC,* 203.

88 "convention-defying" to "and skeptics": *HIG,* 256, 255.

89 "rather fast" to "male drive": ibid., 254; "if it" to "O.U.I": ibid., 256.

90 "The difference" to "and dislikes": MM to *NYHT,* 2/6/64 (unsent draft), MPVC.

90 "the Sphinx . . . smoking-room": ibid., 230.

90–91 "I don't" to "don't certainly": MM to *NYHT,* 2/6/64 (unsent draft).

92 "It's all" to "frightened us": Sheila Tobias, "The 'Group' on Mary McCarthy," *NYHTBR* (1/5/64), 9.

92 "I'm afraid" to "to sue": MM to William Jovanovich, 1/9/64, MPVC.

93 "Lean Year Estimates": *The 1933 Vassarion*, 138, Vassar Collection.

94 "an Irish Jew," *HIG,* 229.

7. STEPPING OUT

98 a "mongoose-and-cobra act" is cited in an earlier letter from MM to Frani Blough, 12/25/31, courtesy of Frani Muser.

100 "I find" to "of letters": MM to Blough, 12/7/33, courtesy of Frani Muser.

100 J. P. Marquand: Susan Edmiston and Linda Cirino, *Literary New York* (Boston: Houghton Mifflin, 1976), 230.

100 "John and I" to "clever dirt": MM to Blough, 12/7/33.

101 "Pyms and Cromwells" to "was established": review of Hilaire Belloc, *Charles the First, King of England, The Nation* (1/3/34), 24.

101 "It is" to "swell" time: MM to Blough, 12/7/33.

101 "just . . . Brownings": ibid.; "tremendous tome" to "is interesting": MM to Blough, 1/6/34, courtesy of Frani Muser.

101–102 "I can" to "above: potty": Harold Johnsrud to Frani Blough, April 1934, courtesy of Frani Muser.

102 "second installment" to "over forty": MM to Blough, April 1934, courtesy of Frani Muser.

102 Comments on *The Children's Hour*: interview with MM, 10/29/85.

102 "pansy joint" to "a degree": MM to Blough, n.d. (1934), courtesy of Frani Muser.

103–104 Kevin McCarthy's trip to New York and personal reminiscence: interview, 1987.

104 "what in" to "professional expenses": MM to Blough, April 1934.

105 Evening at Eunice Clark's, and Johnsrud's flippancy: interview with Muser, 1986.

105 "to escape . . . inevitable things": quoted by Alfred Kazin in *Starting Out in the Thirties* (Boston: Atlantic Monthly Press/ Little, Brown, 1965), 14.

105–106 "on the great . . . weather": ibid., 16.

106 "resembled . . . Gable": ibid., 17.

106 "that he" to "to order": "Fellow Workers," *Granta* (summer 1989), 113.

106–107 "different from" to "its subject": review of *I Went to Pit College, The New Republic* (5/2/34), 338.

107 "The reviewer . . . book": Edmund Wilson, "A Brief Guide for Authors and Editors," *Atlantic Monthly* (June 1935), 606.

107 "a gripping" to "won't you": Otis Ferguson, "P.S. to 'Coalpit College,' " *NR,* 343.

107 "adolescents . . . sound": review of *My Next Bride, The Nation* (12/26/34), 962.

108 "a pale . . . 1935": review of *Marching! Marching!, The Nation* (1/15/35), 82; "buccaneering young" to "turbulent experience": review of *Personal History, The Nation* (3/6/35), 282.

108 "special *vigor*" to "Westminster Bridge": Elizabeth Hardwick, "The Subjection of Women," *A View of My Own* (New York: Ecco Press, 1982), 180–81.

108 "a human being" to "their teachings": review of *Personal History,* 282; reviews of *Honey and the Horn* and *The Black Consul* in *The Nation* (8/28/35 and 3/13/35, respectively).

109 "grand . . . strange": MM to Frani Blough, 9/28/34, courtesy of Frani Muser.

109–110 "observation" to "say, *else*": Harold Johnsrud to Frani Blough, 10/24/34, courtesy of Frani Muser.

110 "He was" to "by you' ": interview with MM, 7/31/85.

110–111 "Would yielding" to "baby teeth": MM to Blough, 9/28/34.

111 "A St. Valentine's . . . critics": "From the Bottom of the Kennel," review of *The Company She Keeps, Time* (6/1/42), 84.

111 "the purpose" to "of taste": "Our Critics, Right or Wrong," Pt. I, *The Nation* (10/ 23/35), 468; " 'I can't . . . cares": Pt. II (11/6/35), 542; "to a quivering . . . emotion": Pt. I, 469; "loves romance . . . 'caster-oil' ": Pt. III (11/20/35), 598.

111–112 "pent-up" to "revolutionary dignity": Pt. IV (12/4/35), 655.

112 "job was" to "the past": Pt. V (12/28/35), 718.

113 "starry-eyed Stalinists": interview with MM, 10/29/85.

113 "to which" to "of it": "My Confession," *OC,* 82.

113 "Well, what's" to "Strike! Strike!": Clurman quoted in *Years of Protest,* eds. Jack Salzman and Barry Wallenstein (New York: Pegasus, 1967), 156.

113 "at the . . . mob": "My Confession," 82.

113–114 "The stock-market" to "Soviet Union": Edmund Wilson, "The Consequences of the Crash," *The Shores of Light: A Literary Chronicle of the 1920s and 1930s* (New York: Farrar, Straus & Giroux, 1952), 496, 498–99.

114 "Culture and the Crisis": cited in Richard H. Pells, *Radical Visions and American Dreams* (New York: Harper & Row, 1985), 77.

114 "make eccentric" to "the nation": Wilson to Theodore Dreiser, 5/2/32, from Edmund Wilson, *Letters on Literature and Politics: 1912–1972,* ed. Elena Wilson (New York: Farrar, Straus & Giroux, 1977), 222.

114–115 Orthodox Jewish boys in Seattle: *HIG*, 46–47.

115 Proust in the *New Masses*: cited by Kazin in *Starting Out in the Thirties*, 4.

115 "that great . . . journalism": Delmore Schwartz to Allen Tate, 6/30/38, from *The Letters of Delmore Schwartz*, ed. Robert Phillips (Princeton: Ontario Review Press, 1984), 54.

115–116 "Long-haired . . . effort": "My Confession," 84.

116 "'class' hardness" to "immediate advantages": Kazin, *Starting Out in the Thirties*, 88–89.

116–117 "dark, smooth-haired" to "nasal catarrh": "My Confession," 85.

117 "Lovestone . . . Lovestoneite": ibid., 83; "They made" to "seem tawdry": ibid., 86.

117 "Twenties ideology" to "fun too": "Notes for Thirties Panel," undated ms. (probably 1959), MPVC.

118 "a smoothie": interview with Nancy Macdonald, 10/22/85.

118 "amorous women," interview with MM, 7/31/85.

118 "romantic adventure," "pink ears only": MM to Frani Blough, 1/3/35, courtesy of Frani Muser.

118 "a little Stalinist": interview with MM, 10/29/85.

118 "lest I . . . liberal": "My Confession," 88.

118–119 "There was" to "an alias": ibid., 87.

119 "Most ex-Communists" to "little embarrassment": ibid., 84.

119 "if everybody . . . began": Sidney Alexander, "Mary, Mary, Quite Contrary," review of *The Stones of Florence, The Reporter* (1/21/60), 44.

119–120 "He looked . . . politics": Hannah Arendt, "The Ex-Communists," *Commonweal* (3/20/53), 597.

120 "There was" to "Mount Sinai": Malcolm Cowley, in Warren Susman, *Culture as History* (New York: Pantheon, 1984), 169.

120 "She liked" to "about it": interview with Nancy Macdonald, 1985.

120–121 "a thrill" to "favorable light": "My Confession," 90–91.

8. A TURN WITH TROTSKY

122 "I felt" to "about me": interview with MM, 7/31/85.

123 "Names . . . reality": MM to Elizabeth Biship, 10/28/79, MPVC.

125 "returnable": "Ghostly Father, I Confess," *CSK*, 278.

126 "an absolutely" to "Fred MacMurray": interview with MM, 7/31/85; "If the Man" to "to them": "Cruel and Barbarous Treatment," *CSK*, 20.

126 the sorry tale: "Fellow Workers," *Granta*, 118–22.

127 "A Divorcee on Gay Street: Meetings and Memories," was first published in *Interview* (February 1988).

127 "slightly scared" to "known one," ibid., 89.

128 "Our Actors and the Critics," Pts. I and II, *The Nation* (5/8/37 and 5/15/37).

128 "just . . . world": Farrell quoted in Gelderman, *Mary McCarthy*, 74.

129 "smart . . . hostesses": "My Confession," *OC*, 94; "the only . . . room": "Divorcee," 89; "in lively . . . Museum": "The Genial Host," *CSK*, 146.

130 "Farrell would" to "Carr stories": interview with MM, 7/31/85.

130 Gossip as a form of social history: cited in James Atlas, *Delmore Schwartz: The Life of an American Poet* (New York: Harvest/HBJ, 1977), 102.

131 "I knew . . . to one": MM to James Farrell, 10/5/57, MPVC.

131 "'Trotsky denies the charges'" to "disciplined formations": "My Confession," 96–98.

132 "the most . . . Union": Earl Browder, quoted in Harvey Klehr, *The Heyday of American Communism* (New York: Basic Books, 1984), 360.

132 "the only . . . inquiry": "My Confession," 99.

132–133 "a man" to "is empty": ibid., 104–05.

133 "the whims . . . design": ibid., 105.

133–134 "classic scheme" to "human beings": "Minority Report," *The Nation* (3/11/36), 326–27.

134 "brilliant character" to "in miniature": Alan M. Wald, *James T. Farrell: The Revolutionary Socialist Years* (New York: New York University Press, 1981), 139.

134 "Marxism . . . will": quoted by Edmund Wilson, in "André Malraux," *NR* (8/9/33), 346.

134 "The author . . . general": Malcolm Cowley, "The Art of Insurrection," *NR* (4/12/33), 248.

134 "although Communism . . . Rousseau": Wilson to John Peale Bishop, 9/20/32, from Edmund Wilson, *Letters on Literature and Politics: 1912–1972*, ed. Elena Wilson (New York: Farrar, Straus & Giroux, 1977), 225.

135 "I knew . . . history": "My Confession," 99.

135 "A Plea to Progressives": quoted by Lionel Trilling in *A Gathering of Fugitives* (Boston: Beacon Press, 1956), 50.

135 "dancing . . . honey": "My Confession," 100.

135 "a vaguely . . . personality": Brock Brower, "Mary McCarthyism," *Esquire* (July, 1962), 64.

9. GIRL FRIDAY AMONG THE PIRATES

136 "The unity . . . myth": Leon Trotsky, letter from Prinkipo, Turkey, in *NR* (7/5/33), 201.

136 "straight into" to "to work": "Mary McCarthy Said," interview by, Peter Duvall Smith *Vogue* (10/15/63), 98; "Marxism" to "ballet-dancing": "My Confession," 102.

137 "Mary got" to "went along": interview with William Phillips, 10/25/88.

137 "manic-impressive": quoted in Barrett, *Truants*, 38.

137 " 'They're looking' " to "bloody shirt' ": interview with MM, 8/18/88.

137 "capitalist system," to "rapidly crumbling": Philip Rahv, "Two Years of Progress," *PR* (Spring 1938), 24.

138 "Within the" to "in fascism": ibid., 24, 26.

138 Views on Lewis and Sinclair: Robert Cantwell, "Sinclair Lewis," in *After the Genteel Tradition,* ed. Malcolm Cowley (New York: W. W. Norton, 1937), 119.

138–139 "little corners" to "organism seriously": Edmund Wilson, "Dos Passos and the Social Revolution," *Shores of Light,* 433–34.

139 "The greater art" to "write sonnets": Michael Gold, in *Years of Protest,* 309; "The upper class" to "two nations": Cowley, *Genteel Tradition,* 181–82.

139 The link between commitment and acquiescence is explored by Warren Susman in *Culture as History,* 180. For novelists such as Dos Passos, Farrell, Conroy, Cantwell, Steinbeck, and Richard Wright, however, commitment to a radical vision of American society occasioned their best work. None of these writers wrote firstrate novels during the years of their disillusion.

140 "Stalinism" to "unruffled serenity": "My Confession," 103.

141 "narrow, uncultivated" to "childish": Dwight Macdonald, *Memoirs of a Revolutionist* (New York: Farrar, Straus and Cudahy, 1957), 8.

141 "the *Fortune*" to "have withheld": Wolcott Gibbs, "Time . . . Fortune . . . Life . . . Luce," in *Parodies: An Anthology from Chaucer to Beerbohm—and After,* ed. Dwight Macdonald (New York: Random House, 1960), 344.

142 "I leaned . . . 'doing something' ": *Memoirs of a Revolutionist,* 10.

142–143 "protofascism" to "a baby": ibid., 11.

143 "fellow-traveling" to "Bloody Sunday": cited in Stephen J. Whitfield, *A Critical American* (New York: Oxford, 1985), 11; and William Phillips, *A Partisan View* (New York: Stein and Day, 1983), pp. 47–48.

143–144 "comrade Macdonald's" to "own subconscious": Leon Trotsky, letter in *The New International* (July 1938), reprinted in *Memoirs of a Revolutionist,* 19.

144 "Art . . . itself": Leon Trotsky, "Art and Politics," *PR* (Aug./Sept. 1938), 10; see also Irving Howe, *A Margin of Hope,* (New York: Harcourt Brace Jovanovich, 1982), 148–49.

144 "*Marxism . . . art*": *Truants,* 11.

145 "pontificating young" to "Land Busy": Mary McCarthy, "Philip Rahv, 1908–1973," *OP, 4.*

146 "My . . . lover": interview with MM, 8/18/87.

146 "Two persons" to "for wonder": "Philip Rahv," 4.

146 "menacing" to "to him": Barrett, *Truants,* 34; " 'Yes . . . Ripper' ": quoted in *Truants,* 39.

146 "Philip does" to "his way": quoted in Atlas, *Delmore Schwartz,* 98.

146 "sectarian thirties" to "and arguing": "Notes for Thirties Panel," 3, MPVC.

146–147 "More and" to "profoundest need": quoted in *Delmore Schwartz,* 99.

147 WPA Federal Writers' Project salary cited in Edmiston and Cirino, *Literary New York,* 220. William Phillips, Lionel Abel, and Harold Rosenberg were also employed by the WPA Writers' Project.

147 "He had . . . we walked": "Divorcée," *Interview,* 89.

147 "compromised" to "one apartment": interview with MM, 7/31/85.

147–148 "How describe" to "a feel' ": *Truants,* 6–7.

148 "To make" to "was pretty": interview with Stwertka, 1985; " 'all . . . girls' ": McCarthy, "Divorcée," 100; "Mary . . . man": interview with Stwertka, 1985.

149 "go back . . . livelihood": *NR* (5/15/37), 567.

149 "a veteran" to "to inconsequentiality": "Two Bad Cases of Social Conscience," *Mary McCarthy's Theatre Chronicles, 1937–1962* (New York: Farrar, Straus and Co., 1963), 5–6.

149–150 "unwillingly . . . behalf": ibid., ix.

150 "Mary McCarthy" to "scare me": telephone interview with Alfred Kazin, 7/1/85.

10. SEDUCTION AND BETRAYAL

151 "I remember . . . prose style": "Edmund Wilson," *The Paris Review* (Summer 1991), 71. According to James Atlas, it was Delmore who maintained that Rahv had been so vehement in praising Wilson's critical abilities that McCarthy took him to heart and shifted her allegiances: *Delmore Schwartz,* 100.

151 slinky black dress, etc.: account of first meeting with Wilson from interview with MM, 7/31/85.

151 "short, stout" to "reddish-brown eyes": "Edmund Wilson," *Paris Review,* 12.

151 "more suited . . . magazine": "Divorcée," *Interview,* 100.

152 "Rahv's alter-Iago": quoted in Barrett, *Truants*, 39.

152 "there is . . . bombing plane": "Communist Criticism," *NR* (1/20/37) reprinted in *Shores of Light*, 645.

152 "literary in" to "the Elizabethans": "Edmund Wilson," 13.

152 "Waterloo": interview with MM, 7/31/85; "Mr. Wilson . . . past": "Our Critics, Right or Wrong," Pt. V, *The Nation* (12/18/35), 719.

152–153 "There was" to "bed—*Margaret*": interview with MM, 7/31/85; Marshall as Wilson's "cover": ibid., 8/20/86.

154 "nothing had happened": ibid., 8/20/86.

154 "How shameful . . . is": "Edmund Wilson," 28.

154 "everybody opens" to "any more": Mary McCarthy to Edmund Wilson, 11/29/37: unless otherwise noted, letters from MM to EW are deposited in the Edmund Wilson Collection, Beinecke Library, Yale University (WCYU); "I am" to "you, too": MM to EW, 11/30/37; *"distraite . . . bearings"*: MM to EW, 12/1/37; "the letters . . . *savante"*: MM to EW, 12/1/37; "Last night . . . nun retract": MM to EW, 11/30/37.

155 "a frivolous" to "the mind": MM to EW, 12/1/37.

155 "has been" to "do so": Edmund Wilson to Mary McCarthy, 12/1/37 and 12/2/37; letters from EW to MM in McCarthy Papers, Vassar College (MPVC).

155–156 "Imagine my" to "about it": Wilson to Dawn Powell, 10/4/43, from Wilson, *Letters on Literature*, 397.

156 "Critipher Ichorword's" to "without dope": Wilson to Louise Bogan, n.d. (1938), ibid., 182.

156 "star pupil": Elizabeth Frank, *Louise Bogan: A Portrait* (New York: Alfred A. Knopf, 1985), 74.

156 "sitting at" to "a teacher": quoted in Frank, *Louise Bogan*, 90.

156 "priestly . . . explicators": ibid., 375.

156 "socially, sexually" to "the world": Wilson to Louise Bogan, in *Louise Bogan*, 138.

157 "pretty pontifical" to "a Bacchante": Bogan's and Wilson's letters to Morton Zabel quoted in *Louise Bogan*, 288.

157 "MacSlush": ibid., 291.

157 Wilson and Bogan in bed: interview with MM, 7/31/85.

157 "I hardly" to "they belong": Wilson to Allen Tate, 4/30/37, from *Letters on Literature*, 292.

158 "You sound" to "stuff, too": Wilson to Malcolm Cowley, 4/15/37, from *Letters on Literature*, 286–87.

158 "nothing . . . opinions": Edmund Wilson, "Flaubert's Politics," *The Partisan Reader* (New York: Dial Press, 1946), 298.

158 "and suddenly" to "animal paws": Wilson, *The Thirties*, ed. Leon Edel (New York: Farrar, Straus & Giroux, 1980), 660–61.

158 "queer pleasure" to "and appearances": Warner Berthoff, *Edmund Wilson* (Minneapolis: University of Minnesota Press, 1968), 41, 44.

159 "the sovereign" to "the new": Edmund Wilson, "The Old Stone House," *The Portable Edmund Wilson*, ed. Lewis M. Dabney (New York: Viking, 1983), 16, 19.

160 "the train" to "Oh, very": MM to EW, December 1937.

160 "This . . . painful": MM to EW, 1/7/38; " 'You will' " to "in it": MM to EW, 1/17/38; "Daisy was" to "from Proust": EW to MM, 12/2/37.

161 "I want" to "Miss Marshall": MM to EW, December 1937.

161 "a good move": "Edmund Wilson," 28.

161 "tried [her]" to "for explanations": MM to EW, 11/30/37.

161 "delighted" to "nothing exciting": EW to MM, 12/1/37.

161 "innumerable . . . articles": EW to MM, January 1938; "thought constantly" to "of bed": EW to MM, 1/27/38.

161–162 "a dreadful . . . Positivism": MM to EW, 12/1/37; "I dreamed . . . Stamford": MM to EW, December 1937.

162 "only . . . and me": MM to EW, 12/9/37; "how . . . letters": MM to EW, 1/20/38.

162–163 "to have . . . clerk," "Ghostly Father, I Confess," *CSK*, 293.

163 "picturesque account": MM to EW, December 1937.

163 "they did . . . narrative": "Yellowstone Park," *MCG*, 188.

163 "turn . . . heart": Edith Wharton, *New Year's Day* in *Old New York* (New York: D. Appleton & Co., 1924), 73.

163–164 "for Stanislaus . . . nothing": *Delmore Schwartz*, 99.

164 "Possibly I" to "tell Philip": "Edmund Wilson," 26.

164 "surprised by" to "rescue me": ibid., 21.

164–165 "brokenhearted, and" to "damn thing": interview with MM, 10/29/85.

166 "Your two . . . love": MM to EW, 1/19/86; "so damned" to "old age": MM to EW, 1/2/38.

166 "It will" to "talk about": MM to EW, 1/17/38; "When my" to "his ways": interview with MM, 10/29/85.

166 "Mary" to "stops talking": Telephone interview with Kazin, 7/1/85.

167 " 'What . . . right' ": MM, "Notes for Thirties Panel," 3, MPVC.

167 dialectical tournaments: figure used by Irving Howe in *A Margin of Hope*, 52.

167 " 'the labor of the negative' ": *Margin of Hope*, 41.

167 Bogan on anti-Stalinists, *Louise Bogan*, 300.

167 "new works . . . bale": "Notes for Thirties Panel," 3.

168 " 'Midtown' " to "ghetto-like mentality": *Truants*, 111.

168 "He is" to "indecent solecism": MM to EW, 12/3/37; "the fear" to "late thirties": "Notes for Thirties Panel," 3–4.

169 "We . . . defeat": quoted by Andrew James Dvosin in "Literature in a Political World: The Career and Writings of Philip Rahv," Ph.D. dissertation, NYU, 1977.

169 "I just . . . Rahv": interview with Phillips, 1988.

169 "She began . . . childhood": Delmore Schwartz, In Dreams Begin Responsibilities, and Other Stories (New York: New Directions, 1978), 105.

169 " 'Bunny, how' " to "squeaky voice": quoted in Louise Bogan, 224.

169 "economic slavery" to "at all' ": MM to EW, 1/19/38.

170 "The great" to "their accomplishment": Byron, quoted in Introduction to The Letters of Lord Byron, ed. R. G. Howarth (London: J. M. Dent, 1936), ix.

170 "reading poetry" to "horse-back riding": interview with MM, 8/17/88.

11. AT HOME WITH EDMUND WILSON

173 "I had" to "the pregnancy": MM to EW, 6/16/38, WCYU.

173 "About this" to "other things": EW to MM, 6/17/38, MPVC.

174–174 "As for" to "a seizure": MM to EW, 6/16/38.

174 "as a" to "was alarmed": interview with MM, 8/17/88.

174 "I did" to "insane daughter": Wilson, unpublished ms. of The Forties, ed. Leon Edel, (New York: Farrar, Straus & Giroux, 1983), 114, MPVC.

174 "Of course . . . thing": interview with MM, 8/17/88.

175 "fits of" to "about it": Wilson, ms. of Forties, 116.

175 "such a" to "the edge": interview with MM, 8/17/88.

176 "drinking binge": ibid.

176 "confined . . . time": Wilson deposition, MPVC.

176 "the almost-cured floor": interview with MM, 8/17/88; "Tonight we" to "a genius": MM to EW, 6/16/38; "The metabolism" to "you think": ibid.

177 "He was" to "was sane": interview with MM, 8/17/88.

177 "You oughtn't" to "loving husband": EW to MM, 6/17/38.

177 "I miss" to "things easy": EW to MM, June 1938.

178 moths and frogs: Wilson, Thirties, 706.

178 "It is" to "the world": Vladimir Nabokov to Edmund Wilson, 8/9/42, from The Nabokov-Wilson Letters, ed. Simon Karlinsky, (New York: Harper & Row, 1979), 69.

179 "the desperate" to "female neuroses": Wilson, "Homage to Edith Wharton," The Wound and the Bow (Boston: Houghton Mifflin, 1941), 196–97. Wharton's biographer, R. W. B. Leavis, disputes Wilson's contention.

179 "the Owl and the Pussycat": EW to MM, 1/18/38.

179 "apparent assumption" to "somewhat excessive": Wilson to Maxwell Perkins, 10/18/38, from Letters on Literature, 312; "'The Short" to "was bad": ibid., 10/25/38, 313.

179–180 "Edmund was" to "no waste": Eileen Simpson, Poets in Their Youth, A Memoir (New York: Random House, 1982), 184.

180 " 'I think . . . stories' ": interview with MM, 7/31/85.

180 "Finally, she" to "that way' ": Mary Meigs, Lily Briscoe: A Self-Portrait (Vancouver: Talonbooks, 1981), 22.

180–181 "although I" to "your problems": interview with MM, 8/20/86.

181 "somewhat . . . body": interview with MM, 7/31/85.

181 "horrified . . . there": interview with Nancy Macdonald, 1985.

181 "I left" to "little different": interview with Muser, 1986.

181 "new girl . . . businessman": Wilson to Christian Gauss, 10/27/38, from Letters on Literature, 313.

181 "colossal . . . touching": interview with MM, 8/20/86.

182 "intellectual conscience": quoted in Barnett, Truants, 59.

182 Wilson's vaudeville: reported by Burton Rascoe in A Bookman's Daybook and cited in Edmiston and Cirino, Literary New York, 77.

182 "Marxism is" to "corrupts absolutely": postcards from Wilson to the Dos Passoses, May 1938, from Wilson, Letters on Literature, 302.

182 "serious . . . Post": Wilson, Thirties, 706.

182 "He looked" to "squared-off": interview with MM, 8/20/86.

182 "He . . . sober": Wilson to John Peale Bishop, 2/1/39, from Letters on Literature, 314.

183 Pineville incident described in letter from Wilson to John Dos Passos, 2/29/32, from Letters on Literature, 221–22.

183 "It seems" to "human effort": Wilson to Allen Tate, 8/16/31, ibid., 220.

183 "when for" to "has lived": Edmund Wilson, To the Finland Station: A Study in the Writing and Acting of History (New York: Doubleday/Anchor, 1953), 467–68.

183 "Edmund" to "theoretical reasoning": interview with MM, 7/31/85; "Marx's carbuncles" to "the cowbarn": interview with MM, 8/20/86.

184 " 'Wilson is' " to "no ideas": quoted in *Truants*, 57.

184 Rousuck's bribe and threatened suit: MM to author, 6/27/88.

185 "Partisansky Review": cited in Phillips, *Partisan View*, 63.

185 "I've thought" to "*Republic* editorials": Wilson to F. W. Dupee, 5/16/40, from *Letters on Literature*, 360.

185 "the dullness" to "at all": Wilson to Allen Tate, 9/28/43, ibid., 399.

185 "regular job" to "regular way": Wilson to Christian Gauss, 10/27/38, ibid., 313.

186 Chicago lectures described in 2/23/39 letter to Gauss, ibid., 317; "awfully let" to "little tributes": EW to MM, 8/26/39.

186 "ritualistic visit" to "elicit something": MM to EW, August 1939.

186 "mad about" to "his crib": ibid.

186 "Maybe . . . mentioned it" EW to MM, 8/14/39.

187 "INFANT . . . SAFELY": MM to EW, 8/1/39.

187 "awfully . . . for days": MM to EW, August 1939.

187–188 "Grandmother is" to "into account": ibid.

188 "though I" to "strange people": EW to MM, 8/19/39.

188 "delirious": EW to MM, 8/14/39; "in a" to "miss you": EW to MM, 7/31/39; "Celibacy" to "on me": EW to MM, 8/14/39.

189 "Darling" to "see me" MM to EW, August 1939.

189 "awful words" to " 'miss you' ": Meigs, *Lily Briscoe*, 24.

189–190 "relapsed Communist": *Thirties*, 708; "I knew . . . once": ibid., 717; "I think . . . Roosevelt": ibid., 722.

190 "for the" to "human race": Wilson to Morton Zabel, 11/26/39, from *Letters on Literature*, 322.

190 "an old-fashioned" to "socialist trimmings": interview with MM, 7/31/85.

191 "for most" to "other way": "I Was There But I Didn't See It Happen," *NR* (11/4/40), 633–34.

191 "Please tell" to "less honey": Dwight Macdonald to Edmund Wilson, 3/1/40, WCYU.

192 "third-rate" to "of life": "Saroyan, an Innocent on Broadway," *PR* (Mar.–Apr. 1940), reprinted in *MMTC*, 46–47, 50–52.

12. WRITING WELL IS THE BEST REVENGE

193 "Your following" to "more complex": Dwight Macdonald to MM, 1/26/40, MPVC.

193 "not to" to "the time": EW to MM, 9/13/41, MPVC.

194 "I couldn't" to "when drinking": interview with MM, 9/25/80.

194 "the daytime" to "Minotaur": Meigs, *Lily Briscoe*, 24–25.

194 " 'in a' to "and satirical' ": quoted in Gelderman, *Mary McCarthy*, 107–08.

194 "I finally" to "of it": interview with MM, 9/25/80.

194 "I would . . . him": ibid.

195 "perpetual Guggenheim": Barrett interviewed by Andrew Dvosin in "Literature in a Political World," 103.

197 George North: identified in interview with MM, 10/25/85.

198 "Yes . . . face": Wharton, *New Year's Day*, 72; "only accomplishment": ibid., 73.

200 "But . . . excrement": W. B. Yeats, "Crazy Jane Talks with the Bishop," *Selected Poems and Two Plays of William Butler Yeats*, ed. M. L. Rosenthal (New York: Collier Books, 1962), 143.

201 "It kept . . . story": letter to Fred Dupee, n.d. (1943), F. W. Dupee Papers, Butler Library, Columbia University (DPCU).

206 "Tidings . . . Whore": quoted in Barrett, *Truants*, 67.

206 "brilliant writing" to "some humiliation": Robert Penn Warren to MM, 1/7/41, MPVC.

206 Mr. Breen as Wendell Willkie: interview with Lionel Abel, 9/30/85.

206–207 "You don't" to "complement her": William Carlos Williams to Simon & Schuster, 5/6/42, MPVC.

207 "From the" to "loose woman": Eleanor Widmer, "Finally a Lady: Mary McCarthy," in *The Forties: Fiction, Poetry, Drama*, ed. Warren French (Deland, Florida: Everett Edwards, 1969), 97.

207–208 "save" to "her character": Malcolm Cowley to Rene Blanc-Roos, 6/5/42, MPVC.

13. WAR BABIES

209 "In my . . . Dostoyevskian": Delmore Schwartz to R. P. Blackmur, 1/22/43, from *Letters of Delmore Schwartz*, 150.

209 "truculantly silent," Barrett, *Truants*, 63.

209 "Mr. Schwartz" to "their work": Schwartz to Gertrude Buckman, n.d. (1943), from *Letters of Delmore Schwartz*, 163.

209 "post-Munich . . . feeling": Schwartz, "New Year's Eve," *In Dreams Begin Responsibilities*, 113.

209–210 "withdrawing . . . features": Schwartz to Buckman, 5/19/43, from *Letters of Delmore Schwartz*, 69.

210 "Am . . . down": interview with MM, 8/18/88.

210 "Uncertain . . . good": W. H. Auden, "September 1, 1939," in *Years of Protest*, 226.

210 "the rooms . . . seen": Louise Bogan to Morton Zabel, 5/24/44, from *What the Woman Lived: Selected Letters of Louise Bogan, 1920–1970*, ed. Ruth Limmer

(New York: Harcourt Brace Jovanovich, 1973), 239.

210 "all the" to "symbolic murders": Malcolm Cowley to Edmund Wilson, n.d. (1940) from Malcolm Cowley, *And I Worked at the Writer's Trade, Chapters of Literary History, 1918–1978* (New York: Viking, 1978), 156; "Stalinist . . . sort": Wilson to Cowley, 1/26/40, from Wilson, *Letters on Literature,* 356.

211 "They would" to "state apparatus": Cowley to Wilson, n.d. (1940), from *And I Worked at the Writer's Trade,* 156.

211 "compared . . . Kant": Schwartz to Buckman, September 1943, from *Letters of Delmore Schwartz,* 192.

211 "When the Depression . . . selection": Atlas, *Delmore Schwartz,* 148.

212 "We loathe" to "the war": in Bloom, *Prodigal Sons,* 126.

212 "The psychology" to "doing this": "Notes for Thirties Panel," 4–5, MPVC.

213 "household deities" to "more familiar": "A Filmy Version of the War," *Town and Country* (April 1944), 111.

213 "true feelings" to "learned ideology": "Notes for Thirties Panel," 4–5.

214 "the bourgeois" to "reservations are": Dwight Macdonald, *PR* (Spring 1939), quoted in Bloom, *Prodigal Sons,* 126.

214 "murdered . . . see": Macdonald, *politics* (March 1945), 26.

214 "systematic mass" to "mass crimes": Hannah Arendt, "Organized Guilt and Universal Responsibility," *Jewish Frontier,* quoted in Howe, *Margin of Hope,* 253.

214 " 'I want" to "to be": Schwartz to Mark Van Doren, 3/22/42, from *Letters of Delmore Schwartz,* 122.

215 "politically amputated" to "American letters": Cowley to Wilson, n.d. (1940), from *And I Worked at the Writer's Trade,* 158.

215 "social consciousness" to "rather uneasy": Wilson to Maxwell Geismar, 6/20/42, from *Letters on Literature,* 385–86.

215 "national" to "MacSlush": Bogan to Dupee, n.d. (1939), DPCU, © Ruth Limmer; "his whole . . . Nature": Schwartz to Allen Tate, 5/18/38, from *Letters of Delmore Schwartz,* 50.

215 "political poetry" to "exacting writer)": quoted in Frank, *Louise Bogan,* 292.

215–216 "Butch Bogan" to "Waste Land' ": Bogan to Dupee, n.d. (1939).

216 "Primary literature" to "of progress": Van Wyck Brooks, in Richard H. Pells, *Radical Visions and American Dreams,* (New York: Harper & Row, 1985), 337.

216 "is a . . . secondary": Dwight Macdonald, "Kulturbolschewismus Is Here," *PR* (Nov.–Dec. 1941), 448–51.

216 "perennial nostalgia" to " 'human nature' ": MM, *"The Skin of Our Teeth,"*

(Jan.–Feb., 1943), reprinted in *MMTC,* 55, 53.

217 " 'What did" to "English language": Schwartz to W. H. Auden, 11/16/43, from *Letters of Delmore Schwartz,* 198.

217 "The old" to "the century": Macdonald, "Kulturbolschewismus Is Here," 452.

217 "It's your" to "his audiences": Dwight Macdonald to Wilson, 11/30/41, WCYU.

218 "It's extremely" to "one's father": Wilson to John Peale Bishop, 1/14/41, from *Letters on Literature,* 329.

218 "high-grade . . . gossip": Clifton Fadiman, *The New Yorker* (5/16/42), 73.

218 "Mary's . . . new": Nabokov to Wilson, 5/6/42, from *Nabokov-Wilson Letters,* 61; "Mary . . . nowadays": Wilson to Nabokov, 6/12/42, ibid., 65.

218 "writing intelligent" to "all afternoon": Randall Jarrell to Wilson, April 1942, from *Randall Jarrell's Letters,* ed. Mary Jarrell (Boston: Houghton Mifflin, 1985), 59.

218 "female Stendahl": MM to Dupee, n.d. (1943), DPCU.

218–219 "had arrived" to "Luce organizations": Edmund Wilson, "Thoughts on Being Bibliographed," in *Portable Edmund Wilson,* 114, 120.

219 "the intellectual" to "except ideas": Philip Rahv, "The Cult of Experience in American Writing," *PR* (Nov–Dec 1940), 414.

220 "anti-Hitlerites": Cowley, *And I Worked at the Writer's Trade,* 149.

220 "children . . . night": Auden, "September 1, 1939."

220 "Now for" to "borrowed light": "Ghostly Father, I Confess," *CSK,* 303.

221 "the sick" to "her victim": Kazin, *Starting Out in the Thirties,* 156, 159.

222 "Most men" to "the world": "Portrait of the Intellectual as a Yale Man," *CSK,* 170.

222 "own identification" to "stomach appeal": John Chamberlain, *A Life with the Printed Word* (Chicago: Regnery Gateway, 1982), 105.

223 Babbitts: Louis Auchincloss, *Pioneers and Caretakers* (Minneapolis: University of Minnesota Press, 1965), 175.

223 "You defend" to "others live' ": Trotsky, letter to *PR* (Jan.–Feb. 1938).

226 "members of" to "human history": Edmund Wilson, "Hemingway: Gauge of Morale," *The Wound and the Bow,* 231–32.

227 "Bob was" to "little Betsy": F. W. Dupee, undated memorandum, DPCU.

228 'choose the West': "I support it critically," Macdonald added; quoted by Peter Coleman in *The Liberal Conspiracy: The Congress for Cultural Freedom and the Struggle for the Mind of Europe* (New York: Free Press, 1989), 75.

228 "when he" to "of them": Cowley to Wilson, n.d. (9140), from *And I Worked at the Writers Trade*, 155.

14. THE WIFE OF BUNNY'S TALE

230 "It's . . . in it": MM, *Vassar Views*, February 1982.

230 "Everything . . . published": Robert Lowell, "Flight to New York," in "2. With Caroline at the Air Terminal," *The Dolphin* (New York: Farrar, Straus & Giroux, 1973), 72.

231 "I used" to "there first": Robert Lowell, "For John Berryman," *Day by Day* (New York: Farrar, Straus & Giroux, 1977), 27. Ian Hamilton reports a malicious rumor, possibly started by Auden, that Berryman left Lowell a note saying, "Your move, Cal": Ian Hamilton, *Robert Lowell* (New York: Random House, 1982), 438.

231 "[A]uthors have" to "son's fiancée": MM, "The Inventions of I. Compton-Burnett," *WW*, 139–40.

231 "Whose will-shot" to "bare air": Lowell, "For Mary McCarthy," *Notebook*, 12.

232 "after all . . . him": interview with MM, 7/31/85.

233–234 "new then" to "amusing": interview with MM, 8/20/86. Remarks about Geismar and Kazin from same interview.

234 "maiden . . . Katz": Wilson, *Thirties*, 726.

234 "a pretty" to "of boredom": interview with MM, 8/20/86; "terrifying" to "very shy": ibid.

234 "first stuttering" to "a quicksand": John Dos Passos, *The Big Money*, third book in *U.S.A.* trilogy (Boston: Houghton Mifflin, 1960), 133.

235 "An intellectual" to "repulsive caricatures": MM, "Two in Our Time," *PR* (Summer 1939), 113.

235 "I think . . . extraversion": Wilson to Dos Passos, 5/3/39, from Wilson, *Letters on Literature*, 317.

235 "a community" to "as Katy": Wilson, *Forties*, 221–22.

236 "joke figures" to "beat-up people": interview with MM, 8/20/86.

236 "The white-nosed" to "'like natives' ": ibid.

236–237 Edmund accused Rado: interview with MM, 8/17/88; "a fatal" to "with sex": interview with MM, 8/20/86.

237 "I was" to "quite inngenious": MM to author, 6/27/88.

237 "Her selling . . . Edmund Wilson": Eve Stwertka to author, 11/8/90.

239 "all . . . acceptance": "Ghostly Father, I Confess," *CSK*, 263.

239 "She was" to "familiar demon": ibid., 262–65.

240 She knew more . . . : interview with Simpson, 1987.

240 "Mary . . . worked": Wilson to Nabokov, 1/24/44, from *Wilson/Nabokov Letters*, 128.

240 "an old" to "expensive things": interview with Simpson, 1987.

241 "outraged at" to "old man": interview with Arthur Schlesinger, Jr., 1/6/87.

241 "tremendous egos" to "a lecher": interview with Kazin, 1985.

241 "very angry" to "*improved* it' ": interview with MM, 8/20/86.

241 "sawing motion" to "exquisite music": *Forties*, 25.

242 "probably . . . satisfaction": Wilson to Zabel, 9/10/43, from *Letters on Literature*, 436.

242 "He appreciated" to "chauvinist thing": interview with Daphne Hellman, 7/1/85.

242 "had made . . . Hill": Wilson To Louise Bogan, 3/22/46, from *Letters on Literature*, 438.

242 "He . . . pale-green eyes": *ACL*, 34.

242 "*not* intended" to "red-haired Irishman": quoted in Doris Grumbach, *The Company She Kept* (New York: Coward-McCann, 1967), 121.

242 "I am . . . eyes' ": Wilson to John J. Geoghegan, 9/24/66, MPVC.

242 "Cf. Wilson's" to "E. doesn't": MM's notes on proof page 36, MPVC.

243 "but a" to "those events": MM to Arthur Schlesinger, Jr., 11/13/55, courtesy of Mary McCarthy.

243 "everybody . . . life": quoted in Brock Brower, "Mary McCarthyism," *Esquire* (July 1962), 65.

243–244 "In some" to "would recognize": *The Company She Kept*, 121.

244 "long slim" to "her garden": *Forties*, 26–27.

248 "Sunday afternoon" to "clear-minded, content": ibid., 202–03.

249 "the dread . . . apprehension": MM to Schlesinger, 11/13/55.

250 "Everybody . . . car": quoted in *The Company She Kept*, 117.

251 "an amusing" to "absolutely nightmarish": *Thirties*, 703–704.

251 "It was" to "Scott Fitzgerald": interview with MM, 7/31/85.

251 "sinking . . . insanity": interview with MM, 7/31/85.

251–252 "Plaintiff . . . happened": Wilson's 1945 deposition was not filed, MPVC.

252 "psychoneurosis": Abraham Kardiner, deposition submitted 3/14/45 for separation hearing, MPVC.

15. THE BREAKUP

253 "There is . . . best": EW to MM, 7/13/44, MPVC.

253–254 "I'm afraid . . . away": MM to EW, n.d., MPVC.

254 "not drink" to "two months": EW to MM, 7/13/44.

254 "And all" to "keep Reuel": interview with MM, 7/31/85.

254 "I am" to "of thousand": EW to MM 1/17/45.

255 " 'the deal is off' ": interview with MM, 7/31/85.

255 "the war" to "military correspondent": Barrett, Truants, 60. Wilson appeared to Nabokov in a dream around this time as Winston Churchill.

255 "Even though" to "in aggression": Anaïs Nin, The Diary of Anaïs Nin, 1944–1947, vol. 4 (New York: Harcourt Brace Jovanovich, 1971), 41.

255–256 "form" to "for him": ibid., 79, 83.

256 "been . . . defendant": MM, plaintiff's statement, Wilson vs. Wilson, 3/14/45 (Supreme Court of the State of New York, County of New York), MPVC.

256 "at no" to "toward me": Wilson, defendant's statement, ibid.

256 "bamboozled" to "her illness": Rosalind Baker Wilson to author, 7/5/92 and 7/9/92.

257 "violent . . . jealousy": Liston M. Oak, deposition filed 3/14/45, ibid.

257 "clandestine meeting": Adelaide Walker, deposition filed 3/14/45, ibid.

257 "I had" to "break with": interview with MM, 8/19/85.

257 "Sir . . . DT": (DT: delerium tremens, etc.) Schwartz to Dwight Macdonald, 12/19/42, from Letters of Delmore Schwartz, 146.

258 "ruling class" to "of gold": Clement Greenberg, "Avant-Garde and Kitsch," The Partisan Reader, 382.

259 "very sadistic" to "a dictator": interview with MM, 8/19/85.

259 "That may" to "male rivalry": ibid.

260 "always true" to "she comes": EW to MM, 7/13/44.

260 Rosalind preferred Dawn Powell: telephone conversation with Rosalind Wilson, 7/7/92.

260 "needed an" to "two children": Wilson, unpublished ms. of The Forties, 117, MPVC.

260 "abortive leavetakings" to "the warmth": Rosalind Baker Wilson, Near the Magician (New York: Grove Weidenfeld, 1989), 111.

261 "necessary . . . myself": Wilson, defendant's statement, March 1945.

261 "blind drunk" to "to cope": interview with MM, 7/31/85.

262 "native . . . deny it": Mary McCarthy, "The Weeds," Cast a Cold Eye (New York: New American Library/Signet, 1963), 20.

262 "The problem" to "formidable stupidity": EW to MM, 8/6/44.

262 "Any woman" to "than this": Elizabeth Hardwick, "The Subjection of Women," A View of My Own, 176.

262–263 "mess" to "your forties": EW to MM, 7/13/44.

263 "Princeton did" to "to this": Wilson to Christian Gauss, 5/15/44, from Letters on Literature, 335.

263–264 "I want" to "you are": EW to MM, 7/13/44.

264 "Mary's childish" to "collapses tragic": Wilson, unpublished ms. of Forties, 117.

264 "One of" to "was fashioning": MM to Ben O'Sullivan, 5/13/82, MPVC.

264–265 "always took" to "with him": Nathalie Rahv, deposition filed 3/14/45.

265 "Formidable and" to "not friendly": interview with Kevin McCarthy, 1987.

265 "almost entirely" to "you mad": MM to O'Sullivan, 5/13/82.

265 "[A]n established" to "new sum": Berthoff, Edmund Wilson, 36.

265 "Mary . . . you": Adelaide Walker to Wilson, 9/12/47, WCYU.

266 "hysteric of" to "quite inappropriate": unpublished ms. of Forties, 116–17.

266 "Finally . . . your" to "apparently indifferent": "Ghostly Father, I Confess," CSK, 298.

267 "just the same": ibid. 294.

16. A TIME OF LIBERATION

271 "When . . . void": Jean-Paul Sartre, quoted by Hannah Arendt in Men in Dark Times (New York: Harcourt, Brace & World, 1968), 228.

271 "Ideology . . . bloomed": Howe, Margin of Hope, 133.

271 "Hiroshima summer" to "strange, bittersweet": interview with MM, 10/29/85; "a dividing-line": chronology in 2/22/66 letter to Grumbach, MPVC.

271 "But I" to "genuine radicalism": "Notes for Thirties Panel," 5–6, MPVC.

272 "discovered . . . adopted": Barrett, Truants, 90.

272–273 "was" to "not so dramatic": interview with MM, 9/25/80.

273 "He represented" to "had introduced": interview with Phillips, 1988.

273 "being totally" to "of events": Nicola Chiaromonte, "Albert Camus," Dissent (Summer 1960), reprinted in The Worm of Consciousness and Other Essays, ed. Miriam Chiaromonte (New York: Harcourt Brace Jovanovich, 1976), 52.

273 "a groping" to "the Absolute": Truants, 91–92.

274 " 'We were' " to "fought it' ": Camus quoted in "Albert Camus," 52.

274 "notion of" to "Bauhaus furniture": MM to Hannah Arendt, 10/7/52, MPVC.

274–275 "very quick" to "believed in": interview with MM, 9/25/80.

275–276 "you had" to "back to": interview with MM, 7/31/85.

276 "coiffed like" to "should look": Simpson, *Poets in Their Youth,* 161–62.

277 "I . . . exist": interview with MM, 7/31/85.

277 "the author" to "vigorous thought": Nicola Chiaromonte, "Simone Weil's *Iliad,*" *Il Mondo* (5/30/53), reprinted in *Worm of Consciousness,* 184.

277–278 " 'it is" to "of it' ": ibid., 185.

278 'alien and impervious': Chiaromonte, "Albert Camus," 52.

278 "that was . . . Europe": Brightman, "Mary, Still Contrary," *The Nation,* 619.

278–279 "A satire" to "romantic episode": "The Novels That Got Away," *NYTBR* (11/25/79), 9.

279 "to lead" to "and Reuel": Bowden Broadwater to MM, August 1945, MPVC.

279 "that is" to "his education": EW to MM, 9/11/45, MPVC.

280 "like wasp-cells" to "a moment": Wilson, *Forties,* 47.

280 "she has" to "airplanes range": ibid., 47; "It must" to "Nazi exploit": ibid, 45–46.

280 "I have . . . . another": ibid., 52–53.

281 "suffocating, stultifying": ibid, 158; "queer getting" to "atomic bomb": Wilson to Mamaine Paget, 9/11/45, from *Letters on Literature,* 427.

281 "You . . . me": EW to MM, 9/11/45.

281 "kidnapping" to "return him": interview with MM, 7/31/85.

17. BARD, BOWDEN, AND BROADWAY

282 "Dearest . . . class": Bowden Broadwater to MM, 9/30/45, MPVC.

282 "Miss McCarthy" to "terrific woman": interview with Stwertka, 1985.

282 "a cow-country . . . yourself": MM to Fred Dupee, 2/19/52, DPCU.

283 " 'It was" to "could be' ": comments quoted in Gelderman, *Mary McCarthy,* 126.

283 "guiding light": telephone interview with Norman Mailer, 4/5/91.

283 "very . . . pretty": interview with Stwertka, 1985.

283 "In those" to "to hear": ibid.

283 Lowell and Stafford turned down at Bard: BB to MM, 5/9/45.

284 "holding . . . hand": BB to MM, 3/5/46.

285 "loved this" to "of education": Bard honorary degree speech, 1976, MPVC.

285 "Kierkegaardian law" to "to do": interview with MM, 7/31/85.

285–286 "a smouldering" to "Tolstoy think": Mary McCarthy, *The Groves of Academe* (New York: Harcourt, Brace and Co., 1952), 199, 37.

286–287 "unobserved, Cousin" to *"very* much": BB to MM, 5/25/46, 11/1/45;

"Le Monstre" to 'through *whom"*: BB to MM, 10/7/43 and 10/15/45; "my father-in-law": interview with Simpson, 1987; "Last night . . . all": BB to MM , 12/11/45.

287 "the Master" to "delicate green": BB to MM, 11/2/45.

287 "best stuff": BB to MM, 10/15/45.

287 "got on" to "were ferocious": interview with Simpson, 1987.

287 "very . . . suits": Eve Stwertka to author, 10/18/90.

287–288 "Pvt. Greengroin's" to "to *me"*: BB to MM, 2/27/46.

288 " 'I would . . . him": interview with MM, 8/19/85.

288 "by . . . best": Phillips, *Partisan View,* 143.

288 "I think . . . things": interview with MM, 8/19/85.

289 "Dear . . . desserts": BB to MM, 2/14/46.

289 "He was" to *"Rahvian"* sofa: interview with MM, 8/18/88.

289 "You are" to "mostly hyperbole": BB to MM, 11/15/45; "the shoe" to "loved one": BB to MM, 4/29/60.

290 "Sweet Bowden" to "dematerialized": MM to BB, 2/28/46, MPVC (a package of Mary's letters to Bowden from these years, torn into little pieces, was returned to McCarthy in 1985 via a mutual friend, without explanation).

290 "What a . . . *slim"*: letter from Stwertka to author, 10/18/90.

290 "so surrounded . . . love": BB to MM, 2/28/46.

290 "He was" to "believe it": interview with Simpson, 1987.

290–291 "Appropriately . . . friends": MM to author, 6/27/88.

291 "What passes" to "not ourselves": "The Friend of the Family," *CCE,* 42.

291 "play doctors" to "of democracy": "We Must Have Faith," *PR* (Winter 1945), reprinted in *MMTC,* 76, 79.

291 "incorrigibly concrete" to "and ambiguity": ibid, 30.

292 "O indispensable . . . world": Edmund Wilson, "The Pleasures of Literature," *The Nation* (1/29/38), reprinted in *Shores of Light,* 712.

292 "The G.I's" to "and adventurous": "Five Curios," *PR* (Jan.–Feb. 1947), reprinted in *MMTC,* 89–91.

292 "To audiences" to "sentimental occasion": "Eugene O'Neill: Dry Ice," *PR* (Nov.–Dec. 1946), reprinted in *MMTC,* 81.

293 "reddened by" to "of sex": review of *A Moon for the Misbegotten, NYTBR* (8/31/52), reprinted in *MMTC,* 86–87.

293 "thing that" to "of hatred": "Eugene O'-Neill: Dry Ice," *MMTC,* 83, 82.

293 "to perform" to "the study": interview with MM, 8/17/88.

294 "terrible drinker" to "you children' ": interview with MM, 8/17/88.

295 "remember the" to "of persecution": Harry McCarthy to MM, 3/8/52, quoted in *Mary McCarthy*, 32–33.

295 "I don't" to "against me": MM to Harry McCarthy, 4/5/52, ibid., 34–35.

296 *"looking . . . figure"*: MCG, 50.

296 "I more . . . it": interview with MM, 8/17/88.

296 "belligerent catholic" to "licked trying": Harry McCarthy to MM, *Mary McCarthy*, 33.

296–297 "[D]espite the" to "the world": review of *A Moon for the Misbegotten*, MMTC, 88, 87.

18. INTELLECT ABROAD

298 "America, I" to "crude society": CBC interview with Mary McCarthy at Vassar College, October 1982, Vassar Collection.

298–299 "How can" to "internment" camp: quoted by Elizabeth Young-Bruehl in *Hannah Arendt: For Love of the World* (New Haven: Yale University Press, 1982), 196–97.

299 "her astonishing" to "means uneroticaly": Alfred Kazin, "Woman in Dark Times," *NYRB* (6/24/82), 3.

299 "Hannah Arendt" to "humble, deferential": interview with Kazin, 1985.

299–300 " 'jelled' " to "same thought": interview with MM, 8/29/85.

300 "anti-Stalinist celebrity": interview with Phillips, 1988.

300 "incredibly beautiful": conversation with David Bazelon, 3/22/86.

301 "Here alliances" to "intellectual conversation": Howe, *Margin of Hope*, 119.

301 "suddenly froze" to "her whips": Barrett, *Truants*, 67.

301 "He made" to "more success": interview with MM, 11/19/87.

301 "Lizzie was" to "the disinclination": interview with MM, 8/18/88.

301 " 'Mary got" to "got tits' ": telephone interview with John Marquand, 11/9/91.

302 "who never" to "this nonsense' ": Phillips, *Partisan View*, 134.

303 "Die Freiheit" to "the offensive": Mamaine Koestler, *Living with Koestler, Letters 1945–51*, ed. Colin Goodman (London: Weidenfeld & Nicolson, 1985), 145.

303–304 "People began" to "real homesickness": "Notes for Thirties Panel," 6, MPVC.

304 "the origin" to "Hotel Carlyle": MM, "A Letter to the Editor of *politics*" (November 1946), reprinted in *OC*, 23.

304 "Was Gandhi" to "last straw": MM, "Gandhi," *politics* (Winter 1949), reprinted in *OC*, 23, 22.

304 "actually . . . looked": interview with Nancy Macdonald, 1985.

304–305 "as a" to "bomb exploded": "Letter to the Editor of *politics*," OC, 4.

305 Groupes de Liaison International and Europe-America Groups discussed in Herbert Lottman, *Albert Camus* (New York: Doubleday, 1979), 158–61.

306 "We tended" to "'helping people' ": interview with Phillips, 1988.

306 "it became . . . time": "Notes for Thirties Panel," 6.

306 "I refused" to "this thing": telephone interview with Abel, 9/24/85.

306 "Nancy . . . intellectuals": interview with Kazin, 1985.

306 " 'Standard' Book Bundle": list courtesy of Miriam Chiaromonte.

307 "who were" to "each other": draft of EAG charter, courtesy Miriam Chiaromonte.

307 "If I" to "new left' ": Nicola Chiaromonte to MM, 7/9/48, courtesy Miriam Chiaromonte and Yale University Library.

307 "almost . . . efforts: MM to Dwight and Nancy Macdonald, July 1948, courtesy Miriam Chiaromonte and Yale University Library.

307 "preventive war": Bertrand Russell's view given by Barrett in *Truants,* 106. After Hiroshima, Lionel Abel recalls Russell urging that the U.S. use atomic weapons "just once more"—against the Soviet Union, before the latter developed its own bomb: Abel, *The Intellectual Follies* (New York: W. W. Norton, 1984), 150.

308 "acting . . . agency": "Europe-America Groups," draft of manifesto, courtesy Miriam Chiaromonte.

308 "We figured" to "Mr. Kaplan": interview with MM, 9/25/80.

308–309 "being what" to "Cold War": interview with MM, 8/19/85.

309 "Master": Miriam Chiaromonte to MM, 7/14/48, courtesy Miriam Chiaromonte and Yale University Library; "Professor Hook" to "right place": ibid.

309 *"droit de veto"* to "latter's war": Koestler, Living with Koestler, 152.

310 "Sidney Hook" to "Van Doren": interview with MM, 8/19/85.

310 "I think" to "dirty trick": ibid.

311 "unbelievable . . . Groups": interview with Kazin, 1985.

311 " 'you have . . . man's' ": interview with Stwertka, 1985.

19. BAD GIRL

313 " 'Do . . . *myself* '": quoted in Brower, "Mary McCarthyism," *Esquire,* 65.

313 "My God . . . Yahoo": Mary McCarthy: *The Oasis* (New York: Random House, 1949), 7.

313 "Was Dwight" to "by anybody": interview with Nancy Macdonald, 1985.

314 special attachment: Delmore's view reported by Barrett in *Truants*, 44.

314 "really . . . Rahv": interview with MM, 8/19/85.

314 "she . . . feelings": interview with Nancy Macdonald, 1985.

314 " 'Are you . . . yourself' ": Dwight Macdonald quoted in Gelderman, *Mary McCarthy*, 146.

314–315 "and when" to "his enemy": interview with MM, 8/19/85.

316 "You have" to "different level": Arendt to MM, 3/10/49.

316 "the mothball . . . words": Dawn Powell, "Reader Left Parched in McCarthy 'Oasis' " *New York Post* (1949, undated clip), MPVC.

316 "The dictators" to "of value": *Oasis*, 21, 19.

316 "concept of" to "than himself": Mary McCarthy, "Artists in Uniform," *OC*, 61.

316–317 "there were" to "the magazine": interview with Stwertka, 1985.

317 "wholly . . . mind": Kazin, *Starting Out in the Thirties*, 154.

317–318 "neo-Right" to "way through": interview with Kazin, 1985.

318 " 'an intellectual . . . man' ": Reuel quoted in letter from MM to EW, 3/30/61, WCYU.

318 "Edmund would" to "by millionaires": interview with Kazin, 1985.

318 "the feeling . . . YPSL's": MM to Richard Rovere, 12/4/52, courtesy Mary McCarthy.

318–319 "very political-minded" to "new country' ": interview with Kazin, 1985.

319 "When the" to "ran out": interview with MM, 8/19/85.

319–320 "If you" to "thrown in": MM to the Macdonalds, July 1948, Dwight Macdonald Papers, Sterling Library, Yale University (MPYU).

320 "Nobody . . . vacation": interview with Abel, 1985.

320 "all these . . . clearly": letter to author from Eve Stwertka, 10/18/90.

320 "some attempt" to "obvious solution": MM to the Macdonalds, July 1948.

320 "old time syndicalists": Nicola Chiaromonte to MM, 7/9/48.

321 "certain tentative" to "the way": MM to the Macdonalds, July 1948.

322 "to counter . . . organizations": Cord Meyer, *Facing Reality: From World Federalism to the CIA* (New York: Harper, 1980), 62.

322 " 'the language . . . accent' ": letter to *The New Statesman*, 12/11/51.

322 "Mary was" to "only halfhearted": Dwight Macdonald to Nicola Chiaro-

monte, 12/10/48, quoted in *Mary McCarthy*, 142.

322–323 In Paris, such mammoth conferences came in pairs: In the spring of 1949, the anti-Communist "International Day of Resistance to Dictatorship and War," with Max Eastman, James Farrell, and Sidney Hook as guest speakers, was immediately followed by the pro-Communist "Resistance Day" Congress, both held at the Sorbonne.

323 "humorless . . . menace": Dwight Macdonald, "The Anti-Communist Left Takes the Offensive," *politics* (Winter 1949), quoted by Michael Wreszin in a letter to *Salmagundi* (Spring–Summer 1984), 188.

323 " 'If she . . . politics' ": MM letter to *Salmagundi* (Spring–Summer 1984), 186, re Michael Wreszin's "Arthur Schlesinger, Jr., Scholar-Activist in Cold War America: 1946," in previous issue.

324 bring umbrellas, etc.: interview with MM, 7/7/85.

324 "how . . . had": reported by Irving Howe in *Margin of Hope*, 157.

324 "a . . . Sinatra": Broadwater quoted in Peter Manso, *Mailer: His Life and Times* (New York: Simon & Schuster, 1985), 187.

324 "I have" to "on writing": Norman Mailer, quoted in *Margin of Hope*, 159.

325 "upset all" to "from politics": Phillips, *Partisan View*, 149.

325 "She had" to "hard time": interview with Robert Silvers, 5/8/89.

325 "sold out" to "the food": interview with MM, 4/21/86.

325 "couldn't bear" to "his food' ": MM to Ben O'Sullivan, 8/23/80, MPVC. According to Stephen Spender, the confrontation took place at his house, where students had gathered to talk to the two female writers they had told Spender they most wanted to meet. "[B]eing Lillian," he commented later, "she imagined we had invited her worst enemy, Mary McCarthy . . . out of malice," which suggests that in 1948 the enmity was already established (Spender quoted in William Wright, *Lillian Hellman*, p. 189).

326 "just a slander" to "jangling noise": interview with MM, 4/21/86.

20. THE EXISTENTIALISTS ARE COMING! THE EXISTENTIALISTS ARE COMING!

327 "I scarcely . . . Village": Simone de Beauvoir, *Force of Circumstance*, trans. by Richard Howard (New York: G. P. Putnam, 1965), 126. At Vassar, de Beauvoir lectured on the political and moral power of literature, drawing from her book *The Ethics of Ambiguity*.

327 "[w]e . . . on": Mary McCarthy, "America the Beautiful," *OC*, 18.

327 "Victors in" to "a princess": Mary McCarthy, "The Cicerone," CCE, 58.

328 Bowden and Mary at Café Flore, etc: MM to author, 4/25/89.

328 "pope of existentialism," etc.: cited by Claude Francis and Fernande Gontier in Simone de Beauvoir, A Life . . . a Love Story, trans. by Lisa Nesselson (New York: St. Martin's, 1985), 225.

328–329 "pleased to" to "but inconvenient": Force of Circumstance, 46, 52–53.

329 "Around PR" to "an Eye": MM to author, 4/25/89.

329 "the most" to "manner generally": interview with Abel, 1985.

329 "inordinately . . . women": Phillips, Partisan View, 132.

329 Camus and Humphrey Bogart: resemblance cited by Herbert Lottman in Albert Camus, 393; Camus reportedly delighted in it.

329–330 "I would" to "athletic nun": MM to author, 4/25/89.

330 "Toward us" to "'that clear' ": Barrett, Truants, 115.

330 "American conditions" to "about America": interview with Miriam Chiaromonte, 9/18/85.

330 "advanced paranoics" to "Truman's speeches": Force of Circumstance, 123.

330 "American dynamism" to "of man": de Beauvoir, NYT Magazine (5/25/47), quoted by Francis and Gontier, Simone de Beauvoir, 233.

330 " 'The trouble" to "with her' ": interview with Phillips, 1988.

331 "Flanner liked" to "intellectual circles' ": quoted by Francis and Gontier in Simone de Beauvoir, 233.

331 "A wood" to "un-American": MM to author, 4/25/89.

331 "amazing agreement" to "did not": Force of Circumstance, 39.

332 'blasting . . . effort': Sartre quoted in Arendt, Men in Dark Times, 228.

332–333 "Rediscovery" to "and curios": "Notes for Thirties Panel," 6, MPVC.

334 "I want . . . them": de Beauvoir, America Day by Day, quoted by Francis and Gontier, Simone de Beauvoir, 235.

335 "republic" to "of Spam": "America the Beautiful," 12.

335–336 "capitalism, certainly" to "the stove": ibid., 12, 16.

336 "I would . . . that": interview with MM, 7/31/85.

337 "Given a" to "the corner": "America the Beautiful," 18–19.

338 "Crushed between" to "this conviction": MM to Dwight Macdonald, 10/14/52, MPVC.

339 "problem" to "and senses": "Mlle. Gulliver en Amérique," OC, 30.

339 "middle-class suburbs" to "exhilarating discovery": MM to Elizabeth Hardwick, 8/22/49, quoted in Gelderman, Mary McCarthy, 158.

339 "Bohemian . . . whatever": MM to Dwight Macdonald, n.d. (1949).

340 "more . . . month": Dwight Macdonald to MM, 12/1/49, MPVC.

340 "The classic" to "Girl": MM to Dwight and Nancy Macdonald, 11/20/49.

340 "terribly reactionary" to "social change": MM to Dwight Macdonald, n.d.(1949).

340 "unfortunate experience" to "probably did": interview with MM, 10/29/85.

340–341 "fascinated" to "tropical fashion": MM to Elizabeth Hardwick, 8/22/49, quoted in Mary McCarthy,, 158.

341 "fearfully . . . never did": Nicholas King, memorial address, Morgan Library, New York City, November 8, 1989.

341 "dangerous . . . people' ": Bogan's observation, made in a 1939 PR Symposium: "The Situation in American Writing," is quoted in Frank, Louise Bogan, 298.

21. BIG WOMEN (A POSTSCRIPT)

342 'Prettiest Existentialist': Janet Flanner quoted by Francis and Gontier, Simone de Beauvoir, 233

342 "deprived because" to "at all": Brightman, "Mary, Still Contrary," 617, 614.

343 "is bad" to "cribbing": ibid., 616–17.

343 "trust" to "from God": Simone de Beauvoir, Prime of Life, trans. by Peter Green (New York: World Publishing Co., 1962), 27.

343 "In fact" to "her case": "Mary, Still Contrary," 617.

343 "The emancipated" to "as man": Simone de Beauvoir, The Second Sex, trans. by H. M. Parshley (New York: Random House, 1974), 676.

343–344 "I've always" to "pitied [de Beauvoir]": "Mary, Still contrary," 617.

344 "[T]o live" to "quite touching": HA to MM, 4/2/65, MPVC.

344 "together . . . reveal": Simone de Beauvoir, She Came to Stay, quoted in Francis and Gontier, Simone de Beauvoir, 169; "In this" to "real crime": de Beauvoir quoted, ibid.

345 "harder to" to "in it": Vassar Views (February 1982).

345 "for her" to "through pity": "Mary, Quite Contrary," 617.

345 "She had" to "rescue her": Wilson, The Thirties, 704.

345 "I owe" to "to do": Jean-Paul Sartre, interview trans. in Vogue (July 1965), quoted in Axel Madsen, Hearts and Minds, The Common Journey of Simone de Beauvoir and Jean-Paul Sartre (New York: William Morrow, 1977), 181–82.

346 "that beautiful . . . career": Simone de Beauvoir, *America Day by Day,* quoted in Madsen, *Hearts and Minds,* 138

346 " 'I never' to "wasn't important": telephone interview with Dierdre Bair, 6/12/91.

346 "intellectual criticism" to "imperialist policy": John Gerassi, letter to *The Nation* (6/23/84), 754.

348 "tall . . . lisping": *The Groves of Academe,* 13.

348 "To do" to "of mind": interview with MM, 10/25/86.

348–349 " 'Alone . . . herself' ": de Beauvoir, *She Came to Stay,* quoted by Mary Evans, *Simone de Beauvoir: A Feminist Mandarin* (London: Tavistock, 1985), 37.

349 "nothing . . . herself": ibid., 37.

350 "rationalist-voluntarist position": *Force of Circumstance,* 23.

350 "Of course" to "of it": "Miss McCarthy Explains," interview by Jean-François Revel, *NYTBR* (5/16/71), 28.

350 "had the . . . ours": *L'Humanité* (10/27/89), 1 (my translation).

350 "Looking at" to "I did": MM to Grumbach, 2/22/66, MPVC.

22. THAT OTHER McCARTHY

351 "[F]or . . . only": letter to *The New Statesman,* 12/11/51, courtesy Mary McCarthy.

351 "cosmopolis of" to "France unthinkable": Lionel Trilling, "Our Country and Our Culture," symposium, *PR* (May–June 1952), 319.

352 judge she knew: This was John Biggs, an old friend of Edmund Wilson's, and then Chief Judge of the Court of Appeals of Philadelphia's First District.

352 "My new" to "next year": MM to Arthur Schlesinger, Jr., 7/11/52, courtesy Mary McCarthy.

352 "an ideologized world": MM to AS, n.d. (1952).

353 "tinniness of" to "self-loving": Brightman, "Mary, Quite Contrary," 611.

353 "Senator McCarthy" to "public domain": MM to AS, n.d. (1953).

353 "Red . . . manner": Joseph McCarthy, quoted in Walter Lafeber and Richard Polenberg, *The American Century* (New York: John Wiley, 1975), 348; "indivisible": ibid., 309.

354 "position of" to "traitorous actions": ibid., 348.

354 "[J]ust when" to "for a while": Howe, *Margin of Hope,* 214.

354 "opposition . . . Left": Barrett, *Truants,* 189–90.

355 "counter-conference" to "*cultural* freedom": MM to HA, 3/14/52, MPVC.

355 "cultural freedom" to "from without": Mary McCarthy, "No News, *or,* What Killed the Dog," *OC,* 41.

355 "[F]ar from" to "popular-front period": Mary McCarthy, "The Contagion of Ideas," *OC,* 49.

355 "didn't . . . 1952": conversation with MM, 7/26/89.

355–356 " 'germ' theory" to "rightly, dread": "The Contagion of Ideas," 51–53.

357 "rather on" to "than today": MM to HA, 3/14/52, MPVC.

357 "[t]hus . . . camp": Barrett, *Truants,* 82.

357–358 "And what" to "true reportage": MM to Richard Rovere, 12/4/52, courtesy Mary McCarthy.

358 " 'between all stools' ": Arendt, quoted in Young-Bruehl, *Hannah Arendt,* 287.

358–359 "totalitarian elements" to "is dwindling": MM to Rovere, 12/4/52.

359 "might . . . project": ibid. At the same time, Wilson let it be known that he thought *The Groves of Academe* "in some ways, the best thing [Mary] has done": Wilson to Nabokov, 2/25/52, from *Wilson/Nabokov Letters,* 273 (Nabokov didn't agree). Bowden's proposed contribution was to be "an occasional box called *Eisenhowlers*": MM to Rovere, 12/4/52.

359 "a sort" to "in *vacuo*": MM to AS, 12/7/49.

359 "[A]nalytic and" to "the large": MM to Rovere, 12/4/52.

359–360 "the Average" to "me Jack' ": MM to AS, 4/17/53; "somebody . . . politics' ": ibid.

360 "Have you" to "putrefying undergraduates": MM to HA, 9/10/53.

360 "mediocrities . . . help": MM to AS, 3/6/53; "drowning . . . sauce": MM to AS, 4/17/53; "About the" to "editing either": MM to AS, 10/28/53.

361 "[T]he rich . . . breed": MM to AS, 3/20/53; "she requires . . . politically": MM to AS, 2/18/53; "intensely . . . people": MM to AS, 4/21/53.

361 "strategic and" to "or foolishness": MM to AS, 2/20/53.

23. HAVE PEN, WILL TRAVEL

365 "I get . . . solitude": quoted in "Lady with a Switchblade," *Life,* 62.

365–366 "only half-aware" to "are wearing": MM to HA, 6/4/55, MPVC.

366 Bowden's affair with Carmen Angleton: conversation with MM, 7/26/89.

366 "It was" to "horribly translated": Brightman, "Mary, Still Contrary," 611.

367 "my capital" to "went home": interview with MM, 9/25/80.

367 "conspicuous solitude" to "*una persona*": MM to Carmen Angleton, 9/2/55, from Gelderman, *Mary McCarthy,* 193.

368 "The Lesbian . . . ": MM to AS, 2/20/50, courtesy of Mary McCarthy.

368 "the shattered" to "bohemianized people": MM to HA, 8/10/54.

368–369 "The ideologue" to "as un-American": "Greenwich Village at Night," part one, *New York Post* (2/20/50), 3, 7.

369 "a Negro" to "off alone": in *Mary McCarthy*, 162.

369 "[V]ery fond" to "Bowden around": Dwight Macdonald to Nicola Chiaromonte, 12/50/50, MPYU.

370 "the shattered . . . epistomology": MM to HA, 8/10/54; "ritual of doubt": HA to MM, 8/20/54; "act of munificence": MM to HA, 9/16/54; "a real" to "of intellectuals": HA to MM, 8/20/54.

370–71 "the thinker to "much amused": HA to MM, 8/20/54.

371 "Our defenses" to "horribly nervous": MM to HA, 8/10/54.

371 "My wise counselor": interview with MM, 8/19/85.

371–372 "I didn't" to "Senator McCarthy": ibid. In his contribution to the "Our Country and Our Culture" symposium, Rahv contended that "anti-Stalinism has become almost a professional stance, . . . a total outlook on life," and he scorned those anti-Stalinists who found it "easy to put up with the vicious antics of a political bum like Senator McCarthy, even as they grow more . . . intolerant of any basic criticism of existing social arrangements." By contrast, the "old anti-Stalinism of the independent Left" had played a "vanguard role," he argued, because its spokesmen were the first to "discern the totalitarian essence of the Soviet myth": *Partisan Review* (May–June, 1952), 307.

372 "not unfriendly" to "of politics": MM to HA, 8/10/54; "You are" to "do you": HA to MM, 8/20/54.

372 "leading him" to "handsome man' ": Barrett, *Truants*, 105, 102.

373 "acting . . . possible": HA to MM, 8/20/54.

373 "funny picture": MM to HA, 8/10/54; "You will . . . one . . . etc": HA to MM, 8/20/54.

373 "disagreeable role": interview with MM, 8/19/85; "more or" to "any better": HA to MM, 8/20/54; "turned upside" to "be fabricated": Arendt, "The Ex-Communists," *Commonweal*, 595, 599.

373–374 "eerie" to "an actress": MM to HA, 8/10/54; "generally . . . others": HA to MM, 8/20/54.

374 "the case . . . government": MM to HA, 8/10/54; "wise up" to "our age": HA to MM, 8/20/54.

374 "your value" to "peaceful again": MM to HA, 8/10/54.

374–375 "Don't you" to "that over": HA to MM, 8/20/54; "hurricanes, illness" to "days off": MM to HA, 9/16/54.

375 "is just . . . tourists": MM to HA, 6/4/55.

375–376 " 'inevitable Bennington-type' " to " 'like Provincetown' ": MM to Dwight Macdonald, 4/9/55, MPYU.

376 "I really" to "situation": MM to AS, 11/13/55.

376–377 'personal' note to "don't know' ": MM to HA, 12/8/54.

377 "treat herself" to "deprivation": conversation with Reuel Wilson, 10/7/89.

378 "wonderful time" to "a magnet": MM to HA, 12/8/54.

378 "aunt" to "intellectual conscience": conversation with Reuel Wilson, 1989; "Mary's exalted" to "to work": interview with Schlesinger, 1987.

378 "Hannah . . . feeling": interview with Silvers, 1989.

378 "When she" to "of them": McCarthy's memorial address quoted in NYT (12/9/75), 32.

24. VENICE UNBOUND

380 "a regular" to "quietly' here": MM to HA, 9/29/55, MPVC.

380 " 'I couldn't" to "against her": MM to BB, 9/28/56, MPVC.

380–381 "parvenu art" to "her presence": Mary McCarthy, *Venice Observed* (New York: Bernier, 1956), 44, 6.

381 "[T]hat modern" to "classic experience": ibid., 20.; "the spirit" to "Sleeping Beauty": ibid., 50.

381 " 'nothing left" to "enormous saloon' ": ibid., 15.

381–382 "to hold" to "the same": interview with MM, 8/29/85.

382 "the overflow" to "anti-anti-Communist": MM to HA, 9/29/55.

382 ACCF severed relations with CCF: Mary Sperling McAuliffe, *Crisis on the Left, Cold War Politics and American Liberals, 1947–1954* (Amherst: University of Massachusetts Press, 1978), 121.

382 "a refuge . . . government": interview with Schlesinger, 1987.

383 "the marble" to "bedraggled": VO, 44, 50.

383–384 "To the medieval" to "from them": ibid., 52, 70.

384–385 "a commercial" to "robber's den": ibid., 37, 43.

385 "a commercial" to "dream incarnate": ibid., 50.

385 "a miser's" to "fairy tales": ibid., 50.

385 "I feel" to "ludicrous role" MM to BB, 9/29/56.

386 "The text" to "fashion enterprise": MM to Bernard Berenson, 2/25/57, from Gelderman, *Mary McCarthy*, 198.

386 " 'It seems . . . like it' ": ibid.

386 "She's been" to "amateur's painter' ": Sacheverell Sitwell, review of *Venice Observed*, NYTBR (11/18/56), 1; "enhanced

. . . world": VO, 116; "is there . . . ink-
pot": Sitwell, 1.

386 "bounder" to "English cigarette": "The
Cicerone," CCE, 57.

387 "was not" to "on Venice": Rosamond Bernier Russell, in Mary McCarthy, 199.

387 "Veronese painted" to "the compositions": André Chastel, Notes on the Plates,
in Venice Observed, 193.

388 "Painting has" to "civic": Brightman,
"Mary, Still Contrary," 611.

388 "Only the" to "in brogue": MM to BB,
10/10/56. Broadwater often served
McCarthy as wardrobe mistress, airmail-
ing her "Jackson Pollock dress" to Tripoli
in 1959, along with chiffon slips for
her "Pirovano and Galanos" (MM to BB,
10/27/59).

388–389 "I hope": to "after all": MM to BB,
9/14/57.

389 "The absence" to "Venetian painting":
VO, 126.

389 "more amused" to "like Venice": Mary
McCarthy, 197.

389 "architectural purists" to "universal maxims": VO, 113.

25. SCOUNDREL TIME

390 "had a" to "in himself": MM to HA, 7/30/
56, MPVC.

390–391 "puritan" to "Greek Gods": MM to
BB, May 1956.

391 Tillich's foot fetish: interview with MM,
8/29/85.

391 "the prosperity-version" to "pure Stieglitz": MM to BB, May 1956.

391–393 "An awful" to "God's hands": MM to
BB, 5/5/57, MPVC.

393 " 'I've wanted" to "like you?' ": MM to
John Davenport, 6/26/56, from Gelderman, Mary McCarthy, 202; "This is" to
"of imprisonment": MM to John Davenport, 7/3/56, ibid.

394 "to come" to "a thorn": MM to Carmen
Angleton, 8/9/56, in Mary McCarthy, 203.

394 Dwight Macdonald: In Venice Observed,
Dwight, who also visited Mary in 1955, is
the American who wonders why the Venetians don't "motorize" their gondolas.
McCarthy scoffed at this, but ten years
later the canals wewre buzzing with vapo-
retti.

394 "resolve . . . how": MM to Angleton,
8/9/56, Mary McCarthy, 203.

394 "This has" to "captive canary": MM to
HA, n.d. (1956, probably October).

395 "darling" to "broken heart": conversation
with MM, 7/26/89. Writing Edmund Wilson on 3/30/61, after he had suffered an
angina attack, McCarthy said she had had
one in 1957.

395–396 "fortunate thing" to "the Crown":
MM to HA, 5/21/57.

396 "It is . . . pursuits": Letters of Lord Byron, ix.

396 "Dinah . . . unfaithful": quoted in Atlas,
Delmore Schwartz, 259.

396 "bad blow" to "tell you": MM to HA,
5/21/57.

396–397 " 'What distinguishes" to "dramatic
quality' ": Arendt's letter supporting
McCarthy's 1959 application for a Guggenheim Foundation grant, from Young-
Bruehl, Hannah Arendt, 196–97.

397 "nearly fainting" to "and drinking": MM
to HA, 5/21/57, MPVC.

397 "He looked" to "was sex": conversation
with MM, 7/26/89.

397–398 "undeception . . . regarding" to "German-Swiss doctor": MM to BB, 5/17/57.

398 "He lives" to "blood transfusion": MM to
HA, 5/21/57.

398–399 "which will" to "lost generation": HA
to MM, 6/7/57.

399 "one shouldn't . . . seriously": Arendt,
Men in Dark Times, 211; "Alas, we" to
"with forbearance": Brecht quoted in Men
in Dark Times, 224–25.

399 "Certainly, there" to "of it": HA to MM,
6/7/57.

400 "The level . . . lives": HA to Hilde Frankel,
3/20/50, from Hannah Arendt, 247; "[a]s
always . . . can": Arendt to Kurt Blumen-
feld, 4/1/51, ibid., 69.

400 "it is" to "the nose": Arendt to Karl Jaspers, 11/1/61, ibid., 307.

400 "Grand . . . masterpieces": Balzac quoted
in Hannah Arendt, 247.

400 "Wisdom is" to "nor prudent": Arendt,
"Isak Dinesen," Men in Dark Times, 109.

401 "I see . . . Tucci": MM to BB, 10/10/56.

401 "obviously . . . here": MM to HA, n.d.
(1956).

401–402 "I feel" to "angst again": MM to BB,
5/18/56.

402 "immediately slipped" to "next summer":
MM to BB, 9/28/56.

402 "morbid condition" to "long last": MM to
BB, 9/29/56.

402 "but feel . . . degradation": MM to BB,
5/18/56.

403 "here . . . hotel": MM to BB, 5/30/57.

403 waking up as George Weidenfeld: MM to
BB, 5/20/57.

403 "I can't to "feel causeless": MM to author,
3/21/88.

26. CHASE AWAY CARE

404 "The apple . . . mellow": Robert Lowell,
"Florence," Selected Poems (New York:
Farrar, Straus & Giroux, 1977), 106.

404 "Whenever . . . Florence": Paris Review
interview reprinted as "Mary McCarthy"
Writers at Work (New York: Viking Press,
1963), 313.

404 "You could" to "and rich": interview with
MM, 9/25/80.

404 "a multiplied" to "old friends": MM to HA, 7/30/56, MPVC.

404–405 " 'But . . . Florence' ": Mary McCarthy, "Brunelleschi's Dome," *Harper's Bazaar* (September 1959), 234.

405 "B.B., greedy" to "queer charm": MM to BB, 9/23/57, MPVC.

405–406 "Took Mary" to "using them": Bernard Berenson, *Sunlight and Twilight: The Diaries of 1947–58* (New York: Harcourt Brace Jovanovich, 1963), 435.

406 "delicate . . . *élégant*": Alfred Kazin, "From an Italian Journal," *PR* (Nov.–Dec. 1948), reprinted in *The New Partisan Review Reader, 1945–53*, eds. William Phillips and Philip Rahv (New York: Harcourt Brace & Co., 1953), 265.

406 " 'Oh, dear' " to "*everybody* Jewish' ": MM to HA, 5/11/74.

406 "like some . . . bottle": MM to HA, 6/23/58; "[I]f I . . . anything": MM to BB, 5/29/57.

406 "I wish" to "reforestation program": MM to BB, 10/14/57.

407 "a consistently" to "shock-absorbers": MM to BB, 5/18/56.

407 "Florentine history" to "its past": MM to HA, 8/9/56.

408 "more . . . beautiful": MM to BB, 5/30/57.

408 "bristling prepotent" to "human ego": Mary McCarthy, *The Stones of Florence* (New York: Harcourt, Brace & Co., 1959), 64.

408 "Dull, dry" to "universal deluge": ibid., 3–4.

409 "*New Yorker* touch": Berenson's and McCarthy's responses reported by Gelderman, *Mary McCarthy*, 216.

409 "Horns . . . sing": *SF*, 7.

410 "sentimental twaddle": quoted in *Mary McCarthy*, 216.

410 "scrappy and nondescript": *Writers at Work*, 313.

410 "Being alone" to "young": MM to BB, 5/29/57.

410 "to Florence" to "for it": ibid.

410 "almost sinister beauty": *SF*, 65.

411 "Miss McCarthy . . . herself": W. T. Scott, review of *MCG* in *NYHTBR* (5/26/57), 3.

411 "up like . . . balloon": MM to BB, 5/25/57.

411 "most as" to "into tears": HA to MM, 6/7/57, MPVC.

411 "ultrasmart": Macdonald expressed his enthusiasm for *MCG* in a letter to Nicola Chiaromonte, 3/21/57, MPYU; "felt for" to "fictional character": ibid.

412 "not interested" to "it's knowable": *Writers at Work*, 314–15.

412 "irreducible facts" to "eternal essences": MM to BB, 10/3/57; "very affirmatively": *Writers at Work*, 314.

413 "*candore* and" to "through it": MM to BB, 10/3/57.

413 "just . . . severe": *MCG*, 166; "republican . . . plainness": *SF*, 100.

413 "*The injustices*" to "*encountered it*": *MCG*, 167.

413 her grandfather: with the death of her Seattle grandmother, Harold Preston rescued McCarthy again in a sense, when she inherited "the Preston money" (as she called it), around $30,000 in stocks.

414 "revolted by" to "by Christmas": MM to BB, 9/14/57. Ginsberg didn't write novels; perhaps it is the "hipsters" in the long poem *Howl* she refers to here.

415 "A strange . . . man": MM to author, 3/21/88.

415 "did not" to "you know": MM to BB, 10/3/57.

415 "I consider" to "a play": Nicola Chiaromonte to MM, 11/15/59, MPVC.

415 "many . . . foolishness": Nicola Chiaromonte to Dwight Macdonald, 11/15/59, MPYU.

415–416 "an insect" to "a crook": MM to BB, 10/3/57.

416 "as though . . . river": *SF*, 31.

417 "He must . . . horribly": ibid., 91.

417 "Homosexuality or" to "transvestite's . . . dream": ibid., 94–95; "*Michelangelo . . . cesello*": ibid., 95.

417–418 "The humanists" to "classic style": ibid., 96.

418 "A tame" to "cat-like": ibid., 93–94.

418 "Nature's . . . 'mistakes' ": ibid., 62.

418 "bait": MM to author, 3/21/88.

419 " 'those . . . people' ": MM to BB, 9/23/57.

419 "a handful" to "twenty divas": MM to HA, 6/14/58.

419–420 "one of" to "asset": interview with MM, 4/21/86; this story is also told in a letter to the author, 3/21/88.

420 "highland blood" to "Montenegrin blood": telephone conversation with Julian Muller, 3/4/91.

420 "playing a" to "this friendship": interview with MM, 4/21/86.

420 " 'You have . . . portrait' ": interview with MM, 8/29/85; "you are . . . way": HA to MM, 8/28/59.

420 "never existed" to "and sculpture": *SF*, 100.

421 "a far . . . discourse": MM to Katharine White, 8/7/57, from *Mary McCarthy*, 214.

421 " 'proof of' " to "of law": *SF*, 99.

27. JUMPING SHIP

425 "the boys . . . Bridges": interview with MM, 8/29/85.

425 "one of . . . career": HA to MM, 6/7/57.

426 "a national . . . fight": MM to Bernard Berenson, 3/22/58, from Gelderman, *Mary McCarthy*, 211.

426 "fix up" to "a bakery": interview with MM, 8/19/85.

427 "Miss Arendt" to "common sense": Mary McCarthy, "The *Vita Activa*," *The New Yorker* (10/18/58), 198.

427 "We both" to "common sense": interview with MM, 8/29/85.

428 "memory-jogger" to "each other": "The *Vita Activa*," 199.

428 "that curiously . . . society": Hannah Arendt, *The Human Condition* (Chicago: University of Chicago Press, 1958), 35.

428 "the first . . . Marx": A. Alvarez, review of *The Human Condition The New Statesman* (3/7/59), 336.

428 "behavior" to "public realm": Arendt, *The Human Condition*, 45.

428 Arendt's affair with Rosenberg mentioned in interview with MM, 8/29/85.

428 "the bold . . . Rosenberg": Mary McCarthy, "An Academy of Risk," *PR* (Summer 1959), reprinted in *OC*, 242.

429 "talked . . . art": HA to MM, 5/20/62.

429 " 'it would" to "abolish it": "An Academy of Risk," 274.

429 "culture . . . whorehouse": interview with MM, 7/31/85. "Western literature is the mirror on the ceiling of the whorehouse," was the actual quote: *Time* (7/4/60), 17.

429 "Cultural Freedom . . . Berlin": MM to HA, 6/29/60, MPVC.

430 "an act" to "your taste": "An Academy of Risk," 248.

430 "Those who . . . normal": Mary McCarthy, "A New Word," *Harper's Bazaar* (May 1958), reprinted in *MMTC*, 204.

431 *"Another vicious"* to "a gangster": MM to HA, 6/28/59.

432 "I had" to "much worse": HA to MM, 7/27/59.

432 "a sort" to "'leftist' note": MM to HA, 6/28/59.

432 "the Pod": BB to MM, 2/15/60, MPVC.

432–433 "partly by" to "shatter morale": MM to HA, 8/17/59.

433 "something . . . England": MM to HA, 6/28/59.

433 "phony scientificality" to "every stone": HA to MM, 8/28/59.

433 "He says" to "a grasshopper": MM to HA, 8/17/59.

433–434 "[D]on't think" to "I doubt": HA to MM, 8/28/59.

434 "compendious history" to "of distortion": McCarthy's Guggenheim application, 1/28/59, in *Mary McCarthy*, 254.

434 "two domesticated" to "and cooking": MM to HA, 6/28/59.

434–435 "bound together" to "silently rebellious": Meigs, *Lily Briscoe*, 148.

435 "made . . . life": ibid., 147.

435 "snug . . . games": MM to HA, 5/15/60.

435 "So far . . . thought of": MM to HA, 6/28/59.

435–436 "I would" to "a way": interview with Daphne Hellman, 1985.

436–437 "an extra" to "Dolly Lamb": *Lily Briscoe*, 148, 152.

437 "He was . . . priapic": conversation with Elizabeth Hardwick, 4/4/91.

437 "the air . . . again": interview with MM, 10/25/85.

437 "a sepulchral . . . hell": interview with MM, 10/25/85.

437 "I think . . . West": Reuel Wilson quoted in chronology contained in 2/22/66 letter to Doris Grumbach, MPVC.

437 "And that . . . bizarre": MM to HA, 5/15/60.

28. LOVE, MARY

438 "Loving . . . time": Hannah Arendt, *Rahel Varnhagen: The Life of a Jewish Woman*, trans. by Richard and Clara Winston (New York: Harcourt Brace Jovanovich), 1974, 71.

438 "It was . . . room": USIA report, 4/23/62, MM's FBI files, MPVC.

438 "The report" to "his 'anti-Communism' ": MM to Edmund Wilson, 3/30/61, MPVC.

438 "feels the" to "old woman": MM to HA, 11/23/60, MPVC.

439 "is a very" to "White circle": MM to EW, 3/30/61.

439 "Commie *voyageurs*": conversation with James West, 4/16/90.

439 "He is" to "strong-willed": MM to EW, 3/30/61.

440 "Bellow is" to "isn't All": Dwight Macdonald to F. W. Dupee, 9/11/61, DPCU.

440 "When Mary . . . man": interview with Carmen Angleton, 4/20/86; "A husband-type husband": Hardwick quoted by Eileen Simpson, 11/21/87.

441 " 'keep up appearances' ": MM to HA, 11/23/60.

441 "remote traveling" to "Secret Police": ibid.

441 "The house" to "was fun": MM to HA, 10/26/60.

442 " 'an embarrassment . . . Embassy' ": MM to HA, 11/23/60.

442 *"persona non"* to "and light' ": ibid.

442–443 " 'Why do" to "his mistress' ": interview with MM, 8/29/85.

443 *"quantité négligeable"*: HA to MM, 9/16/60, MPVC.

443 "as you . . . time": Dwight Macdonald to MM, 11/3/61, MPYU.

443 "It's odd" to "surprises came": Robert Lowell to MM, 10/21/61, MPVC.

444 "The staple" to "self-flattery": Mary McCarthy, "The Fact in Fiction," *OC*, 251, 267.

444 "if the . . . gossip": "The Fact in Fiction," 265; "The worst . . . writer": ibid, 268–69; "We . . . imagine it": ibid., 270.

444–445 "It is" to "often beautifully": HA to MM, 8/22/60.

445   "who niggled" to "with familiarity": MM to HA, 8/30/60.

445   "vacation" to "affectionate place": ibid.

445   "It was . . . hurt": interview with Daphne Hellman, 1985.

445   "not a" to "high society": MM to HA, 8/30/60.

445   "a little . . . Carmen": HA to MM, 5/18/60.

446   "I can't" to "unprincipled": MM to HA, 8/30/60.

446   "Carmen's gossip" to "make mistakes": HA to MM, 9/16/60.

446–447 " 'Sorry, the" to "of kindness": MM to HA, 10/2/60.

447   "had no . . . diplomat": interview with Angleton, 1986.

447   "enchantment and" to "to follow": BB to MM, 4/29/60.

447   "You are . . . Rome": BB to MM, 4/19/60, MPVC.

447   "We were" to "something eventually": BB to MM, 6/4/60.

448   "drawing out" to "awkward interval": BB to MM, 5/19/60.

448   "in all" to "to them": MM to BB, 5/27/60, MPVC; "attitudinizing" to "withering element": MM to BB, 11/25/60.

448–449 "he never" to "partly paralyzed": MM to HA, 5/15/60.

449   "You will . . . you": MM to BB, 5/27/60; "Can't . . . you": MM to BB, 5/15/60; "There's no" to "I am": BB to MM, 5/19/60.

449   "crooked, like" to "own orphaning": MM to BB, 5/15/60.

449   "identity" to "motor responses": MM to BB, 5/3/60.

449   "chatty . . . disillusioning": BB to MM, 1/4/61. "[A]las the emotional aridity and the egotism of Margaret Sargent was not . . . a stylization," Bowden wrote Mary after he had been moved to reread the first chapter of The Company She Keeps, "Cruel and Barbarous Treatment."

449–450 "My 'I' " to "soul for": MM to HA, 1/17/61.

450   "made Rome . . . basement": MM to BB, 5/15/60; "'right part' . . . swim": MM to BB, 9/28/60.

451   "gathering-in" to "such Congresses": MM to HA, 6/29/60.

451   "West Berlin" to "this winter": HA to MM, 7/25/60.

451–452 "Shakespeare, if" to "divine mission": MM to HA, 6/29/60.

452   "If he . . . insane": HA to MM, 7/25/60.

452   "Communism" to "at all": Time (7/4/60), 17.

452–453 "real, pretty" to "not true": MM to HA, 6/29/60.

453   "The mother . . . children": MM to HA, 5/18/60.

453   "any traditional" to "a fact": MM to HA, 6/29/60.

453   "harrowing" to "is right": MM to HA, 10/7/60; "I am . . . people": MM to HA, 10/26/60.

454–455 "condoned" to "ridiculous one": HA to MM, 11/11/60.

455   "Thank you" to "four walls": MM to HA 11/23/60.

455   "colorless . . . streets": ibid.

455   "I would" to "reading Hegel": Brightman, "Mary, Still Contrary," 611.

456   "It's rather . . . advancing": MM to BB, 7/28/60.

456   "From then" to "in the Grand Hotel": interview with MM, 10/25/85.

29. ON THE ROAD

457   "All of . . . incomprehensibly are": Randall Jarrell, Pictures from an Institution, quoted in Young-Bruehl, Hannah Arendt, 438.

457   "leafy . . . millinery": MM to HA, 4/2/61, MPVC.

457   "perpetual motion machine": MM to HA: 3/11/61.

457–458 "a kind" to "gloomy monster": ibid.

458   "a sub-literary . . . truth": Philip Rahv to MM, 1/8/61, MPVC.

458   "there . . . generation": Rahv to MM, 1/8/61.

458   "the question" to "him finally": "Mary McCarthy," Writers at Work, 301.

458   "I'm not" to "and swoop": ibid., 310.

458   "a writer's witchcraft": Meigs, Lily Briscoe, 150.

458–459 "all essentially" to "[her] novels": Writers at Work, 309.

459   "be some . . . work": ibid., 301.

459   "to write" to "in Italy": Mary McCarthy, "Drapes," PR (Winter 1962), reprinted in MMTC, 232–33.

459   " 'Isn't it" to "do it' ": Hardwick and McCarthy's exchange quoted in Brower, "Mary McCarthyism," Esquire, 58.

460   "Whose bark" to "kitchen knives": Jarrell, Pictures from an Institution, 51.

460   "Who would've" to "him mortally": "Mary McCarthyism," 58.

460   "the same" to "she's Gertrude": Randall Jarrell to Philip Rahv, August 1953, from Randall Jarrell's Letters, 383.

460   "subtle . . . intelligences": "Mary McCarthyism," 58.

460   "crotchets" to "excited performances": "Drapes," 233, 230.

460   "These pissass . . . sneak": Norman Mailer, "The Mary McCarthy Case," NYRB (10/17/63), 3.

460–461 "No author . . . self-parody": "Drapes," 231.

461 "The technical" to "is congratulations": Elizabeth Hardwick to MM, 8/3/63, MPVC.

461 "wedding shopping" to "school pageant": MM to Carmen Angleton, 4/2/61, from Gelderman, *Mary McCarthy*, 235.

461 "What . . . you out?": interview with MM, 10/25/85.

462 " '*fête champêtre*' . . . Mary": Dwight Macdonald to Nicola Chiaromonte, 4/23/61; "She is . . . Consort": Nicola Chiaromonte to Dwight Macdonald, 5/9/61, from *Mary McCarthy*, 237.

462 "James" to "my dear?": author's visits with the Wests in Castine, Maine.

463 "a brief" to "United States": Arthur Schlesinger, Jr., to Jacob Beam, 3/15/61, MPVC.

463 "sad and" to "desperately poor": MM to EW, 12/28/61, WCYU.

463 "at a" to "for housing": MM to HA, 3/28/62.

463 "Gertrude . . . about": *Pictures from an Institution*, 190.

464 "That's why" to "New York": interview with MM, 7/7/85.

464 "I think . . . sex": *Look Magazine* (2/25/64).

464 "the most" to "Maine woods": MM to HA, 1/17/61.

464 "Sensibility writers" to "sensibility": Smith, "Mary McCarthy Said," *Vogue* (10/15/63), 99.

464 "Sense and" to "Vassar Girl": interview with MM, 7/7/85.

465 "fat and fair": *Group*, 11.

465 "It was" to "mass-produced": Mary McCarthy, "The Hounds of Summer," *The Hounds of Summer and Other Stories* (New York: Avon/Bard, 1981), 194–96.

466 " 'old' summer" to "through ownership," Mary McCarthy, "The Appalachian Revolution," *HS*, 183.

466 "the 'Germans' " to " '*c'était beau*' ": *HS*, 239–40.

467 "expert buck-passer": Mary McCarthy, "General Macbeth," *WW*, 10.

467 "When did . . . know?": HA to MM, 6/7/62, MPVC.

467 "very viperish . . . pleasure": MM to HA, 6/1/62, MPVC.

467 "between the . . . perpetrated them": Hannah Arendt, *A Report on the Banality of Evil: Eichmann in Jerusalem* (New York: Penguin Books, 1983), 54.

467 "terrific . . . groupiness": MM to HA, 6/1/62.

468 "*Pale Fire*" to "are divided": Mary McCarthy, "A Bolt from the Blue," *WW*, 15.

468 "everything . . . itself": MM to HA, 6/1/62.

468 "terribly funny" to "of art": ibid.

468 "the American" to "more Americanized": *Writers at Work*, 287.

468 "There is" to "with it": HA to MM, 6/7/62.

468–469 "couldn't . . . fanfare": DM to MM, 6/27/62.

469 "epic sweep" to "displaced person": MM to HA, 9/28/62.

469 "an artificial" to "a bore": HA to MM, 10/30/62.

469 "a 'circle' " to "quality, frankly": MM to HA, 6/1/62.

469 "They hanged" to "more gone": MM to HA, ibid.

469–470 "I am" to " 'unimaginative' ": HA to MM, 6/7/62.

471 "and became" to "like it": HA to MM, 4/4/62.

471 "You should" to "grown back": ibid.

471 "turbanwise" to "no whig": HA to MM, 5/20/62.

471 "in great" to "social side": MM to HA, 3/28/62.

471 "the attention" to "was literary": interview with Eileen Finletter, 3/22/86.

472 "like a" to "of life": MM to HA, 5/4/62.

472 "hysterical and" to "*vous savez*' ": MM to HA, tktktk.

472 "cute weekend . . . 'coquettes' ": MM to HA, 5/4/62.

472 "the only" to "never exposed": HA to MM, 6/7/62.

472 "so much" to "the French": MM to HA, 3/11/61.

473 "old . . . *Entertainer*": MM to BB, 2/10/60, MPVC

30. BEAUTY AND THE PRIEST: THE BURROUGHS CONNECTION

474 " 'So . . . climax' ": quoted by Mary McCarthy in "Burroughs' *Naked Lunch*," *NYRB* (February 1963), reprinted in *WW*, 47. This review, in the maiden issue of the *NYRB*, was originally titled "*Déjeuner sur l'Herbe*."

474 "Edinburgh . . . me": interview with MM, 7/7/85.

474 "Registered Heroin Addict": MM to HA, 10/30/62.

474–475 "peculiarly American" to "and riots": "Burroughs' *Naked Lunch*," 49–50.

475 "Passages of" to "the same": ibid., 46.

475 "really . . . five-year-plan": MM to HA, 1/11/62.

476 "was the" to "it enormously": MM to HA, 10/30/62.

476 " 'they . . . *two*' ": ibid.

476 "Our age" to "asses' milk": MM to HA, 10/30/62.

476 " 'Who pays . . . anyway?' ": quoted in Hamilton, *Robert Lowell*, 299.

476–477 "our side's" to "lieutenant": ibid., 300–02.

477 "His head . . . beat it": Saul Bellow, *Humboldt's Gift,* (New York: Viking Press, 1973), 141.

477 "East River gray": Atlas, *Delmore Schwartz,* 375.

478 "If Lenin" to "it stinks": William Phillips to MM, 1/15/63.

478 "a chronic . . . Nantucket": "Burroughs' *Naked Lunch,* 42.

478 "fight . . . McCarthy": telephone interview with Norman Mailer, 1991.

478 "wouldn't be" to "another interview": MM to HA, 10/30/62.

478 " 'You're the . . . regent' ": interview with MM, 7/7/85.

478 "like an" to "a war": Norman Mailer, "General Marijuana," *Advertisements for Myself* (New York: G. P. Putnam's Berkley Medallion Edition, 1959–1966), 258, 277.

479 "our lit" to "lady-book": Mailer, "The Mary McCarthy Case," NYRB, 1.

479 "a shot" to "story hot": "Burroughs *Naked Lunch,* 443–44.

479 "ordinary men" to "all constipated' ": ibid., 47.

479 "Mary's . . . ridiculous": "The Mary McCarthy Case," 3.

479 "taken with" to "rough ore": interview with MM, 4/21/86.

480 " 'Patience . . . else' ": "The Inventions of I. Compton-Burnett," WW, 126; "Only . . . himself": ibid., 121.

480 "coterie literature": "Burroughs' *Naked Lunch,*" 50.

480 "a non-novel . . . extravagance": Philip Rahv, review of Leslie Fiedler's *Waiting for the End,* NYRB (7/9/64), 7.

31. THE BOOK THAT ROARED

481 "I awoke . . . famous": Lord Byron, journal entry after publication of *Childe Harold's Pilgrimage,* in Bartlett's *Familiar Quotations* (Boston: Little, Brown, 1938), 361.

481 "Women's secrets" to "V. strange!": Louise Bogan to Ruth Limmer, 9/8/63, from *What the Woman Lived,* 353.

481 "a kind . . . scorn": MM to Elizabeth Bishop, 10/28/79, MPVC.

482 Finch as Hatton: MM to author, 3/5/87.

482 "real . . . McAusland: Dick Rovere to MM, 6/26/63, MPVC.

482 "[A]s an author" to "he knows' ": Mary McCarthy, "On *Madame Bovary,*" PR (Spring 1964), reprinted in WW, 73.

482 " 'She stood" to "or nothing' ": in Sheila Tobias, "The Group on Mary McCarthy," NYHTBR, 9.

482 "that bit" to "the present": Frani Muser to MM, 3/13/64, MPVC.

482 "awful Harald" to "Johnsrud's cap' ": memorial reading of *The Group* at Vassar College, 9/18/88.

482 "rich . . . beauty": Mailer, "The Mary McCarthy Case," 2.

483 "corrupt and corrupting": Bogan to Limmer, 9/8/63.

483 "is a" to "the book": interview with MM, 10/25/85.

483 "Madonna from" to "of pain": *Group,* 12.

483 "cloistered, pastoral" to "the wilderness": Robert Lowell to MM, 8/7/63, MPVC.

483 "narrative mimicry": Robert Keily, review of *The Group* in *The Nation* (9/21/63), from Mathewson, "The Vassar Joke," *Columbia University Forum,* 10.

483–484 "profound materiality" to "secret ambitions": "Mary McCarthy Case," 3.

484 "No male . . . art": MM to Henry Moe, of the Guggenheim Foundation, 1/28/59, from Gelderman, *Mary McCarthy,* 253.

484 "the sixties" to "the sixties": Podhoretz interviewed in Manso, *Mailer,* 473.

484 "to slice . . . tatters": review of *The Group, Newsweek,* 9/2/63, clip in MPVC.

484 "foolishness and" to "lady-writer's novel": Podhoretz quoted by Mailer in "Mary McCarthy Case," 1.

484 "major triumph" to "turn[ed] quaint": Widmer, "Finally a Lady," *The Forties: Fiction, Poetry, Drama,* 101.

485 'the vulgarity of making good': from MM's review of John Osborne's *Epitaph for George Dillon,* "Odd Man In," MMTC, 205.

485 "fitted" to "of her": Philip Roth, *Goodbye, Columbus,* from Brower, "Mary McCarthyism," 65.

486 "What kind . . . 'The Group' ": reader's letter to MM, 11/24/64; "I believe . . . book?": letter to MM, 5/22/64, both in MPVC.

486 "disappointed . . . court": MM to Ian Turner, 5/21/64, MPVC. In 1964, Turner, an Australian historian, had interested himself in *The Group*'s defense.

486 " 'The Group' " to "Sidney Lumet": Kevin McCarthy to MM, 3/10/66, MPVC.

486 Mary quite enjoyed it: interview with King, 1990.

486–487 "whopper, not" to "the decade": Haydn Carruth, review of *The Group, Chicago Daily News* (8/31/63).

487 "It had . . . stand": "Mary McCarthy Case," 1.

487 "men . . . Scout": Clifton Fadiman, review of *The Group, Holiday* (September 1963), clip in MPVC.

487 "the highbrow's highbrow": Granville Hicks, review of *The Group, Saturday Review* (8/31/63), clip in MPVC.

487 " 'Say, listen" to "dollar measure' ": Bellow, *Humboldt's Gift,* 375.

487 "bad": Lowell to MM, 10/2/63, MPVC; "She is . . . yet": "Mary McCarthy Case,"

3; "with that" to "own work": Lowell to MM, 10/2/63.

488 "treachery of" to "announced enemy": MM to HA, 10/24/63, MPVC.

488 "loyal . . . one": Lowell to MM, 10/2/63.

488 "I don't" to "have met": interview with Silvers, 1989.

488 "Lady M." to "the novel": "Mary McCarthy Case," 3.

488 "I can't" to "stupid invectives": HA to MM, Fall 1963, MPVC.

488 "clearly not . . . better": interview with Silvers, 1989.

488 "he couldn't" to "the time": interview with MM, 10/25/85.

488 "one of" to "the King": telephone interview with Mailer, 1991.

488–489 "that Elizabeth" to "stab-in-the-back": HA to MM, Fall 1963.

489 "Maisie . . . defloratio": Xavier Prynne (Elizabeth Hardwick), "The Gang," NYRB (9/26/63), 22.

489 "perhaps . . . told me": MM to HA, 10/24/63.

489 "was meant" to "answer this": Elizabeth Hardwick to MM, 11/30/63, MPVC.

489 "I think" to "downward direction": MM to Lowell, 1/6/64, from Mary McCarthy, 260.

489 "they are . . . years". Hardwick, "Mary McCarthy," A View of My Own, 38.

489–490 "autumn of" to "one another": Lowell to MM, 10/2/63.

490 "mob": HA to MM, 10/3/63.

490 "If I" to "piety . . . provided": MM to HA, 10/24/63.

490–491 "over-rated" to "you kids": Sontag and Macdonald quoted in letter from Lenny Green to author, 3/20/64.

491 "Middleclassicism . . . is in": Philip Rahv to MM, 4/25/65; "Susan . . . square": Rahv to MM, 4/9/65, both MPVC.

491 "psychopath" to "establishment": Rahv to MM, 4/25/65.

491 "substitution of" to "come through": Rahv to MM, 5/18/73.

491 "desire to" to "circus ring": MM to HA, 10/24/63.

491 "Dwight . . . that": quoted in letter from Lenny Green to author, 11/18/63.

491 "Mary . . . together": Dwight Macdonald to Nicola Chiaromonte, 10/9/63, from Mary McCarthy, 259.

491 "It was" to "the flux": Dwight Macdonald to MM, 9/24/63, MPYU.

492 "A lot" to "did not": Green to author, 11/18/63.

492 " 'educated banal' ": William Abrahams, review of The Group, PR (Jan.–Feb. 1964), 107; "deteriorated . . . style": Green to author, 11/18/63.

492–493 "premature suburbanites" to "has root": "Mary McCarthy Case," 2.

493 "She steers" to "novel should": interview with Stwertka, 1985.

493 "She was" to "by compassion": Gore Vidal, quoted by Lorna Gage in The Independent (10/28/89).

494 "some . . . endeavor": quoted in Frank, Louise Bogan, 247.

494 "enormously . . . sociology": "Mary McCarthy Case," 2.

494 "then the . . . Group": Abrahams, PR, 109.

494 "that should . . . up": Green to author, 11/18/63.

495 "outrageous but articulate": interview with Daphne Hellman, 1985.

495 "To make" to "there before": CBS interview at Vassar College, 10/2/85, Vassar Collection.

32. FUNNY MONEY

496 "A novelist . . . forget": "On Madame Bovary," 77.

496 "Meanwhile . . . time": Louise Bogan to Ruth Limmer, 9/8/63, from What the Woman Lived, 353.

496 " 'Maturity' . . . set in": Lenny Green to author, 11/18/63.

496 "seeming, when" to "graceful physically": telephone interview with Kevin McCarthy, 5/2/87.

497 "yeoman loveliness": Lowell, "For Mary McCarthy," Notebook, 12.

497 "surreptitiously backed" to "by it": MM to HA, 10/24/63, MPVC.

497 "Yes, fame . . . tiring": HA to MM, Fall 1963, MPVC; "that you" to "be happy": HA to MM, 9/16/63.

497 "Je ne" to "the fence": interview with MM, 7/31/85.

497–498 " 'mon chou-chou' " to "smitten": interview with MM, 4/21/86.

498 "Nobody on" to "could have": interview with MM, 7/31/85.

499 "Whoever was" to "imagine": ibid.

499 "obviously was" to "in it": interview with MM, 8/18/88.

500 some money from the State Department: telephone interview with Abel, 1985. " 'Here, give this to intellectuals there who are favorable to us,' " Abel recalls hearing that a State Department official said; and Phillips replied, " 'You can't just buy people like that,' and suggested instead that the government support magazines and organizations. Thus, in his own way," Abel proposes, "Phillips 'founded' the CIA's program of support for the Congress and its magazines."

500 "big jump . . . tour": Phillips, Partisan View, 221. For Phillips, the 1950 trip marked "the end of the isolation and purity we had enjoyed as a dedicated intellectual minority" (221).

500   "a combination . . . in": William Phillips to MM, 5/21/62, MPVC.

500   "Does anyone . . . Medicare": Thomas W. Braden, "I'm Glad the CIA Is 'Immoral,' " *The Saturday Evening Post* (May 1967), 10.

500   "Cultural . . . CIA": Paul Goodman, "The Devolution of Democracy," *Dissent* (Winter 1962), 7.

500   "deny the" to "self-improving units": Nicholas Nabokov, letter to *Dissent* (Summer 1962), 306.3.

500   "Nicky . . . CIA": interview with Silvers, 1989.

500   "since the" to "innocent person": interview with MM, 11/20/87.

501   "It was" to "were doing": interview with MM, 4/21/86.

501   "the general" to "*Preuves* has": Nicola Chiaromonte to MM, 3/29/67, MPVC.

501   "the most" to "forbidden territory": interview with Silvers, 1989.

501   " 'almost John . . . self-lacerating' ": Kristol quoted in Coleman, *The Liberal Conspiracy*, 58; "front-office Metternichs": Macdonald, quoted in *Liberal Conspiracy*, 78.

502   "the individual" to "the law": Stephen Spender, letter to the *New York Times*, 3/24/67.

502   " 'Limit . . . policy' ": quoted in Braden, "I'm Glad the CIA Is 'Immoral,' " 11.

502   Josselson and Lasky's history recounted in Bloom, *Prodigal Sons*, 161–62, and in *Liberal Conspiracy*, 15–19, 94. Lasky's CIA ties also reported in Richard H. Pells, *The Liberal Mind in a Conservative Age*, 129.

502   "a team . . . occasions": Spender to author, 8/11/92.

502   "the 'other" to "false story": interview with MM, 7/31/85. Macdonald, whose tenure was cut short at *Encounter* for general incompatibility with the Congress, was the least likely candidate for Braden's 'agent'; "utterly uncontrollable," McCarthy described him, "even for good reasons, let alone for bad ones" (interview, 7/31/85). "equally . . . gull' ": Spender to author, 8/13/92.

503   "shrewd . . . semi-intellectual": interview with MM, 11/20/87.

503   "because he" to "Forget it' ": ibid. 1964 was when public allegations of CIA subsidies led *Encounter*'s editors to negotiate a business relationship with a *Daily Mirror* group (*Liberal Conspiracy*, 186).

503   "catastrophic . . . deceiver": interview with MM, 7/31/85.

503   "regular subsidization" to "to individuals": "A Statement on the CIA," *PR* (Summer 1967), 463.

504   "Since the" to "capitalist society": Mary McCarthy, *Hanoi*, in *The Seventeenth Degree* (New York: Harcourt Brace Jovanovich, 1974), 313.

504   "socialists . . . communism": Braden, 10.

504   "The fact" to "to Congress": Podhoretz, *Making It* (New York: Random House/Bantam, 1969), 136.

505   "agree[d] with" to "national history": Josselson quoted in *Liberal Conspiracy*, 221.

505   "detachment . . . objectivity": *Hanoi, SD*, 312; "looking . . . interest": Mary McCarthy, *Vietnam, SD*, 63.

506   "brusqueness": Goldman quoted in Hamilton, *Robert Lowell*, 320.

507   "stolen . . . 'Justice' ": Braden, 11.

507   For her, the tie was worth it: interview with MM, 11/20/87.

507   "The CIA's" to "of action": Gloria Steinem quoted in *Time* (2/24/67), 15.

507–508   "other kinds" to "to lie": interview with Silvers, 1989.

508   "Like you . . . Grand": Kevin McCarthy to MM, December 1966, MPVC.

508   "dream . . . it": interview with MM, 7/31/85.

508   "an historical" to "of government": Diana Trilling, "On Withdrawing from Vietnam: An Exchange," *NYRB* (1/18/68), reprinted in *SD*, 173.

508   "The WASPs . . . Fleas": Edward Shils quoted in *Liberal Conspiracy*, 238.

33. PRINCESS IN PARIS

512   "[T]he whirling . . . ravager": Henry James quoted by Wharton's biographer Cynthia Griffin Wolff, and cited in *The Norton Anthology of Literature by Women*, eds. Sandra M. Gilbert and Susan Gubar (New York: W. W. Norton, 1985), 1167.

512   'aussi Sartre': de Gaulle's words, "*Sartre est aussi la France*," quoted in McCarthy's 12/22/64 letter to Arendt.

512   "both fairies" to "sweet ones": MM to HA, 12/22/64, MPVC.

512   "life companion": Mary McCarthy "Crushing a Butterfly," *Encounter* (March 1965), reprinted in *WW*, 100.

512   "*cause célèbre*": MM to HA, 12/22/64.

512   "a plain" to "literary commitment": "Crushing a Butterfly," 96.

513   "Language, for" to "no meaning": ibid., 97; " 'committed literature' " to "the Left": ibid., 99–101.

513   "The sad . . . good": MM to HA, 12/22/64.

514   "a little" to "pro tem": ibid.

514   "*Dans son . . . litterature*": "La mort de Mary McCarthy," *Le Monde* (10/27/89), 22.

514   "She was . . . Paris": interview with King, 1990.

514   "standard people" to "much better": interview with MM, 8/19/85.

514–515   "In Paris" to "anti-clique": interview with Kot Jelenski, 4/19/86.

515   "Each one . . . writers": interview with MM, 8/19/88.

515   "New York" to "the veldt": Hardwick to MM, 2/9/70, MPVC.

515   "a way . . . one": MM to HA, 4/30/71.

Then she was on her way to the Nice Festival du Livre with Stephen Spender.

515 "In London . . . could work": interview with Eileen Finletter, 3/22/86.

515–516 "a very" to "look-at-your-watch life": interview with MM, 8/19/85.

516 "sickening telegram" to "the end": interview with Nicholas King, 1990.

516 "personal . . . convey": ibid.

516 "hoax" to "in literature": Symposium: "On the New Cultural Conservatism," PR (Summer 1972), 434.

516 "because she" to "which she [wasn't]": interview with Finletter, 1986.

516 accent was "appalling": interview with Frances FitzGerald, 1/30/86.

517 "she [didn't]" to "another language": interview with Finletter, 1986.

517 "their . . . American-in-Paris": Jane Kramer, "The Private Mary McCarthy: Unfinished With Life," International Herald Tribune (10/31/89), 19.

517 "a lady . . . club": telephone interview with Jessie Wood, 11/8/91.

518 "full of" to "a minority": MM to HA, 1/18/65.

518–519 "There is" to "believe it": interview with MM, 4/21/86; dining room incident confirmed by Kot Jelenski, 4/19/86.

519 "Vous avez" to "possible, regret": MM to HA, 3/7/68.

519 "solitary people" to "bad word": interview with Jelenski, 1986.

519 "rough . . . her": interview with MM, 4/21/86; "it was" to "smoothed over": interview with Silvers, 1989.

519 "She wanted" to "a reason": interview with MM, 4/21/86, "one could" to "really herself": interview with Jelenski, 1986.

519 "passionate partisanship" to "miracle": MM to HA, 9/23/69.

519–520 "if one" to "qua Jewess": HA to MM, 10/17/69, MPVC.

521 "closest . . . years": Arendt quoted in Young-Bruehl, Hannah Arendt, 56.

521–522 " 'I always" to "communications industry": Mary McCarthy, "Hanging by a Thread," WW, 173–75.

522 "Insofar . . . commodity": ibid., 178.

522 "She was" to "go on": interview with MM, 4/21/86.

523 "The traditional . . . demolition": MM to HA, 1/18/65.

523 "horrible blanks" to "social silence": MM to HA, 6/9/64.

524 "Dear Hannah . . . friends": MM to HA, 1/18/65; "Dearest . . . t'embrasse": HA to MM, 4/28/65; "no-letter": HA to MM, 10/20/65.

524 "spectre of equality" to "to him": MM to HA, 6/9/64.

525 "But to" to "awkward question": "How It Went," SD, 23.

525 "superiors" to "from home": MM to HA, 6/9/64.

525 "a catalogue . . . there": interview with King, 1990; "old American virtues": interview with Cees Nooteboom, 4/22/86.

525 "bright topicality" to "lived experience": Helen Vendler, review of Birds of America, NYTBR (5/16/71), 1.

527 "now that . . . ordination": Prynne (Hardwick), "The Gang," NYRB (9/26/63), 22.

527 "Wasp-cells . . . moment": Wilson, Forties, 47.

528 "but because" to "be multiplying": "On the New Cultural Conservatism," 437.

528–529 "no one . . . book": HA to MM, 5/28/71.

529 "weirdly personal" to "personal enemies": MM to HA, 5/18/71.

529 "MARY . . . VILLAIN": blurb for Vendler review, NYTBR, 1.

529 "[T]he amount" to "the author": HA to MM, 5/28/71.

530 "opposition of" to "our civilization": HA to MM, ibid.

531 "Last night" to "checked cap": MM to HA, 4/30/71.

34. HANOI GOTHIC

532 "I am . . . Vietnam": "Hanoi," SD, 317.

532 her taxes: U. S. taxes for Americans living abroad are due June 15.

532 " 'If you" to "in Saigon' ": "How It Went," SD, 15.

532 "rather hard-line . . . Vietnam": MM to Robert Silvers, 1/28/67, MPVC; "when you . . . anyway": "How It Went," SD, 14–15; Bohlen responded "gallantly": MM to Silvers, 1/28/67.

533 "Cleared for" to "invariably true": ibid.

533–534 "A rather" to "or discouragement": ibid.

534 "great moment" to "an omen": "How It Went," 14.

534 "protesters": interview with King, 1990; mothers' mink coats: interview with Finletter, 1986.

534 " 'Hell . . . me' ": "How It Went," 14.

535 Naturally they hadn't: Thorkild Christiansen later told Jim West that Mary was a "brave woman": interview with West, 7/26/89.

535 "peace" to "confess to": "Hanoi," 322.

535 "I confess . . . official": "Vietnam," SD, 63.

535 " 'How dare" to "Mary's way": interview with King, 1990.

535 "show" to "stand behind": "How It Went," 17.

535 " 'refugees' " to "free enterprise' ": "Vietnam," 79.

535 "like FBI agents": "Vietnam," 92.

536 " 'no more" to "Communist ideology": Edmund Wilson, The Cold War and the Income Tax: A Protest (New York: Farrar, Straus and Co., 1963), 75.

536–537 "would not" to "to curb": "Vietnam," 20–21.

537 position "shaky": "How It Went," 17.
537 "anxious and hamstrung" to "his job": MM to HA, 4/2/65, MPVC.
538 " 'good' Germans": "How It Went," 10.
538 "There isn't" to "their characters": William Jovanovich to MM, 12/16/65, MPVC.
538 "a betrayal . . . too": MM to Jovanovich, 1/30/67, MPVC; "It would" to "a novel": Brightman, "Mary, Quite Contrary," 613.
538–539 "a sort" to " 'final favor' ": MM to Jovanovich, 5/11/67.
539 "annoyed" to "natural enough": Jovanovich to MM, 5/18/67.
539 "They will . . . book": Jovanovich to MM, 10/5/68; "take out . . . again": MM to Jovanovich, 11/4/68, MPVC.
539 risked her " 'position' ": Nicola Chiaromonte to MM, 3/9/68, MPVC.
540 "live under . . . term": "How It Went," 46.
540 "the idea" to "your room": "Hanoi," 316.
540 "might at . . . right' ": ibid., 317; "chiefly for" to "interlocutor: oneself": ibid., 316.
541 "religious freight": interview with King, 1990.
541 "I was . . . Vietnamese": interview with Kazin, 1985; "Mary . . . politically": interview with Phillips, 1988.
541 "only to . . . mirror": "Hanoi," 52.
541 "[L]ike most" to "prominent figures": ibid., 314–15.
541 "My dear . . . suitcases": interview with MM, 8/19/85.
542 "a man" to "vast proscenium": "Hanoi," 303, 305.
542 "automobile-TV culture" to "happy agreement": ibid., 308.
542 "old revolutionaries" to "in Paris": ibid., 297.
542 "a delicate-featured . . . ancestry": ibid., 277; "large village" to "small craftsmen": ibid., 301.
542–543 "après guerre" to "campaign buttons": ibid., 305, 309.
543 "somehow this" to "wore off": "Mary, Quite Contrary," 613–14.
543 "the idea . . . rehabilitation": "Hanoi," 281.
544 "had no . . . society": ibid., 313; "perhaps . . . 'practicing' ": "Mary, Quite Contrary," 613.
544 "[c]onversion, from" to "unilateral de-escalation' ": "Hanoi," 281–83.
544 " 'volunteers' " to "other side": ibid., 283.
544 "at once" to "to it": ibid., 282; "Freedom . . . dissent": Hannah Arendt, "Crises of the Republic," The Partisan Review Reader, 221; "license to . . . system": "Hanoi," 314.

35. CRIME AND PERDITION

545 "Ever since . . . atonement": Mary McCarthy, The Mask of State: Watergate Portraits (New York: Harvest/Harcourt Brace Jovanovich, 1974), 30.
545 "Tuscans" to "[their] past": "Hanoi," 300–01.
545 "A virtuous" to "and morals": MM to Dwight Macdonald, 8/13/69, MPYU.
545 "too far . . . left": interview with MM, 8/18/88; "This doesn't" to "even alluring": MM to DM, 8/13/69.
545–546 "North Vietnam" to "be modern": "Hanoi," 203–04.
546 "I'm for" to "in politics": DM to MM, 9/12/69, MPVC.
546 "soul," "appeased": MM to DM, 4/4/67, "must DO . . . way": DM to MM, 3/27/67, " 'for his" to "earning power": MM to DM, 4/4/67.
546 "You could . . . down": "How It Went," 39.
547 "They were" to "about this' ": ibid., 40–41.
547 "[B]ox-office turkey" to "seemed stale' ": Mary McCarthy, "Medina," SD, 332.
547 "was not" to "lost it": interview with Margo Viscusi, 6/14/90.
547–548 "Leaving out" to "the guilty": "Medina," 384.
548–549 "yawned, stretched" to "child's game": ibid., 327–28.
549 "My Lai was" to "the Army": ibid., 335, 345.
549 " 'destroy . . . moved' " ": ibid., 345.
549–550 "We had" to "attacked us": "How It Went," 80.
550 "I would . . . more": MM to HA, 4/2/65, MPVC.
550 "one of" to "start negotiating": HA to MM, 4/28/65, MPVC.
550 "Let us" to "camp follower": "On Withdrawing from Vietnam: An Exchange," NYRB (1/18/68), 175–76.
551 "Were the" to "they don't": "Medina," 404–05.
552 "studded, like" to "of power": Mary McCarthy, "Sons of the Morning," SD, 413.
552 "[N]ot brains" to " 'scientists' ": ibid., 428–29.
553 " 'world Communist threat' " to "is injurious": ibid, 436–37.
553–554 " 'muscle' " to "of confrontations": ibid., 438.
554 "Actually . . . mystery": ibid., 433.
554 "press's 'objective' " to "the millions": "How It Went," 27.
554–555 "lack of" to "husband's story": James Fallows, "The Blinders She Wears," Washington Monthly (May 1974), 12–13.
555 "[O]nly by . . . reach them": ibid., 13.
555 "Publish in . . . Books": "How It Went," 6.
555 McCarthy's 270,000 royalties: Jovanovich to MM, 10/22/68, MPVC.
555 "So it" to "the combination": "How It Went," 5.
555 "[t]he whole . . . obvious": HA to MM, 12/21/68.

36. THE DUCHESS OF CASTINE

556 "Five nations . . . here!": Robert Lowell, "Fourth of July in Maine," *Selected Poems*, 145.

556 "Bit by . . . lives": "How It Went," *SD*, 42.

556 "[I]f I" to "Archimedean lever": interview with MM, 8/19/85.

556 "Here goes" to "the country": HA to MM, 5/19/69, MPVC.

556–557 "a real . . . village": MM to William Jovanovich, 7/12/67, from Gelderman, *Mary McCarthy*, 284.

557 "Come to" to "colonial times": MM to DM, 8/6/67, MPYU.

558 "one of" to "the Lowells": MM to HA, 9/12/67, MPVC.

558 "The Wests" to "is heard": Robert Lowell to Elizabeth Bishop, 7/30/68, Bishop Papers, Special Collections, Vassar College.

558 "Your eight-inch" to "a duchess": Lowell, "For Mary McCarthy," *Notebook*, 12.

559 "defected" to "a few": MM to HA, 6/26/70.

559 "imaginary country": Mary McCarthy, *Cannibals and Missionaries* (New York: Harcourt Brace Jovanovich, 1979), xi.

559 "recent outbreaks" to "years ago": MM to HA, 9/12/67.

560 " 'A bit" to "could be": William Jovanovich to MM, 8/17/88.

560 "to get . . . advice": telephone interview with Sally Austin, 6/7/91.

561 "pretty vigorous": telephone interview with Kevin McCarthy, 5/2/87.

561 "she thought" to "to eat": telephone interview with Kate McCarthy, 5/2/87.

561–562 "If everything" to "certain hierarchy": telephone interview with Kevin McCarthy, 5/2/87.

562 "If it" to "ELECTIONS TRAHISON": MM to HA, 6/18/68.

562 "exquisitely beautiful" to "jelly-making time": MM to HA, 7/17/69; "From here" to "fixed up": MM to HA, 5/22/69.

563 "a splendid" to "public thing": HA to MM, 2/4/70.

564 "Women's Lib" to "finish last": Elizabeth Hardwick to MM, 6/11/71, MPVC.

564 "no creature" to "a novelist": Vendler, review of *Birds of America*, *NYTBR*, 1. After *The Group*, even an unsuccessful novel such as *Birds of America* sold nearly 400,-000 copies in its various editions—HBJ, The Literary Guild, NAL, and Avon.

564 "She missed" to "to Paris": Fallows, "The Blinders She Wears," *Washington Monthly*, 11.

564–565 "still slogging" to "the reason": MM to Elizabeth Hardwick, 12/9/71, MPVC.

565 "[P]erhaps I" to "with communication": MM to HA, 9/3/72.

565 *"there"* to "Rosie's death": MM to HA, 1/19/72.

565 "She let" to "taken away": Margo Viscusi to author, 10/22/90.

565 Nicola's death was "hateful": MM to HA, 1/19/72; "Mary, look" to "on living": HA to MM, 1/25/72.

566 "I have" to "my calendar": MM to HA, 4/5/72; "feeling . . . journey": MM to Elizabeth Hardwick, 12/9/71.

566 "I suddenly" to "covered eyes": Jim West to Mary and Tommy Thomas, 2/10/72, courtesy of Jim West.

567 "I find" to "in them": MM to HA, 4/5/72.

567 "What kind . . . people": George Meany quoted by Lafeber and Polenberg in *The American Century*, 477.

567 "civic conscience" to "a gesture": MM to HA, 9/3/72.

567 "bussing" to "of bussing": Mary McCarthy, "Imagination, Anyone?" *Newsweek*, 7/10/72, 23–24.

568 "assistant" to *"you* in": interview with Viscusi, 1990.

568 "I just" to "the *Queen":* interview with MM, 4/21/86.

569 "Inside are . . . bark": *MS*, 50; "[w]ith his . . . *Cleopatra":* ibid., 9; "zeal . . . personality": ibid., 13; "the 'old' . . . America": ibid., 32; "honest . . . rustics": ibid., 10.

569 "something turnipy" to "wintering potato": Anthony Howard, "Morality Stories," review of *The Mask of State* in *The New Statesman* (6/28/74), 923.

570 "a great equalizer": *MS*, 7.

570 "their soap . . . characters": MM to HA, 8/10/73.

570 "The contrast . . . year": ibid.

570 " 'rural idiocy' ": Rahv quoted in MM to HA, 7/20/75.

571 "fired with" to "long run": MM to HA, 8/5/75.

573 "The social" to "the referendum": interview with MM, 9/25/80.

573 "I'm going . . . you": interview with MM, 4/21/86.

573–574 "American tincture" to "campus intellectual": interview with MM, 9/25/80.

37. HOW THEY GO

575 "One more" to "a name": E. J. Rousuck to MM, 2/19/62, MPVC.

575 *"A prancing . . . Christmas":* MM to Rousuck, 11/4/65, MPVC; " 'Just give . . . Cooper-Henderson' ": *HIG*, 249.

575 " 'Mannie . . . getter' ": MM to Rousuck, 11/4/65.

576 "He trusted" to " 'an affair' ": *HIG*, 248.

576 slept with over one hundred men: according to Robert Silvers, McCarthy said this to Morton Zabel (Silvers' note on draft ms. of Chapter 11 of *Writing Dangerously*).

576 "intimate friends" to "intellectual pursuits": *HIG*, 249.

576 "I had . . . sense": Rousuck to MM, undated.

576 "the deflating" to "American genius": Elizabeth Hardwick, "Presentation Address," *Colony Newsletter*, 3.

576   "Dear . . . apartment": *HIG, 249.*

577   "I can't" to "ghastly state": Hardwick to MM, 12/27/73, MPVC.

577   "astounding news": ibid.

577   "a strange . . . *never":* interview with Fitz-Gerald, 1986.

578   "one of . . . state": McCarthy, "Divorcée on Gay Street," 100.

578   "utter *'isolation' "* to "on to him": MM to HA, 3/1/74 MPVC; "scandalous . . . play-wright": Frankie Fitzgerald to MM, 2/5/74, MPVC; "as if . . . aspect": MM to HA, 3/1/74.

578   "So he's" to "susceptible, confiding": McCarthy, "Philip Rahv," *OP,* 3.

578   "The best . . . him, *ever":* interview with FitzGerald, 1986.

578   "the real . . . politics": conversation with Dan Rosen, 2/16/88.

578–579   "Jaunty . . . irony": Mary McCarthy, "F. W. Dupee, 1904–1979," *OP,* 43.

579   "There's a" to "of immortality": MM to Frani Muser, 11/11/79, MPVC.

579   "did not . . . dead' ": Hardwick to MM, 12/27/73.

579   "I find" to "I couldn't": MM to HA, 3/1/74.

579–580   "possible themes" to "about Jews": Philip Rahv to MM, 11/26/71, MPVC; "unless . . . abstract": MM to Rahv, 12/9/71 MPVC.

580   "It's strange" to "of *him":* MM to HA, 3/1/74.

580   "I long" to "fact? Astounding": Rahv to MM, 5/18/73.

580   "rather blah": MM to HA, 3/1/74.

580   because she had been "drunk"; it was Philip she loved, *etc.:* "Edmund Wilson," *Paris Review,* 10, 17, reprinted in *Intellectual Memoirs: New York 1936–1938.*

580   *Kein Mitleid":* quoted in Young-Bruehl, *Hannah Arendt,* 467.

581   "still thinking" to "for shelter": HA to MM, 9/30/73, MPVC.

581   "sympathetic to" to "of duty": Stephen Spender to author, 8/11/92.

581   "Homer said" to " 'lucky' ": HA to MM, 9/30/73.

582   "the usual" to *"tant pis":* HA to MM, 12/8/71.

582   "suddenly . . . before": HA to MM, 8/22/75.

582   'deforestation process': HA to MM, 12/23/73.

583   "peculiar, in" to "own ribs": MM to HA, 9/30/74.

583   "tainted witness" to "no feminist": ibid.; "speechless" to "it, *please":* HA to MM, 9/12/74.

584   "the tone" to "am not": MM to HA, 11/20/74; "I am . . . side": MM to HA, 2/17/75.

584   "dark . . . soft": *CM,* 3; "happy . . . bow-tie": ibid., 9.

584   "not waiting . . . snuffer": ibid., 6.

584   "Scylla and" to "not mocked": MM to HA, 2/17/75.

585   "temptation . . . girl": ibid.

585   "high piercing voice": *CM,* 107.

585–586   "my occupational" to "the artist": MM to Rowland Burdon-Mueller, 8/6/79.

586   "felt completely" to "book better": Burdon-Mueller to MM, 9/2/79, both MPVC.

586   "meritorious . . . civilization": Thor A. Bak (Sonning Foundation official) to Arendt, 2/13/75, MPVC.

586   "years of aberration": *Hannah Arendt,* 464.

587   "gastronomic points": MM to HA, 2/17/75.

587   "He and" to "my story": MM to HA, 11/12/75.

588   "good old" to "a butterfly": HA to MM, no date (1975).

588   "impatient propitiatory offerings": "Saying Good-bye to Hannah," *OP,* 41.

589   "To the . . . questions": HA to MM, 8/17/73.

589   "the dark" to "characteristic processes" "Saying Good-bye," 36–38; "physical being" to "stage diva": ibid., 38–39.

590   "Bernhardt or" to "elegant feet": ibid., 39.

590   "a bit" to "was saying": interview with Angleton, 1986.

590   "feminist patriotism" to "intellectual superiority": interview with Jelenski, 1986.

590   "pure" to "lived simply": interview with Elizabeth Hardwick, 3/12/86.

590   "power of" to "an actor": "Saying Good-bye," 40.

590   "elegant woman" to "with Mary": interview with Jelenski, 1986.

590–591   "privileged conceit" to *"moral* quality": interview with Hardwick, 1986.

591   " 'crazy' " to "gruesome *voyeur":* MM to HA, 10/11/66.

591   "it was . . . did she": MM to HA, 12/19/67.

591   "She wanted" to "for me' ": interview with MM, 4/21/86.

593   "plausibility . . . fiction": A. B. Guthrie, quoted in *The Portland Press Herald* (3/5/90).

593   "You're . . . meant to": Brightman, "Mary, Still Contrary," 613; "the emotional" to "precludes identification": MM to author, 4/28/81; "absolutely astonished" to "that sense": interview with MM, 9/25/80; "If there" to "provisional defense": MM to author, 4/28/81.

594   "Today . . . differently": interview with Angélique Levi, 4/19/86.

594   *"de haut en bas":* Benjamin DeMott, "Tales of Two Writers" (includes review of *CM*), *The Saturday Review* (12/19/79).

594–595   "Actually, what" to "repeat, *yes":* "Mary, Still Contrary," 612.

595 "underground railroad" to "the slaughter": MM to HA, 10/4/73.

595 "Den Uyl . . . will": *CM,* 350.

595 "streams of experience": *HIG,* 251.

596 "which led . . . *Republic":* ibid.

38. WITH MALICE TOWARD ONE

597 "Who steals . . . indeed": *Othello,* Act III, Scene 3, line 155.

597 "Anger . . . essence": Hersey quoted in Wright, *Lillian Hellman,* 424.

597 "There's . . . them": CBS interview, 10/85, Vassar College videotape.

597 "to change" to "on television": interview with Simpson, 1987.

598 "the more . . . work": Wilson, "Justice to Edith Wharton," *Wound and the Bow,* 195.

598–599 "genius [which] may" to "this sense": ibid., 208.

599 "seems at" to "flexible steel": ibid., 208–09.

599 "grand old" to "goading her": interview with Viscusi, 1990.

599 "was on" to "about Hellman": interview with Simpson, 1987.

600 "overrated, and" to "writer anymore?": Dick Cavett, transcript of 10/18/79 interview, quoted in McCarthy's June 1983 motion for summary judgment, MPVC, 3; "At least" to "the past": Mary McCarthy, transcript, ibid., 2–3; "What . . . Hellman?" Cavett, ibid., 3; *"Everything"* to "and 'the' ": McCarthy, ibid., 3.

600 "it all" to "tell you": interview with Simpson, 1987.

600 "I'm sure" to "Hellman lately": Cavett, p. 3.

600 "Jim . . . died": interview with Simpson, 1987.

600 "pure hyperbole" to "a thing": interview with Viscusi, 1990.

600 "made no . . . broadcast": Herbert Mitgang, "Book Ends," *NYT* (2/16/80), 12.

600 "Please. . . . scared": MM to Ben O'Sullivan, 2/20/80, MPVC.

601 "false . . . professionally": plaintiff's complaint quoted in Wright, *Lillian Hellman,* 386.

601 "what in" to "is perceptible": MM to William Jovanovich, 2/26/80, MPVC.

601 "the question" to "right away": interview with Muser, 1986.

601 "The fact . . . figure": Macdonald quoted by Michiko Kakutani, "Hellman-McCarthy Libel Suit Stirs Old Antagonisms," *NYT* (3/19/80), C21.

601 "literary criticism" to "such evidence": McCarthy's motion for summary judgment, 2.

602 "distort events" to "pervasive falsity": ibid., 5. "The case is very interesting, gets

more so almost every day as more lies come to light," McCarthy wrote Muriel Gardiner on August 27, 1980 (MPVC).

602 "rhetorical hyperbole," "expression of opinion": Ben O'Sullivan to MM, 6/13/80, MPVC.

602 "I don't" to "her work": transcript of McCarthy's 8/12/81 deposition with Ephraim London, MPVC.

602 "a terrific slam": Kevin McCarthy's interview with MM for *People Weekly,* (October 1979), unpublished part, MPVC.

602 "looking silly" to "moral arbiter": telephone interview with Mailer, 1991.

603 "to call . . . ideas' ": Judge Harold Baer, Jr., *NYT* (5/11/84), C3.

603 "general notoriety" to "or controversy": ibid.

604 "I mean . . . almost": interview with MM, 10/29/85.

604 " 'Thank . . . do it' ": *Lillian Hellman,* 253.

605 "I cannot" to "political group": Hellman quoted in *Lillian Hellman,* 246–47.

605 "Each had" to "have produced": ibid., 381.

606 "[s]ome *were . . .* about it": Phillips quoted in *Lillian Hellman,* 362.

606 "virtually unreconstructed" to "of 'integrity' ": MM to Walter Goldwater, 8/7/80, MPVC.

606 "Lillian was" to "give satisfaction": telephone interview with Mailer, 1991.

607 "would amount . . . game": Lillian Hellman, *Scoundrel Time* (New York: Little, Brown & Co., 1976), 60.

607 "the sins" to "hereditary enemies": ibid., 40; " 'sins' " to "and crimes": Hook quoted in *Lillian Hellman,* 361–62.

607 "raised a" to "hereditary enemies": *Scoundrel Time,* 40; "historically . . . meanness": Kazin quoted in *Lillian Hellman,* 362.

607–608 "The children" to "millionaire waiters": *Scoundrel Time,* 40–41.

608 "raised in" to "Christian honor": quoted in *Lillian Hellman,* 247.

608 "either by" to "injure them": *Scoundrel Time,* 40.

608 "long-standing" to "Cavett Show": MM to O'Sullivan, 4/21/80.

608–609 "she had" to "of society": interview with MM, 4/21/86.

609 "Maybe she" to "she achieved": Schapiro quoted in *NYT* (3/19/80), C21.

609 "She's an . . . quality": interview with Simpson, 1987.

609 "Here was" to "was not": interview with Viscusi, 1990.

609 " 'Missionaries and" to "more successful": London quoted in *NYT* (3/19/80), C21.

610 "I think" to "popped up": interview with MM, 4/21/86.

610 "She knew" to "of course": interview with Muser, 1986.

610   "If something" to "by it": interview with Stwertka, 1985.

610   " 'Don't . . . *schtick'* ": quoted in *Lillian Hellman,* 434.

610   "may have" to "her taste": interview with Stwertka, 1985.

611   "remember[ed] the" to "the years": Lillian Hellman to Stephen Spender, 9/1/83, MPVC.

611   "Lillian . . . lawsuit": telephone interview with Mailer, 1991.

611   "angelic intervention": McCarthy quoted in Gelderman, *Mary McCarthy,* 339. McCarthy had already paid out $23,000 in legal fees.

611   "She was" to "a distraction": interview with Viscusi, 1990.

611   "The power . . . service": Elizabeth Hardwick to MM, undated "autumn foliage note," probably 1976, MPVC.

612   "Lillian . . . known": Trilling quoted in *Lillian Hellman,* 373.

612   "the oily . . . Saroyan": "Eugene O'Neill— Dry Ice," *MMTC,* 81; "[e]xcept . . . dignity": "Five Curios," *MMTC,* 91.

612   "I couldn't be bothered": MM to author, 3/4/88.

612   "Anything in" to "in terms": Mary McCarthy, "The Reform of Dr. Pangloss," *NR* (12/17/56), 383.

612   " 'You! You" to "at Mary": interview with Simpson, 1987.

613   "a reluctance . . . Boy": MM to O'Sullivan, 5/11/84.

613   " 'to extrude" to "public opinion": MM to Jovanovich, November 1980.

613   "confronting [Hellman's] political" to "be heard": MM to O'Sullivan, 5/11/84.

613–614   "Hellman was" to "a liar": Carl Rollyson, *Lillian Hellman, Her Legend and Her Legacy* (New York: St. Martin's Press, 1988), 513.

614   "Her incomprehension . . . idiocy": Gellhorn quoted in Rollyson, *Lillian Hellman,* 514.

614   "The only" to "plaintiff herself": pretrial deposition, MPVC.

615   "Miss Hellman" to "anti-Hellman group": Hellman to Spender, 8/4/83, MPVC.

615   " 'She's a . . . lady' ": telephone conversation with Lady Stephen Spender, 8/14/92.

615   "the painter" to "seeing again": Lillian Hellman, *Pentimento* (New York: Little, Brown, 1973), 3.

616   "It's no" to "with truth": Lillian Hellman, *Maybe* (Boston: Little, Brown, 1980), 51.

616   " 'bring up . . . that' ": Rauh quoted in *Lillian Hellman,* 390.

616   "Mary's . . . aside": Cowley quoted in *NYT* (3/19/80), C21.

616   "hatchet woman" to "deserves this": interview with Simpson, 1987.

617   "[i]f Lillian" to "a brutality": Norman Mailer, "An Appeal to Lillian Hellman and Mary McCarthy," *NYTBR* (5/11/80), 3.

617   "There was" to "she created": telephone interview with Mailer, 1991.

617   "blarney" to "we invent": Mailer, "Appeal to Lillian Hellman and Mary McCarthy," 3, 33.

617   "absolutely appropriate" to "the heap": Plimpton quoted in Manso, *Mailer,* 612.

617–618   "not dishonest" to "the truth": "Appeal to Lillian Hellman and Mary McCarthy," 3.

618   "About truth . . . monotheistic": *HIG,* 199.

618   "We do" to "are fiction": telephone interview with Mailer, 1991.

618   "A much-damaged" to "longer see": "Appeal to Lillian Hellman and Mary McCarthy," 3.

618   "maudlin appeals" to "literary ratings": Richard Poirier, letter to *NYTBR* (5/25/80), 33.

618   "I have . . . quoted Holmes": Norman Mailer to Poirier, 6/16/80 (unpublished), MPVC.

619   "Normie": telephone interview with Mailer, 1991.

619   "There could" to "genuinely sorry": Lillian Hellman to Mailer, 7/5/80, MPVC.

619   "jockeying for" to "kill you' ": Feiffer quoted in *Mailer,* 53–54.

619   "a coupla . . . out": interview with Muser, 1986.

619   "one's attitude" to "20th century": Howe quoted in *NYT* (3/19/80), C21.

619–620   "You knew" to "yourself loveability": interview with MM, 4/21/86.

620   "Lillian Hellman" to "more interesting": *Lillian Hellman,* 433.

620   "only wanted" to "avoid retiring": "Edmund Wilson," *Paris Review,* 20–21.

620   "was hell-bent" to "no premonition": ibid., 24; "my punishment . . . here": ibid., 22.

621   "other reasons" to "evolve into": ibid., 23–24.

621   "vividly . . . words": ibid., 17; "ungrateful" to "particularly grateful": ibid., 25.

621–622   "the Marxist" to "word rate": ibid., 25.

622   "Born in . . . *Penitent*": Daniel Defoe, *Moll Flanders* (Oxford: Oxford University Press, 1990), iii.

EPILOGUE

623   "So we'll . . . night": Lord Byron, letter to Thomas Moore, 2/28/1817, *The Letters of Lord Byron,* 157.

623   "She was" to "life completed": Jane Kramer, "The Private Mary McCarthy: Unfinished Woman," *International Herald Tribune,* 10/31/89, 18.

624   "a bit" to "ultra-accurate test": MM to author, 5/23/86.

624   "She much . . . educational": telephone conversation with Margo Viscusi, 1/4/89.

625   "a hundred . . . right": MM to author, 2/5/88; "With a . . . now": 5/7/88.

625   "The more" to "she became": Jane Kramer, Vassar memorial address, 5/5/90, Vassar College videotape.

626   "an international man": Mary McCarthy, Introduction to Niccolò Tucci's *The Rain Came Last* (New York: New Directions, 1990), x.

626   "the fish house": ibid., ix.

626–627   "there was" to "in it": ibid., ix.

627   "on a" to "for her": Kramer, "The Private Mary McCarthy," 18.

627–628   "We all" to "of citizens": acceptance address, MacDowell Award Ceremony, *Colony Newsletter*, 4; "the slightest" to *"The Group"*: ibid.

628   "felt . . . skin": telephone interview with Jessie Wood, 1991.

629   " 'never been . . . something": conversation with Eve Stwertka, 10/31/89.

629   " 'I used" to "of Man' ": letter to Elizabeth and Robert Lowell, quoted in Gelderman, *Mary McCarthy*, 295.

631   "People can" to "there's hope": Dorothy Richardson, "Death," in *The Norton Anthology of Literature by Women*, 1293.

631   "I cannot . . . destroyed": telephone conversation with James West, 11/19/89.

631   "a touch" to "ferocious": telephone conversation with James West, 10/23/89.

632   "Sing . . . distress": Auden's line from "In Memory of W.B. Yeats," quoted in Young-Bruehl, *Hannah Arendt*, 455.

632   terminating the life support system: conversations with Kate McCarthy, 10/31/89, and James West, 12/31/91.

632   "Insofar as" to "his church": Mary McCarthy, untitled ms. submitted to *Boston College Magazine* in the summer of 1988; "I wish" to "brotherly love": ibid. In view of McCarthy's ties to Boston Col-

lege—she spoke there on several occasions, and gave both encouragement and assistance to the Jesuit scholar Father James W. Bernauer in his edition of *Amor Mundi: Explorations in the Faith and Thought of Hannah Arendt* (1987)—it is surprising the magazine didn't find a way to publish this provocative reflection.

633   "I still haven't *succeeded!*" interview with MM, 8/19/85.

633   "You can't" to "has vanished": Annie Dillard, "To Fashion a Text," *Inventing the Truth, The Art and Craft of Memoir,* ed. William Zinsser (Boston: Houghton Mifflin Co., 1987), 70.

633   "the thirties" to "you wrote": MM to Muser, 8/16/79, courtesy of Frani Muser.

633   "Being the . . . all": "Edmund Wilson," *Paris Review*, 28; "whether I . . . spared it": ibid., 29.

634   "She didn't . . . character": interview with MM, 8/20/86; "It pains" to "must quote' ": MM to Mary Meigs, 4/14/82, MPVC.

634   "the ridiculous" to "of things": Levi quoted in *Mary McCarthy*, 190; "a sort . . . bias": "The Art of Fiction," *Writers and Work*, 310.

634   "Freedom . . . fact": "The Fact in Fiction," *OC*, 259.

634–635   "The McCarthy" to "voluminous drapery": Constance Hunting, "Some Sort of Joy," *Puckerbrush Review* (Winter, 1982), 7.

635   "Surrounded . . . thought": "Saying Goodbye to Hannah," *OP*, 37; "thought . . . experience": ibid., 37–38.

635   " 'Waugh' " to *"Main Street' "*: The exchange occurred over dinner at Harold Acton's, who reported it to McCarthy at I Tatti in 1956. She passed it on in a letter to Bowden Broadwater on 5/18/56, MPVC.

636   "The world . . . oppose it": Goethe, quoted in *Hannah Arendt*, 473.

Photograph Credits

Acknowledgments

This book was a long time in the making, and my debt to the variety of people who helped me bring it to term is really incalculable. Some benchmarks: In 1984, when Mary McCarthy won the National Medal for Literature, my colleague at *GEO*, Ellen Boddie, prompted me to turn the forty-three-page interview I conducted with McCarthy in 1980 into a shorter one, then published in *The Nation*. At *The Nation*, Elizabeth Pochoda convinced me of the commercial potential of a biography of Mary McCarthy at a time when I needed convincing. At home, my partner, Michael Uhl, had already put the fearsome word *biography* before me, which I rejected out of hand (though I had proposed something like it to McCarthy herself in 1979), no doubt, because the closer I came to *writing* it, the safer it seemed to deny it.

Nor, at first, was Mary McCarthy a willing subject. In our initial transatlantic conversation in the spring of 1984, she tried to talk me out of it; she was already being written about, she told me (by Carol Gelderman), and claimed to regret it. I should wait until she was dead, she said; then, oddly, "Why don't you write about Susan Sontag?" When she understood I wasn't a professional biographer staking out a subject, but was bent on writing about *her* life and times, with or without her permission, she came around.

Once I wrote the proposal, it was my agent, Lucy Kroll, who must be thanked for more than selling the book. From the beginning, she conveyed an excitement and confidence in the ultimate outcome of the project that kept me going during the lean years of research and writing. When the book went into production, her partner Barbara Hogenson took care of business with dispatch. It was through my old friend Janie Glaeser West that I first met Lucy Kroll and the Clarkson Potter editor, Carol Southern, who took the book on. "Call Carol Brightman," Janie (Jane, at the office) told Carol Southern in 1977, when Potter, whose publisher she was, was looking for someone to work with Larry Rivers on what became *Drawings and Digressions*. I was then writing occasional art reviews, and Janie, who knew my interest in painting went way back, and wished I was less *occasional* and more professional about writing, put Carol on my trail. When

Jane West died of cancer in 1981, I lost a friendship that started at Saints Faith, Hope and Charity in Winnetka, Illinois, continued at New Trier High School, and flourished at Vassar. If I've often thought about her while writing this book, it's because of what she alone might have read between the lines.

There are other friends who stepped in as readers along the way, whose comments and suggestions were always helpful: Joan Grant, Gordon Quinn, Meg Gerken, Dan Rosen, Vickie Berning, Gwenda Blair, Richard Levy, not to mention Michael Uhl, whose criticism was most pertinent. John Gliedman and Gordon taught me how to use a computer, without which . . . (etc., etc.). My uncle, John Hancock (Jack, to me), read each chapter in manuscript and gave me the benefit of his good sense as an editor and his ample knowledge of the history, politics, and literature of the 1930s, '40s, and '50s. The Biographical Glossary was his idea, and he is "Gilbert Grail" (one of his many pseudonyms from the novels of George Gissing). Another volunteer critic was Robert B. Silvers of *The New York Review of Books,* whose reservations about my treatment of Edmund Wilson might still stand, but whose suggestion that I look at *The Wound and the Bow* for insight into Wilson's psychoanalytic approach to his marital problems with Mary McCarthy I did follow, with illuminating results.

As the book's editor, Carol Southern is to be thanked for pulling my prose back from the brink of obscurity again and again, and for her stubborn attention to detail. At Clarkson Potter, Mark McCauslin was an unflappable production editor, and Eliza Scott, Southern's assistant, a patient troubleshooter. Carol Edwards's copyediting was both painstaking and thoughtful. Thanks also to designer Howard Klein and production supervisor Joan Denman, and to Renato Stanisic, who laid out the pictures.

I am most indebted to all those friends, family members, and acquaintances of Mary McCarthy who gave generously of their time in taped interviews and conversations: Lionel Abel, Carmen Angleton, Sally Austin, David Bazelon, Ann Birstein, Philip Booth, Miriam Chiaromonte, Elizabeth Daniels, Barbara (Andy) Dupee, Eileen Finletter, Frances FitzGerald, Elizabeth Hardwick, Daphne Hellman, Irving Howe, Kot Jelenski (deceased), John Jewett, Alfred Kazin, Nicholas King, Barbara Dole Lawrence, Patsy Leo, Angelique Levi, Nancy Macdonald, Kevin and Kate McCarthy, Norman Mailer, John Marquand, Julian Muller, Frani Muser, Cees Nooteboom, William Phillips, Dorothy Plotz, Robert Pounder, Jess Rosenberg, Dixie Sheridan, Robert Silvers, Eve Stwertka, Margo Viscusi, James West, Reuel Wilson,

Clement and Jessie Wood, and others who prefer to remain unnamed.

I am particularly grateful to Frani Muser for copies of her correspondence with Mary McCarthy from the 1930s and later; to Miriam Chiaromonte for letters and documents pertaining to the Europe-America Groups in 1948; and to Andy Dupee for access to F. W. Dupee's letters and journals at Columbia University (and to the Columbia University Libraries for authorization to quote from these materials). Ruth Limmer kindly permitted me to quote from the published letters of Louise Bogan. I was privileged to draw from the letters of many more people than I can acknowledge here, but special thanks go to Hannah Arendt's literary trustee, Lotte Kohler, for permission to quote extensively from Arendt's correspondence; to Robert Giroux for permission to quote from the poems and letters of Robert Lowell; to Elizabeth Hardwick and to William Jovanovich—whose correspondence with Mary McCarthy, like Hannah Arendt's, reads like a book. Thanks, too, to Lenny Green, who kept me apprised of what Mary and the boys were up to in New York thirty years ago, and whose long letters re-create the scene of several tumultuous readings and debates at the Ninety-second Street Y in the early 1960s.

I began the background reading for the book in the Allen Room of the New York Public Library, a congenial place to work, but the lion's share of my research was conducted in the Rare Book Room at the Vassar College Library, which houses the Mary McCarthy Papers. In the beginning, before the seventy-odd cartons of letters, manuscripts, and photographs were catalogued, I was ably assisted by Vassar's Curator of Special Collections, Lisa Browar, and then by her successor, Nancy MacKechnie, and Nancy's stoic assistant, Melissa O'Donnell. Their help and gracious good humor throughout was a godsend.

I am grateful to Margo Viscusi and Eve Stwertka, Mary McCarthy's literary trustees, for granting permission to quote from material copyrighted by Mary McCarthy and from McCarthy's unpublished letters, interviews, and manuscripts; and to Special Collections, Vassar College Libraries, for authorization to publish material from the Mary McCarthy Papers, as well as a letter from the Elizabeth Bishop Papers. After McCarthy's death in October 1989, Margo Viscusi and Eve Stwertka stepped in as readers and consultants; and many times they buoyed me up when the pressures mounted. The warm hospitality that Mary and Jim West showed me in Castine and Paris was extended later by Margo and Anthony Viscusi in New York, and by Jim West and his new wife in Castine, when I was working on the book.

At the Beinecke Rare Book and Manuscript Library of Yale University, I was aided by the Curator of American Literature, David Schoonmaker, his successor Patricia Willis, and by William Massa and Judith Schiff in the Manuscripts and Archives division of the Yale University Library. For permission to quote from the letters and manuscripts of Edmund Wilson, I am grateful to his daughter, Helen Miranda Wilson; to Roger Straus, Jr., and Erica Seidman of Farrar, Straus & Giroux, Inc.; and to the Yale University Library for authorization to publish material from both the Wilson Collection and the Dwight Macdonald Papers.

Without the generous support of two arts organizations, the Ragdale Foundation in Lake Forest, Illinois, and the Virginia Center for the Creative Arts in Sweet Briar, which gave me the opportunity to work uninterrupted on several occasions, this book would have taken longer to complete than it did. My favorite chapters were written at both places, and reading them aloud at after-dinner gatherings of fellow scribblers and artists was a break in the long Siberian night of working alone. So, too, was meeting with the "group" in New York when I came down from Maine: Jane Ciabattari, Ann Banks, Grace Lichtenstein, Robin Reisig, Marilyn Webb, Gwenda Blair, and Kate Breslin.

A kind of monomania overtakes the writer who enters another life and time, as in the summer of 1988 when I was working over the Riverview Market in Pemaquid, Maine, and thought I'd never get out of the 1940s; it's an occupational hazard of biography-writing that comes down hardest on one's family. "Modem," my twelve-year-old son, Simon, called me a few years ago, after seeing me glued to the word processor month after month. His father and I work elbow to elbow at our workstations in the study, but Michael, who has managed to produce four travel books, plus updates, during the eight years I have been writing dangerously, keeps the home fires burning. To him, to Simon, and to Sarabinh, my daughter, and to my mother Lucy Brightman (who has heard it all), I offer my heartfelt thanks.

Index

Clark, Eunice:
 as fictional model, 92–93, 345
 Johnsrud's affair with, 122, 345
 in New York social circles, 102, 105, 112
 at Vassar, 72, 76, 77
 on Wilson, 169
Clark, Ramsey, 551, 595
Clay, Lucius, 352
Clift, Montgomery, 310, 320
Clurman, Harold, 113
Cocteau, Jean, 214
Code Name Mary (Gardiner), 614–615
Cohen, Elliot, 303, 373
COINTELPRO, 507
Colby, William, 587
Colby College, 625
Cold War and the Income Tax, The
 (Wilson), 536
Coleridge, Samuel Taylor, 80
Colson, Charles W., 569
Columbia Pictures, 100
Columbia University, 167, 303
comic characters, 458–459
Commentary, 303, 334, 367, 372, 431–432,
 484, 614
Commission for Jewish Cultural
 Reconstruction, 588
Committee for Public Justice, 603
Common Market, 463, 471, 475
Common Sense, 102, 112, 128, 482
Commonweal, 273
communism:
 of kibbutzim, 520
 neutral alternative to, 305–306
 see also anticommunism
Communist Manifesto (Marx and Engels),
 219–220
Communist party:
 activism of, 142
 anti-fascist focus of, 137–138, 140
 in election of 1932, 114
 John Reed Clubs and, 128, 139, 140
 literary focus advocated by, 112, 138–139,
 140
 New York intellectuals in, 110, 132,
 605–606
 organizational hierarchy in, 118
 Partisan Review and, 128, 132, 140, 159
 prestige of, 118, 120
 Progressives linked with, 310
 recruiting efforts for, 116, 120–121
 secrecy within, 118–120
 in Spanish Civil War, 120, 234
 Theatre Union and, 113
 Vassar students in, 72
Communists:
 anti-Stalinism and, 130–136, 603
 congressional hearings on, 119, 604–608
 European, 330
 fanaticism of, 116–117
 in Hollywood, 182
 moral authority of, 117, 120
 of North Vietnam, 542, 553
 as Russian nationalists, 218–219

Company She Keeps, The (McCarthy),
 196–208
 critical reactions to, 111, 185, 206–208,
 218
 de Beauvoir's She Came to Stay vs., 344,
 348, 349
 heroine's duality in, 60, 84, 170, 349
 later work vs., 290, 316
 marriage portrayed in, 241
 MM's fictional alter ego in, 35, 52,
 238–239
 preface to, 196
 prose style of, 599
 psychological aspects of, 84, 170, 220, 267
 publication of, 193
 rights sold for, 237
 self-examination in, 84, 196, 220, 412
 self-invention in, 94, 198, 267
 sexual candor in, 283
 on socialist snobbery, 341
 stories collected in, 125, 129, 185, 193,
 196, 219, 224, 229; see also specific
 stories
 success of, 283
Company She Kept, The (Grumbach), 242,
 243
"Complete Adventuress, The" (Schwartz),
 146–147
Compton-Burnett, Ivy, 44, 231, 396, 480
Congress, U.S.:
 HUAC hearings held by, 323, 352, 354,
 604–608
 Marshall Plan funds from, 307
Congress for Cultural Freedom (CCF), 307,
 322, 474, 582
 CIA backing for, 303, 308, 381, 382, 498,
 499–500, 501
 dissolution of, 505, 506
 executive committee of, 309
 international conferences of, 137, 381–382,
 429, 451–452, 497, 498–499
 Sartre criticized by, 513–514
 in South America, 476–477
 staff for, 451, 462
 Vietnam War and, 505
Congress of Industrial Organizations (CIO),
 142, 303
Connecticut College, 486
Connolly, Cyril, 302, 328
Conrad, Joseph, 626
Conroy, Jack, 108, 139
conservative social thought,
 cultural criticism espoused in, 339
Con Spirito, 76–79, 90, 93, 97, 105, 145, 481
consumerism, 333–337, 427–428
Contagion of Ideas, The (McCarthy),
 355–356
containment doctrine, 322
Cook, Jig, 235
Cornell, Katharine, 148
Corso, Gregory, 394, 445
Council for the Free World, 319
Covici-Friede, 147, 154, 165, 168
Coward, Noel, 441